T0188901

# Lecture Notes in Artificial Intelligence    13074

Subseries of Lecture Notes in Computer Science

Series Editors

Randy Goebel
*University of Alberta, Edmonton, Canada*

Yuzuru Tanaka
*Hokkaido University, Sapporo, Japan*

Wolfgang Wahlster
*DFKI and Saarland University, Saarbrücken, Germany*

Founding Editor

Jörg Siekmann
*DFKI and Saarland University, Saarbrücken, Germany*

More information about this subseries at https://link.springer.com/bookseries/1244

André Britto · Karina Valdivia Delgado (Eds.)

# Intelligent Systems

10th Brazilian Conference, BRACIS 2021
Virtual Event, November 29 – December 3, 2021
Proceedings, Part II

 Springer

*Editors*
André Britto 🆔
Universidade Federal de Sergipe
São Cristóvão, Brazil

Karina Valdivia Delgado 🆔
Universidade de São Paulo
São Paulo, Brazil

ISSN 0302-9743          ISSN 1611-3349 (electronic)
Lecture Notes in Artificial Intelligence
ISBN 978-3-030-91698-5          ISBN 978-3-030-91699-2 (eBook)
https://doi.org/10.1007/978-3-030-91699-2

LNCS Sublibrary: SL7 – Artificial Intelligence

This Springer imprint is published by the registered company Springer Nature Switzerland AG
The registered company address is: Gewerbestrasse 11, 6330 Cham, Switzerland

# Preface

The Brazilian Conference on Intelligent Systems (BRACIS) is one of Brazil's most meaningful events for students and researchers in artificial and computational intelligence. Currently in its 10th edition, BRACIS originated from the combination of the two most important scientific events in Brazil in artificial intelligence (AI) and computational intelligence (CI): the Brazilian Symposium on Artificial Intelligence (SBIA), with 21 editions, and the Brazilian Symposium on Neural Networks (SBRN), with 12 editions. The conference aims to promote theory and applications of artificial and computational intelligence. BRACIS also aims to promote international-level research by exchanging scientific ideas among researchers, practitioners, scientists, and engineers.

BRACIS 2021 received 192 submissions. All papers were rigorously double-blind peer reviewed by an international Program Committee (with an average of three reviews per submission), which was followed by a discussion phase for conflicting reports. At the end of the reviewing process, 77 papers were selected for publication in two volumes of the Lecture Notes in Artificial Intelligence series, an acceptance rate of 40%.

We are very grateful to Program Committee members and reviewers for their volunteered contribution in the reviewing process. We would also like to express our gratitude to all the authors who submitted their papers, the general chairs, and the Local Organization Committee for supporting the conference during the COVID-19 pandemic. We want to thank the Artificial Intelligence and Computational Intelligence commissions from the Brazilian Computer Society for the confidence they placed in us serving as program chairs for BRACIS 2021.

We are confident that these proceedings reflect the excellent work in the artificial and computation intelligence communities.

November 2021

André Britto
Karina Valdivia Delgado

# Organization

## General Chairs

Reinaldo A. C. Bianchi      Centro Universitário FEI and C4AI, Brazil
Zhao Liang      Universidade de São Paulo and C4AI, Brazil

## Program Committee Chairs

André Britto      Universidade Federal de Sergipe, Brazil
Karina V. Delgado      Universidade de São Paulo, Brazil

## Steering Committee

Leliane Barros      Universidade de São Paulo, Brazil
Denis Deratani Maua      Universidade de São Paulo, Brazil
Felipe Rech Meneguzzi      Pontifícia Universidade Católica do Rio Grande do Sul, Brazil
Jaime Sichman      Universidade de São Paulo, Brazil
Maria Viviane de Menezes      Universidade Federal do Ceará, Brazil
Tatiane Nogueira Rios      Universidade Federal da Bahia, Brazil
Solange Rezende      Universidade de São Paulo, Brazil
Gina Oliveira      Universidade Federal de Uberlândia, Brazil
Anisio Lacerda      Universidade Federal de Minas Gerais, Brazil
Helida Salles      Universidade Federal do Rio Grande, Brazil
João Xavier-Jr.      Universidade Federal do Rio Grande do Norte, Brazil
Ricardo Prudêncio      Universidade Federal de Pernambuco, Brazil
Renato Tinós      Universidade de São Paulo, Brazil

## Program Committee

Adenilton da Silva      Universidade Federal de Pernambuco, Brazil
Adriane Serapião      Universidade Estadual Paulista, Brazil
Adriano Oliveira      Universidade Federal de Pernambuco, Brazil
Adrião Duarte Dória Neto      Universidade Federal do Rio Grande do Norte, Brazil
Alexandre Delbem      Universidade de São Paulo, Brazil
Alexandre Ferreira      Universidade Estadual de Campinas, Brazil
Aline Paes      Universidade Federal Fluminense, Brazil

| | |
|---|---|
| Daniel Araújo | Universidade Federal do Rio Grande do Norte, Brazil |
| Daniel Dantas | Universidade Federal de Sergipe, Brazil |
| Danilo Sanches | Universidade Tecnológica Federal do Paraná, Brazil |
| Denis Fantinato | Universidade Federal do ABC, Brazil |
| Denis Mauá | Universidade de São Paulo, Brazil |
| Dennis Barrios-Aranibar | Universidad Católica San Pablo, Peru |
| Diana Adamatti | Universidade Federal do Rio Grande, Brazil |
| Diego Furtado Silva | Universidade Federal de São Carlos, Brazil |
| Edson Gomi | Universidade de São Paulo, Brazil |
| Edson Matsubara | Fundação Universidade Federal de Mato Grosso do Sul, Brazil |
| Eduardo Borges | Universidade Federal do Rio Grande, Brazil |
| Eduardo Costa | Corteva Agriscience, Brazil |
| Eduardo Gonçalves | Escola Nacional de Ciências Estatísticas, Brazil |
| Eduardo Palmeira | Universidade Estadual de Santa Cruz, Brazil |
| Eduardo Spinosa | Universidade Federal do Paraná, Brazil |
| Edward Hermann Haeusler | Pontifícia Universidade Católica do Rio de Janeiro, Brazil |
| Elizabeth Goldbarg | Universidade Federal do Rio Grande do Norte, Brazil |
| Elizabeth Wanner | Centro Federal de Educação Tecnológica de Minas Gerais, Brazil |
| Emerson Paraiso | Pontificia Universidade Catolica do Parana, Brazil |
| Eraldo Fernandes | Universidade Federal de Mato Grosso do Sul, Brazil |
| Erick Fonseca | Real Digital, Brazil |
| Evandro Costa | Universidade Federal de Alagoas, Brazil |
| Everton Cherman | Universidade de São Paulo, Brazil |
| Fabiano Silva | Universidade Federal do Paraná, Brazil |
| Fabrício Enembreck | Pontifícia Universidade Católica do Paraná, Brazil |
| Fabricio Olivetti de França | Universidade Federal do ABC, Brazil |
| Fábio Cozman | Universidade de São Paulo, Brazil |
| Felipe França | Universidade Federal do Rio de Janeiro, Brazil |
| Fernando Osório | Universidade de São Paulo, Brazil |
| Fernando Von Zuben | Universidade Estadual de Campinas, Brazil |
| Flavio Tonidandel | Centro Universitário FEI, Brazil |
| Flávio Soares Corrêa da Silva | Universidade de São Paulo, Brazil |
| Francisco Chicano | University of Málaga, Spain |
| Francisco De Carvalho | Universidade Federal de Pernambuco, Brazil |
| Gabriel Ramos | Universidade do Vale do Rio dos Sinos, Brazil |
| George Cavalcanti | Universidade Federal de Pernambuco, Brazil |

| | |
|---|---|
| Gerson Zaverucha | Universidade Federal do Rio de Janeiro, Brazil |
| Giancarlo Lucca | Universidade Federal do Rio Grande, Brazil |
| Gina Oliveira | Universidade Federal de Uberlândia, Brazil |
| Gisele Pappa | Universidade Federal de Minas Gerais, Brazil |
| Gracaliz Dimuro | Universidade Federal do Rio Grande, Brazil |
| Guilherme Barreto | Universidade Federal do Ceará, Brazil |
| Guilherme Derenievicz | Universidade Federal do Paraná, Brazil |
| Guillermo Simari | Universidad Nacional del Sur in Bahia Blanca, Argentina |
| Gustavo Giménez-Lugo | Universidade Tecnológica Federal do Paraná, Brazil |
| Gustavo Paetzold | University of Sheffield, UK |
| Heitor Lopes | Universidade Tecnológica Federal do Paraná, Brazil |
| Helena Caseli | Universidade Federal de São Carlos, Brazil |
| Helida Santos | Universidade Federal do Rio Grande, Brazil |
| Heloisa Camargo | Universidade Federal de São Carlos, Brazil |
| Huei Lee | Universidade Estadual do Oeste do Paraná, Brazil |
| Humberto Bustince | Universidad Pública de Navarra, Spain |
| Humberto César Brandão de Oliveira | Universidade Federal de Alfenas, Brazil |
| Ivandré Paraboni | Universidade de São Paulo, Brazil |
| Jaime Sichman | Universidade de São Paulo, Brazil |
| Joéo Balsa | Universidade de Lisboa, Portugal |
| Joéo Bertini | Universidade Estadual de Campinas, Brazil |
| Joéo Papa | Universidade Estadual Paulista, Brazil |
| Joéo C. Xavier-Júnior | Universidade Federal do Rio Grande do Norte, Brazil |
| Joéo Luís Rosa | Universidade de São Paulo, Brazil |
| Jomi Hübner | Universidade Federal de Santa Catarina, Brazil |
| Jonathan Andrade Silva | Universidade Federal de Mato Grosso do Sul, Brazil |
| José Antonio Sanz | Universidad Pública de Navarra, Spain |
| José Augusto Baranauskas | Universidade de São Paulo, Brazil |
| Jose Eduardo Ochoa Luna | Universidad Católica San Pablo, Peru |
| Juan Pavón | Universidad Complutense Madrid, Spain |
| Julio Nievola | Pontifícia Universidade Católica do Paraná, Brazil |
| Karla Lima | Universidade de São Paulo, Brazil |
| Kate Revoredo | Vienna University of Economics and Business, Austria |
| Krysia Broda | Imperial College, UK |
| Leandro dos Santos Coelho | Pontifícia Universidade Catálica do Paraná, Brazil |
| Leliane Nunes de Barros | Universidade de São Paulo, Brazil |

| | |
|---|---|
| Leonardo Emmendorfer | Universidade Federal do Rio Grande, Brazil |
| Leonardo Matos | Universidade Federal de Sergipe, Brazil |
| Leonardo Filipe Ribeiro | Technische Universitat Darmstadt, Germany |
| Li Weigang | Universidade de Brasília, Brazil |
| Livy Real | B2W Digital and Universidade de São Paulo, Brazil |
| Lucelene Lopes | Universidade de São Paulo, Brazil |
| Luciano Digiampietri | Universidade de São Paulo, Brazil |
| Luis Antunes | Universidade de Lisboa, Portugal |
| Luis Garcia | Universidade de Brasília, Brazil |
| Luiz Carvalho | Universidade Tecnológica Federal do Paraná, Brazil |
| Luiz Coletta | Universidade Estadual Paulista, Brazil |
| Luiz Henrique Merschmann | Universidade Federal de Lavras, Brazil |
| Luiza de Macedo Mourelle | Universidade Estadual de Rio de Janeiro, Brazil |
| Marcela Ribeiro | Universidade Federal de São Carlos, Brazil |
| Marcella Scoczynski | Universidade Tecnológica Federal do Paraná, Brazil |
| Marcelo Finger | Universidade de São Paulo, Brazil |
| Marcilio de Souto | Université d'Orléans, France |
| Marco Cristo | Universidade Federal do Amazonas, Brazil |
| Marcos Domingues | Universidade Estadual de Maringá, Brazil |
| Marcos Quiles | Universidade Federal de São Paulo, Brazil |
| Maria do Carmo Nicoletti | Universidade Federal de São Carlos, Brazil |
| Marilton Aguiar | Universidade Federal de Pelotas, Brazil |
| Marley M. B. R. Vellasco | Pontifícia Universidade Católica do Rio de Janeiro, Brazil |
| Marlo Souza | Universidade Federal da Bahia, Brazil |
| Mauri Ferrandin | Universidade Federal de Santa Catarina, Brazil |
| Márcio Basgalupp | Universidade Federal de São Paulo, Brazil |
| Moacir Ponti | Universidade de São Paulo, Brazil |
| Murillo Carneiro | Universidade Federal de Uberlândia, Brazil |
| Murilo Naldi | Universidade Federal de São Carlos, Brazil |
| Myriam Delgado | Universidade Tecnológica Federal do Paraná, Brazil |
| Nádia Felix | Universidade Federal de Goiás, Brazil |
| Norton Roman | Universidade de São Paulo, Brazil |
| Nuno David | Instituto Universitário de Lisboa, Portugal |
| Patrícia Tedesco | Universidade Federal de Pernambuco, Brazil |
| Patricia Oliveira | Universidade de São Paulo, Brazil |
| Paulo Cavalin | IBM Research, Brazil |
| Paulo Ferreira Jr. | Universidade Federal de Pelotas, Brazil |

| Paulo Quaresma | Universidade de Évora, Portugal |
| Paulo Henrique Pisani | Universidade Federal do ABC, Brazil |
| Paulo T. Guerra | Universidade Federal do Ceará, Brazil |
| Petrucio Viana | Universidade Federal Fluminense, Brazil |
| Priscila Lima | Universidade Federal do Rio de Janeiro, Brazil |
| Rafael Bordini | Pontifícia Universidade Católica do Rio Grande do Sul, Brazil |
| Rafael Giusti | Universidade Federal do Amazonas, Brazil |
| Rafael Gomes Mantovani | Universidade Tecnológica Federal do Paraná, Brazil |
| Rafael Parpinelli | Universidade do Estado de Santa Catarina, Brazil |
| Rafael Rossi | Universidade Federal de Mato Grosso do Sul, Brazil |
| Reinaldo Bianchi | Centro Universitário FEI, Brazil |
| Renata Wassermann | Universidade de São Paulo, Brazil |
| Renato Assuncao | Universidade Federal de Minas Gerais, Brazil |
| Renato Krohling | Universidade Federal do Espírito Santo, Brazil |
| Renato Tinos | Universidade de São Paulo, Brazil |
| Renê Gusmão | Universidade Federal de Sergipe, Brazil |
| Ricardo Cerri | Universidade Federal de São Carlos, Brazil |
| Ricardo Marcacini | Universidade de São Paulo, Brazil |
| Ricardo Prudêncio | Universidade Federal de Pernambuco, Brazil |
| Ricardo Rios | Universidade Federal da Bahia, Brazil |
| Ricardo Suyama | Universidade Federal do ABC, Brazil |
| Ricardo Tanscheit | Pontifícia Universidade Católica do Rio de Janeiro, Brazil |
| Ricardo Fernandes | Universidade Federal de São Carlos, Brazil |
| Roberta Sinoara | Instituto Federal de Ciência, Educação e Tecnologia de São Paulo, Brazil |
| Roberto Santana | University of the Basque Country, Spain |
| Robson Cordeiro | Universidade de São Paulo, Brazil |
| Rodrigo Barros | Pontifícia Universidade Católica do Rio Grande do Sul, Brazil |
| Rodrigo Wilkens | University of Milano-Bicocca, Italy |
| Ronaldo Prati | Universidade Federal do ABC, Brazil |
| Ronnie Alves | Instituto Tecnologia Vale, Brazil |
| Roseli Romero | Universidade de São Paulo, Brazil |
| Rui Camacho | University of Porto, Portugal |
| Sandra Sandri | Instituto Nacional de Pesquisas Espaciais, Brazil |
| Sandra Venske | Universidade Estadual do Centro-Oeste, Brazil |
| Sandro Rigo | Universidade do Vale do Rio dos Sinos, Brazil |
| Sarajane Peres | Universidade de São Paulo, Brazil |

Sílvia Maia                     Universidade Federal do Rio Grande do Norte,
                                  Brazil
Sílvio Cazella                  Universidade Federal de Ciências da Saúde de
                                  Porto Alegre, Brazil
Solange Rezende                 Universidade de São Paulo, Brazil
Sylvio Barbon Junior            Universidade Estadual de Londrina, Brazil
Tatiane Nogueira                Universidade Federal de Bahia, Brazil
Teresa Ludermir                 Universidade Federal de Pernambuco, Brazil
Thiago Covoes                   Universidade Federal do ABC, Brazil
Thiago Pardo                    Universidade de São Paulo, Brazil
Tiago Almeida                   Universidade Federal de São Carlos, Brazil
Valdinei Freire                 Universidade de São Paulo, Brazil
Valerie Camps                   Paul Sabatier University, France
Valmir Macario                  Universidade Federal Rural de Pernambuco,
                                  Brazil
Vasco Furtado                   Universidade de Fortaleza, Brazil
Viviane Torres da Silva         IBM Research, Brazil
Vladimir Rocha                  Universidade Federal do ABC, Brazil
Wagner Botelho                  Universidade Federal do ABC, Brazil
Wagner Meira Jr.                Universidade Federal de Minas Gerais, Brazil
Yván Túpac                      Universidad Católica San Pablo, Peru

## Additional Reviewers

Alexis Iván Aspauza Lescano
André Carvalho
Antonio Parmezan
Bernardo Scapini Consoli
Caetano Ranieri
Cristina Morimoto
Daniel Pinheiro da Silva Junior
Daniela Vianna
Daniela Fernanda Milon Flores
Dimmy Magalhães
Eliton Perin
Eulanda Santos
Felipe Serras
Felipe Zeiser
Fernando dos Santos
Guillermo Simari
Hugo Valadares Siqueira
Italo Oliveira
Jefferson Souza
Jhonatan Alves

Joel Costa Júnior
Juliana Wolf
Kristofer Kappel
Lucas Evangelista
Lucas Navarezi
Lucas Rodrigues
Luciano Cota
Luiz Fernando Oliveira
Maicon Zatelli
Marcia Fernandes
Mariane Regina Sponchiado Cassenote
Matheus Pavan
Maurício Pamplona Segundo
Mohamed El Yafrani
Murilo Falleiros Lemos Schmitt
Nauber Gois
Nelson Sandes
Newton Spolaôr
Rafael João
Rafael Katopodis

Rafhael Cunha
Rodolfo Garcia
Sérgio Discola-Jr.
Tauã Cabreira
Thiago Homem

Thiago Miranda
Vítor Lourenço
Wesley Santos
Wesley Seidel

# Contents – Part II

**Neural Networks, Deep Learning and Computer Vision**

**Text Mining and Natural Language Processing**

# Contents – Part I

## Knowledge Representation, Logic and Fuzzy Systems

## Machine Learning and Data Mining

# Multidisciplinary Artificial and Computational Intelligence and Applications

# A Heterogeneous Network-Based Positive and Unlabeled Learning Approach to Detect Fake News

Mariana C. de Souza[1]([⊠])(iD), Bruno M. Nogueira[2](iD), Rafael G. Rossi[3](iD),
Ricardo M. Marcacini[1](iD), and Solange O. Rezende[1](iD)

[1] Department of Computer Science, University of São Paulo, São Carlos, Brazil
`mariana.caravanti@usp.br`, {`ricardo.marcacini,solange`}`@icmc.usp.br`
[2] Federal University of Mato Grosso do Sul, Campo Grande, Brazil
`bruno@facom.ufms.br`
[3] Federal University of Mato Grosso do Sul, Três Lagoas, Brazil
`rafael.g.rossi@ufms.br`

**Abstract.** The dynamism of fake news evolution and dissemination plays a crucial role in influencing and confirming personal beliefs. To minimize the spread of disinformation approaches proposed in the literature, automatic fake news detection generally learns models through binary supervised algorithms considering textual and contextual information. However, labeling significant amounts of real news to build accurate classifiers is difficult and time-consuming due to their broad spectrum. Positive and unlabeled learning (PUL) can be a good alternative in this scenario. PUL algorithms learn models considering little labeled data of the interest class and use unlabeled data to increase classification performance. This paper proposes a heterogeneous network variant of the PU-LP algorithm, a PUL algorithm based on similarity networks. Our network incorporates different linguistic features to characterize fake news, such as representative terms, emotiveness, pausality, and average sentence size. Also, we considered two representations of the news to compute similarity: term frequency-inverse document frequency, and Doc2Vec, which creates fixed-sized document representations regardless of its length. We evaluated our approach in six datasets written in Portuguese or English, comparing its performance with a binary semi-supervised baseline algorithm, using two well-established label propagation algorithms: LPHN and GNetMine. The results indicate that PU-LP with heterogeneous networks can be competitive to binary semi-supervised learning. Also, linguistic features such as representative terms and pausality improved the classification performance, especially when there is a small amount of labeled news.

Supported by Coordenação de Aperfeiçoamento de Pessoal de Nível Superior [10662147/D], Fundação de Amparo à Pesquisa do Estado de São Paulo [2019/25010-5, 2019/07665-4], and Conselho Nacional de Desenvolvimento Científico e Tecnológico [426663/2018-7, 433082/2018-6, and 438017/2018-8].

© Springer Nature Switzerland AG 2021
A. Britto and K. Valdivia Delgado (Eds.): BRACIS 2021, LNAI 13074, pp. 3–18, 2021.
https://doi.org/10.1007/978-3-030-91699-2_1

**Keywords:** Fake news · One-class learning · Positive and unlabeled learning · Transdutive semi-supervised learning · Graph-based learning

## 1   Introduction

Detecting fake news is a challenging task since fake news constantly evolves, influencing the formation of the opinion of social groups as accepted [6]. To minimize the effects of disinformation provided by fake news, Machine Learning algorithms have been proposed in the literature, which learn classification models to discriminate true and fake content [4,22]. The most common way to deal with this problem is to characterize the fake news detection as a supervised binary or multiclass classification problem [22]. However, labeling real and fake news to cover different subjects, sources, and falsity levels, as well as updating the classification model are costly processes [4]. All of these challenges drive the investigation of more appropriate models for representing and classifying news.

Positive and Unlabeled Learning (PUL) algorithms can be good alternatives in this scenario [3]. PUL algorithms learn models considering little labeled data of the interest class and use the unlabeled data to increase classification performance [9]. Therefore, PUL eliminates the need to label a large number of news of the uninteresting classes. Due to the suitability of PUL to fake news detection scenario, in this paper, we proposed an approach based on the algorithm Positive and Unlabeled Learning by Label Propagation [9] (PU-LP), a network-based semi-supervised transductive learning algorithm. PU-LP has been little explored for text classification, despite its good performance in numerical datasets. PU-LP infers reliable sets of interest (fake news) and not interest (true news) using a small number of labeled data, Katz index and a $k$-Nearest Neighbor ($k$-NN) network. Then, a label propagation algorithm is used to label the remaining unlabeled objects as interest or not interest.

Representing news using traditional models, i.e., Bag-of-Words or embeddings, may not be discriminative enough to distinguish fake and real content [17,21]. Thus, an important challenge for automatic fake news detection is to assemble a set of features that efficiently characterize a false content in a dynamic scenario. This set may contain features about creator or spreader, the target victims, the news content and the social context [22]. In this work, we propose using content-based features in a domain-independent fake news detection approach based on the PU-LP algorithm. Our network use linguistic features such as representative terms, news emotiveness, average number of words per sentence, and pausality as network objects, thus making a heterogeneous network [12]. These features have proven to be relevant for news classification [13]. Also, the presence of different objects and relations in the network allows for representing different patterns on data [15]. To create the $k$-NN news network, we represent the text with Bag-of-Words (BoW) and Doc2Vec (D2V) models to compute the similarity between the news. To the best of our knowledge, heterogeneous networks and PUL have not been explored in the literature to detect fake news.

We evaluated different combinations of features to measure the impact of these features in the classification performance. Our experiments used relatively small sets of labeled fake news: from 10% to 30% of the fake news set. The heterogeneous network was compared with the $k$-NN networks, used in the original proposal of PU-LP. Two Portuguese datasets and four English datasets were used, containing only one or more subjects. For the label propagation, we used two well-established algorithms: Label Propagation Through Heterogeneous Networks [12] and GNetMine [7]. We evaluated the algorithms considering the $F_1$ measure of the fake news class. The results obtained the proposed approach were compared with a semi-supervised binary baseline, and demonstrate competitiveness even with half the news initially labeled and without the labeling of real news. This paper is organized as follows: Sects. 2 and 3 present related work. Section 4 describes the proposed approach. Section 5 presents experimental evaluation and discussions. Section 6 presents conclusions and future works.

## 2 Related Work

Existing methods for news classification, in general, represent news in a structured way using traditional models such as BoW, word (or document) embeddings or networks [22]. However, these models are not discriminative enough to capture the nuances to distinguish fake from real news, requiring the investigation of textual and contextual features that can be incorporated into the representation model [17,21,22]. Contextual features are extracted from the news environment, such as post, source, and publisher related information [21]. Textual features involve lexical, syntactic and semantic aspects of the news content. Lexical features are related to frequency statistics of words, which can be done using $n$-gram models, able to identify, for example, the presence of vague, doubt or sensationalist expressions [4]. Syntactic features are related to the presence and frequency of Part-Of-Speech patterns, like subjects, verbs and adjectives [17]. At the semantic level, meanings are extracted from terms, where methods like Linguistic Inquiry and Word Count (LIWC) [10] can be used to estimate emotional, cognitive and structural components present in the written language.

In [17], authors proposed representation models for the Fake.BR dataset that combine BoW and linguistic features, such as pausality, emotiveness, and uncertainty. The authors reached 96% of macro $F_1$ considering two thirds of the data as training. In [18], the authors proposed a multimodal representation that combines text and images information. For each news, 124 textual features (81 of them with LIWC) and 43 image features are collected. The approach achieves 95% accuracy with Random Forest using approximately 7,000 news documents and 90% of data in the training set.

Some works use networks as a representation model to detect false information. [13] proposes a knowledge network for fact-checking, in which the entry is a triple (subject, predicate, object). The network is constructed with information from Wikipedia, in which given a sentence, if it exists within the knowledge network, it is considered authentic. The approach achieves approximately 74% accuracy. [21] proposes a diffuse neural network graph for inferring the credibility of news, creators and subjects. The graph has approximately 14,000 news items, 3,600 creators and 152 subjects. The approach achieves the best overall performance in the binary classification compared to SVM, Deep Walk and a neural network. [11] proposes an Adversarial Active Learning Heterogeneous

Graph Neural Network to detect fake news. A hierarchical attention mechanism is used to learn nodes' representations, and a selector is responsible for consulting high-value candidates for active learning. The authors evaluate two datasets: the first containing 14,055 news, 3,634 creators and 152 subjects, and the second containing 182 news, 15,257 twitter users and 9 publishers. With 20% of real and fake news labeled, the algorithm reaches respectively 57% and 70% of macro $F_1$. [19] proposes IARNet, an Information Aggregating and Reasoning Network to detect fake news on heterogeneous networks. The network contains the post source, comments and users as nodes and interactions between them as edges. The authors evaluated two datasets, Weibo and Fakeddit, and 70% of the labeled news for training. The algorithm achieved 96% accuracy.

To avoid real news labeling efforts, [5] proposes the DCDistanceOCC, a One-class Learning (OCL) algorithm to identify false content. For each news item, linguistic characteristics are extracted, such as number of words per sentence and sentiment of the message. A new example is classified as the interest class if its distance to the class vector is below a threshold. The algorithm is executed using 90% fake news to train the model. The approach reaches an average $F_1$ that ranges from 54% to 67%, especially considering the Fake.BR dataset.

It is possible to observe that most of the existing work for fake news detection adopts binary supervised learning approaches, which requires labeling news considering the real and fake classes. Additionally, the broad spectrum of real news also makes the generation of a representative labeled training set difficult. On the other hand, the PUL algorithms, which mitigate the drawback of binary supervised learning algorithms in fake news detection, are scarce in this scenario. Also, the use of heterogeneous networks, which usually are more adequate in semi-supervised text classification [12], has not been explored in the literature for detecting fake news. Considering these gaps, in this paper we propose a PUL algorithm for fake-news detection, which is based on a heterogeneous network composed of news, terms, and linguistic features. Our approach uses only information that can be collected in the publication's content, not depending on external information. The proposed approach is detailed in the next sections.

## 3   Positive and Unlabeled Learning Algorithms

PUL algorithms learn models considering a set of labeled documents of an interest class and unlabeled documents to train a classifier (inductive semi-supervised learning) or to classify unlabeled known documents (transductive semi-supervised learning) [3]. The purpose of using unlabeled documents during learning is to improve classification performance. Besides, since the unlabeled documents are easy to collect and a user has to label only a few documents of the interest class, PUL has gained attention in the last years [3,9].

The most common PUL approaches are those which perform learning in two stages. In the first stage, a set of non-interest documents is generated by extracting reliable outliers documents to be considered as non-interest class. In addition, the set of interest documents can also be increased with reliable interest documents. Once there are interest, non-interest, and unlabeled documents, a transductive learning algorithm is applied to infer the label to the remaining unlabeled documents in the second stage [3]. Generally, the PUL algorithms based on this framework include the application of self-training in some or all of the steps, which can be computationally costly and do not improve the classification performance [12]. We can observe the use of algorithms based on vector-space model, such as Rocchio or Expectation Maximization, also demonstrated lower performances than other approaches in text classification [12,20].

Despite the benefits of network-based approaches in semi-supervised learning scenarios, there are few PUL proposals based on networks, such as *Positive documents Enlarging PU Classifier* (PE-PUC) [20] and *Positive and Unlabeled Learning by Label Propagation* (PU-LP) [9]. PE-PUC uses network representations only to increase the set of interest documents with reliable positive documents. The network is not used in the classification step. The remaining steps consider Bayesian classifiers, which have been shown to perform poorly when the labeled training data set is small [12]. The use of networks allows to extract patterns of the interest class even they are given by different distributions, densities on regions in the space [15]. As PU-LP is entirely network-based, achieving good performance in [9], we propose to use it for news classification. Next section describes the proposed approach.

## 4  Proposed Approach: PU-LP for Fake News Detection

Considering that PUL algorithms can reduce labeling effort for news classification, the benefits of network-based representations for semi-supervised learning, and that adding extra information to the network can contribute to differentiating real and fake content, we propose an approach based on PU-LP algorithm applied to fake news detection. After PU-LP infer interest and non-interest news sets in the news network, we add relations (edges) between news, relevant terms and linguistic features making a heterogeneous network. Thus, a label propagation is applied to classify the unlabeled news. We compared different proposed heterogeneous networks with the traditional PU-LP algorithm considering only the news network. We use different parameters, label propagation algorithms, and representation models for unstructured data to assess the algorithms' behavior. Figure 1 presents the proposed approach of PU-LP for semi-supervised fake news detection. The next subsections presents details of each stage of the proposed approach.

### 4.1  News Collection and Representation Model

Let $\mathcal{D} = \{d_1, \ldots, d_l, d_{l+1}, \ldots, d_{l+u}\}$ be a news set and $\mathcal{C} = \{interest, not\ interest\}$, i.e., $\mathcal{C} = \{fake, real\}$, be a set of class labels. The first $l$ elements of $\mathcal{D}$ are fake labeled news, composing the interest labeled set $\mathcal{D}^+$. The remaining $u$ elements are unlabeled news (fake and real), composing the set $\mathcal{D}^u$, and $u \gg l$ (Fig. 1 - Stage 1). The news dataset must be pre-processed, and a representation model, such as BoW or document embedding [1] must be adopted to transform

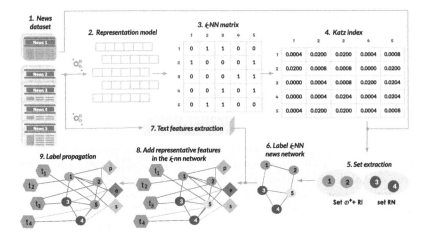

**Fig. 1.** Proposed approach for detecting fake news based on the semi-supervised PU-LP algorithm. Circular nodes represent news, nodes with the letter $t$ are representative unigrams and bigrams, nodes with the letter $p$ correspond to pausality, $e$ emotiveness, and $s$ the average number of words per sentence.

news into structured data (Fig. 1 - Stage 2). Next, PU-LP builds an adjacency matrix with the complete set of examples, $\mathcal{D}$, detailed below.

### 4.2   $k$-NN Matrix, Katz Index and Sets Extraction

The representation model and a chosen distance metric are used to calculate an adjacency matrix. In this matrix, news with similar content has a low distance between them. The adjacency matrix is used as a basis for building a $k$-Nearest Neighbors ($k$-NN) matrix, called $A$, so that $A_{i,j} = 1$ if the news $d_j$ is one of the $k$ nearest neighbors to the news $d_i$, and $A_{i,j} = 0$ otherwise (Fig. 1 - Stage 3). Through the $k$-NN matrix, a heterogeneous network $\mathcal{N}$ is also created. The heterogeneous network can be defined as a triple $\mathcal{N} = \langle \mathcal{O}, \mathcal{R}, \mathcal{W} \rangle$, in which $\mathcal{O}$ is the set of objects, $\mathcal{R}$ is the set of relations between objects, and $\mathcal{W}$ is the set of weights of these relations. Given two pairs of objects $o_i, o_j \in \mathcal{O}$, the relationship between them is $r_{o_i,o_j}$ and the weight of a relation $r_{o_i,o_j}$ is given by $w_{o_i,o_j} \forall o_i, o_j \in \mathcal{O}$. In $\mathcal{N}$, objects are news, the relationships between news are created according to the $k$-NN matrix, and the weights $w_{o_i,o_j}$ are the cosine similarity between news. Although the cosine is a good local similarity measure, its performance as a global similarity measure is not good enough. To consider local paths in the news network that involve neighboring news in common, [9] propose using the Katz Index. The basic idea is that if two news have many neighbors in common, they are likely to be of the same class. Katz index is a global similarity measure that calculates the similarity between pairs of nodes considering all possible paths in a graph that connect them. Thus:

$$sim(d_i, d_j) = \sum_{h=1}^{\infty} \alpha^h \cdot |path_{d_i, d_j}^{<h>}| = \alpha A_{i,j} + \alpha^2 (A^2)_{i,j} + \alpha^3 (A^3)_{i,j} + ..., \quad (1)$$

in which $\alpha$ is a parameter that controls the influence of paths. With a very small $\alpha$, the long paths contribute very little. In the Katz index, when $\alpha < 1/\epsilon$, being $\epsilon$ the biggest eigenvalue for the matrix $A$, Eq. 1 converges and can be calculated as follows: $S = (I - \alpha A)^{-1} - I$, which $I$ denotes the identity matrix and $S$ has dimnesions $|\mathcal{D}| \times |\mathcal{D}|$. Thus, $S_{i,j} \in \mathbb{R}$ denotes the similarity between the nodes $d_i$ and $d_j$ according to Katz index (Fig. 1 - Stage 4). The labeled news in $\mathcal{D}^+$ and the similarity matrix $S$ are used to infer two sets: the set of reliable interest news $RI$ and reliable non-interest news $RN$ (Fig. 1 - Stage 5). The set $RI$ contains news from set $\mathcal{D}^u$ that are most similar to examples from $\mathcal{D}^+$, and $RN$ will contain news from $\mathcal{D}^u - RI$ that are most dissimilar to the set $\mathcal{D}^+ \cup RI$.

For the inference of the $RI$ set, an iterative method is applied. The task is divided into $m$ iterations. In each of the $m$ iterations, the total number of reliable interest news that will be extracted is $(\lambda/m) \times |\mathcal{D}^+|$, which $\lambda$ controls the set's size. The news in $\mathcal{D}^u$ are ranked according to their average similarities for all news in $\mathcal{D}^+$ based on $S$. The $(\lambda/m)|\mathcal{D}^+|$ most similar news are taken from $D^u$ and added into $RI'$. At the end of each iteration, $RI$ is incremented with the elements in $RI'$ ($RI \leftarrow RI \cup RI'$) [9].

For the inference of the reliable non-interest set, news in $\mathcal{D}^u - RI$ are ranked according to their average similarities (based on $S$) for all news in $\mathcal{D}^+ \cup RI$. The algorithm extracts the $|\mathcal{D}^+ \cup RI|$ most dissimilar news, forming the set $RN$. After getting the set $RN$, the sets $\mathcal{D}^+ \cup RI$, $RN$, and $\mathcal{D}^u \leftarrow (\mathcal{D}^u - RI - RN)$ are used as input by label propagation algorithms based on transductive semi-supervised learning. More details about the algorithm can be seen in [9].

### 4.3 Adding Features in the News Network

Considering that the PU-LP algorithm is entirely based on networks, we propose adding new features as nodes into the news network $\mathcal{N}$ that has been shown to be relevant in [2,17] in news classification:

- incertainty = total number of modal verbs and passive voice
- non immediacy = total of singular first and second personal pronoun
- emotiveness (emo) = $\frac{\text{total number of adjectives} + \text{total number of adverbs}}{\text{total number of nouns} + \text{total number of verbs}}$
- pausality (pau) = $\frac{\text{total number of punctuation marks}}{\text{total number of sentences}}$
- average words sentence (avgws) = $\frac{\text{total number of words}}{\text{total number of sentences}}$

Among the features considered, we compute for each dataset which ones had the highest correlation with the target attribute and appeared in more than one dataset. The characteristics chosen to be included in the network were: pausality, emotiveness, and average words per sentence. Table 1 shows the correlations values. The features are added to the news network $\mathcal{N}$ as new unlabeled nodes

$f_j$, $0 < j < $ total features. New edges between news and the features are added, whose weights $w_{d_i,f_j}$ correspond to normalized values of the feature $f_j$ for the news $d_i$, according to the equation: $w_{d_i,f_j} = \frac{w_{d_i,f_j}}{\max_{d_k \in \mathcal{D}} w_{d_k,f_j}}$. We also considered other linguistic features extracted by LIWC [10], such as counting personal pronouns, prepositions, verbs, nouns, adjectives and quantitative words, use of affective words, positive and negative emotions, and anxiety, but they did not demonstrated to be relevant in our proposal.

**Table 1.** Correlations of the main linguistic features considering all news datasets.

|  | FCN | FBR | FNN | FNC1 | FNC2 | FNC3 |
|---|---|---|---|---|---|---|
| Emotiveness | 0.1749 | 0.1314 | 0.0899 | 0.0696 | 0.1504 | 0.0390 |
| Pausality | −0.2851 | −0.4733 | −0.0224 | −0.4727 | −0.4889 | −0.4719 |
| avg_words_sentence | −0.1888 | −0.5833 | 0.0039 | −0.3273 | −0.2247 | −0.3204 |

In addition to the linguistic characteristics, we also considered terms as network nodes since news terms are widely used in researches for discrimination of true and false content. They also demonstrated to be useful in label propagation for text classification [12]. To select terms, stopwords were removed and the terms were stemmed. Then, the single terms and sequences of two terms, i.e., unigrams and bigrams, are selected to be network nodes if they respect a minimum document frequency of 2 documents and their term frequency - inverse document frequency (tf-idf) value in a document is above a threshold $\ell$.

**Table 2.** List of characteristics included in each proposed heterogeneous networks.

| Feature/Network | 1 | 2 | 3 | 4 | 5 | 6 | 7 | 8 | 9 | 10 | 11 | 12 |
|---|---|---|---|---|---|---|---|---|---|---|---|---|
| News | ✓ | ✓ | ✓ | ✓ | ✓ | ✓ | ✓ | ✓ | ✓ | ✓ | ✓ | ✓ |
| Representative terms |  | ✓ |  |  |  | ✓ | ✓ | ✓ | ✓ | ✓ | ✓ | ✓ |
| Emotiveness |  |  | ✓ |  |  | ✓ |  |  | ✓ | ✓ |  | ✓ |
| Pausality |  |  |  | ✓ |  |  | ✓ |  | ✓ |  | ✓ | ✓ |
| avg_words_sentence |  |  |  |  | ✓ |  |  | ✓ |  | ✓ | ✓ | ✓ |

Twelve different heterogeneous networks were created, considering the combination of all features. Table 2 presents the networks and features included in each one. After adding all the features as nodes into the network $\mathcal{N}$, we perform the normalization of network relations in order to mitigate possible distortions due to different ranges of the different types of relations. The relations are normalized considering each relation type. Thus, the edge weight for an object $o_i \in \mathcal{O}_l$ and and object $o_j \in \mathcal{O}_m$ is given by Eq. 2:

$$w_{o_i,o_j} = \frac{w_{o_i,o_j}}{\sum_{o_k} w_{o_i,o_k}}, o_i \in \mathcal{O}_l, o_j \in \mathcal{O}_m, \text{ and } o_k \in \mathcal{O}_m \qquad (2)$$

After building the news and terms network, the next stage (Fig. 1 - Stage 9) is to carry out the label propagation using transductive learning algorithms for heterogeneous networks.

## 4.4 Label Propagation

We propose using regularization-based transductive algorithms for heterogeneous networks to classify the unlabeled news as fake or real. The regularization-based algorithms satisfy two premises: (i) the class information of neighboring objects must be similar; (ii) and the class information of the labeled objects assigned during the classification process must be similar to the real class information [12]. The two algorithms considered in this paper are: Label Propagation through Heterogeneous Networks (LPHN) [12] and GNetMine (GNM) [7].

In order to explain the regularization functions of both algorithms, let $\mathbf{f}_{o_i} = \{f_{interest}, f_{not\text{-}interest}\}$ be the class information vector, which gives how much an object $o_i$ belongs to each of the classes, and let $\mathbf{y}_{o_i}$ be the real class information vector $\mathbf{f}$, in which the position of the vector corresponding to its class is filled with 1. Thus, only labeled objects have values for vector $\mathbf{y}$. The term $w_{o_i,o_j}$ is the weight of the edge connecting object $o_i$ to object $o_j$, and $\mathcal{O}^L$ refers to the set of labeled objects. The regularization function to be minimized by LPHN is given by:

$$Q(\mathbf{F}) = \sum_{\mathcal{D,T} \in \mathcal{O}} \frac{1}{2} \sum_{o_i \in \mathcal{O}_i} \sum_{o_j \in \mathcal{O}_j} w_{o_i,o_j} (\mathbf{f}_{o_i} - \mathbf{f}_{o_j})^2 + \lim_{\mu \to \infty} \sum_{o_i \in \mathcal{O}^L} (\mathbf{f}_{o_i} - \mathbf{y}_{o_i})^2. \quad (3)$$

We can observe that the different relations have the same importance and that $\lim_{\mu \to \infty}$, which forces that $\mathbf{f}_i = \mathbf{y}_i, \forall o_i \in \mathcal{O}^L$, i.e., the class information of label object do not change. After inferring the $\mathbf{f}$ vectors of the unlabeled objects, the Class Mass Normalization (CMN) [23], and then the objects are classified according to the arg-max of the corresponding $\mathbf{f}$ vector.

In GNetMine [7], the relations between different objects have different importance. The label of an object $o_i \in \mathcal{O}^L$ can be changed during the classification process if information from neighboring objects diverges from the class of the object initially labeled. The regularization performed by GNetMine is given by:

$$Q(\mathbf{F}) = \sum_{\mathcal{O}_i, \mathcal{O}_j \subset \mathcal{O}} \lambda_{\mathcal{O}_i, \mathcal{O}_j} \sum_{o_k \in \mathcal{O}_i} \sum_{o_l \in \mathcal{O}_j} w_{o_k,o_l} \left\| \frac{\mathbf{f}_{o_k}(\mathcal{O}_i)}{\sqrt{\sum_{o_m \in \mathcal{O}_j} w_{o_k,o_m}}} - \frac{\mathbf{f}_{o_l}(\mathcal{O}_j)}{\sqrt{\sum_{o_m \in \mathcal{O}_i} w_{o_l,o_m}}} \right\|^2$$
$$+ \sum_{o_j \in \mathcal{O}^L} \alpha_{o_j} (\mathbf{f}_{o_j} - \mathbf{y}_{o_j}) \quad (4)$$

in which $\lambda_{\mathcal{O}_i, \mathcal{O}_j} (0 \geq \lambda_{\mathcal{O}_i, \mathcal{O}_j} \geq 1)$ is the importance given to the relationship between objects of the types $\mathcal{O}_i$ and $\mathcal{O}_j$, and $\alpha_{o_i} (0 \geq \alpha_{o_i} \geq 1)$ is the importance given to the real class information of an object $o_j \in \mathcal{O}^L$ (set of labeled objects). The documents are classified considering the arg-max of the final value of $\mathbf{f}_{d_i}$ vectors for $d_i \in \mathcal{D}^u$.

# 5    Experimental Evaluation

In this section, we present the experimental configuration used in the experiments, the datasets and an analysis of the results achieved. Our goal is to encourage the study of PUL approaches to fake news detection, which perform well using little labeled data. Furthermore, we want to demonstrate that with little labeled fake news data, structured in a network, it is possible to achieve reasonable classification performance, which can be improved by adding extra information, taken from the news textual content.

## 5.1    News Datasets

In this paper, six news datasets[1] were evaluated, four of them are in English and two are in Portuguese. Table 3 presents detailed information about language, subject and amount of real and fake news present in each dataset. Fact-checked news (FCN) was collected from five Brazilian journalistic fact-checking sites to evaluate our approach. The second portuguese dataset is Fake.BR (FBR), the first reference corpus in Portuguese for fake news detection [17]. The third dataset was acquired from FakeNewsNet repository (FNN) [16], which contains news of famous people fact-checked by the *GossipCop* website. FakeNewsNet is the one with the greatest unbalance in the distribution of classes. The last three datasets are also written in English. The news was taken randomly from the FakeNewsCorpus dataset[2] (FNC0, FNC1, FNC2), an open source dataset composed of millions of news, collected from 1001 domains. Fake and real news were selected, and stopwords were extracted that could induce the behavior of classification algorithms, such as links and names of serious publication vehicles.

**Table 3.** Detailed information about news datasets.

| Dataset | FCN | FBR | FNN | FNC0 | FNC1 | FNC2 |
|---------|-----|-----|-----|------|------|------|
| Language | Portuguese | Portuguese | English | English | English | English |
| Subject | Politics | Politics, technology, daily life, celebrities, economics, religion | Celebrities | Multiple domains | Multiple domains | Multiple domains |
| Fake news | 1,044 | 3,600 | 1,705 | 3,000 | 3,000 | 3,000 |
| Real news | 1,124 | 3,600 | 5,298 | 3,000 | 3,000 | 3,000 |

---

[1] All datasets and source codes used in this paper are available in our public repository: https://github.com/marianacaravanti/A-Heterogeneous-Network-based-Positive-and-Unlabeled-Learning-Approach-to-Detecting-Fake-News.

[2] https://github.com/several27/FakeNewsCorpus.

## 5.2   Experimental Setup and Evaluation Criteria

This section presents the experiment configuration and evaluation criteria for the PU-LP and the baseline algorithms. After pre-processing, feature vectors for news representation were obtained considering two strategies: (i) A traditional BoW, with *tf-idf* as the term-weighting scheme; and (ii) D2V (Paragraph Vectors). In D2V we used the union of the models Distributed Memory and Distributed Bag-of-Words to generate the document embeddings. For training each of these models, we consider the average and concatenation of the word vectors to create the hidden layer's output. Also, we employed the range of the maximum number of epochs $\in \{100, 1000\}$, $\alpha = 0.025$ and $\alpha_{min} = 0.0001$, number of dimensions of each model $= 500$, window size $= 8$, and minimum count $= 1$ [8]. For the $k$-NN matrix used in PU-LP, we used $k = [5, 6, 7]$ and cosine as similarity measure. For the extraction of reliable interest and non-interest sets, we use: $m = 2$, $\lambda = [0.6, 0.8]$, and $\alpha = [0.005, 0.01, 0.02]$. These values were chosen as suggested in [9].

For the selection of representative unigrams and bigrams, we use $\ell = 0.08$. The parameter $\ell$ was chosen after a statistical analysis of the sample, indicating that about 25% of bag-of-words terms had tf-idf greater than 0.08. For the label propagation stage, as suggested in [14], we used a convergence threshold $= 0.00005$ and a maximum number of iterations $= 1,000$. For the GNM $\alpha = \{0.1, 0.5\}$ and $\lambda = 1$ was considered.

A 10-fold cross-validation adapted to OCL and PUL problems was used as a validation scheme. In this case, the set of fake news ($\mathcal{D}^+$) was randomly divided into 10 folds. In order to simulate a semi-supervised learning environment, in which the number of labeled examples is higher than the unlabeled examples, i.e., $|\mathcal{D}^+| \gg |\mathcal{D}^u|$, we carried out different experiments considering as labeled data 1, 2 or 3 folds. The remaining folds and the real news are: (i) considered as test documents for the OCL algorithm; (ii) considered as unlabeled and test documents for the PUL algorithms.

We proposed a baseline approach using binary semi-supervised learning to assess the labeling procedure of reliable-interest and reliable-non-interest examples in PU-LP. For this analysis, the set of real news was randomly divided into ten subsets. In the cross-validation scheme, for each fake news fold used to train the algorithm, one fold of real news was used. From the network obtained by $\mathcal{N}$ in PU-LP, and considering the training set as the set of labeled nodes, label propagation algorithms infer the class of the remaining news from the network. We considered the values of $k$ ranging in the interval $[5, 7]$. The propagation algorithms and their respective configurations are the same as the experiments performed with PU-LP.

As evaluation measure, we used $F_1 = (2 \cdot precision \cdot recall)/(precision + recall)$ considering the fake news as the positive class (interest-$F_1$)[3]. In the next section, the results of the experiments are presented.

## 5.3 Results and Discussions

Tables 4 and 5 present the the the best results for the interest-$F_1$ that each network reached considering BoW and D2V representation models for both PU-LP and binary semi-supervised baseline, the experimental configuration defined in Sect. 5.2, and the news datasets. Due to space limitations, we present the results obtained only with the GNM algorithm, which obtained better overall performance. The complete table of results is available in our public repository. 10%, 20%, and 30% indicate the percentage of news used to train the algorithms. Networks 1 to 12 have a combination of the features proposed in Sect. 4.3 (see Table 2). Table 6 presents the average ranking and standard deviation analysis of the proposed heterogeneous networks.

**Table 4.** Interest-$F_1$ of the PU-LP and binary baseline approaches with Bag-of-Words representation model, using GNetMine as label propagation.

| Bag-of-Words | | | | | | | | | | | | | | | | | |
|---|---|---|---|---|---|---|---|---|---|---|---|---|---|---|---|---|---|
| FNC | | | FBR | | | FNN | | | FNCO | | | FNC1 | | | FNC2 | | |
| 10% | 20% | 30% | 10% | 20% | 30% | 10% | 20% | 30% | 10% | 20% | 30% | 10% | 20% | 30% | 10% | 20% | 30% |
| Net | Positive and Unlabeled Learning by Label Propagation | | | | | | | | | | | | | | | | |
| 1 | 0.862 | 0.868 | 0.864 | 0.647 | 0.657 | 0.650 | 0.472 | 0.467 | 0.441 | 0.822 | 0.831 | 0.839 | 0.817 | 0.824 | 0.831 | 0.811 | 0.828 | 0.835 |
| 2 | **0.869** | **0.875** | **0.875** | **0.650** | **0.670** | 0.665 | 0.483 | 0.479 | 0.450 | 0.828 | 0.839 | 0.844 | **0.827** | **0.835** | 0.840 | **0.820** | 0.837 | 0.843 |
| 3 | 0.747 | 0.814 | 0.840 | 0.514 | 0.533 | 0.675 | 0.459 | 0.503 | 0.423 | 0.815 | 0.826 | 0.836 | 0.812 | 0.816 | 0.825 | 0.806 | 0.828 | 0.838 |
| 4 | 0.793 | 0.843 | 0.870 | 0.514 | 0.563 | 0.589 | 0.470 | 0.467 | 0.440 | 0.814 | 0.841 | 0.848 | 0.677 | 0.755 | 0.786 | 0.688 | 0.759 | 0.790 |
| 5 | 0.836 | 0.865 | 0.874 | 0.498 | 0.541 | 0.571 | 0.476 | 0.473 | **0.451** | 0.759 | 0.828 | 0.849 | 0.769 | 0.823 | 0.840 | 0.738 | 0.817 | 0.837 |
| 6 | 0.839 | 0.868 | 0.856 | 0.586 | 0.583 | **0.676** | 0.512 | **0.512** | 0.436 | 0.821 | 0.828 | 0.836 | 0.820 | 0.826 | 0.830 | 0.815 | 0.830 | 0.838 |
| 7 | 0.861 | 0.873 | 0.873 | 0.622 | 0.664 | 0.659 | 0.477 | 0.475 | 0.445 | **0.848** | **0.866** | **0.869** | 0.811 | 0.835 | **0.845** | 0.812 | **0.842** | **0.850** |
| 8 | 0.863 | 0.871 | 0.871 | 0.616 | 0.660 | 0.658 | 0.477 | 0.475 | 0.447 | 0.821 | 0.840 | 0.846 | 0.822 | 0.833 | 0.838 | 0.814 | 0.834 | 0.844 |
| 9 | 0.793 | 0.856 | 0.862 | 0.578 | 0.580 | 0.671 | **0.514** | 0.508 | 0.437 | 0.842 | 0.857 | 0.862 | 0.817 | 0.831 | 0.835 | 0.815 | 0.834 | 0.844 |
| 10 | 0.797 | 0.857 | 0.858 | 0.577 | 0.580 | 0.670 | 0.494 | 0.502 | 0.436 | 0.820 | 0.833 | 0.838 | 0.820 | 0.827 | 0.830 | 0.813 | 0.830 | 0.839 |
| 11 | 0.855 | 0.871 | 0.869 | 0.592 | 0.651 | 0.655 | 0.476 | 0.474 | 0.445 | 0.834 | 0.859 | 0.864 | 0.805 | 0.828 | 0.840 | 0.798 | 0.834 | 0.846 |
| 12 | 0.778 | 0.852 | 0.864 | 0.578 | 0.579 | 0.665 | 0.500 | 0.502 | 0.438 | 0.834 | 0.851 | 0.859 | 0.815 | 0.827 | 0.833 | 0.806 | 0.830 | 0.842 |
| Net | Binary Baseline with Semi-supervised Learning | | | | | | | | | | | | | | | | |
| 1 | 0.810 | 0.886 | 0.791 | 0.642 | 0.552 | 0.521 | 0.383 | 0.419 | 0.402 | 0.709 | 0.841 | 0.681 | 0.747 | 0.713 | 0.679 | 0.747 | 0.749 | 0.763 |
| 2 | **0.892** | **0.912** | **0.920** | **0.768** | 0.736 | 0.751 | 0.456 | 0.454 | 0.433 | **0.847** | **0.864** | **0.872** | **0.845** | **0.865** | **0.876** | **0.859** | **0.874** | **0.883** |
| 3 | 0.871 | 0.906 | 0.918 | 0.727 | 0.756 | 0.777 | 0.184 | 0.188 | 0.082 | 0.828 | 0.852 | 0.866 | 0.830 | 0.853 | 0.867 | 0.837 | 0.861 | 0.875 |
| 4 | 0.839 | 0.887 | 0.902 | 0.532 | 0.613 | 0.636 | 0.479 | **0.526** | **0.512** | 0.795 | 0.825 | 0.838 | 0.678 | 0.759 | 0.791 | 0.711 | 0.786 | 0.813 |
| 5 | 0.862 | 0.897 | 0.910 | 0.516 | 0.589 | 0.610 | 0.229 | 0.134 | 0.142 | 0.768 | 0.822 | 0.844 | 0.771 | 0.821 | 0.842 | 0.781 | 0.834 | 0.853 |
| 6 | 0.883 | 0.906 | 0.917 | 0.743 | **0.764** | **0.783** | 0.373 | 0.359 | 0.369 | 0.842 | 0.858 | 0.871 | 0.840 | 0.859 | 0.873 | 0.851 | 0.868 | 0.880 |
| 7 | 0.875 | 0.901 | 0.912 | 0.737 | 0.705 | 0.706 | **0.524** | 0.507 | 0.471 | 0.831 | 0.855 | 0.870 | 0.810 | 0.842 | 0.858 | 0.825 | 0.857 | 0.870 |
| 8 | 0.879 | 0.904 | 0.914 | 0.730 | 0.705 | 0.697 | 0.401 | 0.399 | 0.371 | 0.832 | 0.853 | 0.867 | 0.833 | 0.853 | 0.868 | 0.843 | 0.864 | 0.877 |
| 9 | 0.879 | 0.901 | 0.912 | 0.723 | 0.752 | 0.772 | 0.445 | 0.425 | 0.456 | 0.833 | 0.855 | 0.869 | 0.822 | 0.846 | 0.862 | 0.828 | 0.857 | 0.873 |
| 10 | 0.879 | 0.902 | 0.913 | 0.720 | 0.750 | 0.771 | 0.368 | 0.359 | 0.358 | 0.833 | 0.852 | 0.867 | 0.835 | 0.854 | 0.867 | 0.843 | 0.862 | 0.876 |
| 11 | 0.869 | 0.897 | 0.909 | 0.717 | 0.687 | 0.675 | 0.475 | 0.463 | 0.410 | 0.818 | 0.849 | 0.866 | 0.801 | 0.836 | 0.856 | 0.812 | 0.851 | 0.868 |
| 12 | 0.877 | 0.899 | 0.910 | 0.695 | 0.735 | 0.761 | 0.421 | 0.408 | 0.426 | 0.821 | 0.849 | 0.866 | 0.813 | 0.842 | 0.859 | 0.816 | 0.852 | 0.869 |

---

[3] We also evaluate the average of $F_1$ for both classes (macro-averaging $F_1$). Due to space limitations, the complete results are available in our public repository: https://github.com/marianacaravanti/A-Heterogeneous-Network-based-Positive-and-Unlabeled-Learning-Approach-to-Detecting-Fake-News/tree/main/Results.

On network 1 (Net 1), built only with news, we can see that overall PU-LP behaves better than the binary baseline, even using half of the labeled news. When exceptions occur, the results obtained tend to be very close, with less than 2% of difference. This demonstrates that identifying reliable fake news and inferring a real news set using the initially interest labeled set and Katz index, can be a promising strategy for news classification. In particular, using only 10% of labeled fake news and representation models that consider semantic relations such as D2V, can provide results as efficient as using larger training sets, which favors the dynamic scenario of news classification.

Including terms (Net 2) in the news network tends to improve classification performance in general, especially when news are represented with BoW (Table 4 and Table 5). Table 6 also shows that Net 2 obtained a better average ranking, with a low standard deviation, in relation to the other networks proposed. For BoW with 20% and 30% labeled data, including also pausality achieved better results (Net 7). The term selection considering the tf-idf measure above a threshold seems to contribute to distinguishing real and fake news by propagation algorithms, increasing the algorithm's accuracy.

**Table 5.** Interest-$F_1$ of the PU-LP and binary baseline approaches with Doc2Vec representation model, using GNetMine as label propagation.

| Doc2Vec | | | | | | | | | | | | | | | | | |
|---|---|---|---|---|---|---|---|---|---|---|---|---|---|---|---|---|---|
| FNC | | | FBR | | | FNN | | | FNCO | | | FNC1 | | | FNC2 | | |
| 10% | 20% | 30% | 10% | 20% | 30% | 10% | 20% | 30% | 10% | 20% | 30% | 10% | 20% | 30% | 10% | 20% | 30% |
| **Net** | **Positive and Unlabeled Learning by Label Propagation** | | | | | | | | | | | | | | | | |
| 1 | **0.911** | **0.916** | **0.921** | 0.598 | 0.636 | 0.642 | 0.511 | 0.508 | 0.496 | **0.901** | **0.908** | 0.905 | **0.886** | 0.875 | 0.876 | **0.881** | **0.895** | **0.899** |
| 2 | 0.904 | 0.913 | **0.921** | 0.622 | **0.659** | **0.667** | **0.527** | 0.518 | 0.503 | 0.889 | 0.906 | 0.906 | 0.883 | 0.875 | 0.879 | 0.872 | 0.892 | 0.897 |
| 3 | 0.798 | 0.855 | 0.834 | 0.491 | 0.528 | 0.634 | 0.479 | 0.519 | 0.521 | 0.881 | 0.894 | 0.895 | 0.867 | 0.862 | 0.865 | 0.854 | 0.877 | 0.885 |
| 4 | 0.814 | 0.878 | 0.901 | 0.536 | 0.563 | 0.570 | 0.493 | 0.485 | 0.472 | 0.860 | 0.876 | 0.884 | 0.777 | 0.846 | 0.877 | 0.788 | 0.850 | 0.873 |
| 5 | 0.848 | 0.893 | 0.907 | 0.526 | 0.546 | 0.555 | 0.491 | 0.499 | 0.490 | 0.861 | 0.889 | 0.895 | 0.868 | **0.877** | 0.881 | 0.859 | 0.871 | 0.867 |
| 6 | 0.870 | 0.904 | 0.868 | 0.562 | 0.576 | 0.634 | 0.519 | **0.529** | **0.531** | 0.881 | 0.896 | 0.896 | 0.875 | 0.867 | 0.871 | 0.863 | 0.880 | 0.889 |
| 7 | 0.883 | 0.901 | 0.914 | 0.596 | 0.637 | 0.643 | 0.512 | 0.497 | 0.479 | 0.893 | 0.907 | **0.909** | 0.870 | 0.875 | **0.884** | 0.863 | 0.876 | 0.886 |
| 8 | 0.888 | 0.902 | 0.914 | 0.591 | 0.633 | 0.641 | 0.517 | 0.503 | 0.481 | 0.878 | 0.896 | 0.900 | 0.875 | 0.872 | 0.875 | 0.864 | 0.879 | 0.888 |
| 9 | 0.842 | 0.894 | 0.858 | 0.551 | 0.571 | 0.634 | 0.515 | 0.515 | 0.516 | 0.885 | 0.895 | 0.901 | 0.872 | 0.871 | 0.875 | 0.862 | 0.872 | 0.883 |
| 10 | 0.843 | 0.895 | 0.859 | 0.550 | 0.570 | 0.634 | 0.508 | 0.517 | 0.525 | 0.878 | 0.894 | 0.895 | 0.875 | 0.868 | 0.870 | 0.862 | 0.875 | 0.885 |
| 11 | 0.875 | 0.897 | 0.910 | 0.577 | 0.623 | 0.634 | 0.511 | 0.497 | 0.475 | 0.881 | 0.900 | 0.904 | 0.866 | 0.873 | 0.881 | 0.858 | 0.868 | 0.882 |
| 12 | 0.828 | 0.889 | 0.855 | 0.549 | 0.568 | 0.634 | 0.507 | 0.511 | 0.513 | 0.880 | 0.891 | 0.897 | 0.872 | 0.870 | 0.875 | 0.860 | 0.866 | 0.879 |
| **Net** | **Binary Baseline with Semi-supervised Learning** | | | | | | | | | | | | | | | | |
| 1 | 0.831 | 0.833 | 0.822 | 0.470 | 0.471 | 0.471 | 0.139 | 0.157 | 0.157 | 0.905 | 0.905 | 0.930 | 0.814 | 0.814 | 0.730 | 0.894 | 0.904 | 0.901 |
| 2 | **0.929** | **0.932** | **0.940** | 0.716 | 0.739 | 0.727 | 0.292 | 0.304 | 0.320 | **0.931** | 0.929 | **0.939** | **0.922** | **0.924** | **0.932** | **0.908** | **0.922** | **0.929** |
| 3 | 0.859 | 0.909 | 0.931 | 0.721 | 0.738 | 0.755 | 0.160 | 0.081 | 0.043 | 0.921 | 0.921 | 0.931 | 0.907 | 0.907 | 0.919 | 0.893 | 0.907 | 0.917 |
| 4 | 0.854 | 0.893 | 0.913 | 0.570 | 0.570 | 0.589 | 0.408 | **0.443** | **0.459** | 0.887 | 0.887 | 0.898 | 0.848 | 0.848 | 0.877 | 0.779 | 0.853 | 0.880 |
| 5 | 0.876 | 0.906 | 0.921 | 0.544 | 0.544 | 0.558 | 0.133 | 0.063 | 0.029 | 0.905 | 0.905 | 0.920 | 0.900 | 0.900 | 0.914 | 0.876 | 0.899 | 0.913 |
| 6 | 0.917 | 0.921 | 0.936 | **0.741** | **0.748** | **0.758** | 0.307 | 0.332 | 0.315 | 0.922 | 0.921 | 0.932 | 0.910 | 0.911 | 0.924 | 0.898 | 0.911 | 0.921 |
| 7 | 0.911 | 0.914 | 0.929 | 0.683 | 0.690 | 0.711 | **0.463** | 0.452 | 0.447 | 0.917 | 0.916 | 0.930 | 0.903 | 0.905 | 0.918 | 0.885 | 0.905 | 0.918 |
| 8 | 0.913 | 0.917 | 0.930 | 0.644 | 0.682 | 0.674 | 0.292 | 0.317 | 0.310 | 0.919 | 0.918 | 0.929 | 0.909 | 0.910 | 0.922 | 0.896 | 0.909 | 0.921 |
| 9 | 0.915 | 0.918 | 0.932 | 0.705 | 0.725 | 0.726 | 0.422 | 0.409 | 0.413 | 0.915 | 0.914 | 0.928 | 0.903 | 0.904 | 0.916 | 0.886 | 0.902 | 0.915 |
| 10 | 0.915 | 0.919 | 0.932 | 0.697 | 0.720 | 0.719 | 0.334 | 0.347 | 0.322 | 0.917 | 0.916 | 0.927 | 0.906 | 0.907 | 0.918 | 0.894 | 0.905 | 0.916 |
| 11 | 0.906 | 0.911 | 0.926 | 0.694 | 0.663 | 0.719 | 0.416 | 0.403 | 0.406 | 0.911 | 0.909 | 0.925 | 0.898 | 0.899 | 0.913 | 0.875 | 0.897 | 0.911 |
| 12 | 0.912 | 0.917 | 0.930 | 0.658 | 0.687 | 0.690 | 0.405 | 0.394 | 0.396 | 0.911 | 0.910 | 0.924 | 0.886 | 0.906 | 0.922 | 0.878 | 0.897 | 0.911 |

Among the news datasets, only the FNN is unbalanced. FNN has only celebrity news, of which fake news is a minority making up only 24.3% of the dataset. For this dataset, the interest-$F_1$ always tends to be lower. However, we can notice that our proposal performed better than the binary baseline, which also points out the utility of PUL for fake news detection.

Lower results also occur in the FBR datasets. This behavior also happened in [5], in which 67% of the interest-$F_1$ was obtained using 90% labeled fake news and one-class learning algorithms. The hypothesis is that since this collection in composed of 6 different subjects, fake news from different subjects are spread along with the space, making it difficult to infer reliable negative documents. Therefore, we conclude that to achieve more promising results, the best way is to classify the news considering one subject at a time. Although the results achieved with these datasets are inferior, we can observe that the addition of extra information in the heterogeneous network was beneficial, especially for the baseline, which increases its interest-$F_1$ by more than 10%.

PU-LP obtained great results for FCN, FNC0, FNC1 and FNC2 news datasets. Using D2V as the representation model, the results ranged from 87 to 92% interest-$F_1$ only with news and terms on the network. These results are relevant, mainly because they consider an initially small set of labeled data, different from the vast majority of methods proposed in the literature for news classification.

**Table 6.** Average ranking and standard deviation analysis for the proposed heterogeneous networks.

| Average ranking analysis | | | | | | | | | | | |
| PU-LP | | | | | | Binary baseline | | | | | |
| BoW | | | D2V | | | BoW | | | D2V | | |
| Net 10% | 20% | 30% | 10% | 20% | 30% | 10% | 20% | 30% | 10% | 20% | 30% |
|---|---|---|---|---|---|---|---|---|---|---|---|
| 1 5.5 ± 2.9 | 8.0 ± 2.8 | 8.5 ± 1.9 | 2.0 ± 2.0 | 2.8 ± 2.4 | 3.5 ± 2.5 | 10.7 ± 1.5 | 10.7 ± 2.4 | 11.2 ± 2.0 | 10.3 ± 2.7 | 10.5 ± 2.0 | 10.3 ± 2.7 |
| 2 **2.3 ± 2.1** | 3.0 ± 2.7 | 4.0 ± 2.8 | **1.8 ± 0.7** | **2.3 ± 0.8** | **2.8 ± 1.8** | **1.5 ± 1.2** | **2.2 ± 1.8** | **2.3 ± 2.2** | **2.6 ± 3.0** | **2.5 ± 3.2** | **2.3 ± 2.4** |
| 3 10.2 ± 1.6 | 9.8 ± 3.5 | 9.7 ± 3.9 | 10.7 ± 1.9 | 8.3 ± 4.1 | 8.3 ± 3.9 | 7.0 ± 2.8 | 5.3 ± 3.2 | 5.5 ± 3.7 | 5.8 ± 3.4 | 5.7 ± 3.6 | 5.2 ± 3.1 |
| 4 11.2 ± 0.8 | 10.3 ± 2.7 | 8.8 ± 3.2 | 11.2 ± 0.9 | 11.5 ± 0.8 | 9.7 ± 2.9 | 9.7 ± 3.8 | 9.2 ± 4.0 | 9.2 ± 4.0 | 10.0 ± 3.0 | 9.7 ± 3.8 | 9.5 ± 4.2 |
| 5 10.3 ± 2.0 | 9.8 ± 1.5 | 5.5 ± 4.5 | 9.7 ± 1.6 | 8.3 ± 3.7 | 8.3 ± 3.9 | 10.7 ± 0.8 | 10.8 ± 1.0 | 10.2 ± 0.8 | 10.2 ± 1.5 | 10.3 ± 1.2 | 10.2 ± 1.5 |
| 6 4.7 ± 2.3 | 6.5 ± 3.3 | 8.5 ± 3.9 | 4.7 ± 1.5 | 4.7 ± 3.1 | 6.3 ± 3.5 | 3.2 ± 2.9 | 3.2 ± 3.4 | 3.2 ± 2.9 | 2.7 ± 2.2 | 2.8 ± 2.1 | 2.8 ± 2.6 |
| 7 5.0 ± 2.9 | **2.7 ± 2.7** | **3.0 ± 2.5** | 4.3 ± 2.1 | 4.7 ± 3.6 | 3.7 ± 3.4 | 5.3 ± 2.7 | 5.6 ± 2.5 | 5.7 ± 2.5 | 5.8 ± 2.6 | 5.3 ± 2.3 | 5.2 ± 2.3 |
| 8 4.2 ± 2.0 | 4.3 ± 1.7 | 5.2 ± 1.9 | 4.2 ± 2.4 | 5.3 ± 1.6 | 5.8 ± 2.2 | 4.3 ± 1.5 | 5.4 ± 2.0 | 5.2 ± 2.3 | 5.4 ± 2.7 | 5.3 ± 2.3 | 6.3 ± 2.5 |
| 9 4.5 ± 3.3 | 5.2 ± 2.8 | 5.5 ± 2.9 | 6.2 ± 1.9 | 6.9 ± 2.2 | 7.0 ± 2.2 | 5.2 ± 1.0 | 5.2 ± 1.5 | 4.7 ± 1.5 | 5.0 ± 2.0 | 5.7 ± 2.3 | 5.5 ± 2.1 |
| 10 6.5 ± 2.4 | 6.7 ± 1.2 | 8.5 ± 2.5 | 7.5 ± 1.8 | 7.4 ± 3.1 | 7.5 ± 3.1 | 5.3 ± 2.7 | 5.2 ± 2.1 | 5.5 ± 2.3 | 4.8 ± 1.2 | 4.8 ± 1.2 | 5.9 ± 1.7 |
| 11 7.0 ± 2.7 | 4.7 ± 2.4 | 4.5 ± 2.7 | 7.3 ± 2.6 | 7.0 ± 3.4 | 6.2 ± 3.1 | 7.8 ± 2.4 | 7.8 ± 2.4 | 8.7 ± 1.4 | 7.5 ± 2.7 | 8.5 ± 2.4 | 7.8 ± 2.4 |
| 12 6.7 ± 3.1 | 7.0 ± 2.5 | 6.3 ± 1.6 | 8.5 ± 1.0 | 8.3 ± 2.2 | 8.3 ± 2.2 | 7.3 ± 1.2 | 7.5 ± 1.0 | 6.8 ± 1.5 | 7.8 ± 1.9 | 6.8 ± 1.9 | 7.0 ± 2.8 |

## 6   Conclusion and Future Work

This paper proposed a new approach for detecting fake news based on PU-LP. Our main contributions were a heterogeneous network using content-based features resulting in a domain-independent fake news detection approach and a performance assessment of different linguistic features for fake news detection.

PU-LP achieves good classification performance using a low amount of labeled data from the interest class and uses unlabeled data to improve classification performance, minimizing the news labeling effort. Furthermore, since PU-LP is a PUL approach based on network, it allows the easy incorporation of other features to perform learning. We assessed the performance of a heterogeneous network that incorporates combinations of four different features based on terms and linguistic characteristics.

The results of our experimental analysis in six datasets from different languages and subjects indicate that our proposal can provide good classification performance even with a small amount labeled fake news. Incorporating additional linguistic information such as representative terms and pausality into the network improved classification performance. Our approach achieved performance similar to a binary classifier in all datasets, even requiring much lesser effort for data labeling. Future work intends to consider more powerful representation models, such as context-based, and use more efficient label propagation algorithms, such as those based on neural networks. We also intend to apply our approach to new datasets, which will allow us to perform statistical significance tests to better assess the results.

# References

1. Aggarwal, C.C.: Machine Learning for Text. Springer Publishing (2018). https://doi.org/10.1007/978-3-319-73531-3
2. Vargas, F.A., Pardo, T.A.S.: Studying dishonest intentions in Brazilian Portuguese texts. arXiv e-prints (2020)
3. Bekker, J., Davis, J.: Learning from positive and unlabeled data: a survey. Mach. Learn. **109**(4), 719–760 (2020). https://doi.org/10.1007/s10994-020-05877-5
4. Bondielli, A., Marcelloni, F.: A survey on fake news and rumour detection techniques. Inf. Sci. **497**, 38–55 (2019)
5. Faustini, P., Covões, T.F.: Fake news detection using one-class classification. In: 2019 8th Brazilian Conference on Intelligent Systems, pp. 592–597. IEEE (2019)
6. Greifeneder, R., Jaffe, M., Newman, E., Schwarz, N.: The Psychology of Fake News: Accepting, Sharing, and Correcting Misinformation. Routledge, Milton Park (2021)
7. Ji, M., Sun, Y., Danilevsky, M., Han, J., Gao, J.: Graph regularized transductive classification on heterogeneous information networks. In: European Conference on Machine Learning and Knowledge Discovery in Databases, pp. 570–586 (2010)
8. Le, Q., Mikolov, T.: Distributed representations of sentences and documents. In: International Conference on Machine Learning, pp. 1188–1196 (2014)
9. Ma, S., Zhang, R.: PU-LP: a novel approach for positive and unlabeled learning by label propagation. In: 2017 IEEE International Conference on Multimedia & Expo Workshops (ICMEW), pp. 537–542. IEEE (2017)
10. Pennebaker, J.W., Boyd, R.L., Jordan, K., Blackburn, K.: The development and psychometric properties of liwc2015. University of Texas, Technical report (2015)
11. Ren, Y., Wang, B., Zhang, J., Chang, Y.: Adversarial active learning based heterogeneous graph neural network for fake news detection. In: 2020 IEEE International Conference on Data Mining (ICDM), pp. 452–461. IEEE (2020)
12. Rossi, R.G.: Automatic text classification through network-based machine learning. Ph.D. thesis, University of São Paulo, Doctoral thesis (2016). (in Portuguese)
13. Santos, R.L.S., Pardo, T.A.S.: Fact-checking for Portuguese: knowledge graph and google search-based methods. In: Quaresma, P., Vieira, R., Aluísio, S., Moniz, H., Batista, F., Gonçalves, T. (eds.) PROPOR 2020. LNCS (LNAI), vol. 12037, pp. 195–205. Springer, Cham (2020). https://doi.org/10.1007/978-3-030-41505-1_19

14. Santos, B.N.: Transductive classification of events using heterogeneous networks. Master's Thesis - Federal University of Mato Grosso do Sul (2018). (in Portuguese)
15. Heterogeneous Information Network Analysis and Applications. DA. Springer, Cham (2017). https://doi.org/10.1007/978-3-319-56212-4_9
16. Shu, K., Mahudeswaran, D., Wang, S., Lee, D., Liu, H.: FakeNewsNet: a data repository with news content, social context, and spatiotemporal information for studying fake news on social media. Big Data 8(3), 171–188 (2020)
17. Silva, R.M., Santos, R.L., Almeida, T.A., Pardo, T.A.: Towards automatically filtering fake news in Portuguese. Expert Syst. Appl. **146**, 113–199 (2020)
18. Singh, V.K., Ghosh, I., Sonagara, D.: Detecting fake news stories via multimodal analysis. Assoc. Inf. Sci. Technol. **72**(1), 3–17 (2021)
19. Yu, J., Huang, Q., Zhou, X., Sha, Y.: IARnet: an information aggregating and reasoning network over heterogeneous graph for fake news detection. In: 2020 International Joint Conference on Neural Networks (IJCNN), pp. 1–9. IEEE (2020)
20. Yu, S., Li, C.: PE-PUC: a graph based PU-learning approach for text classification. In: Perner, P. (ed.) MLDM 2007. LNCS (LNAI), vol. 4571, pp. 574–584. Springer, Heidelberg (2007). https://doi.org/10.1007/978-3-540-73499-4_43
21. Zhang, J., Dong, B., Philip, S.Y.: Deep diffusive neural network based fake news detection from heterogeneous social networks. In: Big Data 2019: International Conference on Big Data, pp. 1259–1266. IEEE (2019)
22. Zhang, X., Ghorbani, A.A.: An overview of online fake news: characterization, detection, and discussion. Inf. Process. Manage. **57**(2), 102025 (2020)
23. Zhu, X., Ghahramani, Z., Lafferty, J.D.: Semi-supervised learning using gaussian fields and harmonic functions. In: Proceedings of the 20th International Conference on Machine Learning (ICML-2003), pp. 912–919 (2003)

# Anomaly Detection in Brazilian Federal Government Purchase Cards Through Unsupervised Learning Techniques

Breno Nunes[1] , Tiago Colliri[2]([✉]) , Marcelo Lauretto[3] , Weiguang Liu[4], and Liang Zhao[5]

[1] Brazilian Office of the Comptroller General (CGU), Brasilia, Brazil
breno.nunes@cgu.gov.br
[2] Department of Computer Science, University of Fortaleza (UNIFOR), Fortaleza, Brazil
tcolliri@alumni.usp.br
[3] School of Arts, Science and Humanities, University of Sao Paulo, Sao Paulo, Brazil
marcelolauretto@usp.br
[4] School of Computer Science, Zhongyuan University of Technology, Zhengzhou, China
weiguang.liu@zut.edu.cn
[5] Faculty of Philosophy, Science and Letters, University of Sao Paulo, Ribeirao Preto, Brazil
zhao@usp.br

**Abstract.** The Federal Government Purchase Card (CPGF) has been used in Brazil since 2005, allowing agencies and entities of the federal public administration to make purchases of material and provision of services through this method. Although this payment system offers several advances, in the technological and administrative aspect, it is also susceptible to possible cases of card misuse and, consequently, waste of public funds, in the form of purchases that do not comply with the terms of the current legislation. In this work, we approach this problem by testing and evaluating unsupervised learning techniques on detecting anomalies in CPGF historical data. Four different methods are considered for this task: K-means, agglomerative clustering, a network-based approach, which is also introduced in this study, and a hybrid model. The experimental results obtained indicate that unsupervised methods, in particular the network-based approach, can indeed help in the task of monitoring government purchase card expenses, by flagging suspect

This research was funded by CEPID-CeMEAI – Center for Mathematical Sciences Applied to Industry (grant 2013/07375-0, Sao Paulo Research Foundation–FAPESP), and was carried out at the Center for Artificial Intelligence (C4AI-USP), with also support from the Sao Paulo Research Foundation (FAPESP) under grant number: 2019/07665-4 and by the IBM Corporation. This work is also supported in part by FAPESP under grant numbers 2015/50122-0, the Brazilian National Council for Scientific and Technological Development (CNPq) under grant number 303199/2019-9, and the Ministry of Science and Technology of China under grant number: G20200226015

A. Britto and K. Valdivia Delgado (Eds.): BRACIS 2021, LNAI 13074, pp. 19–32, 2021.
https://doi.org/10.1007/978-3-030-91699-2_2

transactions for further investigation without requiring the presence of a specialist in this process.

**Keywords:** Anomaly detection · Government purchase cards · Unsupervised learning · Complex networks.

# 1   Introduction

In the last years, the credit card market has been rapidly increasing in Brazil and worldwide, trading a total amount of more than R$ 1.1 trillion in 2019, only in Brazil, which represents a growth of almost 20% over the previous year [1]. The availability of easy to use and practicality led government agencies from several countries to also adopt the use of this payment method. However, with the credit card market transacting increasingly larger volumes, the detection of fraud and anomalies has become one of the biggest challenges faced by companies in this branch [18]. It is estimated that, annually, fraud and anomalies in the use of credit cards generate losses of billions of dollars worldwide.

In Brazil, the Federal Government Purchase Card (CPGF, in Portuguese) was instituted in 2001 by means of a presidential decree, but its use only started in 2005 when it was regulated by another presidential decree [17]. The CPGF allows agencies and entities of the federal public administration that are part of the fiscal budget and of the social security to make purchases of material and provision of services, under the terms of the current legislation. The CPGF is issued in the name of the management unit of each agency, with the nominal identification of its bearer. Due to its specificity, the main concern regarding the CPGF is not related to fraud – in the sense of theft and/or cloning cases – but in the detection of possible anomalies that can help to identify expenses not covered by the current legislation, thus raising possible misuse of CPGF and, consequently, public funds. In this sense, in an attempt to bring transparency to CPGF expenses, the Brazilian Transparency Portal [19] presents a series of information regarding its transactions, such as: expenses by type of card, by cardholders and favored. Nevertheless, despite the efforts from the Brazilian Transparency Portal to transform the public spending technical data, especially expenses made on the CPGF, into information intelligible to the society in general, this promotion of social control does not fully achieve its objective, since this information, as it is currently presented, does not point out possible anomalies in the application of public resources. Therefore, studies detecting possible anomalies in these data can help to identify non-compliant transactions and potential misuse of the CPGF.

Machine learning techniques for detecting fraud/anomalies can be divided into two main approaches: *supervised* and *unsupervised* ones [18]. In the supervised approach, the dataset used to train the model needs to be labeled as legitimate or fraudulent transactions. In the case of credit cards, such labels often do not exist in the dataset, and the suggested approach, in this case, is the unsupervised one. Several studies have been developed over the years, in different areas, on the identification of anomalies using unsupervised machine learning models. One of these works [14], which can be applied in different areas such as financial transactions and industrial machines, focus on the detection of anomalies in time series, proposing a fast and efficient anomaly detection scheme focusing on fluctuation features, thus being capable of handling non-extreme fluctuation anomalies involved in periodic patterns. In the specific area of fraud detection in financial transactions, an unsupervised deep learning model was used to classify Brazilian exporters regarding the possibility of committing fraud in exports [16]. There is also a study [8] which combines unsupervised and supervised learning, in a complementary form: while supervised techniques learn from the fraudulent behaviors of the past, unsupervised techniques are aimed at detecting new types of fraud in the present. Another particularly related study [3] proposes a methodology for detecting anomalies in government purchases, in the form of public bids, through the use of frequent pattern mining, temporal correlation and joint multi-criteria analysis, obtaining results that are in line with those previously and independently gathered by specialists from the Office of the Comptroller General (CGU), through former audits and inspections.

In this work, we investigate anomalies detection in an unsupervised manner, by using real data from CPGF with the main objective of public transparency, i.e., in an attempt to identify purchases that do not comply with the current legislation for the set of goods and services that can be purchased through this payment method. To this end, four different machine learning techniques are tested: two clustering methods (K-means and agglomerative clustering), a network-based approach, which is also introduced in this work, and a hybrid model, based both on networks and the K-means method. We apply these techniques on historical CPGF expenses real data from Brazilian public agencies, occurred in 2018 and 2019. The experimental results obtained indicate that unsupervised methods have the potential to help in the task of monitoring government purchase card expenses, by flagging suspect transactions for further investigation without requiring the presence of a specialist in this process.

## 2   Materials and Methods

The dataset used in this study was built from original data obtained in the Brazilian Transparency Portal [19], comprising a total amount of R\$ 55,048,553 in CPGF expenses, from 211,896 different transactions, performed by 175 public agencies, in 2018 and 2019. We focus our analyses on data from two public agencies which were among the top largest spenders during this period: Army Command and Ministry of Agriculture, Livestock and Food Supply (Table 1).

In Fig. 1, we show the frequency histogram of all values and also the ones from the 10 most frequent types of expense, from Ministry of Agriculture CPGF data. One can observe, from this figure, that the values are concentrated in smaller transactions. We also note that, overall, the values do not seem to follow a normal distribution, and may present different curve shapes, according to the expense type.

**Table 1.** Summary of the data used in the analysis

| Public agency | Transactions | Total amount (R$) |
|---|---|---|
| Army command | 13,550 | 5,478,177 |
| Ministry of agriculture | 9,450 | 2,930,626 |

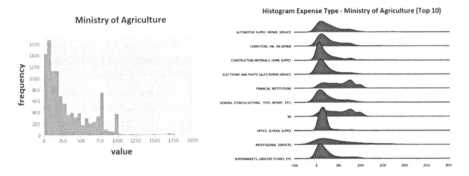

**Fig. 1.** Frequency histogram of all values and of the 10 most frequent types of expense, from Ministry of Agriculture CPGF data.

For the anomaly detection task, four different unsupervised techniques are tested: K-means [15], agglomerative clustering [12], a network-based approach, also introduced in this study, and a hybrid model, based on complex networks and the K-means method. Following, we describe each one of them in more details.

### 2.1 K-Means Method

The idea of the K-means algorithm is to group $n$ objects of a sample into $k$ clusters by minimizing the moment of inertia of each cluster, i.e., by making the data within each cluster as close as possible. K-means uses the squared Euclidean distance to calculate the inertia or, as it is also known, the Within-Cluster Sum of Square - WCSS. Therefore, the total inertia of a dataset can be denoted as follows:

$$\sum_{i=1}^{k} \sum_{x \in C_i} \|x - \mu_i\|^2 \quad , \tag{1}$$

which means that for all points $x$ that are in cluster $C_i$, the square of the distances from each point to the center of the cluster $\mu_i$ is summed up, and to find the total inertia, we just sum all the inertia values of each of the $k$ clusters in the dataset.

One of the problems of the K-means algorithm is that it is extremely sensitive to the centroids starting conditions. This problem can be addressed through the initialization scheme called K-means $^{++}$ [6]. In this method, the first centroid is selected randomly, and the others are selected based on the distance to the first one. In this way, K-means [++] reduces the likelihood of bad starting conditions by selecting the initial centroids that are usually far from each other. The best number of clusters $k$ in this technique is found using the elbow method [4], and the initialization parameter is adjusted by the K-means [++] technique.

## 2.2  Agglomerative Clustering Method

Agglomerative clustering is a bottom-up hierarchical clustering algorithm where the hierarchy of clusters is represented as a tree, called a dendrogram. The root of the dendrogram is the single cluster that contains all the samples, whereas the leaves are the clusters where each sample would be considered as a cluster. In this study, the dendrogram is created by using the Ward linkage method [20], that seeks to minimize the sum of the square of the differences within all clusters. This is an approach which minimizes the variance and, in this respect, is somewhat similar to the K-means function, but from a hierarchical perspective.

For determining the number of clusters to be considered for this technique, we set a threshold value and draw a horizontal line that cuts the tallest vertical line in the dendrogram, and take the number of vertical lines which are intersected by the line drawn using the threshold as the number of clusters to be used in the analysis. In this case, as one can observe from Fig. 2, the number of clusters has been defined as 3, both for Ministry of Agriculture and Army Command data.

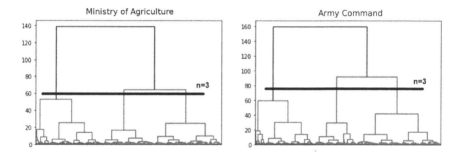

**Fig. 2.** Dendrograms generated from Ministry of Agriculture (left) and Army Command data (right), for the hierarchical agglomerative clustering analysis.

## 2.3  Network-Based Approach

In the last years, driven by technological advances and by the increase in the number of data available to be analyzed, the area of *complex networks* has emerged as a topic capable of unifying complex systems, and is currently present in several branches of science [5]. A network can be defined as a graph $\mathcal{G} = (\mathcal{V}, \mathcal{E})$, where $\mathcal{V}$ is a set of nodes, $\mathcal{V} = \{v_1, v_2, ..., v_n\}$, and $\mathcal{E}$ is a set of tuples, $\mathcal{E} = \{(i, j) : i, j \in \mathcal{V}\}$, representing the edges between each pair of nodes. One of the most evident characteristics in complex networks is the presence of communities. The notion of community is straightforward: each community is defined as a subgraph (or subnet) whose vertices are densely interconnected and, at the same time, these vertices have little connection with the rest of the network. A traditional way of detecting communities in a network is through the use of the *modularity* measure, which, broadly speaking, compares the number of connections between vertices which share a same characteristic with the expected number of connections when occurred randomly [7]. The *fast greedy* algorithm [9], for example, determines the optimal number of communities in the network by maximizing the modularity score of the graph.

Although there are currently already different graph-based methods for detecting anomalies [2], for this study, we have opted for developing and testing a novel one for the considered task. The network-based approach introduced in this work is inspired on a technique originally conceived for detecting periodicity in time series, such as in weather-related data [13]. The same technique had also already inspired the developing of a network-based model to identify up and down price trend patterns in the stock market, using real data [10,11] and, in this study, we adapt it in order to detect anomalies in Federal Government Payment Cards (CPGF) data.

We start by grouping the daily CPGF expenses data, in the form of weekly averaged values, considering only the days where there were at least one card transaction. Afterwards, we calculate the variations in the weekly time series, using a sliding window, in the form of an array $X$. This array is then sorted in ascending order, by weekly variations, and split into $n$ ranges with the same length $l$. In the original study [13], $l$ is defined as $\sqrt{t}$, where $t$ is the total length of $X$ and, in this work, we opt to set $l = \sqrt[3]{t}$, thus increasing the number of ranges $n$ in the series, to better adapt the technique for the outlier detection task. These ranges can be represented by a list $R = [r_0, r_1, r_2..., r_{n-1}]$ ordered from low to high ranges. More specifically, each range $r_q \in R$ is an interval defined as follows:

$$r_q = \begin{cases} [\min(X), X_{[1/n]}] & \text{if } q = 0; \\ ]X_{[(q-1)/n]}, X_{[q/n]}] & \text{if } q \in (1, \ldots, n-2); \\ ]X_{[(q-1)/n]}, \max(X)] & \text{if } q = n-1, \end{cases} \qquad (2)$$

where $X_{[qt]}$ denotes the empirical $qt$-quantile of $X$, $qt \in [0, 1]$.

Every range $r_q \in R$ will be mapped as a vertex $v_q \in \mathcal{V}$ in the network $\mathcal{G}(\mathcal{V}, \mathcal{E})$. For this end, we label every range of $R$ as a sequence of integers $[0, 1, 2..., n-1]$ in the same order they appeared in $R$, that will be used to represent the indexes of an adjacency matrix $A$, and also to store the variation ranges in $R$ as node attributes in the set of nodes $\mathcal{V}$, from network $\mathcal{G}$. Initially, $A$ is considered a null matrix, of size $n \times n$. Two vertices $v_q$ and $v_w$ will become connected if there are two consecutive observations $x_i$ and $x_{i+1}$ in the series located in the different ranges $r_q$ and $r_w$, i.e., if they ever appeared consecutively in the series, chronologically. In this case, we have that $A_{q,w} = A_{w,q} = 1$. The graph resulting from repeating this process to all pairs of consecutive observations in $X$ is an undirected one. The overall procedure for generating the network is described in Algorithm 1.

---

**Algorithm 1.** Adjacency matrix A generation.

---

    **Input:** CPGF spending data $X$, with weekly variations
    **Output:** adjacency matrix $A$
1: **procedure** GET ADJACENCY MATRIX A($X$)
2:    $X \leftarrow$ sort by weekly variation, in ascending order
3:    $R \leftarrow \text{ranges}(X, n)$, with same length $l$ and values rounded down
4:    $X \leftarrow$ sort again by chronological order
5:    $A \leftarrow$ zero matrix $(n \times n)$
6:    $t \leftarrow$ length of $X$
7:    **for** $i = 0$ to $t - 1$ **do**
8:        $r1 \leftarrow \text{range}(R, x_i)$
9:        $r2 \leftarrow \text{range}(R, x_{i+1})$
10:       **if** $r1 \neq r2$ **then**
11:         $A_{r1,r2} = 1$
12:         $A_{r2,r1} = 1$
    **return** $A$

---

In Fig. 3, we provide an illustration showing the application of the network-based technique on a simple time series, comprising only 12 observed weekly values. In this case, the array is divided into 6 equal parts with two observations in each of them, i.e., $\sqrt[3]{12}$, creating variation ranges $R = [r_0, r_1, r_2, r_3, r_4, r_5]$. These values are then mapped as nodes in the network $\mathcal{G}$, with the links between them being generated according to whether they ever appeared consecutively in the original time series, pairwise. Please note that, according to this rule, the node 4 is the one with highest degree in the network.

The resulting network $\mathcal{G}$ can be used to identify anomalies and spending oscillation patterns in the CPGF time series, based on the topological structure of the data. Given that two vertices in the network $\mathcal{G}$ will be connected by a link only if they are immediately next to each other, chronologically, at any point in the weekly time series, then the variation ranges in $\mathcal{G}$ will indicate how distant a certain weekly spending value is from the weekly spending value from a certain number of weeks ago, used as sliding window, and the network topological structure will reflect the overall spending oscillation pattern for the CPGF data, with subsequent and similar variation ranges tending to be connected and closer to each other. In this way, most weekly variation values in $X$ will be less or equal the highest range returned by the nodes in $\mathcal{G}$. When there is an exception to this rule, i.e., when a spending data instance in $X$ presents a weekly variation bigger than the variation ranges represented in $\mathcal{V}$, then it will be labeled as an outlier in the results output. This procedure is described in Algorithm 2.

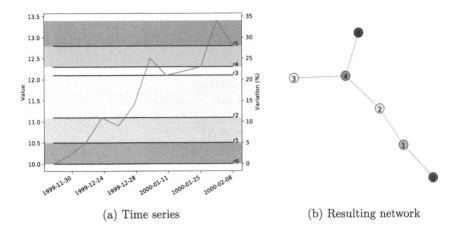

(a) Time series          (b) Resulting network

**Fig. 3.** Example demonstrating how the variation ranges in the original dataset $X$ are defined and then mapped as nodes in the network $\mathcal{G}$, in the network-based approach. For the sake of simplification, there are only 12 weekly observations in this time series, and the variations are calculated based on the initial value, instead of on a sliding window. (a) After sorting the series by variation values, in ascending order, the array is split into 6 equal parts, hence delimiting the ranges $r_0$ to $r_5$. (b) Each range will become a node in the network $\mathcal{G}$, and two nodes will be connected only if they ever appeared consecutively in the original time series, chronologically.

---

**Algorithm 2.** Anomaly detection.

---

    **Input:** CPGF weekly spending data $X$, variation ranges network $\mathcal{G}(\mathcal{V}, \mathcal{E})$
    **Output:** Data instances' labels list
1: **procedure** GET LABELS($X$)
2:     $l \leftarrow [\ ]$
3:     $t \leftarrow$ length of $X$
4:     **for** $i = 0$ to $t - 1$ **do**
5:         **if** $x_i \leq$ max of variation ranges represented in $\mathcal{V}$ **then**
6:             $l_i \leftarrow$ corresponding variation range $r_v$ in $\mathcal{V}$
7:         **else**
8:             $l_i \leftarrow$ outlier label
    **return** $l$

---

It is also worth mentioning that, since the variation ranges in $R$ are generated based on a sliding window, there is the possibility of regulating the model's sensitivity when detecting sudden or progressive spending increases, with smaller window values resulting in a higher sensitivity to detect possible anomalies over time. Another useful feature of the proposed approach is in the fact that the communities detected in the resulting network $\mathcal{G}$ can be used as some sort of spending variation "thermometer", so to speak, such that by looking at which community a certain spending value belongs to, then one can use it as an indicator of how far its variation is from the spending average from a certain number of weeks ago, used as sliding window.

## 2.4  Hybrid Approach

We also test a hybrid model in the anomaly detection task on CPGF data, consisting of taking the weekly averaged values and variation ranges generated by the network-based approach, pairwise, and grouping them using the K-means algorithm. For this end, as preprocessing, all variation values are converted to the logarithmic scale. In this approach, the best number of clusters $k$ is achieved using the elbow method [4] as well, being defined as $k = 4$. To reduce the sensibility to the centroids starting condition, the K-means $^{++}$ method is also used to adjust the initialization parameter.

# 3  Experimental Results

In this section, we present the results obtained when applying the four techniques to detect anomalies in the CPGF data.

We start by showing the results obtained from the K-means and agglomerative clustering techniques, in Fig. 4. In both of these methods, the identification of points of attention as possible anomalies in the use of CPGF had been pointed out by specialists from the business area, who are familiar with the purchasing process in this modality, through the analysis of the generated plots. In this manner, the points identified in red are those that can be further investigated as possible cases of CPGF misuse. As one can observe, the clusters and anomalies returned by the two grouping approaches for the considered period are very alike, with the main difference between them being in the number of clusters generated.

From the results obtained by both K-means and agglomerative clustering techniques, the specialists from the business area were able to identify a total of 10 transactions as possible cases of CPGF misuse for the Army Command, with two of them amounting to around R$ 30,000 each. As for the results obtained for the Ministry of Agriculture, the specialists were able to identify 5 transactions as suspected, with values around R$ 2,000 each. It is also worth noting that the clusters generated by these techniques were more influenced by the transaction values than by the type of expenditure, as can be observed by their flat shape in Fig. 4.

With regard to the network-based approach, we present, in Fig. 5, the variations range networks resulting from the application of this method on the CPGF time series, using a 12-weeks sliding window, i.e., around 3 months of card transactions. Each node in these networks corresponds to one variation range in the time series. For detecting communities in the network, we use the fast greedy algorithm [9]. Both networks, in this case, present 3 communities, which can be used as some sort of "thermometer" to indicate how far a certain weekly value is from the weekly average from 12-weeks ago. In this way, for monitoring purposes, values from communities with higher variation ranges would trigger more attention than values from lower and in-between communities.

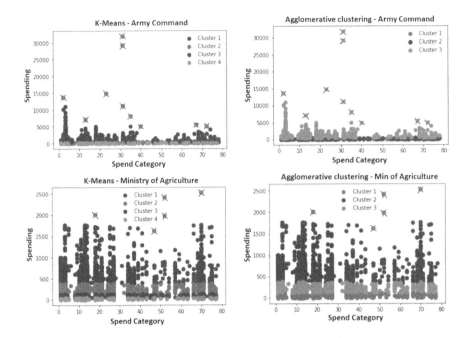

**Fig. 4.** Results obtained with the K-means and agglomerative clustering techniques. The highlighted values indicate possible anomalies in the use of CPGF, identified by specialists from the business area.

In Fig. 6, we present the results obtained with the network-based approach, showing the CPGF weekly time series, for each public agency, and respective outliers detected during the considered period. The main difference we note in these results, when compared to the ones provided by the K-means and agglomerative clustering methods, is that this method was able to point out, regardless of the identification from specialists in the business area, values considered outliers in the time series, based on the chosen 12-weeks sliding window variation. This feature is important as it can contribute to optimize the anomalies-identification process in this area, thus allowing the specialists team to have more focus on monitoring and investigation activities.

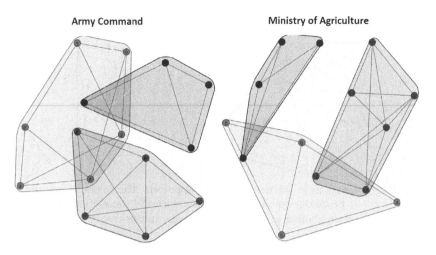

**Fig. 5.** Variation ranges networks resulting from CPGF data of Army Command and Ministry of Agriculture.

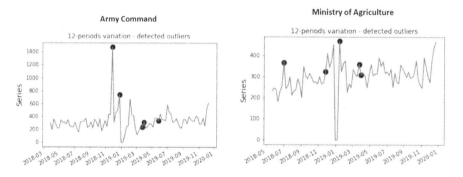

**Fig. 6.** Results obtained with the network-based approach, using a 12-weeks sliding window. The points in black indicate possible anomalies in the use of CPGF returned by the model for the considered period.

In Fig. 7, we show the weekly variations and the communities identified in the CPGF time series, still according to the chosen 12-weeks sliding window. As mentioned earlier, this plot, with the identification of communities, can be used as an alert indicator for certain values of the time series, where communities with higher variation ranges would raise the alert level for possible suspect transactions, with values increasingly becoming more distant from the average of 12 weeks ago. Hence, this type of representation, which is also provided in the results from the network-based approach, can be helpful, as an additional graphical resource, in the activity of monitoring the CPGF transactions.

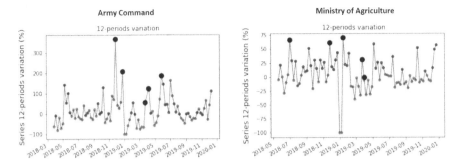

**Fig. 7.** Weekly variations in the network-based approach. The colors denote the communities, that can be used as an indicator of how much the transaction values deviate from those of a certain number of weeks ago (12 weeks, in this case, which is the chosen sliding window).

Finally, we show, in Fig. 8, the results obtained with the hybrid approach, which consists of taking the information generated by the network-based method, i.e., the weekly averaged values and variation ranges, pairwise, and grouping them using the K-means algorithm. In this technique, the values highlighted can be considered outliers. However, in the same manner of the grouping models, this identification had been carried out by specialists from the business area.

## 4   Final Remarks

In this work, four different unsupervised learning techniques were tested and evaluated on detecting anomalies in data from Brazilian Federal Government purchase cards (CPGF). The obtained experimental results indicate that the K-means and agglomerative clustering methods were not able to provide a clear output, in terms of information to help in the identification of values that can configure possible misuse of the card. On the other hand, the network-based approach, also introduced in this study, demonstrated to be more successful in this task, as it was the only technique able to automatically infer some points of attention that can be used as a starting point for further investigations. The hybrid model obtained more clear results when compared to the first two clustering techniques, and has potential to be used as well in the initial process of identifying misuse of CPGF.

It is important to note that the results obtained in the anomaly detection task, in this case, depend heavily on the definition of some factors inherent to the knowledge of the business areas from the Controller General office, such as: what are the more suitable sliding window values to make comparisons, what are the more suitable grouping periods for transactions (weekly, biweekly etc.) and what would be the threshold, for each public agency, to define which payments worth a deeper investigation and which ones can be neglected. All of these parameters have proved to be relevant to the results obtained in this study.

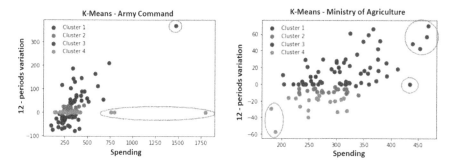

**Fig. 8.** Results obtained with the hybrid approach. The highlighted values indicate possible anomalies in the use of CPGF, identified by specialists from the business area.

We believe that one of the strengths of this research lies in its social contribution aspect, especially when we consider that currently only a few amount of people know how to properly use the Brazilian Transparency Portal and gather relevant information from this source. Therefore, we expect that our work can contribute to improve this scenario, by bringing more attention to the importance of this tool for the population in general, in order to increase the government accountability level in Brazil.

Finally, from the values identified as outliers in the models, especially those returned by the network-based and hybrid approaches, one can evolve to develop a more detailed measurement in order to ascertain whether in fact these identified transactions represent a misuse of the CPGF. In this way, the overall process could hence evolve to a semi-supervised learning approach and, later, to supervised models.

# References

1. ABECS: Brazilian association of credit card and services companies. www.abecs. org.br. Accessed 2 July 2020
2. Akoglu, L., Tong, H., Koutra, D.: Graph based anomaly detection and description: a survey. Data Mining Knowl. Disc. **29**(3), 626–688 (2015)
3. de Andrade, P.H.M.A., Meira, W., Cerqueira, B., Cruz, G.: Auditing government purchases with a multicriteria anomaly detection strategy. J. Inf. Data Manage. **11**(1), 50–65 (2020)
4. Bholowalia, P., Kumar, A.: EBK-means: a clustering technique based on elbow method and k-means in WSN. Int. J. Comput. Appl. **105**(9) (2014)
5. Bornholdt, S., Schuster, H.G.: Handbook of graphs and networks. From Genome to the Internet, Willey-VCH (2003 Weinheim) (2001)
6. Bradley, P.S., Fayyad, U.M.: Refining initial points for k-means clustering. In: ICML, vol. 98, pp. 91–99. Citeseer (1998)
7. Brandes, U., et al.: On modularity clustering. IEEE Trans. Knowl. Data Eng. **20**(2), 172–188 (2007)

8. Carcillo, F., Le Borgne, Y.A., Caelen, O., Kessaci, Y., Oblé, F., Bontempi, G.: Combining unsupervised and supervised learning in credit card fraud detection. Inf. Sci. **557**, 317–331 (2019)
9. Clauset, A., Newman, M.E., Moore, C.: Finding community structure in very large networks. Phys. Rev. E **70**(6), 066111 (2004)
10. Colliri, T., Zhao, L.: A network-based model for optimizing returns in the stock market. In: 2019 8th Brazilian Conference on Intelligent Systems (BRACIS), pp. 645–650 (2019). https://doi.org/10.1109/BRACIS.2019.00118
11. Colliri, T., Zhao, L.: Stock market trend detection and automatic decision-making through a network-based classification model. Nat. Comput. 1–14 (2021). https://doi.org/10.1007/s11047-020-09829-9
12. Day, W.H., Edelsbrunner, H.: Efficient algorithms for agglomerative hierarchical clustering methods. J. Classif. **1**(1), 7–24 (1984)
13. Ferreira, L.N., Zhao, L.: Detecting time series periodicity using complex networks. In: 2014 Brazilian Conference on Intelligent Systems, pp. 402–407. IEEE (2014)
14. Li, J., Di, S., Shen, Y., Chen, L.: FluxEV: a fast and effective unsupervised framework for time-series anomaly detection. In: Proceedings of the 14th ACM International Conference on Web Search and Data Mining, pp. 824–832 (2021)
15. Likas, A., Vlassis, N., Verbeek, J.J.: The global k-means clustering algorithm. Pattern Recogn. **36**(2), 451–461 (2003)
16. Paula, E.L., Ladeira, M., Carvalho, R.N., Marzagao, T.: Deep learning anomaly detection as support fraud investigation in Brazilian exports and anti-money laundering. In: 2016 15th IEEE International Conference on Machine Learning and Applications (ICMLA), pp. 954–960. IEEE (2016)
17. Republica, P.: Decreto 5.355 de 25 de janeiro de 2005. www.planalto.gov.br/ccivil03/ato2004-2006/2005/decreto/d5355.htm. Accessed 7 May 2021
18. Rezapour, M.: Anomaly detection using unsupervised methods: credit card fraud case study. Int. J. Adv. Comput. Sci. Appl. **10**(11), 1–8 (2019)
19. da Uniao, B.C.G.: Portal da transparencia. Gastos por cartoes de pagamento. www.portaltransparencia.gov.br/cartoes?ano=2019. Accessed 27 June 2020
20. Ward, J.H., Jr.: Hierarchical grouping to optimize an objective function. J. Am. Stat. Assoc. **58**(301), 236–244 (1963)

# De-Identification of Clinical Notes Using Contextualized Language Models and a Token Classifier

Joaquim Santos[1], Henrique D. P. dos Santos[2]([⊠]), Fábio Tabalipa[3],
and Renata Vieira[1]

[1] CIDEHUS, University of Évora, Évora, Portugal
d47240@alunos.uevora.pt, renatav@uevora.pt
[2] Institute of Artificial Intelligence in Healthcare, Porto Alegre, Brazil
henrique@noharm.ai
[3] Memed, Clinical Intelligence Department, São Paulo, Brazil
fabio.tabalipa@memed.com.br

**Abstract.** The de-identification of clinical notes is crucial for the reuse of electronic clinical data and is a common Named Entity Recognition (NER) task. Neural language models provide a great improvement in Natural Language Processing (NLP) tasks, such as NER, when they are integrated with neural network methods. This paper evaluates the use of current state-of-the-art deep learning methods (Bi-LSTM-CRF) in the task of identifying patient names in clinical notes, for de-identification purposes. We used two corpora and three language models to evaluate which combination delivers the best performance. In our experiments, the specific corpus for the de-identification of clinical notes and a contextualized embedding with word embeddings achieved the best result: an F-measure of 0.94.

**Keywords:** De-identification · Clinical notes · Language model · Token classifier

## 1 Introduction

With the growth of Artificial Intelligence, predictions based on Electronic Health Records (EHRs) are becoming increasingly viable. As EHRs consolidate information from all patient timelines, they may be processed as input for machine learning models to build Clinical Decision Support Systems (CDSS), to improve hospital workflows. Several studies show the potential of using EHR data for comorbidity index prediction [24], fall event detection [26], and bringing smart screening systems to pharmacy services [23], along with many other possibilities [13].

This work was partially supported by Institute of Artificial Intelligence in Healthcare, Memed, Google Latin America Research Awards, and by FCT under the project UIDB/00057/2020 (Portugal).

© Springer Nature Switzerland AG 2021
A. Britto and K. Valdivia Delgado (Eds.): BRACIS 2021, LNAI 13074, pp. 33–41, 2021.
https://doi.org/10.1007/978-3-030-91699-2_3

Removing patient-identifiable health information is a prerequisite to conduct research over clinical notes [5]. In the United States, the Health Insurance Portability and Accountability Act (HIPAA) listed 18 types of personally identifiable information (PII) [7]. De-identification is the process of finding and removing PII from electronic health records.

De-identification is a typical Named Entity Recognition (NER) problem, part of the Natural Language Processing (NLP) field. The current state-of-the-art approach for NER problems is Bi-LSTM-CRF (bidirectional long-short-term-memory conditional random fields) [2], evaluated over a standard CoNLL-2003 corpus [19].

In this paper, we evaluate the use of neural network topology of Bi-LSTM-CRF using two corpora of patient name recognition in Portuguese. One patient-name-recognition corpus was annotated with 5 thousand names in 15 thousand sentences. Besides, a standard NER corpus was used to evaluate overfitting. Our approach focuses on the identification of the best cutoff point of the de-identification training set.

The rest of this paper is organized as follows: Sect. 2 presents previous works on the de-identification of clinical notes. Section 3 describes the datasets, language models, and neural network topology. We present the results in Sect. 4. Finally, in Sect. 5, we conclude and present future work.

## 2   Related Work

The de-identification of clinical notes has become a common task in the health information research field since the adoption of electronic health records [14]. Datasets such as i2b2 [29] and CEGS N-GRID [28] enable shared tasks in this research field, only for the English language.

In a recent survey, Leevy et al. [12] performed a systematic review of de-identification tasks in clinical notes using Recurrent Neural Networks (RNNs) and Conditional Random Fields (CRFs). They found 12 papers that used RNNs, 12 others that used CRFs, and finally 5 types of research that combine both approaches. Also, the authors consider that overfitting may be an issue when customized de-identification datasets are used during model training.

Most researches found in the survey lack the use of contextualized embeddings for the proposed task. The only exception is the work by Lee et al. [11]. In this investigation, they evaluate the de-identification performance of Gated Recurrent Units (GRUs) versus LSTM topologies, with a final CRF layer, with three types of embeddings: word-level embeddings, character-level embeddings, and contextualized embeddings.

To the best of our knowledge, no previous studies address the detection of patient names based on contextualized embeddings and token classification for the Portuguese language. We also evaluate the overfitting problem employing a non-customized corpus used for entity recognition in the general domain. In the next section, we cover the dataset, the neural network, and the language models (embeddings) used in the experiments.

# 3   Materials and Methods

In this section, we present the corpora used in the experiments, the neural network topologies, and the language models used in the neural networks for the representation of words. Besides, we describe how we evaluate the de-identification task.

The data used in the experiments we conducted for this article came from a project developed with several hospitals. Ethical approval to use the hospitals datasets in this research was granted by the National Research Ethics Committee under the number 46652521.9.0000.5530.

## 3.1   Data Source

We used two sources of Named Entity Recognition (NER) corpora for the sequence labeling task. The corpora are listed below:

**EHR-Names Corpus:** This corpus was built by collecting clinical notes from the aforementioned hospital (HNSC). We randomly selected 2,500 clinical notes for each hospital, totaling 15,952 sentences. The annotation process was performed by two annotators in the Doccano annotation tool [16]. The annotated dataset includes 12,762 tokens; 4,999 of them were labeled as a named entity.

**HAREM Corpora:** The HAREM corpora was an initiative of the Linguateca consortium. The first HAREM corpus [21] was published in 2006 with a human-made gold standard of named entities. The second HAREM corpus [20] was made available in 2008 with basically the same purpose. However, being a more recent contribution, the gold standard for the second HAREM consists in a slightly better test case. The HAREM corpora classify the named entities into ten categories. Nevertheless, for the purposes of our comparison, only the "Person" category was taken into account. Considering the "Person" category, the number of named entities is 1,040 for the first HAREM and 2,035 for the second HAREM.

## 3.2   Neural Network

In this section, we present the neural networks used for the downstream task evaluated in this study. For the neural networks, we used the FLAIR framework [1], developed in PyTorch[1]; it has all the features of parameter tuning for model regulation. All our experiments were performed in NVIDIA T4 GPU.

**BiLSTM-CRF:** As [2], we used a traditional *sequence labeling* task to learn how to detect names at the token level. Our *sequence labeling* is the product of training a BiLSTM neural network with a final CRF layer for token labeling. Bidirectional Long Short-Term Memory (BiLSTM) networks have achieved state-of-the-art results in NLP downstream tasks, mainly for sequential classifications [9,17,27].

---

[1]  https://pytorch.org.

Recurrent neural networks have proven to be an effective approach to language modeling, both in sequence labeling tasks such as part-of-speech tagging and in sequence classification tasks such as sentiment analysis and topic classification [10]. When it receives a sentence, this network topology concatenates information in both directions of the sentence. This makes the network have a larger context window, providing greater disambiguation of meanings and more accurate automatic feature extraction [8].

### 3.3   Language Models

**WE-NILC:** These are pre-computed language models that feature vectors generated from a large corpus of Brazilian Portuguese and European Portuguese, from varied sources and genres. Seventeen different corpora were used, totaling 1.3 billion tokens [6].

**WE-EHR-Notes:** For our experiments, we used a Word Embedding (WE) language model to vectorize the tokens of the clinical notes. We used a WE model that was previously trained by [22], where the authors reported the best results when using this WE trained with the neural network FastText [3]. The model was developed with 603 million tokens from clinical notes extracted from electronic medical records. The generated model has 300 dimensions per word. This model resulted in a vocabulary of 79,000 biomedical word vectors.

**FlairBBP:** This is a pre-trained model taught [25] with three corpora totaling 192 thousand sentences and 4.9 billion tokens in Portuguese. This language model was trained using Flair Embedding [2]. Flair is a contextual embedding model that takes into account the distribution of sequences of characters instead of only sequences of words, as is the case for Skip-gram and CBOW language models. Additionally, Flair Embeddings combine two models, one trained in a forward direction and one trained in a backward direction.

**FlairBBP$_{FnTg}$:** This model was built using the aforementioned model FlairBBP fine-tuned by using the EHR-Names Corpus as input.

### 3.4   Design of the Experiments

Our evaluations were made within two sets of experiments: $i$) Stacking embeddings and $ii$) Corpus addition.

Experiments from set $i$ aim to find the best combination of Language Models covered by this study. Therefore, we started by evaluating a BiLSTM-CRF neural network with shallow Word Embeddings only; then we employed FlairBBP, which is a contextualized language model; we stacked FlairBBP with a WE; and finally, we performed the experiments with the stacking of the fine-tuned FlairBBP with a WE.

Then, we performed set $ii$ to evaluate the best cutoff point concerning the size of the training corpus of the model. Our strategy was to take several pieces of the corpus and train a model with each of these pieces in a cumulative sequence. In

**Table 1.** Number of sentences per training split

| Corpus | Split | Sentences |
|---|---|---|
| ERH-Names | 1 | 709 |
| | 2 | 1,418 |
| | 3 | 2,127 |
| | 4 | 2,836 |
| | ⋮ | ⋮ |
| | 18 | 12,762 |
| ERH-Names + HAREM | 19 | 13,100 |
| | 20 | 13,809 |
| | 21 | 14518 |

other words, we did these experiments by adding a corpus. This means that we divided the Corpus EHR-Names into 18 parts with 709 sentences each. Additionally, we added three more parts that are formed by the union of the EHR-Names corpus and one part of the HAREM corpus. Each part of HAREM also has 709 sentences. The corpora were added cumulatively, that is, the first split has 709 sentences, the second has 1,418, the third, 2.836, and so on. Each split corresponds to a trained model to find out which are the best metrics concerning the size of the corpus. Table 1 shows details of the sizes.

## 4   Results

**Table 2.** Results of stacking embeddings. PRE = Precision; REC = Recall; F1 = F-measure

| Language models | PRE | REC | F1 |
|---|---|---|---|
| WE-NILC (W2V-SKPG) | 0.8813 | 0.8859 | 0.8836 |
| WE-EHR-Notes (W2V-SKPG) | 0.8135 | 0.7984 | 0.8059 |
| FlairBBP | 0.9173 | 0.9416 | 0.9293 |
| FlairBBP + WE-NILC (W2V-SKPG) | **0.9256** | **0.9576** | **0.9413** |
| FlairBBP + WE-EHR-Notes (W2V-SKPG) | 0.9199 | 0.9443 | 0.9319 |
| FlairBBP$_{FnTg}$ + WE-NILC (W2V-SKPG) | 0.9158 | 0.9523 | 0.9337 |
| FlairBBP$_{FnTg}$ + WE-EHR-Notes (W2V-SKPG) | 0.9227 | 0.9496 | 0.9359 |

Experiments from set $i$ are shown in Table 2. In all the experiments in set $i$, we used *Word2Vec Skip-Gram (W2V-SKPG)* [15] Word Embeddings. Experiments from set $ii$ are summarized in a plot in the image 1. Below we present our results and their interpretations from the comparison of the F1 metrics.

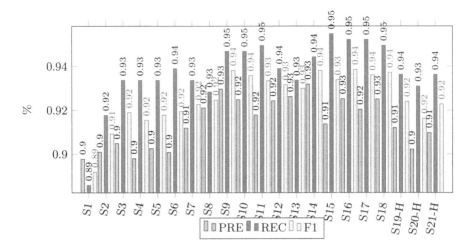

**Fig. 1.** Experimental results by splits. PRE = Precision; REC = Recall; F1 = F-measure

With the first set of experiments, we can see the impact of contextualized language models: the contextualized model $FlairBBP$ outperforms WE-NILC by +0.0457 and WE-EHR-Notes by +0.1234. Another important aspect of the Contextualized Language Models is the potential combination with a Shallow WE, forming a final embedding with a high representational power of the language. Therefore, we managed to overcome both language models alone and we arrived at the best result of $F_1 = 0.9413$, using $FlairBBP$ stacked with WE-NILC. Our best result and consequently our best combination of embeddings were also found in [22,25].

In addition, our results with the stacks using FlairBBP$_{FnTg}$ performed close to the average of the four stacks and both were slightly better than the stack of FlairBBP + WE-EHR-Notes.

From the second set of experiments, in which we looked for the best number of sentences for training, we found that the metrics PRECISION, RECALL, and F1 tend to grow up to split nine. After this split, there is a greater oscillation, as we can see in the graph of Fig. 1. Analyzing all the splits, we can see that split nine is the best, as it demands fewer corpus resources, naturally reduces the effort of the manual annotation of texts, and also reduces the computational cost, since the corpus is smaller.

Regarding the last three splits—which use the HAREM corpus—we can see that there is a significant drop in the metrics. We understand that the main reason for this is the difference in textual style between a medical record and the HAREM texts, extracted from magazines, newspapers, and interviews, among other genres, which are not related to health.

# 5    Conclusion

This paper presents an experimental study on the de-identification of patient names in electronic medical records. For the anonymization process, we manually developed a corpus in Portuguese with around 2,526 named entities and added the traditional HAREM corpus to our experiments. We used a BiLSTM-CRF neural network to train a de-identifier model and concluded that using Contextualized Language Models stacked with Word Embedding models produces cutting-edge results.

Additionally, our results show that it is not always necessary to have the entire training corpus to obtain the best predictor model and also that mixing very different textual genres can hinder the performance of the model. As future work, we plan to run experiments in generating language models, such as T5 [18] and GPT-3 [4].

All the content of the work (algorithm, sample dataset, language models, and experiments) is available at the project's GitHub Page[2] in order to be easily replicated.

**Acknowledgments.** We thank Dr. Ana Helena D. P. S. Ulbrich, who provided the clinical notes dataset from the hospital, for her valuable cooperation. We also thank the volunteers of the Institute of Artificial Intelligence in Healthcare Celso Pereira and Ana Lúcia Dias, for the dataset annotation.

# References

1. Akbik, A., Bergmann, T., Blythe, D., Rasul, K., Schweter, S., Vollgraf, R.: FLAIR: an easy-to-use framework for state-of-the-art NLP. In: Proceedings of the Conference of the North American Chapter of the Association for Computational Linguistics, pp. 54–59. Association for Computational Linguistics, Minneapolis, Minnesota, June 2019. https://doi.org/10.18653/v1/N19-4010, https://www.aclweb.org/anthology/N19-4010
2. Akbik, A., Blythe, D., Vollgraf, R.: Contextual string embeddings for sequence labeling. In: Proceedings of the 27th International Conference on Computational Linguistics, pp. 1638–1649 (2018)
3. Bojanowski, P., Grave, E., Joulin, A., Mikolov, T.: Enriching word vectors with subword information. Trans. Assoc. Comput. Linguist. **5**, 135–146 (2017)
4. Brown, T.B., et al.: Language models are few-shot learners. In: Larochelle, H., Ranzato, M., Hadsell, R., Balcan, M., Lin, H. (eds.) Proceedings of the 33th Annual Conference on Neural Information Processing Systems (2020)
5. El Emam, K.: Guide to the De-identification of Personal Health Information. CRC Press, Boca Raton (2013)
6. Hartmann, N., Fonseca, E., Shulby, C., Treviso, M., Silva, J., Aluísio, S.: Portuguese word embeddings: evaluating on word analogies and natural language tasks. In: Proceedings of the 11th Brazilian Symposium in Information and Human Language Technology, pp. 122–131 (2017)

---

[2] https://github.com/noharm-ai/noharm-anony.

7. Hash, J., Bowen, P., Johnson, A., Smith, C., Steinberg, D.: An introductory resource guide for implementing the health insurance portability and accountability act (HIPAA) security rule. US Department of Commerce, Technology Administration, National Institute of . . . (2005)
8. Hochreiter, S., Schmidhuber, J.: Long short-term memory. Neural Comput. **9**(8), 1735–1780 (1997)
9. Jiang, Y., Hu, C., Xiao, T., Zhang, C., Zhu, J.: Improved differentiable architecture search for language modeling and named entity recognition. In: Proceedings of the 2019 Conference on Empirical Methods in Natural Language Processing, pp. 3585–3590. Association for Computational Linguistics, Hong Kong, China (2019)
10. Jurafsky, D., Martin, J.H.: Speech and Language Processing, vol. 3. Pearson, London, United Kingdom (2014)
11. Lee, K., Filannino, M., Uzuner, Ö.: An empirical test of GRUs and deep contextualized word representations on de-identification. In: MedInfo, pp. 218–222 (2019)
12. Leevy, J.L., Khoshgoftaar, T.M., Villanustre, F.: Survey on RNN and CRF models for de-identification of medical free text. J. Big Data **7**(1), 1–22 (2020)
13. Magboo, Ma. Sheila A.., Coronel, Andrei D..: Data mining electronic health records to support evidence-based clinical decisions. In: Chen, Yen-Wei., Zimmermann, Alfred, Howlett, Robert J.., Jain, Lakhmi C.. (eds.) Innovation in Medicine and Healthcare Systems, and Multimedia. SIST, vol. 145, pp. 223–232. Springer, Singapore (2019). https://doi.org/10.1007/978-981-13-8566-7_22
14. Meystre, S.M., Friedlin, F.J., South, B.R., Shen, S., Samore, M.H.: Automatic de-identification of textual documents in the electronic health record: a review of recent research. BMC Med. Res. Methodol. **10**(1), 1–16 (2010)
15. Mikolov, T., Chen, K., Corrado, G., Dean, J.: Efficient estimation of word representations in vector space. In: Bengio, Y., LeCun, Y. (eds.) Proceedings of the 1st International Conference on Learning Representations (2013)
16. Nakayama, H., Kubo, T., Kamura, J., Taniguchi, Y., Liang, X.: doccano: text annotation tool for human (2018). software available from https://github.com/doccano/doccano
17. Peters, M.E., et al.: Deep contextualized word representations. In: Proceedings of the Conference of the North American chapter of the association for computational linguistics: human language technologies, pp. 2227–2237 (2018)
18. Raffel, C., et al.: Exploring the limits of transfer learning with a unified text-to-text transformer. J. Mach. Learn. Res. **21**, 140:1–140:67 (2020)
19. Sang, E.F., De Meulder, F.: Introduction to the CoNLL-2003 shared task: language-independent named entity recognition. arXiv preprint cs/0306050 (2003)
20. Santos, D., Freitas, C., Oliveira, H.G., Carvalho, P.: Second harem: new challenges and old wisdom. In: International Conference on Computational Processing of the Portuguese Language. pp. 212–215. Springer (2008). https://doi.org/10.1007/978-3-540-85980-2_22
21. Santos, D., Seco, N., Cardoso, N., Vilela, R.: Harem: An advanced NER evaluation contest for Portuguese. In: quot; In: Calzolari, N., et al. (ed.) Proceedings of the 5th International Conference on Language Resources and Evaluation (LREC 2006), Genoa Italy 22–28 May 2006 (2006)
22. dos Santos, H.D.P., Silva, A.P., Maciel, M.C.O., Burin, H.M.V., Urbanetto, J.S., Vieira, R.: Fall detection in EHR using word embeddings and deep learning. In: 2019 IEEE 19th International Conference on Bioinformatics and Bioengineering (BIBE), pp. 265–268, October 2019. https://doi.org/10.1109/BIBE.2019.00054

23. dos Santos, H.D.P., Ulbrich, A.H.D., Woloszyn, V., Vieira, R.: DDC-outlier: preventing medication errors using unsupervised learning. IEEE J. Biomed. Health Inform. **23**, 8 (2018)
24. dos Santos, H.D.P., Ulbrich, A.H.D., Woloszyn, V., Vieira, R.: An initial investigation of the Charlson comorbidity index regression based on clinical notes. In: 2018 IEEE 31st International Symposium on Computer-Based Medical Systems (CBMS), pp. 6–11. IEEE (2018)
25. Santos, J., Consoli, B.S., dos Santos, C.N., Terra, J., Collovini, S., Vieira, R.: Assessing the impact of contextual embeddings for Portuguese named entity recognition. In: Proceedings of the 8th Brazilian Conference on Intelligent Systems, pp. 437–442 (2019)
26. Santos, J., dos Santos, H.D., Vieira, R.: Fall detection in clinical notes using language models and token classifier. In: 2020 IEEE 33rd International Symposium on Computer-Based Medical Systems (CBMS), pp. 283–288. IEEE (2020)
27. Straková, J., Straka, M., Hajic, J.: Neural architectures for nested NER through linearization. In: Proceedings of the 57th Annual Meeting of the Association for Computational Linguistics, pp. 5326–5331. Association for Computational Linguistics (2019)
28. Stubbs, A., Filannino, M., Uzuner, Ö.: De-identification of psychiatric intake records: overview of 2016 CEGS N-GRID shared tasks track 1. J. Biomed. Inform. **75**, S4–S18 (2017)
29. Stubbs, A., Uzuner, Ö.: Annotating longitudinal clinical narratives for de-identification: The 2014 i2b2/UThealth corpus. J. Biomed. Inform. **58**, S20–S29 (2015)

# Detecting Early Signs of Insufficiency in COVID-19 Patients from CBC Tests Through a Supervised Learning Approach

Tiago Colliri[1]([✉]) [iD], Marcia Minakawa[2] [iD], and Liang Zhao[3] [iD]

[1] Dept. of Computer Science, University of Fortaleza (UNIFOR), Fortaleza, Brazil
tcolliri@alumni.usp.br
[2] Faculty of Public Health, Univ. of Sao Paulo, Sao Paulo, Brazil
marciaenf@alumni.usp.br
[3] Faculty of Philosophy, Science and Letters, Univ. of Sao Paulo,
Ribeirao Preto, Brazil
zhao@usp.br

**Abstract.** One important task in the COVID-19 clinical protocol involves the constant monitoring of patients to detect possible signs of insufficiency, which may eventually rapidly progress to hepatic, renal or respiratory failures. Hence, a prompt and correct clinical decision not only is critical for patients prognosis, but also can help when making collective decisions regarding hospital resource management. In this work, we present a network-based high-level classification technique to help healthcare professionals on this activity, by detecting early signs of insufficiency based on Complete Blood Count (CBC) test results. We start by building a training dataset, comprising both CBC and specific tests from a total of 2,982 COVID-19 patients, provided by a Brazilian hospital, to identify which CBC results are more effective to be used as biomarkers for detecting early signs of insufficiency. Basically, the trained classifier measures the compliance of the test instance to the pattern formation of the network constructed from the training data. To facilitate the application of the technique on larger datasets, a network reduction option is also introduced and tested. Numerical results show encouraging performance of our approach when compared to traditional techniques, both on benchmark datasets and on the built COVID-19 dataset, thus indicating that the proposed technique has potential to help medical workers in the severity assessment of patients. Especially those who work in regions with scarce material resources.

This work was carried out at the Center for Artificial Intelligence (C4AI-USP), with support by the São Paulo Research Foundation (FAPESP) under grant number: 2019/07665-4 and by the IBM Corporation. This work is also supported in part by the Coordenação de Aperfeiçoamento de Pessoal de Nível Superior - Brasil (CAPES) - Finance Code 001, FAPESP under grant numbers 2015/50122-0, the Brazilian National Council for Scientific and Technological Development (CNPq) under grant number 303199/2019-9, and the Ministry of Science and Technology of China under grant number: G20200226015.

A. Britto and K. Valdivia Delgado (Eds.): BRACIS 2021, LNAI 13074, pp. 42–57, 2021.
https://doi.org/10.1007/978-3-030-91699-2_4

**Keywords:** Complex networks · Classification · High-level data pattern characterization · COVID-19 prognosis · Insufficiency detection · Biomarkers · CBC tests

# 1   Introduction

Since the COVID-19 outbreak, advanced machine learning techniques have been applied in the development of clinical decision support tools, to help medical workers on guiding the monitoring and treatment of affected patients. Examples of these studies include the automation and introduction of new methods for routine medical activities, such as: the analysis of computed tomography (CT) images [21], COVID-19 diagnosis and screening [27], detection of new viral species and subspecies [15], medication [2], and patients monitoring through biomarkers, such as the ones provided by blood samples [26].

When a new COVID-19 case is confirmed, the clinical protocol involves an initial assessment, made by healthcare professionals, to classify its severity as mild, moderate or grave, followed by a monitoring activity to evaluate the progression of the disease [20]. This procedure, although it may slightly vary, depending on the region, usually includes specific tests, such as creatinine, lactic dehydrogenase and blood urea nitrogen, as well as a Complete Blood Count (CBC), which is a series of tests used to evaluate the composition and concentration of cellular components in the blood. Such type of testing, as the CBC, is widely used because it can be easily collected at any place, even in situations of medical resource scarcity. Moreover, it is usually processed in a matter of minutes, up to two hours. Therefore, it is considered as a fast, low-cost and reliable resource to assess the patient's overall conditions. During the monitoring process, healthcare professionals then need to decide whether to order complementary tests for detecting possible signs of hepatic, renal or respiratory insufficiency. Considering that progressive respiratory failure is the primary cause of death from COVID-19, this monitoring activity hence is critical for the patient. However, we must face the problem that such complementary tests incur high costs, and may not be available in some specific places due to scarcity of material and human resources.

In this study, we present a technique that may assist medical professionals on this monitoring activity, by detecting early signs of insufficiency in COVID-19 patients solely based on CBC test results. Specifically, our approach can help to identify the level of risk and the type of insufficiency for each patient. We start by building a training dataset comprising results from both CBC and specific tests used to detect signs of hepatic, renal and respiratory insufficiency, from a total of 2,982 COVID-19 patients, who received treatment in the Israelite Albert Einstein Hospital, from Sao Paulo, Brazil [10]. In this process, we identify which CBC tests are more effective to be used as biomarkers to detect signs from each type of insufficiency. The dataset resulting from this analysis is then delivered to a modified network-based high-level classification technique, also introduced in this study. The obtained results present competitive performance of the proposed technique compared to classic and state-of-the-art ones, both on benchmark classification datasets and on the built COVID-19 dataset.

Real-world datasets usually contain complex and organizational patterns beyond the physical features (similarity, distance, distribution, etc.). Data classification, which takes into account not only physical features, but also the organizational structure of the data, is referred to as *high level* classification. Complex networks are suitable tools for data pattern characterization due to their ability of capturing the spatial, topological, and functional relationship among data [1,6,22,23]. In this study, we present a modified high-level classification technique based on complex network modeling. It can perform classification tasks taking into account both physical attributes and the pattern formation of the data. Basically, the classification process measures the compliance of the test instance to the pattern formation of each network constructed from a class of training data. The approach presented in this work is inspired by the high-level data classification technique introduced in previous works [6,8,22], and here it is modified in terms of the network building parameters automation method, the topological measure used for characterizing the data pattern structure, and the inclusion of a network reduction option, to facilitate its application on larger datasets by saving processing and memory resources.

The main contributions of this work are summarized as follows:

- Building a training dataset from unlabeled original data, comprising medical tests from almost 3,000 de-identified COVID-19 patients, provided by a hospital in Brazil, which will be made publicly available to be used in other relevant researches,
- Introducing a network-based high level classification technique, based on the betweenness centrality measure, with a network reduction option included in the training phase, to make the technique faster and to facilitate its application on larger datasets, and
- Applying the proposed technique both on benchmark classification datasets and on the built dataset, and comparing the results with those achieved by other traditional classification techniques, on the same data, to evaluate the possibility of detecting early signs of insufficiency in COVID-19 patients solely based on CBC tests, used as biomarkers.

## 2   The Proposed MNBHL Technique

In this section we describe the proposed modified network-based high level (MNBHL) classification technique. All implementations are made using the igraph Python package [9].

In classic *supervised learning*, initially we have an input dataset comprising $n$ instances in the form of an array $X_{train} = [x_1, x_2, ..., x_n]$, where each instance $x_i$ itself is a $m$-dimensional array, such that $x_i = [x_{i,1}, x_{i,2}, ..., x_{i,m}]$, representing $m$ features of the instance. Correspondingly, the labels of the instances are represented by another array $Y = [y_1, y_2, ..., y_n]$, where $y_i \in \mathcal{L} = \{L_1..., L_C\}$, and $L_i$ is the label of the $i$th class. The objective of the *training phase* is to construct a classifier by generating a mapping $f : X_{train} \xrightarrow{\Delta} Y$. In the *testing phase*, this mapping is used to classify data instances without label. The test dataset is denoted by $X_{test}$.

A network can be defined as a graph $\mathcal{G} = (\mathcal{V}, \mathcal{E})$, where $\mathcal{V}$ is a set of nodes, $\mathcal{V} = \{v_1, v_2, ..., v_n\}$, and $\mathcal{E}$ is a set of tuples, $\mathcal{E} = \{(i, j) : i, j \in \mathcal{V}\}$, representing the edges between each pair of nodes. In the proposed modified high-level classification technique, each node in the network represents a data instance $x_i$ in the dataset, and the connections between nodes are created based on the their similarity in the attribute space, pairwise. In the *training phase*, one network component is constructed for the data instances of each class. Afterwards, there is an option to reduce the built network, by preserving only its $r\%$ most central nodes, according to a selected centrality index. In the *testing phase*, each data instance is inserted as a new node in the network, one at a time, by using the same rules from the training phase. In case only one network component is affected by the insertion, then its label will be equal to the respective class of that component. In case more than one component is affected by the insertion, then its label will be given by the class whose component is the least impacted by the new node's insertion, in terms of the network topological structure.

## 2.1   Description of the Training Phase

The training phase starts by balancing the values in $X_{train}$, for dealing with unbalanced datasets. For this end, we introduce a list $\alpha$, where each element is given by:

$$\alpha^{(L)} = \frac{|X_{train}^{(L)}|}{|X_{train}|} \quad , \forall L \in \mathcal{L} \quad , \tag{1}$$

where $|X_{train}|$ is the total number of elements of the training set and $|X_{train}^{(L)}|$ is the number of elements in the subset $X_{train}$ whose corresponding class label in $Y$ is $L$. These values are also normalized, assuming $\alpha_i = \frac{\alpha_i}{\sum_i^n \alpha_i}$.

The edges between nodes in the network are generated by measuring the pairwise similarity of the corresponding data instances in the attribute space through a combination of two rules: $k$NN and $\epsilon$-radius. The $\epsilon$-radius rule is used for dense regions, while the $k$NN is employed for sparse regions. The value of $\epsilon$ is yielded by:

$$\epsilon = Q(D, p) \quad , \tag{2}$$

where $D_i$ is a 1d vector containing the Euclidean distances between each element and element $x_i$ in $X_{train}$, and $Q$ is a function which returns the $p$-th quantile of the data in $D$. For the second rule used for generating the edges in the network, the $k$NN, we opt to set the initial value for the parameter $k$ as the $\min(\min v, p\bar{v})$, where $v$ is a vector containing the number of data instances per each class in the dataset. Hence, the maximum possible value for $k$ will be the average number of data instances per class in the dataset multiplied by the same parameter $p$ used for returning the quantile from the $\epsilon$-radius technique. By proceeding this way, we are therefore linking the value of $k$ to the value of $\epsilon$ and, consequently, to the characteristics of each dataset (here represented by $\bar{v}$). This is also a novelty introduced in this technique, compared to its previous versions [8,22], with the aim of avoiding exaggerated disproportions between the number of edges yielded by the two rules.

With the initial values of $\epsilon$ and $k$ being set, the model then proceeds to generate the edges of the network $\mathcal{G}$. The neighbors to be connected to a training node $x_i$ are yielded by:

$$N(x_i) = \begin{cases} \epsilon\text{-radius}(x_i, y_i), & \text{if } \epsilon\text{-radius}(x_i, y_i) > k \\ k\text{NN}(x_i, y_i), & \text{otherwise} \end{cases} \quad (3)$$

where $y_i$ denotes the class label of the training instance $x_i$, $\epsilon$-radius$(x_i, y_i)$ returns the set $\{x_j, \forall j \in \mathcal{V} \mid dist(x_i, x_j) \leq \epsilon \wedge y_i = y_j\}$, and $k$NN$(x_i, y_i)$ returns the set containing the $k$ nearest vertices of the same class of $x_i$.

A common issue regarding the application of network-based techniques on larger datasets is that, depending on the available computational resources, the process may become too expensive, both in terms of processing power and memory consumption. For this reason, in this study, we introduce an option to reduce the number of vertices in the network, for the sake of saving processing time and memory resources, both in the training and testing phases. There are different possible strategies for reducing a network [24] and, in this work, we opt for one which consists in keeping only the nodes that occupy more central positions in it, measured in terms of the *betweenness centrality* [3]. This measure, broadly speaking, estimates the extent to which a vertex lies on paths between other vertices, and is considered essential in the analysis of complex networks. In a network that does not present communities, the nodes with higher betweenness centrality are among the most influential ones [7], while in networks that present communities, these nodes are the ones which usually work as links between the communities. We chose to use this measure for believing that it is able to identify the most representative nodes in the network, such that only these selected nodes can be used in the classification task.

For controlling this option, we add a reduction parameter $r \in [0, 1]$ in the model, such that when its value is set as less than 1, only the ratio of $r$ vertices with higher betweenness centrality are kept in the network. In this case, the values in $X_{train}$ and $Y$ are also reduced, accordingly. The value of $\epsilon$ is updated, and the network edges are generated again, by using the same rules provided in Eq. 2 and Eq. 3. If, after this procedure, the number of components in the network is higher than the number of classes in the dataset, then the value of $k$ is increased by 1, and the edges are updated again. This step can be repeated more times, if necessary, until we have, at the end, one component in the network per class in the dataset.

The complete process of the training phase is outlined in Algorithm 1. In line 2, there is the balancing task, in which the parameter $\alpha$ is generated. Then, in line 3, the network $\mathcal{G}$ is built, by using the values of parameters $\epsilon$ and $k$. In lines 4–7, there is the optional procedure to reduce the network, by leaving only its $r\%$ most central nodes. In lines 8–10, we have the validation of whether the

---

**Algorithm 1.** Training phase

---

1:  **procedure** FIT($X, Y$)
2:      $\alpha \leftarrow$ fraction of items per class (balancing parameter)
3:      $G \leftarrow$ initial network, resulted from $\epsilon$ and $k$
4:      **if** network reduction is opted **then**
5:          $vs \leftarrow$ the $r\%$ most central nodes in $G$
6:          $G \leftarrow$ reduced version of $G$, leaving only $vs$
7:          $X, Y \leftarrow$ reduced versions of $X, Y$
8:      **while** number of components in $G >$ number of classes in $Y$ **do**
9:          $k+ = 1$
10:         $G \leftarrow$ network resulted from $\epsilon$ and $k$

---

number of network components is equal to the number of classes in the dataset, with the parameter $k$ and the network $\mathcal{G}$ being updated, if necessary.

## 2.2 Description of the Testing Phase

In the testing phase, the data instances from $X_{test}$ are inserted as new vertices in the network $\mathcal{G}$, one at a time, and the model then needs to infer the label of each testing instance. The model extracts two groups of network measures for each component, before and after the insertion of a testing instance, respectively. The testing instance is classified to the class of the component which its insertion caused the smallest variation in the network measures. In other words, a testing instance is classified to a certain class because it conforms the pattern formed by the training data of that class. In this way, the data instances from $X_{test}$ are inserted in the network, to be classified, one by one.

The new node's insertion is made by using the same rules described in Eq. 3 for generating the edges between the new node and the other nodes in the network. The only difference now is that, since we do not know the class of the new data instance $x_i$, the "same label" restriction is removed from the procedure, so that the nodes to be connected to $x_i$ are yielded by:

$$N(x_i) = \begin{cases} \epsilon\text{-radius}(x_i), \text{ if } \epsilon\text{-radius}(x_i) > k \\ k\text{NN}(x_i), \text{ otherwise} \end{cases} \tag{4}$$

where $\epsilon$-radius($x_i$) returns the set $\{x_j, \forall j \in \mathcal{V} \mid dist(x_i, x_j) \leq \epsilon\}$, and $k$NN($x_i$) returns the set containing the $k$ nearest vertices of $x_i$.

The model will assign the label for the new node according to the number of components affected by the node's insertion in the network. In case only one component is affected by its insertion, i.e., when all the target nodes of its edges belong to the same component, then the model will assign the class of this component for the new node. On the other hand, when more than one component is affected by the insertion, then the model will extract new measures of the affected components and assign a class label to the testing data instance as the label of the component less impacted by the insertion, in terms of the network topology. In this work, we use *betweenness centrality* for measuring these impacts.

The overall impact $I^{(L)}$ on each affected component of class $L$, caused by the insertion of the testing instance, is calculated and balanced according to:

$$I^{(L)} = \alpha^{(L)} \frac{M_1^{(L)} - M_0^{(L)}}{M_0^{(L)}} \quad , \tag{5}$$

where $M_0^{(L)}$ and $M_1^{(L)}$ are the extracted network measures for the component representing class $L$, before and after the insertion of the testing instance, respectively. The probability $P(x_i^{\hat{y}_i=L})$ of the testing instance $x_i$ to belong to class $L$ is given by the reciprocal of the value in vector $I$, in the normalized form, as in:

$$P(x_i^{\hat{y}_i=L}) = \begin{cases} \frac{1/I^{(L)}}{\sum_L 1/I^{(L)}} & , \text{ if } C^{(L)} \text{ is affected} \\ 0, & \text{ otherwise,} \end{cases} \tag{6}$$

where $C^{(L)}$ is the network component representing class $L$. Finally, the label $\hat{y}_i$ to be assigned for the testing instance $x_i$ is yielded by:

$$\hat{y}_i = \underset{L}{\operatorname{argmax}} P(x_i^{\hat{y}_i=L}) \quad . \tag{7}$$

The complete process of the testing phase is described in Algorithm 2. In lines 2–3, an initial empty list is created to store the predicted labels for each data instance in $X_{test}$, and the current measures of each network component are extracted. In lines 4–13, the model generates a label for each testing instance, one by one. In case only one component is affected by the insertion of the testing data, then its label will be this component's class. In case more than one component is affected by the insertion, then the testing data is classified to that class whose component is least impacted by the insertion, in terms of topological structure. In line 14, the classification list is updated with each predicted label.

---

**Algorithm 2.** Testing phase

---
```
 1: procedure PREDICT(X)
 2:     Ŷ ← [ ]
 3:     M₀ ← initial measures of each component in G
 4:     for x in X do
 5:         insert x in G, using ϵ and k
 6:         if x affects only one component in G then
 7:             ŷ ← class of affected component
 8:         else
 9:             M₁ ← new measures of each component in G
10:             I ← α · abs(M₁ − M₀)/M₀
11:             P ← 1.0/I
12:             P ← P/sum(P)
13:             ŷ ← class of argmax(P)
14:         Ŷ ← append ŷ
15: return Ŷ
```
---

# 3   Materials and Methods

We first evaluate the performance of the proposed MNBHL model by apply-ing it to well-known benchmark classification datasets, both artificial and real ones. Afterwards, we apply the MNBHL model to a dataset specially built for this work, obtained from the analysis of publicly available data of de-identified COVID-19 patients from one of the main hospitals in Brazil. Each dataset is processed 20 times by all models, each time having their data items shuffled by using a different random seed. The final accuracy scores are the averaged ones achieved by each model, on each dataset. For splitting each dataset into 2 subdatasets, for training and testing purposes, we make use of a function that returns a train-test split with 75% and 25% the size of the inputs, respectively.

**Table 1.** Meta information of the datasets used in the experimental results

|            |               | N° of Samples | N° of Features | N° of Classes |
|------------|---------------|---------------|----------------|---------------|
| Artificial | Circles_00    | 100           | 2              | 2             |
|            | Circles_02    | 100           | 2              | 2             |
|            | Moons_00      | 100           | 2              | 2             |
|            | Moons_02      | 100           | 2              | 2             |
| Real       | Breast Cancer | 569           | 30             | 2             |
|            | Digits        | 1,797         | 64             | 10            |
|            | Iris          | 150           | 4              | 3             |
|            | Wine          | 178           | 13             | 3             |
|            | Zoo           | 101           | 16             | 7             |

A succinct meta-information of the benchmark datasets used for obtaining the experimental results is given in Table 1. Circles_00 and Circles_02 datasets are two concentric circles without noise and with a 20% noise, respectively. Moons_00 and Moons_02 datasets are two moons without noise and with a 20% noise, respectively. For a detailed description of the real datasets, one can refer to [14].

We built the COVID-19 dataset from originally unlabeled data [10] collected from COVID-19 patients of the Israelite Albert Einstein Hospital, located in Sao Paulo, Brazil. The original database comprises a total of 1,853,695 results from 127 different medical tests, collected from 43,562 de-identified patients, who received treatment in the hospital from January 1, 2020 until June 24, 2020. Firstly, we identify the patients who tested positive in at least one of the following COVID-19 detection tests: polymerase chain reaction (PCR), immunoglobulin M (IgM), immunoglobulin G (IgG) and enzyme-linked immunosorbent assay (ELISA). Next, we filter the patients and left in the dataset only the ones who have made at least one complete blood count (CBC) test, in a date no earlier than the date to be tested positive for COVID-19. In case a patient has made more than one CBC test, we then consider only the results of the first test

**Table 2.** Tests considered for identifying signs of insufficiency in patients and respective CBC tests considered for detecting those signs

| Insufficiency | Tests considered for detecting signs (for labels generation) | Biomarkers considered (predictive attributes) | | | | | |
|---|---|---|---|---|---|---|---|
| | | Age | Neutrophils | Basophils | Lymphocytes | Eosinophils | RDW |
| Hepatic | • transaminase TGO (AST)<br>• transaminase TGP (ALT)<br>• alkaline phosphatase<br>• gamma-glutamyl transpeptidase (GGT) | x | x | x | x | x | |
| Renal | • creatinine clearance (urine test)<br>• creatinine (blood test)<br>• blood urea nitrogen (BUN) | x | x | | x | | |
| Respiratory | • arterial blood gas<br>• respiratory pathogen panel<br>• lactate<br>• ionized calcium<br>• potassium | x | | x | x | | |
| Any | | x | x | x | x | | x |

for predicting early signs of insufficiency. We adopt this procedure because we aim to make predictions based on *early* signs of insufficiency, hence the use of only the first CBC test for the predictions. Afterwards, we run an algorithm to automatically label each patient of the dataset as presenting or not signs from each type of insufficiency, strictly according to results from specific tests, listed in the second column of Table 2, and using their respective reference values provided in the same original database, which are standardized in the medical literature.

After the data cleansing, we end up with a total of 2,982 different patients in the dataset, with each of them belonging to one of the following 4 classes: Healthy, Hepatic Insufficiency Signs, Renal Insufficiency Signs, and Respiratory Insufficiency Signs. For determining the predictive attributes (or biomarkers) for each type of insufficiency, we make use of the *Pearson correlation coefficient* [16], to select the CBC tests that are most correlated to the labels, i.e., to each type of insufficiency. At the end, the following biomarkers were used for this end: age, neutrophils, basophils, lymphocytes, eosinophils and red cell distribution width (RDW). In Table 2, we provided an overview of how the COVID-19 dataset has been built, showing all tests considered, both for the labels and predictive attributes generation. The details regarding all patients in the dataset are summarized in Table 3.

**Table 3.** Overview of the patients in the built COVID-19 dataset

| Age | Total | Healthy | With Signs of Insufficiency | | |
|-----|-------|---------|---------|-------|-------------|
| | | | Hepatic | Renal | Respiratory |
| 00–20 | 57 | 25 | 19 | 22 | 9 |
| 21–40 | 830 | 467 | 258 | 191 | 134 |
| 41–60 | 1279 | 516 | 554 | 404 | 373 |
| 61–80 | 688 | 135 | 388 | 377 | 404 |
| 80+ | 128 | 5 | 84 | 98 | 88 |
| Total | 2982 | 1148 | 1303 | 1092 | 1008 |

The models performances on the COVID-19 dataset are evaluated by the following indicators: accuracy (ratio of true predictions over all predictions), precision, sensitivity/recall and F1 score, as defined below:

$$\text{Precision} = \frac{\text{TP}}{\text{TP} + \text{FP}}, \text{Recall} = \frac{\text{TP}}{\text{TP} + \text{FN}}, \text{F1} = \frac{2 \times \text{Precision} \times \text{Recall}}{\text{Precision} + \text{Recall}} \quad (8)$$

where TP, TN, FP and FN stand for true positive, true negative, false positive and false negative rates, respectively.

For the application, we set the parameter $p$ from the proposed technique, responsible for the network edges generation, as $p = 0.01$ when processing the benchmark datasets, and $p = 0.02$ when processing the COVID-19 dataset. Regarding the network reduction option, we set $r = 0.1$ (10%) when processing the Digits dataset and the COVID-19 dataset and, for the others, we do not make use of this resource, since they are smaller ones. For the sake of comparison, the following traditional classification models are applied on all datasets: Decision Tree [19], Logistic Regression [12], Multilayer Perceptron (MLP) [13], Support Vector Machines (SVM) with an RBF kernel [25] and Naive Bayes [18]. We also apply the following ensemble methods: Bagging of MLP [4], Random Forest [5] and AdaBoost [11]. All models were implemented through Scikit-learn [17], by using their respective default parameter values, in all tests performed.

## 4    Tests Performed on Benchmark Datasets

In Table 4, we present the obtained results, in terms of average accuracy, from the application of the proposed MNBHL model to the benchmark datasets, as well as the comparison with the performances achieved by traditional models. These results indicate that the model's overall performance is competitive, being ranked as second one when compared to traditional techniques, in the average rank. We highlight the good performance achieved on the Moons_00 and Moons_02 datasets, in which it was the only model that obtained an 100% accuracy in all 20 classification tasks processed. This result, in particular, is a strong sign that the model is able to correctly capture the topological pattern present in these two datasets, as expected in high level techniques. Observing the running times of all considered models, we can say that the MNBHL is quite competitive on that aspect as well.

In Fig. 1, we show the effect of the network reduction option on the MNBHL model performance, in terms of average accuracy and processing time, on two benchmark datasets. Each dataset is processed 10 times for obtaining these values, each time using a different random seed. As one can note, from this figure, when the network built for the Digits dataset is reduced in 90%, i.e., to only 10% of the training data, the average accuracy rate decreases from around 0.955 to around 0.905, thus with a negative variation of about 5%, while the average processing time decreases from 55 s to only 2 s, thus with a negative variation of about 96%. As for the Wine dataset, there is an initial improvement in the accuracy, when using a 30% reduction option, which is somewhat surprising, with a later decrease, as the reduction increases. Overall, on the two datasets considered, a 90% network reduction option has a negative impact of around 4%

**Table 4.** Experimental results: average accuracy rates (%) obtained by the following models, in that order: MNBHL, AdaBoost, Bagging of MLP, Decision Tree, Logistic Regression, MLP, Naive-Bayes, Random Forest and SVM. The values between parenthesis indicate the rank achieved and the average running time (in seconds), respectively, including the training and testing phases, on each dataset.

| | MNBHL | Ada | BagMLP | DT | LR | MLP | N-B | RF | SVM |
|---|---|---|---|---|---|---|---|---|---|
| Breast Cancer | 94.6 (3, 0.2) | **95.6** (1, 0.2) | 92.7 (5, 5.1) | 92.2 (6, 0.0) | 95.2 (2, 0.0) | 91.5 (7, 0.5) | 94.5 (4, 0.0) | 95.2 (2, 0.1) | 65.3 (8, 0.1) |
| Circles_00 | 81.5 (4, 0.1) | **94.2** (1, 0.1) | 50.5 (6, 1.2) | 89.8 (2, 0.0) | 35.6 (9, 0.0) | 55.6 (5, 0.1) | 50.2 (8, 0.0) | 87.6 (3, 0.0) | 50.5 (7, 0.0) |
| Circles_02 | 72.7 (3, 0.1) | **89.8** (1, 0.1) | 65.5 (6, 1.2) | 85.1 (2, 0.0) | 41.1 (8, 0.0) | 70.2 (4, 0.1) | 67.3 (5, 0.0) | 85.1 (2, 0.0) | 52.4 (7, 0.0) |
| Digits | 90.3 (5, 2.5) | 24.7 (9, 0.3) | **97.6** (1, 21.9) | 84.0 (7, 0.0) | 95.6 (3, 0.3) | 97.2 (2, 2.6) | 85.4 (6, 0.0) | 93.7 (4, 0.1) | 47.6 (8, 0.8) |
| Iris | 96.5 (4, 0.2) | 95.2 (6, 0.1) | 97.8 (2, 1.5) | 95.6 (5, 0.0) | 94.3 (7, 0.0) | 96.9 (3, 0.2) | 96.5 (4, 0.0) | 95.6 (5, 0.0) | **97.8** (1, 0.0) |
| Moons_00 | **100.0** (1, 0.1) | 98.9 (2, 0.1) | 85.8 (7, 1.2) | 93.5 (5, 0.0) | 85.5 (8, 0.0) | 86.2 (6, 0.1) | 86.2 (6, 0.0) | 94.2 (4, 0.0) | 95.3 (3, 0.0) |
| Moons_02 | **100.0** (1, 0.0) | 95.6 (3, 0.1) | 87.3 (7, 1.2) | 95.3 (4, 0.0) | 86.9 (8, 0.0) | 88.0 (5, 0.0) | 87.6 (6, 0.0) | 97.1 (2, 0.0) | 97.1 (2, 0.0) |
| Wine | 94.8 (2, 0.1) | 85.6 (4, 0.1) | 63.7 (6, 0.5) | 91.9 (3, 0.0) | **95.9** (1, 0.0) | 74.4 (5, 0.1) | **95.9** (1, 0.0) | **95.9** (1, 0.0) | 42.6 (7, 0.0) |
| Zoo | 92.9 (4, 0.1) | 73.7 (7, 0.1) | 94.2 (3, 1.6) | **94.9** (1, 0.0) | 89.7 (5, 0.0) | 94.9 (2, 0.2) | **94.9** (1, 0.0) | 94.2 (3, 0.0) | 86.5 (6, 0.0) |
| Average rank | 2nd | 3rd | 7th | 4th | 9th | 5th | 6th | 1st | 8th |

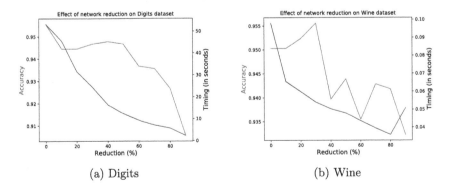

(a) Digits     (b) Wine

**Fig. 1.** Effect of the network reduction option on the average accuracy and processing time, on two benchmark classification datasets. Each dataset is processed 10 times for obtaining these values, with a different random seed.

on the average accuracy rate and of around 80% on the average running time. Therefore, this resource can be used in situations when one needs to process larger datasets using a network-based approach and needs to adapt the problem to locally available computational resources, both in terms of memory and processing capacity, as it is the case in this study.

## 5    Experimental Results

We start this section by showing an example of different processing stages from the proposed technique, when applied to detect respiratory insufficiency signs. In Fig. 2(a), there is the initial network built by the model, i.e., the network formed by all training data instances. This network has 2.236 nodes in total (representing the patients), and two classes (with and without insufficiency signs), denoted by the orange and blue colors. In Fig. 2(b), we have the reduced version of this network, with only the 10% of nodes (223 in total) with the highest betweenness values. In this example, the new node's insertion during the classification phase, in Fig. 2(c), affected both network components, and hence its label will be yielded by the class whose component is least impacted, in terms of betweenness centrality.

(a) Initial network

(b) Reduced network

(c) New data instance insertion

**Fig. 2.** Plots showing three different processing stages from the proposed MNBHL technique, when applied to detect respiratory insufficiency signs.

In Table 5, we display the results obtained by all classification models considered, in terms of accuracy, on detecting early signs of each type of insufficiency, on the built COVID-19 dataset. Overall, all models are more successful on detecting signs of respiratory insufficiency over other types, with most of them achieving an accuracy of more than 70% on this task, while the most difficult signs to be detected are those regarding the hepatic insufficiency. The proposed MNBHL model is the one that achieved the best performance, considering all tasks, followed by Logistic Regression and the BagMLP model, respectively. It is worth noting that the results achieved by the MNBHL model were obtained by using a network reduction option of 90%, i.e., with only 10% of the training data being preserved for testing purposes. Hence, it is expected that these accuracy rates should increase, if one can process the same data without using the network reduction resource.

**Table 5.** Average accuracy rates (%) and standard deviations for each insufficiency type, obtained by each classification technique. The values between parenthesis indicate the rank achieved by each technique, in each row.

|  | MNBHL | Ada | BagMLP | DT | LR | MLP | N-B | RF | SVM |
|---|---|---|---|---|---|---|---|---|---|
| Any | **68.4** ± .01 (1) | 67.4 ± .01 (5) | 67.9 ± .01 (3) | 61.9 ± .02 (9) | 67.6 ± .01 (4) | 67.1 ± .02 (6) | 67.9 ± .02 (2) | 64.8 ± .02 (7) | 63.5 ± .01 (8) |
| Hepatic | **64.9** ± .02 (1) | 64.4 ± .01 (3) | 64.1 ± .01 (4) | 56.0 ± .03 (9) | 64.8 ± .02 (2) | 63.7 ± .02 (5) | 62.9 ± .01 (6) | 60.0 ± .03 (7) | 58.8 ± .01 (8) |
| Renal | 70.4 ± .01 (3) | 69.9 ± .01 (6) | 70.3 ± .01 (4) | 60.5 ± .01 (9) | **70.9** ± .01 (1) | 70.1 ± .02 (5) | 70.6 ± .01 (2) | 66.9 ± .01 (7) | 65.6 ± .02 (8) |
| Respiratory | 75.9 ± .01 (3) | 75.3 ± .01 (6) | **76.0** ± .01 (1) | 65.3 ± .01 (9) | **76.0** ± .01 (2) | 75.9 ± .01 (4) | 75.5 ± .01 (5) | 71.5 ± .01 (8) | 72.0 ± .01 (7) |
| Avrg rank | 1st | 5th | 3rd | 8th | 2nd | 5th | 4th | 6th | 7th |

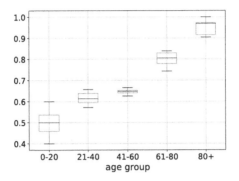

**Fig. 3.** Boxplots of the overall performance, in terms of accuracy, achieved by the proposed model on detecting early signs from any type of insufficiency in COVID-19 patients, grouped by age.

Given the nature of the COVID-19 dataset, the input data may become more or less unbalanced in each age group. In this sense, younger patients, from age groups 00–20 and 21–40 years old, are expected to present a lower incidence of insufficiency cases than older patients, from age groups 60–80 and 80+ years old (see Table 3). For analyzing how such differences may affect the model's performance, we present, in Fig. 3, the overall accuracy obtained by the MNBHL

**Table 6.** Precision, sensitivity and F1 score achieved by each model, when detecting signs from any type of insufficiency in COVID-19 patients over 60 years old.

|  | Precision | Sensitivity | F1 score |
|---|---|---|---|
| MNBHL | 0.886 | 0.983 | 0.931 |
| Ada | 0.881 | 0.989 | 0.930 |
| BagMLP | 0.882 | 0.995 | 0.933 |
| DT | 0.897 | 0.881 | 0.888 |
| LR | 0.884 | 0.990 | 0.933 |
| MLP | 0.884 | 0.991 | 0.933 |
| N-B | 0.893 | 0.963 | 0.926 |
| RF | 0.895 | 0.928 | 0.911 |
| SVM | 0.880 | 0.982 | 0.927 |

model on detecting early signs from any type of insufficiency, on each age group. The boxplots indicate that the model is able to achieve higher performances when analyzing data from older patients, reaching an average accuracy of more than 90% for the 80+ years old age group.

People who are older than 60 years are in the high risk group for COVID-19. If any sign of insufficiency is detected in patients from this group, prompt measures should be taken by healthcare professionals, oftentimes by making use of mechanical ventilation. For this reason, we also evaluate, in Table 6, how the models perform, in terms of precision, sensitivity and F1 score, specifically on data from this group, when detecting signs from any type of insufficiency. From this table, we see that the proposed MNBHL model again obtains competitive results in comparison to classic ones.

## 6   Final Remarks

In this work, we evaluate the possibility of predicting early signs of insufficiency in COVID-19 patients based only on CBC test results, used as biomarkers, through a supervised learning approach. For this end, a training dataset has been built, from original data of de-identified COVID-19 patients who received treatment in one of the main hospitals in Brazil. Additionally, for processing the built dataset, we use a modified network-based high-level classification technique, with novelties including the method used for automating the network building parameters, the measure used for capturing the data pattern structure, and the inclusion of a network reduction option, to facilitate its application on larger datasets. The proposed technique is evaluated by applying it firstly on benchmark classification datasets, and then on the built COVID-19 dataset, as well as by comparing its performance with those achieved by other traditional techniques, on the same data. The experimental results are encouraging, with the proposed technique obtaining competitive performance, both on the benchmark datasets and on the built COVID-19 dataset. Moreover, the considered models were particularly successful on data regarding patients from the risk group, who are older than 60 years old. Therefore, we believe the method proposed in this study can be potentially used as an additional tool in the severity assessment of COVID-19 patients who have higher risk of complications, thus helping healthcare professionals in this activity. Especially the ones who work in regions with scarce material and human resources, as in some places of Brazil.

As future research, we plan to explore the possibility of extending the classification technique by using additional centrality measures, in a combined form, both in the network reduction method and for the new node's insertion impact evaluation. We also plan to make applications on larger datasets, such as X-ray and CT images, to further assess the model's robustness on different type of data.

# References

1. Anghinoni, L., Zhao, L., Ji, D., Pan, H.: Time series trend detection and forecasting using complex network topology analysis. Neural Netw. **117**, 295–306 (2019)
2. Beck, B.R., Shin, B., Choi, Y., Park, S., Kang, K.: Predicting commercially available antiviral drugs that may act on the novel coronavirus (SARS-CoV-2) through a drug-target interaction deep learning model. Comput. Struct. Biotechnol. J. **18**, 784–790 (2020)
3. Brandes, U.: A faster algorithm for betweenness centrality. J. Math. Sociol. **25**(2), 163–177 (2001)
4. Breiman, L.: Bagging predictors. Mach. Learn. **24**(2), 123–140 (1996)
5. Breiman, L.: Random forests. Mach. Learn. **45**(1), 5–32 (2001)
6. Carneiro, M.G., Zhao, L.: Organizational data classification based on the importance concept of complex networks. IEEE Trans. Neural Netw. Learn. Syst. **29**(8), 3361–3373 (2017)
7. Chen, D., Lü, L., Shang, M.S., Zhang, Y.C., Zhou, T.: Identifying influential nodes in complex networks. Phys. A: Stat. Mech. Appl. **391**(4), 1777–1787 (2012)
8. Colliri, T., Ji, D., Pan, H., Zhao, L.: A network-based high level data classification technique. In: 2018 International Joint Conference on Neural Networks (IJCNN), pp. 1–8. IEEE (2018)
9. Csardi, G., Nepusz, T., et al.: The Igraph software package for complex network research. Int. J. Complex Syst. **1695**(5), 1–9 (2006)
10. Fapesp: Research data metasearch. https://repositorio.uspdigital.usp.br/handle/item/243. Accessed 1 Feb 2021
11. Freund, Yoav, Schapire, Robert E..: A desicion-theoretic generalization of on-line learning and an application to boosting. In: Vitányi, Paul (ed.) EuroCOLT 1995. LNCS, vol. 904, pp. 23–37. Springer, Heidelberg (1995). https://doi.org/10.1007/3-540-59119-2_166
12. Gelman, A., Hill, J.: Data Analysis Using Regression and Multilevel Hierarchical Models, vol. 1. Cambridge University Press, New York (2007)
13. Hinton, G.E.: Connectionist learning procedures. Artif. Intell. **40**(1–3), 185–234 (1989)
14. Lichman, M.: UCI machine learning repository (2013). http://archive.ics.uci.edu/ml
15. Metsky, H.C., Freije, C.A., Kosoko-Thoroddsen, T.S.F., Sabeti, P.C., Myhrvold, C.: CRISPR-based surveillance for COVID-19 using genomically-comprehensive machine learning design. BioRxiv (2020)
16. Pearson, K.: Note on regression and inheritance in the case of two parents. Proc. Royal Soc. London **58**(347–352), 240–242 (1895)
17. Pedregosa, F., et al.: Scikit-learn: machine learning in Python. J. Mach. Learn. Res. **12**, 2825–2830 (2011)
18. Rish, I.: An empirical study of the Naive Bayes classifier. In: IJCAI 2001 Workshop on Empirical Methods in Artificial Intelligence, vol. 3(22) (2001), IBM New York
19. Safavin, S.R., Landgrebe, D.: A survey of decision tree classifier methodology. IEEE Trans. Syst., Man, Cybern. **21**(3), 660–674 (1991)
20. Secr. Saude SP: prefeitura.sp.gov.br/cidade/secretarias/saude/vigilancia_em_saude/. Accessed 9 May 2021
21. Shan, F., et al.: Lung infection quantification of COVID-19 in CT images with deep learning. arXiv preprint arXiv:2003.04655 (2020)

22. Silva, T.C., Zhao, L.: Network-based high level data classification. IEEE Trans. Neural Netw. Learn. Syst. **23**(6), 954–970 (2012)
23. Strogatz, S.H.: Exploring complex networks. Nature **410**(6825), 268–276 (2001)
24. Valejo, A., Ferreira, V., Fabbri, R., Oliveira, M.C.F.d., Lopes, A.D.A.: A critical survey of the multilevel method in complex networks. ACM Comput. Surv. (CSUR) **53**(2), 1–35 (2020)
25. Vapnik, V.N.: The Nature of Statistical Learning Theory. Springer, New York (2000). https://doi.org/10.1007/978-1-4757-3264-1
26. Yan, L., et al.: An interpretable mortality prediction model for COVID-19 patients. Nat. Mach. Intell. **2**(5), 1–6 (2020)
27. Zoabi, Y., Deri-Rozov, S., Shomron, N.: Machine learning-based prediction of COVID-19 diagnosis based on symptoms. npj Digital Med. **4**(1), 1–5 (2021)

# Encoding Physical Conditioning from Inertial Sensors for Multi-step Heart Rate Estimation

Davi Pedrosa de Aguiar$^{(\boxtimes)}$ ⓘ and Fabricio Murai ⓘ

Universidade Federal de Minas Gerais, Belo Horizonte, Brazil
{daviaguiar,murai}@dcc.ufmg.br

**Abstract.** Inertial Measurement Unit (IMU) sensors are present in everyday devices such as smartphones and fitness watches. As a result, the array of health-related research and applications that tap onto this data has been growing, but little attention has been devoted to the prediction of an individual's heart rate (HR) from IMU data, when undergoing a physical activity. Would that be even possible? If so, this could be used to design personalized sets of aerobic exercises, for instance. In this work, we show that it is viable to obtain accurate HR predictions from IMU data using Recurrent Neural Networks, provided only access to HR and IMU data from a short-lived, previously executed activity. We propose a novel method for initializing an RNN's hidden state vectors, using a specialized network that attempts to extract an embedding of the physical conditioning (PCE) of a subject. We show that using a discriminator in the training phase to help the model learn whether two PCEs belong to the same individual further reduces the prediction error. We evaluate the proposed model when predicting the HR of 23 subjects performing a variety of physical activities from IMU data available in public datasets (PAMAP2, PPG-DaLiA). For comparison, we use as baselines the only model specifically proposed for this task and an adapted state-of-the-art model for Human Activity Recognition (HAR), a closely related task. Our method, PCE-LSTM, yields over 10% lower mean absolute error. We demonstrate empirically that this error reduction is in part due to the use of the PCE. Last, we use the two datasets (PPG-DaLiA, WESAD) to show that PCE-LSTM can also be successfully applied when photoplethysmography (PPG) sensors are available, outperforming the state-of-the-art deep learning baselines by more than 30%.

**Keywords:** Heart rate estimation · IMU sensors · Photoplethysmography · Neural networks

## 1 Introduction

In the recent years there has been an ever increasing usage of sensor-equipped devices, such as smartphones, smartwatches and fitness watches. These sensors can be used to track user behavior and health-related measurements. Among

ⓒ Springer Nature Switzerland AG 2021
A. Britto and K. Valdivia Delgado (Eds.): BRACIS 2021, LNAI 13074, pp. 58–72, 2021.
https://doi.org/10.1007/978-3-030-91699-2_5

the most common types are the Inertial Measurement Units (IMU), composed primarily of accelerometers and gyroscopes.The use of photoplethysmography (PPG) sensors to track heart rate (HR) is also becoming ubiquitous, especially in devices targeting fitness conscious consumers, such as the Apple Watch, Fit-Bit and Samsung SimBand [1]. To promote an effective fitness training, it is necessary to induce an optimal cardiovascular response, making it essential to model and predict individual HR responses [2].

Several methods have been designed to predict the HR under the influence of physical activity. Most of them are based on differential equations [3,4], Hammerstein and Wiener models [5] or Neural Networks. Among the latter, some predict many steps into the future [6,7], and others use IMU signals as input [7,8] but only the model proposed in [7] does both, to the best of our knowledge.

Despite the recent advances in neural networks, the problem of multi-step HR estimation from IMU sensor data remains little explored. In this paper, we investigate neural architectures that could be used for this task. To benchmark our model, in addition to using the model from [7], we adapt a network proposed for a closely related task called Human Activity Recognition (HAR), where the goal is to identify the activity being performed by a person (e.g., running, walking, swimming) given some sensor data (mostly, IMU) as input.

Recurrent Neural Networks (RNNs) are widely used for multi-step predictions because they can carry information regarding the "hidden" state of a sequence through time as vectors. Although the performance of RNNs can be highly dependent on the initialization of these vectors, most often they are simply set to zero. Sometimes, the RNNs are set up so that the state vectors go through some iterations (washout period) before the first prediction can be returned. In the context of aerial vehicle dynamics, [9] proposes an approach to initialize these vectors by using features and labels from a previous interval.

In a similar spirit, based on the premise that different subjects will display different HR levels when performing the same exercises depending on their physical conditioning, we propose a novel neural architecture that attempts to encode that attribute given IMU and HR data collected from a previous, short-lived, activity performed by an individual. This attribute is extracted by a CNN network as a vector dubbed *physical conditioning embedding* (PCE). The PCE is used, in turn, to set the initial values of the hidden and cell states of an LSTM responsible for outputting the HR predictions. Our proposed method, PCE-LSTM, differs from [9] in several ways, markedly, (i) it uses a discriminator to improve the ability of the network to capture the inherent characteristics of the subjects based on previous activities and (ii) it is able to improve predictions over windows of up to 2 h. This corroborates the idea that PCE-LSTM is encoding physical conditioning, rather than information about specific physical activities.

Although PPG sensors for tracking HR are becoming more common, they are prone to measurement errors due to motion-related artifacts. In this case, data from other sensors can be used to correct the HR measurements. This task, called PPG-based HR estimation, has been explored in [1,10,11]. To show that the proposed architecture can also be used for this task, we adapt PCE-LSTM to incorporate the PPG signal as an additional input and show that it can also outperform the state-of-the-art in this task. In sum, our main contributions are:

A **new model** to predict the HR from IMU-sensor signals, which outperforms state-of-the art baselines; An **ablation study** on the contribution of the PCE subnetwork to the performance of the model; A demonstration that PCE-LSTM estabilishes the **new deep learning SOTA of PPG-based HR estimation**.[1]

*Outline.* Section 2 describes datasets and pre-processing used in this work. Section 3 details the proposed method, PCE-LSTM, and the key hypothesis we investigate. Section 4 discusses the reference methods for the HR estimation task. Section 5 presents the evaluation results. The related work is reviewed in Sect. 6. Last, Sect. 7 discusses the significance and impact of this work.

## 2  Methodology

This work addresses the problem of predicting the heart rate $H_t$ of an individual at time $t = 1, \ldots$, given IMU sensor data gathered up to time $t$ and HR values from an initial, short lived period, $H_1 \ldots H_I$, with $I < t$. We refer to this task as **IMU-based multi-step HR estimation**. For this study, we use the PAMAP2 and PPG-DaLiA datasets (Sect. 2.1), which are among the very few publicly available sets containing both IMU and HR signals from individuals performing a variety of activities. PPG-DaLiA also has data from PPG sensors, which is disregarded in this first task.

We address the case where PPG sensors are available (in addition to IMU) as a secondary prediction task, referred as **PPG-based multi-step HR estimation**. Since PPG data are HR measurements that can be perturbed by movement, this task consists of correcting such measurements based on IMU data. For this task, we use the (complete) PPG-DaLiA [1] and WESAD [12] datasets. We show that it is possible to adapt the architecture proposed for the first to the second task with minor changes. Below we describe the datasets and the pre-processing techniques used throughout this work.

### 2.1  Datasets

**The PAMAP2 Dataset.** [13] consists of data from 40 sensors (accelerometers, gyroscopes, magnetometers, thermometers and HR sensor) sampled 100 Hz of 9 subjects performing 18 different activities (e.g., rope jumping, running, sitting). There is a single time series of sensor signals per subject, each performing a sequence of activities. Later on we explain that the time series for 1 of 9 the individuals is too short for training the models.

**The PPG-DaLiA Dataset.** [1] is composed of signals from two devices, a chest-worn device which provides accelerometer and ECG data; and a wrist-worn device measuring the PPG and triaxial acceleration, sampled 32 Hz. It also includes HR series computed from the ECG signals. This dataset contains a contiguous time series of sensor signals from 15 individuals performing 8 activities. We dub DaLiA, the subset of this dataset which does not include the PPG signals (to use in the IMU-based multi-step HR estimation task).

---

[1] We released all our code at https://github.com/davipeag/HeartRateRegression.

D. Aguiar, F. Murai

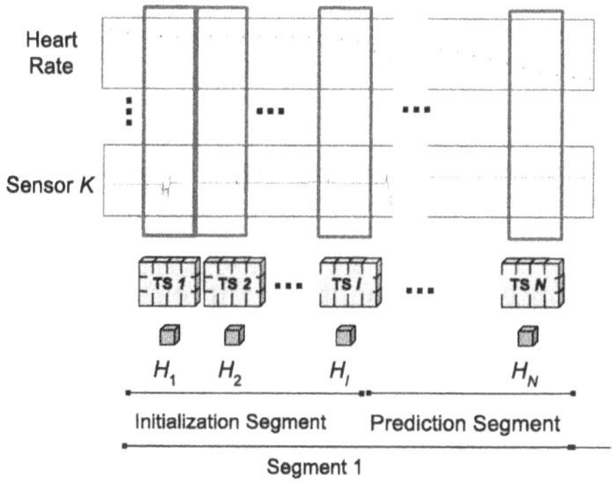

**Fig. 1.** Time Snippet Representation

**The WESAD Dataset.** [12] consists of data from 15 subjects wearing the same sensors available in PPG-DaLiA, but the individuals remain seated/standing during the whole study while going through different affective states (neutral, stress, amusement). Unlike PPG-DaLiA, WESAD does not provide precomputed HR series, therefore we used the heartpy library [14] to extract HR measurements from the ECG signals. Although subjects are indexed up to number 17, the dataset does not include subject identifiers 1 and 12.

In total, we use data from 23 (resp. 30) subjects for IMU-based (resp. PPG-based) multi-step HR estimation task.

### 2.2 Pre-processing

**Basic Preprocessing.** We upsample the HR signal using linear interpolation in all datasets to make its sampling rate consistent with the other signals. Only PAMAP2 contains a few missing data points, which we handle by local averaging the data around the missing point using a 0.4s window [15]. To make the use of the PAMAP2 and PPG-DaLiA datasets more consistent, we use only the accelerometer signals of the chest and wrist, and downsampled the signals 32 Hz. All signals $\mathbf{s}$ are z-normalized, i.e., $\hat{\mathbf{s}} = (s - \mu(\mathbf{s}))/\sigma(\mathbf{s})$, where $\mu$ stands for the mean operator and $\sigma$ for the standard deviation operator.

**Time Snippet Discretization.** Like most works based on this data, we discretize the time series signals into **time snippets** (TS), i.e., partially overlapping windows of fixed duration $\tau_{TS}$ and overlap ratio $r_{TS}$ (task-dependent). Figure 1 illustrates this procedure for the case when $r_{TS} = 0$. Each time snippet $TS_t$ is a matrix where each row represents a sensor. Time snippets determine the granularity of the predictions. Accordingly, we define the average HR $H_t$ for each time snippet $TS_t$ as the response to be predicted.

**Time Series Segmentation.** In order to create a fixed-length training set, we segment the time series of each individual in a sequence of $N$ contiguous time snippets of fixed duration. Each segment is partitioned into two smaller segments. The first, called **Initialization Segment**, contains the IMU and HR signals for the first $I = 12$ time snippets, and can be used by a neural network (NN) to encode a "state" specific to that time series. The second, called **Prediction Segment**, contains the IMU, but does not contain the HR, as it is used by a (possibly different) NN to output predictions for each time snippet. Figure 1 illustrates the subdivision of a segment, in the case where $r_{TS} = 0$. Note that the NN used for processing the first segment can also be used for processing the second segment by replacing the HR signal in the latter by zeroes.

## 3   The Physical Conditional Embedding LSTM Model

Here we describe PCE-LSTM, our proposed neural network architecture for HR prediction. PCE-LSTM is composed of convolutional and LSTM layers, similarly to the state-of-the-art techniques for the closely related task of HAR. The main novelty of this model is discussed below.

Recurrent Neural Networks (RNNs) have been especially designed to work with time series data. They are composed by cells with shared parameters, which process units of the input sequentially, using one or more vectors to carry state information through time. In particular, the unidirectional LSTM (long short-term memory) cell uses two vectors – the hidden state and the cell state – which are received from the previous iteration, updated based on the input for that time and passed onto the next iteration. The first iteration, however, receives these vectors as they were initialized, typically as zero vectors. The implicit assumption is that the network will gradually be able to encode the correct state from the inputs as the vectors are passed through the cells.

For HR prediction, we argue that if some data on the relationship between the input and output signals is available prior to the prediction, it can be beneficial to use a specialized network to encode this relationship as the RNN initial state. This initial state should contain information about physical conditioning: a more fit individual is able to sustain similar movement levels with smaller increase in HR. Thus, the main hypothesis investigated here can be stated as

> **Hypothesis:** *It is possible to encode information about physical conditioning from an individual's sensor data as a vector and use it as the initial state of a RNN to improve HR predictions.*

This is the rationale behind the main difference between our approach and similar ones, namely the initialization of the RNN hidden vectors using a specialized network, which we call the Physical Conditioning Encoder.

Figure 2 shows the high level structure of our architecture, which is made of five components: the **Time Snippet Encoder** (TS Encoder), a convolutional network which encodes the 2-dimensional TS into a vector; the **Physical Conditioning Encoder** (PC Encoder), a convolutional network which extracts, from signals of the Initialization Segment (including HR), a Physical

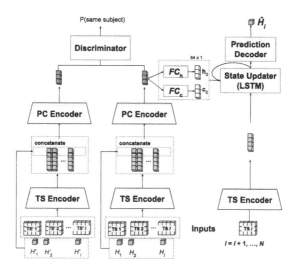

**Fig. 2.** PCE-LSTM (proposed architecture).

Conditioning Embedding (PCE) used for initializing the LSTM's hidden vectors; the **Discriminator**, used to force the PCE of a given subject to be similar across time segments; the **State Updater**, a LSTM which maintains and updates the subject's state, encoded in its hidden vectors; and the **Prediction Decoder**, a Fully-Connected network which decodes the HR prediction from the state tracked by the State Updater. We emphasize that instances of the same module shares the same weights. Each component is described in detail below.

**TS Encoder:** extracts features from one time snippet. We reckon the role of each sensor in the description of the intensity of an activity as being equivalent to role of each RGB channel in the description of a picture. Hence, it is reasonable to combine them early in the NN. To do so, we use 1D convolutions along the time dimension, with the sensors stacked along the channel dimension. This approach differs from the most well known architectures in the literature [1, 16,17] which keep the transformations on each sensor's signals separate during the convolutional section of their architectures by the use convolutional kernels spanning a single sensor, only combining them later on.

The TS Encoder comprises multiple layers, each made of a 1D convolution followed by a Leaky Rectified Linear Unit activation and a dropout layer of rate $\text{TSE}_{\text{dropout}}$. After each layer, the tensor length $\ell$ is reduced to $\lfloor \ell/2 \rfloor$ by filters of size 3 and stride 2 (when $\ell$ is even, we use padding $= 1$), except when the the tensor length is 2, in which case we use a filter of size 2 without padding. All layers have $\text{TSE}_F$ filters, except the last layer, which has $\text{TSE}_{\text{out}}$ filters. The number of layers is $\text{TSE}_N = \lfloor \log_2(\text{TS}_L) \rfloor$, where $\text{TS}_L$ is the length of the time dimension of the TS, so as to transform the size of the time dimension to one.

The vectors extracted from each time snippet of the Initialization Segment are concatenated along the time dimension, and the HR of each TS is concatenated along the feature dimension before being passed onto the next component.

**PC Encoder:** takes the vectors concatenated in the previous step and extracts a **physical conditioning embedding** (PCE). It is a multi-layer convolutional network that transforms the 2D-input ( (TSE$_{\text{out}}$ + 1) × $I$) into a single vector of length PCE$_{\text{out}}$. Its convolutional architecture is designed with the same principles as the TS Encoder. Figure 2 shows the PC Encoder in detail.

From the PCE, the LSTM's hidden state and cell state vectors are computed using a single linear layer each, represented in Fig. 2 by FC$_h$ and FC$_c$.

**State Updater:** is a standard LSTM with both state vectors (cell and hidden state's) of size LSTM$_H$, and input of size TSE$_{\text{out}}$. These state vectors are initialized by the PC Encoder using only signals from the Initialization Segment. The LSTM is then fed with the deep attributes extracted by the TS Encoder from each time snippet.

**Prediction Decoder:** takes the hidden state representation for each time snippet from the State Updater and computes the prediction from these representations. It is made of three fully connected layers, where the first two layers have 32 neurons, each followed by a ReLU activation function, and the last layer have LSTM$_H$ neurons, without activation function, outputting the predicted HR. We use the mean absolute error ($\ell_1$ loss) as the cost function $L_{\text{HR}}$ associated with this output because using the $\ell_2$ loss hampers training as larger differences between the predicted and actual HR have an out-sized impact on the loss, according to our preliminary experiments.

**Discriminator:** Given the benefits of multi-task learning we propose the simultaneous training of the model on a constructed task in which the PCE is used to distinguish between individuals. Assuming a subject's physical conditioning as constant in the short term, we reason that employing a network to discriminate whether two PCEs belong to same person will foster better embeddings, when trained jointly with PCE-LSTM[2]. To train the Discriminator, for each segment in the training set, we sample another segment from the same individual with probability 0.50 and from a different individual with probability 0.50. For each pair, we measure the cross entropy as the loss function ($L_D$). We set the weight of the discrimination loss to 10% of the total loss.[3] Hence, the total loss $L_{\text{total}}$ is given by $L_{\text{total}} = 0.9 L_{\text{HR}} + 0.1 L_D$. This component is the head of a Siamese network and is completely optional, being used exclusively to improve the performance of the model. The Discriminator's chosen architecture is comprised of 5 fully connected linear layers, each with 64 neurons and followed by ReLU activation function and a dropout rate of 0.15, except for the last layer, which uses a sigmoid activation function. This network receives two PCEs (concatenated) and outputs a probability.

### 3.1 Adaptations for PPG-Based HR Estimation

The task of PPG-based HR estimation has 3 main distinctions from the IMU-only HR estimation and hence requires a few adaptations to our method. First,

---

[2] We avoid overfitting by using disjoint sets of subjects for training and validation.

[3] Alternatively, losses' weights can be set by hyperparameter tuning, but since we use a single subject for validation, we fixed the weights to $(0.9, 0.1)$ to avoid overfitting to the validation subject.

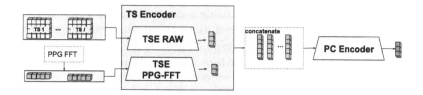

**Fig. 3.** PPG-adapted PCE

the PPG signal is best represented in the frequency domain; second, the PPG signal is more important than the other signals since it is a rough estimate of the HR; third, for PPG-based HR estimation, a ground truth HR is not usually available. To deal with these differences, we modified the TS Encoder sub-network to comprise two TS Encoder architectures, one for the raw PPG and IMU signals ($\text{TSE}_{\text{raw}}$) and another for the Fast Fourier the Transformed PPG signal ($\text{TSE}_{\text{PPG-FFT}}$). These outputs are concatenated and returned by the new sub-network. The $\text{TSE}_{\text{PPG-FFT}}$ is smaller, with $[\text{TSE}_{\text{PPG-FFT}}]_{\text{out}} = 12$. We also modified the PC Encoder slightly, so that it only receives as input the concatenated outputs of the TSE (without the HR). Figure 3 illustrates the changes to the PCE-LSTM architecture for the secondary task.

## 4   Reference Methods

To the best of our knowledge, the task of predicting multiple steps of HR given IMU signals has only been attempted by [7], which used in their experiments a dataset not publicly available. In addition to using their model as a baseline, we also adapt a model [17] designed for similar tasks (HAR) in order to benchmark our method. In this section we describe each of these models, the task they were designed to address and the minor changes required to adapt the models for the task at hand. More recent architectures for the HAR task, such as [16], were not used as baselines because they were not designed for multi-step predictions over time series and, as such, would require significant changes.

**FFNN.** [7] is a feed-forward recursive architecture with skip connections using data from a wrist-worn 3-axial accelerometer. The model uses the average measurement of each sensor in a non-overlapping window of 30 s. As the architecture details were not reported, we set the layer size to 16 and ReLU as the activation function for each layer based on random search optimization. We adapted their architecture, using a time window of $\tau_{\text{TS}} = 4$ s, to make it more comparable to our method (testing with $\tau_{\text{TS}} = 30$ s as in the original work yielded worse results). We train the network using Adam, instead of the genetic algorithms used in that study.

**DeepConvLSTM.** [17] performs a sequence of convolutions on the input series. The deep features from each time entry feed a LSTM. From each LSTM hidden vector, a prediction is computed using a single linear layer. In our adapted version, we add padding to the convolutions to maintain the length of the tensor and select only the outputs corresponding to the last time input of each time snippet, as we have one label per time snippet. As in [17], we downsampled the input signals 30 Hz, and set time snippets' length to $\tau_{TS} = 3s$.

## 5   Empirical Evaluation

In this section we describe the experiments conducted to evaluate PCE-LSTM and their results. We begin with an overview of the experimental setup. Next, we present the IMU-based HR prediction experiments (the primary prediction task) and an ablation study on the PCE's impact on performance. Last, we describe the PPG-based HR estimation (the secondary prediction task).

### 5.1   Experimental Setup

We evaluate the IMU-based multi-step HR estimation results w.r.t. Mean Absolute Error (MAE), Root Mean Squared Error (RMSE) and Maximum Error ($\ell_1$) as evaluation metrics. For the PPG-based HR estimation, however, we consider only MAE, since we transcribe the results from the paper where the baseline method was proposed [1], which did not include another evaluation metric.

**Train-Test Split.** We create several train-test splits using a "leave one subject out strategy", which mimics a realistic setting where the model would be applied to individuals not contained in the training set, as is the case for most models trained offline [18]. In a dataset with $S$ subjects, each of the subjects is used once as the test subject and the remaining $S - 1$ subjects' time series are split into training segments of $N = 50$ time snippets each and then randomly assigned to Train/Validation sets using an 80/20 split. For test, we use the whole series of each subject, which represents around one or two hours for most subjects in the PAMAP2 and DaLiA datasets respectively. With each of the $S$ subjects as the test subject, we perform 7 executions, with different Train/Validation splits and different neural network weight initialization, as done in [1].

**Hyperparameter Tuning.** In order to choose PCM-LSTM' and the optimizer's (Adam) hyperparameters, we applied a random search using the results on PAMAP2's subject 5 as reference, following [17]. The following hyperparameters were selected: $PCE_F = 64$, $I = 12$, $\tau_{TS} = 4$, $r_{TS} = 0.5$, $TSE_{out} = 128$, $TSE_F = 16$, $LSTM_H = 64$, $PCE_{out} = 64$, $TSE_{dropout} = 0.15$, learning rate $= 0.005$, weight decay $= 0.00005$.

**Training Setup.** All the models are optimized with Adam using the $\ell_1$ loss as the cost function associated with the HR predictions. In each epoch, we compute the validation loss. After training is complete, we load the model weights that yielded the lowest validation loss. Training was done using a batch size of 64 over 100 epochs for PCE-LSTM and DeepConvLSTM. FFNN showed slower convergence and hence was trained for 200 epochs. Subject 9 of the PAMAP2

**Table 1.** Error metrics on the DaLiA dataset (best shown in bold)

| Model | MAE by test subject [beats/minute] | | | | | | | | | | | | | | | | RMSE | ℓ₁ |
|---|---|---|---|---|---|---|---|---|---|---|---|---|---|---|---|---|---|---|
| | 1 | 2 | 3 | 4 | 5 | 6 | 7 | 8 | 9 | 10 | 11 | 12 | 13 | 14 | 15 | Avg. | Avg. | Avg. |
| FFNN (mean) | 13.2 | 10.5 | 12.9 | 9.0 | 45.0 | **32.1** | 13.7 | 16.0 | **12.3** | 11.9 | **22.2** | 17.8 | 17.2 | 12.7 | 14.0 | 17.4 | 21.8 | 64 |
| DeepConvLSTM (mean) | 9.8 | 7.7 | 16.1 | 12.9 | 44.1 | 34.9 | 15.8 | **9.2** | 14.8 | 13.2 | 25.5 | **11.3** | 15.3 | 13.6 | 11.2 | 17.0 | 22.2 | 69 |
| PCE-LSTM (mean) | 9.3 | **6.5** | 12.2 | 8.7 | 42.0 | 34.7 | **11.3** | 12.2 | 13.6 | 12.2 | 22.4 | 15.1 | **10.9** | 11.5 | 9.2 | 15.5 | 18.5 | **51** |
| FFNN (ens.) | 12.2 | 8.0 | 11.4 | 7.7 | 45.0 | **31.4** | 12.4 | 14.5 | 11.5 | 8.6 | 22.1 | 17.3 | 15.0 | 11.2 | 10.6 | 15.9 | 19.5 | 60 |
| DeepConvLSTM (ens.) | 9.2 | 7.1 | 15.3 | 12.7 | 43.9 | 34.7 | 15.4 | **6.9** | 13.9 | 12.9 | 25.4 | **10.7** | 15.1 | 13.2 | 10.5 | 16.5 | 20.6 | 68 |
| PCE-LSTM (ens.) | **8.4** | **5.1** | **7.8** | **6.6** | 41.9 | 34.4 | **7.4** | 8.9 | **11.4** | **8.4** | **19.6** | 14.9 | 9.3 | 9.8 | **8.5** | **13.5** | **16.2** | **49** |

**Table 2.** Error metrics on PAMAP2 (best shown in bold)

| Model | MAE by test subject [bpm] (mean) | | | | | | | | | RMSE | ℓ₁ | MAE by Test Subject [bpm] (ensemble) | | | | | | | | | RMSE | ℓ₁ |
|---|---|---|---|---|---|---|---|---|---|---|---|---|---|---|---|---|---|---|---|---|---|---|
| | 1 | 2 | 3 | 4 | 5 | 6 | 7 | 8 | Avg. | Avg. | Avg. | 1 | 2 | 3 | 4 | 5 | 6 | 7 | 8 | Avg. | Avg. | Avg. |
| FFNN | 24.9 | 18.3 | 10.5 | **17.2** | 18.6 | 14.7 | 21.6 | 33.7 | 19.9 | 26.1 | 72 | 23.2 | 14.2 | 9.5 | **15.8** | 17.8 | 13.4 | 20.3 | 23.9 | 17.3 | 22.1 | 64 |
| DeepConvLSTM | **14.7** | 11.4 | **8.8** | 18.7 | 11.9 | 13.9 | 20.0 | 14.9 | 14.3 | 17.9 | 52 | **11.8** | 10.6 | **8.3** | 18.4 | 9.3 | 13.1 | 19.5 | 13.3 | 13.0 | 15.8 | 46 |
| PCE-LSTM | 16.6 | **10.7** | 9.0 | 19.5 | **9.6** | 9.9 | **12.6** | 14.8 | **12.9** | 16.4 | 49 | 16.5 | **9.5** | 8.4 | 16.7 | **8.4** | **8.8** | **10.8** | 13.2 | **11.5** | 14.6 | **45** |

dataset was not included in the analysis because the corresponding time series is shorter than the length of the training segment (102 s).

**Mean vs. Ensemble Performance.** Each method is trained 7 times for each test subject (using different train-validation splits). We compute a "mean" performance by averaging the errors of individual models and an "ensemble" performance by averaging the predictions and then computing the resulting error.

## 5.2    IMU-Based Multi-step HR Estimation

We begin by analyzing the performance metrics. Table 1 and 2 shows the Mean and the Ensemble performances w.r.t. MAE by test subject and MAE averages for PCE-LSTM and the baselines, on DaLiA and PAMAP2 respectively. Due to space limitations, we only report $\ell_1$ and RMSE averages, but the complete results can be found in our technical report [19]. We note that the series of subjects 5 and 6 of DaLiA dataset can be regarded as outliers as none of the methods performed well on them. As expected, ensembles tend to outperform their standalone counterparts. Considering the ensemble performances, out of 23 subjects, FFNN, DeepConvLSTM and PCE-LSTM achieve the lowest errors for 2, 4 and 17 subjects, respectively. The lowest average error is obtained by the PCE-LSTM ensemble, with over 11.5% lower MAE and 7.3% lower RMSE than the next best method. In relation to the maximum error, our method was over 18% better than the next best method in the DALIA dataset, but just slightly better than the second best on the PAMAP2 dataset.

For a qualitative evaluation, we plot the predictions of each model. Figure 4 shows the ensemble predictions for the complete series of five representative test subjects in the DaLiA and PAMAP2 datasets. We observe that DeepConvLSTM fails to capture the variance of the HR series: although the predictions are correlated with changes in HR, they tend to remain close to an "average" HR. FFNN, in turn, exhibits more variance, but cannot accurately capture the amplitude of

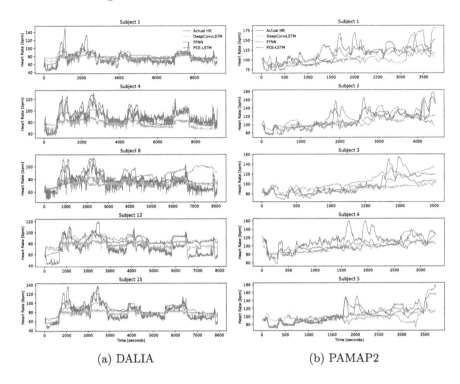

(a) DALIA                     (b) PAMAP2

**Fig. 4.** Long-term IMU-based HR estimation

the peaks and sometimes overestimates the HR. In contrast, PCE-LSTM (our method) can capture both peaks and valleys more accurately than the baselines.

### 5.3 Performance Impact of PCE-LSTM's Hidden State Initialization

In this section we conduct an ablation study to demonstrate that PCE-LSTM's strategy for initializing hidden state vectors is key to boosting the model's performance. For conciseness, we limit this study to the DaLiA dataset, which contains nearly twice the number of subjects, and a longer series per subject. A typical strategy to extract a hidden state is to use the LSTM itself to encode the relationship between sensor data and HR. In contrast, our model initializes the LSTM's hidden state vectors by passing the sensor and HR data corresponding to the first $I = 12$ time snippets (26 s) of the series through the Physical Conditioning Encoder (PC Encoder). As we assume that the PCE partially encodes an individual's physical conditioning, we expect that the joint training of the PCE-LSTM regression and the Discriminator will improve the regression predictions by promoting a better training of the PC Encoder subnetwork.

To quantify the performance impact of the proposed initialization and of using the discriminator, we conduct additional experiments with alternative initialization strategies. In what follows, "with discr." indicates the joint training

**Table 3.** Ablation: error results for variations of the PCE-LSTM model on DaLiA

| | MAE by test subject [beats/minute] | | | | | | | | | | | | | | | | RMSE | $\ell_1$ |
|---|---|---|---|---|---|---|---|---|---|---|---|---|---|---|---|---|---|---|
| | 1 | 2 | 3 | 4 | 5 | 6 | 7 | 8 | 9 | 10 | 11 | 12 | 13 | 14 | 15 | Avg. | Avg. | Avg. |
| LSTM self-encode (ens.) | 11.0 | 7.6 | **7.1** | 7.4 | 48.6 | 33.6 | 10.7 | 15.6 | 11.5 | 9.3 | 21.2 | 15.2 | 10.7 | 10.7 | 10.4 | 15.4 | 18.3 | **44** |
| Without discr. (ens.) | 10.5 | 5.9 | 13.7 | 7.6 | 43.7 | **29.5** | 7.8 | 14.3 | **9.4** | 9.5 | **18.8** | **13.6** | 9.1 | 11.4 | **7.7** | 14.2 | 16.8 | 46 |
| With discr. (ens.) | **8.4** | **5.1** | 7.8 | **6.6** | **41.9** | 34.4 | **7.4** | **8.9** | 11.4 | **8.4** | 19.6 | 14.9 | 9.3 | **9.8** | 8.5 | **13.5** | **16.2** | 45 |

**Table 4.** PPG-based HR estimation experiments

| | PPG-DaLiA: MAE by test subject [beats/minute] | | | | | | | | | | | | | | | |
|---|---|---|---|---|---|---|---|---|---|---|---|---|---|---|---|---|
| Model | 1 | 2 | 3 | 4 | 5 | 6 | 7 | 8 | 9 | 10 | 11 | 12 | 13 | 14 | 15 | Avg. |
| [1] | 7.73 | 6.74 | 4.03 | 5.90 | 18.51 | 12.88 | 3.91 | 10.87 | 8.79 | 4.03 | 9.22 | 9.35 | 4.29 | 4.37 | 4.17 | 7.65 |
| PCE-LSTM | **5.53** | **3.77** | **2.54** | **5.41** | **10.96** | **5.54** | **2.61** | **9.09** | **6.57** | **2.62** | **5.47** | **8.47** | **2.73** | **3.71** | **3.36** | **5.22** |
| | WESAD: MAE by test subject [beats/minute] | | | | | | | | | | | | | | | |
| Model | 2 | 3 | 4 | 5 | 6 | 7 | 8 | 9 | 10 | 11 | 13 | 14 | 15 | 16 | 17 | Avg. |
| [1] | 5.07 | 14.48 | 7.84 | 7.70 | 3.88 | 6.78 | **4.27** | 3.99 | 8.89 | 11.07 | 6.52 | 5.26 | 4.18 | 12.78 | 9.36 | 7.47 |
| PCE-LSTM | **3.59** | **9.83** | **3.46** | **4.65** | **2.65** | **4.58** | 4.61 | **3.03** | **4.91** | **7.06** | **4.77** | **4.67** | **3.51** | **4.91** | **8.35** | **4.97** |

with the discriminator, "without discr." indicates that the discriminator is not used; and "LSTM self-encode", indicates that hidden state vectors are initialized by feeding the HR to the network as an additional input channel in the TS of the Initialization Segment (replaced by zeros during the prediction segment).

Table 3 shows the prediction results for these experiments on DaLiA. PCE-LSTM's outperforms an LSTM self-encode initialization strategy even without a discriminator, but using the discriminator further reduces the error.

### 5.4 PPG-Based HR Estimation

We adapt PCE-LSTM for PPG-based HR estimation. While similar to the IMU-based HR estimation, the former task has been better explored in the literature and has, therefore, well established baselines. For this reason, we compare PCE-LSTM to the SOTA method based on deep learning [1]. This method is based on CNNs and will be referred simply as CNN.

To match the length and step size of each time snippet in [1], we set $\tau_{TS} = 8$ and $r_{TS} = 0.75$ for this task. Table 4 shows the ensemble performance for each method on PPG-DaLiA and WESAD, when the individual designated in the column is the test subject. The results of CNN were transcribed directly from [1]. The last column shows the row average. On both datasets, PCE-LSTM provides error reductions of approximately 32% when compared to the SOTA method. Another advantage of PCE-LSTM is that it has 2 orders of magnitude less parameters than the CNN – approx. 120k parameters for PCE-LSTM vs. approx. 8.5M parameters for the CNN model.

## 6    Related Work

Few studies used IMU sensors to predict the heart rate. [8] used a simple Feed-Forward Neural Network to predict the HR one step ahead, given its value and the average signal of each IMU sensor on the previous step. Quite similarly, [7] performed a multi-step HR prediction by repeatedly using the HR computed for step $t$ to predict the HR for step $t+1$. Their experiments demonstrated promising results, but had some notable deficiencies: they used data from a single individual in his daily activities, hence without much variation in HR values.

Also on multi-step HR estimation, but using speed and acceleration as inputs, [6] proposed a Bayesian combined predictor, where one estimator was a linear regression and the other, a neural network similar to that of [7]. In their experiments, data from multiple individuals performing running sessions was used, thus addressing some of the shortcomings in [7]. However, the proposed method required calibration with actual HR data every 90 s, hindering its practical use.

For HAR, a task where the use of IMU data is widespread, [20] studied the performance of Deep Feed-Forward Networks (DNNs), CNNs and LSTMs, demonstrating that CNN and LSTM based models outperform DNNs and, among them, the best performing model was very dependent on the dataset used.

The hybrid CNN and LSTM model proposed by [17], achieved good results but was surpassed by the CNN-based architecture of [16]. More recently, some works proposed the use of self-attention based architectures for this task [21,22]. The model proposed by [16] outperformed the one proposed by [21] in the datasets that were common to both works. [22] proposed a deep attention model that was able to surpass [16] in some, but not all datasets. A more extensive survey was conducted by [23], where the authors note the variety of neural network architectures proposed for this task, such as CNNs, DNNs, RNNs, Stacked Auto Encoders and hybrid approaches.

A few studies have proposed methods for initializing state vectors of RNNs. To regularize and improve the dynamics of an RNN, [24] proposed initializing the RNN with a vector proportional to the backpropagated errors. [25] showed that using contextual information to initialize the RNN hidden state improved the convergence rate, but not the final accuracy of the networks on some constructed problems. In modeling an aerial vehicle dynamics, [9] showed that passing an initial segment of the data through a custom network to set the hidden state vectors reduces errors, especially in the first iterations of predictions. Our work differs from theirs in several ways. Most markedly, (i) it uses a discriminator to improve the ability of the network to capture the subjects' inherent characteristics based on previous activities and (ii) it is able to improve predictions over windows of up to 2 h. This corroborates the idea that PCE-LSTM is encoding physical conditioning, rather than information about specific physical activities.

## 7    Conclusions

We investigated the much neglected task of predicting HR from IMU sensor data. We started from the premise that, depending on their physical conditioning, different people will display different HR levels when performing the same exercises. We proposed a neural architecture dubbed Physical Conditioning Embedding

LSTM (PCE-LSTM) that employs a convolutional network to extract vectors which carry information about the relationship between sensor measurements and the HR for a specific individual, thus representing his/her physical conditioning. These vectors are used as the initial state vectors for a LSTM network that outputs HR predictions from sensor data. We evaluate the prediction accuracy of PCE-LSTM w.r.t. MAE and RMSE using public datasets (PAMAP2, PPG-DaLiA, WESAD). Moreover, we compare PCE-LSTM with 2 baselines: one model proposed for this task (FFNN) and one minimally-adapted state-of-the-art model (DeepConvLSTM) originally proposed for the closely related task known as Human Activity Recognition.

PCE-LSTM yields over 10% (resp. 30%) lower MAE in the IMU-based (resp. PPG-based) HR estimation task. Last, we conduct additional experiments to show that the performance gains achieved by our method are, in part, due to the strategy used to initialize the hidden vectors. Specifically, using the outputs of the PCE network applied to the data from the previous 12 time snippets of the subject's time series is helpful and works better than using the LSTM itself to output hidden vectors from the same data, especially when using the PCE discriminator during training.

We have highlighted the potential of neural network approaches to tackle this problem. Some questions are left open for future work, such as whether these results are accurate enough to be successfully used in real-world applications or whether the metrics used best represent the suitability of a model. We hope that this work can foster the development of new methods and metrics for this task, bringing about a practical use for the method in medical or fitness applications.

# References

1. Reiss, A., Indlekofer, I., Schmidt, P., Van Laerhoven, K.: Deep PPG: large-scale heart rate estimation with convolutional neural networks. Sensors **19**(14), 3079 (2019)
2. Ludwig, M., Hoffmann, K., Endler, S., Asteroth, A., Wiemeyer, J.: Measurement, prediction, and control of individual heart rate responses to exercise-basics and options for wearable devices. Front. Physiol. **9**, 778 (2018)
3. Cheng, T.M., Savkin, A.V., Celler, B.G., Wang, L., Su, S.W.: A nonlinear dynamic model for heart rate response to treadmill walking exercise. In: IEEE IEMBS, pp. 2988–2991 (2007)
4. Hunt, K.J., Fankhauser, S.E.: Heart rate control during treadmill exercise using input-sensitivity shaping for disturbance rejection of very-low-frequency heart rate variability. Biomed. Signal Process. Control **30**, 31–42 (2016)
5. Mohammad, S., Guerra, T.M., Grobois, J.M., Hecquet, B.: Heart rate control during cycling exercise using Takagi-Sugeno models. IFAC Proc. **44**(1), 12783–12788 (2011)
6. Zhang, H., Wen, B., Liu, J.: The prediction of heart rate during running using Bayesian combined predictor. In: IEEE IWCMC, pp. 981–986 (2018)
7. Xiao, F., Yuchi, M., Ding, M., Jo, J.: A research of heart rate prediction model based on evolutionary neural network. In: IEEE ICBMI, pp. 304–307 (2011)

8. Yuchi, M., Jo, J.: Heart rate prediction based on physical activity using feedforwad neural network. In: IEEE ICHIT, pp. 344–350 (2008)
9. Mohajerin, N., Waslander, S.L.: Multistep prediction of dynamic systems with recurrent neural networks. **30**(11), 3370–3383 (2019)
10. Salehizadeh, S., Dao, D., Bolkhovsky, J., Cho, C., Mendelson, Y., Chon, K.: A novel time-varying spectral filtering algorithm for reconstruction of motion artifact corrupted heart rate signals during intense physical activities using a wearable photoplethysmogram sensor. Sensors **16**(1), 10 (2016)
11. Schäck, T., Muma, M., Zoubir, A.M.: Computationally efficient heart rate estimation during physical exercise using photoplethysmographic signals. In: EUSIPCO, pp. 2478–2481 (2017)
12. Schmidt, P., Reiss, A., Duerichen, R., Marberger, C., Van Laerhoven, K.: Introducing WESAD, a multimodal dataset for wearable stress and affect detection. In: ACM ICMI, pp. 400–408, New York, NY, USA (2018). Association for Computing Machinery
13. Reiss, A., Stricker, D.: Introducing a new benchmarked dataset for activity monitoring. In: IEEE ISWC, pp. 108–109, June 2012
14. van Gent, P., Farah, H., van Nes, N., van Arem, B.: Analysing noisy driver physiology real-time using off-the-shelf sensors: heart rate analysis software from the taking the fast lane project. J. Open Res. Softw. **7**(1) (2019)
15. Eyobu, O.S., Han, D.S.: Feature representation and data augmentation for human activity classification based on wearable IMU sensor data using a deep LSTM neural network. Sensors **18**(9), 2892 (2018)
16. Rueda, F.M., Grzeszick, R., Fink, G.A., Feldhorst, S., Hompel, M.T.: Convolutional neural networks for human activity recognition using body-worn sensors. Informatics **5**(2), 26 (2018)
17. Ordóñez, F.J., Roggen, D.: Deep convolutional and LSTM recurrent neural networks for multimodal wearable activity recognition. Sensors **16**(1), 115 (2016)
18. Jordao, A., Nazare Jr, A.C., Sena, J., Schwartz, W.R.: Human activity recognition based on wearable sensor data: a standardization of the state-of-the-art. arXiv e-prints, page arXiv:1806.05226, June 2018
19. de Aguiar, D.P., Murai, F.: Am I fit for this physical activity? Neural embedding of physical conditioning from inertial sensors (2021)
20. Hammerla, N.Y., Halloran, S., Plötz, T.: Deep, convolutional, and recurrent models for human activity recognition using wearables. In: IJCAI, pp. 1533–1540 (2016)
21. Vaswani, A.: Attention is all you need. In: NeurIPS, pp. 5998–6008 (2017)
22. Wu, N., Green, B., Ben, X., O'Banion, S.: Deep transformer models for time series forecasting: the influenza prevalence case. arXiv e-prints, page arXiv:2001.08317, January 2020
23. Wang, J., Chen, Y., Hao, S., Peng, X., Lisha, H.: Deep learning for sensor-based activity recognition: a survey. Patt. Recogn. Lett. **119**, 3–11 (2019)
24. Zimmermann, H., Grothmann, R., Schaefer, A., Tietz, C.: 8 modeling large dynamical systems with dynamical consistent neural networks. In: Haykin, S., Principe, J.C., Sejnowski, T.J., McWhirter, J. (eds.) New Directions in Statistical Signal Processing: From Systems to Brains, chapter 8. The MIT Press (2006)
25. Wenke, S., Fleming, J.: Contextual recurrent neural networks (2019)

# Ensemble of Protein Stability upon Point Mutation Predictors

Eduardo Kenji Hasegawa de Freitas⬤, Alex Dias Camargo⬤,
Maurício Balboni⬤, Adriano V. Werhli⬤,
and Karina dos Santos Machado$^{(\boxtimes)}$⬤

Computational Biology Laboratory - COMBI-LAB, Centro de Ciências
Computacionais, Universidade Federal do Rio Grande - FURG,
Av. Itália, km 8, Rio Grande, RS, Brazil
karina.machado@furg.br

**Abstract.** Computational determination of protein stability upon point mutations is very useful in a wide field of applications. The reliability of such computational predictions is essential. Unfortunately, existing computational tools frequently disagree in their results. In the present study, the usage of Ensemble Learning Algorithms to aggregate the results from different stability prediction tools is investigated. Techniques of Stacking, Bagging, and Boosting as well as different Machine Learning algorithms as combiner function are explored. All the investigation is carried out in real dataset ProTherm for which experimental results are known. The proposed methodology was validated considering two different experiments according to the training set. Results show that our proposed ensemble approach is appropriate to predict the effect of point mutations on protein stability showing more reliable results than the individual tools improving overall accuracy, precision, and/or recall.

**Keywords:** Ensemble learning · Bioinformatics · Protein stability · Point mutations

## 1 Introduction

The latest research and development in biological experiments and techniques have created a deluge of experimental data. To deal with this quantity and variety of data the necessity of computational methods and tools is obvious. In some cases, the use of Data Science methodology is mandatory.

In all living species, biological information is stored in the DNA (deoxyribonucleic acid). DNA can be seen as the source code that contains all the instructions to create and sustain life. To transform the information contained in the DNA into functioning parts, DNA is transcript as RNA (ribonucleic acid) which is then translated into proteins. Proteins are the principal biological elements

This study was supported by CAPES Edital Biologia Computacional (51/2013), CAPES Financial Code 001 and CNPq (439582/2018-0).

A. Britto and K. Valdivia Delgado (Eds.): BRACIS 2021, LNAI 13074, pp. 73–88, 2021.
https://doi.org/10.1007/978-3-030-91699-2_6

responsible for executing biological functions. Proteins can be thought of as the compiled result of the information stored in the DNA [23]. Moreover, proteins are the most abundant organic molecules in living systems and have the widest range of functions among macro-molecules. These functions can be structural, regulatory, contracting, or protective. Furthermore, they can serve as transport, storage, or membranes, as well as being enzymes or toxins. Each cell in a living system has thousands of proteins where each one has a function, making their structures very varied.

Proteins are the biological elements that execute functions and frequently they are modified (mutated) to achieve specific goals. These designed changes, mutations, are carried out in specific parts of the DNA using for example site-directed mutagenesis. These mutations can produce a strong impact on the structure and function of proteins [17,19]. However, due to the vast number of possibilities, it is impractical to experimentally evaluate the impact of all possible mutations on protein structure and function [25].

A series of computational tools have been developed, with the common objective of predicting the effect of point mutations on the structure of a protein. In general, prediction tools are developed and used by professionals from different areas who, generally, do not access the same tools for their analysis, which implies discrepancies in results and difficulties in interpretation, as they will have different results for the same data entries. Among the many tools available we can cite: Dmutant [30], FoldX [12], I-Mutant2.0 [4], CUPSAT [17], Eris [28], I-Mutant3.0 [5], PoPMuSiC [7], SDM [25], mCSM [18], MUpro [6], MAESTRO [14], and DUET [19].

This computationally predicting the impact on proteins structure, and function, upon point mutations is of great scientific and commercial interest. One way of performing such predictions is to compute the $\Delta\Delta G$ (variation in the variation of the free energy). However, the existing methods and tools do not always obtain similar results for the same entries. This differences in results obtained from distinct tools might impact negatively in the experiments carried out by researchers. The resulting $\Delta\Delta G$ from the computational tools is usually discretized in Stabilizing and Destabilizing and this is an important information to define whether a mutation is viable or not.

In this context, where we have several answers for the same problem, Ensemble Learning techniques can be a good alternative. Ensemble learning aims to aggregate predictions from different classifier models in just one result. These combinations can be achieved in many different ways, e.g., average, major voting, etc. The resulting ensemble classifier usually obtains better results than the individual results of the classifiers used in the combination [27].

Therefore, the present work proposes the application of Ensemble Learning to aggregate the protein stability predictions of individual tools. Techniques of Stacking, Bagging, and Boosting as well as different Machine Learning algorithms as combiner function are explored. The ensemble models were trained and validated using data from ProTherm [2], a database composed by sequence and structural information obtained from experimental methods for wild-type and mutant proteins. The paper is organized as follows: Sect. 2 presents bioinformatics and machine learning brief concepts related to this purpose; Sect. 3 detailed the individual tools used on the ensemble; Sect. 4 describes the proposed methodology; Sect. 5 presents the results and discussion and finally Sect. 6 concludes the paper and show some future work.

## 2    Background

### 2.1    Point Mutations and Their Effects on Protein Structures

DNA is formed by a sequence of molecules, or base pairs. Some parts of DNA are transcript as RNA which in turn is translated as a protein. In translation, each three bases of RNA is translated as one amino acid. The order of amino acids determines the 3D structure and consequently the function of proteins.

A point mutation is when a single base pair is exchanged [1,29]. They can be: i) **silent:** when the resulting amino acid is the same, no changes in the resulting protein; ii) **missense:** when the resulting amino acid is different from the original hence the protein is different and iii) **nonsense:** the resulting mutations indicate a stop signal, again the result is a modified protein. In this study, the focus is on point mutations that results in an exchange of amino acids and thus in a modified protein.

### 2.2    Gibbs Free Energy (G)

Gibbs free energy is stabilized when the protein is in constant equilibrium, both in pressure and temperature. Therefore, the protein in its native state (or wild type, WT) has a certain amount of energy $G_{WT}$. When the protein folding process occurs, the Gibbs free energy undergoes a variation, providing a variation of energy $\Delta G_{WT}$. In the same way that, if we analyze the same protein in a mutated state, we have, in its equilibrium, an energy $G_{mutant}$ and, when this mutated protein folds, we can calculate the $\Delta G_{mutant}$.

Then, with the folding of the native and mutant proteins, one can calculate the $\Delta\Delta G$, which is calculated using the Eq. 1 [10,21]. The $\Delta\Delta G$ is a metric for predicting how a single-point mutation affects protein stability. With this, the present work uses the $\Delta\Delta G$ as the main attribute to be evaluated, where the unit kcal/mol is used for the quantitative values.

$$\Delta\Delta G = \Delta G_{WT} - \Delta G_{mutant} \tag{1}$$

### 2.3    Supervised Machine Learning

Machine learning (ML) investigates how computers can learn based on data and has proven to be of great practical value in a variety of application domains [13]. Supervised learning is the ML task of learning a model (or function) that maps an input to an output based on example input-output pairs. Thus, the objective of these tasks is to predict the value of a particular attribute (target) based on the values of other attributes (explanatory or independent variables) [22].

Since the data considered in this work has a target value, the $\Delta\Delta G$, we are applying supervised ML. This target is discretized between *Stabilizing* or *Destabilizing* (Sect. 2.2). In this way, we are applying as meta-classifiers in ensemble learning tasks the classification algorithms Decision Trees (DT), Multilayer perceptron (MLP), Naive Bayes (NB) and Support Vector Machines (SVM).

## 2.4   Ensemble Learning

Ensemble learning is a popular method that combines multiple algorithms to make a decision usually in supervised ML [8]. Ensembles have been applied in several research areas as economy, logistic, medicine, education and so on. In Bioinformatics, it has been applied in different contexts as reviewed by Yang [26]. In Eickhotl & Cheng [9], the authors proposed to apply boosting ensembles of deep networks for a sequence based prediction of protein disorder. Mendonza *et al.* [15] discuss the use of ensemble-based solutions for inference of gene regulatory networks and prediction of microRNAs targets. Saha *et al.* [20] applied an Ensemble Learning method on majority voting on datasets of protein-protein interactions data.

The main premise of this method is that by combining multiple models, the errors of a single predictor can be compensated by others [8]. Moreover, the objective of ensemble methods is not only to improve the predictions but also to enhance their capability of generalization. An ensemble method for classification consists in a set of $k$ models, $M_1, M_2, \ldots, M_k$, used to build an improved predictive model. A dataset $D$ is used to obtain $k$, $D_1, D_2, \ldots, D_k$ datasets in which $D_i$ $(1 \leq i \leq k\text{-}1)$ is used to build the classification model $M_i$ [13]. There are several methodologies for forming an ensemble considering the $k$ induced models: modifying the $D_1, D_2, \ldots, D_k$ datasets (sub-sampling, bagging, randomly sampling, etc.), modifying the learning task, exploiting the predictive algorithms characteristics and so on. Thus, given a new instance to classify, each one of the induced models contributes to compose the final decision of the ensemble. Combining the predictive models can reduce the risk to choose a bad result since the result of the combination usually is better than the best induced model. The definition of the best combination of classifiers is a combinatorial problem and there are different implementations of ensemble methods. In this paper we propose to generate stacking [16] , bagging [3] and boosting [11] ensemble models combining different classification algorithms.

Stacking [16] is a heterogeneous ensemble method where the models are obtained considering different algorithms and one unique dataset. Then the answers of the predictive models are combined in a new dataset [31] and a meta-classifier is introduced. Bagging and Boosting are homogeneous ensemble methods. In Bagging [3], the individual models are built parallel, are different from each other and all the instances have the same weight. In Boosting [11] individual models are built sequentially where the outputs of the first model is used on the next and so on. So, during training, the algorithm defines weights for the instances and the ensemble models are incrementally built.

# 3   Individual Tools for Predicting the Effects of Point Mutations in Protein Stability

There are many tools for predicting the effects of point mutations in protein stability. In this work we have chosen the tools based on the following characteristics: they produce a numerical prediction of $\Delta\Delta G$; their response time should be short; they consider protein structure as input; they permit automatic submission and license of use for academic purposes is available. In doing so, the selected tools are: CUPSAT [17], SDM [25], mCSM [18], DUET [19], MAESTRO [14] and PoPMuSic [7]. Besides, these tools have similar input forms and therefore similar outputs, which allow us to better manipulate the data.

## 3.1   CUPSAT

CUPSAT (Cologne University Protein Stability Analysis Tool) [17] is a web tool that analyzes and predicts protein stability changes for point mutations. It uses the specific structural environment of potential atoms and potential torsion angles, in the unwinding, to predict the $\Delta\Delta G$. Their results consist of informing the structural characteristics about the mutation of this location, such as: solvent accessibility, secondary structure and torsion angles.

It also looks at the ability of mutated amino acids to adapt to twist angles. It uses several validation tests (split-sample, jack-knife and k-fold) to guarantee the reliability, accuracy and transferability of the prediction methods, which guarantee an accuracy of more than 80% on their tests [17].

## 3.2   SDM

Site Directed Mutator (SDM) [25] web tool is a potential energy statistical function with the aim of predicting the effect that single nucleotide polymorphisms will have on protein stability. Using amino acid substitution frequencies in specific environments within protein families, the tool calculates a stability score that is analogous to the variation in free energy between the native and mutant state of the protein.

## 3.3   mCSM

Mutation Cutoff Scanning Matrix (mCSM), is a predictor that uses structural graph-based signatures of proteins to study the impact of mutations [18]. mCSM signatures were derived from the graph-based concept of Cutoff Scanning Matrix (CSM), originally proposed to represent network topology by distance patterns in the study of biological systems. In mCSM each mutation is represented by a pharmacophore vector that is used to train and test machine learning prediction methods, both in regression and predictive classification.

On their proposed algorithm, first mCSM signature is calculated using a set of mutations, wild-type structure, the atomic categories (or pharmacophore) to be considered, and a cutoff range and step. For each mutation, based on the cutoff, the residue environment is calculated, followed by the determination of a distance matrix of the pairwise distances between all pairs of atoms of the residue environment. Then, the distance matrix is scanned using the cutoff range and step generating a cumulative distribution of the distances by atomic category. Finally, the pharmacophoric changes between wild-type and mutant residue are appended to the signature. This signatures are used for training the predictive models.

### 3.4   DUET

The DUET [19] tool is an integrated computational approach available online, which aims to predict the impact of mutations in protein stability. Given a single point mutation, DUET combine/consensus the predictions of two other tools SDM and mCSM in a non-linear way, similar to the ensemble learning method, to make predictions and optimize results using Support Vector Machines (SVMs) with radial basis function kernel.

As a filtering step, residue relative solvent accessibility (RSA) is used to optimize the standard SDM predictions using a regression model tree (M5P algorithm) before combining it with mCSM. Then, the mCSM an optimized SDM predictions, together with secundary structure from SDM and pharmacophore vector from mCSM are used as input for SVM generating the combined DUET output. All their training was carried out by data sets with little redundancy and validated with random data sets.

### 3.5   MAESTRO

In order to predict changes in stability on point mutations of proteins, MAE-STRO [14] is based on the structure of the protein and, although it has a predictive similar to other methods, it differs because of the following points: it implements a multi-agent system for learning; provides in-depth mutation scanning at various points where mutation types can be comprehensively controlled; and provides a specific mode for stabilizing disulfide bond predictions.

MAESTRO is based on two different machine learning approaches: artificial neural networks (ANN) and SVM (Gaussian Kernel), and also on multiple linear regression (MLR). In order to improve generalization, a set of ANNs is utilized rather than a single one.

### 3.6   PoPMuSic

PopMuSic [7] is a web server for predicting thermodynamic changes in point mutations of proteins, which uses a linear combination of statistical potentials whose coefficients depend on the solvent accessibility of the mutated residue.

It is a fast tool that allows you to make predictions for all possible mutations of a protein, average size, in less than a minute. It has the ability to detect which and how optimal the amino acids are in each protein, so that mutation experiments can be carried out, also demonstrating structural weaknesses by quantifying how much these sites are optimized for protein function, rather than stability.

# 4    Proposed Methodology

Our proposed methodology is presented in Fig. 1. We are applying Stacking and Bagging/Boosting ensemble learning on the results of six protein stability changes upon point mutations predictors: CUPSAT [17], SDM [25], mCSM [18], DUET [19], MAESTRO [14] and PopMuSic [7].

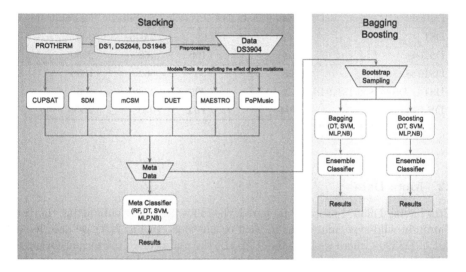

**Fig. 1.** Proposed methodology of ensemble learning applied on protein stability changes upon point mutations predictors.

## 4.1    Input Data

The first step on our proposed methodology is to prepare the input dataset. In this paper we are considering as input data sets of proteins from which we can obtain the experimental value of Gibbs free energy ($\Delta\Delta G$) between wild-type and mutants (our target attribute on ensemble learning). This thermodynamic experimental data was obtained from ProTherm [2]. ProTherm is a database containing several thermodynamic parameters along with sequence and structural information, experimental methods and conditions parameters for wild-type and mutant proteins.

The non-disjoint datasets DS1, DS2648 and DS1948, Table 1 lines 1–3, are taken from ProTherm [2] and considered in the individual tools for training their models. DS1 and DS2648 were used by PoPMuSic [7], SDM [25] and MAESTRO [14], while DS1948 was used by I-Mutant [4] tool. These three datasets DS1, DS2648 and DS1948 have different formats for presenting their data, in addition to containing several duplicates. Thus, we unified and preprocess all these data totaling 7244 instances (4th line on Table 1). After preprocessing all these data, we remove duplicates of the same protein experimental results resulting in our final input dataset DS3904 (highlighted on Table 1).

**Table 1.** Input datasets: number of instances, number of unique proteins, number of stabilizing mutations and number of destabilizing mutations.

| Dataset | Total of instances | Proteins | Stabilizing | Destabilizing |
|---|---|---|---|---|
| DS1 | 2648 | 99 | 2.046 | 602 |
| DS2648 | 2648 | 100 | 568 | 2080 |
| DS1948 | 1948 | 58 | 562 | 1386 |
| DS1 ∪ DS2648 ∪ DS1948 | 7244 | 298 | 3738 | 4068 |
| **DS3904** | **3904** | **151** | **951** | **2953** |

### 4.2   Meta Data

After having DS3904 properly prepared, the following step is submitting this list of protein wild-type/mutations in each of the tools. In Fig. 2(A) we describe a part of DS3904 where we have the PDB ID, the mutation in the format Original residue type - position - mutation and the experimental $\Delta\Delta G$. For example, the first line, PDB ID 1A23 has as original residue in position 32 a Histidine (H) that when mutated to a Leucine (L) has an experimental $\Delta\Delta G$ of 4.6.

In order to obtain the predicted $\Delta\Delta G$ of each tool to generate our meta data we would need to manually submit each entry of DS3904 to the tools. To perform this task in batch we use a browser plugin called iMacros. iMacros is a scripting language that allows users to simulate online activities for filling out forms, uploading and downloading images and files, or even importing and exporting information from databases, CSV files, XML files, among others. PopMusic is different of the other tools since it allows the user to inform the PDB code for each of the 151 proteins of DS3904 (and their specific mutation positions) in a list.

The results were properly stored in a local database generating our meta data (Fig. 2(B)) where we have as predictive attributes the predicted $\Delta\Delta G$ by the tools and as target attribut the experimental $\Delta\Delta G$ discretized as *Destabilizing* ($\Delta\Delta G < 0$) or *Stabilizing* ($\Delta\Delta G \geq 0$).

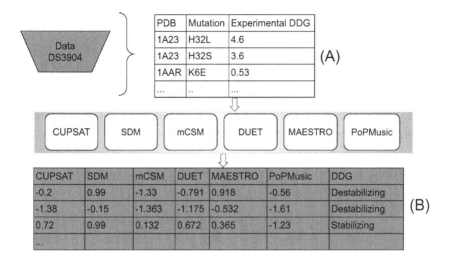

**Fig. 2.** Part of input data. (A) DS3904 (B) Meta data.

### 4.3  Ensemble Learning - Stacking

Considering as input the meta data generated by heterogeneous predictive tools in the previous step we performed stacking ensemble learning considering as meta classifiers: Random Forest (RF), Decision Trees (DT), Support Vector Machines (SVM), Multilayer Perceptron - Radial basis function (MLP) and Naive Bayes (NB). The parameters of these algorithms were set as default values: DT (maxDepth = unlimited; numFeatures = unlimited; numTrees = 100), SVM (degree of the kernel = 3; kernel type = radial; eps = 0.001), MLP (autoBuild = true; decay = false; hiddenLayers = 'a'; learningrate = 0.3; momentum = 0.2; validationThreshold = 20) and NB (useKernelEstimator = false and useSupervisedDiscretization = false). We evaluate all the generated ensemble models using accuracy, precision, recall and F-measure.

### 4.4  Ensemble Learning - Bagging/Boosting

In order to evaluate the impact of ensemble learning not only with stacking configuration we decided to also apply bagging and boosting. We have performed different configurations for this ensemble experiments: Bagging and Boosting. The parameters of these algorithms were set as default values: Bagging (bagSizePercent = 100; calcOutofBag = false; Classifiers = SVM, DT, MLP and NV - same parameters used in Stacking; numIterations = 10), Boosting (numIterations = 10; Classifiers = SVM, DT, MLP and NV - same parameters used in Stacking; useResampling = false; weightThreshold = 100). The stacking, bagging and boosting ensemble learning algorithms were performed using WEKA 3.8 [24].

## 5    Results and Discussion

To evaluate our proposed methodology of ensemble learning for this problem we performed two experiments: *Experiment* 1 considers a balanced training dataset from where 500 random instances where selected from DS3904 for each target value *Stabilizing* and *Destabilizing*; in *Experiment* 2 we divided DS3904 in 70% (Training) and 30% (Testing), and we have not balanced training/testing datasets. Table 2 describes the datasets for *Experiments* 1 and 2.

**Table 2.** Training and testing datasets for *Experiments* 1 and 2.

| Experiment | Training | | | Testing | | |
|---|---|---|---|---|---|---|
| | Stabilizing | Destabilizing | Total | Stabilizing | Destabilizing | Total |
| 1 | 500 | 500 | 1000 | 451 | 2453 | 2904 |
| 2 | 666 | 2066 | 2732 | 285 | 887 | 1172 |

### 5.1    Experiment 1: Balanced Training Dataset

DS3904 is unbalanced according to the target attribute. Although it is common in real datasets can cause some problems in generating predictive models as being highly specialized (specially to detect the rare class) or susceptible to presence of noise [22]. Thus, we decided to train the stacking and bagging/boosting ensemble models in *Experiment* 1 with 500 random instances of each class, totaling 1000 instances for training. The remaining 2904 instances are part of the test set. In order to compare the results of the generated ensemble models with the individual Tools we calculated the metrics accuracy, precision, recall and F-measure for the test set for all.

First, we evaluate the individual tools considering the test set with 2904 instances (see Table 2)and comparing the predicted $\Delta\Delta G$ with the experimental value from ProTherm (Table 3). We can observe that all tools obtained good accuracy values but with low values for precision. It is important to mention that our test set probably was used by the tools to train their models.

Both Stacking (Table 4), and Bagging/Boosting ensemble models (Table 5), obtained good values of accuracy and precision. From these results, we can highlight SVM , Multilayer Perceptron and Random Forest close to mCSM Tool. From the Experiment 1 results we can notice that better precision measures were obtained if we compare with individual tools.

The predictions about point mutation effects on protein structures are going to be used in the decision of generating experimentally some proposed protein mutations, which is expensive in terms of time and costs. Considering *Stabilizing* as a positive class, *false positives* are mutations predicted as *stabilizing* but they are *destabilizing*. This error can make the laboratory spends money and time on

Table 3. Evaluation of individual tools in Experiment 1.

| Individual tools | Accuracy | Precision | Recall | F-measure |
|---|---|---|---|---|
| CUPSAT | 0.75 | 0.31 | 0.54 | 0.39 |
| SDM | 0.65 | 0.23 | 0.60 | 0.33 |
| mCSM | 0.81 | 0.35 | 0.31 | 0.34 |
| DUET | 0.78 | 0.34 | 0.58 | 0.43 |
| MAESTRO | 0.70 | 0.24 | 0.53 | 0.34 |
| PoPMusic | 0.78 | 0.29 | 0.35 | 0.32 |

Table 4. Evaluation of stacking ensemble in Experiment 1.

| Stacking ensemble: meta classifiers | Accuracy | Precision | Recall | F-measure |
|---|---|---|---|---|
| Naive Bayes (NB) | 0.63 | 0.84 | 0.26 | 0.40 |
| Multilayer Perceptron (MLP) | 0.74 | 0.76 | 0.32 | 0.46 |
| SVM (radial) | 0.75 | 0.76 | 0.34 | 0.47 |
| Decision Trees (DT) | 0.76 | 0.70 | 0.35 | 0.47 |
| Random Forest (RF) | 0.80 | 0.70 | 0.40 | 0.51 |

a not viable protein. On the other side, *false negatives* are mutations predicted as *destabilizing* but they are *stabilizing*. These errors can discard some important mutation that impacts on the protein function of interest, for example. Both errors can impact experimental laboratory activities according to the project. So, we expect to achieve good values for *precision* and *recall* since it is important to guarantee that the *stabilizing* or *destabilizing* predictions are correct.

Table 5. Evaluation of Bagging/Boosting in Experiment 1.

| Bagging/Boosting ensemble | Accuracy | Precision | Recall | F-measure |
|---|---|---|---|---|
| Bagging (SVM) | 0.75 | 0.76 | 0.35 | 0.48 |
| Bagging (DT) | 0.75 | 0.76 | 0.34 | 0.47 |
| Bagging (MLP) | 0.74 | 0.75 | 0.33 | 0.46 |
| Bagging (NB) | 0.63 | 0.84 | 0.26 | 0.40 |
| Boosting (SVM) | 0.70 | 0.79 | 0.30 | 0.44 |
| Boosting (DT) | 0.75 | 0.71 | 0.33 | 0.45 |
| Boosting (MLP) | 0.74 | 0.76 | 0.33 | 0.46 |
| Boosting (NB) | 0.69 | 0.80 | 0.30 | 0.43 |

## 5.2   Experiment 2: Unbalanced Training Set

In Experiment 2 we are training the ensemble models with unbalanced dataset randomly dividing the DS3904 into 70% of for training and the remaining 30% of the instances for testing.

Table 6 presents the results of the individual tools. It is observed that although they present good accuracy, the values for precision and recall varies. Some tools (mCSM and PoPMuSic) have better Recall values, while SDM and MAESTRO have better precision (around 0.6).

**Table 6.** Evaluation of individual tools in Experiment 2.

| Individual tools | Accuracy | Precision | Recall | F-measure |
|---|---|---|---|---|
| CUPSAT | 0.72 | 0.43 | 0.51 | 0.47 |
| SDM | 0.66 | 0.38 | 0.60 | 0.47 |
| mCSM | 0.78 | 0.57 | 0.36 | 0.45 |
| DUET | 0.77 | 0.52 | 0.59 | 0.56 |
| MAESTRO | 0.68 | 0.40 | 0.60 | 0.48 |
| PoPMusic | 0.75 | 0.49 | 0.42 | 0.45 |

Tables 7 and 8 present the Ensemble learning models evaluation for Experiment 2. We can observe better accuracy, recall and precision values. Boosting (SVM) model has the best accuracy (0.84) and good recall (0.77). We can see similar results for Stacking learning (MLP, SVM, DT and RF), Bagging (SVM, DT and MLP) and also Boosting (MLP).

**Table 7.** Evaluation of stacking ensemble in Experiment 2.

| Stacking ensemble: meta classifiers | Accuracy | Precision | Recall | F-measure |
|---|---|---|---|---|
| NaiveBayes (NB) | 0.73 | 0.78 | 0.46 | 0.58 |
| Multilayer Perceptron (MLP) | 0.83 | 0.43 | 0.77 | 0.56 |
| SVM (radial) | 0.84 | 0.47 | 0.79 | 0.59 |
| Decision Trees (DT) | 0.82 | 0.35 | 0.77 | 0.49 |
| Random Forest(RF) | 0.84 | 0.40 | 0.85 | 0.55 |

These are good models for avoiding to incorrectly predict as destabilizing a stabilizing mutation (*falses negatives*). On the other side, Stacking learning, Bagging and Boosting with Naive Bayes (NB) also have good accuracy but presented better precision values. It means that ensemble models with NB can be good options for avoiding to predict destabilizing mutations as stabilizing (*falses positives*).

**Table 8.** Evaluation of Bagging/Boosting in Experiment 2.

| Bagging/Boosting esemble | Accuracy | Precision | Recall | F-measure |
|---|---|---|---|---|
| Bagging (SVM) | 0.84 | 0.45 | 0.80 | 0.57 |
| Bagging (DT) | 0.84 | 0.52 | 0.74 | 0.61 |
| Bagging (MLP) | 0.84 | 0.56 | 0.73 | 0.63 |
| Bagging (NB) | 0.73 | 0.78 | 0.46 | 0.58 |
| Boosting (SVM) | 0.85 | 0.52 | 0.77 | 0.62 |
| Boosting (DT) | 0.82 | 0.60 | 0.63 | 0.62 |
| Boosting (MLP) | 0.83 | 0.44 | 0.78 | 0.56 |
| Boosting (NB) | 0.80 | 0.67 | 0.58 | 0.62 |

# 6    Conclusion

The knowledge about the impact on proteins stability upon point mutations is an important scientific and commercial research topic. One way is to computationally predict the variation of the free energy $\Delta\Delta G$ and its consequently impact on protein stability. There are different methods and tools for this purpose that do not always obtain similar results for the same entries.

Besides, these predictions are used to define point mutations on protein structures that are experimentally generated, which is expensive in terms of time and costs. Errors on this predictions can have important impacts. For example, consider a point mutation as *destabilizing* but when it is *stabilizing* can discard this candidate. At the same time that a wrong prediction of *stabilizing* when the mutation destabilizes the protein structure can made the laboratory spends money and time on a not viable protein. Thus, in this paper we propose to aggregate the results from different stability prediction tools using Stacking, Bagging/Boosting Ensemble Learning techniques achieving to obtain models with not only good accuracy but also good precision and/or recall.

In our proposed methodology we are considering six individual $\Delta\Delta G$ predictors: CUPSAT [17], SDM [25], mCSM [18], DUET [19], MAESTRO [14] and PoPMuSic [7]. We prepared an input dataset from ProTherm [2] with 3,904 instances about wild-type and mutation proteins. After submitting this list to the tools we obtained our meta-data composed by their $\Delta\Delta G$ predictions. Having this meta-data, we applied Stacking ensemble with meta-classifiers (RF, DT, SVM, MLP and NB), Bagging (SVM, DT, MLP and NV) and Boosting .

For both ensemble techniques we validated considering two different experiments according to the training set. In Experiment 1 (balanced training set) results we can observe that even all individual tools obtained good accuracy values, they presented low precision. On the other side, both Stacking and Bagging/Boosting ensemble models obtained also good accuracy but with better precision.

In Experiment 2 (unbalanced training set) results we can observe better accuracy, recall and precision values for ensemble models. Boosting(SVM) obtained the best accuracy (0.84) and good recall (0.77). We can see similar results for Stacking learning (MLP, SVM, DT and RF), Bagging (SVM, DT and MLP) and also Boosting (MLP). These are good models for avoiding to incorrectly predict as destabilizing a stabilizing mutation. On the other side, Stacking learning, Bagging and Boosting with Naive Bayes (NB) also have good accuracy but presented better precision values. It means that ensemble models with NB can be good options for avoiding to predict destabilizing mutations as stabilizing.

Thus, according with the results, our proposed ensemble approach is appropriate to predict the effect of point mutations on protein stability showing more reliable results than the individual tools. As future work, we can combine the individual tools using genetic algorithms to determine the weight of each $\Delta\Delta G$ predicted and also include more tools in the ensemble. In addition, other balancing strategies can be performed on the training datasets.

# References

1. Auclair, J., et al.: Systematic mRNA analysis for the effect of MLH1 and MSH2 missense and silent mutations on aberrant splicing. Hum. Mutat. **27**(2), 145–154 (2006). https://doi.org/10.1002/humu.20280
2. Bava, K.A., Gromiha, M.M., Uedaira, H., Kitajima, K., Sarai, A.: ProTherm, version 4.0: thermodynamic database for proteins and mutants. Nucleic Acids Res. **32**(1), 120–121 (01 2004). https://doi.org/10.1093/nar/gkh082
3. Breiman, L.: Bagging predictors. Mach. Learn. **24**(2), 123–140 (1996)
4. Capriotti, E., Fariselli, P., Casadio, R.: A neural-network-based method for predicting protein stability changes upon single point mutations. Bioinformatics **20**(Suppl 1), i63–i68 (2004). https://doi.org/10.1093/bioinformatics/bth928
5. Capriotti, E., Fariselli, P., Rossi, I., Casadio, R.: A three-state prediction of single point mutations on protein stability changes. BMC Bioinform. **9**(Suppl 2) (2008). https://doi.org/10.1186/1471-2105-9-s2-s6
6. Cheng, J., Randall, A., Baldi, P.: Prediction of protein stability changes for single-site mutations using support vector machines. Prot. Struct. Function Bioinform. **62**(4), 1125–1132 (2005). https://doi.org/10.1002/prot.20810
7. Dehouck, Y., Kwasigroch, J.M., Gilis, D., Rooman, M.: PoPMuSiC 2.1: a web server for the estimation of protein stability changes upon mutation and sequence optimality. BMC Bioinform. **12**(1) (2011). https://doi.org/10.1186/1471-2105-12-151
8. Dong, X., Yu, Z., Cao, W., Shi, Y., Ma, Q.: A survey on ensemble learning. Front. Comput. Sci. **14**(2), 241–258 (2020)
9. Eickholt, J., Cheng, J.: DNdisorder: predicting protein disorder using boosting and deep networks. BMC Bioinform. **14**(1), 1 (2013)

10. Fersht, A.R.: Protein folding and stability: the pathway of folding of Barnase. FEBS Lett. **325**(1–2), 5–16 (1993)
11. Freund, Y., Schapire, R.E., et al.: Experiments with a new boosting algorithm. In: ICML, vol. 96, pp. 148–156 (1996)
12. Guerois, R., Nielsen, J.E., Serrano, L.: Predicting changes in the stability of proteins and protein complexes: a study of more than 1000 mutations. J. Mol. Biol. **320**(2), 369–387 (2002). https://doi.org/10.1016/s0022-2836(02)00442-4
13. Han, J., Pei, J., Kamber, M.: Data Mining - Concepts and Techniques. Morgan and Kaufmann, San Francisco (2006)
14. Laimer, J., Hofer, H., Fritz, M., Wegenkittl, S., Lackner, P.: Maestro - multi agent stability prediction upon point mutations. BMC Bioinform. **16**(1) (2015). https://doi.org/10.1186/s12859-015-0548-6
15. Mendoza, M.R., Bazzan, A.L.C.: The wisdom of crowds in bioinformatics: what can we learn (and gain) from ensemble predictions? In: Proceedings of the Twenty-Seventh AAAI Conference on Artificial Intelligence, pp. 1678–1679 (2013)
16. Noçairi, H., Gomes, C., Thomas, M., Saporta, G.: Improving stacking methodology for combining classifiers; applications to cosmetic industry. Electron. J. Appl. Stat. Anal. **9**(2), 340–361 (2016)
17. Parthiban, V., Gromiha, M.M., Schomburg, D.: CUPSAT: prediction of protein stability upon point mutations. Nucl. Acids Res. 34(Web Server), January 2006. https://doi.org/10.1093/nar/gkl190
18. Pires, D.E.V., Ascher, D.B., Blundell, T.L.: mcSM: predicting the effects of mutations in proteins using graph-based signatures. Bioinformatics **30**(3), 335–342 (2013). https://doi.org/10.1093/bioinformatics/btt691
19. Pires, D.E., Ascher, D.B., Blundell, T.L.: DUET: a server for predicting effects of mutations on protein stability using an integrated computational approach. Nucl. Acids Res. **42**(W1), W314–W319 (2014)
20. Saha, I., Zubek, J., Klingström, T., Forsberg, S., Wikander, J., Kierczak, M., Maulik, U., Plewczynski, D.: Ensemble learning prediction of protein-protein interactions using proteins functional annotations. Mol. BioSyst. **10**(4), 820–830 (2014)
21. Sugita, Y., Kitao, A.: Dependence of protein stability on the structure of the denatured state: free energy calculations of I56V mutation in human lysozyme. Biophys. J. **75**(5), 2178–2187 (1998)
22. Tan, P.N., Steinbach, M., Kumar, V.: Introduction to Data Mining. Pearson Education, London (2016)
23. Verli, H.: Bioinformática: da biologia à flexibilidade molecular. Sociedade Brasileira de Bioquímica e Biologia Molecular (2014)
24. Witten, I.H., Frank, E., Hall, M.A.: Data Mining Practical Machine Learning Tools and Techniques Third Edition. Morgan Kaufmann, Burlington (2016)
25. Worth, C.L., Preissner, R., Blundell, T.L.: SDM-a server for predicting effects of mutations on protein stability and malfunction. Nucl. Acids Res. **39**(suppl_2), W215–W222 (2011)
26. Yang, P., Yang, Y.H., Zhou, B.B., Zomaya, A.Y.: A review of ensemble methods in bioinformatics. Current Bioinform. **5**(4), 296–308 (2010)
27. Yang, Y.: Temporal Data Mining via Unsupervised Ensemble Learning. Elsevier, Amsterdam (2016)
28. Yin, S., Ding, F., Dokholyan, N.V.: Eris: an automated estimator of protein stability. Nat. Meth. **4**(6), 466–467 (2007). https://doi.org/10.1038/nmeth0607-466
29. Zhang, Z., Miteva, M.A., Wang, L., Alexov, E.: Analyzing effects of naturally occurring missense mutations. Comput. Math. Meth. Med. **2012**, 1–15 (2012). https://doi.org/10.1155/2012/805827

30. Zhou, H., Zhou, Y.: Distance-scaled, finite ideal-gas reference state improves structure-derived potentials of mean force for structure selection and stability prediction. Prot. Sci. **11**(11), 2714–2726 (2009). https://doi.org/10.1110/ps.0217002
31. Zhou, Z.H.: Ensemble Methods: Foundations and Algorithms. Chapman and Hall/CRC, Boca Raton (2019)

# Ethics of AI: Do the Face Detection Models Act with Prejudice?

Marcos Vinícius Ferreira[1,2]($\boxtimes$), Ariel Almeida[1], João Paulo Canario[1], Matheus Souza[3], Tatiane Nogueira[1], and Ricardo Rios[1]

[1] Federal University of Bahia, Salvador, Brazil
{marcosvsf,arielalmeida,joao.canario,tatiane.nogueira,ricardoar}@ufba.br
[2] Neodados, Salvador, Brazil
marcos.ferreira@neodados.com
[3] Integra - Association of Public Transportation Companies, Salvador, Brazil
matheus.souza@gevan.com.br

**Abstract.** This work presents a study on an ethical issue in Artificial Intelligence related to the presence of racist biases by detecting faces in images. Our analyses were performed on a real-world system designed to detect fraud in public transportation in Salvador (Brazil). Our experiments were conducted by taking into account three steps. Firstly, we individually analyzed a sample of images and added specific labels related to the users' gender and race. Then, we used well-defined detectors, based on different Convolutional Neural Network architectures, to find faces in the previously labeled images. Finally, we used statistical tests to assess whether or not there is some relation between the error rates and such labels. According to our results, we had noticed important biases, thus leading to higher error rates when images were taken from black people. We also noticed errors are more likely in both black men and women. Based on our conclusions, we recall the risk of deploying computational software that might affect minority groups that are historically neglected.

**Keywords:** Face detection · Racism · Ethic · Deep learning

## 1 Introduction

The face detection approaches have been widely adopted in several applications to create biometric markers in social networks, smart devices, surveillance systems, fraud detection, and so on [15,20,25]. In summary, face detection is a subarea of object detection, devoted to finding regions in images that contain faces [22,25].

The advances in the Artificial Neural Networks (ANN) [9], especially with the Convolutional Neural Networks (CNN) [14], have improved the face detection performances and made its usage more usual in many real-world scenarios. Nowadays, state-of-the-art manuscripts report relevant performances by finding faces with different positions and rotations, occlusions, expressions, scales, and localization [23,25].

© Springer Nature Switzerland AG 2021
A. Britto and K. Valdivia Delgado (Eds.): BRACIS 2021, LNAI 13074, pp. 89–103, 2021.
https://doi.org/10.1007/978-3-030-91699-2_7

Despite the theoretical and scientific advances, scientists are concerned about the fairness in AI models, which is a current hot topic in computer vision, aiming at better understand the robustness of such AI models across important human features as, for example, age, gender, and race [5]. Due to ethical issues, some commercial systems designed by important companies (e.g. IBM, Microsoft, and Clarifai) were discontinued due to the high error rates in specific groups as black women, possibly presenting a racist bias [7]. Recently, in New York, scientists have asked to interrupt the usage of face recognition in some situations due to errors associated with gender, race, and ethnicity [4]. The most important factor related to this issue is that, even in systems with high accuracy rates, small errors may strongly affect the life of minorities who are historically oppressed [2,15].

An alert was recently triggered when several researchers have emphasized that classification errors are more likely when people of color are under scrutiny [4]. The reason why such errors happen is still being assessed. According to the scientists, it can be driven by the own methods and/or the dataset used during the training process, thus requiring a careful evaluation when deployed in a scenario characterized by different groups [16].

In our context, the problem came up during the development of an AI-based system to detect fraud in public transportation in Salvador (Brazil). Before the pandemic outbreak, more than 1,1 million passengers used to take buses per day in Salvador (average calculated between 2016 and 2019). Our system analyzes all images taken when the passengers cross the turnstile by running two steps. Firstly, we execute a face detection step in the usage images and, then, we compare the estimated face along with the users' profiles. The fraud usually happens when users have some benefits like student discounts. In this situation, the students share their discount cards with others. In case of confirmed fraud, the card is blocked.

By considering Salvador is the Brazilian city with the highest percentage of black people (about 80%), any error may affect a significant number of users, leading to a high number of false positives. In our scenario, due to the absence of images with appropriate labels to describe users by gender and race, we used pre-trained face detectors, published by the original authors. Thus, we created an empirical setup to assess whether the detectors have gender and race biases, before deploying our system. Aiming at reaching this goal, we firstly created a specialist committee to label our images. Then, we analyzed the errors produced by every detector by taking into account different groups of genders and races. As discussed later, we have indeed found a race bias in our environment.

This manuscript is organized as follows: Sect. 2 shows a set of related work; Sect. 3 introduces our methodology and tools considered to conduct our study; The experimental results are presented in Sect. 4; Finally, concluding remarks and future directions are given in Sect. 5, which is followed by a list of references.

## 2    Background

This section presents studies related to the investigation of ethical issues caused by gender and race biases that influence the performance of Artificial Intelligence methods. In this sense, Farinella and Dugelay (2012) [6] published a manuscript focused on understand whether gender and ethnicity affect each other during the classification process. According to the authors, these features are not affected by themselves.

Furl, Phillips, and O'Toole (2002) [7] designed a study to verify the precision of face recognition models by dealing with different ethnicities. The results were focused on Caucasians and Asians. Phillips et al. (2011) [16] have discussed the risks of using faces with different characteristics during the training and test phases.

Similar work was published by Klare et al. (2012) [13], in which the main contribution was extend the analysis to different demographic features as gender, race, and age. According to the authors, black and young women have presented the highest error rates. To overcome this situation, the authors recommend balanced datasets with data sampled from the population where the system will be deployed. The authors also suggest an effort to create public datasets support systems that will be implemented in similar scenario.

More recent manuscripts show contributions in the organization of datasets as well as investigation of the existence of a racist bias. In that sense, Karkkainen and Joo (2021) [12] focused on developing a balanced dataset, named FairFace, which has information about seven race groups: White, Black, Indian, East Asia, Southeast Asia, Middle East, and Latino. This dataset was compared with others in the literature and used in commercial APIs, bringing improvements in the race classification task.

Buolamwini and Gebru (2018) [2] explored three models created to detect faces used in commercial solutions (Microsoft, IBM, Face++) to evaluate the presence of gender and race prejudice. Their most important contribution to the literature was the creation of a dataset, by integrating other public images, balanced by gender and ethnicity. Results presented by the authors show higher errors were obtained from the group composed of black women.

Wang et al. (2019) [21] have evaluated the racist bias in races/ethnicities by developing a dataset and a model capable of reducing racist bias in facial recognition. The dataset created, named Racial Faces in-the-Wild (RFW), has Caucasian, Indian, Asian and African ethnicities. The experiments have shown that the facial recognition of Africans has error rates twice as high as the facial recognition of Caucasians.

Raji et al. (2020) [17] have investigated ethics in facial processing technologies developed by Amazon, Microsoft and Clarifai, verifying the accuracy of their systems in classifying people according to race, gender, age, expression, and face detection. All experiments were performed on a dataset created by the authors, which is made up only of celebrities. The main result of such research is the alert about the importance of correctly analyzing ethical issues in the considered models.

## 3   Methodology

As previously mentioned, the main objective of this work is to assess whether or not the mostly-adopted face detection methods present similar performance to classify real-world images regardless of the users' gender and race. The analyzed images were collected by the consortium Integra, formed by the four companies responsible for public transportation in Salvador (Bahia – Brazil).

Aiming at reaching this objective, we defined the following hypothesis: Do the pre-trained face detection models act with prejudice? This hypothesis was analyzed by using validation metrics, usually adopted in ML problems, under a null hypothesis ($H_0$) that supports the statement there is no difference between metrics when compared users by gender and race. In turn, our alternative hypothesis was used to illustrate when $H_0$ is rejected, which might call our attention to biases that affect the expected face detection behavior.

To better define the scope of our analyses, we have selected images from the Integra databases and three well-defined face detectors: i) Yolo Faces [18]; ii) Multitask Cascaded Convolutional Networks (MTCNN) [26]; and iii) ResNet [10]. The following sections detail our scope, the experimental setup and the methodology considered to assess our hypothesis.

### 3.1   Dataset

The images considered in our experiments were collected from public transportation in Salvador. When a passenger crosses the turnstile inside the buses, four pictures are taken and stored in a database. From this database, we have randomly selected 10, 000 images captured on December 10, 2019. This date was a usual workday and was considered without any relevant reason, but the fact of being before the COVID-19 pandemic outbreak to avoid analyzing images of users wearing masks, which might affect the performance of the selected face detectors.

We also created a tool to support specialists during the tasks of setting the gender and race labels and validating the face detector results, as shown in Fig. 1. As one may notice, as a specialist sets the gender and race, the percentage of each label is updated to keep the dataset balanced. Consequently, the final set of images contains a similar amount of users according to their gender and race. We emphasize that, although we are aware of the different classes of gender and race adopted by IBGE (Brazilian Institute of Geography and Statistics), the scope of this study was limited to man/woman and black/white, respectively. The final dataset is composed of instances with the following class rates: i) black – 569 (56.50%); ii) white – 438 (43.50%); iii) male – 407 (40.42%); and iv) female – 600 (59.58%).

Another important feature implemented in this tool is the validation of the face detectors. Once pre-trained models are used, we show to the specialists a face and the bounding boxes produced by all detectors, thus selecting their performances based on four possibilities. True Positive (TP) happens when the bounding box highlights an actual face. In turn, if a bounding box is drawn on

**Fig. 1.** GUI Interface for target imagens and models predictions.

a region without a face, the specialists set it as False Positive (FP). A True Negative option is used to confirm when no bounding box is drawn on an image without a face. It usually happens when the camera is wrongly positioned or triggered. Finally, False Negative characterizes situations when the face detectors do not find an existing face. After performing this step, we have a contingency matrix, which is considered to assess our hypothesis.

Aiming at respecting the users' privacy and due to the Brazilian General Personal Data Protection Law (LGPD), the resultant dataset cannot be shared. We emphasize all images were manipulated by authorized employees from Integra and the researchers associated with this researcher, respecting the LGPD requirements. If the reviewers deem it is necessary to audit the dataset, the program chairs of the conference can contact us to have access to images, bounding boxes, and labels, always respecting the LGPD requirements.

## 3.2   Face Detection Models

The detection of faces in images is a challenging task in the Computer Vision area and is considered an instance of object detection in general. Recent advances in this area, especially with the advent of Convolutional Neural Networks (CNNs), have allowed performing this task with great performance, even in a situation characterized by, for example, face rotation, and occlusion (e.g. hat, cap, and glass). Based on the literature, approaches designed to detect face are, usually, less complex than those considered to look for several objects in images. Next, we show three models widely used to do so.

The first approach considered in our experiments was YOLO (You Only Look Once) [18], which is a CNN with 26 convolutional, 4 pooling, and 2 full connected layers. The face detection is essentially performed by a fast regression task, which provides high performance. In summary, YOLO analyzes the image as a grid, in which every piece is considered to predict a bounding box and define a confidence level to estimate the presence of objects. The pre-trained model considered in our evaluation was based on the Wider Face dataset [24].

The second approach is called Multi-Task Cascaded Convolutional Neural Network (MTCNN) [26], which is based on 3 steps. The fist one, referred to as P-Net, contains three convolutional layers with 10, 16, and 32 filters and a pooling layer. The second one is called R-Net and composed of three convolutional layers with 28, 48, and 64 filters, two pooling layers, and a full-connected layer. Finally, the last step, known as O-Net, is characterized for presenting four convolutional layers along with 32, 64, 64, and 128 filters. Moreover, it has 3 pooling and 1 full-connected layers. P-Net is designed to detect candidate faces initially and its results are refined by R-Net that removes regions whose presence of faces is highly unlikely. Then, O-Net detects the faces and provides five reference points. In our scenario, we have considered a pre-trained model that was adjusted on the datasets Face Detection Benchmark [11] and Wider Face [24].

The third approach used in our experiments was ResNet-33 [10], which is based on Region Proposal Network (RPN) to define bounding boxes and reference points. The architecture considered by ResNet uses a shared memory strategy, aiming at making the face map available to all convolutional layers. Firstly, there is a fast ZF-Net(Zeiler and Fergus model) with five convolutional and three full-connected layers. Then, there is a VGG-16 architecture [19] with 13 convolutional and 3 full-connected layers. The model used in our analyses was previously trained on the dataset Wider Face, as well.

### 3.3   Validation Metrics

Aiming at assessing the contingency matrix produced by comparing the results obtained by the face detectors and specialists, we used six validation metrics widely adopted by the ML area: Sensitivity, Specificity, Accuracy, Matthews Correlation Coefficient (MCC), Kappa Coefficient, and F1-Score.

Sensitivity, defined in Eq. 1, calculates the true positive rate between the correctly-detected and missing faces. The true negative rate is measured by the Specificity as shown in Eq. 2, i.e., the total of images correctly classified as without faces and wrong bounding boxes. Accuracy is responsible for calculating the total number of correct classifications, i.e. right bounding boxes and total of images without faces and bounding boxes, as depicted in Eq. 3. In contrast, Precision counts the total of correctly detected faces among all bounding boxes produced by the detectors, Eq. 4. We also used F-Score, Eq. 5, which calculates a harmonic mean between Precision and Sensitivity (Recall). In our analyses, we have considered Precision and Sensitivity to have the same weight and are equally important.

$$\text{Sensitivity} = \frac{TP}{TP + FN} \tag{1}$$

$$\text{Specificity} = \frac{TN}{FP + TN} \tag{2}$$

$$\text{Accuracy} = \frac{TP + TN}{FP + TN + TP + TN} \tag{3}$$

$$\text{Precision} = \frac{TP}{FP + TP} \tag{4}$$

$$\text{F1-Score} = \frac{2 * (\text{precision} * \text{sensitivity})}{\text{precision} + \text{sensitivity}} \tag{5}$$

The Kappa Coefficient ($\kappa$), Eq. 6, is calculated between the observed $P_o$ classification and the agreement that would be expected to occur by chance $P_e$, as shown in Eq. 7. For all metrics presented so far, the greater the value, the better the classification is.

$$\text{Kappa} = \kappa = (P_o - P_e)/(1 - P_e) \tag{6}$$

$$P_o = \sum_{i=1}^{C} p_{ii}, \quad P_e = \sum_{i=1}^{C} p_{i.}p_{.i} \tag{7}$$

The last measure used in our experiments is MCC (Matthews Correlation Coefficient), Eq. 8, which uses a contingency matrix to compare classifiers similarly to the Pearson's correlation coefficient. The coefficient can be interpreted by the interval $[-1, +1]$, in which $+1$ represents a perfect mach between expected and predicted labels. When it is equal to 0, learning models are confirmed to provide random predictions. Values approaching $-1$ suggest a total disagreement between expected and predicted labels.

$$MCC = \frac{TP \times TN - FP \times FN}{\sqrt{(TP + FP)(TP + FN)(TN + FP)(TN + FN)}} \tag{8}$$

### 3.4 Hypothesis Test

The validation metrics aforementioned were considered to verify the agreement between the bounding boxes produced by the face detectors and the presence of actual faces. Next, we need to verify whether or not the classifier performances vary depending on the users' gender and race.

In this way, we start from the assumption that the data distribution follows a discrete sequence of independent Bernoulli random variables with probability $p$ for Class 1 and probability $q = 1 - p$ for Class 0. Thus, the expected value of the i-*th* Bernoulli random variable is $E(X_i) = p$ and its variance is defined by $\mathrm{Var}(X_i) = p(1 - p)$ [8]. In our context, by calculating the probability of success for the gender and race labels, the confidence interval approaches a binomial proportion, which is used to calculate the test statistics.

From this perspective, we evaluate whether there are significant differences among outcomes yielded from the combination of different pairs of experiments considering users' gender and race. In this sense, we used the two proportion z-test to assess the presence of biases affecting the face detection process. The null hypothesis $(H_0)$ states there is no significant difference between proportions $(p_1 - p_2 = 0)$. On the other hand, the alternate hypothesis $(H_1)$ states the proportions are not the same, i.e., we reject $H_0$ with a significance level $\alpha = 0.05$ in case of $p_1 - p_2 > 0$. Equation 9 calculates the statistic used in our test.

$$Z = \frac{p_1 - p_2}{\sqrt{\dfrac{p \cdot (1 - p)}{n_1} + \dfrac{p \cdot (1 - p)}{n_2}}}; p = \frac{n_1 \cdot p_1 + n_2 \cdot p_2}{n_1 + n_2}; \tag{9}$$

As one may notice, we focused our analysis on the upper-tailed test, in which a $Z$ value greater than 1.645 leads to rejecting $H_0$. By choosing $\alpha = 0.05$, there is a 5% probability of getting pairs of value by chance and the results present, indeed, type I error (false positive) [3]. Next section, we show the obtained results and our analyses performed to assess our hypothesis.

## 4    Experimental Results

Before proceeding with our statistical analyses, we have to confirm that the detectors are suitable to find faces in images from our database. As previously mentioned, we are processing real-world images collected from passengers while using public transportation in Salvador. The analyses of such images are very challenging due to the dynamic environment, i.e., pictures taken inside the buses are affected by cameras with low quality, current weather, road condition, natural movements, and different illumination, thus producing, for example, underexposed, overexposed, and blurry images.

Firstly, we have run the three detectors on our complete dataset. As a consequence, every detector produced new images with bounding boxes drawn on regions where faces were estimated. Figure 1 illustrates three images along with bounding boxes produced by the detectors. In this figure, there is also a button called "No clear face" that is used to remove the image from our analyses. This is especially important when, for example, the images have low quality or the specialists are not completely confident about the most appropriate label. In summary, if a human specialist has any doubt, then the image must be disregarded to avoid propagating a classification error.

Aiming at verifying the performances of the selected detectors, the human specialists had two main tasks. The first one was to check the bounding boxes, by choosing one of the following options for the contingency matrix: TP (true positive – the face was correctly detected), FN (false negative – no face was found), FP (false positive – a bounding box was drawn on a region with no face), and TN (true negative – no bounding box was drawn on an image with no face). The second task is to set gender and race labels for the users. Therefore, the final dataset contains 1,038 images correctly classified by a specialist committee. Figure 2 presents all contingency matrices calculated based on the agreement between the face detectors (rows) and the specialists' opinion (columns).

By considering the resultant contingency matrices, we calculated the validation metrics (see Sect. 3.3) as shown in Table 1. According to such results, we notice the best overall result was produced by MTCNN. We emphasize that, as expected, our dataset is imbalanced, presenting more images with faces (positive). For this reason, we have also selected metrics that verify results by chance. Concerning the classes based on gender and race, the dataset is balanced as presented in Sect. 3.1. Once we use pre-trained models published by the original authors, all these images were used as a test fold, whose results are presented in this section.

**Table 1.** Validation metrics: Positive – 97.27% and Negative 2.73%.

| Model | Measures | | | | | |
|---|---|---|---|---|---|---|
| | Accuracy | Sensibility | Specify | MCC | Kappa | F1 |
| *MTCNN* | **0.95** | **0.95** | 0.89 | **0.55** | **0.49** | **0.98** |
| YoloFaces | 0.83 | 0.82 | 0.96 | 0.32 | 0.19 | 0.90 |
| ResNet | 0.61 | 0.60 | 1 | 0.20 | 0.7 | 0.75 |

After demonstrating the general performance of the detectors, we start assessing our hypothesis that, essentially, raises the following question: "Are the face detectors influenced by the users' gender and race?". To systematically answer this question, we have hypothesized the following assumptions:

– $H_0$: the error proportions are the same regardless of the users' gender and/or race: $p_1 - p_2 = 0$;
– $H_1$: the error proportions are not the same, thus there is difference based on the users' gender and/or race: $p_1 - p_2 > 0$.

The first step towards performing this analysis was to find the error proportions $p$ and the number $n$ of sample per class, as shown in Table 2. For example, by considering this table, we notice the detection error in black users is greater when compared to white people. However, can this difference be considered significant?

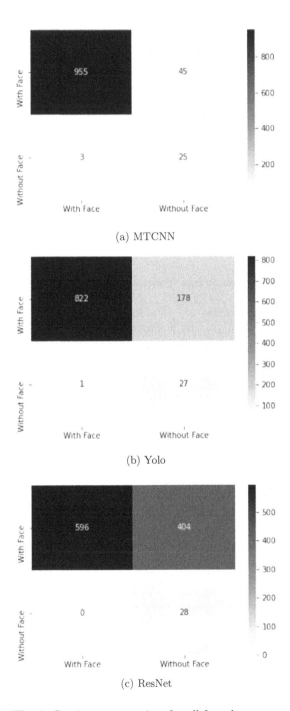

(a) MTCNN

(b) Yolo

(c) ResNet

**Fig. 2.** Contingency matrices for all face detectors.

**Table 2.** Error proportions (%) between classes.

| Population | | Models | | |
| --- | --- | --- | --- | --- |
| | $n$ | MTCNN | YOLO | ResNet |
| Woman | 593 | 3.54 | 15.18 | 39.46 |
| Man | 401 | 5.99 | 21.70 | 41.15 |
| Black | 560 | 6.25 | 21.61 | 45.89 |
| White | 434 | 2.30 | 12.90 | 32.72 |
| Black/Woman | 348 | 4.89 | 18.39 | 44.25 |
| White/Woman | 245 | 1.63 | 10.61 | 32.65 |
| Black/Man | 212 | 8.49 | 26.89 | 48.58 |
| White/Man | 189 | 3.17 | 15.87 | 32.80 |

In the next step, by only considering images with faces according to the specialists, we computed $Z_{obs}$, $\alpha_{obs}$, and the (lower and upper) confidence intervals (CI) from the error proportions between a different combination of gender and races. In the following tables, results with significant differences were highlighted in bold.

In Table 3, we show the comparison between errors from different combinations of classes, based on the face detection task performed by MTCNN. As one may notice, although there are different error rates in Table 2, the statistical tests reject the null hypothesis in three situations: Black × White, Black/Woman × White/Woman, and Black/Man × White/Man. Therefore, by considering the alternative hypothesis, the error is greater when black users are the analyzed passenger. In this experiment, we have noticed no significant difference when the passengers are compared by gender.

**Table 3.** Test statistic for MTCNN.

| Hypothesis : $p_1 > p_2$ | Statistical parameters | | |
| --- | --- | --- | --- |
| | $Z$ | $\alpha_{obs}(\%)$ | CI 95% |
| $\epsilon(\textbf{Black}) > \epsilon(\textbf{White})$ | 2.971 | 0.15 | [0.019, 0.06] |
| $\epsilon(\text{Woman}) > \epsilon(\text{Man})$ | −1.822 | 96.58 | [−0.048, −0.001] |
| $\epsilon(\textbf{Black/Woman}) > \epsilon(\textbf{White/Woman})$ | 2.114 | 1.72 | [0.009, 0.056] |
| $\epsilon(\textbf{Black/Man}) > \epsilon(\textbf{White/Man})$ | 2.242 | 1.25 | [0.015, 0.091] |
| $\epsilon(\text{White/Woman}) > \epsilon(\text{White/Man})$ | −1.061 | 85.57 | [−0.04, 0.009] |
| $\epsilon(\text{Black/Woman}) > \epsilon(\text{Black/Man})$ | −1.707 | 95.61 | [−0.073, 0.001] |
| $\epsilon(\text{Black/Woman}) > \epsilon(\text{White/Man})$ | 0.940 | 17.36 | [−0.011, 0.046] |

Next, we repeated the same analyses on images processed by YOLO. Regardless of the classification metrics, we decided to assess whether the errors produced by this detector were also influenced by gender and race. According to the results summarized in Table 4, we noticed the face detection errors have ratified the results produced by MTCNN. As shown in bold, there are significant differences when race is assessed. The face detection with YOLO also produced worse results when the passengers are black.

**Table 4.** Test statistic for Yolo.

| Hypothesis : $P(A) > P(B)$ | Statistical Parameters | | |
|---|---|---|---|
| | $Z$ | $\alpha_{obs}(\%)$ | CI 95% |
| $\epsilon$(**Black**) > $\epsilon$(**White**) | 3.560 | 0.02 | [0.048, 0.126] |
| $\epsilon$(Woman) > $\epsilon$(Man) | −2.636 | 99.58 | [−0.107, −0.024] |
| $\epsilon$(**Black/Woman**) > $\epsilon$(**White/Woman**) | 2.600 | 0.47 | [0.031, 0.125] |
| $\epsilon$(**Black/Man**) > $\epsilon$(**White/Man**) | 2.673 | 0.38 | [0.044, 0.177] |
| $\epsilon$(White/Woman) > $\epsilon$(White/Man) | −1.621 | 94.75 | [−0.107, 0.002] |
| $\epsilon$(Black/Woman) > $\epsilon$(Black/Man) | −2.371 | 99.11 | [−0.146, −0.024] |
| $\epsilon$(Black/Woman) > $\epsilon$(White/Man) | 0.734 | 23.15 | [0.03, 0.081] |

In our last analysis, we have also compared the results produced by ResNet. Although this detector has presented the worst results, we decided to perform a close examination on the error proportions produced by it according to the different classes. The final results, presented in Table 5, also ratifies the previous analyses, in which the error proportions are significant when users are compared by their race. Moreover, the errors produced by this detector were statistically different when black woman results are compared to a white man. Despite the users' race, we cannot affirm, at least in our scenario and experiments, there is a significant difference by comparing the users' gender.

**Table 5.** Test statistic for ResNet.

| Hypothesis: $P(A) > P(B)$ | Statistical parameters | | |
|---|---|---|---|
| | $Z$ | $\alpha_{obs}(\%)$ | CI 95% |
| $\epsilon$(**Black**) > $\epsilon$(**White**) | 4.201 | 0.00 | [0.081, 0.182] |
| $\epsilon$(Woman) > $\epsilon$(Man) | −0.533 | 70.31 | [−0.069, 0.035] |
| $\epsilon$(**Black/Woman**) > $\epsilon$(**White/Woman**) | 2.846 | 0.22 | [0.05, 0.182] |
| $\epsilon$(**Black/Man**) > $\epsilon$(**White/Man**) | 3.205 | 0.07 | [0.078, 0.237] |
| $\epsilon$(White/Woman) > $\epsilon$(White/Man) | −0.033 | 51.32 | [−0.076, 0.073] |
| $\epsilon$(Black/Woman) > $\epsilon$(Black/Man) | −0.997 | 84.07 | [−0.115, 0.028] |
| $\epsilon$(**Black/Woman**) > $\epsilon$(**White/Man**) | 2.584 | 0.49 | [0.043, 0.186] |

# 5 Conclusion

In this work, we decided to investigate an ethical issue that has been calling the attention of several AI researchers and practitioners. In 2020, a letter signed by several mathematicians had explicitly pointed out the risks of using AI-based technologies without carefully examining whether their decision processes are implicitly working as expected [5]. The Mathematics Community has not criticized the advances of AI, which are important and necessary to the wellness of our society as the contribution in areas as, for example, medicine and ecology. However, can we work in such direction without propagating to our algorithms (and data) historical errors as structural and explicit racism?

This situation is strongly relevant in the Computer Vision area, especially by working on tasks related to face recognition. Are our data and algorithms performing as expected regardless of users' race? Can the algorithm produce more errors when black people are under analysis? As discussed by Nick Bostrom in the preface of his book on superintelligence with the fable "The Unfinished Fable of the Sparrows", an important part of the AI advances is performed by researchers interested in studies about the risks of deploying them incautiously [1].

This issue motivated us during the design of a solution to identify fraud in the usage of benefit cards in public transportation in Salvador (Brazil). Aiming at identifying whether or not the cards were being used by the actual owner, we created a fraud detection system that uses Artificial Neural Networks to identify when the users' pictures taken inside the bus were different from their registered profiles.

The experimental setup created in this work was based on the application of models, published to detect faces in images, on our dataset, which is composed of millions of pictures daily taken inside the buses. In summary, we evaluated the errors produced by MTCNN, YOLO, and ResNet by comparing different groups according to the users' gender and race. According to our analyses, we have noticed significant differences when the passengers' race is analyzed. All results consistently highlighted detection errors were greater with black passengers. Moreover, we have noticed this problem also happened when we subsampled the data by the users' gender. In summary, errors with black woman and man were greater than those obtained from white woman and man, respectively.

This bias found in our experiments was strongly important to emphasize the need for better models to detect fraud before deploying our system. The main limitation of our work is the usage of pre-trained model, although it is a common practice in commercial applications, especially when the availability of labeled data is limited. Finally, we recall the results obtained in this work shows this undesired bias to our unspecific application and illustrates the risks, in which similar applications may suffer in real-world scenarios. Thus, as future work, we plan to increase our dataset with more gender and race labels, aiming at retraining the face detectors, and updating their parameters and hyper-parameters. Then, we will draw stronger conclusion about whether the problem happens due to the ANN architectures, our data used in the test phase, or the requirement of retraining the models with more appropriated (fair) datasets. In the future, we also plan to evaluate other users' labels.

**Acknowledgment.** This work was partially supported by CAPES (Coordination for the Improvement of Higher Education Personnel – Brazilian Federal Government Agency). We gratefully acknowledge the support of NVIDIA Corporation with the donation of the Titan V GPU used for this research. Finally, we also thank the company Integra, responsible for the public transportation in Salvador, for support this work. Any opinions, findings, and conclusions or recommendations expressed in this material are those of the authors and do not necessarily reflect the views of CAPES, NVIDIA, and Integra.

# References

1. Bostrom, N.: Superintelligence: Paths, dangers, strategies (2014)
2. Buolamwini, J., Gebru, T.: Gender shades: intersectional accuracy disparities in commercial gender classification. In: Conference on Fairness, Accountability and Transparency, pp. 77–91. PMLR (2018)
3. Casella, G., Berger, R.L.: Statistical inference. Cengage Learning (2021)
4. Castelvecchi, D.: Is facial recognition too biased to be let loose?, vol. 587. Nature, https://doi.org/10.1038/d41586-020-03186-4 (2020). https://www.nature.com/articles/d41586-020-03186-4
5. Castelvecchi, D.: Mathematicians urge colleagues to boycott police work in wake of killings. Nature **582**, 465 (2020). https://doi.org/10.1038/d41586-020-01874-9
6. Farinella, G., Dugelay, J.L.: Demographic classification: do gender and ethnicity affect each other? In: 2012 International Conference on Informatics, Electronics & Vision (ICIEV), pp. 383–390. IEEE (2012)
7. Furl, N., Phillips, P., O'Toole, A.J.: Face recognition algorithms and the other-race effect: computational mechanisms for a developmental contact hypothesis. Cogn. Sci. **26**(6), 797–815 (2002). https://doi.org/10.1016/S0364-0213(02)00084-8, https://www.sciencedirect.com/science/article/pii/S0364021302000848
8. Grinstead, C.M., Snell, J.L.: Introduction to probability. Am. Math. Soc. (2012)
9. Haykin, S.: Neural Networks: A Comprehensive Foundation, 1st edn. Prentice Hall PTR, Upper Saddle River (1994)
10. He, K., Zhang, X., Ren, S., Sun, J.: Deep residual learning for image recognition. In: Proceedings of the IEEE Conference on Computer Vision and Pattern Recognition, pp. 770–778 (2016)
11. Jain, V., Learned-Miller, E.: FDDB: a benchmark for face detection in unconstrained settings. Technical report, UMass Amherst technical report (2010)
12. Karkkainen, K., Joo, J.: FairFace: face attribute dataset for balanced race, gender, and age for bias measurement and mitigation. In: Proceedings of the IEEE/CVF Winter Conference on Applications of Computer Vision (WACV), pp. 1548–1558, January 2021
13. Klare, B.F., Burge, M.J., Klontz, J.C., Vorder Bruegge, R.W., Jain, A.K.: Face recognition performance: role of demographic information. IEEE Trans. Inf. Foren. Secur. **7**(6), 1789–1801 (2012). https://doi.org/10.1109/TIFS.2012.2214212
14. LeCun, Y., Bottou, L., Bengio, Y., Haffner, P.: Gradient-based learning applied to document recognition. Proc. IEEE **86**(11), 2278–2323 (1998)

15. Najibi, A.: Racial discrimination in face recognition technology. 24, October 2020. https://sitn.hms.harvard.edu/flash/2020/racial-discrimination-in-face-recognition-technology

16. Phillips, P.J., Jiang, F., Narvekar, A., Ayyad, J., O'Toole, A.J.: An other-race effect for face recognition algorithms. ACM Trans. Appl. Percept. (TAP) **8**(2), 1–11 (2011)

17. Raji, I.D., Gebru, T., Mitchell, M., Buolamwini, J., Lee, J., Denton, E.: Saving face: investigating the ethical concerns of facial recognition auditing. https://doi.org/10.1145/3375627.3375820 (2020)

18. Redmon, J., Divvala, S., Girshick, R., Farhadi, A.: You only look once: unified, real-time object detection. In: Proceedings of the IEEE Conference on Computer Vision and Pattern Recognition, pp. 779–788 (2016)

19. Simonyan, K., Zisserman, A.: Very deep convolutional networks for large-scale image recognition. arXiv preprint arXiv:1409.1556 (2014)

20. Snow, B.J.: Amazon's face recognition falsely matched 28 members of congress with mugshots. 26, July 2018 (June 2018), technology & Civil Liberties Attorney, ACLU of Northern California

21. Wang, M., Deng, W., Hu, J., Tao, X., Huang, Y.: Racial faces in the wild: reducing racial bias by information maximization adaptation network. In: Proceedings of the IEEE/CVF International Conference on Computer Vision, pp. 692–702 (2019)

22. Yang, M.H., Kriegman, D.J., Ahuja, N.: Detecting faces in images: a survey. IEEE Trans. Patt. Anal. Mach. Intell. **24**(1), 34–58 (2002)

23. Yang, S., Luo, P., Loy, C.C., Tang, X.: From facial parts responses to face detection: a deep learning approach. In: Proceedings of the IEEE International Conference on Computer Vision, pp. 3676–3684 (2015)

24. Yang, S., Luo, P., Loy, C.C., Tang, X.: WIDER FACE: a face detection benchmark. In: IEEE Conference on Computer Vision and Pattern Recognition (CVPR) (2016)

25. Zhang, C., Zhang, Z.: A survey of recent advances in face detection. Technical report. MSR-TR-2010-66, June 2010. https://www.microsoft.com/en-us/research/publication/a-survey-of-recent-advances-in-face-detection/

26. Zhang, K., Zhang, Z., Li, Z., Qiao, Y.: Joint face detection and alignment using multitask cascaded convolutional networks. IEEE Signal Process. Lett. **23**(10), 1499–1503 (2016)

# Evaluating Topic Models in Portuguese Political Comments About Bills from Brazil's Chamber of Deputies

Nádia F. F. da Silva[1,2(✉)], Marília Costa R. Silva[1], Fabíola S. F. Pereira[1,3], João Pedro M. Tarrega[1], João Vitor P. Beinotti[1], Márcio Fonseca[4], Francisco Edmundo de Andrade[4], and André C. P. de L. F. de Carvalho[4]

[1] Institute of Mathematics and Computer Science, University of São Paulo, São Carlos, SP 13566-590, Brazil
nadia.felix@ufg.br,
{marilia.costa.silva,fabiola.pereira,joao.tarrega,joaobeinotti}@usp.br
[2] Institute of Informatics, Federal University of Goiás, Goiânia, Go, Brazil
[3] Federal University of Uberlândia, Uberlândia, Brazil
[4] Câmara dos Deputados - Palácio do Congresso Nacional - Praça dos Três Poderes Brasília, Brasília, DF, Brazil
{marcio.fonseca,francisco.edmundo}@camara.leg.br, andre@usp.br

**Abstract.** The popular participation in Law-making is an important resource in the evolution of Democracy and Direct Legislation. The amount of legislative documents produced within the past decade has risen dramatically, making it difficult for law practitioners to attend to legislation and still listen to the opinion of the citizens. This work focuses on the use of topic models for summarizing and visualizing Brazilian comments about legislation (bills). In this paper, we provide a qualitative evaluation from a legal expert and compare it with the topics predicted by our model. For such, we designed a specific sentence embedding technique able to induce models for Portuguese texts, and we used these models as topic model, obtaining very good results. We experimentally compared our proposal with other techniques for multilingual sentence embeddings, evaluating them in three topical corpora prepared by us, two of them annotated by a specialist and the other automatically annotated by hashtags.

**Keywords:** Topic models · Language models · Natural language processing · Sentence embeddings

## 1 Introduction

The popular participation in the definition of public policy is inherent to a democratic state, and it comprises more than electoral processes. The Information and Communication Technologies (ICTs) provide a means for citizens to manifest their options in social media and government platforms [31]. Furthermore,

A. Britto and K. Valdivia Delgado (Eds.): BRACIS 2021, LNAI 13074, pp. 104–120, 2021.
https://doi.org/10.1007/978-3-030-91699-2_8

the citizens can effectively contribute to better public policies and government decision-making [41]. In Brazil, the Chamber of Deputies has an online platform that enables all Brazilian citizens to interact and express their opinions concerning bills being discussed by the parliament [12].

One of the main sources of public opinion data are the social engagement platforms, such as Twitter[1]. In 2019, approximately 500 million tweets were daily generated in the world [47]. Relying exclusively on human judgment as a tool for the analysis of very large public opinion data streams regarding the Brazilian e-democracy is not feasible. The design and use of new computational tools able to extract relevant and useful information from the opinions of the population regarding new bills can result in more accepted and embraced legislation.

As means to reliably process opinions, and ensure that citizens have their freedom of speech respected and equally considered, text analytic techniques [18] emerge as tools for the e-democracy [17]. It is important to observe that the objects (opinions) received in these data streams are mostly unlabeled. *Ergo*, unsupervised and semi-supervised learning approaches, such as clustering and topic models algorithms, can be more suitable to extract relevant information from these data.

Text clusterization and topic modeling techniques, which are often used in text mining, have been frequently adopted for text data analysis [17]. Previous studies, such as Evangelopoulos and Visinescu [17], successfully applied clustering algorithms for topic modeling using the analysis of citizens' opinions in the e-democracy. Topic modeling techniques can extract from texts information to support semantic analyses. This paper investigates a similar application, using topic modeling as the core method to extract key information about the Brazilians' political opinions for any proposed legislation publicly available in stances in the Chamber of Deputies online platform. This work focuses on a very specific instrument of citizen participation in the law-making process: comments related to the bills, in particular, those collected from the polls in the Chamber of Deputies web portal (refer to Sect. 3 for details). While there is a vast literature exploring the analysis of social media influence in politics [5,30], our comments dataset is more structured and focused on specific bills. The research reported in this paper has the following contributions:

- We adapted the **BERTopic topic mining tool** [21] to extract topics from political comments from [11];
- We applied an unsupervised deep learning based embedding technique [19] to train a Brazilian Portuguese Legislative Sentence based-Embedding, and this resulting model is available at https://github.com/nadiafelix/Bracis2021;
- We compared the performance of BERTopic by leveraging Portuguese and multilingue sentence embedding models. The sentence embeddings are used by topic models as input features in the clustering approach;
- We described and made available three topical corpora, two of them annotated by a specialist and the other automatically annotated by hashtags;

---

[1] https://twitter.com/.

- We performed a dynamic topic modeling presenting a timeline of evolution;
- We evaluated a topic model, before evaluated only for English, for Brazilian Portuguese corpora.
- Our work, to the best of our knowledge, is the first open source approach in Brazilian Portuguese to analyze user-generated content from the parliament platform about bills.

This work is organized as follows. The second section provides an overview about related works. Section 3 outlines the corpora and exploratory analyses. The fourth section introduces the methodology. Section 5 presents the experimental evaluation. The following section comprises the discussions and concludes the work, summarizing the findings, advantages, limitations, contributions and research opportunities.

## 2   Related Work

**Legal Text Analysis.** Recent advances in natural language processing techniques led to a surge in the application of text analysis in legal domains. In private law practice, the *legal analytics* tools impact areas such as legal research, document retrieval, contract review, automatic document generation, and custom legal advice [14,39]. Recent surveys indicate that the adoption of these tools results is not only in a significant reduction in time to deliver the services but also improves the predictability and trust in the litigation process [3].

Beyond assisting legal practitioners, textual analysis has been increasingly adopted in the legislative process. Before a law comes into force, a bill (law proposal) is subject to extensive technical analysis and discussion, which often allows the participation of civil organizations and the general public. During this process, a plethora of textual documents is generated, including technical reports, transcribed speeches, project amendments, among others. The availability of these documents in open formats [10] spurred the development of approaches to extract insights including the analysis of parliamentary debates [1] and prediction of bill enactment probabilities [27].

Among those legislative documents, this work focuses on a very specific instrument of citizen participation in the lawmaking process: comments related to the law proposals, in particular, those collected from the polls in the Chamber of Deputies web portal (refer to Sect. 3 for details). While there is a vast literature exploring the analysis of social media influence in politics [5,30], our comments dataset is more structured and focused on specific bills.

**Text Clustering.** Text clusterization is a data mining task that consists of grouping instances according to their characteristics, and the Curse of Dimensionality also jeopardizes the clustering performance [28]. However, short texts, such as tweets, lead to more sparse vectors, which may require compression. The clusterization has hierarchical approaches [45]. The first is top-down and consists of an initial cluster with the entire dataset that is successively divided [2]. The bottom-up approach considers at first that each instance constitutes a cluster, and the most similar (the algorithm sets up first similarity measures) instances are agglomerated [2]. The distance-based clusterization, such as KMeans, can start with k clusters, each one with one centroid, and these centroids gather the other instances according to a distance metric [6], such as cosine similarity, euclidean distance, Jaccard distance and so forth. Finally, density-based methods (such as Density-Based Spatial Clustering of Applications with Noise (DBSCAN)) start clustering the instances that have more neighbors [40].

Topic models and text clustering have analogous purposes. Both of them aim to group text instances based on their similarity [24, 26]. Nonetheless, whereas clustering algorithms mostly have a deterministic approach, topic models premises include stochastic assumptions [2]. Moreover, interpretable topic models extract from each group the latent semantic-based n-grams that most represent the topic [26], in contrast to clustering algorithms that only gather instances without summarizing the inherent characteristics of each group.

**Topic Modeling.** Topic models are widely used to analyze large text collections. They represent a suite of unsupervised learning algorithms whose purpose is to discover the thematic structure in a collection of documents. Several researchers have studied topic modeling. Originally, Probabilistic Latent Semantic Indexing [23] and Latent Semantic Indexing [29] paved the way for the creation of the Latent Dirichlet Allocation (LDA) [7] which is the most commonly implemented topic modeling algorithm in use today. In recent years, researchers have started to develop topic modeling algorithms that have achieved state of the art performance by leveraging word embeddings [15, 25, 34].

Lda2vec [26], Embedded Topic Model (ETM) [16], and Deep Latent Dirichlet Allocation (DLDA) [13] are three examples of topic models that extend LDA. The lda2vec is an unsupervised topic model, which combines Latent Dirichlet Allocation and Word Embeddings (word2vec - skipgram) [26]. This method generates context vectors combining word vectors and document vectors [26]. The second model incorporates word embeddings and LDA [16]. The ETM keeps its performance even in large vocabularies. In addition, the topics are represented as vectors in the semantic space, and the topic embeddings generate context vectors. This method leads to interpretable topics, regardless the inclusion or removal of stopwords. The third work, DLDA, uses sample strategies that provide scalability to single or multilayered methods. Besides, the DLDA can have multiple learning rates (based on topics and layers), and is a generalization of LDA. In contrast to the two previous models, the DLDA uses count vectors. The three models lose semantic context due to the embedding approach. This issue is partially solved by methods that consider sentence embeddings such as BERT [15].

Top2Vec [4] and BERTopic [21] proposed the use of distributed representations of documents and words due to their ability to capture the semantics of words and documents. They emphasize that before their approaches it was necessary to have the number of topics as input to the topic model algorithms, and with Top2Vec and BERTopic, this parameter is found by their approaches. The first work proposes that topic vectors be jointly embedded with the document and word vectors with distance between them representing semantic similarity. BERTopic is a topic modeling technique that leverages sentences based BERT embeddings [15] and a class-based TF-IDF [36] to create dense clusters allowing for interpretable topics whilst keeping important words in the topic descriptions.

As this paper focuses on topic models, we compare these previous described in Table 1 (The columns #Topics and Dynamic express whether the approach uses the number of topics and dynamic topic modeling, respectively). This table shows, e.g., that BERTopic [21] can use different topic modeling techniques (value "yes", in the column #Topics) and uses dynamic topic modeling (value "yes", in the column Dynamic), a collection of techniques that analyze the evolution of topics along the time, generating the topic representations at each timestamp for each topic. These methods help to understand how a topic changes during a period of time. Furthermore, it provides other forms of topic modeling, not explored in this study, such as semi-supervised learning.

**Table 1.** Topic model approaches. *Hierarchical density-based spatial clustering of applications with noise [8]

| Approach | Clustering algorithm | Feature engineering | #Topics | Dynamic |
|----------|---------------------|---------------------|---------|---------|
| Lda2vec [26] | Generative probabilistic model | Embeddings of words | Yes | No |
| DLDA [13] | Generative probabilistic model | Count vectors | Yes | No |
| ETM [16] | Generative probabilistic model | Embeddings of words and topics | Yes | No |
| Topic2Vec [4] | HDBSCAN*[8] | Sentence or word embeddings, like BERT [15] or Sentence-based BERT | No | No |
| BERTopic [21] | HDBSCAN*[8] | Sentence or word embeddings (ex. BERT [15] or Sentence-based BERT) | No | Yes |

## 3    Portuguese Political Comments

The Chamber of Deputies Board of Innovation and Information Technology provided the dataset used in this study, which is available at [11]. This dataset consists of information classified by the user commentary for the bill, including counter of comments, date, opinion on the bill (positive or negative) and the commented proposition.

The user can make its participation through the website [11]. In order to organize the commentaries, since there are several law projects and constitutional amendment propositions, the user can choose a specific proposition, whether his/her stand is for or against the legal document, as well as formulate the comment itself. A feature was implemented to "like" a certain commentary, simulating a social network, with the purpose of emphasizing the popularity of a certain point of view.

An exploratory data analysis was performed on the dataset prior to the experimental evaluation. For every comment we calculated its word count, character count, and mean word length (characters per word). These metrics can be visualized in Fig. 1. Metadata with the number of likes of each comment, as well as its perception by the user as a positive or negative aspect of the legal document were also included in the analysis.

The majority of comments have none or few likes, which is expected since the most liked comments are shown to the user in the voting page. As such, with more visibility this creates a snowball effect in which they attain more votes. This is seen in both bills and positive/negative opinions.

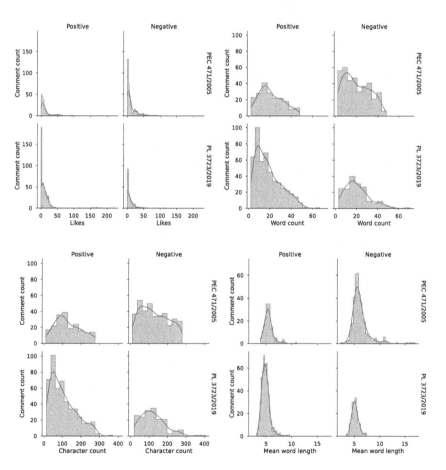

**Fig. 1.** Textual metrics distribution in our corpora. The blue horizontal line represents the kernel density function approximation of the data. (Color figure online)

In word and character count, the density distribution of the variables differs slightly in shape between the projects and opinions, although their medians remain close to each other. The mean word length presents a normal-like distribution in all categories. Extracted comments with at least 2 words were kept in the corpora and had URL links removed.

### 3.1   Corpora

For our experiments, we considered all comments associated with the two bills (PL 3723/2019 and PL 471/2005), and the set of all comments that have a hashtag in their content (Hashtag Corpus). Below, we briefly detail these scenarios.

**PL 3723/2019.** The *PL 3723/2019* Bill changes the Law No. 10.826, of December 22, 2003, which deals with registration, possession and sale of firearms and ammunition, and defines crimes. The *PL 3723/2019 corpus* was collected from National Congress Polls[2], in which the citizens are asked about the positive and negative parts of this bill. This corpus is composed of 195 negative and 530 positive comments. For our experiments, we considered the total number of comments (i.e., 725 comments).

**PEC 471/2005.** The *PL 471/2005* Bill establishes the effectiveness for the current responsible and substitutes for the notary services, invested according to the law. Known as *"PEC dos Cartórios"*, the *PL 471/2005 corpus* was collected from National Congress Polls[3], in which the citizens were asked about the positive and negative parts of this bill. This corpus is composed of 383 negative and 205 positive comments. For our experiments, we considered the total number of comments, i.e., 588 comments.

**Hashtag Corpus.** This corpus is composed of 522 comments, which contain at least 16 comments with hashtags [11]. There are 189 bills with hashtags. We considered the top ten bills with more comments. The top ten bills with more comments and hashtags are: PEC 32/2020, PL 318/2021, PL 3019/2020, PDL 232/2019, PL 2893/2019, PEC 135/2019, PEC 101/2003, PL 4425/2020, PEC 6/2019, and PL 1577/2019. More details are shown in Table 2.

---

[2] https://forms.camara.leg.br/ex/enquetes/2209381.
[3] https://forms.camara.leg.br/ex/enquetes/304008.

**Table 2.** Hashtag corpus

| Bill | Examples of hashtags | Example of comments | Total of comments |
|---|---|---|---|
| PEC 32/2020 | #NãoAoFimDaEstabilidade #contraareforma #estabilidadesim, #valorizaçãodoservidor, #naoapec32, #servicopublicodequalidade, #valorizeoservidor, #pecparaospoliticos | A estabilidade do servidor é um direito e garante a prestação de um serviço justo e sem interferência de terceiros. #EstabilidadeSIM. | 159 |
| PL 318/2021 | #todasasvidasimportam, #ChegaDeMausTratos, #CadeiaParaMausTratosDeAnimais #naopl318 #PrisãoAQuemMaltrataOsAnimais #ChegaDeTortura | Basta!! Chega de explorar os animais!! A mãe natureza não aguenta mais tanto retrocesso!! E nós também !!#naopl318 | 127 |
| PL 3019/2020 | #ditaduranuncamais, #ditadurafascistanuncamais #AntifaTERRORISTA, #foraSobrenome1 #AntifasNao | Direito legítimo de manifestação. Os fascistas se articulam incorporando as palavras de ordem da oposição.#ditadurafascistanuncamais | 45 |
| PDL 232/2019 | #euapoioodecretodearmas, #ArmasPelaVida, #REFERENDO2005, #LegitimaDefesa | DIREITO à legítima defesa. O Estado faz a defesa social, eu QUERO TER O DIREITO de defender meu corpo físico, bem como meu espaço de moradia e trabalho. #ArmasPelaVida | 42 |
| PL 2893/2019 | #SalvemosAsDuasVidas, #AbortoNãO, #simavida, #naoaoaborto, #justiçaporMariBFerrer, #PelosDireitosDasMulheres,#direitoaoaborto | Apenas a mulher que sofreu a violência tem direito de decidir se quer ou não prosseguir com a gestação. #direitoaoaborto | 37 |
| PEC 135/2019 | #votoimpresso, #VotoImpressoJá, #VotoImpressoEm2022, #PEC135JÁ | Quero ter a certeza de que o voto que digitei na urna eletrônica realmente foi computado para meus candidatos. Até jogo do bicho tem comprovante impresso. Porque o voto, que define o futuro de um país não pode ter comprovante? #VotoImpressoJá | 28 |
| PEC 101/2003 | #ForaSobrenome2, #ForaSobrenome3, #NãoAPEC101, #Sobrenome4InimigoDoBrasil | Sou Totalmente contra, a Pec 101 é uma Afronta à constituição, ninguém tem o direito de se perpetuar no poder #NãoAPEC101 | 26 |
| PL 4425/2020 | #CriminalizaçãodoComunismoJa, #PL4425, #PL5358CriminalizacaoDoComunismo, #ComunismoMata, #NazismoNÃO, #ComunismoNão | O Brasil tem que criminalizar essas ideologias nefastas urgentemente, isso visa até o fortalecimento de nossa democracia. #NazismoNÃO #ComunismoNão | 22 |
| PEC 6/2019 | #NovaPrevidênciaÉParaTodos, #EuApoioNovaPrevidencia, #ninguémacimadoteto #OBrasilQuerReforma, #ReformaDaPrevidência | Sem a reforma o Brasil quebra. Não queremos virar uma Grécia! Pensem no Brasil, e não no poder. #NovaPrevidênciaÉParaTodos | 20 |
| PL 1577/2019 | #somosGamersNãoAssassinos,#EuTenhoODireitoDeJogar, #somosgamersnaoassassinos,#gamenaomata | Jogos não são um tutorial de como matar pessoas e como conseguir armas na vida real, são mídias de entretenimento, tanto que ajudam a desestressar. #somosGamersNãoAssassinos | 16 |

# 4    Methodology

We summarize the methodology for topic modeling in Fig. 2. First we obtain the comments of citizens about a bill, next we chose a sentence embedding that will convert the comments into a vector representation. Next, the clustering algorithm takes care of obtaining clusters based on spatial density.

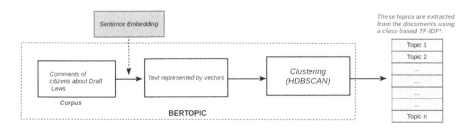

**Fig. 2.** Methodology for topic modeling. ∗TF-IDF (Term Frequency-Inverse Document Frequency).

## 4.1 Sentence Embeddings

A common method to address clustering and semantic search is to map each sentence to a vector space as semantically similar sentences are close. Researchers have started to input individual sentences into BERT [15] and to derive fixed-length sentence embeddings. The most commonly used approach is to average the BERT output layer (known as BERT embeddings) or by using the output of the first token (the [CLS] token). As it was shown by [33], this practice yields rather bad sentence embeddings, often worse than averaging static word embeddings (for example, Glove [32]). In this work, we evaluate three sentence embeddings: (i) Universal Sentence Encoder [9]; (ii) Multilingual Universal Sentence Encoder for Semantic Retrieval (distiluse-base-multilingual-cased-v2) [48]; and (iii) a Portuguese Legislative Sentence Embedding [19] trained by us.

(i) *Universal Sentence Encode (USE)*[4]: It is an encoder of greater-than-word length text trained on a variety of data [9], in a variety of languages (Arabic, Chinese-simplified, Chinese-traditional, English, French, German, Italian, Japanese, Korean, Dutch, Polish, Portuguese, Spanish, Thai, Turkish, Russian) i.e., it is a cross-lingual sentence representation. Unsupervised training data for the sentence encoding models are drawn from web sources of Wikipedia[5], web news, web question-answer pages and discussion forums. The authors mention that augment unsupervised learning with training on supervised data from the Stanford Natural Language Inference corpus (SNLI)[6].

(ii) *Multilingual Universal Sentence Encoder for Semantic Retrieval* (distiluse-base-multilingual-cased-v2): It is a multilingual knowledge distilled version of the multilingual Universal Sentence Encoder. This version supports 50+ languages, including Portuguese. Training data consists of mined question-answer pairs from online forums including Reddit[7], StackOverflow[8], YahooAnswers[9], and translation pairs, MultiNLI [46], an extensive corpus,

---

[4] https://tfhub.dev/google/universal-sentence-encoder-multilingual-large/1.
[5] https://www.wikipedia.org/.
[6] https://nlp.stanford.edu/projects/snli/.
[7] https://www.reddit.com/.
[8] http://stackoverflow.com/.
[9] https://help.yahoo.com/kb/answers.

which contains examples from multiple sources is also used. The number of mined question-answer pairs also varies across languages with a bias toward a handful of top tier languages. To balance training across languages, the authors used Google's translation system to translate SNLI to the other languages.

(iii) *Portuguese Legislative Sentence Embedding*: We trained our sentence embedding using a contrastive learning[10] framework [19] coupled with the Portuguese pre-trained language model named BERTimbau [37]. This proposal advances the state-of-the-art sentence embeddings using only unsupervised learning, and the authors named SimCSE [19]. We use the same hyperparameters, and the training set is described next: (**1**) From [12], we used the column *Conteudo* with 215,713 comments. We removed the comments from PL 3723/2019, PEC 471/2005, and Hashtag Corpus, in order to avoid bias. (**2**) From [12], we also used 147,008 bills. From these projects, we used the summary field named *txtEmenta* and the project core text named *txtExplicacaoEmenta*. (**3**) From Political Speeches[11], we used 462,831 texts, specifically, we used the columns: *sumario*, *textodiscurso*, and *indexacao*. These corpora were segmented into sentences and concatenated, producing 2,307,426 sentences.

## 4.2   Topic Models

BERTopic [21] is a topic modeling technique that leverages sentence embeddings transformers and c-TF-IDF, a Class-based TF-IDF (Term Frequency-Inverse Document Frequency) to create dense clusters, allowing for interpretable topics whilst keeping important words in the topic descriptions. The algorithm makes an assumption that many semantically similar documents can indicate an underlying topic. This approach automatically finds the number of topics, no stop word lists are required, no need for stemming/lemmatization, and works on short text [21].

## 5   Experimental Evaluation

### 5.1   Quantity and Quality Evaluation

The unsupervised nature of topic model makes the evaluation task difficult [43]. We use the topic coherence evaluation [38] to decide which sentence embedding has better interpretability.

---

[10]   Contrastive learning is a machine learning technique used to learn the general features of a dataset without labels by teaching the model which data points are similar or different [20].

[11]   Available at https://github.com/nadiafelix/Bracis2021.

**Topic Coherence Evaluation.** The goal of topic coherence is to automate the evaluation of the interpretability of latent topics and the underlying idea is rooted in the distributional hypothesis of linguistics [22] – words with similar meanings tend to occur in similar contexts [38]. There have been approaches that confirmed a positive correlation with human interpretability and have been applied to evaluate the effectiveness of advances in the field of topic modeling. In order to evaluate our models, we used the coherence measurement $C_V$ from the literature [35]. $C_V$ is the most accurate measure according to M. Röder et al. [35], and is calculated as follows. The top $N$ words of each topic are selected as the representation of the topic, denoted as $W = \{w_1, ..., w_N\}$. Each word $w_i$ is represented by an $N$-dimensional vector $v(w_i) = \{NPMI(w_i, w_j)\}_{j=1,...,N}$, where $j$th-entry is the *Normalized Pointwise Mutual Information* (*NPMI*) between word $w_i$ and $w_j$, i.e. $NPMI(w_i, w_j) = \frac{log P(w_i, w_j) - log(P(w_i)P(w_j))}{-log P(w_i, w_j)}$. $W$ is represented by the sum of all word vectors, $v(W) = \sum_{j=1}^{N} v(w_j)$. The calculation of NPMI between word $w_i$ and $w_j$ involves the marginal and joint probabilities $P(w_i), P(w_j), P(w_i, w_j)$. For each word $w_i$, a pair is formed $(v(w_i), v(W))$. A cosine similarity measure $\phi_i(v(w_i), v(W)) = \frac{v(w_i)^T v(W)}{\|v(w_i)\|\|v(W)\|}$ is then calculated for each pair. The final $C_V$ score for the topic is the average of all $\phi$'s.

**Human Evaluation.** Each performance metric has distortions and limitations. This metric, in the context of unsupervised learning, could mislead results. Thus, an expert also evaluated qualitatively the datasets. The specialist defined the key topics of the corpora without knowing how many are or without any clue.

## 5.2   Setup

We used the BERTopic [21] topic modeling tool[12] with the default parameters, and n-gram ranging from 2 to 20. The n-gram range corresponds to the number of terms that composes each topic. We reported results with 5 runs, showing the mean and standard deviation for topics ranging from 2 to 46 in increments of 2.

We trained our Portuguese Legislative Sentence Embedding based in Sim-CSE[13] with train batch size = 128, number of epochs = 1, max sequence length = 32, and Portuguese pre-trained language model named BERTimbau [37]. Sim-CSE is based on Huggingface's transformers package[14], and we take 5e−5 as the learning rate with the unsupervised learning approach.

## 5.3   Results

**Coherence of Topics.** In first experiment, we analyze the number of topics versus $C_V$ coherence score for the three corpora. As we can see on Figs. 3a, 3b,

---

[12] https://github.com/MaartenGr/BERTopic.
[13] https://github.com/princeton-nlp/SimCSE.
[14] https://huggingface.co/.

and 3c, the Portuguese Legislative Sentence Embedding presents the best results in all experiments.

We emphasize that although we analyze the coherence of topics as a function of the number of topics, this metric was not used to decide the optimal number of topics. This is because the clustering algorithm used to learn the model infers automatically the number of topics through the spatial density of the sentences represented by the embeddings[15].

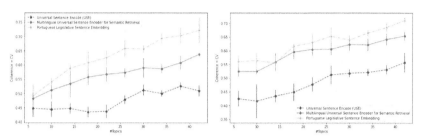

(a) Coherence Score with $C_V$ measure for PL 3723/2019

(b) Coherence Score with $C_V$ measure for PEC 471/2005

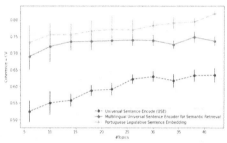

(c) Coherence Score with $C_V$ measure for Hashtag Corpus

**Fig. 3.** BERTopic coherence analysis

**Real and Predicted Topics.** The second experiment carried out is the comparison of the topics inferred by the best BERTopic configuration (with Portuguese Legislative Sentence Embedding) and the topics noted by the domain specialist. We pair the most similar ones in Table 3 showing that the approach proposed by BERTopic is indeed efficient. We report the real topics and respective predicted topics only for PL 3723/2019, for reasons of space in the paper[16]. It is important to note that the topics raised by the expert are not the only and definitive ones. For this experiment, we asked her to raise the obvious topics. Another observation is that the expert did not know how many topics were

---

[15] To analyze the coherence in function of topics we enter with the number of topics.

[16] We report the real Topics and respective predicted topics for PEC 471/2005 and Hashtag corpus in https://github.com/nadiafelix/Bracis2021.

inferred by BERTopic and did not have previous access to them, so that there is no bias in her answers.

**Table 3.** Real Topics and respective predicted topics for PL 3723/2019

| #Topics | Predicted topics | Topics extracted by specialist |
|---|---|---|
| 1 | proteção vida garantido conforme cf88 garante meu direito legítima defesa pessoal direito de proteção vida garantido conforme cf88 | Legítima defesa |
| 2 | familia propriedade devolve direito ao cidadão de se defender defender-ser onipresente direito do cidadão defender vida família | Proteção preventiva da vida da família |
| 3 | liberdade do cidadão sério honesto poder ter posse de arma de fogo | Liberdade individual |
| 4 | finalmente estamos regulamentando relação aquisição grande restrição em relação ao porte de arma rastreabilidade | Armas legais são rastreáveis |
| 5 | segurança pública correm os mesmos riscos que agentes prisionais ou mais defesa pois como socioeducativos do qual são alvos de constantes ameaças efetiva necessidade | Necessidade de acréscimo de profissões entre as de risco |
| 6 | arma de fogo em sua maioria possuem mais preparo que muitos policiais lei do desarmamento mas infelizmente nunca ouve regulamentação os cacs para manusearem arma de fogo em sua maioria possuem mais lei aguardando apenas regulamentação quando se faz leitura da l13502 | |
| 7 | seu art 6° inciso ix concede porte de armas | Segurança jurídica |
| 8 | direito do cidadão de escolha de porta ou não arma | Direito constitucional |
| 9 | opinião do povo que rejeitou lei do desarmamento no referendo popular | Referendo / plebiscito de 2005 já garantia o porte de arma |
| 10 | porte funcional de diversas categorias relacionadas persecução criminal restringe muito para os cacs ainda sim contem restrições quanto quantidades categorias | Necessidade de acréscimo de profissões entre as de risco |
| 11 | atiradores desportivos como categoria que tem direito ao porte federal | |
| 12 | um crime povo precisa de educação investir em escolas | População deveria ser educada |
| 13 | bens família garante minha segurança de minha familia proteção minha | |
| 14 | cidadão comum que não tem suficiente proteção estatal que estado incapaz de prover total segurança estado não cumpre | Estado não é onipresente |
| 15 | familiaridade com armas de fogo necessário garantir direito de transporte quando da eventual necessidade de utilização mais categorias atividades poderiam de arma para os vigilantes categorias de risco de fato de arma para esta categoria será importante para efetivação | |
| ⋮ | ⋮ | ⋮ |
| 26 | ... | ... |

**Example 1.** *Defesa, pois como vigilante tenho o direto de defesa. Trabalho com risco de vida. E também não estamos seguros. O governo não nos da segurança.*

The BERTopic models the Example 1 on Fig. 4, in which one can see that topic 10 is more significant. The relevant keywords from this topic are 'armas', 'não', 'direito', 'de fogo', 'cidadão', 'defesa'. The other topics are still relevant as: topic

8 is about 'arma de fogo', 'uma arma de fogo'; topic 9 is about 'advogados', 'categorias', 'risco', 'de risco', 'arma', 'porte de arma'.

**Fig. 4.** Topics probability distribution

## 6 Discussion

This work has presented a fully automated approach for identifying topics in Brazilian comments about legislation (bills). The BERTopic together with Portuguese Legislative Sentence Embedding got the best result. This work is an early indication as to how legal practitioners can identify salient and coherent topics using automatic topic modeling tools and how can this ensure greater citizen participation.

In sentence embeddings context, we experiment an unsupervised training approach, which takes an input sentence and predicts itself in a contrastive objective, with only standard dropout used as noise [19]. This simple method works well, performing on par with previous supervised counterparts [19]. We intend to train other unsupervised models for Portuguese in this legal domain, as in [44], evaluating in topic model, and in other tasks.

Regarding topic model experiments, we intend to analyze other coherence measures, as well as human evaluation. Besides that, we intend to develop a protocol of annotation for the corpora, and with this identify the topics and have a more accurate evaluation with supervised measures [42].

## References

1. Abercrombie, G., Batista-Navarro, R.: Sentiment and position-taking analysis of parliamentary debates: a systematic literature review. J. Comput. Soc. Sci. **3**(1), 245–270 (2020)
2. Allahyari, M., et al.: A brief survey of text mining: classification, clustering and extraction techniques (2017)
3. Andrade, M.D.D., Rosa, B.D.C., Pinto, E.R.G.D.C.: Legal tech: analytics, inteligência artificial e as novas perspectivas para a prática da advocacia privada. Revista Direito GV **16**(1) (2020)
4. Angelov, D.: Top2Vec: distributed representations of topics (2020). https://arxiv.org/abs/2008.09470

5. Barberá, P., Rivero, G.: Understanding the political representativeness of Twitter users. Soc. Sci. Comput. Rev. **33**(6), 712–729 (2015)
6. Basu, S., Banerjee, A., Mooney, R.J.: Active semi-supervision for pairwise constrained clustering. In: Proceedings of the 2004 SIAM, International Conference on Data Mining. Society for Industrial and Applied Mathematics, April 2004
7. Blei, D.M., Ng, A.Y., Jordan, M.I.: Latent Dirichlet allocation. J. Mach. Learn. Res. **3**, 993–1022 (2003)
8. Campello, R.J.G.B., Moulavi, D., Zimek, A., Sander, J.: Hierarchical density estimates for data clustering, visualization, and outlier detection 10(1) (2015)
9. Chidambaram, M., et al.: Learning cross-lingual sentence representations via a multi-task dual-encoder model (2019)
10. Câmara dos Deputados: Dados Abertos da Câmara dos Deputados (Open Data of the Chamber of Deputies, when translated to English). https://dadosabertos.camara.leg.br (2021). Accessed 8 June 2021
11. Câmara dos Deputados (Brazilian Chamber of Deputies, when translated to English): Enquetes (polls, when translated to English). https://www.camara.leg.br/enquetes. Accessed 5 May 2021
12. Câmara dos Deputados (Brazilian Chamber of Deputies, when translated to English): Popular participation. https://www2.camara.leg.br/transparencia/servicos-ao-cidadao/participacao-popular (2021). Accessed 5 May 2021
13. Cong, Y., Chen, B., Liu, H., Zhou, M.: Deep latent Dirichlet allocation with topic-layer-adaptive stochastic gradient Riemannian MCMC. In: Proceedings of the 34th International Conference on ML , vol. 70, pp. 864–873. ICML 2017, JMLR.org (2017)
14. Dale, R.: Law and word order: NLP in legal tech. Nat. Lang. Eng. **25**(1), 211–217 (2019)
15. Devlin, J., Chang, M., Lee, K., Toutanova, K.: BERT: pre-training of deep bidirectional transformers for language understanding. In: Proceedings of the 2019 Conference of the North American Chapter of the Association for Comp. Linguistics: Human Language Tech, pp. 4171–4186. Minnesota, June 2019
16. Dieng, A.B., Ruiz, F.J.R., Blei, D.M.: Topic modeling in embedding spaces. Transactions of the Association for Computational Linguistics **8**, 439–453 (2020)
17. Evangelopoulos, N., Visinescu, L.: Text-mining the voice of the people. Commun. ACM **55**(2), 62–69 (2012)
18. Gandomi, A., Haider, M.: Beyond the hype: big data concepts, methods, and analytics. Int. J. Inf. Manage. **35**(2), 137–144 (2015)
19. Gao, T., Yao, X., Chen, D.: SimCSE: simple contrastive learning of sentence embeddings. https://arxiv.org/abs/2104.08821 (2021). Accessed 5 May 2021
20. Giorgi, J., Nitski, O., Wang, B., Bader, G.: DeCLUTR: deep contrastive learning for unsupervised textual representations (2021)
21. Grootendorst, M.: BERTopic: leveraging BERT and c-TF-IDF to create easily interpretable topics. https://doi.org/10.5281/zenodo.4381785, note = Accessed 5 May 2021
22. Harris, Z.: Word **10**(2–3), 146–162 (1954)
23. Hofmann, T.: Probabilistic latent semantic indexing. In: Proceedings of the 22nd Annual International ACM SIGIR Conference on Research and Development in Information Retrieval. SIGIR 1999, pp. 50–57. Association for Computing Machinery, New York, NY, USA (1999)

24. Mahyoub, M., Hind, J., Woods, D., Wong, C., Hussain, A., Aljumeily, D.: Hierarchical text clustering and categorisation using a semi-supervised framework. In: 2019 12th International Conference on Developments in eSystems Engineering (DeSE). IEEE, October 2019

25. Mikolov, T., Chen, K., Corrado, G., Dean, J.: Efficient estimation of word representations in vector space (2013)

26. Moody, C.E.: Mixing Dirichlet topic models and word embeddings to make lda2vec (2016)

27. Nay, J.J.: Predicting and understanding law-making with word vectors and an ensemble model. PLoS ONE **12**(5), e0176999 (2017)

28. Nebu, C.M., Joseph, S.: Semi-supervised clustering with soft labels. In: 2015 International Conference on Control Communication & Computing India (ICCC). IEEE, November 2015

29. Papadimitriou, C., Raghavan, P., Tamaki, H., Vempala, S.: Latent semantic indexing: a probabilistic analysis. J. Comput. Syst. Sci. **61**(2), 217–235 (2000)

30. Parmelee, J.H., Bichard, S.L.: Politics and the Twitter Revolution: How Tweets Influence the Relationship Between Political Leaders and the Public. Lexington books, Lanham (2011)

31. Pavan, J.N.S., Pinochet, L.H.C., de Brelàz, G., dos Santos Júnior, D.L., Ribeiro, D.M.N.M.: Study of citizen engagement in the participation of elective mandate actions in the Brazilian legislature: analysis of the use of political techs. Cadernos EBAPE.BR **18**(3), 525–542, September 2020

32. Pennington, J., Socher, R., Manning, C.: GloVe: global vectors for word representation. In: Proceedings of the 2014 Conference on Empirical Methods in Natural Language Processing (EMNLP), pp. 1532–1543. Association for Computational Linguistics, Doha, Qatar, October 2014

33. Reimers, N., Gurevych, I.: Sentence-BERT: sentence embeddings using Siamese BERT-networks. In: Proceedings of the 2019 Conference on Empirical Methods in NLP and the 9th International Joint Conference on NLP (EMNLP-IJCNLP), pp. 3982–3992. ACL, Hong Kong, China, November 2019

34. Reimers, N., Gurevych, I.: Making monolingual sentence embeddings multilingual using knowledge distillation. In: Proceedings of the 2020 Conference on Empirical Methods in NLP. ACL, November 2020

35. Röder, M., Both, A., Hinneburg, A.: Exploring the space of topic coherence measures. In: Proceedings of the 8a ACM International Conference on Web Search and Data Mining, pp. 399–408. WSDM 2015, New York, NY, USA (2015)

36. Sammut, C., Webb, G.I. (eds.): TF-IDF, pp. 986–987. Springer, US, Boston, MA (2010)

37. Souza, F., Nogueira, R., Lotufo, R.: BERTimbau: pretrained BERT models for Brazilian Portuguese. In: 9th Brazilian Conference on Intelligent Systems, BRACIS, Rio Grande do Sul, Brazil, 20–23 October 2020. (to appear)

38. Stevens, K., Kegelmeyer, P., Andrzejewski, D., Buttler, D.: Exploring topic coherence over many models and many topics. In: Proceedings of the 2012 Joint Conference on Empirical Methods in Natural Language Processing and Computational Natural Language Learning, pp. 952–961. Association for Computational Linguistics, Jeju Island, Korea, July 2012

39. Sugathadasa, K., et al.: Legal document retrieval using document vector embeddings and deep learning. In: Arai, Kohei, Kapoor, Supriya, Bhatia, Rahul (eds.) SAI 2018. AISC, vol. 857, pp. 160–175. Springer, Cham (2019). https://doi.org/10.1007/978-3-030-01177-2_12

40. Thaiprayoon, S., Unger, H., Kubek, M.: Graph and centroid-based word clustering. In: Proceedings of the 4th International Conference on NLP and Information Retrieval. ACM, December 2020. https://doi.org/10.1145/3443279.3443290
41. United Nations: Inclusion and more public participation, will help forge better government policies: Guterres. https://news.un.org/en/story/2020/09/1073742, September 2020. Accessed 5 May 2021
42. Vinh, N.X., Epps, J., Bailey, J.: Information theoretic measures for clusterings comparison: Is a correction for chance necessary? In: Proceedings of the 26th Annual International Conference on Machine Learning, pp. 1073–1080. ICML 2009. Association for Computing Machinery, New York, NY, USA (2009)
43. Wallach, H., Murray, I., Salakhutdinov, R., Mimno, D.: Evaluation methods for topic models. In: Proceedings of the 26th Annual International Conference on ML (ICML 2009), pp. 1105–1112. ACM (2009)
44. Wang, K., Reimers, N., Gurevych, I.: TSDAE: using transformer-based sequential denoising auto-encoder for unsupervised sentence embedding learning (2021)
45. Willett, P.: Recent trends in hierarchic document clustering: a critical review. Inf. Process. Manage. **24**(5), 577–597 (1988)
46. Williams, A., Nangia, N., Bowman, S.: A broad-coverage challenge corpus for sentence understanding through inference. In: Proceedings of the 2018 Conference of the North American Chapter of the Association for Computational Linguistics: Human Language Technologies, vol. 1, pp. 1112–1122. Association for Computational Linguistics, New Orleans, Louisiana, June 2018
47. World Economic Forum: How much data is generated each day? https://www.weforum.org/agenda/2019/04/how-much-data-is-generated-each-day-cf4bddf29f/ (2019). Accessed 5 May 2021
48. Yang, Y., et al.: Multilingual universal sentence encoder for semantic retrieval (2019)

# Evaluation of Convolutional Neural Networks for COVID-19 Classification on Chest X-Rays

Felipe André Zeiser, Cristiano André da Costa$^{(\boxtimes)}$, Gabriel de Oliveira Ramos, Henrique Bohn, Ismael Santos, and Rodrigo da Rosa Righi

Graduate Program in Applied Computing, Universidade do Vale do Rio dos Sinos, São Leopoldo, Brazil
{felipezeiser,hbohn,ismael}@edu.unisinos.br,
{cac,gdoramos,rrrighi}@unisinos.br

**Abstract.** Early identification of patients with COVID-19 is essential to enable adequate treatment and to reduce the burden on the health system. The gold standard for COVID-19 detection is the use of RT-PCR tests. However, due to the high demand for tests, these can take days or even weeks in some regions of Brazil. Thus, an alternative for detecting COVID-19 is the analysis of Digital Chest X-rays (XR). Changes due to COVID-19 can be detected in XR, even in asymptomatic patients. In this context, models based on deep learning have great potential to be used as support systems for diagnosis or as screening tools. In this paper, we propose the evaluation of convolutional neural networks to identify pneumonia due to COVID-19 in XR. The proposed methodology consists of a preprocessing step of the XR, data augmentation, and classification by the convolutional architectures DenseNet121, InceptionResNetV2, InceptionV3, MovileNetV2, ResNet50, and VGG16 pre-trained with the ImageNet dataset. The obtained results for our methodology demonstrate that the VGG16 architecture presented a superior performance in the classification of XR, with an Accuracy of 85.11%, Sensitivity of 85.25%, Specificity of 85.16%, F1-score of 85.03%, and an AUC of 0.9758.

**Keywords:** COVID-19 · Chest X-Rays · Deep learning · Convolutional neural network

## 1 Introduction

Severe Acute Respiratory Syndrome Coronavirus 2 (SARS-CoV-2) is a new beta-coronavirus first identified in December 2019 in Wuhan Province, China [3]. Since the initial outbreak, the number of patients confirmed with COVID-19 has exceeded 178 million in the world. More than 3.85 million people have died as a result of COVID-19 (June 19, 2021) [11]. These numbers can be even higher due to asymptomatic cases and flawed tracking policies. In Brazil, a study points to seven times more infections than that reported by the authorities [12].

© Springer Nature Switzerland AG 2021
A. Britto and K. Valdivia Delgado (Eds.): BRACIS 2021, LNAI 13074, pp. 121–132, 2021.
https://doi.org/10.1007/978-3-030-91699-2_9

SARS-CoV-2 shares 79.6% of the SARS-CoV base pairs genome [37]. Despite its resemblance to the 2002 SARS-CoV virus, SARS-CoV-2 has rapidly spread across the globe challenging health systems [28]. The burden on healthcare systems is due to the high rates of contagion and how SARS-CoV-2 manifests itself in the infected population [22]. According to data from epidemiological analyses, about 20% to 30% of patients are affected by a moderate to severe form of the disease. In addition, approximately 5% to 12% of infected patients require treatment in the Intensive Care Unit (ICU). Of those admitted to ICUs, about 75% are individuals with pre-existing comorbidities or older adults [8].

In Brazil, the first case was officially notified on February 25, 2020 [5]. Since then, due to the continental proportions of Brazil, several measures to contain and prepare the health system have been carried out in the Federative Units [24]. Brazil went through two delicate moments for the health system, with hospitals without beds and even the lack of supplies for patients in some regions of the country [33].

Currently, reverse transcription polymerase chain reaction (RT-PCR) is the test used as the gold standard for the diagnosis of COVID-19 [20,32]. However, due to difficulties in purchasing inputs, increases in the prices of materials and equipment, the lack of laboratories and qualified professionals, and the high demands for RT-PCR tests, the diagnosis can take days or even weeks in some cities in Brazil [20]. This delay can directly impact the patient's prognosis and be associated with a greater spread of SARS-CoV-2 in Brazil [7].

As alternatives to RT-PCR, radiological exams as Computed Tomography (CT) and Digital Chest Radiography (XR) are being used as valuable tools for the detection and definition of treatment of patients with COVID-19 [9]. Studies show equivalent sensitivities to the RT-PCR test using CT images [2,35]. Lung alterations can be observed even in asymptomatic patients of COVID-19, indicating that the disease can be detected by CT even before the onset of symptoms [19].

XR has lower sensitivity rates compared to CT. However, due to some challenges in CT use, health systems adopted XR in the front line of screening and monitoring of COVID-19 [4]. The main challenges in using CT compared to XR are: (i) exam cost, (ii) increased risk for cross-infection, and (iii) more significant exposure to radiation [34]. Furthermore, in underdeveloped countries, the infrastructure of health systems generally does not allow RT-PCR tests or the acquisition of CT images for all suspected cases. However, devices for obtaining radiographs are now more widespread and can serve as a fundamental tool in the fight against the epidemic in these countries [9].

In this perspective, artificial intelligence techniques have shown significant results in the processing of large volumes of information in various pathologies and have significant potential in aiding the diagnosis and prognosis of COVID-19 [10,16,18,36]. Thus, this work aims to explore the application of Deep Learning (DL) techniques to detect pneumonia caused by COVID-19 through XR images. In particular, our objective is to evaluate the performance and provide a set of pre-trained Convolutional Neural Network (CNN) models for use as diagnostic support systems. The CNN architectures evaluated in this article are: DenseNet121 [15], InceptionResNetV2 [30], InceptionV3 [31], MovileNetV2 [27], ResNet50V2 [13], and VGG16 [29].

The study is organized into five sections. In Sect. 2, we present the most significant related works for the definition of the work. Section 3 presents the methodology of the work. Section 4 details the results. Finally, Sect. 5 presents the conclusions of the work.

## 2   Related Work

Artificial intelligence has made significant advances motivated by large data sets and advances in DL techniques. These advances have allowed the development of systems to aid in analyzing medical images with a precision similar to healthcare specialists. Furthermore, machine learning or data mining techniques extract relevant features and detect or predict pathologies in the images. Therefore, this section describes some relevant works in the literature to detect pneumonia and COVID-19 in XR images.

Since the initial outbreak of COVID-19, studies applying CNNs have been used to detect COVID-19 in XR images. However, at the beginning of the outbreak, the lack of positive XR images was a problem. In [14], the performance of seven CNNs using fine-tuning was compared in a set of 50 XR, 25 positive cases, and 25 negative cases for COVID-19. However, the few images used, the lack of a test set, and the learning graphs presented indicate that the models could not generalize the problem.

In the work proposed by [1], a CNN-based Decompose, Transfer, and Compose (DeTraC) model is used for COVID-19 XR classification. The model consists of using a pre-trained CNN for the ImageNet set as a feature extractor. Selected features go through Principal Component Analysis (PCA) to reduce dimensionality. These selected characteristics are then classified by a CNN into COVID-19 or not. The proposed model reached an accuracy of 93.1% and sensitivity of 100% for the validation set.

DarkCovidNet, a convolutional model based on DarkNet, is used for the COVID-19 detection task in XR [21]. The authors used seventeen DarkNet convolutional layers, achieving an accuracy of 98.08% for binary classification and 87.02% for multi-class classification. In [17] it is proposed to use the pre-trained CNN Xception for the ImageNet dataset for the classification of images into normal, bacterial, viral, and COVID-19 pneumonia. The study achieved an average accuracy of 87% and an F1-Score of 93%.

Another alternative for detecting COVID-19 in XR is detection in levels using VGG-16 [6]. At the first level, XRs are analyzed to detect pneumonia or not. In the second level, the classification of XRs in COVID-19 or not is performed. Finally, on the third level, the heat maps of the activations for the COVID-19 XRs are presented. The accuracy of the study, according to the authors, is 99%.

In summary, several recent works have investigated the use of CNNs for the COVID-19 XR classification. However, most of these works were based on small datasets, performed evaluations directly on the validation sets, and only a few performed the multiclass classification. Therefore, these studies lack evidence on their ability to generalize the problem, making it unfeasible to be used as an aid system for the radiologist. Thus, our contribution to these gaps is the proposal to evaluate six convolutional models in a dataset with more than five thousand XR. We evaluated models on a set of XRs not used in training and validation.

## 3    Materials and Methods

An overview of the methodology employed in this work is presented in Fig. 1. The methodology is divided into four stages: preprocessing, data augmentation, training, and testing. Image preprocessing consists of image resizing and contrast normalization (Sect. 3.2). The data augmentation step describes the methods used to generate synthetic images (Sect. 3.3). In the training stage, the CNN models and the parameters used are defined (Sect. 3.4). Finally, in the test step, we performed the performance evaluation of the CNN models (Sect. 3.4).

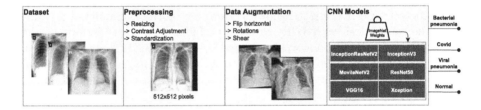

**Fig. 1.** Diagram of the proposed methodology.

### 3.1    Dataset

We use XRs from the Curated Dataset for COVID-19 [26]. The dataset is a combination of chest XR images from different sources. The dataset has XRs for normal lung, viral pneumonia, bacterial pneumonia, or COVID-19. The authors performed an analysis of all images to avoid having duplicate images. In addition, for the final selection of images, the authors used a CNN to remove images with noise, such as distortions, cropped, and with annotations [26]. In Table 1 we present the number of images used in our work.

### 3.2    Preprocessing

In this step, we resize the XRs to $512 \times 512$ pixels. This size limitation is imposed by available computing power. To avoid distortions in the XR, a proportional reduction was applied to each of the dimensions of the images. We added a

**Table 1.** Public dataset of chest XR used in this article.

| Pathology | Number of images |
|---|---|
| COVID-19 | 1,281 |
| Normal | 1,300 |
| Viral | 1,300 |
| Bacterial | 1,300 |

black border to complement the size for the dimension that was smaller than 512 pixels.

As radiographic findings are often low contrast regions, contrast enhancement techniques can be used in XR images. The application of techniques such as Contrast-Limited Adaptive Histogram Equalization (CLAHE) to breast and chest radiography images helped in the generalization of convolutional models and an increase in performance metrics [23,36]. Therefore, we use CLAHE to enhance XR images. CLAHE subdivides the image into sub-areas using interpolation between the edges. To avoid noise increase, uses a threshold level of gray, redistributing the pixels above that threshold in the image. CLAHE can be defined by:

$$p = [p_{max} - p_{min}] * G(f) + p_{min} \tag{1}$$

where $p$ is the pixel's new gray level value, the values $p_{max}$ and $p_{min}$ are the pixels with the lowest and highest values low in the neighborhood and $G(f)$ corresponds to the cumulative distribution function [38]. In Fig. 2 we present an example with the original and preprocessed image.

(A) (B)

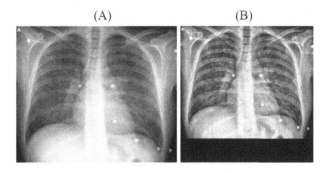

**Fig. 2.** (A) original XR image with COVID-19; (B) preprocessed image.

Finally, we use stratified K-fold cross-validation as a method for evaluating the models, with K=10. With a 10-fold we train the models 10 times for each model. At the end of the training, we calculated the mean and standard deviation of the results for the defined metrics.

## 3.3   Data Augmentation

A technique that helps in the convergence and learning of CNN is the use of data augmentation. Thus, we use the ImageDataGenerator class from Keras to perform on-the-fly data augmentation. We apply a horizontal flip, rotations of up to 20°C, and shear in the training set for each fold. We do not apply transformations on XRs in the validation and test set.

## 3.4   Convolutional Architectures

We use six CNN architectures for chest XR classification: DenseNet121 [15], InceptionResNetV2 [30], InceptionV3 [31], MovileNetV2 [27], ResNet50V2 [13], and VGG16 [29]. We use the pre-trained weights provided by Keras for the ImageNet dataset for each model. This process of initializing pre-trained weights speeds up the convergence process of the models. Table 2 presents the hyper-parameters used for each of the architectures evaluated in this work.

**Table 2.** Parameters used for each of the CNN architectures.

| Architecture | Learning rate | Batch size | Trainable params | Non-trainable params | Depth |
|---|---|---|---|---|---|
| DenseNet121 [15] | $5 \times 10^{-7}$ | 16 | 11 149 444 | 83 648 | 121 |
| InceptionResNetV2 [30] | $5 \times 10^{-7}$ | 4 | 57 816 420 | 60 544 | 572 |
| InceptionV3 [31] | $5 \times 10^{-7}$ | 4 | 26 488 228 | 34 432 | 159 |
| MovileNetV2 [27] | $5 \times 10^{-7}$ | 4 | 7 468 036 | 34 112 | 88 |
| ResNet50V2 [13] | $1 \times 10^{-6}$ | 16 | 31 909 252 | 45 440 | 50 |
| VGG16 [29] | $5 \times 10^{-7}$ | 16 | 48 231 684 | 38 720 | 23 |

In the training stage, we use categorical cross-entropy as the loss function. The categorical cross-entropy measures the log-likelihood of the probability vector. To optimize the weights of the models, we use the Adam algorithm. At the end of each epoch, we used the validation set to measure the model's accuracy in an independent set and obtain the best training weights.

# 4   Results and Discussion

In this section, we present and evaluate the results obtained using the proposed convolutional models.

## 4.1   Models Training and Validation

We train the models for 100 epochs for each fold. We evaluate each model at the end of training in the validation set. The choice of the best set of weights was performed automatically based on the error for the validation set. Figure 3, presents the confusion matrices for each of the models.

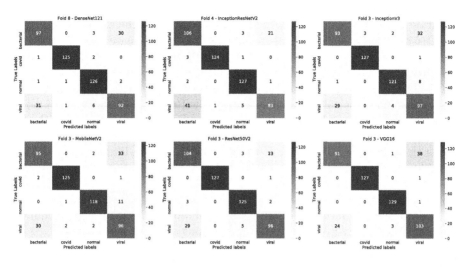

**Fig. 3.** Confusion matrices of each model for the best test fold set. Dark colors represent a greater number of cases. Light colors represent a smaller amount of cases.

Analyzing the confusion matrices (Fig. 3), we can see that all classifiers could correctly classify the vast majority of cases. We can highlight the tendency to classify cases of viral pneumonia as bacterial and bacterial pneumonia as viral. This trend may indicate that the number of viral and bacterial pneumonia cases was insufficient for an optimized generalization for these two classes. As for the classification of normal cases, the ResNet50V2 model had the highest rate of misclassification. The classification of pneumonia due to COVID-19 showed similar success rates. The highest false-negative rate for COVID-19 was presented by the InceptionResNetV2 model, with 4 cases. The lowest rate of false negatives was presented by the InceptionV3, ResNet-50, and VGG16 models, with 1 cases.

From the confusion matrix, we can calculate the performance metrics of the models [25]. Table 3 presents the values obtained for the evaluation metrics in the test fold based on the confusion matrices presented in Fig. 3.

**Table 3.** Results for the test fold for each model.

| Model | Accuracy | Sensitivity | Specificity | F1-score | AUC |
|-------|----------|-------------|-------------|----------|-----|
| DenseNet121 [15] | 81.28 ± 2.27% | 81.40 ± 2.23% | 81.33 ± 2.26% | 81.22 ± 2.32% | 0.9620 |
| InceptionResNetV2 [30] | 84.16 ± 1.42% | 83.49 ± 1.52% | 84.10 ± 1.47% | 84.16 ± 1.42% | 0.9707 |
| InceptionV3 [31] | 83.14 ± 1.01% | 83.34 ± 1.09% | 83.20 ± 1.00% | 83.22 ± 1.04% | 0.9704 |
| MovileNetV2 [27] | 82.04 ± 1.33% | 82.55 ± 1.34% | 82.10 ± 1.39% | 82.21 ± 1.28% | 0.9655 |
| ResNet50V2 [13] | 85.08 ± 1.62% | **85.36** ± 1.54% | 85.12 ± 1.61% | **85.06** ± 1.60% | 0.9748 |
| VGG16 [29] | **85.11** ± 1.30% | 85.25 ± 1.27% | **85.16** ± 1.30% | 85.03 ± 1.42% | **0.9758** |

Analyzing the results, it is clear that there was relative stability in the performance metrics analyzed for each model. For accuracy, the largest standard deviation was ±2.27%, and the largest difference between the models was 3.83% (VGG16 and DenseNet121). These results indicate an adequate generalization of each model for detecting pneumonia due to COVID-19. As for sensitivity, which measures the ability to classify positive classes correctly, the models differ by 3.96%. The maximum variation between models for specificity was 3.83%.

In general, for the chest XR classification, the ResNet50V2 and VGG16 models showed the best results. This better performance can be associated with the organizations of the models. For ResNet50V2, we can highlight the residual blocks that allow an adaptation of the weights to remove filters that were not useful for the final decision [13]. As for VGG16, the performance may indicate that the classification of XR resources from lower levels, such as more basic forms, is better to differentiate viral pneumonia, bacterial pneumonia, COVID-19, and normal. However, the VGG16 is computationally heavier and requires more training time. Also, VGG16 has a vanishing gradient problem.

Figure 4 presents the ROC curves for each fold and model in the test fold. When comparing the accuracy, sensitivity, specificity, and F1-score metrics, the Area under the ROC Curve (AUC) showed the greatest stability, with a variation of only ±0.80%.

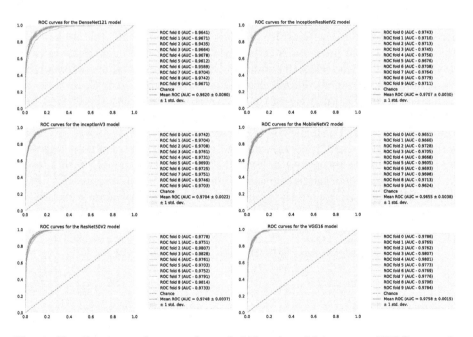

**Fig. 4.** Classification performance for each fold and model in terms of ROC curves in the test fold.

## 4.2   Comparison with Related Work

A direct quantitative comparison with related works is difficult. Due to private datasets, methodologies with different image cuts, selecting specific aspects of the datasets, removing some images, and with different classification objectives. In this way, we organized in Table 4 a quantitative comparison with similar works.

**Table 4.** Comparison with the related works. *Acc* is the Accuracy, *Sen* is the Sensitivity, *Spe* is Specificity, *F1* is the F1-Score, and *AUC* is the area under the ROC curve.

| Study | Goal | Dataset size | Acc | Sen | Spe | F1 | AUC |
|-------|------|--------------|-----|-----|-----|-----|-----|
| Hemdan et al. 2020 [14] | Comparison of convolutional architectures for binary classification of XR in COVID or not | 50 | 90.0 | – | – | 91.0 | 0.90 |
| Abbas et al. 2021 [1] | Extract features using CNN with dimensionality reduction using PCA to classify XR into COVID-19, SARS, and normal | 196 | 93.10 | 100 | 85.18 | – | – |
| Ozturk et al. 2020 [21] | Use of DarkNet for multiclass classification of XRs in no findings, pneumonia, and COVID-19 | 1127 | 87.02 | 85.35 | 92.18 | 87.37 | – |
| Khan et al. 2020 [17] | Classification of XR into four classes using a pre-trained Xception | 1251 | 89.60 | 89.92 | 96.4 | 89.80 | – |
| Brunese et al. 2020 [6] | Binary classification of XR in COVID-19 or not at two levels | 6523 | 98.00 | 87.00 | 94.00 | 89.00 | – |
| *Our Method* | *Evaluation of CNNs for classification of chest XR into COVID-19, viral pneumonia, bacterial pneumonia and normal* | 5184 | 85.11 | 85.25 | 85.16 | 85.03 | 0.9758 |

In general, the convolutional architectures evaluated in our work achieved performance similar to the works that perform multiclassification [1,17,21]. If compared to works that perform binary classification, the difference for accuracy is ±13%. However, the work with the best accuracy uses a reduced set of positive images for COVID-19 (250 images) out of a total of 6523 [6]. Thus, the dataset used in the work is not balanced and may indicate a bias in the study. This bias may be associated with a lower sensitivity (87.00%) of the study compared to other metrics.

The sensitivity was similar to the other studies, except for the work with 100% sensitivity [1]. However, the size of the dataset used in the study (196 XR images) can influence the results of the method. In addition, the method proposed by [1] is more complex compared to the proposed in our study. In this way, we can highlight that our method use a balanced dataset. We also use stratified K-fold cross-validation for models training. In this way, we can assess the stability of the assessment metrics and the confidence interval. Finally, the trained models and source code is available on GitHub [Hidden ref.].

## 5  Conclusion

This article compared six convolutional architectures for the detection of pneumonia due to COVID-19 in chest XR images. In order to improve the generalizability of the results, we apply a set of preprocessing techniques. We use several models with pre-trained weights for the ImageNet dataset, and we propose the classification in normal cases, viral pneumonia, bacterial pneumonia, or COVID-19.

The main scientific contribution of this study was the performance comparison of the DenseNet121, InceptionResNetV2, InceptionV3, MovileNetV2, ResNet50, and VGG16 convolutional architectures for the detection pneumonia due to COVID-19. These pre-trained models can serve as a basis for future studies and provide a second opinion to the radiologist during XR analysis.

As future work, we intend to analyze the influence of datasets on the characteristics learning of COVID-19 XR images, analyzing whether CNNs can generalize characteristics for different datasets. Furthermore, we hope to investigate Explainable Artificial Intelligence approaches to convey specialists the features present in the images used to form the diagnostic suggestion. Finally, using multimodal methodologies, for example, using clinical data and images, can be helpful in the transparency of diagnostic recommendations.

**Acknowledgements.** We thank the anonymous reviewers for their valuable suggestions. The authors would like to thank the Coordination for the Improvement of Higher Education Personnel - CAPES (Financial Code 001), the National Council for Scientific and Technological Development - CNPq (Grant numbers 309537/2020-7), the Research Support Foundation of the State of Rio Grande do Sul - FAPERGS (Grant numbers 08/2020 PPSUS 21/2551-0000118-6), and NVIDIA GPU Grant Program for your support in this work.

## References

1. Abbas, A., Abdelsamea, M.M., Gaber, M.M.: Classification of covid-19 in chest x-ray images using DeTraC deep convolutional neural network. Appl. Intell. **51**(2), 854–864 (2021)
2. Ai, T., et al.: Correlation of chest CT and RT-PCR testing for coronavirus disease 2019 (covid-19) in china: a report of 1014 cases. Radiology **296**(2), E32–E40 (2020). https://doi.org/10.1148/radiol.2020200642
3. Andersen, K.G., Rambaut, A., Lipkin, W.I., Holmes, E.C., Garry, R.F.: The proximal origin of SARS-CoV-2. Nat. Med. **26**(4), 450–452 (2020)
4. Borghesi, A., Maroldi, R.: Covid-19 outbreak in Italy: experimental chest x-ray scoring system for quantifying and monitoring disease progression. La radiologia medica **125**(5), 509–513 (2020)

5. Brasil, M.D.S.: Boletim epidemiológico especial: Doença pelo coronavírus covid-19 (2020). https://saude.gov.br/images/pdf/2020/July/22/Boletim-epidemiologico-COVID-23-final.pdf
6. Brunese, L., Mercaldo, F., Reginelli, A., Santone, A.: Explainable deep learning for pulmonary disease and coronavirus covid-19 detection from x-rays. Comput. Methods Program. Biomed. **196**, 105608 (2020)
7. Candido, D.S., et al.: Evolution and epidemic spread of SARS-CoV-2 in Brazil. Science **369**(6508), 1255–1260 (2020)
8. CDC COVID-19 Response Team: Severe outcomes among patients with coronavirus disease 2019 (covid-19)-united states, February 12-march 16, 2020. MMWR Morb. Mortal Wkly. Rep **69**(12), 343–346 (2020)
9. Cohen, J.P., et al.: Covid-19 image data collection: Prospective predictions are the future (2020)
10. De Fauw, J., et al.: Clinically applicable deep learning for diagnosis and referral in retinal disease. Nat. Med. **24**(9), 1342–1350 (2018)
11. Dong, E., Du, H., Gardner, L.: An interactive web-based dashboard to track covid-19 in real time. Lancet. Infect. Dis **20**(5), 533–534 (2020)
12. EPICOVID: Covid-19 no brasil: várias epidemias num só país (2020). http://epidemio-ufpel.org.br/uploads/downloads/276e0cffc2783c68f57b70920fd2acfb.pdf
13. He, K., Zhang, X., Ren, S., Sun, J.: Deep residual learning for image recognition. In: Proceedings of the IEEE Conference on Computer Vision and Pattern Recognition, pp. 770–778 (2016)
14. Hemdan, E.E.D., Shouman, M.A., Karar, M.E.: Covidx-net: A framework of deep learning classifiers to diagnose covid-19 in x-ray images. arXiv preprint arXiv:2003.11055 (2020)
15. Huang, G., Liu, Z., Van Der Maaten, L., Weinberger, K.Q.: Densely connected convolutional networks. In: Proceedings of the IEEE Conference on Computer Vision and Pattern Recognition, pp. 4700–4708 (2017)
16. Jatobá, A., Lima, L., Amorim, L., Oliveira, M.: CNN hyperparameter optimization for pulmonary nodule classification. In: Anais do XX Simpósio Brasileiro de Computação Aplicada à Saúde, pp. 25–36. SBC, Porto Alegre, RS, Brasil (2020). https://doi.org/10.5753/sbcas.2020.11499, https://sol.sbc.org.br/index.php/sbcas/article/view/11499
17. Khan, A.I., Shah, J.L., Bhat, M.M.: Coronet: a deep neural network for detection and diagnosis of covid-19 from chest x-ray images. Comput. Methods Program. Biomed. **196**, 105581 (2020)
18. Lakhani, P., Sundaram, B.: Deep learning at chest radiography: automated classification of pulmonary tuberculosis by using convolutional neural networks. Radiology **284**(2), 574–582 (2017)
19. Lee, E.Y., Ng, M.Y., Khong, P.L.: Covid-19 pneumonia: what has CT taught us? Lancet. Infect. Dis **20**(4), 384–385 (2020)
20. Marson, F.A.L.: Covid-19 - 6 million cases worldwide and an overview of the diagnosis in brazil: a tragedy to be announced. Diagn. Microbiol. Infect. Dis. **98**(2), 115113 (2020)
21. Ozturk, T., Talo, M., Yildirim, E.A., Baloglu, U.B., Yildirim, O., Rajendra Acharya, U.: Automated detection of covid-19 cases using deep neural networks with x-ray images. Comput. Biol. Med. **121**, 103792 (2020)
22. Pascarella, G., et al.: Covid-19 diagnosis and management: a comprehensive review. J. Internal Med. **288**(2), 192–206 (2020)

23. Pooch, E.H.P., Alva, T.A.P., Becker, C.D.L.: A deep learning approach for pulmonary lesion identification in chest radiographs. In: Cerri, R., Prati, R.C. (eds.) BRACIS 2020. LNCS (LNAI), vol. 12319, pp. 197–211. Springer, Cham (2020). https://doi.org/10.1007/978-3-030-61377-8_14

24. Rafael, R.D.M.R., Neto, M., de Carvalho, M.M.B., David, H.M.S.L., Acioli, S., de Araujo Faria, M.G.: Epidemiologia, políticas públicas e pandemia de covid-19: o que esperar no brasil?[epidemiology, public policies and covid-19 pandemics in brazil: what can we expect?][epidemiologia, políticas públicas y la pandémia de covid-19 en brasil: que podemos esperar?]. Revista Enfermagem UERJ **28**, 49570 (2020)

25. Ruuska, S., Hämäläinen, W., Kajava, S., Mughal, M., Matilainen, P., Mononen, J.: Evaluation of the confusion matrix method in the validation of an automated system for measuring feeding behaviour of cattle. Behav. Process. **148**, 56–62 (2018). https://doi.org/10.1016/j.beproc.2018.01.004

26. Sait, U., et al.: Curated dataset for covid-19 posterior-anterior chest radiography images (x-rays). (September 2020). https://doi.org/10.17632/9xkhgts2s6.3

27. Sandler, M., Howard, A., Zhu, M., Zhmoginov, A., Chen, L.C.: Mobilenetv 2: inverted residuals and linear bottlenecks. In: Proceedings of the IEEE Conference on Computer Vision and Pattern Recognition, pp. 4510–4520 (2018)

28. Shereen, M.A., Khan, S., Kazmi, A., Bashir, N., Siddique, R.: Covid-19 infection: origin, transmission, and characteristics of human coronaviruses. J. Adv. Res. **24**, 91–98 (2020)

29. Simonyan, K., Zisserman, A.: Very deep convolutional networks for large-scale image recognition. arXiv preprint arXiv:1409.1556 (2014)

30. Szegedy, C., Ioffe, S., Vanhoucke, V., Alemi, A.: Inception-v4, inception-resnet and the impact of residual connections on learning. In: Proceedings of the AAAI Conference on Artificial Intelligence (2017)

31. Szegedy, C., Vanhoucke, V., Ioffe, S., Shlens, J., Wojna, Z.: Rethinking the inception architecture for computer vision. In: Proceedings of the IEEE Conference on Computer Vision and Pattern Recognition, pp. 2818–2826 (2016)

32. Tang, Y.W., Schmitz, J.E., Persing, D.H., Stratton, C.W.: Laboratory diagnosis of covid-19: current issues and challenges. J. Clin. Microbiol. **58**(6) (2020). https://doi.org/10.1128/JCM.00512-20, https://jcm.asm.org/content/58/6/e00512-20

33. Taylor, L.: Covid-19: Is manaus the final nail in the coffin for natural herd immunity? bmj 372 (2021)

34. Wong, H.Y.F., et al.: Frequency and distribution of chest radiographic findings in patients positive for covid-19. Radiology **296**(2), E72–E78 (2020)

35. Xie, X., et al.: Chest CT for typical coronavirus disease 2019 (covid-19) pneumonia: Relationship to negative RT-PCR testing. Radiology **296**(2), E41–E45 (2020)

36. Zeiser, F.A., et al.: Segmentation of masses on mammograms using data augmentation and deep learning. J. Digital Imaging 1–11 (2020)

37. Zhou, P., et al.: A pneumonia outbreak associated with a new coronavirus of probable bat origin. Nature **579**(7798), 270–273 (2020)

38. Zuiderveld, K.: Graphics gems iv. In: Heckbert, P.S. (ed.) Graphics Gems, chap. Contrast Limited Adaptive Histogram Equalization, pp. 474–485. Academic Press Professional Inc, San Diego, CA, USA (1994)

# Experiments on Portuguese Clinical Question Answering

Lucas Emanuel Silva e Oliveira[1,2]([✉]) [iD], Elisa Terumi Rubel Schneider[1] [iD],
Yohan Bonescki Gumiel[1] [iD], Mayara Aparecida Passaura da Luz[1] [iD],
Emerson Cabrera Paraiso[1] [iD], and Claudia Moro[1] [iD]

[1] Pontifícia Universidade Católica Do Paraná, Curitiba, Brazil
lucas.oliveira@pucpr.br
[2] Comsentimento, NLP Lab, São Paulo, Brazil

**Abstract.** Question answering (QA) systems aim to answer human questions made in natural language. This type of functionality can be very useful in the most diverse application domains, such as the biomedical and clinical. Considering the clinical context, where we have a growing volume of information stored in electronic health records, answering questions about the patient status can improve the decision-making and optimize the patient care. In this work, we carried out the first experiments to develop a QA model for clinical texts in Portuguese. To overcome the lack of corpora for the required language and context, we used a transfer learning approach supported by pre-trained attention-based models from the Transformers library. We fine-tuned the BioBERTpt model with a translated version of the SQuAD dataset. The evaluation showed promising results when evaluated in different clinical scenarios, even without the application of a clinical QA corpus to support a training process. The developed model is publicly available to the scientific community.

**Keywords:** Question answering · Electronic health records · Transfer learning

## 1 Introduction

Question answering (QA) is a task that seeks to automatically answer questions asked in natural language by humans, with a combination of Information Retrieval (IR) and Natural Language Processing (NLP) techniques. QA systems have been applied in multiple domains of knowledge, as they can facilitate access to information by reasoning and inferring it from a large volume of data stored as natural language [1].

There has been a growth in interest in the use of QA in the biomedical context, including efforts to create biomedical and clinical QA corpora [8,12,18, 23] and the realization of shared tasks such as BioASQ 8 [9]. The possibility of finding answers to questions in the growing volume of data available in the

© Springer Nature Switzerland AG 2021
A. Britto and K. Valdivia Delgado (Eds.): BRACIS 2021, LNAI 13074, pp. 133–145, 2021.
https://doi.org/10.1007/978-3-030-91699-2_10

scientific literature and patients' medical records evidence the potential of these systems for practical use. Therefore, QA systems can assist both the medical research community (e.g., researching disease treatments and symptoms) and healthcare professionals (e.g., clinical decision support).

Specifically in the clinical context, when we work with patient's data, the QA research has few initiatives if compared to other domains, mainly in languages other than English [10,12]. The lack of studies may be due to the required medical expertise and the ethical/legal restrictions, which limits the data access [7]. Another aspect that hinders the research of clinical QA is the complexity of the data that are stored in the patient's Electronic Health Records (EHR). The longitudinal and unstructured nature of the clinical notes, high use of medical terminology, temporal relations between multiple clinical concepts (e.g., medications, diseases, symptoms), text misspellings, frequent redundancy, and implicit events make text comprehension much more complex for the machine, and make it difficult to apply baseline NLP tools [2].

Currently, health professionals manually browse or use a simple search algorithm to find answers about patients, and often they are unable to reach the information they need. A QA system can provide a much more intuitive interface for this task, allowing humans to "talk" to the EHR asking questions about patient's status and health condition, generating a much more fluid and human interaction [12,16,18].

Nevertheless, how to develop a clinical QA system for Portuguese if we do not have a large corpus of questions and answers that support most of the current QA methods? A well-established strategy in the NLP community is the use of transfer learning, which consists of using a pre-trained language model in a large dataset and then fine-tune it for a specific task in a smaller dataset. For example, one can use a large attention-based model [19] available in Transformers library[1], such as BERT [3], and fine-tune it for a specific NLP task, such as Named Entity Recognition [17]. We can go beyond that, like Jeong and colleagues [7], who fine-tuned two different QA corpora (one open-domain and the other biomedical) to achieve superior performances in biomedical QA.

In this work, we present the first glance of experiments on a QA system used to answers questions about patients in Portuguese. We developed a biomedical QA model for the Portuguese language based on the fine-tuning of the BioBERTpt model [15] using the SQuAD QA dataset translated into the Portuguese language. We evaluate the performance in a small set of different clinical contexts with multiple types of clinical notes. Finally, we discuss our preliminary results, main findings, and future work. The model is publicly available for use.

## 2    Related Work

In this section, we present important QA corpora development initiatives. Moreover, we introduce the transfer learning method, which is one of the solutions

---

[1] https://github.com/huggingface/transformers/.

used to overcome the lack of domain-specific corpora. Furthermore, we highlight biomedical and clinical QA studies based on Transformers models and transfer learning.

## 2.1 Corpora

In the literature, we can find several QA datasets, most of them covering open-domain questions and answers, as the Stanford Question Answering Dataset (SQuAD) [14]. SQuAD is a reading comprehension dataset consisting of English questions and answers from a set of Wikipedia articles. This dataset is present in a QA format, where the answer to each question is a segment of text from the reading passage (see Fig. 1). The SQuAD 1.1 contains more than 100,000 question-answer pairs on approximately 500 articles, all of them manually annotated.

In meteorology, precipitation is any product of the condensation of atmospheric water vapor that falls under gravity. The main forms of precipitation include drizzle, rain, sleet, snow, graupel and hail... Precipitation forms as smaller droplets coalesce via collision with other rain drops or ice crystals within a cloud. Short, intense periods of rain in scattered locations are called "showers".

What causes precipitation to fall?
gravity

What is another main form of precipitation besides drizzle, rain, snow, sleet and hail?
graupel

Where do water droplets collide with ice crystals to form precipitation?
within a cloud

**Fig. 1.** Example of answers annotated within the text in SQuAD corpus. Image from [14]

Regarding the biomedical context, we need to mention the PubMedQA, a corpus with the objective of answering research questions with "yes", "no" and "maybe". It consists of 1,000 expert-annotated QA pairs and 211,300 artificially generated QA pairs. All the answers were annotated in PubMed scientific paper abstracts [8].

In the clinical domain, we highlight the following recent initiatives. Yue and colleagues [23] developed a corpus with 1,287 expert-annotated QA pairs, originated from 36 discharge summaries from the MIMIC-III dataset[2]. The emrQA

---

[2] https://physionet.org/content/mimiciii/1.4/.

corpus [12] has minimal expert involvement, as they generated the QA pairs using an automated method that leverages annotations from shared i2b2 datasets[3], resulting in 400,000 QA pairs.

It is worth noting the discrepancy of manually annotated QA pairs from SQuAD and the biomedical and clinical corpora, which affects directly the development of QA algorithms for these specific domains.

## 2.2  Transfer Learning

Transfer learning is a method focused on the reuse of a model trained for a specific task, by applying and adjusting it (i.e., fine-tuning) to a different but related task. Several studies have already proven the efficacy of transfer learning when using deep learning architectures [13], especially the pre-trained attention-based models available in the Transformers library.

The BioBERTpt [15] is an example of how transfer learning can result in models with low computational cost and at the same time extremely useful. BioBERTpt was generated from the fine-tuning of the multilingual version of BERT[4] in clinical and biomedical documents written in Portuguese. The model was also adjusted for the named entity recognition (NER) task, which achieved state-of-the-art results in the SemClinBr corpus [11].

## 2.3  Biomedical and Clinical QA

Considering the current availability of domain-specific corpora for the QA task, many studies focused on transfer learning to take advantage of the huge amount of annotated data in open-domain resources, as the SQuAD. Furthermore, due to the state-of-the-art results obtained by architectures based on the attention mechanism on several NLP tasks, most studies explore the fine-tuning of pre-trained models available in the Transformers library.

Wiese and colleagues [20] transferred the knowledge from the SQuAD dataset to the BioASQ dataset. In Yoon's work [22], they executed a sequential transfer learning pipeline exploring BioBERT, SQuAD, and BioASQ. In [7], the authors used sequential transfer learning as well but trained BioBERT on the NLI dataset. Finally, Soni and Roberts [16] performed experiments on multiple Transformers models and fine-tuned them with multiple QA corpora combinations. They found that a preliminary fine-tuning on SQuAD improves the clinical QA results across all different models. Due to the unavailability of a clinical QA corpus in Portuguese and the good results obtained when using transfer learning based on an open-domain QA corpus (i.e., SQuAD), we decided to follow a similar development protocol.

---

[3]  https://www.i2b2.org/NLP/DataSets/Main.php.

[4]  https://huggingface.co/bert-base-multilingual-cased.

# 3    Materials and Methods

This section describes the development of our Transformer-based QA model, including all the steps of execution and details regarding the data used. Next, we present the evaluation setup used to assess our approach.

## 3.1    BioBERTpt-squad-v1.1-portuguese: A Biomedical QA Model for Portuguese

As seen in the previous section, the use of transfer learning supported by contextual embedding models, pre-trained on large-scale unlabelled corpora, combined with the transformer architecture, has proven to reach state-of-the-art performance on NLP tasks. Then, our method will focus on these pre-trained models and the consequent fine-tuning of the QA task.

The method is composed of the following general phases:

1. Obtain a model for biomedical Portuguese texts
2. Obtain a dataset for QA in Portuguese
3. Fine-tune the biomedical model to QA task

For our first phase, we needed a model capable of processing Portuguese biomedical texts, and for that, we used the BioBERTpt model. The BioBERTpt is a deep contextual embedding model for the Portuguese language to support clinical and biomedical tasks. The authors fine-tuned the multilingual BERT on clinical notes and biomedical literature, resulting in a Portuguese medical BERT-base model. In this paper, we used the BioBERTpt(all) version[5], which includes both biomedical and clinical texts.

As the second phase, we used the automatically translated version of the SQuAD dataset, shared by the Deep Learning Brasil group[6], which we will call SQuADpt from now on. They used Google-powered machine translation to generate a Portuguese version of SQuAD v1.1, with additional human correction after. It is worth noting the warning made by the authors, in which they state that the dataset could contain a good amount of unfiltered content with potential bias.

In the final phase, we fine-tuned BioBERTpt on the question and answer dataset, the SQuAD-pt, with the following steps:

1. Pre-processing of data (removal of spaces and possible duplicate records);
2. Tokenization of the inputs and converting the tokens to their corresponding IDs in the pre-trained vocabulary, with the Transformers Tokenizer [21];
3. Split of long inputs (longer than the model maximum sequence length) into several smaller features, overlapping some features if the answer is at the split point;
4. Mapping of the start and end positions of the answers in the tokens, so the model can find where exactly the answer is in each feature;

---

[5] https://huggingface.co/pucpr/biobertpt-all.
[6] http://www.deeplearningbrasil.com.br/.

5. Padding the text to the maximum sequence length.

Finally, we performed the fine-tuning to the QA task with the Transformers AutoModelForQuestionAnswering class [21], using BioBERTpt pre-trained weights. We trained our Portuguese biomedical QA model for three epochs on a GPU GTX2080Ti Titan 12 GB, with learning rate as 0.00003, and both training and evaluation batch size as 16. All these parameters were recommend for fine-tuning step by [3], at Appendix A.3 of the paper. Table 1 shows the main hyper-parameter settings used to train our model.

In Fig. 2 we can see the BERT model trained for the QA task, where given input with the question and context, the model predicts as output the start and end indices of the probable answer to the question. The resulting model is available at Transformers repository[7].

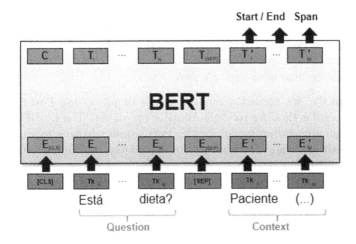

**Fig. 2.** BERT model architecture for QA task, where it is packed both the question and the context (i.e., reference text) into the input and as output, the model predicts the beginning and end spans of the answer. In bold, the expected answer to the input question.

---

[7] https://huggingface.co/pucpr/bioBERTpt-squad-v1.1-portuguese.

**Table 1.** Main hyper-parameter settings of BioBERTpt-squad-v1.1-portuguese training

| Hyper-parameter | Value |
|---|---|
| Number of epochs | 3 |
| Training batch size | 16 |
| Evaluation batch size | 16 |
| Learning rate | 0.00003 |
| Maximum sequence length | 384 |
| Weight decay | 0.01 |

## 3.2 Evaluation Setup

Our model achieved a F1-score of 80.06 when measuring using the SQuAD dataset annotations. However, the goal of our work is to generate a QA model to be used in the clinical domain, therefore, we need to define an assessment protocol that addresses this context. In the following subsections, we describe the selection of the clinical notes and the definition of the questions used to evaluate our model.

**Clinical Notes Selection.** There are many uses of a QA system in the clinical environment, being able to support the entire multidisciplinary health staff. Among the possibilities, the system could help the medical and nursing professionals, who constantly need to retrieve information from the patient's medical record to carry out their interventions. Thinking about these cases, we selected two main categories of clinical notes, nursing notes, and medical notes.

The nursing note is a document that describes the general state of the patient and actions performed by the nurses during the care (e.g., physical examination, medications used, vital signs monitoring). This document is used to compare the patient's clinical condition during the last 24 h and is very useful to determine optimal strategies of care (e.g., new physical examinations) [4]. The medical note contains a narrative regarding the patient's signs, symptoms, comorbidities, diagnosis, prescribed medications, post-surgery data, etc. All this information is written in chronological order, to facilitate the understanding of the history of care and support the decision of the healthcare professionals [5].

The nursing and medical notes were selected from the SemClinBr corpus, prioritizing narrative aspects that would allow the realization of questions, to use the answers to facilitate the elaboration of a Nursing Diagnosis by the nursing team, during the shift. As well as carrying out a quick search by the multidisciplinary team to support the practices to be adopted in the patient's care. Three nursing notes and six medical notes were selected, being three from medical assistance (i.e., hospital admission) and three from ambulatory (i.e., outpatient service).

**Questions Definition.** After defining the clinical notes to be used as the context for our QA model, we defined a set of questions that we would ask the model to try to find the answers to. The questions were based on Nursing Diagnosis, risk factors, and defining characteristics, that is, a set of information that demonstrates signs and symptoms of a given diagnosis. The selected criteria were: physical examination, level of consciousness, circulation and ventilation, procedures/care, nutrition, physiological eliminations, intravenous devices, pain complaints and exams. For nursing notes, ten questions were elaborated and applied. For the medical notes, eight questions were elaborated and applied.

**Evaluation Process and Metrics.** To generate the gold standard of answers, a specialist analyzed all selected clinical notes and annotated the text with the corresponding answers (examples are presented in Fig. 3 and Fig. 4). After the generation of the gold standard, all questions and clinical notes were input to our QA model, so we made a comparison between the model's answers and those generated by the expert. A calculation of Precision, Recall and F1 metrics was performed. We used a partial-match strategy since once the QA system finds and marks the answer in the text, even partially, the user could easily identify the rest of the information in the text. For example, in the gold standard the excerpt of text that answers the *"Has previous diseases?"* question is *"Previously Hypertension/Diabetes/Chronic obstructive pulmonary disease. Stroke with left hemiparesis 2 years ago."*, but the model outputted just a partial match: *"Previously Hypertension/Diabetes/Chronic obstructive pulmonary disease."*. In these cases the partial match approach considers the prediction as a true positive.

It is worth noting that our gold standard was not used for training purposes. We used it only for evaluation, as we exploited the use of transfer learning and already built resources to develop our model.

## 4 Results

The result of the evaluation process is summarized in Table 2, where we can see better results when we process nursing and outpatient notes. In Fig. 5, all items evaluated and the confidence rate given by the model when making the prediction were plotted. In addition to the hits and misses, we also include the situation in which the question asked does not contain an answer in the text, therefore, it is not possible to make a right answer. An analysis of the graph suggests that if we use a threshold of 0.5 when returning the answer to the user ($<0.5$ then No Answer; $\geq 0.5$ then Show Answer) we could avoid several false positives. However, we would also have a reduction of true positives, so a more in-depth analysis of this trade-off is needed.

1- Está aceitando dieta?
2- Possui Lesão por pressão?
3- O curativo está com secreção ou possui sinais flogísticos?
4- Como está a ausculta pulmonar?
5- Quais os parâmetros do ventilador?
6- Qual o Glasgow ou Ramsay do paciente?
7- Quais as condições pupilares?
8- Está com edema?
9- Qual o aspecto do débito da SNG?
10- Diurese ou evacuação presente?

ÀS 11:20: REPASSADO SNE, SEM INTERCORRÊNCIA NO PROCEDIMENTO, AUSCULTA ABDOMINAL POSITIVA, RETIRO FIO GUIA. SOLICITO RAIO-X PARA AVALIAÇÃO DA POSIÇÃO. Cliente intubada com TOT n° 7.5, rima labial 22 cm DIR, VM nos parametros PCV, PI 14 cmH2O, peep 5 cmH2O, FR 11, FiO2 50%, Ramsay 6, pupilas iso / foto +, face corada, mucosa oral hidratada, boa perfusão periferica, no leito com cabeceira elevada á 45°. Mantem com monitorização de multiparametros ECG, PAM em radial ESQ oscilante, SpO2 e PVC (regua), SNG aberta narina ESQ com estase gastrica ++ de coloração biliosa, SNE aberta narina ESQ com dietoterapia em curso BI 40ml/hr, cateter venoso central duplo-lumen em subclavia DIR sem sinais flogisticos e infusão de fentanil + dormonid á 10 ml/hr + eletrolitos á 42 ml/hr em curso BI. Apresenta ausculta cardiaca ritmica e normofonetica, ausculta pulmonar MV + com roncos esparsos, abdomem flacido com RHA +, edemas MMSS e II cacifo I/II, liberação de exudato em MMSS e II, região dorsal, lesão de dermatite em dorso + escapula DIR, ctvos em região femural DIR. Faz uso de SVD aberta com debito diuretico presente ++ de coloração amarelo-claro, eliminação fecal ausente. segue cuidados.

**Fig. 3.** Example of nursing note and questions extracted from the gold standard. The answers to each question are annotated within the text with the corresponding color.

1- Qual o motivo do atendimento?
2- Possui doenças prévias?
3- Em uso de quais medicamentos?
4- Foram solicitados exames?
5- Qual foi a conduta tomada?
6- Quais os resultados dos exames?
7- Qual o histórico familiar do paciente?
8- Qual é a queixa clínica?

# LUCAS, 78 ANOS. SEGUNDA CONSULTA. RETORNO COM EXAMES. # REFERE INCONTINENCIA URINARIA AOS ESFORÇOS, NEGA DEMAIS QUEIXAS URINARIAS. # HAS HA 20 ANOS, DM HA 20 ANOS, DSLP. HISTERECTOMIZADA AOS 45 ANOS, RETIROU OVARIO DIR AOS 19 ANOS. G 1 C 1 A 0. NEGA ALERGIA A MEDICAMENTOS. # AAS 100 MG; LEVOTIROXINA 25MCG; METFORMINA 850MG 1 CP; OMEPRAZOL 20MG 1 CP; LOSARTANA 50MG 12/12; BEZAFIBRATO 200MG; PREMARIN 0,3MG; CITRATO DE CALCIO 600MG; COLECALCIFEROL. # MAE FALECEU AOS 54 POR IAM, PAI FACELEU DE CA PROSTATA AOS 74 ANOS. # LAB: CREAT 1,4; U 68; CKD-EPI 35,9; GLICEMIA 128; K 5,2; URINA LEVEMENTE TURVA, PH 7, LEUC 29; GASO VEN: PH 7,36; PCO2 52,60; HCO3 29. # BEG, LOTE, NORMOCORADA, HIDRATADA. PULMONAR SP. CARDIACO SP. MMII: VARIZES BILAT MAIS PRONUNCIADAS EM MIE. PA 130/80, FC 72. # PEÇO US DE RINS E VIAS URINARIAS, PEÇO LAB, RETORNO EM 6 MESES.

**Fig. 4.** Example of medical ambulatory note and questions extracted from the gold standard. The answers to each question are annotated within the text with the corresponding color. The name appearing in the text is a result of a de-identification process.

**Table 2.** Evaluation results considering the clinical notes types.

| Narrative type | Precision | Recall | F1-score |
|---|---|---|---|
| Nursing note | 0.6333 | 0.7308 | 0.6786 |
| Medical assistance note | 0.2917 | 0.4118 | 0.3415 |
| Medical ambulatory note | 0.5625 | 0.6429 | 0.6 |
| **Overall** | **0.5** | **0.614** | **0.5512** |

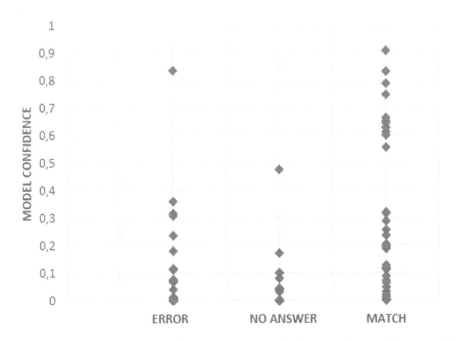

**Fig. 5.** Scatter plot containing all matches, errors and situations in which the text did not contain the answer to the question. The y-axis defines the confidence score of the model when making the prediction.

## 5  Discussion

This work is an initial investigation into the development of a clinical QA system in Portuguese, which could be a powerful resource in clinical decision support and patient care process optimization (e.g., discover information about the patient's condition, optimal shift change). The aim of this article is to carry out preliminary experiments to help define the next steps towards a robust model of clinical QA.

Our findings are in line with other studies [7,16,20,22] regarding the use of transfer learning as a means of overcoming the lack of annotated resources for the desired language/context, as we use the BioBERTpt model, which is a result of the fine-tuning of the multilingual BERT for clinical texts, and we also used the SQuAD, which, despite being an open-domain dataset, helped us to adapt the model for the clinical QA task. However, it is worth emphasizing that, even without quantitative results to benchmark, apparently the results of this process of creating the model for the clinical domain require a little more attention, due to the great differences in vocabulary, questions and specificities of clinical notes. We can find models that followed a similar process of development to our model, working a little more cohesively when applied to the context of questions about medical topics [6].

A more detailed analysis about the use of a threshold in the model output should be carried out, as it is common to have missing data in clinical notes. Furthermore, it is necessary to study the different types of possible questions (i.e., factoid, list, yes/no) in the clinical context, since using all these types of questions considerably increases the complexity of the problem. Moreover, something that is also out of the scope of this article is to understand the use of discontinuous answers, when the response is in multiple parts of the clinical note. As the Transformers model allows returning the top k texts, it might be possible to perform some kind of inference through this list.

We recognize as limitations of this work the size of the dataset used for evaluation, as well as the search for answers about the patient's status in a single patient's clinical note and not in all of its EHR records. As future work, we intend to expand both the dataset size and the exploration of the entire longitudinal aspect of the patient's clinical notes. Finally, since we intend to expand the gold standard for evaluation, a natural step would be to use this corpus to train a model directly from these data and also make it available to the scientific community as well as emrQA[12] and CliCR [18].

## 6   Conclusion

We developed a clinical QA model for the Portuguese language by sequentially fine-tuning attention-based models available in the Transformers library. The model is publicly available to the scientific community. We used the BioBERTpt model with the SQuADpt QA dataset to build a model capable of finding answers about a patient within the clinical notes. Our experiments show promising results, even with the use of resources adapted (i.e., fine-tuned) to the target task, context and language. We plan to expand our experiments in various aspects, as the increase of evaluation dataset size, use of multiple patients' clinical notes, training a model with our own clinical QA corpus, and deepen analysis about the use of thresholds, discontinuous answers and question types. We understand that this work was the first step towards a robust clinical QA system in Portuguese, which could result in more intelligent systems for healthcare professionals and improve the patients' care.

**Acknowledgements.** This study was financed in part by the Coordenação de Aperfeiçoamento de Pessoal de Nível Superior - Brasil (CAPES) - Finance Code 001.

## References

1. Calijorne Soares, M.A., Parreiras, F.S.: A literature review on question answering techniques, paradigms and systems (2020). https://doi.org/10.1016/j.jksuci.2018.08.005
2. Dalianis, H.: Characteristics of patient records and clinical corpora. In: Clinical Text Mining, pp. 21–34. Springer, Cham (2018). https://doi.org/10.1007/978-3-319-78503-5_4

3. Devlin, J., Chang, M.W., Lee, K., Toutanova, K.: BERT: pre-training of deep bidirectional transformers for language understanding. In: Proceedings of the 2019 Conference of the North American Chapter of the Association for Computational Linguistics: Human Language Technologies, Volume 1 (Long and Short Papers), pp. 4171–4186. Association for Computational Linguistics, Minneapolis, Minnesota (June 2019). https://doi.org/10.18653/v1/N19-1423, https://www.aclweb.org/anthology/N19-1423

4. Dias, L.B., Duran, E.C.M.: Análise das evoluções de enfermagem contextualizadas no processo de enfermagem. Revista de Enfermagem UFPE on line (2018). https://doi.org/10.5205/1981-8963-v12i11a234623p2952-2960-2018

5. Garritano, C.R.d.O., Junqueira, F.H., Lorosa, E.F.S., Fujimoto, M.S., Martins, W.H.A.: Avaliação do Prontuário Médico de um Hospital Universitário. Revista Brasileira de Educação Médica (2020). https://doi.org/10.1590/1981-5271v44.1-20190123

6. Guillou, P.: Portuguese bert base cased QA (question answering), finetuned on squad v1.1 (2021). https://huggingface.co/pierreguillou/bert-base-cased-squad-v1.1-portuguese

7. Jeong, M., et al.: Transferability of natural language inference to biomedical question answering. CoRR abs/2007.00217 (2020). https://arxiv.org/abs/2007.00217

8. Jin, Q., Dhingra, B., Liu, Z., Cohen, W.W., Lu, X.: PubMedQA: a dataset for biomedical research question answering. In: EMNLP-IJCNLP 2019–2019 Conference on Empirical Methods in Natural Language Processing and 9th International Joint Conference on Natural Language Processing, Proceedings of the Conference (2020). https://doi.org/10.18653/v1/d19-1259

9. Krallinger, M., Krithara, A., Nentidis, A., Paliouras, G., Villegas, M.: BioASQ at CLEF2020: large-scale biomedical semantic indexing and question answering. In: Jose, J.M., et al. (eds.) ECIR 2020. LNCS, vol. 12036, pp. 550–556. Springer, Cham (2020). https://doi.org/10.1007/978-3-030-45442-5_71

10. Mutabazi, E., Ni, J., Tang, G., Cao, W.: A review on medical textual question answering systems based on deep learning approaches. Appl. Sci. **11**(12) (2021). https://doi.org/10.3390/app11125456, https://www.mdpi.com/2076-3417/11/12/5456

11. e Oliveira, L.E.S., et al.: Semclinbr - a multi institutional and multi specialty semantically annotated corpus for Portuguese clinical NLP tasks (2020). https://arxiv.org/abs/2001.10071

12. Pampari, A., Raghavan, P., Liang, J., Peng, J.: emrQA: a large corpus for question answering on electronic medical records. In: Proceedings of the 2018 Conference on Empirical Methods in Natural Language Processing, pp. 2357–2368. Association for Computational Linguistics, Brussels, Belgium (October-November 2018). https://doi.org/10.18653/v1/D18-1258, https://aclanthology.org/D18-1258

13. Qiu, X.P., Sun, T.X., Xu, Y.G., Shao, Y.F., Dai, N., Huang, X.J.: Pre-trained models for natural language processing: a survey. Sci. Chin. Technol. Sci. **63**(10), 1872–1897 (2020). https://doi.org/10.1007/s11431-020-1647-3

14. Rajpurkar, P., Zhang, J., Lopyrev, K., Liang, P.: SQuad: 100,000+ questions for machine comprehension of text. In: EMNLP 2016 - Conference on Empirical Methods in Natural Language Processing, Proceedings (2016). https://doi.org/10.18653/v1/d16-1264

15. Schneider, E.T.R., et al.: BioBERTpt - a Portuguese neural language model for clinical named entity recognition (2020). https://doi.org/10.18653/v1/2020.clinicalnlp-1.7

16. Soni, S., Roberts, K.: Evaluation of dataset selection for pre-training and fine-tuning transformer language models for clinical question answering. In: LREC 2020–12th International Conference on Language Resources and Evaluation, Conference Proceedings (2020)
17. Souza, J.V.A.D., et al.: A multilabel approach to Portuguese clinical named entity recognition. J. Health Inf. **12** (2021). http://www.jhi-sbis.saude.ws/ojs-jhi/index.php/jhi-sbis/article/view/840. http://www.jhi-sbis.saude.ws/ojs-jhi/index.php/jhi-sbis/issue/view/98/showToc
18. Šuster, S., Daelemans, W.: CliCR: a dataset of clinical case reports for machine reading comprehension. In: Proceedings of the 2018 Conference of the North American Chapter of the Association for Computational Linguistics: Human Language Technologies, Volume 1 (Long Papers), pp. 1551–1563. Association for Computational Linguistics, New Orleans, Louisiana (June 2018). https://doi.org/10.18653/v1/N18-1140, https://aclanthology.org/N18-1140
19. Vaswani, A., et al.: Attention Is All You Need. In: Proceedings of the 31st International Conference on Neural Information Processing Systems, NIPS 2017, pp. 6000–6010 (2017)
20. Wiese, G., Weissenborn, D., Neves, M.: Neural domain adaptation for biomedical question answering. In: CoNLL 2017–21st Conference on Computational Natural Language Learning, Proceedings (2017). https://doi.org/10.18653/v1/k17-1029
21. Wolf, T., et al.: transformers: state-of-the-art natural language processing. In: Proceedings of the 2020 Conference on Empirical Methods in Natural Language Processing: System Demonstrations, pp. 38–45. Association for Computational Linguistics (October 2020). https://www.aclweb.org/anthology/2020.emnlp-demos.6
22. Yoon, W., Lee, J., Kim, D., Jeong, M., Kang, J.: Pre-trained language model for biomedical question answering. In: Communications in Computer and Information Science (2020). https://doi.org/10.1007/978-3-030-43887-6_64
23. Yue, X., Zhang, X.F., Sun, H.: Annotated question-answer pairs for clinical notes in the mimic-iii database (2021). https://doi.org/10.13026/J0Y6-BW05, https://physionet.org/content/mimic-iii-question-answer/1.0.0/

# Long-Term Map Maintenance in Complex Environments

Josias Oliveira[1](✉), Filipe Mutz[2](✉), Avelino Forechi[3](✉), Pedro Azevedo[1](✉), Thiago Oliveira-Santos[1](✉), Alberto F. De Souza[1](✉), and Claudine Badue[1](✉)

[1] Departamento de Informática, Universidade Federal do Espírito Santo, Av. Fernando Ferrari 514, Goiabeiras, Vitória 29075-910, Brazil
{josias,alberto,claudine}@lcad.inf.ufes.br
[2] Coordenação de Informática, Instituto Federal do Espírito Santo, ES-010 Km-6.5, Manguinhos, Serra 29173-087, Brazil
[3] Coordenadoria de Engenharia Mecânica, Instituto Federal do Espírito Santo, Av. Morobá 248, Bairro Morobá, Aracruz 29192-733, Brazil

**Abstract.** As changes in external environments are inevitable, a lifelong mapping system is desirable for autonomous robots that aim at long-term operation. Capturing external environment changes into internal representations (for example, maps) is crucial for proper behavior and safety, especially in the case of autonomous vehicles. In this work, we propose a new large-scale mapping system for our autonomous vehicle or any other. The new mapping system is based on the Graph SLAM algorithm, with extensions to deal with the calibration of odometry directly in the optimization of the graph and to address map merging for long-term map maintenance. The mapping system can use sensor data from one or more robots to build and merge different types of occupancy grid maps. The system's performance is evaluated in a series of experiments carried out with data captured in complex real-world scenarios. The experimental results indicate that the new large-scale mapping system can provide high-quality occupancy grid maps for later navigation and localization of autonomous vehicles that use occupancy grid maps.

**Keywords:** Mapping · SLAM · Map maintenance · Map merging · Autonomous vehicles

## 1 Introduction

Autonomous Vehicles (AVs) typically use maps of the environment to localize themselves and safely navigate in it. In this context, AVs can localize themselves in relation to the map using their sensor measurements (localization problem).

This study was financed in part by Coordenação de Aperfeiçoamento de Pessoal de Nível Superior – Brasil (CAPES) – Finance Code 001; Conselho Nacional de Desenvolvimento Científico e Tecnológico - Brasil (CNPq); and Fundação de Amparo à Pesquisa do Espírito Santo - Brasil (FAPES) – grants 75537958 and 84412844.

© Springer Nature Switzerland AG 2021
A. Britto and K. Valdivia Delgado (Eds.): BRACIS 2021, LNAI 13074, pp. 146–161, 2021.
https://doi.org/10.1007/978-3-030-91699-2_11

When there is no map, they can create a new one also using their sensors. Vehicle poses can be known when creating the map (mapping problem) or can be estimated as the map is built (simultaneous localization and mapping - SLAM - problem [4]).

One of the requirements imposed on AVs is the ability to operate for a long period of time without human intervention. Therefore, AVs must display a life-long mapping capability and promptly update their internal maps whenever the environment changes. In addition, when operating outdoors, AVs face highly dynamic objects (for example, pedestrians and other vehicles) and slightly dynamic objects (for example, parked vehicles and traffic cones). Environments may undergo slower modifications to the infrastructure and, therefore, the AVs' internal maps must be updated accordingly. These issues, altogether, pose the life-long mapping problem, which usually requires merging the current map already built with the new ones from another surveying mission with a single robot or multiple robots at the same time. The map merging problem consists of combining two or more individual maps without a common frame of reference into a larger global map.

One of the main challenges in the map merging problem is illustrated in Fig. 1, where red and green pixels represent obstacles reached by a LiDAR sensor and projected in the ground. Red pixels represent obstacles in a map while green pixels represent obstacles in another. Considering the final map after improper merging, there is a prominent misalignment between the two individual maps.

We have developed a self-driving car (Fig. 2), whose autonomy system follows the typical architecture of self-driving cars [1]. Our self-driving car is based on a Ford Escape Hybrid tailored with a variety of sensors and processing units. Its autonomy system is composed of many modules, which include a localizer [6], a mapper [13], a moving obstacle tracker [15], a traffic signalization

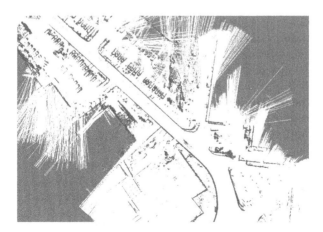

**Fig. 1.** Example of map merging. The lack of loop closure treatment between the sessions results in misalignment between the maps.

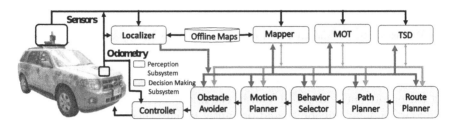

**Fig. 2.** Our self-driving car and its autonomy software system. In light blue, perception modules. In orange, decision making modules. TSD denotes Traffic Signalization Detection and MOT, Moving Objects Tracking. Red arrows show the State of the car, produced by its Localizer module and shared with most modules; blue arrows show the car's internal representation of the environment, jointly produced by several perception modules and shared with most decision making modules. See details in Badue et al. (2020).

detector [14,20], a route planner, a path planner for structured urban areas, a behavior selector, a motion planner [5], an obstacle avoider [10], and a controller [11], among other modules.

In this work, we propose a new mapping system based on graph SLAM for solving the map merging problem in large outdoor environments. The proposed mapping system aims to provide high quality grid maps for autonomous driving. It is also able to calibrate the vehicle odometry using a new method applied in the graph optimization. The system receives as input one or more log files containing the surveying missions (or sessions) from a single or multiple vehicles, and it outputs the AVs' poses in a global coordinate frame, the parameters of the odometry bias calibration for each vehicle and different types of grid maps.

We evaluated the performance of the proposed mapping system on logs containing high and low dynamics in real-world scenarios. The logs were collected using the available sensors in the AV over a period of two years. The new odometry bias calibration method was compared against an odometry calibration based on Particle Swarm Optimization (PSO) proposed by Mutz et al. [13]. The results indicate that the new method provides better calibration values in all logs. The new mapping features were also analyzed through mapping and map merging experiments. The results show that the proposed system is able to correctly estimate the AV poses in a global reference frame, and to correctly merge local maps without drifts and misalignment for all logs.

The remaining sections are organized as follows. In Sect. 2, we present related work. In Sect. 3, we detail the proposed mapping system. In Sect. 4, we describe the experimental methodology and, in Sect. 5, we discuss experimental results. Finally, in Sect. 6, we close with our conclusions and directions for future work.

## 2   Related Work

Progress on the Simultaneous Localization and Mapping (SLAM) problem can be measured in terms of a wide variety of algorithms, techniques and theoretical frameworks that have been developed in last decades. However, unresolved questions remain such as robustness and outlier rejection for long-term operations [4].

The map merging problem addresses theses open issues in different contexts of application, either with multiple robots running synchronously or with only one robot gathering data during multiple sessions. While the first is focused in collaborative strategies to efficient mapping, the later is oriented to long-term map maintenance in order to accommodate infrastructural changes along time. Both share the same main goal which is to produce a final aggregated map alongside the robot trajectories for all sessions.

The common approach in multi-robot scenarios is to fetch all maps using map-matching to find the relative map transformations and merge all maps into one final map alongside the corresponding trajectory of each robot in that map.

A system for real-time multi-robot collaborative SLAM is presented in Deutsch et al. [7]. The distributed robots use their own SLAM system to build local maps, but they also share information (features from images) with a central system, which builds a global pose graph including information from all robots. After the graph optimization, the central system sends the results to all robots, so they keep a consistent local position and map estimates. In contrast, in our solution, maps are built before autonomous operation on outdoor environments. Ours can handle any map size as it depends only in the available storage.

Sun et al. [19] convert the map merging problem into an image registration problem. When two grid maps contains overlapping areas, their approach tries to find the best transformation which aligns the maps. The algorithm extract features from both maps using the Harris corner detector and it uses the selected features to calculate a initial transformation matrix which is later refined by an iterative algorithm. In contrast, our method finds the common reference frame through the graph optimization by making usage of GPS and LiDARs sensors, hence the proper alignments are achieved before the map construction.

The approach in single-robot multi-session scenarios is to use the all maps using map-matching to find the relative map transformations and merge all maps into one final map alongside the corresponding trajectory of each robot in that map

A SLAM system using Normal Distribution Transform (NDT) maps is presented in Einhorn and Gross [9]. The authors propose a modification in the NDT mapping to handle free-space measurements which makes them better suited for SLAM. The map merging is achieved by the alignment of the NDT maps through registration techniques.

Bonanni et al. [3] present a SLAM method that considers the map as a graph of point clouds. In order to merge two maps, it visits each node in the first graph and tries to find the best match in the second graph. Normal Iterative Closest Point (NICP) [17] is used to find the registration between the point clouds. The method is similar to our solution as point clouds are used to provide the correct relationship between sessions. We use GPS and a nearest neighbor algorithm to find the best candidates in the second graph.

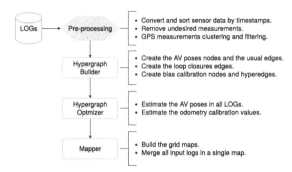

**Fig. 3.** System overview.

The work of Ding et al. [8] is meant for large scale outdoor environments, as ours, and use 3D LiDAR for loop closure detection whilst we use GPS. Their system is capable of building maps using multi-session data as ours. Their approach splits maps into submaps and use an efficient method for loop closure detection using feature vectors and a loop closure database using the kd-tree algorithm. Their method also takes care of loop closure outliers and actively detects changes in the environment (high and low dynamics).

## 3    Large-Scale Mapping System

In this section, we describe the proposed *full* SLAM-based mapping system. Despite being able to build many types of grid maps, the next sections will focus only on OGMs.

Figure 3 shows the architecture of the proposed mapping system. The Pre-processing and the Hypergraph Builder modules are responsible for handling low-level information coming from sensors, removing undesired measurements, and building the hypergraph. The Hypergraph Optimizer is responsible for estimating the AV poses along the sessions while also calibrating the odometry bias. The Mapper module builds and merges the maps.

### 3.1    Pre-processing

The Pre-Processing module sorts all measurements by their timestamps and also discards measurements in which the AV is below a minimum speed $MS$. This module also removes a specific error on GPS measurements as illustrated in Fig. 4. Figure 4(b) shows the poor results after increasing the GPS error variance in a try to solve this issue. Our solution is illustrated on Fig. 4(c). The GPS measurements are clustered together if the distance between immediate neighbors is less than $NeighborDistance$. After clustering, all groups containing fewer elements than $NeighborQuantity$ are removed.

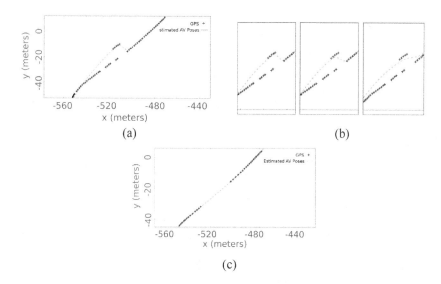

**Fig. 4.** (a) GPS error. (b) Increasing variance from left to right. (c) Clustering GPS and removing small groups.

## 3.2  Hypergraph Building

Nodes in the hypergraph represent AV poses and odometry biases. Edges represent constraints between the nodes.

A pose node $N_i$ is added to the hypergraph for each sensor measurement $z_i$. $N_i$ refers to an unknown pose $x_i$:

$$N_i = x_i = (x_i, y_i, \theta_i) \tag{1}$$

where $(x_i, y_i)$ is the position of the vehicle in the ground plane and $\theta_i$ is its heading.

For each log, the Hypergraph Builder creates odometry edges connecting each pair $N_i$ and $N_{i+1}$. This procedure guarantees that all nodes in the hypergraph are connected by odometry measurements, therefore, there is no need to synchronize the sensors since the odometry is used o join all nodes from the same log. While traversing the nodes in the graph, the system maintains the current command $u_i = (v_i, \varphi_i, \Delta t)$. $\Delta t$ is the time difference between $N_i$ and $N_{i+1}$. The velocity $v_i$ and steering angle $\varphi_i$ are obtained from the last odometry measurement and they are updated at each new odometry measurement. The odometry edge indicates a constraint between the nodes $N_i$ and $N_{i+1}$ through the error function $e^o(x_i, u_i)$.

We also simplify the notation by encoding the involved quantities in the indices of the error function as in [12]:

$$e^o(x_i, u_i) \overset{def.}{=} e_i^o(x, u) \tag{2}$$

The odometry constraint between each node pair is defined as:

$$e_i^o(\boldsymbol{x}, \boldsymbol{u}) = (\boldsymbol{x}_{i+1} \ominus \boldsymbol{x}_i) \ominus K(\boldsymbol{u}_i) \tag{3}$$

where $\ominus$ is the inverse of the motion composition operator $\oplus$ as defined in [18], and $K(.)$ uses the Ackerman steering geometry with understeer corrections [2] to compute a relative movement given the command $\boldsymbol{u}_i \in \boldsymbol{u}$, and $\boldsymbol{u}$ is a vector containing all commands. All odometry edges are combined in:

$$\boldsymbol{J}^o(\boldsymbol{x}, \boldsymbol{u}) = \sum_i^n e_i^o(\boldsymbol{x}, \boldsymbol{u}^\mathsf{T})^\mathsf{T} \hat{\boldsymbol{\Omega}}_i^o e_i^o(\boldsymbol{x}, \boldsymbol{u}^\mathsf{T}) \tag{4}$$

where $\hat{\Omega}_i^o$ is the odometry information matrix at node $\boldsymbol{N}_i$ projected through the non-linear function $K(.)$ via the unscented transformation [22].

Each node $\boldsymbol{N}_i$ created by a GPS measurement $\boldsymbol{z}_i^{GPS}$ receives a unary edge containing the error:

$$e_i^{GPS}(\boldsymbol{x}) = \boldsymbol{x}_i \ominus \boldsymbol{z}_i^{GPS} \tag{5}$$

All GPS edges constraints are combined in the total GPS error:

$$\boldsymbol{J}^{GPS}(\boldsymbol{x}) = \sum_i e_i^{GPS}(\boldsymbol{x})^\mathsf{T} \Omega_i^{GPS} e_i^{GPS}(\boldsymbol{x}) \tag{6}$$

where $\Omega_i^{GPS}$ is the inverse of the GPS covariance matrix at node $\boldsymbol{N}_i$.

We use LiDAR and GPS to compute intra-session loop closures as in [13]. however, we use an ad-hoc method to reduce the number of edges in the graph by only considering a new loop closure if it is at a certain distance from the previous one. We also extend this approach to handle inter-session loop closures. Inter-session loop closures provide the required relationships between the AV poses in multiple logs. A loop closure edge computes the following error:

$$e_{i,j}^L(\boldsymbol{x}) = (\boldsymbol{x}_j \oplus \boldsymbol{s}^L) \ominus (\boldsymbol{x}_i \oplus \boldsymbol{s}^L) \ominus ICP_{i,j}^L \tag{7}$$

where $\boldsymbol{x}_i$ and $\boldsymbol{x}_j$ are the AV poses that are considered as a loop closure, $\boldsymbol{s}^L$ is the pose of the LiDAR sensor in the AV reference frame and $ICP_{i,j}^L$ is a linear transform that aligns the point cloud $\boldsymbol{z}_i^L$ with the point cloud $\boldsymbol{z}_j^L$. We use a custom method based on the Generalized Iterative Closest Point (GICP) [16] algorithm to find the transform. The error below combines the constraints of all loop closure edges:

$$\boldsymbol{J}^L(\boldsymbol{x}) = \sum_i e_{i,j}^L(\boldsymbol{x})^\mathsf{T} \Omega_{i,j}^L e_{i,j}^L(\boldsymbol{x}) \tag{8}$$

where $\Omega_i^L$ is the inverse GICP covariance matrix.

Mutz et al. [13] showed that odometry measurements are subject to biases. This error can be propagated to the edges in the graph if not addressed. The authors proposed a PSO-based optimization method to calibrate the odometry bias before building the graph. The calibration is approximated by the following linear functions:

$$v_i^{'} = v_i b_{mult}^v \tag{9}$$

$$\varphi_i^{'} = \varphi_i b_{mult}^\varphi + b_{add}^\varphi \tag{10}$$

where $b_{mult}^v$ is the velocity multiplicative bias, $b_{mult}^\varphi$ and $b_{add}^\varphi$ are the steering wheel angle multiplicative and additive bias. The authors employed a PSO-based optimization method using a fitness function, which computes the difference between GPS and dead reckoning poses. Each particle contains the odometry bias parameters, $\boldsymbol{B} = (b_{mult}^v, b_{mult}^\varphi, b_{add}^\varphi)$, and the best parameters are used to update all odometry measurements before the AV poses optimization.

We propose a new method, which is performed directly in the hypergraph optimization. A bias calibration node $\boldsymbol{N}_{j:k}^B$ contains the parameters of the Eqs. 9 and 10:

$$\boldsymbol{N}_{j:k}^B = (b_{mult}^v, b_{mult}^\varphi, b_{add}^\varphi)_{j:k} \tag{11}$$

The range subscript $j : k$ indicates that a single bias calibration node $\boldsymbol{N}_{j:k}^B$ can be related to any subgroup of AV poses $\boldsymbol{x}$ containing all consecutive poses from $j$ to $k$.

As each session generates its hypergraph and each hypergraph have at least one bias calibration node, the system can calibrate the odometry bias on each session.

Each pair $(\boldsymbol{N}_i, \boldsymbol{N}_{i+1})$ is linked to a calibration node, forming a hyperedge. We use the following error to calibrate the odometry bias:

$$e_{i,j:k}\left(\boldsymbol{x}, \boldsymbol{B}, \boldsymbol{u}\right) = (\boldsymbol{x}_{i+1} \ominus \boldsymbol{x}_i) \ominus \overline{K}(\boldsymbol{B}_{j:k}, \boldsymbol{u}_i, \Delta t) \tag{12}$$

where $\overline{K}(.)$ is a function that takes the bias parameters $\boldsymbol{B}_{j:k}$ at $\boldsymbol{N}_{j:k}^B$ to update the command $\boldsymbol{u}_i$ through Eqs. 9 and 10, and then it calls $K(.)$ to estimate a relative displacement. The global odometry bias calibration error is defined as:

$$
\begin{aligned}
\boldsymbol{J}^B&(\boldsymbol{x}, \boldsymbol{B}, \boldsymbol{u}) \\
&= \sum_{j:k} \sum_{i=j}^{k-1} e_{i,j:k}\left(\boldsymbol{x}, \boldsymbol{B}, \boldsymbol{u}\right)^\mathsf{T} \hat{\boldsymbol{\Omega}}_i^B e_{i,j:k}\left(\boldsymbol{x}, \boldsymbol{B}, \boldsymbol{u}\right)
\end{aligned} \tag{13}
$$

where $\hat{\boldsymbol{\Omega}}_i^B$ is the odometry information matrix projected through $\overline{K}(.)$ via the unscented transformation. In this case, the projection must be updated when the bias changes substantially.

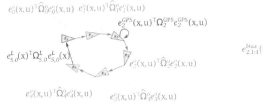

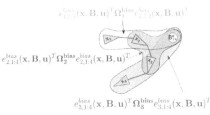

**Fig. 5.** Graph containing edges from odometry, GPS and loop closure.

**Fig. 6.** Odometry bias calibration node and hyperedges.

The resulting hypergraph contains all AV pose nodes, the odometry bias calibration nodes and all required edges to impose the constraints defined in Eqs. 4, 6, 8 and 13. Figure 5 illustrates the relationships between the elements of the hypergraph, including pose nodes, odometry edges, a GPS edge, and a loop closure edge. Figure 6 displays an odometry bias calibration node and some calibration hyperedges represented by regions with different colors for better visualization.

### 3.3  Hypergraph Optimization

The hypergraph optimization is an iterative process limited by a pre-defined number of iterations and it is separated in two main steps. The first step maximizes only the likelihood of the AV poses by combining Eqs. 4, 6 and 8 while excluding Eq. 13:

$$J_1\left(\boldsymbol{x}, \boldsymbol{u}\right) = \boldsymbol{J}^o\left(\boldsymbol{x}, \boldsymbol{u}\right) + \boldsymbol{J}^{GPS}\left(\boldsymbol{x}\right) + \boldsymbol{J}^L\left(\boldsymbol{x}\right) \tag{14}$$

The second step swaps the node update strategy by handling only the odometry bias calibration:

$$J_2 = \boldsymbol{J}^B(\boldsymbol{x}, \boldsymbol{B}, \boldsymbol{u}) \tag{15}$$

When the second step reaches a defined number of iterations, the new odometry biases are used to update all edges related to Eq. 7 by first updating the corresponding commands $\boldsymbol{u}$ using Eqs. 9 and 10. After these updates, the optimization process restarts from the first step. After repeating the two steps for a desired number of iterations, the optimization returns the AVs poses and the odometry calibration biases.

### 3.4  Large-Scale Environment Mapping

The map is represented in log-odds to avoid numerical instabilities [21]. The log-odds of a given cell $\boldsymbol{m}_c$ in the map is defined as:

$$l_c = \log \frac{p\left(\boldsymbol{m}_c|\boldsymbol{x}, \boldsymbol{z}\right)}{1 - p\left(\boldsymbol{m}_c|\boldsymbol{x}, \boldsymbol{z}\right)} \tag{16}$$

where $p\left(\boldsymbol{m}_c | \boldsymbol{x}, \boldsymbol{z}\right)$ is the probability of $\boldsymbol{m}_c$ being occupied given $\boldsymbol{x}$ and $\boldsymbol{z}$.

Initially, all grid cells are set to an invalid state (e.g. -1.0) and, at each time step, if a cell $\boldsymbol{m}_c$ is in the LiDAR perceptual field then it's current log-odds is updated:

$$l_{i,c} = l_{i-1,c} + ISM\left(\boldsymbol{m}_c, \boldsymbol{x}_i, \boldsymbol{z}_i^L\right) - l_0 \tag{17}$$

where $l_{i-1,c}$ is the previous log-odds of the cell $\boldsymbol{m}_c$, $l_0$ is the map prior probability, $\boldsymbol{z}_i^L$ is a LiDAR measurement and $ISM(.)$ is the inverse sensor model function [21].

### 3.5   Large-Scale Map Merging

The Mapper module merges the grids maps in an incremental approach. A first map is created using any of the resulting output files from the hypergraph optimization. While the mapping process evolves, the system saves how many times each cell $\boldsymbol{m}_c$ is reached by the LiDAR rays in the current session. After the first map is complete, the system changes the rule defined in Eq. 17 and then only the cells with the hit counter below a threshold value $K$ are updated:

$$l_{i,c} = \begin{cases} l_{i-1,i} + ISM\left(\boldsymbol{m}_c, \boldsymbol{x}_i, \boldsymbol{z}_i^L\right) - l_0, & hits\left(\boldsymbol{m}_c\right) < K \\ l_{i-1,i}, & otherwise \end{cases} \tag{18}$$

We assume that the LiDAR sensor is reliable and after enough hits the system can freeze the resulting log-odds. This procedure can unintentionally keep the low dynamics fixed in a previous map, but we can easily return to the original update rule defined in Eq. 17 if the difference in time between the sessions are greater than that of parameterized in Sect. 4. Assuming that the main changes in the environment infrastructure takes a time greater than that, then the system can update the current map while discarding most of the undesired changes in the next sessions.

## 4   Experimental Methodology

In this section, we describe each one of the recorded sessions, and the metrics used to compare the odometry calibration methods and to evaluate the estimated AV poses. We also indicate all the experiments that evaluates the main features of the new proposed large-scale mapping system.

We collected data using the IARA platform. The AV was conducted by a human along the beltway of the university campus and within parking lots in it's vicinity. Figure 7(a) shows the beltway (red) and the parking lots 1 (yellow), 2 (dark blue) and 3 (cyan). Log UB1 was acquired along the beltway at night, in the clockwise direction and without moving obstacles. Log UB2 was recorded in the morning, in counterclockwise direction, with moving objects and many parked vehicles. The Logs PL1, PL2 and PL3 are related to the parking lots.

(a)

(b)

**Fig. 7.** Satellite view of the environments. (a) University campus beltway (red), parking lot 1 (yellow), parking lot 2 (dark blue) and parking lot 3 (cyan). (b) Route from the university campus to another city (light blue). (Color figure online)

Finally, Fig. 7(b) shows the route from the campus to another city in which the AV crosses highways, rural and urban streets and a long bridge. The TRVL log was recorded along this route which has about 72 km of extension.

### 4.1   Experiments

We carried out a series of experiments to evaluate the odometry calibration and the map building and merging proposed methods.

The main parameters of the proposed mapping system used in our experiments are the Minimum Speed ($MS$) set to 0.01 ms in the speed filtering, the Neighbor Distance ($ND$) and the Neighbor Quantity ($NQ$) thresholds used in the GPS clustering are set to 1.2 m and 40, respectively. The cell hits threshold ($K$) represented in Eq. 18 is set to 64. The time distance between sessions ($ISTD$) is set to $1month$ for low dynamics consideration.

**Odometry Bias Calibration.** In this experiment, we compare the PSO-based optimization [13] and the proposed hypergraph optimization methods for calibrating odometry biases. We use the mean absolute error (MAE) metric to

**Table 1.** Odometry bias calibration using PSO and hypergraph optimization.

| LOG | Method | $b^v_{mult}$ | $b^\varphi_{mult}$ | $b^\varphi_{add}$ | MAE |
|---|---|---|---|---|---|
| UB1 | **PSO** | 1.03011 | 0.97289 | $-1.412\times10^{-3}$ | 113.30952 |
|  | **Graph** | 0.99663 | 1.02816 | $-1.530\times10^{-3}$ | **38.00164** |
| UB2 | **PSO** | 0.99286 | 0.92143 | $0.499\times10^{-3}$ | 198.21247 |
|  | **Graph** | 0.99647 | 1.00497 | $0.591\times10^{-3}$ | **49.84211** |
| PL1 | **PSO** | 0.99091 | 0.98748 | $0.447\times10^{-3}$ | 5.61165 |
|  | **Graph** | 0.99990 | 0.99752 | $0.747\times10^{-3}$ | **2.35632** |
| PL2 | **PSO** | 1.00082 | 0.98382 | $0.354\times10^{-3}$ | 3.47713 |
|  | **Graph** | 0.99675 | 0.99318 | $0.285\times10^{-3}$ | **1.76424** |
| PL3 | **PSO** | 0.98799 | 0.98748 | $0.542\times10^{-3}$ | 2.08321 |
|  | **Graph** | 0.99350 | 1.00022 | $0.562\times10^{-3}$ | **1.77525** |
| TRVL | **PSO** | 0.97999 | **0.55000** | $-0.304\times10^{-2}$ | $2.708\times10^4$ |
|  | **Graph** | 1.00059 | **0.98049** | $-0.305\times10^{-3}$ | $\mathbf{3.809\times10^3}$ |

compare the paths obtained by both calibration methods (PSO-based and hypergraph) against the GPS. A better odometry calibration should produce lower MAE values as the resulting path should better approximate GPS measurements.

**Map Building and Merging.** In this experiment, we compare the estimated AV poses with the GPS measurements for each log using the MAE metric. We constructed a single map using all logs in order to verify the merging capabilities of the proposed system. We illustrate same obstacles viewed in different visits to the same region with different colors in order to qualitatively evaluate the results of the map merging.

## 5   Results and Discussions

### 5.1   Odometry Bias Calibration

Table 1 compare the MAE results of the calibration using both methods. In all cases, the novel approach has found better parameters since it produces lower MAE values and the recovered paths are closer to GPS than both raw odometry and PSO. Figure 8 compares GPS and raw odometry with the paths computed by the two odometry bias calibration methods in the TRVL log.

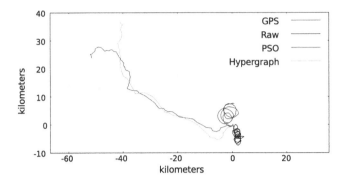

**Fig. 8.** Odometry calibration - TRVL.

## 5.2   Map Building and Merging

Given that our new system exploits all relevant sensor data, additional filtering strategies and LiDAR odometry, it was capable of handling the TRVL dataset and providing the maps in that large-scale context. Figure 9(a) illustrates the absence of a common reference frame while merging UB1 and UB2 without the inter-session loop closures while also using 18. Red pixels are the obstacles found in UB1 and green pixels are obstacles in UB2. Similar errors occur when we merge the remaining logs without using the inter-session loop closure to estimate a good reference frame. Figure 9(b) illustrates the removal of the errors after activating the inter-session loop closures between UB1 and UB2. Figure 9(c) presents the final merged map including all parking lots.

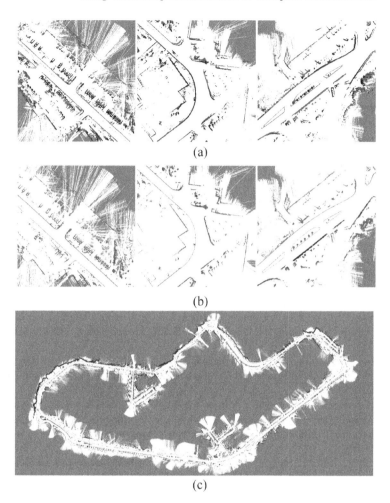

**Fig. 9.** Map merging. (a) Errors in the OGM (UB1 and UB2). (b) Enabling inter-session loop closures. (c) Complete map.

# 6    Conclusions and Future Work

In this work, we presented a new system for long-term map maintenance. The system uses multi-session data with the purpose of building and updating grid maps for posterior autonomous navigation and localization. The system deals with different types of sensors and can handle typical errors found in noisy sensor data. The Hypergraph Builder module includes intra-session and inter-session loop closures in order to estimate the AV poses in a global coordinate frame. The system also uses a new odometry bias calibration method to turn the odometry more reliable in the entire process. The Mapper module uses a custom method to freeze highly observed cells and so handle high and low dynamics in the map merging. We evaluated the system using datasets collected in an university campus and in a travel to another city. Experiments indicate that the new odometry bias calibration method surpass a previous PSO-based and also shows that the system can build and merge submaps into a global map using inter-session loop closures.

Equation 7 is used in Kümmerle et al. [12] to estimate the 2D pose of some laser scanner sensors directly in the hypergraph optimization. We did not obtain same quality results for the Velodyne HDL-32E in our AV. In a future work, we can investigate proper methods to calibrate the extrinsic of our LiDAR and cameras.

# References

1. Badue, C., et al.: Self-driving cars: a survey. Expert Syst. Appl. **165**, 113816 (2020)
2. Bergman, W.: The basic nature of vehicle understeer-oversteer. SAE Trans. **74**, 387–422 (1966)
3. Bonanni, T.M., Corte, B.D., Grisetti, G.: 3-D map merging on pose graphs. IEEE Robot. Autom. Lett. **2**(2), 1031–1038 (2017)
4. Cadena, C., et al.: Past, present, and future of simultaneous localization and mapping: toward the robust-perception age. IEEE Trans. Robot. **32**(6), 1309–1332 (2016)
5. Cardoso, V., et al.: A model-predictive motion planner for the iara autonomous car. In: 2017 IEEE International Conference on Robotics and Automation (ICRA), pp. 225–230 (2017)
6. De Paula Veronese, L., et al.: A light-weight yet accurate localization system for autonomous cars in large-scale and complex environments. In: 2016 IEEE 19th International Conference on Intelligent Transportation Systems (ITSC), pp. 520–525 (2016)
7. Deutsch, I., Liu, M., Siegwart, R.: A framework for multi-robot pose graph SLAM. In: 2016 IEEE International Conference on Real-Time Computing and Robotics, RCAR 2016, pp. 567–572 (2016)
8. Ding, X., Wang, Y., Yin, H., Tang, L., Xiong, R.: Multi-session map construction in outdoor dynamic environment. In: 2018 IEEE International Conference on Real-Time Computing and Robotics, RCAR 2018, pp. 384–389 (2019)
9. Einhorn, E., Gross, H.M.: Generic NDT mapping in dynamic environments and its application for lifelong SLAM. Robot. Auton. Syst. **69**, 28–39 (2015)
10. Guidolini, R., Badue, C., Berger, M., de Paula Veronese, L., De Souza, A.F.: A simple yet effective obstacle avoider for the iara autonomous car. In: 2016 IEEE 19th International Conference on Intelligent Transportation Systems (ITSC), pp. 1914–1919 (2016)
11. Guidolini, R., De Souza, A.F., Mutz, F., Badue, C.: Neural-based model predictive control for tackling steering delays of autonomous cars. In: 2017 International Joint Conference on Neural Networks (IJCNN), pp. 4324–4331 (2017)
12. Kümmerle, R., Grisetti, G., Burgard, W.: Simultaneous parameter calibration, localization, and mapping. Adv. Robot. **26**(17), 2021–2041 (2012)
13. Mutz, F., Veronese, L., Oliveira-Santos, T., Aguiar, E., Cheein, F.A., De Souza, A.: Large-scale mapping in complex field scenarios using an autonomous car. Expert Syst. Appl. **46**, 439–462 (2016)

14. Possatti, L., et al.: Traffic light recognition using deep learning and prior maps for autonomous cars, pp. 1–8 (July 2019)
15. Sarcinelli, R., et al.: Handling pedestrians in self-driving cars using image tracking and alternative path generation with frenét frames. Comput. Graph. **84**, 173–184 (2019)
16. Segal, A., Hähnel, D., Thrun, S.: Generalized-icp (June 2009)
17. Serafin, J., Grisetti, G.: Nicp: dense normal based point cloud registration. In: 2015 IEEE/RSJ International Conference on Intelligent Robots and Systems (IROS), pp. 742–749 (2015)
18. Smith, R., Self, M., Cheeseman, P.: Estimating uncertain spatial relationships in robotics. In: Cox I.J., Wilfong G.T. (eds.) Autonomous Robot Vehicles, vol. 1, pp. 167–193. Springer, New York (July 1990)
19. Sun, Y., Sun, R., Yu, S., Peng, Y.: A grid map fusion algorithm based on maximum common subgraph. In: 2018 13th World Congress on Intelligent Control and Automation (WCICA), vol. 2018-July, pp. 58–63. IEEE (July 2018)
20. Tabelini Torres, L., et al.: Effortless deep training for traffic sign detection using templates and arbitrary natural images. 2019 International Joint Conference on Neural Networks (IJCNN), pp. 1–7 (July 2019)
21. Thrun, S., Burgard, W., Fox, D.: Probabilistic Robotics (Intelligent Robotics and Autonomous Agents). The MIT Press, Cambridge (2005)
22. Uhlman, J.: Dynamic map building and localization for autonomous vehicles. Ph.D. thesis, University of Oxford (1994)

# Supervised Training of a Simple Digital Assistant for a Free Crop Clinic

Mariana da Silva Barros[1]([✉]), Igor de Moura Philippini[1], Ladson Gomes Silva[1],
Antonio Barros da Silva Netto[1], Rosana Blawid[2],
Edna Natividade da Silva Barros[1], and Stefan Blawid[1]

[1] Centro de Informática, Universidade Federal de Pernambuco, Recife, Brazil
{msb4,imp2,lgs3,absn2,ensb,sblawid}@cin.ufpe.br
[2] Departamento de Agronomia, Universidade Federal Rural de Pernambuco,
Recife, Brazil
rosana.blawid@ufrpe.br

**Abstract.** Family farming represents a critical segment of Brazilian agriculture, involving more than 5 million properties and generating 74% of rural jobs in the country. Yield losses caused by crop diseases and pests can be devastating for small-scale producers. However, successful disease control requires correct identification, which challenges smallholders, who often lack technical assistance. The present work proposes a system that detects disease symptoms in images of plant leaves to assist phytopathology experts. The objective is to decrease the experts' workload and enable consulting services for free or at nominal cost. In addition, the required digital communication channel will promote the formation of a caring community ready to offer unpaid advice for family farmers. The machine learning and refinement of the assistance system are described in detail. The developed classification system achieves a recall value of 95%.

**Keywords:** Disease identification · Machine learning · Family farming

## 1 Introduction

There are currently about 5 million properties in Brazil that subsist on family farming, employing more than 10 million people. According to the Brazilian government [1], smallholder farmers represent 84.4% of rural establishments and are responsible for 74% of rural jobs and 33.2% of the agricultural GDP. In Pernambuco, located in the Northeast region of Brazil, family farming employs ca. 83% of the people living in the countryside. However, smallholder farmers are economically vulnerable, especially in a region that still demonstrates one of the highest poverty rates in the country. Moreover, they are strongly affected by a changing climate. Yet today, Pernambuco suffers from major meteorological disasters, especially droughts.

Despite the great importance of family farming, small-scale producers have to face their challenges alone. They lack the financial resources to seek private

A. Britto and K. Valdivia Delgado (Eds.): BRACIS 2021, LNAI 13074, pp. 162–176, 2021.
https://doi.org/10.1007/978-3-030-91699-2_12

agricultural consultants, and governmental support is sparse. According to the Agricultural Census in 2006 and 2017, about 80% of the agricultural establishments declared not having received any technical support required to adopt modern technology and improve productivity. Furthermore, pests and plant diseases can have severe economic impacts, causing losses that reached up to 43% of the annual production in 2016. Significant yield losses are avoidable when caused by the misuse (or lack of usage) of phytosanitary products for disease control. This situation aggravates by the aging and low education level of small-scale producers. 15.6% of the farmers who use phytosanitary products are illiterate [1]. The correct disease identification is vital for any treatment strategy that explicitly targets the causing agents, avoiding the excessive use of non-specified agrochemicals. Access to technical assistance would inform family farmers about the technological and management innovations and empower them to adopt these measures correctly, reducing the risks inherent to agricultural activities.

The present work proposes an assistant system based on deep learning to identify the presence of disease symptoms in images of plant leaves. The assistant was developed in partnership with experts from the Phytosanitary Clinic of Pernambuco (CliFiPe) hosted by the Federal Rural University of Pernambuco (UFRPE). The goal is to provide technical aid in plant disease diagnosis, prevention, and treatment more efficiently to family farmers. Furthermore, the efficiency gain shall enable the experts from CliFiPe to reach out to a more significant part of the local farming community. The system can classify the leaves' images, achieving a recall value of 95%.

## 2   Related Works

The application of technology to agriculture has been approached in several studies that employ mobile services to help smallholder farmers or machine learning to detect diseases.

Baumüller recently reviewed [2] the literature on agriculture-related services offered through mobile phones, recognizing that the strategic application of information and communication technology provides the best opportunity for economic growth and poverty reduction. The review describes four service categories offered through mobile phones (information dissemination, financial services, access to suppliers, and access to output markets). It also takes a critical look at experimental works and the expected impact related to these services. Agricultural mobile services for crop disease monitoring and diagnosis belong to the first category.

In a pioneering work, Mohanty et al. [3] suggested using a deep learning approach based on image classification to identify selected plant diseases through leaf images. To this extent, the authors created a dataset for disease classification [4] composed of 38 classes defined as a pair of crop and illness. Then, they trained a Convolutional Neural Network (CNN) to classify them, achieving an accuracy of over 99%. The dataset includes more than 54000 images from 14 crop species and 26 diseases. Most importantly, the publicly accessible dataset enabled several follow-up studies. In the application scenario envisioned in the here proposed work, the CNN only assists in disease recognition. A human expert takes the final responsibility since false identification can cause severe consequences for a small-scale producer. Moreover, the farmer himself takes pictures of the symptoms and provides crop information. In addition, the images taken by the farmers in the field will not follow any predefined pattern, as opposed to the proposed dataset created in a laboratory. Thus, the CNN needs to be trained with images that match reality and are specific to the crops and diseases encountered in the region where advice shall be provided, here, the state of Pernambuco.

Rangarajan et al. [5] also proposed a system to perform disease classification using plant leaves images. In addition, the study assembled a dataset using pictures from five different diseases of the eggplant crop taken both in a lab and in an actual field. The proposed classifier used VGG16 as a feature extractor and Multi-Class Support Vector Machine to classify the diseases. Even though these techniques are frequently used in image classification tasks, studies indicate that this method produces worse results than using the same network as feature extractor and classifier.

Barbedo [6] introduced a system to identify plant diseases using the public dataset Digipathos [7], created by the Brazilian Agricultural Research Corporation Embrapa. The author also used deep learning to perform the image classification but explored individual lesions and spots rather than considering the entire leaf. Since the Embrapa dataset is not balanced, the segmentation in individual lesions acts as data augmentation. The system is specialized to detect and classify diseases based mainly on these spots. In its current form, our digital assistant suggests to a human expert larger picture segments to provide context and aid in the identification. However, lesion-based segmentation is considered for future work.

## 3 Proposed Approach

### 3.1 System Overview

As mentioned in Sect. 1, the system's objective is to help farmers monitor their plantations and identify whether the plant is diseased. For this purpose, the system uses machine learning and computer vision techniques to analyze leaves images and detect whether they show or not disease symptoms. We also built a digital platform where both farmers and experts can connect and interact. Such a platform facilitates and improves the provided diagnosis and assistance. Figure 1 shows the system's general structure.

The proposed platform is accessible to farmers through a mobile application. The user selects a crop from a predefined collection and takes a picture of a crop leaf. Images are automatically segmented and submitted to the classification system to detect the probability of revealing disease symptoms. All pictures are stored in a database and are used to fine-tune and continuously optimize the classification systems' performance. The app also displays general information about possible diseases to the user, such as its most common symptoms and

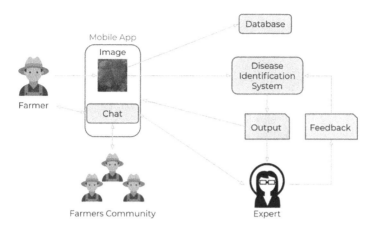

**Fig. 1.** General architecture of the proposed system composed by a mobile app and a digital assistant for a crop clinic

measures for prevention. However, more specific advice on disease control is left to direct communication with a phytopathology expert. The knowledge base is an information database created by experts from CliFiPe.

The mobile app allows the farmer to directly communicate with the experts, exposing doubts and receiving assistance with problems in their crops. The community also grants an opportunity for the farmers to help each other and share knowledge.

Currently, the system is trained to identify symptoms in images of grapes leaves. However, the plant disease diagnosis will focus on the main food crops cultivated in Pernambuco, and later in the Northeast region of Brazil. Therefore, one of the project's goals is to build a dataset of images of the region's most common and essential crops and the diseases affecting them. We also aim to make this dataset available to all researchers who work on improving plant disease management.

### 3.2   Crop Clinic Digital Assistant

To correctly identify the presence of disease symptoms in plant leaves images, we developed a system that generates segments from images of plant leaves and uses deep learning techniques to classify whether they show disease symptoms or not.

Section 2 delineates some examples of works that perform similar tasks. However, images are usually taken in a controlled environment, with supervised conditions and a standard background. Available training datasets, such as the PlantVillage [4] and the Digipathos dataset [7], do not include images with variations in lighting, size, or framing and thus does not reflect actual field conditions. As a result, according to [3], models trained over such datasets achieve only an average precision of 31% when applied to authentic field images. Here we use

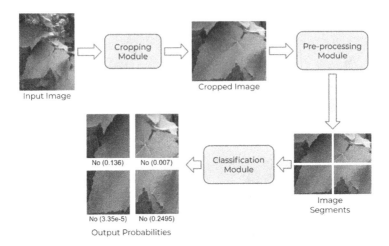

**Fig. 2.** Tasks performed by the digital assistant

photos taken in the field to train the neural network model. Since images taken with a mobile phone by inexperienced users will exhibit similar picture quality and detail variations, the CNN will recognize the presence of disease symptoms more reliably.

Figure 2 shows the general architecture of the digital assistant. The system takes the raw images to be classified as input and consists of three modules:

- **Cropping Module:** Cropping the input image centers the leaf and eliminates parts of the background. Manually cropped images constitute the training and validation data sets to guarantee a certain standard, improving the classification performance of the CNN. However, photos submitted by the users will be cropped automatically once the app is more broadly disseminated. The algorithm will use cropping margins based on typical pictures taken by the app users.
- **Pre-processing Module:** The division of leaves images into segments depends on the frame proportions. Frames with a height-to-width ratio below a certain threshold are separated into four segments, otherwise in six. The chosen threshold value guarantees that each segment shows a similar degree of detail. Segmentation increases the size of the training data set, allowing to exclude parts with limited information. Also, it gives more flexibility in balancing the training data set by selected inclusion of segments of varying exposure conditions and quality. The generated segments are resized using the Bilinear Interpolation technique [8] to match the input shape of the neural network ($256 \times 256 \times 3$).
- **Classification Module:** A Convolutional Neural Network classifies the input segments as showing "Symptoms" or "No symptoms". A CNN is a deep learning technique widely used in pattern recognition that employs a single network to learn and classify the image features [9]. We base our model on the

ResNet50V2 pre-trained model. Details of the image training dataset will be given in Sect. 4. The digital assistant performs only binary classification, and forwards the segments with the most pronounced symptoms (highest probability) for further analysis to a phytopathology expert. Selecting the segments that most clearly demonstrate the disease symptoms is a valuable step in disease identification and agent recognition, either by human experts or another machine learning model.

# 4 Hyperparameter Tuning and Training

We discuss the classification results of the digital assistant in two parts. First, in the present Sect. 4, we will assess the performance of different trained models in the search for a balanced training dataset and optimal hyperparameters. Then, in Sect. 5, the classification of segments from twelve selected leaves images (that were not part of any training dataset) will be discussed in detail for illustration.

## 4.1 Dataset Collection

Currently, some online datasets are available for plant disease classification experiments, e.g., the PlantVillage [4] and the Digipathos dataset [7]. However, their images are usually taken in a lab and do not present variations in lighting, size, or framing, thus not reflecting the field conditions. Therefore, to improve the network performance when applied to images taken in the field, we manually build the dataset used in the network training.

The dataset employed in this study is composed of images collected by us in the region of the Siriji valley, in Pernambuco's countryside. There are several smallholders plantations in the area, and we collected images from plant leaves at some of them. Among the cultivated crops, the most important ones for the region's economy and production include grape, banana, and sugar cane. For this study, we trained a CNN to identify disease symptoms in grape leaves images, but the extension to other crops is straightforward. We took images from leaves in different growth stages, both healthy and diseased, and in different lighting conditions. Then, the photos were annotated by phytopathology experts from CliFiPe, identified as manifesting symptoms or not. After the expert annotation, the dataset size was:

- 1987 images for the class "No symptoms"
- 1302 images for the class "Symptoms"

The collected pictures were then manually cropped and segmented, as described in Sect. 3.2. After this step, they are ready to be divided into subsets and used in the experiments.

## 4.2    Dataset Division

Not all images were used for the training of the CNN. First, we separated a small number of representative images to illustrate how particular image characteristics influence the classification results of selected trained models. To ensure some variability and balancing between classes and conditions, twelve leaves images (six from the class "No Symptoms" and six from the class "Symptoms") were selected for this final case study, exhibiting different illumination, focus, and contrast conditions. The selected images were not used in the training of any of the models and are not used to extract statistics results. The final case study, reported in Sect. 5, only illustrates possible outcomes when the trained models are applied and emulates the challenges of a usage scenario at a large scale.

Second, the remaining images were divided into training and testing subsets in several different ways. This allows the training and verification of distinct neural network models. We will use this approach to estimate the expected performance variability when using these models for the digital assistant in a crop clinic. Moreover, insights into the composition of a well-balanced training dataset are obtained.

After cropping and segmentation of the collected images, the complete dataset contained 5750 images for the class "Symptoms" and 7676 images for the category "No symptoms". The entire dataset is then randomly divided into two groups, one for training (with 75% of the total pictures) and one for testing (with the remaining 25%). After the division, the set sizes are:

- Train set: 10069 images (4312 for the class "Symptoms" and 5757 for the class "No Symptoms")
- Test set: 3357 images (1438 for the class "Symptoms" and 1919 for the class "No Symptoms")

The generated train subset is used for the neural network model training. For this reason, the set must be composed of a sufficient number of images covering a significant variety of segments. The test set is used for the trained model to perform predictions. It allows estimating the performance when used as a digital assistant, classifying pictures taken by the mobile app users. Note that the random division is repeated several times to obtain distinct neural network models.

## 4.3    Model Training

During the training, the model might face learning problems of varying severity. In extreme situations, the model exhibits under- or overfitting. If the model does not learn to generalize well, then it becomes underfitted and will have a poor performance on training data. On the other hand, if the model retains the training dataset pattern too well, including all specific peculiarities, it becomes overfitted. Thus, the learning progress must be monitored by validating the model after each epoch (each training iteration updating the internal network

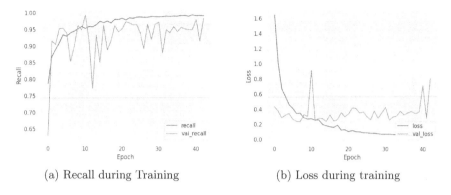

(a) Recall during Training                    (b) Loss during training

**Fig. 3.** Training results for a well performing model.

parameters). To this extent, a certain percentage of the training dataset needs to be separated as a validation set. The model's performance over this subset, evaluated after each epoch, will indicate potential fitting problems. We used 20% of the training set for validation.

Moreover, the remaining 80% of the images (used for training) were carefully balanced according to the number of images belonging to each class. The ratio between the size of the two categories determined the required augmentation of the class with fewer images, which is achieved by image rotation and flipping.

The CNN was configured using a sigmoid activation function in the output layer. During training, binary cross-entropy served as a loss function. The chosen optimizer was Adam, with a learning rate of 0.0001. The evaluation metric most closely observed during training should reflect the desired outcome. In this case, the digital assistant shall forward to experts image segments that possibly show symptoms for further inspection. Thus, ideally, segments with no symptoms will be classified correctly ("true negatives", TN) and not analyzed. Still, any segment possibly showing symptoms need to be inspected, i.e., should not be classified erroneously ("false negatives", FN). Therefore, during training, an essential evaluation metric is the recall metric, computed as $TP/(TP + FN)$. Nevertheless, other evaluation metrics were also computed when applying the model to the test dataset, such as accuracy, precision, F1-score, and average precision. We trained the model using a batch size of 128 and a maximum number of epochs of 100. However, an early stopping criterion was employed to avoid overfitting, with a threshold of 3 epochs with no progress. The classification module was implemented using the Tensorflow framework.

Figure 3 shows the training progress and the validation after each epoch for (a) the recall metric and (b) the loss function. The trained model achieves a high recall score of 95%.

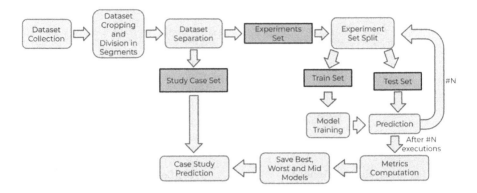

**Fig. 4.** Flow diagram of the performed computational experiments

## 4.4 Prediction

For performance evaluation, the trained model is applied to the images of the test set (not used in training). The prediction returns a probability between 0 and 1, indicating the likelihood of the segment showing disease symptoms. A threshold value of 0.5 separates the classes, i.e., a prediction below 0.5 indicates an image segment with "No Symptoms", otherwise with "Symptoms". Using the confusion matrix resulting from the prediction, we calculated the accuracy, precision (both for the positive and negative classes), recall, true negative rate, F1-score, and average precision for the performance assessment. However, the metric most closely observed is the recall.

## 4.5 Performance Optimization

Different dataset division strategies and hyperparameter value options were tested and evaluated to determine the ones that maximize the model performance. Figure 4 shows a diagram that summarizes the experiment flow. We implemented a script to repeat the complete assessment (training and testing) a certain number of times ($N$) while performing a grid search for high-performance models. For each repetition, the dataset is divided differently (maintaining the ratio of 75/25). Then, the trained model is applied to the respective test dataset of the repetition, and the evaluation metrics are computed. After $N$ assessments, the mean and standard deviation of the predicted recall metric from each execution are calculated. Although not representing a systematic cross-dataset validation, the approach will identify flyers, i.e., models that show atypical performance due to an accidentally introduced bias in the randomly selected training dataset. The script also saves the models that produce the best recall, the worst recall, and the closest recall to the mean. In addition, other prediction measures are also observed to guarantee that the model is behaving as expected. Applying these models to the case study dataset, composed equally of healthy and diseased leaves images with different quality levels, gives further insights

**Table 1.** Assessment results - Group 1

| Execution number | Split category | Dataset size | Mean recall | Max recall | Min recall | Mean precision | Mean accuracy | Mean F1-Score |
|---|---|---|---|---|---|---|---|---|
| 10 | Segments | 14076 | 0.907 | 0.945 | 0.876 | 0.785 | 0.856 | 0.836 |
| 50 | Segments | 14076 | 0.916 | 0.949 | 0.862 | 0.791 | 0.86 | 0.841 |
| 50 | Leaves | 14076 | 0.912 | 0.979 | 0.834 | 0.743 | 0.813 | 0.805 |
| 50 | Leaves | 3650 | 0.863 | 0.923 | 0.770 | 0.927 | 0.858 | 0.882 |
| 50 | Segments | 3650 | 0.863 | 0.910 | 0.811 | 0.931 | 0.871 | 0.894 |

into the strategy for finding a well-performing model. Due to image variability, a suitable dataset for training should not only balance between images showing disease symptoms or not but should also balance between pictures of good and low quality. The training of $N$ distinct models helps to understand both the expected performance, capability, and limitations of the neural network, as well as the impact of the training.

Table 1 summarizes the findings of the first group of assessments. A minimum number of repetitions of dataset splits and model training is required to reliably explore the complete dataset. We found that $N = 50$ is sufficient for the collected data. The mean recall and standard deviation do not change significantly for larger $N$, but the computation time increases. Another interesting finding concerns the dataset division strategy. The data can be divided into train and test sets before or after separating the leaves' pictures into segments. The former approach (before segmentation, defined in the table as the split category "Leaves") ensures that all the parts from a given picture end up in the same group. However, constructing the training set on segment level (splitting after segmentation, defined in the table as the split category "Segments") increases flexibility. This leads to a smaller standard deviation and reduced gap between maximum and minimum recall. Finally, the first group of assessments also included an evaluation of the desirable dataset size. We tested the use of the complete dataset, as opposed to the use of a partial one. As shown in Tab. 1, a training set that is too small leads to a reduced recall mean and maximum value, independently of the division strategy. However, the 14076 images collected in a dedicated field expedition are sufficient to train models with good performance and high evaluation metrics. The table also shows the mean values of the precision, accuracy, and F1-score measured in the experiments.

Table 2 summarizes the findings of the second group of assessments, related to the optimization of the training algorithm. Inside the second group, some experiments were conducted to determine the best weight to be attributed to each of the two classes during training. Choosing different weights for the classes allows to balance them without resampling. In other words, weights can tell the model to pay more attention to the instances of a particular category. Table 2 shows that attributing weight "1" to class "0" ("No symptoms") and weight "2" to class "1" ("Symptoms") gives a higher recall mean. This result is plausible because the importance to the class "Symptoms" is increased, and we are mainly trying to avoid false negatives.

**Table 2.** Assessment results - Group 2

| Weight class "0" | Weight class "1" | Mean recall | Standard deviation recall | Max recall | Min recall | Mean precision | Mean accuracy | Mean F1-Score |
|---|---|---|---|---|---|---|---|---|
| 1 | 2 | 0.928 | 0.024 | 0.969 | 0.857 | 0.7875 | 0.847 | 0.839 |
| 2 | 1 | 0.905 | 0.027 | 0.957 | 0.836 | 0.818 | 0.863 | 0.849 |
| 1 | 1 | 0.911 | 0.026 | 0.962 | 0.832 | 0.819 | 0.861 | 0.849 |
| 1 | 1.34 | 0.919 | 0.024 | 0.955 | 0.844 | 0.829 | 0.873 | 0.859 |

In addition, the evaluation metric and the classification threshold were also analyzed, but are not shown in the table. Some models were trained using the accuracy metric instead of the recall metric. However, they produced too many false negatives, which is not desirable since segments classified as showing no symptoms will not be called for further inspection by a human expert. We also tested different threshold values for the classification but found that the standard choice of 0.5 gives the most reliable prediction.

As mentioned in Sect. 2, the purpose of the present work is to detect the presence of symptoms in the leaf image, which constitutes a different application scenario as discussed in the state-of-the-art literature. Therefore, the implemented neural network model was specifically developed for the present application. Consequently, we cannot compare our model to a reference.

Promising models trained in the various assessments were applied to the (previously separated) case study dataset, giving further insights into the expected classification performance when analyzing leaves images of varying quality.

## 5 Case Study and Discussion

Twelve models were chosen for the final inference study. These models gave the best, worst, and mean recall in the assessments presented in the four last lines of Table 1. As stated in Sect. 4, the case study dataset is composed of images from both classes (showing or not symptoms) for various light, focus, and background conditions and different severity levels of symptoms.

The analysis of the predictions revealed some characteristics present in the inference images that influence the classification accuracy. For example, when the area occupied by the background is small, it is easier for the model to classify the

**Table 3.** Prediction Results of two selected models

| Model ID | Accuracy | Precision positive class | Precision negative class | Recall | True negative rate | F1-score | Average precision |
|---|---|---|---|---|---|---|---|
| 1 | 0.838 | 0.731 | 0.956 | 0.949 | 0.761 | 0.826 | 0.715 |
| 2 | 0.882 | 0.850 | 0.904 | 0.862 | 0.896 | 0.856 | 0.788 |

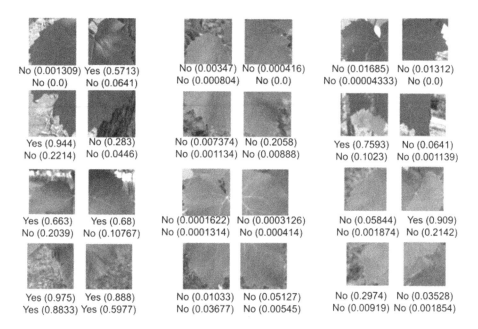

No (0.001309)  Yes (0.5713)
No (0.0)       No (0.0641)

No (0.00347)   No (0.000416)
No (0.000804)  No (0.0)

No (0.01685)   No (0.01312)
No (0.00004333) No (0.0)

Yes (0.944)    No (0.283)
No (0.2214)    No (0.0446)

No (0.007374)  No (0.2058)
No (0.001134)  No (0.00888)

Yes (0.7593)   No (0.0641)
No (0.1023)    No (0.001139)

Yes (0.663)    Yes (0.68)
No (0.2039)    No (0.10767)

No (0.0001622) No (0.0003126)
No (0.0001314) No (0.000414)

No (0.05844)   Yes (0.909)
No (0.001874)  No (0.2142)

Yes (0.975)    Yes (0.888)
Yes (0.8833)   Yes (0.5977)

No (0.01033)   No (0.05127)
No (0.03677)   No (0.00545)

No (0.2974)    No (0.03528)
No (0.00919)   No (0.001854)

**Fig. 5.** Classification results for selected healthy leaves images obtained from two distinct models

leaf segment correctly. However, the classification is more challenging for the model when the sunlight is too bright, or the leaf image does not have enough contrast. Thus, a carefully composed and sufficiently large training dataset is essential. As shown in Table 1, all models trained using a smaller dataset (constituted of about 3600 images) achieved a poor performance, committing many errors (both false positives and false negatives) when applied to the case study dataset (results not shown). Meanwhile, models trained with a more extensive dataset performed better.

However, defining the correct target metrics values for optimal performance is challenging. Table 3 displays the predicted evaluation metrics of two models that produced different recall values, out of $N = 50$ different training and test sets when divided on segment level (second line of Table 1).

The results indicate how the changes in the training dataset are related to the output metrics. For example, the first model achieved better results for metrics indicating the absence of false negatives, like negative precision and recall. On the other hand, the second model performed better for metrics that increase with decreasing false positives, like positive precision and true negative rate. However, this does not necessarily imply that the second model leads to more decisive errors in predicting the negative class ("No Symptoms").

Figure 5 displays the classification results of the two models applied to the images from the case study dataset of healthy leaves. The leaves images are divided into segments and show the model output classification (symptoms "yes"

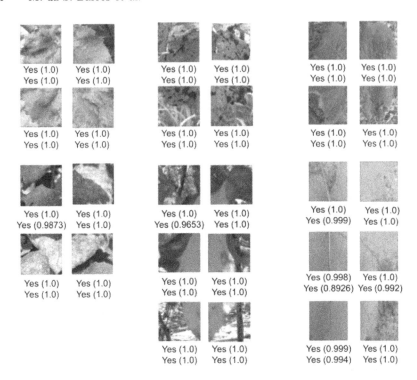

**Fig. 6.** Classification results for selected diseased leaves images obtained from two distinct models

or "no") and the corresponding probability for each of them. The first line under each segment is the prediction obtained from model 1 from Table 3, and the second line is from model 2. Similarly, Fig. 6 shows the diseased leaves images and their classification results when the two models are applied.

As expected, probabilities are higher when predicted by the first model in comparison to the second one. Although it is desirable to avoid false negatives (the objective of the training), model 1 leads to more errors in predicting the negative class, i.e., the model classifies segments without symptoms as presenting them (FP). Table 4 shows the confusion matrices results from the two models when applied to the case study dataset.

The inference study also revealed potential future improvements, such as, for example, the use of multi-label classification. This technique uses the same neural network to classify multiple different labels at the same time. That might allow, for instance, the enhancement of other prediction metrics maintaining the recall values.

**Table 4.** Confusion Matrices for two selected models over the case study dataset

| Model ID | TP | FN | FP | TN |
|----------|----|----|----|----|
| 1 | 28 | 0 | 8 | 16 |
| 2 | 28 | 0 | 2 | 22 |

# 6    Conclusion

The present work proposes using computer vision and machine learning to identify the presence of disease symptoms in plant leaves images. The main objective is to assist experts from the Phytosanitary Clinic of Pernambuco and enable consulting services for free or at a nominal cost offered to small-scale agricultural producers.

The implemented system allows smallholders to communicate with phytopathology experts and the community of users. In addition, the digital assistant successfully solves the problem of classifying whether image segments taken by inexperienced users show disease symptoms or not and, thus, acts as a filter for the subsequent analysis by human experts.

We also tackled the challenge of lacking data for training a Convolutional Neural Network by building our own training set composed of images of essential crops from Pernambuco. The training dataset balances images of good and poor quality to maximize the recall of photos taken from non-experts in the field. The best-performing model could achieve a recall of over 95%. Moreover, the annotated dataset will continuously improve with a growing user community. Test and inference results for distinct trained models gave insights into an ideal training dataset and the influence of exposure conditions when taking the photos to be classified in the field. We also found that models compromising on multiple metrics may give better classification results.

Future works include optimizing the classification system, automatizing identification of the disease-causing agent, and using a multi-label approach to improve the model performance.

**Acknowledgments.** This work was supported by an A.I. for Earth Microsoft Azure Compute Grant. M.B. would like to thank CAPES for the master's degree scholarship. S.B. is a CNPq fellow. The authors also thank the experts from CliFiPe, especially Dr. Jonas Alberto Rios and Dr. André Angelo Medeiros Gomes, for helpful discussion on the working of a crop clinic.

# References

1. IBGE: Agricultural Census 2017. https://censoagro2017.ibge.gov.br/templates/ censo_agro/resultadosagro/index.html. Accessed 1 Mar 2021
2. Baumüller, H.: The little we know: an exploratory literature review on the utility of mobile phone-enabled services for smallholder farmers. In: Journal of International Development, vol. 30, pp. 134–154. Willey Online Library (2018). https://doi.org/ 10.1002/jid.3314

3. Sharada, P.M., David, P.H., Salathé, M.: Using deep learning for image-based plant disease detection. In: Frontiers in Plant Science, vol. 7, pp. 1419. Frontiers (2016). https://doi.org/10.3389/fpls.2016.01419
4. Sharada P.M.: PlantVillage Dataset. https://github.com/spMohanty/PlantVillage-Dataset/tree/master/raw. Accessed 1 Mar 2021
5. Rangarajan, A.K., Purushothaman, R.: Disease classification in eggplant using pre-trained vgg16 and msvm. In: Scientific reports, vol. 10, pp. 1–11. Nature Publishing Group (2020). https://doi.org/10.1038/s41598-020-59108-x
6. Barbedo, J.G.A.: Plant disease identification from individual lesions and spots using deep learning. In: Biosystems Engineering, vol. 180, pp. 96–107. Science Direct (2019). https://doi.org/10.1016/j.biosystemseng.2019.02.002
7. Embrapa: Digipathos Dataset. https://www.digipathos-rep.cnptia.embrapa.br/. Accessed 1 Mar 2021
8. Smith, P.R.: Bilinear Interpolation of Digital Images. In: Ultramicroscopy, vol. 6, pp. 201–204. Science Direct (1981). https://doi.org/10.1016/0304-3991(81)90061-9
9. Voulodimos, A., Doulamis, N., Doulamis, A., Protopapadakis, E.: Deep learning for computer vision: a brief review. In: Computational Intelligence and Neuroscience, vol. 2018, pp. 1–13. Hindawi (2018). https://doi.org/10.1155/2018/7068349

# The Future of AI: Neat or Scruffy?

Bernardo Gonçalves$^{(\boxtimes)}$ (ID) and Fabio Gagliardi Cozman (ID)

Escola Politécnica, Universidade de São Paulo, São Paulo, Brazil
{begoncalves,fgcozman}@usp.br

**Abstract.** The "neat" and "scruffy" portraits have long been painted to describe viewpoints, styles of reasoning and methodologies in AI research. Essentially, the neats defend techniques based on first principles and grounded in mathematical rigor, while the scruffies advocate diversity within cognitive architectures, sometimes meant to be models of parts of the brain, sometimes just kludges or ad-hoc pieces of engineered code. The recent success of deep learning has revived the debate between these two approaches to AI; in this context, some natural questions arise. How can we characterize, and how can we classify, these positions given the history of AI? More importantly, what is the relevance of these positions for the future of AI? How should AI research be pursued from now on, neatly or scruffly? These are the questions we address in this paper, resorting to historical analysis and to recent research trends to articulate possible ways to allocate energy so as to take the field to maximal fruition.

**Keywords:** Neat vs. Scruffy · History of AI · Future of AI · Scientific method · Styles of scientific reasoning

## 1 Introduction

Which architecture should be implemented in a machine to make it best reproduce human intelligence in relevant intellectual tasks? In the history of AI, two answers have often been given to this question by different researchers, who have been labeled either as "neats" or "scruffies." Capturing viewpoints, styles of reasoning and methodologies, these labels have often been used as caricatures of the AI researcher—the analytical, sensible, dry *vs.* the empirical, messy, creative. But is this a fair account of what is at stake?

The debate about which methodologies are best for AI and what AI actually is or should be is an old one. But the advent of deep learning brought it back to the front stage of the discussion about the present and the future of AI. With considerable success in image, speech and natural language processing, AI has increased its social impact. Arguably the question about which architecture is most promising for AI underwent a twist, and it now comes with an attached social concern about the future.

Which future is best for AI? Is it one developed around a (super)intelligence that emerges through learning and that makes its judgements with little oversight? Or is it one based on a useful yet more predictable AI that is managed

© Springer Nature Switzerland AG 2021
A. Britto and K. Valdivia Delgado (Eds.): BRACIS 2021, LNAI 13074, pp. 177–192, 2021.
https://doi.org/10.1007/978-3-030-91699-2_13

more closely? Possible answers to this question are strongly tied to different research directions that have been proposed by the neats, on one side, and by the scruffies, on the other side. Recently hybrid or the so-called neurosymbolic AI has also been proposed as an attempt to leverage on the strengths of both sides. This approach to AI needs to be tested by time and deserves further study. In any case, it shall also benefit from a reflection upon its neat *vs.* scruffy origins.

In this paper we contribute to the discussion with:

1. an in-depth examination of the past through a review of notable neat and scruffy positions in the history of AI up to the present;
2. the identification of three types of attitudes towards AI research from neats and scruffies;
3. the formulation of their implications for the future of AI from the point of view of both research and its social impact.

In Sects. 2, 3 we shall study positions and uses of the "neat" and the "scruffy" terminology through the history of AI in order to arrive in Sect. 4 at three types of attitude towards AI research. Our contributed scheme is aimed at clarifying which notions of the terms have been available. In Sect. 5 we study implications of the three approaches for the future of AI. We conclude the paper in Sect. 6.

## 2   The "neats" Vs. "scruffies" Debate in the History of AI

We start with a review that partly extends a recent survey paper [3]. Our exposition is not chronological.

### 2.1   Marvin Minsky (1985–1995)

Minsky did not explicitly refer to the "neat" vs. "scruffy" dichotomy yet he posited an influential position in the discussion. In his 1985 book *The Society of Mind* and later, Minsky appealed to the complexity of the human mind and/or brain to justify that his explanations "rarely go in neat, straight lines from start to end." He associated it with the very nature of the mind:

> Perhaps the fault is actually mine, for failing to find a tidy base of neatly ordered principles. But I'm inclined to lay the blame upon the nature of the mind: much of its power seems to stem from just the messy ways its agents cross-connect. If so, that complication can't be helped; it's only what we must expect from evolution's countless tricks. [18, p. 18]

A few years later Minsky developed the point in connection with the brain:

> The brain's functions simply aren't based on any small set of principles. Instead, they're based on hundreds or perhaps even thousands of them. In other words, I'm saying that each part of the brain is what engineers call a kludge — that is, a jury-rigged solution to a problem, accomplished

by adding bits of machinery wherever needed, without any general, overall plan: the result is that the human mind — which is what the brain does — should be regarded as a collection of kludges. The evidence for this is perfectly clear: If you look at the index of any large textbook of neuroscience, you'll see that a human brain has many hundreds of parts — that is, subcomputers — that do different things. Why do our brains need so many parts? Surely, if our minds were based on only a few basic principles, we wouldn't need so much complexity [19].

So according to Minsky, one is led to think, AI systems shall be untidy like the brain. But did Minsky suggest that AI as a discipline shall be messy as well? This question will be revisited in a discussion with Yann Lecun in Subsect. 2.6.

## 2.2  Nils Nilsson (2009)

Nilsson addressed Minsky's position that the brain is a kludge so an AI system should be likewise. In his 2009 book *The Quest for Artificial Intelligence*, Nilsson acknowledged the wide disagreement in the field about what AI research should be like. He observed:

> Of course, just because the brain is a kludge does not mean that computer intelligences have to be. Nevertheless, some AI researchers favored systems consisting of collections of experimentally derived, ad hoc routines designed to solve specific problems. These people called themselves "scruffies" to distinguish themselves from the "neats" who favored programs based on theoretically based principles. (These terms were apparently first used by Roger Schank in the 1970s to contrast his approach to building natural language processing systems with the more theoretically based work of McCarthy and others.) In his keynote address at the 1981 annual meeting of the Cognitive Science Society, Robert Abelson compared the two camps by saying "The primary concern of the neat is that things should be orderly and predictable while the scruffy seeks the rough-and-tumble of life as it comes [...]." [20, p. 417]

Nilsson thus resumed to put his own opinion over the issue:

> I believe that both neats and scruffies are needed in a field as immature as AI is. Scruffies are better at exploring frontiers outside the boundaries of well-established theory. Neats help codify newly gained knowledge so that it can be taught, written about, and thus remembered. (*Ibid.*)

So it seems that Nilsson supported the coexistence of both approaches in AI research, each one in its own camp. He suggested that this is particularly important while AI is still a young endeavor.

## 2.3   Herbert Simon (1972)

Simon had received in 1978 the Nobel Prize in Economics for identifying the limited and messy nature of decision making as opposed, say, to idealized metrics of utility. Pamela McCorduck interviewed Simon extensively. She reported:

> Simon also took up the problem that had divided the AI (and cognitive science) community from the beginning: Is thinking best viewed as a process of reasoning from premises (the Neats?) or as a process of selective search through a maze (the Scruffies)? He had no final answer to that when he died in 2001, though we can assume he leaned toward the Scruffy point of view, given his book, Human Problem Solving, that he'd published with Allen Newell in 1972. [15, p. 452-3]

In his theory of human problem solving with Allen Newell, Simon emphasized the role of heuristics. He thus described their famous Logic Theorist (LT) program:

> There were important differences between LT's processes and those used by human subjects to solve similar problems. Nevertheless, in one fundamental respect that has guided all the simulations that have followed LT, the program did indeed capture the central process in human problem solving: LT used heuristic methods to carry out highly selective searches, hence to cut down enormous problem spaces to sizes that a slow, serial processor could handle. Selectivity of search, not speed, was taken as the key organizing principle [...]. Heuristic methods that make this selectivity possible have turned out to be the central magic in all human problem solving that has been studied to date. [29, p. 147]

From a mathematical point of view, heuristics may be considered ad-hoc techniques as it is hard to assign to them accurate theoretical guarantees. This is probably related to what McCorduck meant when classing Simon (and his LT co-designed with Newell) as an example of scruffiness in AI. Now, if the event in the northern summer of 1956 in Dartmouth marks the birth of AI as a discipline, then the scruffy LT can be considered the first AI program.

## 2.4   John McCarthy (1958)

McCarthy was the primary organizer of the Dartmouth workshop [15]. But it was Newell and Simon who seem to have taken most of the attention at Dartmouth, as they were the ones that had something real to show—the LT. McCarthy's reaction would come soon. In 1958, he compared the LT with his own program:

> The *advice taker* is a proposed program for solving problems by manipulating sentences in formal languages. The main difference between it and other programs or proposed programs for manipulating formal languages (the *Logic Theory Machine* of Newell, Simon and Shaw and the Geometry Program of Gelernter) is that in the previous programs the formal system

was the subject matter but the heuristics were all embodied in the program. In this program the procedures will be described as much as possible in the language itself and, in particular, the heuristics are all so described. [14, no emphasis added]

McCarthy's reservations with respect to Newell and Simon's LT had to do with the organization of the knowledge manipulated by the program. For McCarthy, this knowledge—about the world and about the problems the program is expected to solve—should be held transparent in an expressive language. So the language should be "most likely a part of the predicate calculus" (Ibid.).

McCarthy's concern with the knowledge representation language to be used in an AI program seems to have been the core of his research agenda. Further on in his 1958 text he outlined five features that, in his opinion, a system "which is to evolve intelligence of human order" should have at least. He then summarized: "We base ourselves on the idea that: *In order for a program to be capable of learning something it must first be capable of being told it*" (no emphasis added).

McCarthy had also expressed back then his hope to collaborate with Minsky:

The design of this system [so-called "the advice taker"] will be a joint project with Marvin Minsky, but Minsky is not to be held responsible for the views expressed here. [14]

Later on, as of 1996, McCarthy updated his text with a note "[t]his was wishful thinking," for "Minsky's approach to AI was quite different." In fact, McCarthy is seen as perhaps the main advocate of neatness in AI. His divergence with Minsky seems strongly related with our main subject in this paper. And yet it is still hard to pinpoint what exactly their differences were. Before we conclude this review and proceed to address the issue, we shall refer to another AI textbook and to the advent of deep learning as the most recent success in AI.

## 2.5    Russell and Norvig (1995–2020)

In the 1995 (first) edition of their textbook [24], Russell and Norvig reported that AI research had just seen a "sea change in both [its] content and [its] methodology" (p. 25). They referred to "the field of speech recognition" as a paradigmatic example, as it went through a shift from the use of "ad-hoc and fragile architectures and approaches" to eventually find in Hidden Markov Models (HMM's) an approach that is "based on a rigorous mathematical theory" and whose models "are generated by a process of training on a large corpus of real speech data." This, the authors observed, allowed "speech researchers to build on several decades of mathematical results developed in other fields," and ensured "that the performance is robust." They further remarked:

Some have characterized this change as a victory of the *neats* — those who think that AI theories should be grounded in mathematical rigor — over the *scruffies* — those who would rather try lots of ideas, write some programs, and then assess what seems to be working. Both approaches are important. A shift towards increased neatness implies that the field has reached a level of stability and maturity. (Whether that stability will be disrupted by a new scruffy idea is another question.) [24, p. 25, note 17, no emphasis added]

The last phrase, as appearing in this 1995 edition of the book, has been replaced in the 2020 (fourth and latest) edition by this note: "The present emphasis on deep learning may represent a resurgence of the scruffies" [25, p. 24, note 14]. It seems that, for these authors, the advent of deep learning is a result of scruffiness while that of HMM and Bayesian Networks are results of neatness. But to what extent is deep learning not based on mathematical theory?

## 2.6    Yann LeCun (2018)

With the success and also the hype around deep learning, there has been a criticism that machine learning techniques are pseudo-science and that their empirical results are not explainable nor reproducible. A report in *Science* magazine [9] covered the NIPS 2017 "Test-of-Time Award" keynote address by AI researchers Ali Rahimi and Benjamin Recht [23], who made the case that various aspects of machine learning algorithms are so badly understood, even by engineers, that they amount to alchemy. This has triggered a polemic with co-recipient of the 2018 Turing Award and Facebook's VP and chief AI scientist Yann LeCun, who reacted to their talk on the Internet:

> In the history of science and technology, the engineering artifacts have almost always preceded the theoretical understanding: the lens and the telescope preceded optics theory, the steam engine preceded thermodynamics, the airplane preceded flight aerodynamics, radio and data communication preceded information theory, the computer preceded computer science. Why? Because theorists will spontaneously study "simple" phenomena, and will not be enticed to study a complex one until there [is] a practical importance to it. [11]

Along the same lines, LeCun is reported by the *Science* magazine reporter to have said that "shifting too much effort away from bleeding-edge techniques toward core understanding could slow innovation and discourage AI's real-world adoption." He concluded that "It's not alchemy, it's engineering;" and added: "Engineering is messy."

Now, is engineering messy? It seems that it is only in the eyes of the scruffies that it is. We can think of researchers and practitioners who contribute to the field with standards and specification, design theory and so on, and altogether with the tidy application of principles in engineering. In any case, LeCun suggested that deep learning is engineering. And yet there has been no question that deep learning is AI.

We shall then make a detour to inquire about the nature of AI.

# 3 Is AI a Science of Intelligence or a Branch of Engineering?

There is something odd going on here—for Minsky and Simon seem to have thought of AI more as a *science* of intelligence and less as a field of engineering.

Minsky had a point about the possibility of intelligence itself and the brain being messy as products of evolution by natural selection. For him, neuroscience—and AI —, as scientific disciplines, would be accordingly untidy as well. Now, is this reasonable? Let us consider an analogy. Just like the brain, the human organism as a whole is a (messy) biological product of evolution. Yet that did not stop the discovery of the molecular structure of DNA as a unifying principle of all life. So Minsky's point may be seen rather as an *a priori* assumption.

Simon also seems to have thought that brain processes were to some extent messy. But he found in heuristics sort of a unifying principle. Given the initial success achieved by Newell and Simon's heuristics, Minsky himself felt compelled to refer to them in his 1959 paper [16] and in his follow-up survey [17]. Moreover, Simon presented a view of the design of artificial systems as an empirical science, and strove to manage the complexity of large systems [28]. Later in 1995 he even wrote a dedicated piece to show that AI is an empirical science [27]. And yet it is unlikely that he would endorse Minsky's view that AI should be messy. For Simon, AI is a lawful empirical science just as physics is. He wrote:

> The natural laws that determine the structure and behavior of an object, natural or artificial, are its internal constraints. An artificial system, like a natural one, produces empirical phenomena that can be studied by the methods of observation and experiment common to all science. [27, p. 99]

In fact, Simon accepted no significant distinction between natural and artificial objects from the point of view of empirical studies.

But LeCun's point looks really different. He seems to be talking about AI as an engineering discipline, say, such as aerospace engineering. And this connects to an older point about AI but also about computer science more generally. In a 1984 talk "The threats to computer science" [5], the physicist and computer programming pioneer Edsger Dijkstra set out one of his ingenious metaphors:

> The Fathers of the field had been pretty confusing: John von Neumann speculated about computers and the human brain in analogies sufficiently wild to be worthy of a medieval thinker and Alan M. Turing thought about criteria to settle the question of whether Machines Can Think, a question of which we now know that it is about as relevant as the question of whether Submarines Can Swim [5].

Ten years later a variant of the same metaphor was caught by Noam Chomsky and appeared (with no source given) in the May 1994 lectures that further composed his 1995 *Mind* paper [2]. Many of these debates "over such alleged questions as whether machines can think," Chomsky referred (p. 9), "trace back to the classic paper by Alan Turing." They fail to take note, he objected, that Turing himself declared to believe that the question "can machines think?" was "too meaningless to deserve discussion." Chomsky thus concluded:

> It is not a question of fact, but a matter of decision as to whether to adopt a certain metaphorical usage, as when we say (in English) that airplanes fly but comets do not [...] Similarly, submarines set sail but do not swim. There can be no sensible debate about such topics; or about machine intelligence, with the many familiar variants. [2, p. 9]

Overall, Chomsky denied Turing's question to have a seat within the empirical sciences. Given Minsky's position as we have quoted above, it is unlikely that he would agree with Dijkstra and Chomsky. But perhaps LeCun and others would do it, and then the discussion must go back to Turing's 1950 vision of AI [31].

In an influential keynote lecture at IJCAI 1995 [8], Patrick Hayes and Kenneth Ford indirectly associated themselves with Chomsky's variant of Dijkstra's metaphor to argue against "the Turing test vision" of AI (p. 974–5). They complained that AI systems back then (e.g., expert systems) were sufficiently successful as task-specific cognitive artifacts and yet were seen as a failure because of "Turing's ghost" (p. 976). They then urged:

> [I]f we abandon the Turing Test vision, the goal naturally shifts from making artificial superhumans which can replace us, to making superhumanly intelligent artifacts which we can use to amplify and support our own cognitive abilities, just as people use hydraulic power to amplify their muscular abilities. [8, p. 974]

According to the vision laid out by Hayes and Ford, the primary concern of AI should be the engineering of intelligent systems.

Now, it is interesting to note that Patrick Hayes hardly fits in the scruffy portrait. In fact, Hayes' intellectual project in AI had significant overlapping with McCarthy's and can be best seen as a neat one. This shows that the discussion about the nature of AI as a discipline is present among both scruffies and neats. Among neats, however, the science v. engineering question seems much less pronounced. This is perhaps because neats tend to agree on the value of understanding—the logic of intelligent systems must be well-understood. In fact, lack of principles and understanding is the core of most critiques of machine learning today, e.g., Rahimi and Recht's at NIPS 2017 (cf. Subsect. 2.6).

In 2012, Chomsky claimed that AI departed from the tradition of modern science as it gave up the understanding of cognitive phenomena and their rendering in artificial systems. A reporter mentioned AI's recent shift from the so-called "Good Old Fashioned AI" to the use of "probabilistic and statistical models." He was trying to get Chomsky's opinion on what could explain that shift and whether or not it was a step in the right direction. Chomsky answered:

> **Chomsky:** [An] approach, which I think is the right approach, is to try to see if you can understand what the fundamental principles are that deal

with the core properties, and recognize that in the actual usage, there's going to be a thousand other variables intervening — kind of like what's happening outside the window, and you'll sort of tack those on later on if you want better approximations [...That] is what science has been since Galileo, that's modern science. The approximating unanalyzed data kind is sort of a new approach, not totally, there's things like it in the past. It's basically a new approach that has been accelerated by the existence of massive memories, very rapid processing, which enables you to do things like this that you couldn't have done by hand. But I think, myself, that it is leading subjects like computational cognitive science into a direction of maybe some practical applicability...

**Interviewer:** "... in engineering?"

**Chomsky:** ... But away from understanding. [10].

Chomsky's opinion is worth quoting also because Google's director of research Peter Norvig bothered to reply it. Thus wrote Norvig:

> I agree that engineering success is not the goal or the measure of science. But I observe that science and engineering develop together, and that engineering success shows that something is working right, and so is evidence (but not proof) of a scientifically successful model. Science is a combination of gathering facts and making theories; neither can progress on its own. I think Chomsky is wrong to push the needle so far towards theory over facts; in the history of science, the laborious accumulation of facts is the dominant mode, not a novelty. The science of understanding language is no different than other sciences in this respect [21].

Norvig's view seems strongly related with LeCun's.

We shall now be well positioned to characterize types of past and present attitudes towards AI in view of its future as a science and engineering discipline.

# 4    Types of Neat and Scruffy's Attitudes in AI

Considering neat and scruffy approaches to AI and the further heterogeneity that is found within each camp, we shall distinguish three types of attitudes. Although there is some overlapping of concerns in between them, the primary commitment in each type is different and looks clear, as we elaborate next.

## 4.1    Scruffy Type I: The Empirical Scientists

For the scruffies type I, AI should be above all an empirical science of intelligence and of the mind and/or the brain. In short, their primary goal is:

> *Goal: to understand and reproduce the phenomenon of intelligence.*

This attitude was quite strong among influential figures in the early phase of the discipline. We identify it in Minsky and Simon but first, very early on in Turing himself. After World War II, Turing was recruited by the National Physical Laboratory (NPL) near London to build a digital computer that would match US-based initiatives such as the construction of the ENIAC. Turing's first technical report *Proposed Electronic Calculator* in late 1945 is an outcome of his task of specifying a computer architecture. He was engaged in the job of building a computer system ("a machine"). But the historical sources show that, unlike some of his colleagues at the time (e.g., the physicist and computer pioneer Douglas Hartree [7]), Turing's goal was not to enable scientific computing applications but rather to try to imitate the human brain [6, p. 237]. In fact, when he joined the NPL after the northern summer of 1945 he said that he was going to "build a brain" [6, p. 233]. It is possible to identify Turing's shift from neatness to scruffiness—from his seminal *On computable numbers* paper in 1936 and his 1938 doctoral thesis in mathematical logics to codebreaking and empirical problem solving ever since his wartime service in 1939 on [6, p. 230-1]. This illustrates the ambition of the scruffy type I, who will resort to systems building as a means to empirically study natural intelligence and the brain.

The same inclination can be found in Minsky and Simon's intellectual projects. Minsky opened his 1985 *Society of Mind* by positing his goal of explaining "how minds work" straightforwardly and asking "[h]ow can intelligence emerge from non-intelligence?" To answer that, he added, "we'll show that you can build a mind from many little parts, each mindless by itself." [18, p. 17]. As known, Minsky's experimental approach to pursue that project was based on computer techniques and systems. This is described, for example, in his well-known 1961 survey of AI techniques [17].

Simon's take is another example of the scruffy type I. Together with Allen Newell, he developed plenty of computer techniques and software systems in order to test his theories of intelligence. The Logic Theorist as we have seen was the first of the line, and was followed by the General Problem Solver and others.

To mention an active AI researcher that we identify with this type, Rodney Brooks has recently called upon AI to get back at taking the human brain as reference [1].

In short, among scruffies, the *empirical scientist* seems to aim at discovering whatever cognitive architecture and kludges that can be shown to emulate human intelligence. Emphasis is given on the best knowledge then available about the human brain as a product of evolution by natural selection over billions of years.

But in fact, as we have seen (Sect. 3), this is not the only kind of attitude among scruffies. We shall discuss a second position next.

### 4.2   Scruffy Type II: The System Builders

For this other class of scruffies, AI should not be primarily concerned with the deeper mysteries that surround human intelligence.

The *system builders* seem to aim at inventing whatever techniques to achieve or surpass human-level intelligence. If some contribution to the understanding of human intelligence is made in the process, the better. Emphasis is given on leveraging the best computer resources then available. In short, we can write their goal as:

> *Goal: to build intelligent systems that are as autonomous as possible.*

We identify this view in LeCun and Norvig as quoted above. Both posed their commentaries while being in charge of two of the biggest companies that invest in AI today. Their wish to reply to criticisms can also be understood as a defense of the research strategy and methodology underlying the AI systems that have been deployed in society by the companies they represent.

Another AI researcher that seems to express this view is Richard Sutton, Distinguished Research Scientist of the company DeepMind. In a 2019 web commentary [30], he wrote that "[t]he biggest lesson that can be read from 70 years of AI research is that general methods that leverage computation are ultimately the most effective." Sutton called this "the bitter lesson." He was implicitly referring to the recent success of deep learning and suggested that "[t]he ultimate reason for this is Moore's law." He completed: "researchers seek to leverage their human knowledge of the domain, but the only thing that matters in the long run is the leveraging of computation." Now, there is no doubt that the human brain has huge computation power. Yet Sutton's line of thought seems to depart from a concern with discovering the true nature of human intelligence and with imitating it closely. It characterizes most clearly the goal of resorting to whatever techniques are available in order to achieve performance that is compatible with the output of human intelligence.

## 4.3  Neats: The Computer Epistemologists

We have examined the varieties of discourse among neats and found no significant differences. This class may even include logicians and analytic philosophers, as it closely resembles the field of epistemology (or the theory of knowledge) in modern philosophy. But it also includes builders of knowledge bases (KB's), as long as there seems to be a concern with the soundness of both the knowledge that gets into the KB and the knowledge that is derived out of it.

The *computer epistemologists* seem to aim at understanding and developing knowledge management and inference techniques to imitate the rational aspects of human-level intelligence. Emphasis is given on the soundness and effectiveness of reasoning. In short, we can write their goal as:

> *Goal: to understand and reproduce rational aspects of intelligence.*

As mentioned, McCarthy advocated the need to address commonsense knowledge representation and management in view of human-level intelligence early on in the history of AI. He was perhaps the main champion of the neats in AI research. But there is a lot more diversity in this class.

The related tradition of expert systems is also a notable example of the neats at work. Douglas Lenat and Ed Feigenbaum thus tried to summarize their view:

> We articulate the three major findings and hypotheses of AI to date:
> (1) The Knowledge Principle: If a program is to perform a complex task well, it must know a great deal about the world in which it operates. In the absence of knowledge, all you have left is search and reasoning, and that isn't enough.
> (2) The Breadth Hypothesis: To behave intelligently in unexpected situations, an agent must be capable of falling back on increasingly general knowledge and analogizing to specific but superficially far-flung knowledge. (This is an extension of the preceding principle.)
> (3) AI as Empirical Inquiry: Premature mathematization, or focusing on toy problems, washes out details from reality that later turn out to be significant. Thus, we must test our ideas experimentally, *falsifiably*, on large problems. [12, p. 185, no emphasis added]

Considering all three "findings and hypotheses," one may note Lenat and Feigenbaum's concern with justified reasoning through sound knowledge in real-world scenarios. Also, they address the caricature of the neat profile which is often criticized for tackling toy problems.

Lenat's iniative to develop the large-scale commonsense KB he called Cyc was based on an expressive knowledge representation language "involving first-order predicate calculus plus ZF set theory, meta-level assertions, contexts, and modal operators" [13, p. 38]. It did not pay much attention to uncertainty management. But several other approaches to knowledge representation and reasoning have been developed by the neats based on, say, multi-valued logics and probability theory. We identify as neats thinkers such as Isaac Levi and Henry Kyburg, who developed theories of uncertain and approximate reasoning; but also thinkers such as David Lewis who studied causaility and counterfactuals. Other neats are Ronald Fagin and Joseph Halpern, who theorized on reasoning about beliefs; but also Judea Pearl and Adnan Darwiche who contributed to reasoning through graphical models and probability distributions.

Darwiche posited that the results achieved by "function-based" approaches to AI such as deep learning are closer to animal-like abilities" than to "human-level intelligence." He pointed out that the latter requires a "model-based approach" [4]. For Pearl, true AI can only come when a machine is able to test cause-and-effect statements, which would allow it to explain events [22].

## 5   Implications for the Future of AI

Related to the goals of scruffy types I and II and the neats are implications for the future of AI research in society. The discussion between researchers from different categories is often heated as if there was no room for the fellow's approach in AI. In dialogue with the scruffy type II, e.g., Ali Rahimi said at the 2017 of NIPS:

We are building systems that govern healthcare and mediate our civic dialogue. We would influence elections. I would like to live in a society whose systems are built on top of verifiable, rigorous, thorough knowledge, and not on alchemy [23].

But also, in dialogue with the neats Simon had written in 1995:

Artificial objects, including computer programs, are what they are because they were designed to be that way. This fact has led some to claim that there can be no science of artificial objects, but only an engineering technology. Those who hold the most extreme form of this view look to the discovery and proof of mathematical theorems about intelligent systems as the only genuine route to a science of AI, and denigrate the role of system building and experiment as "only engineering." [27, p. 98-9]

Now, in acknowledgement of the values underlying each of the three attitudes let us pack their core values and implications for the future of AI in society.

- **Scruffy type I**. The empirical scientists hold the promise to contribute to an in-depth understanding of the phenomenon of intelligence, perhaps in cross-fertilization with neuroscience, cognitive psychology and the behavioral sciences, psychiatry and human development. This attitude towards AI research was present early on from the beginning with Turing, Minsky and Simon. There is hardly any ethical concern to be brought about in connection with it, and this is particularly true if we consider its software-based (abstract and non-invasive) methodology.[1] As intelligence is distinctive of the human, this approach to AI can in principle deliver an improved understanding of our own nature.
- **Scruffy type II**. The system builders are primarily committed to deliver AI systems that can learn for themselves from experience and change their environment, be it physical or virtual. This form of AI needs essentially two skills: perception or the ability to recognize things, and control or the ability to do things in its environment. So the recent success in image, speech and natural language processing, that is, in the semantic interpretation of opaque data, is for sure a step forward towards it. This attitude towards AI research is more recent and arguably flourished with the emergence of large AI projects in the big tech companies. it holds promise to deliver value by pushing the amount of automation in industry to the next level. It is key for applications such as tumor detection, face and speech recognition, language translation and self-driving cars. It can also replace workers in dangerous jobs. However, hand in hand with this great value there is increasing social concern that it shall lead to significant job losses, privacy risks and concentration of power.

---

[1] And yet, as mentioned, these types of attitude towards AI do have some overlapping. It is worth noting that Simon's RAND-corporation collaboration with DARPA during the Cold War has something of the scruffy type II as well (e.g., cf. [26]).

– **Neats**. The computer epistemologists are primarily concerned with the study of reasoning and the delivery of AI systems that can truly interact with us humans in our own language. This form of AI needs essentially one skill: knowing or the ability to understand and form new ideas and judgements, perhaps even structured theories, which must be communicated and explained in a conversation. This approach to AI is key for achieving non-shallow chatbots and personal assistants, question answering and domain-specific reasoning and decision making in, say, law, science and engineering, healthcare and so on. It is also important, of course, in teaching AI. It has cross-fertilization with analytic philosophy and logics.

We hope that this description of types and their implications for the future of AI can be helpful for the AI community in its reflection about methodologies.

## 6    Conclusion

In the history of AI as a discipline, researchers tended to adopt either a neat or a scruffy (of whatever type) approach and seldom both. It is important to recognize that the forms of AI derived from each of them are in fact essentially different and hard to integrate. In spite of that, recently an approach to AI called hybrid or neurosymbolic AI has been proposed. This purportedly hybrid approach to AI needs to be tested by time and deserves a dedicated study.

In this paper we have striven to describe the state of affairs within AI research. Hopefully this descriptive effort can be of value for the AI community to make a step forward in its own reflection towards the future.

## References

1. Brooks, R.: Is the brain a good model for machine intelligence? Nature **482**, 462–3 (2012). https://doi.org/10.1038/482462a
2. Chomsky, N.: Language and nature. Mind **104**(413), 1–61 (1995). https://doi.org/10.1093/mind/104.413.1
3. Cozman, F.: No canal da Inteligência Artificial: nova temporada dos desgrenhados e empertigados. Estudos Avançados **35**(101), 7–20 (2021). https://doi.org/10.1590/s0103-4014.2021.35101.002
4. Darwiche, A.: Human-level intelligence or animal-like abilities? Commun. ACM **61**(10), 56–67 (2018)
5. Dijkstra, E.: The threats to computing science. In: Talk delivered at the ACM 1984 South Central Regional Conference, November 16–18, Austin, Texas (November 1984). http://www.cs.utexas.edu/users/EWD/transcriptions/EWD08xx/EWD898.html. Accessed 10 Jun 2021
6. Gonçalves, B.: Machines will think: structure and interpretation of Alan Turing's imitation game. Ph.D. thesis, Faculty of Philosophy, Languages and Human Sciences, University of São Paulo, São Paulo (March 2021). http://dx.doi.org/10.11606/T.8.2021.tde-10062021-173217
7. Hartree, D.: Calculating Instruments and Machines. University of Illinois Press, Champaign (1949)

8. Hayes, P., Ford, K.: Turing test considered harmful. In: Proceedings of the 14th International Joint Conference on Artificial Intelligence (IJCAI 1995), pp. 972–7 (1995)
9. Hudson, M.: IA researchers allege that machine learning is alchemy. Science (3 May 2018). http://dx.doi.org/10.1126/science.aau0577
10. Katz, Y.: Noam Chomsky on where artificial intelligence went wrong: An extended conversation with the legendary linguist. The Atlantic (1 Nov 2012) (2012). http://www.theatlantic.com/technology/archive/2012/11/noam-chomsky-on-where-artificial-intelligence-went-wrong/261637/
11. LeCun, Y.: My take on ali rahimi's "test of time" award talk at nips. https://www.facebook.com/yann.lecun/posts/10154938130592143. Accessed 3 June 2021
12. Lenat, D., Feigenbaum, E.: On the thresholds of knowledge. Artif. Intell. **47**(1–3), 185–250 (1991). https://doi.org/10.1016/0004-3702(91)90055-O
13. Lenat, D.: Cyc: a large-scale investment in knowledge infrastructure. Commun. ACM **38**, 33–8 (1995)
14. McCarthy, J.: Programs with common sense. In: Proceedings of the Teddington Conference on the Mechanization of Thought Processes, Her Majesty's Stationery Office, London (December 1958). http://www-formal.stanford.edu/jmc/mcc59.pdf. Accessed 3 June 2021
15. McCorduck, P.: Machines Who think: a Personal Inquiry into the History and Prospects of Artificial Intelligence. A. K. Peters, second edn. CRC Press, Boca Raton (2004 [1979])
16. Minsky, M.: Some methods of heuristic programming and artificial intelligence. In: Blake, D.V., Uttley, A.M. (eds.) Proceedings of the Symposium on Mechanisation of Thought Processes, vol. 2, H. M. Stationery Office, London (1959)
17. Minsky, M.: Steps toward artificial intelligence. Proc. IRE **49**, 8–30 (1961). https://doi.org/10.1109/JRPROC.1961.287775
18. Minsky, M.: The Society of Mind. Simon & Schuster, New York (1985)
19. Minsky, M.: Smart Machines. In: Brockman, J. (ed.) The Third Culture: Beyond the Scientific Revolution, chap. 8. Simon & Schuster, New York (1995)
20. Nilsson, N.: The Quest for Artificial Intelligence. Cambridge University Press, Cambridge (2009)
21. Norvig, P.: On chomsky and the two cultures of statistical learning (2012). http://norvig.com/chomsky.html. Accessed 3 June 2021
22. Pearl, J.: The Book of Why. Basic Books, New York (2019)
23. Rahimi, A., Recht, B.: NIPS "test-of-time award" keynote address (2017). http://www.youtube.com/watch?v=Qi1Yry33TQE. Accessed 3 June 2021
24. Russell, S., Norvig, P.: Artificial Intelligence: a Modern Approach. 1st edn. Prentice Hall, Hoboken (1995), ISBN 0-13-103805-2
25. Russell, S., Norvig, P.: Artificial Intelligence: a Modern Approach. Pearson Series in Artificial Intelligence, Pearson, 4th edn. (2020). ISBN 9781292401133
26. Sent, E.M.: Herbert A. Simon as a cyborg scientist. Perspect. Sci. **8**(4), 380–406 (2000). https://doi.org/10.1162/106361400753373759
27. Simon, H.: Artificial intelligence: an empirical science. Artif. Intell. **77**(1), 95–127 (1995). https://doi.org/10.1016/0004-3702(95)00039-H
28. Simon, H.: The Sciences of the Artificial. 3rd edn. MIT Press, Cambridge (1996 [1969])
29. Simon, H., Newell, A.: Human problem solving: the state of the theory in 1970. Am. Psychol. **26**(2), 141–59 (1971). https://doi.org/10.1037/h0030806

30. Sutton, R.: The bitter lesson. http://incompleteideas.net/IncIdeas/BitterLesson. html. Accessed 15 June 2021
31. Turing, A.M.: Computing machinery and intelligence. Mind LIX (236), 433–60 (1950). https://doi.org/10.1093/mind/LIX.236.433

# Weapon Engagement Zone Maximum Launch Range Estimation Using a Deep Neural Network

Joao P. A. Dantas[1]($\boxtimes$) iD, Andre N. Costa[1] iD, Diego Geraldo[1] iD,
Marcos R. O. A. Maximo[2] iD, and Takashi Yoneyama[3] iD

[1] Decision Support Systems Subdivision, Institute for Advanced Studies,
Sao Jose dos Campos - SP 12.288-001, Brazil
{dantasjpad,negraoanc,diegodg}@fab.mil.br
[2] Autonomous Computational System Lab (LAB-SCA), Computer Science Division,
Aeronautics Institute of Technology, Sao Jose dos Campos - SP 12228-900, Brazil
mmaximo@ita.br
[3] Electronic Engineering Division, Aeronautics Institute of Technology,
Sao Jose dos Campos - SP 12228-900, Brazil
takashi@ita.br
http://www.ieav.cta.br, http://www.comp.ita.br/labsca/,
http://www.ele.ita.br

**Abstract.** This work investigates the use of a Deep Neural Network
(DNN) to perform an estimation of the Weapon Engagement Zone
(WEZ) maximum launch range. The WEZ allows the pilot to identify
an airspace in which the available missile has a more significant probability of successfully engaging a particular target, i.e., a hypothetical
area surrounding an aircraft in which an adversary is vulnerable to a
shot. We propose an approach to determine the WEZ of a given missile
using 50,000 simulated launches in variate conditions. These simulations
are used to train a DNN that can predict the WEZ when the aircraft
finds itself on different firing conditions, with a coefficient of determination of 0.99. It provides another procedure concerning preceding research
since it employs a non-discretized model, i.e., it considers all directions
of the WEZ at once, which has not been done previously. Additionally,
the proposed method uses an experimental design that allows for fewer
simulation runs, providing faster model training.

**Keywords:** Weapon engagement zone · Deep neural network · Air
combat

## 1 Introduction

Within simulated computational environments, military systems must resemble
reality in a level of fidelity that leads to useful conclusions [15]. This is done
through the use of reliable computational models, that are deemed to encompass
the main characteristics of the systems they represent [16].

© Springer Nature Switzerland AG 2021
A. Britto and K. Valdivia Delgado (Eds.): BRACIS 2021, LNAI 13074, pp. 193–207, 2021.
https://doi.org/10.1007/978-3-030-91699-2_14

When dealing with air combat, one of the most critical parts to be modeled is the missile. This is true concerning both the missile system itself and the decision of when to employ it, i.e., to fire. That is even more critical when considering Beyond Visual Range (BVR) air combat since this decision must be taken based only on what the situational awareness systems display to the pilot [11].

In the context of constructive simulations, in which the aircraft behave autonomously, there is a need to provide their controlling algorithms with data similar to what real pilots would receive, so that the behaviors perform in accordance [9]. One of the most important aspects that a pilot can use to decide whether to launch a missile on an opposing aircraft is the Weapon Engagement Zone (WEZ), which, in simple terms, represents the range of the weapon [10]. This definition is discussed with more depth further in Sect. 2.1. The determination of this range is not a simple task, however, since it is influenced by a series of variables from both the shooter and the target. Moreover, it is naturally dependent on the missile itself. In this work, we propose an approach to determine the WEZ of a given missile using a series of simulated launches in variate conditions. These simulations are used to train a machine learning algorithm that can predict the WEZ when the aircraft finds itself on different firing conditions. Previous works have employed some types of Artificial Neural Networks (ANN), such as Wavelet Neural Networks (WNN) [29] and a Multi Layer Perceptron (MLP) with Bayesian Regularization of Artificial Neural Networks (BRANN) [4], to make predictions of the WEZ, also from previously simulated data. Purely mathematical approaches are also available within the literature, such as [14] and [23], but they provide an intermediate step between unrealistic missile models that consider fixed missile ranges and more complex models based on simulations.

Much more research may have been developed within companies and governments concerning WEZ determination [5], but this is still seldom publicly available. The contribution of this work is employing a Deep Neural Network (DNN) with a novel non-discretized model, i.e. the model considers all directions of the WEZ at once, not discretizing the off-boresight angle (Fig. 5) as done previously to the best of our knowledge. Additionally, it uses an experimental design that allows for a lower number of simulation runs, which provides a faster training of the model.

The remainder of this paper is organized as follows. Section 2 provides the background, explaining in more depth the concept of WEZ, as well as presenting the particular missile model employed and the experimental design utilized. In Sect. 3, the proposed methodology is detailed, whereas the results coming from it are presented and analyzed in Sect. 4. Finally, Sect. 5 states the main conclusions of the work and suggests some future developments.

## 2    Background

In this section, we detail the concept of WEZ, present the missile model, and specify the simulation experimental design used within this work.

## 2.1  Weapon Engagement Zone

The term WEZ may present different definitions throughout the military domain. According to the United States Department of Defense [25], WEZ can be described as an "airspace of defined dimensions within which the responsibility for engagement of air threats normally rests with a particular weapon system." Although being a rather broad definition, its focus resides on the responsibility for engagement of target that is inside the zone by a specific system.

In our work, on the other hand, we are more focused on the airspace defined by the range of a weapon system (missile), which is not necessarily responsible for engaging all threats within this zone. This is rather a possibility, that is, the WEZ in our case allows the pilot to identify an airspace in which the missile available has a larger probability of being successful in engaging a particular target. In other words, the definition of WEZ adopted by us is similar to what Portrey *et al.* [27] present: a hypothetical area surrounding an aircraft in which an adversary is vulnerable to a shot. This concept can be found in the literature under different terminologies which may present subtle variations on meaning, such as Launch Acceptability Region (LAR) [29] and Dynamic Launch Zone (DLZ) [2].

Figure 1 presents a simplified depiction of a WEZ, which stretches from the minimum range $R_{min}$ to the maximum range $R_{max}$. The $R_{max}$ is defined by us as the maximum distance in which the missile will hit a non-maneuvering target, that is, if the target performs any maneuver, the missile will most likely miss if fired at this distance. On the other limit of this zone, the $R_{min}$ is the minimum distance required by the missile to be able to properly activate its systems and, therefore, trigger its warhead. Between these two ranges, there is the no-escape zone (NEZ) range ($R_{NEZ}$), which represents a distance within which the target is very unlikely to be able to evade the missile, even when employing a high-performance defensive maneuver.

It is important to point out that the WEZ is also a function of the threat since it takes into consideration the parameters of the target in its calculation. As Portrey *et al.* [27] state, the WEZ is determined by many factors regarding both the shooter and the target, such as "type of weapon, aircraft speed, relative altitudes, and geometry." These factors are used by the authors of [27] to define a metric that allows the pilot to know what is the amount of G-force that must be pulled to escape from an incoming missile. Therefore, their focus was less on the definition of the WEZ per se, but rather on the determination of this particular metric.

On the other hand, Birkmire [5], focuses precisely on the determination of the WEZ for a missile in the context of virtual simulations, i.e., simulations in which real pilots interact with simulated systems. Therefore, his goal was to provide the pilots in virtual environments with a similar estimation of the WEZ as pilots in real aircraft have in their heads-up displays (HUDs) to support their decisions to fire a missile (Fig. 2).

Our work has a slightly different focus since it aims to provide WEZ information to autonomous agents within a constructive simulation environment,

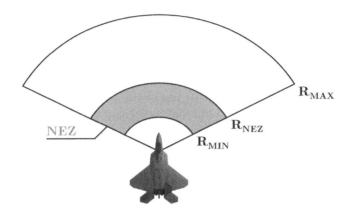

**Fig. 1.** Simplified WEZ representation.

i.e., a simulation in which simulated pilots interact with simulated systems. In addition, we provide a map visualization of the estimated WEZ, which can be valuable within the analysis of this type of simulation.

### 2.2   Missile Model

Since this is not the focus of this work, inasmuch as the methodology presented may be applied to any simulated missile, we just provide a brief overview of the missile model. Our implementation is completely done in the R programming language [19] and it provides a simplified model with 5°C of freedom (5DOF) of a Fox 3 missile-based on [12]. According to [1], Fox is a brevity code that refers to the guidance of a missile, in which type 3 stands for an active radar-guided missile, i.e., a missile which contains a seeker of its own that can track the target autonomously after reaching its activation distance. Still, with regards to its guidance, the missile performs perfect proportional navigation concerning its target, maneuvering to exactly comply with its guidance law, as well as a loft maneuver (i.e., an aggressive climb right after launch) whenever possible, as Fig. 3 shows.

The model simulates the missile trajectory considering either a still or a maneuvering target. To define the NEZ range, the simulation considers a high-performance maneuver of +5 G, which may be employed with a delay from the moment of launch. Some important metrics for the missile flight are provided in Fig. 4.

Referring to Fig. 4, the most straightforward metric is the mass (a). Since the missile operates with a boost-sustain motor [24], its mass decays almost linearly during its boost (burn) phase. Due to the loft maneuver, angle of attack values (b) vary very aggressively at the beginning of the flight, which can also be observed on the pitch angle (theta) chart (c). Concerning heading (psi), there are some maneuvers to respond to the high-performance evasion that the target

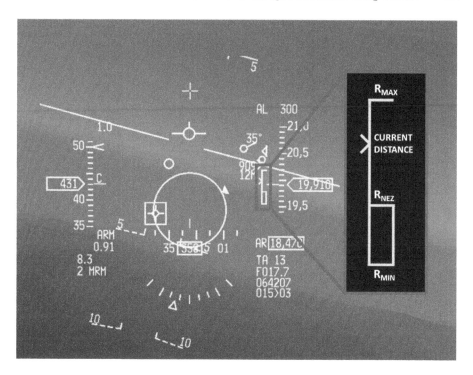

**Fig. 2.** HUD representation with focus on the WEZ indication. Source: Adapted from [22].

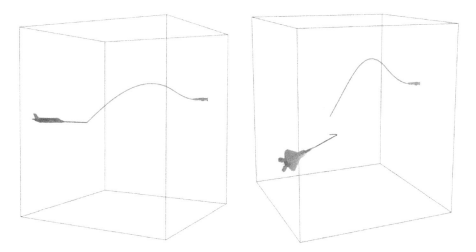

**Fig. 3.** Missile simulated trajectory samples.

employs (d). Accelerations in the East (e) and Down (f) axis in the NED coordinate system [8] are also very abrupt due to the loft maneuver and the target

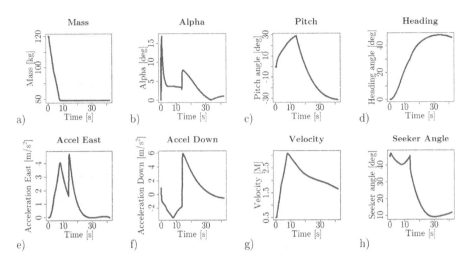

**Fig. 4.** Missile trajectory metrics samples.

response, respectively. The velocity (g) steadily increases during burn time and decays on the sustain phase. Finally, the seeker angle (h) accounts for the proportional navigation, being defined as the deviation of the shooter's longitudinal axis from the off-boresight angle (Fig. 5).

### 2.3   Experimental Design

The parameters used as inputs to our missile model (Table 1) are very similar to the ones presented in [5], which makes it easier to compare our results with the ones obtained by it. However, instead of using an implementation in MATLAB Simulink [21], our model was implemented entirely on R language as aforementioned, which has many prepackaged programs that help to solve analytical problems, prioritizing the simplicity of understanding and the parametrization. To provide a common understanding of the angles used, Fig. 5 provides a depiction of them.

These parameters are selected based on operational experience and the missile model possibilities. The shooter's velocity and altitude are directly related to the energy that will be available to the missile. In particular, the launch altitude also influences the drag to which the missile will be subjected during flight, which is also true concerning the target altitude on the missile final approach. Target's velocity can either help or hinder the missile's effectiveness, depending on its heading. However, heading alone cannot provide a full account with regards to positioning, since this is dependent on the off-boresight angle to determine whether the target aircraft is getting closer to the shooter and, therefore, to the missile itself. At last, the shooter's pitch angle at the moment of launch may help the initial maneuvering of the missile, that is, its loft maneuver.

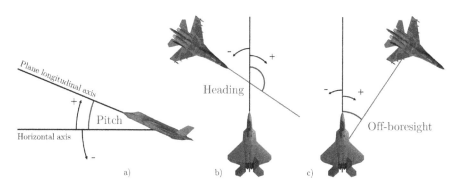

**Fig. 5.** Pitch (a), heading (b), and off-boresight (c) angles with respect to the target aircraft.

Instead of a full factorial experiment as [5] presented, we tried to reduce the number of simulation runs by means of a more sophisticated design that takes into account randomness in its formation. Alternatively of a Monte Carlo simulation (MCS) that simply randomly samples the search space [17], we used the Latin Hypercube Sampling (LHS), which is deemed to be more efficient [13].

The LHS is a near-random method, which aims at a better coverage of the search space, since a purely random approach may concentrate the samples by chance. Its main idea is to divide the multidimensional space so that the random samples are drawn from these subdivisions instead of the whole search space [18]. In our particular case, we employed a maximin algorithm, which attempts to optimize the sample through the maximization of the minimum distance between design points, fulfilling the constraints established by the LHS method. Table 1 presents the intervals for each variable used in the sampling. These limits were defined by subject matter experts, in this case, pilots, which considered meaningful values concerning their operational context.

**Table 1.** Model parameters with the respective intervals considered.

| Parameter | Variable | Min. | Max. | Unit |
|---|---|---|---|---|
| Shooter altitude | Alt_sht | 1,000 | 45,000 | Feet |
| Shooter velocity | Vel_sht | 400 | 600 | Knots |
| Shooter pitch | Pit_sht | −45 | 45 | Degrees |
| Target altitude | Alt_tgt | 1,000 | 45,000 | Feet |
| Target velocity | Vel_tgt | 400 | 600 | Knots |
| Target heading | Hdg_tgt | −180 | 180 | Degrees |
| Target off-boresight | Rgt_tgt | −60 | 60 | Degrees |

# 3  Methodology

This section contains the description of the preprocessing, training and evaluation of the DNN model that is applied on the data coming from the simulation.

## 3.1  Simulation

After creating the input batch files, through LHS and with the limits presented previously, 50,000 simulations were run using 2 Intel Xeon Silver 4210R CPUs with 2.40GHz and 128 GB of RAM. It took approximately 7 h to execute all the simulations, which generated an output file containing the maximum range of the missile for the respective input conditions.

## 3.2  Preprocessing

From that, an Exploratory Data Analysis (EDA) was performed to identify general behaviors of the output data. The methods employed in this analysis were: histogram, boxplots, correlation, and descriptive statistics.

Before performing the training of the ANN, some feature engineering techniques were employed. The first one was a form of encoding to better deal with cyclical features. The angles related to aircraft heading and off-boresight were encoded into their sine and cosine counterparts as done in [26], slightly increasing our model performance.

In addition, a form of handling potential outliers was to perform downsampling of the Latin Hypercube design. This was done because the pre-established intervals generated some improbable conditions. For instance, an aircraft at 1,000 ft firing on a target at 45,000 ft is exceedingly rare from the operational standpoint since a pilot would most likely increase its altitude before launching a missile. Therefore, we removed these undesirable samples, like the one presented, from the whole dataset based on subject matter expert operational knowledge, which can vary according to the mission type.

Lastly, data scaling was performed to equally distribute the importance of each input in the ANN learning process [28]. This was done through a min-max scaler, which individually scales and translates all data features to a range from 0 to 1 [7].

## 3.3  Model Training

Before training the DNN, a train-validate-test split was performed, allocating 80% for training and validation using a 5-fold cross-validation technique, and 20% for testing. This division is done randomly and will allow the evaluation of the machine learning model later. The DNN model was formed by 12 layers of nodes, with the structure represented in Fig. 6. All nodes have a rectified linear activation function (ReLU) [3].

In addition, the Adaptive Moment Estimation (Adam) optimizer was employed, an extremely popular training algorithm for ANN [6]. Adam is a stochastic gradient descent method based on adaptive estimation of first- and second-order moments function [20], which, in our case, aimed to minimize the Mean-Squared Error (MSE) loss. This was monitored by an early stopping method that checked whether the validation set metric had stopped improving (the patience, i.e., the number of epochs to wait before early stop if no progress on the validation set, was set to 20).

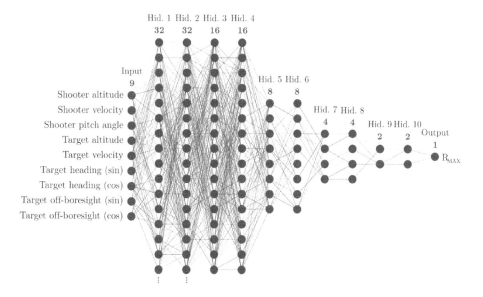

**Fig. 6.** Proposed DNN architecture.

### 3.4   Model Evaluation

As the model being analyzed deals with a regression problem, the evaluation of the model will be carried out observing the following metrics: Mean Absolute Error (MAE), Mean Squared Error (MSE), Root Mean Squared Error (RMSE), and coefficient of determination ($R^2$).

## 4   Results and Analysis

This section examines the exploratory data analysis and the test dataset metrics. Additionally, it provides a Multi-Function Display (MFD) representation, focusing on the WEZ indication based on the proposed model.

### 4.1   Exploratory Data Analysis

Initially, an overview of the descriptive statistics of the model's input and output variables was observed, as shown in Table 2. The input variables of the model follow a uniform distribution since these variables were sampled using the LHS. The model's output variable presents great variability with an average of 12.38 NM and a standard deviation (std) of 9.37 NM. Notice that the mean and median (50%) are varying by 3.24 NM, which indicates a considerable amount of outliers for this variable at the top of the distribution. These outliers will be eliminated from a superior threshold value (33.28 NM), which is not the maximum value (max), but is rather the largest value of the sampling excluding outliers, based on the interquartile range ($75\% - 25\%$). Observing the minimum (min), values of the order of 0.08 NM can be found, which shows that in the dataset there are values in the target variable (`max_range`) that are smaller than the minimum activation distance of the missile modeled. For this case, this distance is considered to be 2 km (1.079 NM), which is the inferior threshold. So that the model would not be harmed in its training to try to predict the maximum missile range distance values, samples in which the model's output variable was smaller than the minimum missile activation distance were removed from the dataset. A histogram and a boxplot were generated together to visualize the distribution and the thresholds of the target variable, which can be seen in Fig. 7.

**Table 2.** Descriptive statistics of the model's input and output variables.

| | alt_sht (ft) | vel_sht (kt) | pit_sht (deg) | alt_tgt (ft) | vel_tgt (kt) | hdg_tgt (deg) | rgt_tgt (deg) | max_range (NM) |
|---|---|---|---|---|---|---|---|---|
| Mean | 23,000.00 | 500.00 | 0.00 | 23,000.00 | 500.00 | 0.00 | 0.00 | 12.38 |
| Std | 12,701.83 | 57.74 | 25.98 | 12,701.83 | 57.74 | 103.92 | 34.64 | 9.37 |
| Min | 1,000.22 | 400.00 | −45.00 | 1,000.82 | 400.00 | −180.00 | −60.00 | 0.08 |
| 25% | 12,000.34 | 450.00 | −22.50 | 12,000.32 | 450.00 | −90.00 | −30.00 | 5.55 |
| 50% | 22,999.96 | 500.00 | 0.00 | 22,999.99 | 500.00 | 0.00 | 0.00 | 9.14 |
| 75% | 33,999.75 | 550.00 | 22.50 | 33,999.76 | 550.00 | 90.00 | 30.00 | 16.64 |
| Max | 44,999.38 | 600.00 | 45.00 | 44,999.42 | 600.00 | 179.99 | 60.00 | 40.87 |

Pearson's correlation analysis of the variables can be seen in the correlation matrix represented in Fig. 8. Notice that none of the model's features has a strong correlation with each other, with the largest absolute value being only 0.30 between shooter's altitude (`alt_sht`) and pitch (`pit_sht`). The performance of the algorithm may deteriorate if two or more variables are tightly related, called multicollinearity. We may also be interested in the correlation between input variables with the output variable (`max_range`) to provide insight into which variables may or may not be relevant as input for developing a model. Only the variables `alt_sht` and `pit_sht` have a slight correlation with the target variable.

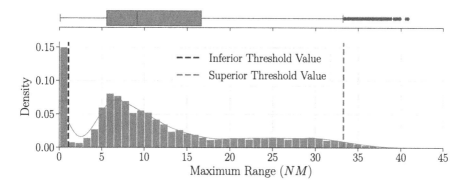

**Fig. 7.** Histogram and boxplot of the target variable.

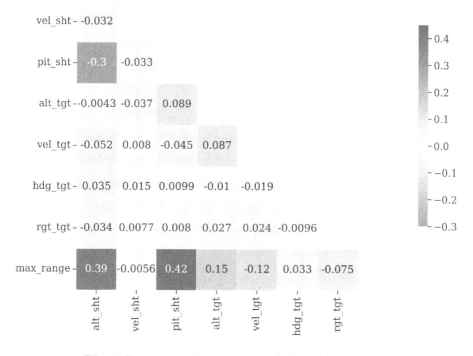

**Fig. 8.** Pearson correlation matrix of all model variables.

## 4.2   Model Predictions

Table 3 shows all the metrics used to evaluate the model with respect to the test set at the end of the training process. Very satisfactory results were found, with a coefficient of determination above 99%, which shows a very consistent model. In addition, note that the MAE was around 0.58 NM, which can be considered a very low value, considering that the values of the target variable have a mean of

13.13 NM with a standard deviation (std) of 8.58 NM. If we consider the RMSE, which penalizes the outliers' effects, the observed value is around 1.10 NM.

Table 3. Metrics used to evaluate the DNN model at the end of the training process.

| MAE (NM) | MSE (NM$^2$) | RMSE (NM) | $R^2$ |
|---|---|---|---|
| 0.58 | 1.23 | 1.10 | 0.99 |

A 5-fold cross-validation was conducted to estimate the skill of a machine learning model on unseen data and will help to better understand our data, giving much more information about our algorithm performance. The metrics of the five-folds were very similar as shown in Table 4. The low variance found between the folds of this sample demonstrates the consistency of the model.

Table 4. 5-fold cross-validations metrics.

|  | MAE (NM) | MSE (NM$^2$) | RMSE (NM) | $R^2$ |
|---|---|---|---|---|
| 1º Fold | 0.54 | 1.06 | 1.03 | 0.99 |
| 2º Fold | 0.62 | 1.22 | 1.10 | 0.99 |
| 3º Fold | 0.71 | 1.39 | 1.18 | 0.98 |
| 4º Fold | 0.52 | 1.08 | 1.04 | 0.99 |
| 5º Fold | 0.57 | 1.34 | 1.16 | 0.98 |
| Mean | 0.59 | 1.22 | 1.10 | 0.99 |
| Std | 0.08 | 0.15 | 0.07 | 0.01 |

### 4.3   Model Representation

We estimated the WEZ Maximum Launch Range from the trained model using one of the samples from the test group. The target's position was varied by changing the off-boresight values from $-60°$ to $+60°$ with steps of $0.5°$. A MFD representation with a focus on the WEZ indication can be seen in Fig. 9. The curve that shows the missile's maximum range proved to be quite consistent, with a continuous aspect throughout the variations of off-boresight angles. Thus, we conclude that employing a different approach, unlike other research, with the incorporation of the off-boresight angle between the reference and the target aircraft as a feature in the model does not affect the performance of the WEZ estimation significantly since the supervised learning model used can be able to generalize well the results obtained in the training dataset to the test dataset.

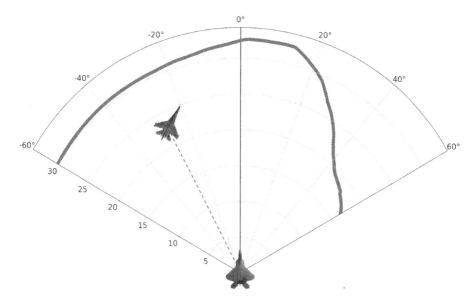

**Fig. 9.** MFD representation with a focus on the WEZ maximum range indication.

# 5   Conclusions and Future Work

Therefore, the main improvements advocated by us with respect to [5] is that, instead of discretizing the WEZ calculation concerning the off-boresight angle between shooter and target (Fig. 4), creating, therefore, several ANNs, we approached the problem considering the whole space defined by the shooter's radar, with only one DNN being able to predict the values of WEZ. In addition, the number of simulation runs was much lower (50,000 runs, as opposed to 222 million in [5]), which was achieved by a more carefully tailored experimental design.

In addition, in this work, a DNN with an MLP architecture was used, and brought better results than an ANN with only one hidden layer, as done in [5], comparing the coefficient of determination of both approaches applied to their respective datasets. In addition, different configurations of training and test groups were used in the dataset using the k-fold cross-validation. For a value of $k = 5$, that is, the training and test group was sampled 5 times, the results found were quite similar among all samples, demonstrating the consistency of the DNN model presented in this work.

The use of feature engineering techniques, with the creation of other model input variables, such as the use of sine and cosine for the variables that represent heading and off-boresight angles, also contributed to greater adequacy of the model to the dataset collected from the simulations. Furthermore, it was observed, with the use of operational knowledge, that some of the samples collected would be unlikely to occur in a real air combat environment. These cases were when, for example, at a given altitude, the speeds of a given agent should meet at certain speed intervals. In the dataset some samples were not respecting these intervals, which could impair the model's performance, trying to predict cases that would most likely not occur in a real situation. To avoid these problems, these samples were eliminated from the dataset.

Future work should investigate how possible improvements in the architecture used for the DNN can bring better results and be more efficient, i.e. with a lower computational cost in the training process. In addition, the results found in this work can be compared with the use of other supervised machine learning techniques. These comparisons will help to determine the most appropriate methodology for calculating WEZ. In addition, in future work, it is possible to carry out calculations not only of the maximum range but also the distances related to the NEZ or even intermediate distances that could provide pilots with more assertive information about the probabilities of a missile reaching its target. Also, more advanced simulation models of the missile may be used in the future to provide better reliability to the presented results.

**Acknowledgments.** This work was supported by Finep (Reference n$^{\underline{o}}$ 2824/20). Takashi Yoneyama is partially funded by CNPq – National Research Council of Brazil through the grant 304134/2-18-0.

# References

1. Air Land Sea Application Center: Brevity: Multi-Service Tactics, Techniques, and Procedures for Multi-Service Brevity Codes (2020)
2. Alkaher, D., Moshaiov, A.: Dynamic-escape-zone to avoid energy-bleeding coasting missile. J. Guidance Control Dyn. **38**(10), 1908–1921 (2015)
3. Bengio, Y., Goodfellow, I., Courville, A.: Deep learning, vol. 1. MIT press Massachusetts, USA (2017)
4. Birkmire, B., Gallagher, J.: Air-to-air missile maximum launch range modeling using a multilayer perceptron. In: AIAA Modeling and Simulation Technologies Conference, p. 4942 (2012)
5. Birkmire, B.M.: Weapon engagement zone maximum launch range approximation using a multilayer perceptron. Master's thesis, Wright State University (2011)
6. Bock, S., Weiß, M.: A proof of local convergence for the Adam optimizer. In: 2019 International Joint Conference on Neural Networks (IJCNN), pp. 1–8. IEEE (2019)
7. Bonaccorso, G.: Machine Learning Algorithms. Packt Publishing Ltd, Birmingham (2017)
8. Cai, G., Chen, B.M., Lee, T.H.: Coordinate Systems and Transformations. In: Unmanned Rotorcraft Systems, pp. 23–34. Springer, London (2011). https://doi.org/10.1007/978-0-85729-635-1_2
9. Costa, A.N.: Sequential Optimization of Formation Flight Control Method Based on Artificial Potential Fields. Master's Thesis, Instituto Tecnológico de Aeronáutica, São José dos Campos, SP, Brazil (2019)
10. Dantas, J.P.A., Costa, A.N., Geraldo, D., Maximo, M.R.A.O., Yoneyama, T.: Engagement decision support for beyond visual range air combat. In: 2021 Latin American Robotics Symposium (LARS), pp. 1–6 (2021), Accepted for publication
11. Dantas, J.P.A.: Apoio à decisão para o combate aéreo além do alcance visual: uma abordagem por redes neurais artificiais. Master's Thesis, Instituto Tecnológico de Aeronáutica, São José dos Campos, SP, Brazil (2018)

12. Departament of Defense: Military Handbook: Missile Flight Simulation Part One: Surface-to-Air Missiles (MIL-HDBK-1211) (1995)
13. Deutsch, J.L., Deutsch, C.V.: Latin hypercube sampling with multidimensional uniformity. J. Stat. Planning Infer. **142**(3), 763–772 (2012)
14. Farlik, J., Casar, J., Stary, V.: Simplification of missile effective coverage zone in air defence simulations. In: 2017 International Conference on Military Technologies (ICMT), pp. 733–737. IEEE (2017)
15. Hancock, P.A., Vincenzi, D.A., Wise, J.A., Mouloua, M.: Human Factors in Simulation and Training. CRC Press, Boca Raton (2008)
16. Hill, R.R., Miller, J.O., McIntyre, G.A.: Applications of discrete event simulation modeling to military problems. In: Proceeding of the 2001 Winter Simulation Conference (Cat. No. 01CH37304), vol. 1, pp. 780–788. IEEE (2001)
17. Homem-de-Mello, T., Bayraksan, G.: Monte carlo sampling-based methods for stochastic optimization. Surv. Oper. Res. Manage. Sci. **19**(1), 56–85 (2014)
18. Husslage, B.G., Rennen, G., Van Dam, E.R., Den Hertog, D.: Space-filling Latin hypercube designs for computer experiments. Optim. Eng. **12**(4), 611–630 (2011)
19. Ihaka, R., Gentleman, R.: R: a language for data analysis and graphics. J. Comput. Graph. Stat. **5**(3), 299–314 (1996)
20. Kingma, D.P., Ba, J.: Adam: a method for stochastic optimization. arXiv preprint arXiv:1412.6980 (2014)
21. Klee, H.: Simulation of Dynamic Systems with MATLAB and Simulink. CRC Press, Boca Raton (2018)
22. Kravchenko, M.: Future UI. https://br.pinterest.com/krava88/future-ui/. Accessed 06 Nov 2021
23. Li, A., Meng, Y., He, Z.: Simulation research on new model of air-to-air missile attack zone. In: 2020 IEEE 4th Information Technology, Networking, Electronic and Automation Control Conference (ITNEC), vol. 1, pp. 1998–2002. IEEE (2020)
24. Noaman, D., Noaman, M., Mahir, D., Rami, A., Faiz, D., et al.: Boost-sustain missile motor performance with fixed predetermined coast time interval. Eur. J. Mol. Clin. Med. **7**(2), 5070–5079 (2020)
25. Office of the Chairman of the Joint Chiefs of Staff, Washington DC: DOD Dictionary of Military and Associated Terms (2021)
26. Petnehází, G.: Recurrent neural networks for time series forecasting. arXiv preprint arXiv:1901.00069 (2019)
27. Portrey, A.M., Schreiber, B., Winston, B.: The pairwise escape-g metric: a measure for air combat maneuvering performance. In: Proceedings of the Winter Simulation Conference, 2005. p. 8. IEEE (2005)
28. Priddy, K.L., Keller, P.E.: Artificial Neural Networks: an Introduction, vol. 68. SPIE Press, Bellingham (2005)
29. Yoon, K.S., Park, J.H., Kim, I.G., Ryu, K.S.: New modeling algorithm for improving accuracy of weapon launch acceptability region. In: 29th Digital Avionics Systems Conference, p. 6-D. IEEE (2010)

# Neural Networks, Deep Learning and Computer Vision

# Code Autocomplete Using Transformers

Gabriel T. Meyrer[1]([✉]) [iD], Denis A. Araújo[1] [iD], and Sandro J. Rigo[2] [iD]

[1] CWI Software, São Leopoldo, Brazil
{gabriel.meyrer,denis.araujo}@cwi.com.br
[2] Applied Computing Graduate Program, UNISINOS, São Leopoldo, Brazil
rigo@unisinos.br

**Abstract.** In software development, code autocomplete can be an essential tool in order to accelerate coding. However, many of these tools built into the IDEs are limited to suggesting only methods or arguments, often presenting to the user long lists of irrelevant items. Since innovations introduced by transformer-based models that have reached the state of the art performance in tasks involving natural language processing (NLP), the application of these models also in tasks involving code intelligence, such as code completion, has become a frequent object of study in recent years. In these paper, we present a transformer-based model trained on 1.2 million Java files gathered from top-starred Github repositories. Our evaluation approach was based on measuring the model's ability to predict the completion of a line, proposing a new metric to measure the applicability of the suggestions that we consider better adapted to the practical reality of the code completion task. With a recently developed Java web project as test set, our experiments showed that in 55.9% of the test cases the model brought at least one suggestion applicable, while the best baseline model presented this in 26.5%.

**Keywords:** Code completion · Deep learning

## 1 Introduction

When building digital solutions, combining good practices of code quality and standardization with fast development is one of the challenges in the field of Software Engineering. In this context of productivity, associated with Integrated Development Environments (IDEs) and often used by developers, code completion can be an essential tool in order to accelerate coding [10].

Many traditional code completion systems works recommending all possible methods or attributes. Although, the list of suggestions is often long, requiring the user to scroll through many irrelevant items. To supply this, intelligent code completion systems propose to reduce these lists to relevant items given the context being edited [1,10,13]. However, many of them work exclusively suggesting only methods or arguments [12], that is, not able to complete longer code sequences by suggesting them both together, increasing productivity.

© Springer Nature Switzerland AG 2021
A. Britto and K. Valdivia Delgado (Eds.): BRACIS 2021, LNAI 13074, pp. 211–222, 2021.
https://doi.org/10.1007/978-3-030-91699-2_15

Since innovations introduced by transformer-based solutions such as Bidirectional Encoder Representations from Transformers (BERT) [2], Generative Pre-trained Transformer (GPT) [11] and XLNet [17], natural language processing (NLP) tasks has significantly expanded its range of possibilities in recent years. Dismissing recurrence or convolutions, the transformers model architecture has reached state of the art results in translation tasks mainly based on attention mechanisms [16]. Thus, the application of these models also in tasks involving code intelligence such as code completion has become a frequent target [3,5,7,12,14].

Even though it has aroused great interest and stimulated much work, there are some open research points in this area. The appropriate use of meaningful datasets for the tasks, modeling and evaluation aspects are among the observed challenges. So our work was developed with this context in perspective. The first contribution of this paper is a transformer-based model trained on 1.2 million Java files focused on code completion. As the second contribution, we point out a new method of evaluating code completion systems, proposing a new metric that we consider closer to measuring the applicability of the suggestion in the real world of software development.

The paper is structured as follows: Sect. 2 discusses the context of related works. After that, Sect. 3 describes our approach for building the corpus, model definition and training. In Sect. 4, we define our model evaluation methodology, and propose a new code completion evaluation metric by arguing how the standard metrics that we are aware of can be problematic in this context. Section 5 presents the results of the experiments and, finally, Sect. 6 concludes this work.

## 2   Related Work

This section summarizes selected papers in the area, highlighting their objectives, results, techniques, and parameters used. The papers were obtained in a non-systematic review considering the main topics involved in Machine Learning applied to code autocomplete tasks.

A challenge when applying standard language models to tasks like code completion consists of out-of-vocabulary (OOV) words, which can be understood as words that were not observed during training and become unpredictable for many models. This problem can strongly affect the performance since the software developers can create any identifier needed on the code, which is not a frequent problem in natural language tasks [4]. Jian Li et al. [6] proposes a solution for that presenting what they called a pointer mixture network. Based on the context, the proposed model learns to regenerate an OOV word locally repeated through a pointer copy mechanism, and generate a within vocabulary word through an RNN component. To build the training corpus, the source codes were represented in the form of abstract syntax tree (AST). It was evaluated different approaches with JavaScript and Python datasets, totaling 150,000 files each stored in the AST format.

Although, as demonstrated by Rafael-Michael Karampatsis et al. [4], advanced approaches such as variations of the Byte-Pair Encoding (BPE) algorithm can not only deal well with the OOV problem, but also reduce the vocabulary size. Having the BPE as a principle of the tokenization strategy, the GPT-2 [11] is a 1.5B parameter Transformer [16] that performs state of the art results in several natural language tasks. Recently, this model started to be widely explored also for code intelligence tasks.

In this context, Alexey Svyatkovskiy et al. [12] introduces GPT-C, which is a variant of GPT-2 trained from scratch using a large set of data files that comprises over 1.2 billion lines of source code in JavaScript, TypeScript, C# and Python. As the evaluation of the model's quality, besides the perplexity, was used another two metrics to capture string similarity between suggested and expected code: ROUGE-L, which consists of a variant of the Recall-Oriented Understudy for Gisting Evaluation (ROUGE) based on the Longest Common Subsequence (LCS), and Levenshtein edit similarity. The authors consider the last one a critical metric in this context by affirming that developers tend to accept suggestions even partially matching the expectation, that is, requiring edits. The best model presented was trained on Python, reaching an average perplexity of 1.82, ROUGE-L of 0.80 and an edit similarity of 86.7%.

In addition, Shuai Lu et al. [7] also proposes a GPT model for code completion and text-to-code generation, named CodeGPT. The authors present pretrained models for both Python and Java, with datasets that includes respectively 1.1M and 1.6M functions. For each programming language, they have used two training approaches. The first approach trains the model from scratch, which means that weights are randomly initialized and the vocabulary is newly obtained. The other approach uses GPT-2 model as starting point, taking advantage of the predefined weights and keeping the same vocabulary. The evaluation of the models is made both in token-level, measuring the accuracy in predicting the next token, and line-level, measuring the exact match (EM) and the edit similarity. Their best model reaches a score average of 71.28.

Finally, based on the GPT-2 model as well, we find Tabnine [14]. Available for several IDEs, this is a plugin that displays code sequences as suggestions according to the context. However, we are not aware about performance metrics of this solution, as much as architecture details.

## 3    Approach

In this session, we describe the construction of our training corpus, as well as detail the model applied and the training process.

### 3.1    Corpus

We built our corpus selecting public Java projects on Github. In order to increase the probability of obtaining a selection of projects with well-written code, we limited our search for repositories with at least 1500 stars, indicating a good relevance in the community. The corpus is structured in a single text file, using special tokens to delimit the beginning and end of a file, as well as the end of each line. After processing these repositories, we reached 8.12G of total data size, comprising over 1.4 million files and 230 million lines of Java source code.

## 3.2 Model

The Transformers [16] is a type of deep neural network that relies on attention mechanisms for sequence processing, dispensing with recurrence or convolutions. This architecture applies multiple heads of what the authors called *self-attention* mechanism, which enables the model to draw complex correlations between tokens in different levels, taking this data into account when predicting the next tokens in a sequence. This type of network overcomes the state of the art approaches such as recurrent neural networks and long short-term memory in many tasks in the field of natural language processing (NLP) and natural language understanding (NLU). In addition, it requires significantly less time to train as it is able to parallelize.

The architecture of our model is the same as the GPT-2 [11], which is an auto-regressive pre-trained model based on 12 layers of Transformer decoders. In order to take advantage of the pre-defined weights and vocabulary, we used the GPT-2 small version pretrained in English as a starting point. This indicates that the resulting model has the original GPT-2 vocabulary and persists the natural language processing skills.

The process of model fine-tuning with the Java Corpus was done with 1 epoch, 1.6 million steps and 96 h of computing time in a single GPU V100. Throughout this article, we'll refer to our model as *Java8G*.

## 4    Evaluation

In this section, we define our evaluation methodology, where we initially propose the creation of a new metric to measure the applicability of the model's suggestions in code completion, and then we detail how we proceed with the experiments.

### 4.1    DG Evaluation Metric

This far we already know that language models can also be applied to problems involving code intelligence. However, when looking for the best metric to evaluate the model code suggestions, we found that the application of standard metrics (e.g. Levenshtein and BLEU) to evaluate natural language tasks could be problematic when applied to code completion tasks, meaning that they may not measure the real applicability of a code hint.

Motivated by this, we propose a new metric we consider better adapted to the context of code completion. Given two strings *expected* and *prediction*, the DG metric, as formally described in Algorithm 1, calculates the sum of equal

---

**Algorithm 1.** DG Metric

---

**Input:** *String expected, String prediction*
**Output:** *Score*
 1: **function** DGMETRIC(*expected, prediction*)
 2:     *matches* ← 0
 3:     *n* ← *length*(*prediction*)
 4:     **for** *k* ← 1 to *n* **do**
 5:         **if** *expected*[*k*] = *prediction*[*k*] **then**
 6:             *matches* ← *matches* + 1
 7:         **else**
 8:             **break**
 9:         **end if**
10:     **end for**
11:     *score* ← *matches* / *n*
12:     **return** *score*
13: **end function**

---

characters until there is a divergence between *expected* and *prediction*, rated by the *expected* length.

To support the proposed metric, in Fig. 1, we present two practical cases simulating the string comparison between an expected code and the model prediction by applying edit similarity, one of the metrics used to evaluate the IntelliCode models [12], against DG metric. As we can see, in the case A, the strings are relatively close by the edit similarity metric, but there's a big difference between them when we talk about the algorithm logic. In such case, we understand that there's a higher chance of the user skipping the suggestion than accept and edit it to meet the expectation, since it tends to be as less productive as writing the entire sequence. In the other way, we have a lower DG score, showing that only 20% of the prediction could be applied without requiring adaptation.

Now, in the case B, we have a situation where the model effectively suggests part of the expected code, meaning that the user could fully accept the suggestion, but we don't have it reflected on the edit similarity metric. Even more problematic, we have two very different situations for the practical reality of the code completion presenting the same edit similarity score (67.6%). That's not the case for DG score where we have a full match, meaning that the suggestion is perfectly applicable.

## 4.2   Methodology

The DG metric creation and evaluation methodology we defined was based on the attempt to get as close as possible to the practical reality of using a code completion tool. For this purpose, our approach was based on submitting the model to try to complete a line given specific previous contexts, and evaluate the applicability of the predictions in the current line using the DG metric.

To base the execution of the tests we selected a real project of an Web API recently developed with Spring Boot, one of the most popular Java Frameworks

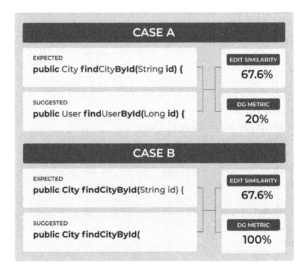

**Fig. 1.** Edit Similarity and DG Metric in code completion

in Web Development. In order to get more insights from the evaluation, we decided to observe the performance in more specific contexts of the project. Thus, we categorized the files in the following groups, which are also often found in other Web API projects: controller, which comprises implementation of classes that handles HTTP requests; service, consisting of classes that implements functionalities and system business rules; test, defining the context of unit testing; generic, for everything else. From this project, we generated 4075 test cases for evaluation.

To define the test cases we worked with the concept of triggers, which can be understood as points of opportunity to display suggestions, like the insertion of characters such as white space, ".", "(" or "@". We consider this examples as triggers for the Java language because we understand them as points where the developer is more likely to seek help from a code completion tool. Therefore, our evaluation system iterates through the project files lines, seeking for triggers to generate test cases, taking what's before the trigger as input and what's next as reference to measure the applicability of the predictions. To exemplify this, the Fig. 2 shows how we structured the test cases. Highlighted in dark gray, we have the marker *endofcontext* right after the trigger "@", meaning that everything before this marker, in white, is the input sent to the model and, in dark green, what will be used as reference for evaluation.

For each test case, we request twice the model to generate two sequences of 16 tokens. For each model prediction, we create two suggestions: the long suggestion (L) and the short suggestion (S). In the Fig. 3 we show highlighted a demonstration of the model suggestions and their types in a plugin developed for IDEA IntelliJ. Therefore, the L suggestions are the complete predictions of the model within the boundary of a line. As an attempt to increase the performance

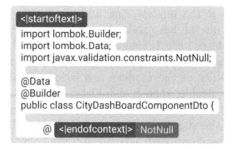

**Fig. 2.** Example of a test case

of the model, the short suggestions presents only a part of the predicted sequence, since we understand that there's a higher probability of the model to correctly predict a short next part of the code than trying to complete the entire line. As shown, the S suggestions are the first alphabetical part of the L suggestions.

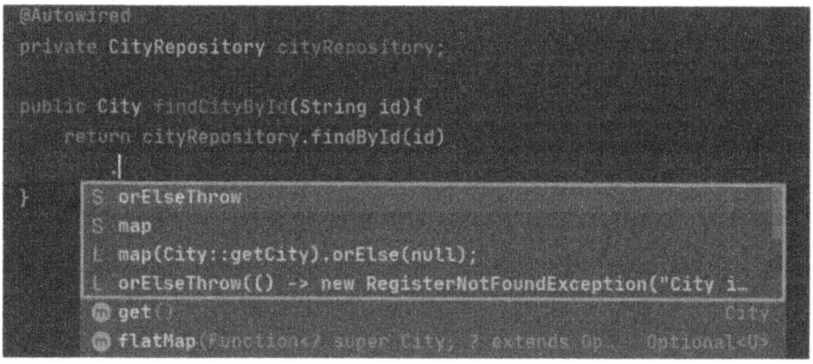

**Fig. 3.** Java8G suggestions on IntelliJ

### 4.3 Baseline

We selected the Microsoft CodeGPT [7] Java model as baseline, since our model is also based on the GPT architecture. We ran the tests with both models versions available on HuggingFace [15]: the CodeGPT [8], which is trained from scratch, and the CodeGPT-Adapted [9], that is pretrained in English as well as our model.

## 5    Results

In this section we present different analyzes and interpretations of the results obtained in the experiments.

In Fig. 4 we present the models long and short suggestions score average in two metrics: DG, on the left, and edit similarity on the right. As we can see, unlike the DG Metric, the L suggestions performed better than S in edit similarity. This highlights the problem of using this metric when you want to measure the applicability of the model's predictions. Since S is part of the L suggestion, if L is applicable, then S should be as well. The opposite happens with the edit similarity because it considers the length of the target to calculate the score, penalizing the suggestion score even with it fully matching a initial part of the target. Therefore, with DG Metric, the S suggestions must have a superior or at least equivalent performance compared to the L suggestion. And, as we can see, the model tends to predict shorter sequences more accurately than longer sequences, meeting the initial expectation regarding the creation of short suggestions.

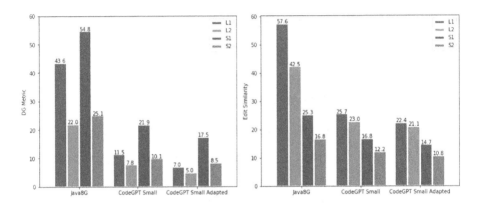

**Fig. 4.** Suggestions DG and Edit Similarity score average

By analysing the Fig. 5, in which we again demonstrate the score average of both DG metric and edit similarity, but this time with the individual results for each code category, we can observe a pattern: in most of the analysis the performance in the controller category presented the best results. Intuitively, by analyzing the code pattern applied in these contexts, we can deduce that, since it is usually formed by blocks of codes that are remarkably often repeated, we understand that it tends to become more easily predictable by the model. The same could explain the lower performance on the service category, where there tend to have fewer patterns or repetitions that can increase the predictive capacity of the model. For ease of reading and comparison, we also present this data in tabular form, in Table 1, adding the average of the metric for each tested model.

Analyzing the average performance of the metrics can give us a good overview of the model's performance. However, since we understand that the developer tends to ignore suggestions that require corrections, the analysis considering partially matching suggestions can be limited. This way, looking deeper into the

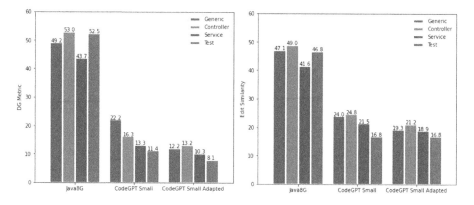

**Fig. 5.** Suggestions DG and Edit Similarity score by category

**Table 1.** Suggestions and Average for DG and Edit Similarity score by category

| Category | Java 8G | | CodeGPT | | CodeGPT-A | |
|---|---|---|---|---|---|---|
| | DG | ES | DG | ES | *DG* | ES |
| Generic | **49.2** | **47.1** | 22.2 | 24.0 | 12.2 | 19.3 |
| Controller | **53.0** | **49.0** | 16.3 | 24.8 | 13.2 | 21.2 |
| Service | **43.7** | **41.6** | 13.3 | 21.5 | 10.3 | 18.9 |
| Test | **52.5** | **46.8** | 11.4 | 16.8 | 8.1 | 16.8 |
| Average | **49.6** | **46.1** | 15.8 | 21.8 | 10.9 | 19.1 |

data, in Fig. 6 we try to answer an important question: of all the test scenarios applied, how many presented at least one full matching suggestion? As we can see, our model in 55% the tests brought at least one full match suggestion, while the best CodeGPT model present this in 26.5% of the cases. Again, we present the view in tabular form in Table 2.

**Table 2.** Presence of full matching suggestions in each test case and Average

| Category | Java 8G | | CodeGPT | | CodeGPT-A | |
|---|---|---|---|---|---|---|
| | DG | ES | DG | ES | DG | ES |
| Generic | **52.9** | **34.3** | 27.3 | 3.0 | 19.1 | 0.1 |
| Controller | **62.3** | **30.4** | 23.8 | 0.1 | 21.6 | 0.3 |
| Service | **50.8** | **21.0** | 19.1 | 2.1 | 16.4 | 2.0 |
| Test | **57.6** | **31.0** | 17.0 | 0.7 | 10.3 | 0.4 |
| Average | **55.9** | **29.2** | 26.5 | 1.5 | 21.0 | 0.7 |

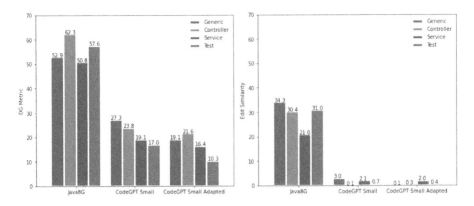

**Fig. 6.** Presence of full matching suggestions in each test case

## 6    Conclusion

We presented a GPT-2 based model trained on 1.2 million Java files focused on code completion. We also introduced the DG Metric, a new approach that we consider closer to measure the applicability of the suggestion in the real world of the software development compared to standard metrics such as Levenshtein that, as we demonstrated, can be problematic.

We also look to run tests on a real and newly developed project, seeking to get a real idea of the model's completion capability in a situation as close to reality as we could simulate. Among different analyzes shown, we demonstrated that our model presented at least one fully applicable suggestion in more than half of the test cases, outperforming in 2 times the baseline models.

The results corroborate, along with other studies in this field, that transformers-based models have great potential in code intelligence tasks. In the future, as also proposed by Alexey Svyatkovskiy et al. [12], we plan to fine-tune the model for user personalization, making the model sensitive to specific standards of each project, enhancing the performance of the suggestions.

## References

1. Bruch, M., Monperrus, M., Mezini, M.: Learning from examples to improve code completion systems. In: Proceedings of the 7th Joint Meeting of the European Software Engineering Conference and the ACM SIGSOFT Symposium on The Foundations of Software Engineering, ESEC/FSE '09, pp. 213–222. Association for Computing Machinery, New York (2020). ISBN 9781605580012, https://doi.org/10.1145/1595696.1595728

2. Devlin, J., Chang, M.W., Lee, K., Toutanova, K.: BERT: pre-training of deep bidirectional transformers for language understanding. In: Proceedings of the 2019 Conference of the North American Chapter of the Association for Computational Linguistics: Human Language Technologies, Minneapolis, Minnesota, vol. 1 (Long and Short Papers), pp. 4171–4186. Association for Computational Linguistics (2019). https://doi.org/10.18653/v1/N19-1423, https://www.aclweb.org/anthology/N19-1423

3. Feng, Z., et al.: CodeBERT: a pre-trained model for programming and natural languages. In: Findings of the Association for Computational Linguistics: EMNLP 2020, pp. 1536–1547. Association for Computational Linguistics (2020). https://doi.org/10.18653/v1/2020.findings-emnlp.139, https://www.aclweb.org/anthology/2020.findings-emnlp.139

4. Karampatsis, R.M., Babii, H., Robbes, R., Sutton, C., Janes, A.: Big code != big vocabulary. In: Proceedings of the ACM/IEEE 42nd International Conference on Software Engineering (2020). https://doi.org/10.1145/3377811.3380342, http://dx.doi.org/10.1145/3377811.3380342

5. Kim, S., Zhao, J., Tian, Y., Chandra, S.: Code prediction by feeding trees to transformers. In: 2021 IEEE/ACM 43rd International Conference on Software Engineering (ICSE), pp. 150–162 (2021). https://doi.org/10.1109/ICSE43902.2021.00026

6. Li, J., Wang, Y., Lyu, M.R., King, I.: Code completion with neural attention and pointer networks. In: Proceedings of the Twenty-Seventh International Joint Conference on Artificial Intelligence (2018). https://doi.org/10.24963/ijcai.2018/578, http://dx.doi.org/10.24963/ijcai.2018/578

7. Shuai, L., et al.: A machine learning benchmark dataset for code understanding and generation, Codexglue (2021)

8. Microsoft Code GPT small Java (2021). https://huggingface.co/microsoft/CodeGPT-small-java, Accessed 18 May 2021

9. Microsoft Code GPT small Java adapted GPT-2 (2021). https://huggingface.co/microsoft/CodeGPT-small-java-adaptedGPT2, Accessed 18 May 2021

10. Proksch, S., Lerch, J., Mezini, M.: Intelligent code completion with bayesian networks. ACM Trans. Softw. Eng. Methodol. 25(1) (2015). ISSN 1049–331X, https://doi.org/10.1145/2744200

11. Radford, A., Wu, J., Child, R., Luan, D., Amodei, D., Sutskever, I.: Language Models are Unsupervised Multitask Learners (2019). https://openai.com/blog/better-language-models/

12. Svyatkovskiy, A., Deng, S.K., Fu, S., Sundaresan, N.: Intellicode compose: code generation using transformer. In: Proceedings of the 28th ACM Joint Meeting on European Software Engineering Conference and Symposium on the Foundations of Software Engineering, ESEC/FSE 2020, New York, NY, USA, pp. 1433–1443. Association for Computing Machinery (2020). ISBN 9781450370431, https://doi.org/10.1145/3368089.3417058

13. Svyatkovskiy, A., Zhao, Y., Fu, S., Sundaresan, N.: Pythia: ai-assisted code completion system. In: Proceedings of the 25th ACM SIGKDD International Conference on Knowledge Discovery & Data Mining (2019). https://doi.org/10.1145/3292500.3330699

14. Tabnine. Code faster with AI completions (2021). https://www.tabnine.com/, Accessed 18 May 2021

15. The AI community building the future (2021). https://huggingface.co/, Accessed 18 May 2021
16. Vaswani, A., et al.: Attention is all you need. In: Proceedings of the 31st International Conference on Neural Information Processing Systems, NIPS'17, Red Hook, NY, USA, pp. 6000–6010. Curran Associates Inc. (2017). ISBN 9781510860964
17. Yang, Z., Dai, Z., Yang, Y., Carbonell, J., Salakhutdinov, R.R., Le, Q.V.: Xlnet: generalized autoregressive pretraining for language understanding. In: Wallach, H., Larochelle, H., Beygelzimer, A., d'Alché-Buc, F., Fox, E., Garnett, R. (eds.) Advances in Neural Information Processing Systems, vol. 32. Curran Associates Inc. (2019). https://proceedings.neurips.cc/paper/2019/file/dc6a7e655d7e5840e66733e9ee67cc69-Paper.pdf

# Deep Convolutional Features
# for Fingerprint Indexing

Leonardo F. da Costa[✉], Lucas S. Fernandes, João P. B. Andrade,
Paulo A. L. Rego, and José G. R. Maia

Federal University of Ceara, Fortaleza, Brazil
{leonardo.costa,lucasdesousafernandes,jpandrade}@alu.ufc.br,
{pauloalr,gilvanm}@ufc.br

**Abstract.** Automatic fingerprint identification systems (AFIS) are among the most used people identification solutions. As the size of fingerprint databases is continuously growing, studying fingerprint indexing mechanisms is desirable to facilitate the search process in a large-scale database. This work presents a method for fingerprint indexing, which uses both exact and approximation methods of nearest neighbors (ANNs), which are very efficient in terms of runtime, even if they sacrifice a little accuracy by presenting approximate solutions. In the presented approach, searches with ANN methods are made from deep embedding vectors extracted from image databases using a convolutional neural network (CNN). In this work, a CNN ResNet18 was used to extract the deep feature embeddings vectors, and the vectors vary in size between 64, 96, and 128. The ANNs methods tested for the query step were ANNOY, NGT, HNSW, and Nanoflann. The results were quite promising when using the FVC fingerprint databases (2000, 2002, and 2004), once we reached 100% hits in the searches with a penetration rate of 1%, with very low run times.

**Keywords:** Fingerprint indexing · Deep feature embedding · CNN · ANN models

## 1 Introduction

The use of fingerprints as a form of authentication and identification has proven to be a robust and efficient method over the past few years. It is assumed that fingerprints are unique to each individual and do not change their shape and texture throughout life. Another positive point for using this type of technology is the low cost and the high quality of fingerprint capture sensors, compared to other biometric sensors. Lines or ridges form fingerprints, and the spaces between these lines are called valleys. Based on features found in the flow of these lines, most automatic fingerprint identification systems (*AFIS*) can distinguish two fingerprints.

Lately, fingerprint inclusion and the massive use of technological devices by governments and private institutions have generated AFIS with large databases

© Springer Nature Switzerland AG 2021
A. Britto and K. Valdivia Delgado (Eds.): BRACIS 2021, LNAI 13074, pp. 223–237, 2021.
https://doi.org/10.1007/978-3-030-91699-2_16

registered with many individuals. In this context, a simple identification query to a system with millions of people can take a completely undesirable time. In this context, AFIS applications usually employ indexing mechanisms when identifying individuals by searching in a subset of the database instead of searching in the entire registered database. Fingerprint indexing can be done using different fingerprint features, such as singular points [25], minutiae [7], and texture [12]. In the latter case, some works have used Convolutional Neural Networks (CNNs) to extract features from fingerprints in recent years.

Generally, indexing mechanisms consist of two steps: indexing and querying. When indexing, the system extracts different kinds of features from fingerprints and stores them according to the method. In the query step, according to a queried fingerprint, the collection of features is generated so that a search is made based on similarity to return the k fingerprints most similar to the query, where k is a previously defined number [8].

In this work, we used approximate nearest neighbor search algorithms (ANN) as an indexing and search technique based on fingerprints' features extracted using a CNN architecture, ResNet18. We used ANN to calculate the $k$ best candidates (i.e., the k most similar) fingerprints. We conducted experiments to evaluate the performance of the proposed solution using FVC (Fingerprint Verification Competition) databases and four ANN methods (ANNOY [2], HNSW [18], NGT [11], and Nanoflann [4]). Our main goal was to study how different parameters influence the system's performance, which is evaluated with time and hit rate metrics.

This work is organized as follows: In Sect. 2, the database used for searches with the presented method was shown. In Sect. 3, concepts to understand this work were described; they are indexing, evaluation, and performance metrics. In Sect. 4, the related works were presented. In Sect. 5, the method presented in this work was described. In Sect. 6, we have the preparations for the performance evaluation tests. In Sect. 7, the results were presented. Furthermore, finally, in Sects. 8 and 9, we have the conclusion and acknowledgments, respectively.

## 2    FVC Databases

The FVC 2000, 2002 e 2004 datasets, described in [21], has a total of 10,560 fingerprint samples divided into different databases (DB1, DB2, DB3, DB4). Each DB has 110 different fingers, and each finger 8 different finger captures, each capture representing a different image of the same finger. Another important piece of information is that within the same year, the same 110 fingers were captured between the different DBs, making it possible to compare the same finger with different equipment, just comparing the same finger id with different DBs of the same finger same year.

There is an internal subdivision for one of the DBs, where for the 110 sets of samples, those numbered from 1 to 100 correspond to DBa, and those numbered from 101 to 110 are part of DBb. Researchers commonly use such division as the split into training and test sets, where DBa is used for training and DBb is used for testing, allowing the results to be compared fairly.

Table 1 presents detailed information about the FVC dataset, such as image dimensions, sensor type for each DB in each year. As we can see in the table, there are optical, capacitive, and thermal sensors, and each type of sensor model results in images with different dimensions. DB4 databases were synthetically generated by the tools described in the "sensor type" column. Figures 1, 2 and 3 shows one sample from each database described in the Table 1.

**Table 1.** Description of FVC databases with the list of sensors.

| FVC | DB | Sensor type | Image dimension |
|---|---|---|---|
| 2000 | DB1 | Optical Sensor "S.D. Scanner" | 300×300 |
| | DB2 | Capacitive Sensor "TouchChip" | 256×364 |
| | DB3 | Optical Sensor "DF-90" | 448×478 |
| | DB4 | Synthetic generator not specified | 240×320 |
| 2002 | DB1 | Optical Sensor "TouchView II" | 388×374 |
| | DB2 | Optical Sensor "FX2000" | 296×560 |
| | DB3 | Capacitive Sensor "100 SC" | 300×300 |
| | DB4 | Synthetic generator "SFinGe v2.51" | 288×384 |
| 2004 | DB1 | Optical Sensor "V300" | 640×480 |
| | DB2 | Optical Sensor "U.are.U 4000" | 328×364 |
| | DB3 | Thermal sweeping Sensor "FingerChip" | 300×480 |
| | DB4 | Synthetic generator "SFinGe v3.0" | 288×384 |

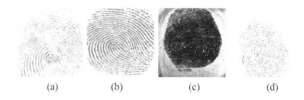

(a)          (b)          (c)          (d)

**Fig. 1.** FVC 2000: (a) 2000_DB1; (b) 2000_DB2; (c) 2000_DB3; (d) 2000_DB4.

# 3   Indexing, Evaluation, and Performance Metrics

The construction of indexes in the fingerprint storage can follow different strategies, among the main ones based on minutiae, singular points, and, more recently, deep features. The indexing process consists of two main steps, the indexing of features and the recovery strategy. When indexing a database of fingerprints, the objective is to optimize searches in large collections of registered individuals, making the identification process less complex, reducing the *1:1* verification needed until finding the searched fingerprint, thus saving considerable time to get an answer.

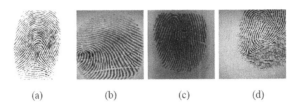

(a)                (b)                (c)                (d)

**Fig. 2.** FVC 2002: (a) 2002_DB1; (b) 2002_DB2; (c) 2002_DB3; (d) 2002_DB4.

(a)                (b)                (c)                (d)

**Fig. 3.** FVC 2004: (a) 2004_DB1; (b) 2004_DB2; (c) 2004_DB3; (d) 2004_DB4.

The set of features consists of a collection of discriminating characteristics extracted by the strategy adopted to differentiate and store the fingerprints in the representation of the index. The recovery step consists of recovering a considerably smaller subset of previously registered fingerprints using some similarity function. Such a smaller subset forms the list of candidate fingerprints, where it is expected that among these is the sought fingerprint.

According to [8] the challenges in indexing fingerprints are: features with high dimensions, features of varying type, unorderable indexes, no pattern in catches of the fingerprints, especially concerning lighting and occlusion, images used in the search may be of low quality or be rotated, and finally the interoperability between capture devices as can be seen in the description of the FVC datasets.

There are different metrics used to evaluate indexing techniques, among which we can mention the hit rate, the penetration rate, and the search time. Defined in the Eq. 1 the hit rate is the percentage of genuine matches between the queried fingerprint and the set $k$ returned by the recovery method concerning all queries. The penetration rate is how much of the search set equals the value of $k$, and usually, this rate varies between 1% and 10% [13,17,22]. Moreover, the search time is equivalent to the total execution time of the respective approximate method responsible for identifying all images from the test set.

$$Hit\_rate = \frac{hits}{queries} \times 100\% \qquad (1)$$

## 4   Related Works

In [6], the authors proposed an indexing mechanism based on CNNs, more precisely using Inception V3 [23]. In the proposed mechanism, fingerprints are aligned in a unified coordinate system, and a dictionary of maps is created from a base of 440 thousand fingerprints. The CNN is used to extract fixed-length features to be indexed and uses consensus similarity metric when querying. Tests were performed using NIST's SD4 and SD14 datasets and demonstrated better performance than state of the art published so far.

An indexing solution was proposed in [22], which is composed of three different CNNs. Being the first network called FingerNet [24] to enhance the fingerprints and extract minutiae, with the minutiae divided by locations in smaller blocks. With another CNN, features are extracted based on texture and minutiae, called Minutia-centred Deep Convolutional (MDC). Finally, the last CNN aggregates the features of the descriptors in the representation end name AMDC or aggregated LCD. The similarity between the indexed features is calculated directly via AMDC, where only a normalization and scalar product between two AMDC features is used. The experiments were carried out with FVC2000 DB2, FVC2000 DB3, NIST SD4, NIST SD4 natural, and NIST SD14, preventing the method's superiority in several studies. However, there were no comparisons with techniques based on CNN.

Some works use variations of Delaunay triangulation for indexing. In [14] this is used with the k-means clustering algorithm for search, performing experiments on the FVC2000, FVC2004, FVC2004, NIST SD4, and NIST SD14 datasets. In [13] an extended triangulation is used and partitioning the triangles into groups, presenting results on the FVC2002 and FVC2004 databases. Improving on the results of these papers, in [17] a new index vector is proposed whose values are spread in index space, with experiments using the datasets FVC2002 and FVC2004, outperforming the state-of-the-art.

The authors of [1] studied fingerprint indexing using information from the fingerprint pores, which requires high-quality images and sensors with a lot of capture capacity. Complete and partial fingerprint pore information is extracted and clustered using K-means. The recovery of fingerprints is made possible by searching for the nearest cluster based on the pores detected in the query image. The results are satisfactory compared to other techniques based on minutiae.

## 5    Proposed Indexing Method

The objective of this work is to evaluate a solution for fingerprint indexing. When performing tests with the FVC 2000, 2002, and 2004 databases, it is possible to evaluate results for different types of sensors. In the following subsections, both the solution and the techniques used in its composition will be detailed.

### 5.1    Architecture

The system to be evaluated consists of two different stages, the fingerprint indexing stage and the indexed fingerprint query stage, like the other indexing systems. It is considered that the input images were captured with fingerprint sensors and preprocessed so that they are used both for indexing and for queries.

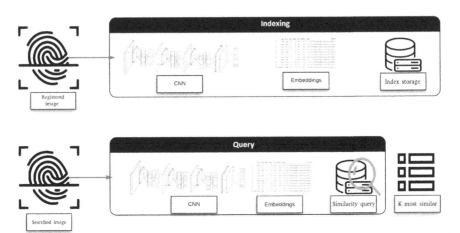

**Fig. 4.** Indexing system architecture

As can be seen in Fig. 4 in the indexing process, the fingerprint is given as an entry in a CNN so that the features can be extracted so that they are stored in an indexing base. The result of this step is an indexing database duly completed and ready to carry out consultations. The networks are trained with different fingerprints than those used in the production environment and evidently need to be trained in a stage before using the approach.

The second and complementary step of the solution is to perform searches with fingerprints so that the subset of fingerprints is considerably smaller than the registered base is returned so that the task of fingerprint identification is more efficient. Each fingerprint consulted is extracted from the embeddings with CNN, and then searches are made using approximate ANN algorithms to define the fingerprint $k$ most similar to the query.

## 5.2 Deep Metric Learning

The generation of embeddings, that is, a set of features is carried out through a convolutional neural network (Convolutional Neural Network, CNN). The chosen CNN is the ResNet18 because it is an architecture with a good trade-off between performance and computational cost. The embeddings are extracted from the neck of the last completely connected layers, with a dimensionality ranging between 64, 96, and 128.

The ResNet18 is a residual neural network, as shown in Fig. 5. Altogether the neural network has 11511784 trainable parameters, requiring a total of 2 GFLOPS for activation. The residual layers, obtained through shortcuts, facilitate the convergence of training and improve the accuracy [10].

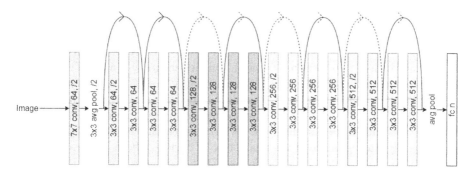

**Fig. 5.** ResNet18 architecture.

The implementation of ResNet18 present in the machine learning DLIB C++ library was used [15]. The loss function used is Coupled Loss (CL), which is the DLIB default, defined in the Eq. 2 [26]. The CL is defined in terms of a global distance threshold $d$ and also by a margin $\epsilon$ added to decide when two embeddings $n$-dimensional, $f(x_1)$ and $f(x_2)$, of two fingerprints, belong to the same identification. Therefore, if the distance between the embeddings is greater than $d$, then they belong to different fingerprints.

$$||f(x_1) - f(x_2)|| < d \qquad (2)$$

The training is carried out with $N$ elements of an image base forming the load tensor, with a dimensionality of 224×224 for the entry of CNNs, resizing the images to this dimension. When using backpropagation, a neural network can only learn from cases where the condition imposed by the loss function is violated. Therefore, example mining similar to [3] is used at the load loss computation level, so the training procedure benefits from difficult negatives, which typically improves quality and convergence. However, difficult negatives are also combined with random specimens, which, unlike [16], also take into account easy negatives.

### 5.3 Approximate Nearest Neighbors

The principle behind Approximate Nearest Neighbors (ANN) is to get a significant improvement in search performance, which comes at the cost of a loss in accuracy, so an approximately correct but fast result is obtained [2,19]. This means that ANN methods can be used for various tasks, such as classification, labeling, and recommendation. In addition, there is evidence in the literature that, for some cases, ANN can also impact an unexpected improvement in results [5,9]. Three state-of-the-art ANN methods have been chosen that are widely used in both research and commercial products: ANNOY, HNSW and NGT. In addition to these, Nanoflann was also used.

ANNOY (Approximate Nearest Neighbors Oh Yeah) [2] was developed by Erik Bernhardsson and is used by Spotify to recommend songs. Its implementation is summarized in a Binary Space Partition (BSP) tree using hyperplanes, similar to those used to render old 3D graphics. A random forest of BSP trees is built to improve search results: the more trees, the greater the accuracy of the results and the less "performance (time) for higher accuracy (quality)". Standard configurations use $2 * D$, where $D$ is dimensionality.

HNSW (Hierarchical Navigable Small World Graphs) [18] is a graph-based method that separates links between nodes in a search graph according to their size scales in different layers, therefore performing searches in a multilayer graph. Consequently, the estimate of the nearest node occurs only in a necessary fixed portion of the connections for each element. The main advantages of the HNSW method are its robustness and its support for continuous incremental indexing.

NGT (Neighborhood Graph and Tree for Indexing Highdimensional Data) is a graph-based ANN method initially proposed to work on a large scale, high-dimensional vector space [11]. NGT improves the graph of k-nearest neighbors (KNNG) by adjusting the path and degree of edges derived from a KNNG, that is, optimization in terms of the number of edges entering and leaving influencing the accuracy and search time, respectively. In particular, the authors describe how an acceleration in performance can be achieved by removing edges that can be replaced by alternative search paths. NGT also supports adding and removing items from the index, which is an important feature for real-world applications. Experimental evaluations show that NGT can compete or even surpass other methods [2,11].

Blanck and Kumar [4] propose nanoflann, based on FLANN [19,20], one of the first libraries to provide ANN methods. This includes several algorithms to search for the nearest neighbor in metric spaces, such as KD-Trees variants. The nanoflann method was proposed for the construction of KD-Trees from databases describing point clouds and rotation groups. However, nanoflann does not focus on searches for approximately closer neighbors but on the exact performance of the closest neighbor based on optimizations, such as adopting quadratic distances and customizable memory access policies.

## 6    Experimental Evaluation

The experiments were carried out on a computer with Linux operating system (Ubuntu 20.04.2 LTS), equipped with an Intel(R) Core(TM) i7-9750H CPU @ 2.60 GHz×12, 16 GB RAM memory, a 512 GB SSD, and NVIDIA GeForce RTX 1660TI graphics card.

For the generation of embeddings, ResNet18 was trained using a synthetic dataset, with 100 identities with ten fingerprint images each, totaling 1000 images. This decision was made to verify the efficiency of generalizing the generation of embeddings to other datasets without the need for new training. The fingerprints were generated using a proprietary tool of a project of which the authors of this paper are members[1]. Figure 6 shows an example of a fingerprint from the synthetic dataset.

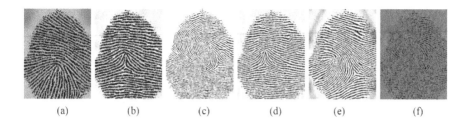

| (a) | (b) | (c) | (d) | (e) | (f) |

**Fig. 6.** Examples of fingerprints from our synthetic dataset.

Regarding the generation of embeddings for search with ANN models, tests were performed using all FVC BDs. First, the bases were separated into search and test sets. The search set corresponds to the sample in which the ANNs models will consult and calculate the nearest neighbors in order to identify each of the elements of the test set.

For comparison with related works, the DBa of the FVC DBs corresponded to the search set, and the DBb was used for the test set. For each of the search and test sets, three sets of embeddings were generated, with their respective sizes of 64, 96, and 128.

Finally, the ANNs models were tested in each of the search and test sets in order to verify which combinations of these models and embedding vector size yield better hit rates. As for the penetration rate, also in order to compare to related works, a minimum of 1% and a maximum of 10% were used. In this work, the penetration rate is directly related to the $k$ value of nearest neighbors used by the ANN models, that is, a penetration rate of 1% indicates that a value equivalent to this rate was used as $k$. So, as the search set has $100 * 8 = 800$ elements, the value corresponds to $k$ with 1% penetration is 8, and the value corresponds to 10% is 80.

Search time was also a metric calculated in the experiments in order to verify the efficiency of the approach in generating good results quickly. It equals the sum of all searches performed in the test set.

## 7   Results

First, the results will be presented regarding the training of ResNet18 to generate deep feature embeddings using the synthetic image dataset. Figure 7 shows the evolution of the curve of mean loss values concerning the CNN training.

---

[1] The synthetic fingerprint base is available at the following link: https://github.com/ LeonardoCosta21/Fingerprint-synthetic-dataset.

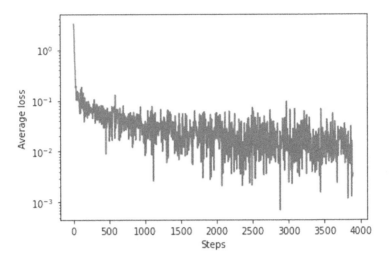

**Fig. 7.** Evolution of average loss for ResNet18 training over our synthetic dataset.

An early stopping strategy was used for stopping training in order to avoid overfitting. Therefore, when stagnation in the loss curve evolution was detected for many epochs, training was manually interrupted. We validated this strategy empirically using increasing volume cuts from the training base. It was found that, in fact, this situation led to a model of poor performance. The results observed from queries based on the deep feature embedding vectors generated by our best model provide evidence that the stopping criterion was well applied.

Table 2 presents the best results obtained in queries with the ANN methods in each of the FVC image databases. The best results were considered in relation to the hit rate of 1% penetration to 10%. That is, whoever obtained better results from 1% penetration is ahead, as the idea is to use the least value of nearest neighbors $k$ for searches. In case of a tie, the combination of the ANN model with the smaller embeddings vector was highlighted since the larger the embeddings vector, the more computational resources are allocated to generate it. If the tie persists, the following criterion was the search time for each of the penetration rates. In all cases, the NGT method was superior in relation to the other ANNs, regarding the Hit rate, therefore, all the results of Table 2 were obtained with the NGT method.

Generally, the larger the vector of embeddings, the better the results found by searches of the ANNs methods, but the longer the search time tends to be. Search time in each search performed presented values so low that the difference between these can be considered disregarded.

Complementing the previous data, Table 3 presents the best results obtained by each of the ANN models.

Interestingly, the best results for each of the ANN models were all relative to searches over FVC's 2004 DB3. There is evidence that this dataset has the most uncomplicated images to identify by the proposed method. As much as

**Table 2.** Results of the best combinations of embeddings vector size for each of FVC 'DBs.

| Dataset | Embeddings | Search time ($\mu s$) | | | Hit rate (%) | | |
|---------|-----------|---------|--------|--------|--------|--------|--------|
| | | Penetration rate | | | | | |
| | | 1% | 5% | 10% | 1% | 5% | 10% |
| 2000_DB1 | 96 | 34870 | 23439 | 19089 | 97.50 | 100.00 | 100.00 |
| 2000_DB2 | 96 | 18001 | 13365 | 27914 | 100.00 | 100.00 | 100.00 |
| 2000_DB3 | 96 | 14302 | 27911 | 27836 | 100.00 | 100.00 | 100.00 |
| 2000_DB4 | 96 | 14837 | 7917 | 28149 | 97.50 | 100.00 | 100.00 |
| 2002_DB1 | 96 | 11758 | 36081 | 29307 | 96.25 | 98.75 | 98.75 |
| 2002_DB2 | 96 | 28563 | 27946 | 27747 | 97.50 | 98.75 | 100.00 |
| 2002_DB3 | 96 | 14618 | 16694 | 23825 | 100.00 | 100.00 | 100.00 |
| 2002_DB4 | 128 | 13381 | 19305 | 13557 | 95.00 | 98.75 | 100 |
| 2004_DB1 | 64 | 12281 | 18509 | 17503 | 95.00 | 97.50 | 97.50 |
| 2004_DB2 | 64 | 12370 | 24317 | 15370 | 100.00 | 100.00 | 100.00 |
| 2004_DB3 | 64 | 12251 | 12472 | 10855 | 100.00 | 100.00 | 100.00 |
| 2004_DB4 | 128 | 15002 | 24310 | 19827 | 98.75 | 100.00 | 100.00 |

**Table 3.** Best results obtained by each of the ANNs models.

| ANN | Dataset | Embeddings | Search time ($\mu s$) | | | Hit rate (%) | | |
|-----|---------|-----------|---------|--------|--------|--------|--------|--------|
| | | | Penetration rate | | | | | |
| | | | 1% | 5% | 10% | 1% | 5% | 10% |
| Annoy | 2004_DB3 | 96 | 13111 | 17568 | 12523 | 96.25 | 98.75 | 100.00 |
| NGT | 2004_DB3 | 64 | 12251 | 12472 | 10855 | 100.00 | 100.00 | 100.00 |
| HNSW | 2004_DB3 | 96 | 20248 | 7733 | 19835 | 95.00 | 98.75 | 100.00 |
| nanoflann | 2004_DB3 | 96 | 6659 | 13218 | 19865 | 95.00 | 98.75 | 100.00 |

the NGT method was superior, it is possible to notice that the other indexing methods do not fall so far behind in terms of accuracy because they still present very competitive results.

The results obtained in this paper were compared with previous results from the literature. For doing so, evaluation was carried out using the same image bases used in the related works. It is worthy of mentioning that all the works considered used the same search and test set separation scheme. The comparisons were made considering the best results of each one for the queries in the respective image database. These comparative results are depicted by Figs. 8, 9, 10 and 11. Bear in mind that some works do not appear in all comparisons, as the authors did not present tests regarding the fingerprints database in their work.

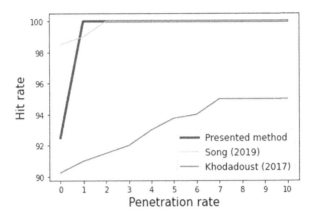

**Fig. 8.** Comparison with other indexing methods with FVC 2000_DB2 dataset.

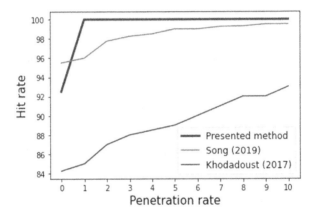

**Fig. 9.** Comparison with other indexing methods with FVC 2000_DB3 dataset.

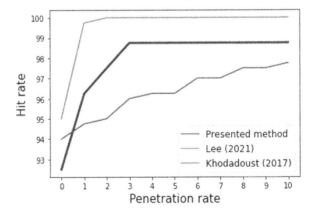

**Fig. 10.** Comparison with other indexing methods with FVC 2002_DB1 dataset.

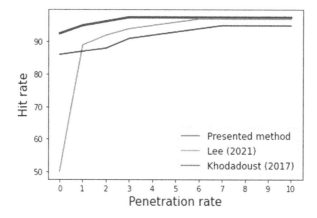

**Fig. 11.** Comparison with other indexing methods with FVC 2004_DB1 dataset.

The search method presented in this work using ANN models presented better results in most cases. Unfortunately, none of the related works discussed in this paper present information on search times for comparison, which would probably enhance the proposal of this work even more. After all, the search times were negligible.

## 8  Conclusion

This work presented a method for fingerprint indexing based on deep embedding vector extraction using CNN and ANNs. We performed several experiments varying the embedding vector size and using four ANNs methods (ANNOY, NGT, HNSW, and Nanoflann). The feature extraction CNN was trained using a synthetic dataset that was applied out-of-the-box to the evaluation datasets constructed with different sensors for real-world fingerprints (see Table 1). Experimental results indicate that the proposed method is competitive compared to other works found in the literature.

On top of that, for several FVC databases, the method achieved 100% hit rate at a low penetration rate of 1%.

It is important to highlight that the CNN used (ResNet18) is simple and fast. This model can be leveraged to run the proposed method on resource-constrained devices, such as smartphones, as well as stated by the tiny search times.

As for future work, it is intended to use other CNNs to compare with the performance of ResNet18. It is intended to use other databases for training CNNs for the indexing stage and also for the query stage. Finally, it is planned to test the solution on smartphones, at least the query step, in order to verify performance on mobile hardware.

**Acknowledgements.** This study was financed in part by the Coordenação de Aperfeiçoamento de Pessoal de Nível Superior - Brasil (CAPES) - Finance Code 001. The authors would like to thank The Ceará State Foundation for the Support of Scientific and Technological Development (FUNCAP) for the financial support (6945087/2019).

# References

1. Anand, V., Kanhangad, V.: Pore-based indexing for fingerprints acquired using high-resolution sensors. Pattern Anal. Appl. **23**(1), 429–441 (2019). https://doi. org/10.1007/s10044-019-00805-3
2. Aumüller, M., Bernhardsson, E., Faithfull, A.: Ann-benchmarks: a benchmarking tool for approximate nearest neighbor algorithms. In: Beecks, C., Borutta, F., Kroger, P., Seidl, T. (eds.) International Conference on Similarity Search and Applications, vol. 10609, pp. 34–49. Springer, Heidelberg (2017). https://doi.org/ 10.1007/978-3-319-68474-1_3
3. Balntas, V., Riba, E., Ponsa, D., Mikolajczyk, K.: Learning local feature descriptors with triplets and shallow convolutional neural networks. In: Bmvc, vol. 1, pp. 1–11 (2016)
4. Blanco, J.L., Rai, P.K.: nanoflann: a c++ header-only fork of flann, a library for nearest neighbor (nn) wih kd-trees (2014)
5. Boytsov, L., Novak, D., Malkov, Y., Nyberg, E.: Off the beaten path: let's replace term-based retrieval with k-nn search. In: Proceedings of the 25th ACM International on Conference on Information and Knowledge Management, pp. 1099–1108 (2016)
6. Cao, K., Jain, A.K.: Fingerprint indexing and matching: an integrated approach. In: 2017 IEEE International Joint Conference on Biometrics (IJCB), pp. 437–445. IEEE (2017)
7. Galton, F.: Finger prints macmillan (1892)
8. Gupta, P., Tiwari, K., Arora, G.: Fingerprint indexing schemes-a survey. Neurocomputing **335**, 352–365 (2019)
9. Gysel, C.V., De Rijke, M., Kanoulas, E.: Neural vector spaces for unsupervised information retrieval. ACM Trans. Inf. Syst. (TOIS) **36**(4), 1–25 (2018)
10. He, K., Zhang, X., Ren, S., Sun, J.: Deep residual learning for image recognition. In: Proceedings of the IEEE Conference on Computer Vision and Pattern Recognition, pp. 770–778 (2016)
11. Iwasaki, M., Miyazaki, D.: Optimization of indexing based on k-nearest neighbor graph for proximity search in high-dimensional data (2018). arXiv preprint arXiv:1810.07355
12. Jain, A.K., Prabhakar, S., Hong, L., Pankanti, S.: Filterbank-based fingerprint matching. IEEE Trans. Image Process. **9**(5), 846–859 (2000)
13. Kavati, I., Prasad, M.V.N.K., Bhagvati, C.: Hierarchical decomposition of extended triangulation for fingerprint indexing. In: Efficient Biometric Indexing and Retrieval Techniques for Large-Scale Systems. SCS, pp. 21–40. Springer, Cham (2017). https://doi.org/10.1007/978-3-319-57660-2_2
14. Khodadoust, J., Khodadoust, A.M.: Fingerprint indexing based on expanded delaunay triangulation. Expert Syst. Appl. **81**, 251–267 (2017)
15. King, D.E.: Dlib-ml: a machine learning toolkit. J. Mach. Learn. Res. **10**, 1755–1758 (2009)
16. Kuma, R., Weill, E., Aghdasi, F., Sriram, P.: Vehicle re-identification: an efficient baseline using triplet embedding. In: 2019 International Joint Conference on Neural Networks (IJCNN), pp. 1–9. IEEE (2019)

17. Lee, S., Jeong, I.R.: Improved fingerprint indexing based on extended triangulation. IEEE Access **9**, 8471–8478 (2021)
18. Malkov, Y.A., Yashunin, D.A.: Efficient and robust approximate nearest neighbor search using hierarchical navigable small world graphs. IEEE Trans. Pattern Anal. Mach. Intell. **42**, 824–836 (2018)
19. Muja, M., Lowe, D.G.: Fast approximate nearest neighbors with automatic algorithm configuration. VISAPP (1) **2**(331–340), 2 (2009)
20. Muja, M., Lowe, D.G.: Scalable nearest neighbor algorithms for high dimensional data. IEEE Trans. Pattern Anal. Mach. Intell. **36**(11), 2227–2240 (2014)
21. Schuch, P., Schulz, S., Busch, C.: Survey on the impact of fingerprint image enhancement. IET Biometrics **7**(2), 102–115 (2017)
22. Song, D., Tang, Y., Feng, J.: Aggregating minutia-centred deep convolutional features for fingerprint indexing. Pattern Recogn. **88**, 397–408 (2019)
23. Szegedy, C., Vanhoucke, V., Ioffe, S., Shlens, J., Wojna, Z.: Rethinking the inception architecture for computer vision. In: Proceedings of the IEEE Conference on Computer Vision and Pattern Recognition, pp. 2818–2826 (2016)
24. Tang, Y., Gao, F., Feng, J., Liu, Y.: Fingernet: an unified deep network for fingerprint minutiae extraction. In: 2017 IEEE International Joint Conference on Biometrics (IJCB), pp. 108–116. IEEE (2017)
25. Wang, S., Zhang, W.W., Wang, Y.S.: Fingerprint classification by directional fields. In: Proceedings, Fourth IEEE International Conference on Multimodal Interfaces, pp. 395–399. IEEE (2002)
26. Weinberger, K.Q., Saul, L.K.: Distance metric learning for large margin nearest neighbor classification. J. Mach. Learn. Res. **10**(2), 207–244 (2009)

# How to Generate Synthetic Paintings to Improve Art Style Classification

Sarah Pires Pérez$^{(\boxtimes)}$ and Fabio Gagliardi Cozman

Escola Politécnica, Universidade de São Paulo, São Paulo, Brazil

**Abstract.** Indexing artwork is not only a tedious job; it is an impossible task to complete manually given the amount of online art. In any case, the automatic classification of art styles is also a challenge due to the relative lack of labeled data and the complexity of the subject matter. This complexity means that common data augmentation techniques may not generate useful data; in fact, they may degrade performance in practice. In this paper, we use Generative Adversarial Networks for data augmentation so as to improve the accuracy of an art style classifier, showing that we can improve performance of EfficientNet B0, a state of art classifier. To achieve this result, we introduce Class-by-Class Performance Analysis; we also present a modified version of the SAGAN training configuration that allows better control against mode collapse and vanishing gradient in the context of artwork.

**Keywords:** Computer vision · GAN · Art style classification

## 1 Introduction

No society, however low it may have been its level of material accomplishment, has ceased to produce art [15]. Art has been, through the ages, a mirror reflecting society; the purpose of art has varied but its importance in capturing society has been constant. One way to discuss the content of artwork is through style categories. Such categories indicate connections between paintings and help us to better understand their meanings. Even if many art theorists look at style categories with reservations,[1] categories provide an important guideline for beginner art aficionados and the general crowd within museums and galleries. Besides, style categories can be used by recommendation tools to improve a museum visitor's experience, either in a traditional physical museum location or in one of the increasingly common digital galleries.

Alas, the current quantity of online art has now surpassed our manual indexing abilities. The field of computer vision has developed artwork style classification tools using a diversity of techniques from feature-based machine learning [2,32] to deep learning [3,10,23]. Beyond the challenge of class imbalance,

---

[1] This feeling can be found in articles on the study of art: https://www.artsy.net/article/alina-cohen-art-movements-matter.

© Springer Nature Switzerland AG 2021
A. Britto and K. Valdivia Delgado (Eds.): BRACIS 2021, LNAI 13074, pp. 238–253, 2021.
https://doi.org/10.1007/978-3-030-91699-2_17

style classification is further complicated by aesthetic diversity, a problem that is not usually met in most image classification models. For instance, the Baroque is directly linked to the historic moment of the Catholic Church struggling against the Protestant Reformation; in an attempt to combat the Protestant faith, the Church announced during the Council of Trent (1545–1563) the dissemination of religious ideas through images to awaken religious fervor—therefore, the Baroque works are very concentrated on the religious theme. Minimalism, on the other hand, does not have a single theme, but it employs a few elements in a distinctive manner [15].

The use of image augmentation is well established in computer vision so as to enhance the content of a training dataset. But usual techniques do not produce good results when applied to artwork; for instance, many of the common image augmentation techniques modify the resulting color of the image, which can be problematic in the case of artwork as colors often have or convey particular meaning. In this paper we propose an artwork style classifier that resorts to Generative Adversarial Networks (GANs) as an image augmentation tool for oversampling.

Artwork generation with GANs is not a direct matter; even high performance GAN architectures did not do well in preliminary experiments, so we had to propose techniques to enhance image quality and diversity. We describe in this paper a methodology for data augmentation that is tuned to the requirements of artwork classification; we also describe a specialized network architecture and an adjusted loss function that both contribute to the overall performance of our proposal. In short, our contributions are both in adopting GANs for data augmentation in the particular context of artwork classification, and in proposing novel techniques that may be of broad interest whenever similar classification problems are met.

The paper is organized as follows. Section 2 analyzes related work on art style classification and Generative Adversarial Networks. Section 3 describes our approach; results and analysis are shown in Sect. 4. Finally, conclusions are presented in Sect. 5.

## 2   Related Work

In this section, we explore relevant efforts on artwork classification. We also present the architectural development of Generative Adversarial Networks (GANs), its use in the art domain and its relevance to image augmentation.

### 2.1   Artwork Classification

Initial research on artwork classification was focused on feature-based machine learning [2,32]. Since the initial success of a convolutional neural network (CNN) in object classification for ImageNet [25], several studies in artwork classification have explored these networks [3,10,16,23]. To improve the performance of the classification of art styles with CNNs, researchers have investigated the benefits of pre-trained weights from the ImageNet Challenge instead of random startups [26, 36].

There has been significant activity in artwork classification in recent years. Cetinic *et al.* expanded artwork classification beyond style, genre, artist and time period classification, examining also nationality and testing scene recognition and sentiment analysis techniques [6]. Chu *et al.* studied the style classification task focusing on describing image texture with deep learning. They investigated the intra-layer and inter-layer correlations in order to create deep features for style classification. [9]. The work of Elgammal *et al.* analyzed the learned representations of a fine-tuned ResNet-152, noting that some of the style patterns designed by Heinrich Wölfflin (1846–1945) correlate with the PCA decomposition of these learned representations [14]. In Rodriguez *et al.*, five image patches of painting were used for training and weights for each patch were optimized in order to improve accuracy of the final model [29]. Sandoval *et al.* also worked with image patches, but in a two-stage deep learning approach, in which these five patches are trained independently at a first step. At the second stage, the outcome of these patches are fused to a second shallow neural network for the final decision [31]. Zhong *et al.* presented a two-channel dual path network and two inputs are used: the RGB image and four-directional gray-level co-occurrence matrix for detecting the brush stroke information [44]. The work of Zhu *et al.* not only trained the Inception V3 network for classifying nine artistic movements, but also used Grad-CAM heat map for visualizing the areas of the images the model was focusing for class prediction [46]. Chen *et al.* presented an adaptive cross-layer correlation for artwork classification, in which it adaptively weights features in different spatial locations based on similarity [7]. Bianco *et al.* studied the advantages of training a model with the full image of the paintings and also its crop at different resolutions [4].

## 2.2  Generative Adversarial Networks

Generative Adversarial Networks (GANs) are built by training two networks with a minimax game framework, where we have a model capable of generating synthetic data (model G) and another model that evaluates whether the data is real or synthetic (model D) [19]. In the work of Mirza and Osindero, an extra parameter was introduced in the GAN architecture so as to allow the generator model to create images according to class labels [27]. Chen *et al.* developed a GAN architecture to learn disentangled representations in an unsupervised manner; they introduced a representation learning algorithm called Information Maximizing Generative Adversarial Networks (InfoGAN), in which an information-regularized minimax game is used in order to train a multi class generative model without the label information [8].

Some work on GANs has focused on the impact of the loss function. Arjovsky *et al.* used the concept of the Earth Mover (EM) distance, also known as Wasserstein-1 distance, as a loss function [1]. Gulrajani *et al.* improved the Wasserstein function loss adding a gradient penalty [20].

An important concept in the evolution of the GAN architecture is the self-attention mechanism. The convolutional architecture processes information in local neighborhoods and it has no mechanism to deal with long distance dependencies. The self-attention enables both the generator and the discriminator to deal with widely separated spatial regions. The work of Zhang *et al.* presented this concept as Self-Attention GAN (SAGAN) [43] and other proposals have used this architecture as a reference [5,11].

The use of synthetic images to improve classifiers has been adopted particularly in the medical field, for instance in simulating lung nodules [21], ECG [42], liver lesions [17], chromosomes [40], skins lesions [28] and Covid-19 results [12,38]. We also mention the work of Suh *et al.*, where classifier loss is included in the GAN training process in order to reduce ambiguity between classes: their classification enhancement generative adversarial networks (CEGAN) consist of three independent networks – a discriminator, a generator and a classifier – using WGAN-GP for classification under imbalanced data conditions [34].

Generative adversarial networks have already been used in the art domain. For instance, one can find a generator for image style transfer (the Cycle-GAN [45]), an Image-to-Image translator from art to real images [18,37], and a model specialized in creating Chinese landscapes [41]. The first, and to the best of our knowledge the only, work aimed at creating artwork with the WikiArt dataset appeared in Ref. [13]. There, Elgammal *et al.* developed the Creative Adversarial Network to creatively generate artwork by maximizing deviation from established styles and by minimizing deviation from art distribution [13]. The authors found that the way to encourage the generator "to be creative" was to penalize it any time in which it was too easy for the Discriminator to identify the synthetic image as being art from a certain style.

## 3   Our Proposal

Simply put, our main goal is to enhance the accuracy of artwork style classification. In pursuing this, we were led to study the potential benefits of synthetic images generated by Generative Adversarial Networks. As noted before, synthetic art generation has been employed only by Elgammal *et al.* (2017), but not with the purpose of enhancing classification; to the best of our knowledge, the latter task has not been investigated yet. In short, our specific goal here is not to make art, but to improve art style classification.

We introduce a strategy that we refer to as Class-by-Class Performance Analysis. In order to start up learning, a baseline model is trained without image augmentation techniques. The next step is to explore the benefit of geometric transformations. We then concentrate on classes with the lowest performance; we want to maximize the information about these classes. Such information is enhanced by a version of GANs with a self-attention mechanism for image diversity that is trained with the Wasserstein with Gradient Penalty loss function for avoiding vanishing gradient.

In addition, classes with low performance may or may not contain a small number of images. Hence, we suggest two strategies when we sample either:

– low quantity classes: add a multiple of the number of original images;
– high quantity classes: add a fraction of the number of original images.

There are many decisions that must be set in implementing this strategy; some of them depend on the particular artwork collection is dealing with. In the following subsections, all relevant aspects of our strategy are discussed: our study of image augmentation, our choices regarding the GAN architecture and the loss function and, finally, the model architecture for our classification task.

### 3.1 Image Augmentation

Data Augmentation is a natural solution to the problem of limited data [33]. With respect to images, augmentation techniques consist of geometric transformations, such as rotation, image cropping, flipping and color conversions [34]. We studied these techniques in the context of art style classification, a setting with many classes and serious class imbalance.

Our first experiment was to ascertain the benefits of rotation, image cropping and flipping. Results can be seen in Table 6. Improvement was obtained by rotating the image between -10 and 10 degrees, horizontal flips and random crops. Alas, traditional image augmentation techniques often generate simple and redundant copies of the original data in many cases [34]. In some cases, data augmentation may not be a profitable idea. For many domains, color conversions offer image diversity; for instance, the object class "bicycle" can be represented with red or blue bicycles. In artwork, however, colors are meaningful and altering them without care can result in an image that lies in a category different from the original one. For example, Pablo Picasso's Blue Period paintings (1901–1904) should always be represented by gloomy shades of grayish blue. The true atmosphere color for Édouard Manet should always be violet and many of his Impressionist colleagues used violet as their main color [24].

### 3.2 Generative Adversarial Network

One of the most challenging tasks for Generative Adversarial Networks is producing a diverse set of synthetic images. Wang *et al.* compare the most influential GAN architectures with respect to image quality, performance against vanishing gradient and ability for mode diversity. In order to create synthetic artwork, where shape must greatly vary and colors are very relevant, we chose to focus on a mechanism proven to excel in diversity; we adopted Self-Attention Generative Adversarial Network (SAGAN) with some modifications which will be explained later. We chose this architecture as the basis of our GAN as the self-attention mechanism helps the GAN to learn global and long-range dependencies across multi-class images [39].

Figure 1 shows a self-attention module. Transformers are used to create the key $f(x)$, query $g(x)$ and value $h(x)$:

$$f(x) = W_f x, \qquad g(x) = W_g x, \qquad h(x) = W_h x.$$

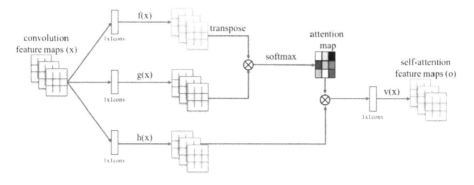

**Fig. 1.** The self-attention mechanism [43]

The attention map is created after applying a softmax to the dot product of the key and the query (Eq. 1). Another dot product is taken between the attention map and the value; the attention map is applied to the value in order to create a self-attention map $(o_j)$ (Eq. 2).

$$\alpha_{j,i} = \text{softmax}(f(x_i)^\top g(x_j)), \tag{1}$$

$$o_j = W_v \left( \sum_{i=1}^{N} \alpha_{j,i} h(x_i) \right). \tag{2}$$

The parameters $W_f$, $W_g$, $W_h$ and $W_v$ are the learned weight matrices.

### 3.3  Adversarial Loss Function

The original version of the SAGAN training configuration used hinge loss. For our dataset, we experienced frequent mode collapse and vanishing gradient with this loss, likely due to our dataset's diversity. Moreover, in order to guarantee this to be $k$-Lipschitz, as needed to prevent mode collapse, a Gradient Penalty was added to the loss function. For this reason, we used the Wasserstein with Gradient Penalty (Wasserstein-GP) loss function so as to have better control of the values for feedback. That is, the loss is:

$$L = \mathop{\mathbb{E}}_{\tilde{x} \sim \mathbb{P}_g} [D(\tilde{x})] - \mathop{\mathbb{E}}_{x \sim \mathbb{P}_r} [D(x)] + \lambda \mathop{\mathbb{E}}_{\hat{x} \sim \mathbb{P}_{\hat{x}}} \left[ (\|\nabla_{\hat{x}} D(\hat{x})\|_2 - 1)^2 \right], \tag{3}$$

where $\mathbb{P}_r$ is the real images distribution, $\mathbb{P}_g$ is the generated images distribution and $\mathbb{P}_{\hat{x}}$ is the sampling uniformly along straight lines between pairs of points sampled from the data distribution $\mathbb{P}_r$ and the generator distribution $\mathbb{P}_g$. In our experiments, the interpolation between a batch of real images and fake images was enforced and the gradient norm of its output was limited at 1. The value of the penalty coefficient $(\lambda)$ was 10, following the original paper [20].

### 3.4 EfficientNet

The EfficientNet B0 architecture was chosen for these experiments due to its high performance and relatively small size. EfficientNet B0 belongs to a family of models known as EfficientNet, presented by Tan and Le [35]. The EfficientNet B0 is the EfficientNet family's baseline, from which all the models from B1 to B7 are scaled up uniformly in dimensions of depth, width and resolution. Table 1 summarizes the stages in the EfficientNet B0. Each stage consists of one or more layers built with blocks of MBConv [30], which are combined with a Squeeze-and-Excitation optimization [22].

**Table 1.** Summary of the composition of the EfficientNet B0

| Stages | Operators | Resolution | # of channels | # of layers |
|--------|-----------|------------|---------------|-------------|
| 1 | Conv3 × 3 | 224 × 224 | 32 | 1 |
| 2 | MBConv1, k3 × 3 | 112 × 112 | 16 | 1 |
| 3 | MBConv6, k3 × 3 | 112 × 112 | 24 | 2 |
| 4 | MBConv6, k5 × 5 | 56 × 56 | 40 | 2 |
| 5 | MBConv6, k3 × 3 | 28 × 28 | 80 | 3 |
| 6 | MBConv6, k5 × 5 | 14 × 14 | 112 | 3 |
| 7 | MBConv6, k5 × 5 | 14 × 14 | 192 | 4 |
| 8 | MBConv6, k3 × 3 | 7 × 7 | 320 | 1 |
| 9 | Conv1 × 1 & Pooling & FC | 7 × 7 | 1280 | 1 |

## 4 Experimental Results

The methods described previously are only useful if they do lead to improvement in realistic circumstances. We developed and tested them by dealing with real artwork and existing datasets. In this section, we present the dataset we used and its characteristics, the training configurations for both GAN and classifier and the results for each step of the Class-by-Class Performance Analysis.

### 4.1 The Wikiart Dataset

We used the Wikiart dataset in our experiments. In fact, the version we used was the one discussed by Elgammal *et al.* [14], from which we adopted the following conventions:

- New Realism and Contemporary Realism were added to Realism;
- Action Painting was added to Abstract-Expressionism;
- Synthetic Cubism and Analytical Cubism were added to Cubism.

Table 2. Dataset used in experiments.

| Art movement | Total of images | Training images |
|---|---|---|
| Abstract expressionism | 2,783 | 2,283 |
| Art nouveau | 4,292 | 3,442 |
| Baroque | 4,241 | 3,448 |
| Color field painting | 1,615 | 1,308 |
| Cubism | 2,417 | 1,942 |
| Early renaissance | 1,391 | 1,134 |
| Expressionism | 6,720 | 5,457 |
| Impressionism | 13,060 | 10,566 |
| Minimalism | 1,258 | 1,009 |
| Naíve art | 2,340 | 1,917 |
| Northern renaissance | 2,552 | 2,084 |
| Pop art | 1,460 | 1,205 |
| Realism | 11,400 | 9,188 |
| Romanticism | 6,963 | 5,640 |
| Ukiyo-e | 1,167 | 940 |

A total of 63,659 images are available there; 10% of them were used for testing and 10% of the remaining dataset was used for validation. The training volumetry of the image distribution is presented in the last column of Table 2. The training dataset is used both in classifier training and in GAN training. The test dataset is the same for all experiments to ensure comparability of results. The class imbalance is apparent with the volumetry varying between 10,566 and 940 images.

### 4.2 GAN Training Configuration

In order to accommodate the training process in 2 GPUs GeForce GTX 1080 Ti (12 GB) to generate images of $128 \times 128$, we lowered the batch size to 32 images (the SAGAN was trained with batch size of 256 images). The process ran for 200.000 epochs (approximately 34 h). Each class was trained independently, using the equivalent training dataset of the classifier. The optimizer setup follows the original SAGAN article: Adam optimizer with $\beta_1 = 0$ and $\beta_2 = 0.9$. The learning rate is constant but specific for each model: for the discriminator is 0.0004 and for the generator is 0.0001 [43].

### 4.3 EfficientNet B0 Training Configuration

Using the ImageNet pretrained model, the fine-tuning for our classification purpose was done by unfreezing each block until there was no further improvement on the validation dataset. The Stochastic Gradient Descent optimizer was used with decay 0.9 and momentum 0.9; initial learning rate of 0.01 with decay after the fifth epoch ($lr = lr * e^{-0.1}$). Images were resized to $224 \times 244$ and batch size was 32 images.

## 4.4   Baseline Results

The result of the EfficientNet B0 baseline trained model and the EfficientNet B0 trained model with geometric augmentation are shown in Table 6 (first and second lines). The performance for each class of the latter is shown in Fig. 2. It is important to highlight that low performance is not correlated to image quantity: the Ukiyo-e movement – the Japanese style – had the least amount of images and the best f1-score. Still, the worst performance was obtained by the Pop Art class with only 1205 images. On the other hand, the second and third worst performances belong to two classes with the largest number of images - Expressionism and Romanticism.

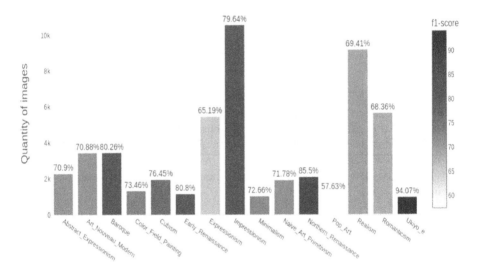

**Fig. 2.** Analysis of the trained EfficientNet B0 with geometric augmentation

## 4.5   Sampling Low Quantity Classes

Pop Art is the fourth lowest class in terms of quantity and images, so the low quantity class sampling strategy was applied. The results are shown in Table 3. The classifier that obtained the best accuracy score is not the same as that obtained the best f1-score for the Pop Art class. This shows that other classes have benefited from the information obtained from the images generated (Tables 4 and 5).

**Table 3.** Summary of experiments with added synthetic Pop Art images

| Synthetic images | class f1-score | Classifier accuracy |
|---|---|---|
| 1205 (1×) | 60.00% | 74.00% |
| 2410 (2×) | 62.07% | 73.83% |
| 3615 (3×) | **65.52%** | 74.05% |
| 4820 (4×) | 62.81% | **74.07%** |

## 4.6 Sampling High Quantity Classes

Both Expressionism and Romanticism classes have a similar behavior to that of our reference model: they have many more images than most of the classes – more than four times Pop Art's image quantity – but low performance. It is interesting to observe that for both classes, the quantity of images that generated the best results was 1/4 of its original training data quantity. The synthetic Romantic class had a better f1-score when 3/4 of the quantity of the original data was added, but still didn't produce a better classifier.

**Table 4.** Summary of experiments with added synthetic Expressionist images

| Synthetic images | class f1-score | Classifier accuracy |
|---|---|---|
| 682 (1/8) | 64.61% | 73.81% |
| 1364 (1/4) | **66.77%** | **74.40%** |
| 2728 (1/2) | 65.62% | 73.96% |
| 4092 (3/4) | 65.67% | 74.11% |

**Table 5.** Summary of experiments with added synthetic Romantic images

| Synthetic images | class f1-score | Classifier accuracy |
|---|---|---|
| 705 (1/8) | 69.67% | 73.69% |
| 1410 (1/4) | 70.38% | **74.27%** |
| 2820 (1/2) | 69.93% | 73.83% |
| 4230 (3/4) | **70.69%** | 74.18% |

## 4.7 Summary of Results

Figure 3 shows how each class performed in the best experiment for each class (Pop Art, Expressionism and Romanticism). Although the classification problem has many classes to be able to point out correlations, it is possible to observe that the Art Nouveau class had its best performance with synthetic images from the Pop Art artistic movement. It is also observed that the Pop Art class itself performs even better when we have the information of the synthetic images of the artistic movements Romanticism and Expressionism.

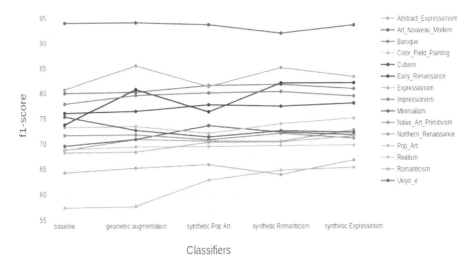

**Fig. 3.** The evolution of performance for each class during experiments.

Table 6 also shows the best result of each EfficientNet B0 model trained with synthetic artwork class. The strategy of Class-by-Class Performance Analysis allowed us to improve the classifier accuracy by almost 2%.

**Table 6.** EfficientNet B0 trained models.

| Experiment | Precision | Recall | Accuracy |
|---|---|---|---|
| Baseline | 73.58% | 73.47% | 72.43% |
| Geometric Augmentation | 74.62% | 74.46% | 73.59% |
| Geometric Augmentation + synthetic Pop Art | 74.89% | 74.50% | 74.07% |
| Geometric Augmentation + synthetic Expressionism | **76.12%** | **75.41%** | **74.40%** |
| Geometric Augmentation + synthetic Romanticism | 75.30% | 75.55% | 74.27% |

## 4.8   Generated Images

Figures 3, 4 and 5 show a sample of the images generated in our experiments. To help in understanding the quality of these generated images, real images of corresponding artistic styles were added above. By visual inspection, it is noticeable that the generated images retain general properties of the styles. For the three depicted artistic styles, it is clear that the models are flawed in terms of shape definition, but they are competent in the choice of colors, even in the variety of colors that a style contains and correctly separating grayscale images from colored images (examples in Figs. 4 and 5) (Fig. 6).

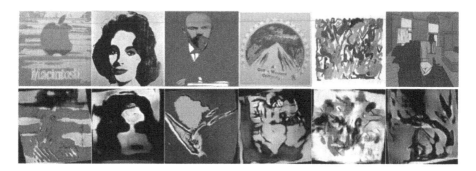

**Fig. 4.** First row of images contains real Pop Art painting and second row contains generated Pop Art painting.

**Fig. 5.** First row of images contains real Expressionist painting and second row contains generated Expressionist painting.

**Fig. 6.** First row of images contains real Romantic painting and second row contains generated Romantic painting.

# 5    Conclusion

Artwork style classification is quite challenging: class imbalance and high diversity within classes and similarities between classes are inevitable given existing art styles. Besides, classification performance does not correlate with dataset size. It is thus natural to look for data augmentation strategies; however, straightforward techniques do not generate images that can help distinguish between class styles.

In this paper we explored GANs for data augmentation in this setting; this is a little explored avenue and one that cannot be taken without some care. To be able to actually use GANs to generate artwork-like images with the desirable properties and diversity, we had to develop a working methodology, a specialized network architecture, and an adapted loss function. These technical contributions should be valuable in other settings where artwork is to be classified; moreover, they should be useful in data augmentation scenarios with many classes that are hard to differentiate and that are sensitive to popular existing techniques such as coloring and rotation.

We found that our approach and methodology can generate better classifiers. In particular, the combination of self-attention for mode diversity and the Wasserstein-GP loss function against vanishing gradient enabled us, in our experiments, to improve the augmentation of the images and consequently increase the accuracy of the model by almost 2 %.

**Acknowledgements.** This work is part of the Center for Data Science with funding by Itaú Unibanco. The first author thanks Itaú Unibanco for its generosity in authorizing research activities that led to this work. The second author was partially supported by Conselho Nacional de Desenvolvimento Científico e Tecnológico (CNPq), grant 312180/2018-7, and by São Paulo Research Foundation (FAPESP), grant 2019/07665-4.

# References

1. Arjovsky, M., Chintala, S., Bottou, L.: Wasserstein gan. arXiv (2017)
2. Arora, R.S., Elgammal, A.: Towards automated classification of fine-art painting style: a comparative study. In: Proceedings - International Conference on Pattern Recognition, pp. 3541–3544 (2012)
3. Bar, Y., Levy, N., Wolf, L.: Classification of artistic styles using binarized features derived from a deep neural network. In: Agapito, L., Bronstein, M.M., Rother, C. (eds.) ECCV 2014. LNCS, vol. 8925, pp. 71–84. Springer, Cham (2015). https://doi.org/10.1007/978-3-319-16178-5_5
4. Bianco, S., Mazzini, D., Napoletano, P., Schettini, R.: Multitask painting categorization by deep multibranch neural network. Expert Syst. Appl. **135**, 90–101 (2019). https://doi.org/10.1016/j.eswa.2019.05.036
5. Brock, A., Donahuey, J., Simonyany, K.: Large scale gan training for high fidelity natural image synthesis, pp. 1–35 (2018). arXiv
6. Cetinic, E., Lipic, T., Grgic, S.: Fine-tuning convolutional neural networks for fine art classification. Expert Syst. Appl. **114**, 107–118 (2018). https://doi.org/10.1016/j.eswa.2018.07.026

7. Chen, L., Yang, J.: Recognizing the style of visual arts via adaptive cross-layer correlation. In: MM 2019 - Proceedings of the 27th ACM International Conference on Multimedia, pp. 2459–2467 (2019). https://doi.org/10.1145/3343031.3350977
8. Chen, X., Duan, Y., Houthooft, R., Schulman, J., Sutskever, I., Abbeel, P.: Infogan: Interpretable representation learning by information maximizing generative adversarial nets. In: Neural Information Processing Systems, pp. 2180–2188 (2016)
9. Chu, W.T., Wu, Y.L.: Image style classification based on learnt deep correlation features. IEEE Trans. Multimedia **20**, 2491–2502 (2018). https://doi.org/10.1109/TMM.2018.2801718
10. Condorovici, R.G., Florea, C., Vertan, C.: Automatically classifying paintings with perceptual inspired descriptors. J. Visual Commun. Image Represent. **26**, 222–230 (2015). https://doi.org/10.1016/j.jvcir.2014.11.016
11. Daras, G., Odena, A., Zhang, H., Dimakis, A.G.: Your local gan: designing two dimensional local attention mechanisms for generative models. Proceedings of the IEEE Computer Society Conference on Computer Vision and Pattern Recognition, pp. 14519–14527 (2020). https://doi.org/10.1109/CVPR42600.2020.01454
12. Eldeen, N., Khalifa, M.: Detection of coronavirus (covid-19) associated pneumonia based on generative adversarial networks and a fine-tuned deep transfer learning model using chest x-ray dataset (2020). http://www.egyptscience.net
13. Elgammal, A., Liu, B., Elhoseiny, M., Mazzone, M.: Can: creative adversarial networks, generating "art" by learning about styles and deviating from style norms, pp. 1–22 (2017). arXiv
14. Elgammal, A., Liu, B., Kim, D., Elhoseiny, M., Mazzone, M.: The shape of art history in the eyes of the machine. In: 32nd AAAI Conference on Artificial Intelligence, AAAI 2018, pp. 2183–2191 (2018)
15. Farthing, S.: Tudo sobre Arte. 2 edn. (2018)
16. Florea, C., Toca, C., Gieseke, F.: Artistic movement recognition by boosted fusion of color structure and topographic description. In: Proceedings - 2017 IEEE Winter Conference on Applications of Computer Vision, WACV 2017, pp. 569–577 (2017). https://doi.org/10.1109/WACV.2017.69
17. Frid-Adar, M., Diamant, I., Klang, E., Amitai, M., Goldberger, J., Greenspan, H.: Gan-based synthetic medical image augmentation for increased CNN performance in liver lesion classification. Neurocomputing **321**, 321–331 (2018). https://doi.org/10.1016/j.neucom.2018.09.013
18. Gao, X., Tian, Y., Qi, Z.: RPD-GAN: learning to draw realistic paintings with generative adversarial network. IEEE Trans. Image Process. **29**, 8706–8720 (2020). https://doi.org/10.1109/TIP.2020.3018856
19. Goodfellow, I., et al.: Generative adversarial networks. Commun. ACM **63**, 139–144 (2014). https://doi.org/10.1145/3422622
20. Gulrajani, I., Ahmed, F., Arjovsky, M., Dumoulin, V., Courville, A.: Improved training of wasserstein gans, vol. 2017-Decem, pp. 5768–5778 (2017)
21. Han, C., et al.: Synthesizing diverse lung nodules wherever massively: 3d multi-conditional gan-based ct image augmentation for object detection. In: Proceedings - 2019 International Conference on 3D Vision, 3DV 2019, pp. 729–737 (2019). https://doi.org/10.1109/3DV.2019.00085
22. Hu, J., Shen, L., Sun, G.: Squeeze-and-excitation networks. In: Proceedings of the IEEE Computer Society Conference on Computer Vision and Pattern Recognition, pp. 7132–7141 (2018). https://doi.org/10.1109/CVPR.2018.00745
23. Karayev, S., et al.: Recognizing image style. In: BMVC 2014 - Proceedings of the British Machine Vision Conference 2014, pp. 1–20 (2014). https://doi.org/10.5244/c.28.122

24. Kastan, D.S., Farthing, S.: On Color. Yale University Press, New Haven (2018)
25. Krizhevsky, A., Sutskever, I., Hinton, G.E.: Imagenet classification with deep convolutional neural networks. Commun. ACM **60**, 84–90 (2012). https://doi.org/10.1145/3065386
26. Lecoutre, A., Negrevergne, B., Yger, F.: Recognizing art style automatically in painting with deep learning. J. Mach. Learn. Res. **77**, 327–342 (2017)
27. Mirza, M., Osindero, S.: Conditional generative adversarial nets, pp. 1–7 (2014)
28. Qin, Z., Liu, Z., Zhu, P., Xue, Y.: A gan-based image synthesis method for skin lesion classification. Comput. Methods Prog. Biomed. **195** (2020). https://doi.org/10.1016/j.cmpb.2020.105568
29. Rodriguez, C.S., Lech, M., Pirogova, E.: Classification of style in fine-art paintings using transfer learning and weighted image patches. In: 2018, 12th International Conference on Signal Processing and Communication Systems, ICSPCS 2018 - Proceedings, pp. 1–7 (2019). https://doi.org/10.1109/ICSPCS.2018.8631731
30. Sandler, M., Howard, A., Zhu, M., Zhmoginov, A., Chen, L.C.: Mobilenetv 2: inverted residuals and linear bottlenecks. In: Proceedings of the IEEE Computer Society Conference on Computer Vision and Pattern Recognition, pp. 4510–4520 (2018)
31. Sandoval, C., Pirogova, E., Lech, M.: Two-stage deep learning approach to the classification of fine-art paintings. IEEE Access **7**, 41770–41781 (2019)
32. Shamir, L., Macura, T., Orlov, N., Eckley, D.M., Goldberg, I.G.: Impressionism, expressionism, surrealism: automated recognition of painters and schools of art. ACM Trans. Appl. Percept. **7** (2010). https://doi.org/10.1145/1670671.1670672
33. Shorten, C., Khoshgoftaar, T.M.: A survey on image data augmentation for deep learning. J. Big Data **6**, 1–48 (2019)
34. Suh, S., Lee, H., Lukowicz, P., Lee, Y.O.: Cegan: classification enhancement generative adversarial networks for unraveling data imbalance problems. Neural Netw. **133**, 69–86 (2021)
35. Tan, M., Le, Q.V.: Efficientnet: rethinking model scaling for convolutional neural networks. In: 36th International Conference on Machine Learning, ICML 2019 2019-June, pp. 10691–10700 (2019)
36. Tan, W.R., Chan, C.S., Aguirre, H.E., Tanaka, K.: Ceci n'est pas une pipe: a deep convolutional network for fine-art paintings classification. In: Proceedings - International Conference on Image Processing, ICIP 2016-August, pp. 3703–3707 (2016). https://doi.org/10.1109/ICIP.2016.7533051
37. Tomei, M., Cornia, M., Baraldi, L., Cucchiara, R.: Art2real: unfolding the reality of artworks via semantically-aware image-to-image translation, vol. 2019-June, pp. 5842–5852 (2019). https://doi.org/10.1109/CVPR.2019.00600
38. Waheed, A., Goyal, M., Gupta, D., Khanna, A., Al-Turjman, F., Pinheiro, P.R.: Covidgan: data augmentation using auxiliary classifier GAN for improved covid-19 detection. IEEE Access **8**, 91916–91923 (2020). https://doi.org/10.1109/ACCESS.2020.2994762
39. Wang, Z., She, Q., Ward, T.E.: Generative adversarial networks: a survey and taxonomy, pp. 1–41 (2019). arXiv
40. Wu, J., Huang, Z., Thoma, J., Acharya, D., Van Gool, L.: Wasserstein divergence for GANs. In: Ferrari, V., Hebert, M., Sminchisescu, C., Weiss, Y. (eds.) ECCV 2018. LNCS, vol. 11209, pp. 673–688. Springer, Cham (2018). https://doi.org/10.1007/978-3-030-01228-1_40
41. Xue, A.: End-to-end chinese landscape painting creation using generative adversarial networks, pp. 3863–3871 (2020). arXiv

42. Özal Yıldırım, Pławiak, P., Tan, R.S., Acharya, U.R.: Arrhythmia detection using deep convolutional neural network with long duration ecg signals (2018)
43. Zhang, H., Goodfellow, I., Metaxas, D., Odena, A.: Self-attention generative adversarial networks. In: Chaudhuri, K., Salakhutdinov, R. (eds.) Proceedings of the 36th International Conference on Machine Learning. Proceedings of Machine Learning Research, vol. 97, pp. 7354–7363. PMLR (2019)
44. Zhong, S., Huang, X., Xiao, Z.: Fine-art painting classification via two-channel dual path networks. Int. J. Mach. Learn. Cybern. **11**, 137–152 (2020)
45. Zhu, J.Y., Park, T., Isola, P., Efros, A.A.: Unpaired image-to-image translation using cycle-consistent adversarial networks, vol. 2017-Octob, pp. 2242–2251 (2017)
46. Zhu, Y., Ji, Y., Zhang, Y., Xu, L., Zhou, A.L., Chan, E.: Machine: the new art connoisseur (2019). http://arxiv.org/abs/1911.10091

# Iris-CV: Classifying Iris Flowers Is Not as Easy as You Thought

Itamar de Paiva Rocha Filho[1(✉)], João Pedro Vasconcelos Teixeira[1],
João Wallace Lucena Lins[1], Felipe Honorato de Sousa[1],
Ana Clara Chaves Sousa[1], Manuel Ferreira Junior[1], Thaís Ramos[2],
Cecília Silva[3], Thaís Gaudencio do Rêgo[1], Yuri de Almeida Malheiros[1],
and Telmo Silva Filho[1]

[1] Universidade Federal da Paraíba, João Pessoa, PB, Brazil
[2] Universidade Federal do Rio Grande do Norte, Natal, RN, Brazil
[3] Universidade Federal de Pernambuco, Recife, PE, Brazil

**Abstract.** The iris flower dataset is a ubiquitous benchmark task in machine learning literature. With its 150 instances, four continuous features, and three balanced classes, of which one is linearly separable from the others, iris is generally considered an easy problem. Hence researchers usually rely on other datasets when they need more challenging benchmarks. A similar situation happens with computer vision datasets such as MNIST and ImageNet, which have been widely explored. The state of the art models essentially solves these problems, motivating the search for more challenging tasks. Therefore, this paper introduces a new computer vision toy dataset featuring iris flowers. Users of a nature photography application took the pictures, thus they include noisy background information. Additionally, certain desirable features are not guaranteed, such as single, similarly-sized objects at the center of each picture, which makes the task more challenging. Our benchmark results show that the dataset can be challenging for traditional machine learning algorithms without any pre-processing steps, while state of the art deep learning architectures achieve around 82% accuracy, which means some effort will be necessary to drive this accuracy closer to what has been accomplished for MNIST and ImageNet.

**Keywords:** Computer vision · Dataset · Machine learning

## 1 Introduction

Since Fisher's original publication in the context of linear discriminant analysis [4], the iris flower dataset turned into one of the most well-known and explored datasets in statistical classification and machine learning (ML), with over 18,000 citations until the date of publication of this work.

The dataset consists of 150 observations, equally divided into three classes (*Iris setosa*, *Iris virginica* and *Iris versicolor*), which are described by four features: the length and the width of the sepals and petals, in centimeters. The

© Springer Nature Switzerland AG 2021
A. Britto and K. Valdivia Delgado (Eds.): BRACIS 2021, LNAI 13074, pp. 254–264, 2021.
https://doi.org/10.1007/978-3-030-91699-2_18

measurements were taken by Edgar Anderson [1], who was interested in measuring the morphological variation of these species, while Fisher was the first to use the dataset in a statistical learning context.

Iris is generally considered an easy classification problem and is frequently used as ML's "hello world" (i.e., as the first example one comes into contact with as a beginner in this area). Most classification techniques have no trouble achieving accuracies well above 90% for iris with various hyperparameter configurations, as shown by multiple benchmark results available at OpenML [17].

In this paper, we introduce a new iris flower toy dataset, which breaks away from the original dataset's simplicity by turning the problem of iris classification into a computer vision (CV) task. Since the rise of deep learning (DL), the literature of CV has seen many of its well-known problems, including MNIST [9], ImageNet [3], and the newer Fashion-MNIST [18], being mostly solved, i.e., there have been models which achieved near-human or even better-than-human accuracy for these tasks.

Hence, this work introduces a dataset which features CV challenges such as fine grained categorization, background noise, real world environment conditions (e.g. lighting variation), as well as different scales and non-centered objects. The main idea is to make this dataset available so that it can be used to validate machine/deep learning approaches considering difficult CV scenarios. The paper also contains the classification results of traditional machine learning algorithms, as well as some state-of-the-art deep learning architectures using the Iris-CV dataset.

The remainder of this paper is organized as follows: Sect. 2 shows some related works using the iNaturalist dataset, Sect. 3 describes our new dataset, Sect. 4 presents benchmark results, including experiments with traditional ML algorithms and state of the art deep neural networks, and finally, Sect. 5 contains our final remarks.

## 2    Related Works

The iNaturalist is a dataset proposed by [16] and has 675,170 images from more than 5 thousand different species of animals and plants. The category of plants has almost 200 thousand images. Those species images were captured from all over the world, with different cameras and image qualities. Also, it has a large class imbalance [16]. This dataset is constantly being updated.

Although iNaturalist is a toy dataset that was used in Kaggle competitions, it was already used in published papers. Some works were focused on detection [16] and others' purposes were to make classifications such as this work.

Plant classification was the focus of a study using the iNaturalist dataset [12], where the authors used a convolutional neural network to classify the plant's subclasses. Data Augmentation was used to reduce overfitting and balance the classes. Then, a transfer learning approach based on ResNet50 was utilized. This work classifies different plant species rather than only iris unlike our work.

Another study used the entire iNaturalist dataset to make both classification and detection [16]. For classification, the following deep network architectures were performed: ResNets, Inception V3, Inception ResNetV2 and MobileNet. From those models, Inception ResNetV2 SE had the best performance. This work also classifies different plant species rather than focusing on iris flowers, and their experiments did not include classic algorithms unlike ours.

This work uses the iNaturalist dataset as a single source, but some other researchers used it combined with different datasets. An example of it was the work proposed by [7]. After selecting different species of plant images from three datasets, they applied deep learning techniques for plant classification. Their goal was to achieve at least 50 percent accuracy as a baseline classification and ResNet50 was able to classify almost half of the iNaturalist observations. The iNaturalist dataset performed better than the Portuguese Flora dataset, but the Google Image Search observations were better than both.

As the purpose of this paper is to classify the different species of Iris, the iNaturalist dataset provided the images necessary to do that. The paper differs from works described in this section since it focuses on benchmark analysis, thus it covers a variety of algorithms and computational cost for each of them. In addition, we focus specifically on iris flowers, whereas the other works used plants in general.

## 3   A New Iris Dataset

Our new iris dataset, called Iris-CV, consists of 5,139 examples extracting from iNaturalist (September 10th 2020). Each example representing an RGB image associated with a label corresponding to five different species: Bearded Iris (**Be**) (*Iris x germanica*, 928 images), Douglas Iris (**Do**) (*Iris douglasiana*, 944 images), Dwarf Crested Iris (**Dw**) (*Iris cristata*, 1290 images), Western Blue Iris (**We**) (*Iris missouriensis*, 1036 images), and Yellow Iris (**Ye**) (*Iris pseudacorus*, 941 images), as shown in Table 1. All images were gathered from iNaturalist [10], a website that provides Creative Commons-licensed pictures of fauna and flora taken by users worldwide.

**Table 1.** Dataset size per class

| Class | Quantity of images |
|---|---|
| Bearded Iris (Be) | 928 |
| Douglas Iris (Do) | 944 |
| Dwarf Crested Iris (Dw) | 1290 |
| Western Blue Iris | 1036 |
| Yellow Iris (Ye) | 941 |
| Total | 5,139 |

After downloading the images, we manually removed photos that had too much noise, i.e., pictures of many different flowers, human hands covering the majority of the frame, and blurry images, which could confuse learning models, resulting in a harder problem.

The original images have different sizes, therefore we resized them to a resolution of 256x256, which maintained the images' main features while avoiding high memory requirements. We also kept the color information, which is coded in three RGB channels, as it can be important to differentiate the classes. Table 2 shows resized examples of each class. The classes show different color patterns, particularly the Yellow Iris, which is appropriately named, and the Dwarf Crested Iris, with its white and orange crests.

**Table 2.** Class names and examples from the Iris-CV dataset.

| Label | Class | Examples |
| --- | --- | --- |
| 0 | Bearded Iris | |
| 1 | Douglas Iris | |
| 2 | Dwarf Crested Iris | |
| 3 | Western Blue Iris | |
| 4 | Yellow Iris | |

The pictures also show heavy background information, thus models must learn how to separate the flowers from the background to perform well. Images may contain multiple and/or non-centered flowers. Additionally, due to the different image and flower sizes, some individuals may become small compared to others after we resize the pictures, as seen in some examples in Table 2. There can also be very different lighting conditions across pictures.

Finally, successful models will have to learn that each species can show different colors, for instance, Dwarf Crested Irises can be lavender, lilac, pale blue, purple, white, or pink. As a result of all these features, Iris-CV can be a challenging computer vision problem.

## 4  Benchmark Results

We begin our experimental analysis by validating our dataset with eight different classic algorithms using scikit-learn and XGBoost libraries, as listed below:

- Decision tree (DT);
- Extra tree (ET);
- Gradient boosting (GB);
- Extreme gradient boosting (XGB);
- Multilayer perceptron (MLP);
- Perceptron;
- Random forest (RF);
- K-nearest neighbors (KNN).

Since these algorithms are not originally equipped to receive pixel matrices as input, we flattened the 256x256x3 images, obtaining vectors with 196,608 dimensions which can then be used as input. After obtaining the input vectors, we rescaled the images by dividing each pixel by 255 before training and testing the algorithms.

Experiments were carried out using 5-fold stratified cross-validation, which maintains class proportions across folds. The code was implemented using python's scikit-learn library [11].

The algorithms and their hyperparameter values were chosen based on their performances on Fashion-MNIST's benchmark [18] and we used several machines to streamline the execution of tasks. Despite each machine has different settings (i.e. processor, graphic cards and memory), it is important to notice that this only affects the training time, not the algorithms overall performance. The best results achieved per classifier can be seen in Table 3.

We tested different values (Table 3) for the following hyperparameters: criterion; objective; splitter; max_depth; loss; n_estimators; activation; hidden_layer_sizes; penalty; n_neighbors; weights; and p. See scikit-learn's documentation [11] for more details about these parameters. In addition, Table 4 describes the hardware resources for each classifier.

Even though most results surpassed the expected accuracy of a random classifier (0.251), the overall performance shows how difficult this problem is for classic methods without any extra preprocessing specifically designed to improve their results. Best results were obtained by XGBoost with 500 estimators, multi:softmax as the split objective, and 3 as the max depth, with a mean accuracy of 0.614. Results were also poor compared to Fashion-MNIST [18] and MNIST [9], where the same algorithms can reach accuracy values over 0.85 and 0.95, respectively.

As mentioned in Sect. 3, our dataset's difficulty can be explained by some factors, such as somewhat high-dimensional images, RGB channels, non-centered images, noisy backgrounds, and petals with different colors within each species. Thus, this problem cannot be tackled by simple approaches.

**Table 3.** Results with standard deviation (Std) of classic algorithms for the Iris-CV dataset using 5-fold cross validation. The time column refers only to training time. Hyperparameter names are shown as they appear in scikit-learn's documentation.

| Classifier | Hyperparameters | | | Accuracy(Std) | Time |
|---|---|---|---|---|---|
| DT | criterion | splitter | max_depth | | |
| | gini | random | 10 | 0.365 (0.015) | 00:11:22 |
| | **entropy** | **best** | **10** | **0.371 (0.016)** | 01:21:39 |
| | entropy | best | 50 | 0.361 (0.007) | 01:41:31 |
| | entropy | best | 100 | 0.363 (0.016) | 01:47:38 |
| | entropy | random | 50 | 0.358 (0.006) | 00:22:12 |
| ET | criterion | splitter | max_depth | | |
| | **gini** | **best** | **10** | **0.353 (0.009)** | 00:00:11 |
| | gini | random | 10 | 0.345 (0.009) | 00:00:06 |
| | entropy | best | 10 | 0.350 (0.010) | 00:00:18 |
| | entropy | best | 50 | 0.342 (0.007) | 00:00:21 |
| | entropy | random | 10 | 0.352 (0.016) | 00:00:06 |
| GB | loss | n_estimators | max_depth | | |
| | deviance | 10 | 3 | 0.460 (0.012) | 12:19:09 |
| | **deviance** | **50** | **3** | **0.538 (0.024)** | 53:08:56 |
| XGB | objective | n_estimators | max_depth | | |
| | multi:softmax | 50 | 3 | 0.561 (0.015) | 00:18:29 |
| | multi:softmax | 100 | 3 | 0.584 (0.016) | 00:36:25 |
| | **multi:softmax** | **500** | **3** | **0.614 (0.019)** | 02:48:48 |
| MLP | activation | hidden_layer_sizes | | | |
| | tanh | (10,) | | 0.275 (0.049) | 00:50:51 |
| | tanh | (100,) | | 0.251 (0.000) | 00:53:32 |
| | tanh | (10, 10) | | 0.251 (0.000) | 00:29:27 |
| | **relu** | **(100,)** | | **0.383 (0.109)** | 02:07:01 |
| | relu | (100, 10) | | 0.251 (0.000) | 01:53:32 |
| Perceptron | penalty | | | | |
| | elasticnet | | | 0.410 (0.068) | 00:08:50 |
| RF | criterion | n_estimators | max_depth | | |
| | gini | 100 | 100 | 0.516 (0.013) | 00:03:03 |
| | entropy | 100 | 50 | 0.504 (0.010) | 00:04:00 |
| | entropy | 100 | 100 | 0.503 (0.008) | 00:03:58 |
| | **gini** | **1000** | **50** | **0.543 (0.015)** | 00:09:35 |
| | gini | 1000 | 100 | 0.539 (0.025) | 00:09:56 |
| KNN | n_neighbors | weights | p | | |
| | 1 | uniform | 1 | 0.299 (0.010) | 00:47:57 |
| | 5 | uniform | 1 | 0.318 (0.021) | 00:47:54 |
| | **5** | **distance** | **1** | **0.321 (0.017)** | 00:48:00 |
| | 9 | uniform | 1 | 0.318 (0.015) | 00:47:46 |
| | 9 | distance | 2 | 0.310 (0.015) | 00:47:45 |

**Table 4.** Hardware settings for training and evaluate each classifier

| Classifier | Hardware |
| --- | --- |
| DT | i7-7700HQ 16 GB RAM |
| ET and MLP | i5-7200U 8 GB RAM |
| GB and KNN | Ryzen 5 3600 16 GB RAM |
| XGB and Perceptron penalty | Ryzen 5 3600X 16 GB RAM |
| RF | i7-8550U 8 GB RAM |

### 4.1 Deep Neural Net Results

We now turn to state-of-the-art Convolutional Neural Network (CNN) architectures, implemented using TensorFlow 2 [5], to see how these techniques performing in the classification of Iris-CV images. We chose to the hyperparameters used in the DenseNet [8] paper, since this is a state-of-the-art network. We trained each network with the stochastic gradient descent (SGD) optimizer, using 0.9 for the Nesterov momentum and 40 epochs. Regarding the learning rate, we chose a starting value of 0.1, decaying at a pace of $10^{-\frac{epoch}{20}}$ as a way of tuning network performance, which was observed empirically. In addition, we used different state-of-the-art architectures such as EfficientNet, MobileNet and ResNet50 to verify if it has any performance improvement regarding state-of-the-art network architectures.

Also, we performed data augmentation to balance the class proportions. We tested several combinations of the parameters of the ImageDataGenerator provided by TensorFlow and Keras, viewing the images we had as a result and choosing the ones that kept most of the original information. Below we list the augmentation parameters:

- **Rescale:** 1/255
- **Rotation Range:** 20°
- **Width Shift Range:** 0.1
- **Height Shift Range:** 0.1
- **Horizontal Flip:** True
- **Shear Range:** 0.1
- **Zoom Range:** 0.4 - 0.5
- **Fill Mode:** nearest

More information about these settings and the process used by ImageData-Generator is available in the official Tensorflow documentation[1]. The trained architectures are listed below:

**DenseNet121.** Proposed by Huang [8], this deep net aims to optimize the flow of information between the layers of the network, making a dependency link between them, trying to minimize convergence time through shorter paths.

---

[1] See Tensorflow documentation for more details.

**EfficientNetB0.** This architecture, introduced by Mingxing Tan [15], is a neural network obtained through a compound scaling method of ConvNets's depth, width, and resolution.

**InceptionV3.** This architecture is a refinement of its antecessors, firstly by the introduction of batch normalization, and later by additional factorization ideas in the third iteration [14].

**MobileNetV2.** This network uses light convolution layers to filter the features in the intermediate layer, is based on a residual inverted structure [13].

**ResNet50.** ResNet [6] is an abbreviation for Residual Networks. This type of deep convolutional neural network uses residual blocks and can work with many layers of depths, avoiding the vanishing gradient problem. Specifically, ResNet50 is a 50-layer residual network.

**Xception.** Xception [2] is a novel deep convolutional neural network architecture inspired by Inception [14], where Inception modules have been replaced with depthwise separable convolutions.

The models were evaluated using 5-fold stratified cross-validation. Table 5 shows that all CNNs outperformed almost all classic algorithms, as expected. Most architectures achieved accuracies over 0.74, except for EfficientNetB3, which achieved the worst performance among the deep learning architectures. Results also show that MobileNetV2 holds the highest accuracy and can be considered the state of the art for the Iris-CV dataset.

In addition to assessing accuracy, we analyzed the confusion matrix that corresponds to the best MobileNetV2 result, so that we can determine which classes the models have the most difficulty in predicting. The confusion matrix is shown in Table 6.

**Table 5.** Results with standard deviation (Std) of Deep Learning architectures for the Iris-CV dataset using 5-fold cross-validation. Columns $B$ and $E$ refer to batch size and number of epochs, respectively. We used different batch sizes considering hardware resources of each machine. The DenseNet121, EfficientNetB0, and MobileNetV2 architectures were trained using RTX 2060 Super, ResNet 50 was trained with RTX 2070, while the remaining ones were trained with a GTX 1660Ti.

| Classifier | $B$ | $E$ | Accuracy | Std | Time |
|---|---|---|---|---|---|
| DenseNet121 | 32 | 40 | 0.751 | 0.032 | 02:36:36 |
| EfficientNetB0 | 32 | 40 | 0.591 | 0.051 | 02:15:39 |
| InceptionV3 | 16 | 40 | 0.653 | 0.202 | 02:03:47 |
| **MobileNetV2** | **32** | **40** | **0.816** | **0.009** | **02:12:21** |
| ResNet50 | 16 | 40 | 0.553 | 0.194 | 02:32:53 |
| Xception | 16 | 40 | 0.760 | 0.032 | 3:16:22 |

**Table 6.** Confusion matrix corresponding to MobileNetV2's best test accuracy – each class is represented by the first two letters in its common name.

|  |  | Predicted label | | | | |
|---|---|---|---|---|---|---|
|  |  | Be | Do | Dw | We | Ye |
| Class label | Be | 148 | 15 | 4 | 9 | 10 |
|  | Do | 23 | 130 | 20 | 14 | 1 |
|  | Dw | 7 | 13 | 230 | 6 | 2 |
|  | We | 7 | 11 | 6 | 184 | 0 |
|  | Ye | 11 | 1 | 1 | 7 | 168 |

The MobileNetV2 confusion matrix shows that the network was good at differentiating Western Iris (We), Yellow Iris (Ye), and Dwarf Crested Iris (Dw) from the other classes, as their precision scores corresponded to approximately 88%, 89%, and 89%, respectively, as shown in Table 7. The other two classes – Bearded Iris (Be) and Douglas Iris (Do) – were not as well discriminated, and the algorithm had some trouble distinguishing them correctly since the flowers belonging to these two classes often have the same color, although they have different petal shapes. The similarity between these two classes can be observed in Table 8. Douglas Iris can also sometimes be confused with Dwarf Crested Irises, due to their white petal markings. As a result, Douglas Irises were the hardest flowers to classify correctly, with only 69% precision.

**Table 7.** Precision, recall and F1-Score corresponding to MobileNetV2's best results in test dataset - each class is represented by the first letters in its common name

| Class | Precision | Recall | F1-Score |
|---|---|---|---|
| Be | 0.79 | 0.75 | 0.76 |
| Do | 0.69 | 0.76 | 0.71 |
| Dw | 0.89 | 0.89 | 0.88 |
| We | 0.88 | 0.83 | 0.85 |
| Ye | 0.89 | 0.92 | 0.89 |

**Table 8.** Examples of Bearded Iris and Douglas Iris flowers showing their similar colors, but different petal structures.

| Class | Examples |
| --- | --- |
| Bearded Iris | |
| Douglas Iris | |

## 5   Conclusion

This paper introduced a new computer vision dataset, called Iris-CV, consisting of five classes of iris flowers. The images show many features that make this dataset a challenging task, such as non-centered flowers, different lighting conditions, multiple flowers per image, and classes that naturally appear with different petal colors. Due to all of these reasons, Iris-CV proved to be too hard for traditional machine learning algorithms, with poorer results than those observed for established benchmark datasets, such as MNIST and Fashion-MNIST.

State-of-the-art deep neural nets also performed worse than current results for MNIST, Fashion-MNIST, and ImageNet, with MobileNetV2 achieving 82% accuracy, which is the best cross-validated result so far. Additionally, an analysis of the best confusion matrix produced by MobileNetV2 showed that three of the classes are more easily classified, namely Dwarf Crested Iris, Western Iris, and Yellow Iris. The remaining two classes – Bearded Iris and Douglas Iris – offered harder challenges, with the latter being the toughest to discriminate.

Since this paper main objective is to propose a new Iris dataset considering computer vision common problems (e.g. occlusion, background noise and fine grained features), we performed a baseline of most used and state-of-the-art algorithms. Future works include further exploration of deep neural net architectures and regularization techniques since the architectures used in this work focused on learning large datasets and some of them overfitted. In addition, hyper parameter tuning is also possible through optimization techniques such as bayesian optimization, grid search or random search, specially classic machine learning approaches which returned worse performed in this dataset. Therefore, our next goal is to improve the current benchmark results, collect more data from different sources, and extract an object detection dataset based on the same images.

# References

1. Anderson, E.: The species problem in iris. Ann. Mo. Bot. Gard. **23**(3), 457–509 (1936). http://www.jstor.org/stable/2394164
2. Chollet, F.: Xception: deep learning with depthwise separable convolutions. In: Proceedings of the IEEE Conference on Computer Vision and Pattern Recognition, pp. 1251–1258 (2017)
3. Deng, J., Dong, W., Socher, R., Li, L.J., Li, K., Fei-Fei, L.: Imagenet: a large-scale hierarchical image database. In: 2009 IEEE Conference on Computer Vision and Pattern Recognition, pp. 248–255. IEEE (2009)
4. Fisher, R.A.: The use of multiple measurements in taxonomic problems. Ann. Eugenics **7**(2), 179–188 (1936). https://doi.org/10.1111/j.1469-1809.1936.tb02137. x, https://onlinelibrary.wiley.com/doi/abs/10.1111/j.1469-1809.1936.tb02137.x
5. Goodfellow, I., et al.: TensorFlow: large-scale machine learning on heterogeneous systems (2015). https://www.tensorflow.org/softwareavailablefromtensorflow.org
6. He, K., Zhang, X., Ren, S., Sun, J.: Deep residual learning for image recognition. In: Proceedings of the IEEE Conference on Computer Vision and Pattern Recognition, pp. 770–778 (2016)
7. Heredia, I.: Large-scale plant classification with deep neural networks. In: Proceedings of the Computing Frontiers Conference, pp. 259–262 (2017)
8. Huang, G., Liu, Z., Van Der Maaten, L., Weinberger, K.Q.: Densely connected convolutional networks. In: Proceedings of the IEEE Conference on Computer Vision and Pattern Recognition, pp. 4700–4708 (2017)
9. LeCun, Y., Bottou, L., Bengio, Y., Haffner, P.: Gradient-based learning applied to document recognition. Proc. IEEE **86**(11), 2278–2324 (1998)
10. Loarie, S.: A community for naturalists (2008). https://www.inaturalist.org/
11. Pedregosa, F., et al.: Scikit-learn: machine learning in Python. J. Mach. Learn. Res. **12**, 2825–2830 (2011)
12. R. Al-Qurran, M.A.A., Shatnawi, A.: Plant classification in the wild: a transfer learning approach. International Arab Conference on Information Technology (ACIT) (2018)
13. Sandler, M., Howard, A., Zhu, M., Zhmoginov, A., Chen, L.C.: Mobilenetv 2: Inverted residuals and linear bottlenecks. In: Proceedings of the IEEE Conference on Computer Vision and Pattern Recognition, pp. 4510–4520 (2018)
14. Szegedy, C., Vanhoucke, V., Ioffe, S., Shlens, J., Wojna, Z.: Rethinking the inception architecture for computer vision. In: Proceedings of the IEEE Conference on Computer Vision and Pattern Recognition, pp. 2818–2826 (2016)
15. Tan, M., Le, Q.: Efficientnet: rethinking model scaling for convolutional neural networks. In: International Conference on Machine Learning, pp. 6105–6114. PMLR (2019)
16. Van Horn, G., et al.: The inaturalist species classification and detection dataset. In: Proceedings of the IEEE Conference on Computer Vision and Pattern Recognition, pp. 8769–8778 (2018)
17. Vanschoren, J., van Rijn, J.N., Bischl, B., Torgo, L.: Openml: networked science in machine learning. SIGKDD Explor. **15**(2), 49–60 (2013). https://doi.org/10.1145/2641190.2641198, http://doi.acm.org/10.1145/2641190.2641198
18. Xiao, H., Rasul, K., Vollgraf, R.: Fashion-mnist: a novel image dataset for benchmarking machine learning algorithms (2017). arXiv preprint arXiv:1708.07747

# Performance Analysis of YOLOv3 for Real-Time Detection of Pests in Soybeans

Fábio Amaral Godoy da Silveira[1]([✉]) [iD], Everton Castelão Tetila[1] [iD],
Gilberto Astolfi[2,3] [iD], Anderson Bessa da Costa[1] [iD],
and Willian Paraguassu Amorim[1] [iD]

[1] Federal University of Grande Dourados, FACET, Dourados 79825-070, Brazil
{evertontetila,andersoncosta,willianamorim}@ufgd.edu.br
[2] Federal Institute of Mato Grosso do Sul, Informática/Eng. de Software,
Campo Grande 79100-510, Brazil
[3] Federal University of Mato Grosso do Sul, Facom, Campo Grande 79070-900, Brazil
http://www.springer.com/gp/computer-science/lncs

**Abstract.** In this work, we evaluate the *You Only Look Once* (YOLOv3) architecture for real-time detection of insect pests in soybean. Soybean crop images were collected on different days, locations, and weather conditions between the phenological stages R1 to R6, considered the period of the high occurrence of soybean pests. For training and testing the neural network, we used 5-fold cross-validation analyzing four metrics to evaluate the classification results: precision, recall, F-score, and accuracy; and three metrics to evaluate the detection results: mean absolute error (MAE), root mean square error (RMSE) and coefficient of determination ($R^2$). The experimental results showed that the YOLOv3 architecture trained with batch size 32 leads to higher classification and detection rates than batch sizes 4 and 16. The results indicate that the evaluated architecture can support experts and farmers in monitoring pest control action levels in soybean fields.

**Keywords:** Deep learning · Object detection · Precision agriculture · Pests in soybeans

## 1 Introduction

Soy (*Glycine max*) is a vegetable crop belonging to the Fabaceae family. It is mainly used for human nutrition (in the form of soybean oil, tofu, soy sauce, soy milk, soy protein, soybeans) and animal nutrition (in the preparation of

We thank the Centro Nacional de Desenvolvimento Científico e Tecnológico (CNPq), the Coordenação de Aperfeiçoamento de Pessoal de Nível Superior (CAPES), NVIDIA Corporation for the graphics card donation, and the Fundação de Apoio ao Desenvolvimento do Ensino, Ciência e Tecnologia do estado de Mato Grosso do Sul (FUNDECT).

A. Britto and K. Valdivia Delgado (Eds.): BRACIS 2021, LNAI 13074, pp. 265–279, 2021.
https://doi.org/10.1007/978-3-030-91699-2_19

animal feed). Additionally, it has an excellent nutritional profile and essential economic support [1]. In the 2019–2020 season, Brazil has once again become the world's largest producer of soybeans, surpassing its main competitor, the United States. For the Brazilian crop in 2020–2021 is expected a record production of 134.45 million tons, representing an increase of 7.7% over the previous crop [2]. The state of Mato Grosso is the largest Brazilian producer, followed by the Rio Grande do Sul, Paraná, Goiás, and Mato Grosso do Sul [3]. It is estimated that most of the direct costs for soybean production are concentrated in fertilizers (27.82%), pesticides (18.24%), machinery operations (9.10%), seeds (7.35%) and depreciation of agricultural machinery and equipment (6.76%) [4]. Therefore, one of the highest costs for soybean production is applying pesticides to control pests that can cause damage to the end product.

Monitoring pests from the beginning of soybean development allows a more efficient application of pesticides. Agricultural inputs can be applied in the correct amount and places, reducing production costs and the environmental impact from the overuse of chemical control. Additionally, contributing to human health and food safety [5]. Sampling methods, visual examination of plants, and examination of soil samples have been used in monitoring pests, and their damage in the crop [6].

Regardless of the method used to assess field pest infestation, the number of insects should be recorded at each sampling point, allowing to determine the level of infestation in each area of the field. The higher the number of samples taken in an area, the more confidence in predicting the level of pest infestation. It is recommended at least six samplings for plots up to 10 ha, eight considering plots up to 30 ha, and ten considering plots up to 100 ha. For larger farms, a division into 100 ha plots is recommended [6].

Digital images collected from the field are an increasingly used alternative to manual sampling methods. Computer vision systems fed with these digital images perform real-time detection of pest insects. Automatically analyzing images is crucial for making these applications viable since many images are captured. In addition, high spatial resolution cameras can be embarked on Unmanned Aerial Vehicles (UAVs) to capture images of the crop on data collection missions, allowing experts and farmers to make better pest management decisions [7]. UAVs can also be programmed to perform automatic flight plan operations, with an autonomy of over 1 h depending on the model, covering average areas that can exceed 1,000 ha per flight [8]. However, few works address the use of digital images to identify insect pests in soybeans. Furthermore, no reports have been found in the literature of pest monitoring in soybean fields using state-of-the-art object detection methods such as YOLOv3 [9], Faster R-CNN [10], and RetinaNet [11].

This paper proposes to evaluate the You Only Look Once (YOLOv3) architecture to detect pest insects in an actual field environment under different lighting conditions, object size, and complex background variations. YOLOv3 is one of the most popular series of object detection models. Its advantage has been to provide real-time detections while approaching the accuracy of state-of-the-art object detection models. Soybean crop images were collected on different days, locations, and weather conditions between the phenological stages R1 to R6, considered the period of the high occurrence of soybean pests. For training and testing the neural network, we used 5-fold cross-validation analyzing four metrics to evaluate the classification results: accuracy, recall, F-score, and precision; and three metrics to evaluate the detection results: mean absolute error (MAE), root mean square error (RMSE) and coefficient of determination ($R^2$). To the best of our knowledge, no papers were found that address state-of-the-art object detection methods for pest detection in soybean.

## 2 Related Work

By using deep learning, the authors in [12] created a framework that identifies ten types of pests of different crops using a manually collected dataset. The dataset was collected by downloading 5,629 images from search engines (Google, Baidu, Yahoo, and Bing) and taking outdoor footage using an iPhone 7 Plus. In the pre-processing phase, data augmentation was used to expand the dataset. Further, the *GrabCut* and *Watershed* algorithms were implemented to remove complex background from the images. In the training phase, VGG-16, VGG-19, ResNet50, ResNet152 and GoogLeNet were used. The GoogLeNet model outperformed other models in terms of accuracy, model complexity, and robustness in the experiments. The original model achieved an accuracy of 93%, while the fine-tuned model achieved an accuracy of 98.91%. On the other hand, GoogLeNet required more computational resources. As a drawback, the complex architecture of Inception-V3 makes it challenging to adjust the layer structure for a specific dataset.

A novel pest detection approach called DeepPest, based on two-stage mobile vision, was proposed in [13] for small-sized pest recognition and multiple species classification in an unbalanced dataset. First, DeepPest extracts multi-scale contextual information from images. Next, a multi-projection pest detection model (MDM) is proposed and trained by crop-related pest images. The MDM function can combine pest contextual information from low-level convolutional layers with high-level layers to generate the super-resolved feature of DeepPest. Experimental results show better performance of DeepPest compared with other state-of-the-art methods. Although the dataset contains 17,192 pest images captured in a field environment with 76,595 pest annotations, the dataset is restricted to wheat and rice crops.

Through the use of Convolutional Neural Network (CNN), the authors in [14] developed a mobile application for detecting pests and diseases in rice. An Inception-v3 model was trained using transfer learning with the weights obtained from Imagenet. The final layer of the model was retrained from scratch using the provided images. Experiments showed that the model achieved an accuracy of 90.9%. The mobile app can display the appropriate description of the pest, its possible damage, and how to control it. Nonetheless, no information about the level of infestation or the number of pests in the crop can be found.

The authors in [15] created and made available a large-scale dataset, called IP102, for pest insect recognition, including over 75,000 images of 102 species. Initially, the performance of classification with shallow approaches was evaluated, comparing six methods: color histogram, Gabor filter, GIST, Scale Invariant Feature Transform (SIFT), Speeded Up Robust Features (SURF), local color histogram; and two classifiers: Support Vector Machine (SVM), k-Nearest Neighbors (k-NN). Next, four Deep Learning approaches were compared: Alexnet, GoogleNet, VGGNet, and ResNet. As a result, the best shallow approach achieved 19.5% accuracy using the combination of SURF and the SVM classifier. Resnet stood out among the deep approaches. Last, five state-of-the-art detection methods were evaluated on IP102: Faster R-CNN, FPN, SSD300, RefineDet, and YOLOv3. The results show that the performance of the two-stage detector (FPN) was better than the one-stage detector (SSD300, RefineDet, and YOLOv3). The experimental results showed low accuracy (<50%) in almost all scenarios, indicating that the shallow and deep methods cannot yet handle pest recognition well on data sets with inter-class and intra-class variance along with data imbalance.

Similarly, using Convolutional Neural Networks (CNN), the authors in [16] evaluated three detection and classification methods to identify five species of insects collected in traps in a factory environment. With a set of 200 original photos of 3,026 insects, the following methods were compared: (1) Adaptive Thresholding combined with VGG-16, (2) Single Shot MultiBox Detector (SSD) developed over VGG16 network but replacing the fully connected layers, (3) VGG16 with Sliding Window approach. SSD produced the best results among the three methods in the experiments, achieving detection and classification rates of 84% and 86%, respectively. In the paper, data augmentation was performed on the training set and test set. Note, however, that data augmentation should be done on the training set only. Otherwise, the visual patterns of an original image learned during training may be the same as those of an augmented image in the test set, causing overfitting and, ultimately, making the data set unreliable.

In Reference [17], an improved network architecture based on VGG19 was implemented for the detection and classification of 24 insect species collected in crop fields such as rice and soybean. The proposed method was implemented by combining VGG19 models and a particular network called Region Proposal Network (RPN). The experimental results showed that the proposed method achieved an accuracy of 89.2% on the MPest dataset and is superior to the traditional state-of-the-art SSD (85.3%) and Fast R-CNN (79.6%) methods. However, there are still some problems with this method, such as target detection errors. Although the paper proposes a CNN to solve the problem of multi-classification of agricultural insects, species frequently found on soybean, such as *euschistus heros*, *edessa meditabunda*, *nezara viridula*, *anticarsia gemmatalis*, *spodoptera* spp. and *diabrotica speciosa*, were not present in the MPest dataset.

The deep residual learning method was used in [18] for identifying ten classes of agricultural pests in images with complex backgrounds. The method's performance was improved after optimizing with deep residual learning the pre-trained

ResNet101 and ResNet50 models in ImageNet. Compared with traditional Support Vector Machines (SVM) and Convolutional Neural Networks (CNN), such as Alexnet, the ResNet-101 model based on deep residual learning achieved 98.67% accuracy in agricultural pest recognition, being significantly higher than traditional SVM and CNN. The deep residual network could be combined with object detection methods such as Faster R-CNN or R-FCN to track pest targets in real-time, providing a practical value of the method in agricultural pest control tasks.

The work in [19] aims to select the best approach for detection and identification of the most harmful pests in greenhouse tomato and pepper crops, *Bemisia tabaci* and *Trialeurodes vaporariorum*. A dataset with many images of infected tomato plants was created to train and evaluate machine learning models (MLP and k-NN) and deep learning models (SSD and Faster R-CNN). Results show that the deep learning models offer a better solution as they achieve the highest accuracy. Results also indicate that egg detection and identification are a significant challenge, as they are similar in color and shape at an early stage. Moreover, adding other metrics to evaluate the models would be interesting, such as accuracy and F-score.

In order to achieve accurate detection and identification of Pyralidae pests, the authors in [20] designed an intelligent robot on an autonomous vehicle to acquire images in the natural farm scene and also presented a Pyralidae pest recognition algorithm to be used on the robot. Precisely, by employing the color and shape features of Pyralidae pests, they proposed a segmentation algorithm using Inverse Histogram Mapping and spatial-constrained OTSU (SC-OTSU) to segment pests. Further, they designed a recognition approach based on Hu's Invariant Moment. The experimental results show that the robot vehicle can automatically capture images of Pyralidae pests in the natural farm scene, achieving 94.3% accuracy in pest recognition. This approach, however, is limited by the time complexity required. The average processing time for each frame is longer than 1 s, leading to a delay in responding to the observation results. In addition, the detection of pests under non-uniform illumination was also not efficient. The local color of the images being too light or too dark made it difficult to determine a stable threshold range in the algorithm.

With the purpose of rapid detection and recognition of ten insect species affecting tea fields in China, the authors in [21] created the SIFT-HMAX model inspired by the mechanism of human visual attention. First, the statistical model Saliency Using Natural (SUN) generated saliency maps and detected the region of interest (ROI) in a pest image. To extract the attributes representing the appearance of the pest, the Hierarchical Model and X (HMAX) was extended. SIFT was integrated into the HMAX model to increase invariance to rotational changes. Meanwhile, Non-negative Sparse Coding (NNSC) was used to simulate the simple cell responses. Texture attributes were extracted based on the Local Configuration Pattern (LCP) algorithm. Finally, the extracted attributes were fed into an SVM to perform the recognition task. The proposed method performed well with a recognition rate of 85.5%, showing an advantage over the compared methods HMAX, Sparse coding, and NIMBLE, but being slightly inferior to a CNN such as MatConvNet (86.9%).

In the work [22] a method based on SVM, MSER and HOG was developed for aphid identification in wheat fields. The method uses a Maximally Stable Extreme Regions (MSER) descriptor to simplify the complex background of the images containing the aphids, and then Histogram Oriented Gradient (HOG) attribute vectors are used in an SVM for aphid classification. This method was compared with five other commonly used methods for aphid detection; its performance was analyzed using images with different aphid densities, colors, and plants' locations. The results showed that the method provides average identification and error rates of 86.81% and 8.91%, respectively, higher than other compared methods including K-means, thresholding, SVM-HOG, SVM, SVM-HOG-Haar, and AdaBoost-Haar-HOG. The authors did not compare the proposed method with state-of-the-art deep learning models.

The authors in [7] evaluated deep learning models trained with different fine-tuning and transfer learning parameters for the tasks of classification and counting of pest insects in soybean. First, an image segmentation stage with the SLIC Superpixels method was considered to segment the images' insects. In the classification stage, three deep learning models were compared: Inception-Resnet-v2, ResNet-50 and DenseNet-201. The approach with the best result was DenseNet-201 (94.89%) using 100% fine-tuning. In the counting experiment, the authors used the weights of the CNN best rated for accuracy in a computer vision system to classify each superpixel segment of the image. The count of pest insects was obtained by adding up the superpixels of each class, thus calculating the infestation level of a crop area. The count results showed that the accuracy decreases to 90.86% when an insect is segmented into two different superpixels. It should be noted that this is an area of research that has been explored but not yet resolved. Moreover, the authors did not compare the results with other state-of-the-art detection methods, such as YOLOv3, Faster R-CNN, and RetinaNet.

## 3    Materials and Methods

### 3.1    Image Acquisition

An experimental area of 2 ha was sown with conventional soybean cultivars and no pesticide application to create a reference collection of soybean pest insects. The agricultural area shown in Fig. 1 is located at the experimental farm of the Federal University of Grande Dourados, located in the municipality of Dourados-MS, Brazil, with geographic coordinates 22°13'57.52" South latitude and 54°59'17.93" West longitude.

In order to collect images of insects present in the experimental area, a Sony DSC-HX300 camera with 20.4 megapixels resolution and a SM-G930F camera with 12.2 megapixels resolution were used. A total of 1,800 images (600x800 pixels) in JPG format were collected from Sep/2017 to Feb/2018 crop during the phenological stages R1 to R6 of the soybean reproductive phase, on different days and weather conditions, between 8 am to 10 am and 5 pm to 6:30 pm. The exposure of pests at the plant's top usually occurs early in the day or late in the afternoon. The recommendation is to sample insects of the aerial part be

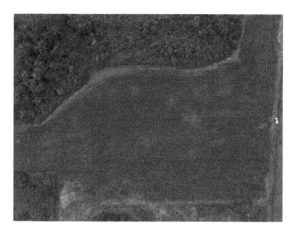

**Fig. 1.** (Color online) Aerial view of the experimental area used for soybean planting.

performed, preferably, in the cooler weather and more humid periods of the day, as reported in [6].

The researcher captured images on-site using a camera 50 cm away from the target of interest and a 90-degree angle of the camera to the ground. The targets, in this case, correspond to the defoliating insects that cause economic damage when found at high levels in soybean fields. Next, each image was annotated in LabelImg[1] with support from an entomologist biologist. Thus building a reference collection for the system's training and test image set (see Fig. 2), named INSECT12C-Dataset and available at [23]. Table 1 presents the total number of insects annotated by species. The unequal number of samples used in the training and test image set reflects the number of occurrences of each pest species under actual field conditions.

### 3.2   You only Look once (YOLOv3)

The YOLOv3 detection method evaluated in this paper is briefly described in the following. The source code used as a basis for our implementation can be found at https://github.com/qqwweee/keras-yolo3.

Unlike Faster-RCNN, which has a region proposal stage, YOLOv3 [9] approaches object detection as a direct pixel regression problem for bounding box coordinates and class probabilities. The input image is divided into $S \times S$ blocks. For each block, YOLOv3 predicts bounding boxes using dimension groups as anchor boxes. The objectivity score is predicted using logistic regression for each bounding box, which indicates the chance that the bounding box has an object of interest. In addition, the probabilities of class $C$ are estimated for each bounding box, indicating the classes it may contain. In our case, each bounding

---

[1] LabelImg is a graphical image annotation tool and label object bounding boxes in images.

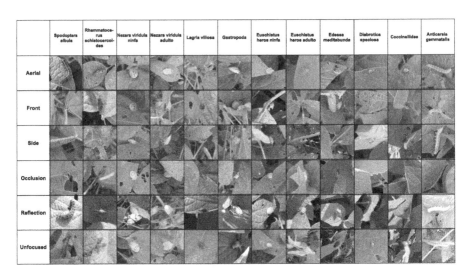

**Fig. 2.** (Color online) Sample images from our dataset, divided into 12 soybean pest species. The images were collected under actual field conditions, which include lighting conditions, object size and positioning, occlusion, complex background variations, and developmental stages.

**Table 1.** The total number of insects noted per species.

| Species | Quantity |
|---|---|
| Anticarsia gemmatalis | 115 |
| Coccinellidae | 120 |
| Diabrotica speciosa | 113 |
| Edessa meditabunda | 112 |
| Euschistus heros adulto | 836 |
| Euschistus heros ninfa | 802 |
| Gastropoda | 170 |
| Lagria villosa | 67 |
| Nezara viridula adulto | 125 |
| Nezara viridula ninfa | 23 |
| Rhammatocerus schistocercoides | 37 |
| Spodoptera albula | 238 |
| **Total** | 2.758 |

box may contain the species of an insect or the bottom of the plantation (uninteresting object). Thus, each prediction in YOLOv3 comprises four parameters for the bounding box (coordinates), the objectivity score, and the $C$ class probabilities. YOLOv3 uses Darknet-53 as its backbone to provide high accuracy, requiring fewer operations than other architectures.

## 3.3   Experimental Design

We adopted 5-fold cross-validation with validation, and test sets in the INSECT12C [23] dataset. In each fold, we set aside the 20% allocated for testing. We then split the 80% allocated for training into two subsets, 60% to be the actual training set and 20% to be the validation set. Thus, in each fold, the dataset was divided into 60% for training, 20% for validation, and 20% for testing, allowing the deep learning model to be iteratively trained and validated on different sets. Finally, the classifier's output is given by the average of the five folds in the test set.

The classification task consists of predicting the class of the object in the image. The problem of identifying the location of the object along with its class is called object detection. Instead of predicting the object class from an image, we now have to train a multi-label classifier to determine the location of objects and predict the class of each object (circumscribed in a rectangle called the bounding box). We consider four metrics to evaluate the classification results: precision, recall, F-score, and accuracy; and three metrics to evaluate the detection results: mean absolute error (MAE), root mean square error (RMSE), and coefficient of determination ($R^2$).

We have calculated the average results of the evaluation metrics for the model studied and the standard deviation. We used the ANOVA hypothesis test to determine statistical significance in the average performance between groups with different batch sizes. We report the *p-value* found for each metric, and the significance level was set at 5%.

In our experiments, we used the open-source implementation of the YOLOv3 [9] recognized by the ImageNet competition [24]. The following input parameters were used: input image width and height set to $608 \times 800$ pixels, batch size by 4, 16, 32 samples, and training with 24,000 iterations. We also used the SGD optimizer [25] with a learning rate set at 0.001 and momentum at 0.9. We employed the data augmentation technique to supplement the training data by applying the random rotation operations between $0°$ and $90°$ clockwise/anticlockwise and changing image brightness from –10% to 10%. This procedure aims to enhance rotation invariance and illumination invariance during detection.

We used Colab, a Google Research service that allows writing code through a browser while providing free GPU resources in all of our experiments. We use the Google Colab Pro version for our work, which provides priority access to more powerful GPU resources and high-memory virtual machines over the free Colab. Additionally, the lifecycle of virtual machines is increased from 12 to 24 h.

## 3.4   Evaluation Metrics

To evaluate the classification results, we use four metrics: Accuracy Eq. (1), Precision Eq. (2), Recall Eq. (3) and F-score Eq. (4). We account for true positive (TP) when the insect is detected in the correct class with a detection score $\geq$ 0.3; and false positive (FP) when some object that is not of interest (leaves or background) is identified as an insect. In cases where the insect was not detected or was detected in the incorrect class, we say it is a false-negative (FN). A true negative (TN) occurs when the network does not detect any insect in the image where there is no insect. Since all images have at least one insect, we have no true negative case in our dataset.

$$Accuracy = \frac{TP + TN}{TP + FP + FN + TN} \tag{1}$$

$$Precision = \frac{TP}{TP + FP} \tag{2}$$

$$Recall = \frac{TP}{TP + FN} \tag{3}$$

$$F - score = \frac{2 * (Recall * Precision)}{(Recall + Precision)} \tag{4}$$

Furthermore, we consider three metrics to evaluate the detection results: mean absolute error (MAE) Eq. (5), root mean square error (RMSE) Eq. (6) and coefficient of determination ($R^2$) Eq. (7).

$$MAE = \frac{1}{n} \sum_{i=1}^{n} |y_i - \hat{y}_i| \tag{5}$$

$$RMSE = \sqrt{\frac{1}{n} \sum_{i=1}^{n} (y_i - \hat{y}_i)^2} \tag{6}$$

$$R^2 = 1 - \frac{\sum_{i=1}^{n}(y_i - \hat{y}_i)^2}{\sum_{i=1}^{n}(y_i - \bar{y})^2} \tag{7}$$

where $y_i$ is the observed value, $\hat{y}_i$ is the predicted value, $\bar{y}$ is the mean of the observation, and $n$ is the number of observations.

## 4    Results and Discussion

*Classification Evaluation.* The classification results obtained by YOLOv3 for precision, recall, F-measure, and accuracy are presented in Table 2. The values in percentages represent the average of the five folds in the test set. Regarding accuracy, the experiment with batch size 4 obtained a higher result than size 32, resulting in fewer false positives during detection. However, YOLOv3 achieved the best results with batch size 32 for the other metrics, showing that the proportion of predicted insects were true-positives in most cases.

Note that batch size 32 results in fewer false negatives than batch size 4 and batch size 16. Overall, this is the most critical measure for the studied problem since its occurrence implies the lack of agricultural product application in an area with the presence of pest insects.

**Table 2.** Classification results obtained by YOLOv3 in average percentage on the INSECT12C dataset.

| Architecture | Batch | Precision (%) | Recall (%) | F-score (%) | Accuracy (%) |
|---|---|---|---|---|---|
| YOLOv3 | 4 | **97,85** ± .0049 | 51,24 ± .0334 | 67,21 ± .0288 | 50,67 ± .0326 |
| | 16 | 95,47 ± .0171 | 70,65 ± .0109 | 81,20 ± .0126 | 68,36 ± .0178 |
| | 32 | 95,15 ± .0060 | **75,79** ± .0234 | **84,35** ± .0133 | **72,96** ± .0200 |

The results of the ANOVA test indicate that there is evidence of a statistical significance in mean performance between the groups of batch sizes at a significance level of 5%, using the precision ($p$-value $= 2.46e^{-04}$), recall ($p$-value $= 7.99e^{-09}$), F-score ($p$-value $= 2.3e^{-08}$) and accuracy ($p$-value $= 1.37e^{-08}$) as metrics.

*Insect Pest Detection in Soybeans.* Table 3 presents the measured values of the three configurations proposed. In the experiments, batch size 32 produced the best results among the sizes evaluated, obtaining MAE and RMSE rates of 0.41 and 0.83, respectively. The results show low mean error rates in almost all scenarios, indicating that the YOLOv3 architecture can handle multi-species pest detection well, even in unbalanced datasets with interclass and intraclass variance. Some examples of insect-pest detection in YOLOv3 are shown in Fig. 3. The bounding boxes are true positive with a detection score $\geq 0.3$.

**Table 3.** Insect pest detection on the INSECT12C dataset for YOLOv3.

| Architecture | Batch | RMSE | MAE | $R^2$ |
|---|---|---|---|---|
| YOLOv3 | 4 | 1,25 ± .0788 | 0,77 ± .0654 | 0,14 ± .0254 |
| | 16 | 0,92 ± .0829 | 0,48 ± .0460 | 0,47 ± .0440 |
| | 32 | **0,83** ± .0606 | **0,41** ± .0386 | **0,58** ± .0446 |

However, YOLOv3 presented false negatives (insects not detected or detected incorrectly) and false positives (when some object that is not of interest is identified as an insect), showing that detections fail under certain field conditions such: non-uniform illumination on the insect, complex insect-like background (e.g., herbivory and lesions on leaves), partial occlusion of the insect, and mainly low representativity of species with few samples (Fig. 4).

**Fig. 3.** (Color online) Examples of pest-insect detection in the YOLOv3 architecture with batch size set at 32 samples. The cases are true positive with a detection score ≥ 0.3.

**Fig. 4.** (Color online) Examples of pest insect detection failures in the YOLOv3 architecture with batch size set at 32 samples. Subfigures in the first row have examples of false negatives and in the second row false positives.

## 5    Conclusion

In this paper, we evaluated the performance of the YOLOv3 architecture for the real-time detection of soybean pest insects. We also defined a baseline for soybean pest detection by publishing a new dataset called INSECT12C, consisting of 2,758 annotated insects from 12 species. Experimental results showed that YOLOv3 architecture trained with batch size 32 leads to higher classification and detection rates compared to batch sizes 4 and 16; however, the method failed in some cases: areas with complex lighting conditions, herbivory and leaf injuries, partial insect occlusion, and low species representativeness with few samples. The ratio of true positives to the total predicted positives achieved did not show significant distortions, indicating that YOLOv3 allows tracking pest targets in real-time, offering additional practical value of the method in agricultural pest control tasks.

We plan to evaluate new state-of-the-art object detection architectures with higher resolution cameras onboard the UAV as future work. We also intend to make use of the oversampling technique in order to solve class unbalances. Finally, we plan to implement automatic counting of detected insects by species.

# References

1. Hou, J., et al.: Association analysis of vegetable soybean quality traits with ssr markers. Plant Breed. **130**(4), 444–449 (2011). https://doi.org/10.1111/j.1439-0523.2011.01852.x
2. CONAB, Acompanhamento da safra brasileira grãos V. 8 - SAFRA 2020/21 - N. 3 - Terceiro levantamento (2020). https://www.conab.gov.br/info-agro/safras/graos/boletim-da-safra-de-graos. ISSN: 2318–6852
3. —, Acompanhamento da safra brasileira grãos V. 6 - SAFRA 2018/19 - N. 12 - Décimo segundo levantamento (2019). https://www.conab.gov.br/info-agro/safras/graos/boletim-da-safra-de-graos/item/download/28484_9a9ee12328baa359b3708d64e774e5d8. ISSN 2318–6852
4. —, Compêndio de estudos conab: Evolução dos custos de produção de soja no brasil, **2** (2016). https://www.conab.gov.br/institucional/publicacoes/compendio-de-estudos-da-conab/item/download/2512_c2638f76696e3b926ab22e93f9549d21. ISSN 2448–3710
5. Tetila, E.C., Machado, B.B., Belete, N.A., Guimarães, D.A., Pistori, H.: Identification of soybean foliar diseases using unmanned aerial vehicle images. IEEE Geosci. Remote Sens. Lett **14**(12), 2190–2194 (2017). https://doi.org/10.1109/LGRS.2017.2743715
6. Hoffmann-Campo, C.B., Corrêa-Ferreira, B.S., Moscardi, F.: Soja: manejo integrado de insetos e outros Artrópodes-praga., Embrapa Soja (2012). http://www.cnpso.embrapa.br/artropodes/Capitulo9.pdf. ISBN 978-85-7035-139-5
7. Tetila, E.C., Machado, B.B., Menezes, G.V., de Souza Belete, N.A., Astolfi, G., Pistori, H.: A deep-learning approach for automatic counting of soybean insect pests. IEEE Geosci. Remote Sens. Lett **17**, 1–5 (2019). https://doi.org/10.1109/LGRS.2019.2954735
8. Tetila, E.C.: Detecção e classificação de doenças e pragas da soja usando imagens de veículos aéreos não tripulados e técnicas de visão computacional. Ph.D. dissertation, Universidade Católica Dom Bosco (2019). http://repositorio.ufgd.edu.br/jspui/handle/prefix/2385
9. Redmon, J., Farhadi, A.: Yolov3: an incremental improvement (2018). CoRR, vol. abs/1804.02767, http://arxiv.org/abs/1804.02767
10. Ren, S., He, K., Girshick, R.B., Sun, J.: Faster R-CNN: towards real-time object detection with region proposal networks (2015). CoRR, vol. abs/1506.01497, http://arxiv.org/abs/1506.01497
11. Lin, T.-Y., Goyal, P., Girshick, R., He, K., Dollár, P.: Focal loss for dense object detection. IEEE Trans. Pattern Anal. Mach. Intell. **42**(2), 318–327 (2020)
12. Li, Y., Wang, H., Dang, L.M., Sadeghi-Niaraki, A., Moon, H.: Crop pest recognition in natural scenes using convolutional neural networks. Comput. Electron. Agric. **169**,(2020). https://doi.org/10.1016/j.compag.2019.105174. ISSN 0168–1699
13. Wang, F., Wang, R., Xie, C., Yang, P., Liu, L.: Fusing multi-scale context-aware information representation for automatic in-field pest detection and recognition. Comput. Electron. Agric. **169**,(2020). https://doi.org/10.1016/j.compag.2020.105222. ISSN 0168–1699
14. Mique, E.L., Palaoag, T.D.: Rice pest and disease detection using convolutional neural network. In: Proceedings of the 2018 International Conference on Information Science and System, Series ICISS '18, pp. 147–151. Association for Computing Machinery, New York (2018). https://doi.org/10.1145/3209914.3209945. ISBN 9781450364218

15. Wu, X., Zhan, C., Lai, Y., Cheng, M., Yang, J.: Ip102: a large-scale benchmark dataset for insect pest recognition. In: 2019 IEEE/CVF Conference on Computer Vision and Pattern Recognition (CVPR), pp. 8779–8788 (2019). https://doi.org/10.1109/CVPR.2019.00899
16. Nam, N.T., Hung, P.D.: Pest detection on traps using deep convolutional neural networks. In: Proceedings of the 2018 International Conference on Control and Computer Vision, Series ICCCV '18, pp. 33–38. Association for Computing Machinery, New York (2018). https://doi.org/10.1145/3232651.3232661
17. Xia, D., Chen, P., Wang, B., Zhang, J., Xie, C.: Insect detection and classification based on an improved convolutional neural network. Sensors **18**(12), 4169 (2018). https://doi.org/10.3390/s18124169. ISSN 1424–8220
18. Cheng, X., Zhang, Y., Chen, Y., Wu, Y., Yue, Y.: Pest identification via deep residual learning in complex background. Comput. Electron. Agric. **141**, 351–356 (2017). https://doi.org/10.1016/j.compag.2017.08.005
19. Gutierrez, A., Ansuategi, A., Susperregi, L., Tubío, C., Rankić, I., Lenža, L.: A benchmarking of learning strategies for pest detection and identification on tomato plants for autonomous scouting robots using internal databases (2019). https://doi.org/10.1155/2019/5219471
20. Liu, B., Hu, Z., Zhao, Y., Bai, Y., Wang, Y.: Recognition of pyralidae insects using intelligent monitoring autonomous robot vehicle in natural farm scene (2019). CoRR, vol. abs/1903.10827, http://arxiv.org/abs/1903.10827
21. Deng, L., Wang, Y., Han, Z., Yu, R.: Research on insect pest image detection and recognition based on bio-inspired methods. Biosyst. Eng. **169**, 139–148 (2018). https://doi.org/10.1016/j.biosystemseng.2018.02.008. ISSN 1537–5110
22. Liu, T., Chen, W., Wu, W., Sun, C., Guo, W., Zhu, X.: Detection of aphids in wheat fields using a computer vision technique. Biosyst. Eng. **141**, 82–93 (2016). https://doi.org/10.1016/j.biosystemseng.2015.11.005. ISSN 1537–5110
23. Tetila, E.C.: INSECT12C-Dataset - Conjunto de Imagens de Insetos e outros Invertebrados da Cultura da Soja, UFGD (2021). http://evertontetila.ws.ufgd.edu.br/INSECT12C-Dataset.zip
24. Russakovsky, O., et al.: ImageNet large scale visual recognition challenge. Int. J. Comput. Vision **115**(3), 211–252 (2015). https://doi.org/10.1007/s11263-015-0816-y
25. Bottou, L., Bousquet, O.: The tradeoffs of large scale learning. In: Platt, J., Koller, D., Singer, Y., Roweis, S. (eds.) Advances in Neural Information Processing Systems, vol. 20. Curran Associates Inc. (2008). https://proceedings.neurips.cc/paper/2007/file/0d3180d672e08b4c5312dcdafdf6ef36-Paper.pdf

# Quaternion-Valued Convolutional Neural Network Applied for Acute Lymphoblastic Leukemia Diagnosis

Marco Aurélio Granero[1] [iD], Cristhian Xavier Hernández[2] [iD],
and Marcos Eduardo Valle[3]([✉]) [iD]

[1] Instituto Federal de Educação, Ciência e Tecnologia de São Paulo,
São Paulo, Brazil
granero@ifsp.edu.br
[2] Escuela Superior Politécnica del Litoral, Guayaquil, Ecuador
[3] Universidade Estadual de Campinas, Campinas, Brazil
valle@ime.unicamp.br

**Abstract.** The field of neural networks has seen significant advances in recent years with the development of deep and convolutional neural networks. Although many of the current works address real-valued models, recent studies reveal that neural networks with hypercomplex-valued parameters can better capture, generalize, and represent the complexity of multidimensional data. This paper explores the quaternion-valued convolutional neural network application for a pattern recognition task from medicine, namely, the diagnosis of acute lymphoblastic leukemia. Precisely, we compare the performance of real-valued and quaternion-valued convolutional neural networks to classify lymphoblasts from the peripheral blood smear microscopic images. The quaternion-valued convolutional neural network achieved better or similar performance than its corresponding real-valued network but using only 34% of its parameters. This result confirms that quaternion algebra allows capturing and extracting information from a color image with fewer parameters.

**Keywords:** Quaternion algebra · Hypercomplex number · Neural network · Quaternion neural network · Classification problem

## 1 Introduction

In recent years, machine learning has influenced how we solve a variety of real-world problems. Indeed, artificial neural networks (NN) outperformed many state-of-the-art approaches in several applications with the development of deep neural networks (DNN) and convolutional neural networks (CNN) architectures.

This work was supported in part by Coordenação de Aperfeiçoamento de Pessoal de Nível Superior - Brasil (CAPES) - Finance Code 001.

A. Britto and K. Valdivia Delgado (Eds.): BRACIS 2021, LNAI 13074, pp. 280–293, 2021.
https://doi.org/10.1007/978-3-030-91699-2_20

Most neural network architectures are real-valued neural networks (RVNN). In such architectures, the input data is arranged into real-valued vectors, matrices, or tensors to be processed by the neural network. In some sense, this approach assumes that all the input data components have equal importance and, thus, they are all evaluated in the same way. However, in some cases, the data sets contain multidimensional information that requires a specific approach to treat them as single entities. For example, a pixel's color is obtained by combining the red, green, and blue components in image processing. The three coordinates position in the color space represents a plethora of colors such as pink or brown, and the color information is lost if the components are treated separately [38]. In some practical image recognition tasks, the complexity of the color space needs to be captured by the neural networks to generalize well and represent the multidimensional nature of the colors [20,27]. Indeed, Parcollet et al. showed that RVNNs might fail to capture the color information [39]. Also, Matsui et al. remarked that RVNNs are not able to preserve the 3D shape of an input object when transformed into the 3D space [30]. From these remarks, neural networks based on hypercomplex numbers, such as complex and quaternions, have been proposed and extensively investigated in the last years.

## 1.1 Complex and Quaternion-Valued Neural Networks

A complex-valued neural network (CVNN) is based on the algebra of complex numbers, which allows preserving or treating the relationship between magnitude and the phase information during the learning [38]. Furthermore, the algebraic structure of complex numbers yields CVNNs better generalization capability [17] besides being easier to train [35]. As long as the processed information are correlated two-dimensional data, CVNNs mostly outperformed or at least matched the real-valued ones [3,4,16,29,48].

The encouraging performance of CVNNs inspired the development of quaternion-valued neural networks (QVNNs). QVNNs use quaternion algebra and can represent colors efficiently, with the advantage of fully representing colors through unique structures [6].

As far as we know, the first QVNN has been introduced by Arena et al. [6], who developed a specific backpropagation algorithm able to learn the local relations that exist between quaternions. Furthermore, like the real-valued neural networks, single hidden layer QVNNs are universal approximators [6]. An extensive list of applications and investigations with different QVNN architectures can be found in references [7,11,36–38,40,46]. A detailed up-to-date review on quaternion-valued neural networks, including some of their successful applications, can be found at [38].

In contrast to RVNN, which represented color channels as independent variables, QVNN can benefit from representing colors as single quaternions. For example, Greenblatt et al. applied a QVNN model to prostate cancer [13]. Gaudet and Maida investigated the use of quaternion-valued convolutional neural networks (QVCNN) for image processing [11]. Pavllo et al. modeled human

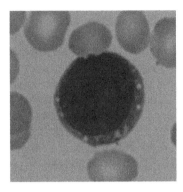

**Fig. 1.** Candidate cell to be a lymphoblast, from ALL-IDB dataset [28].

motion using QVNNs [41]. Zhu et al. proposed a QVCNN for color image classification and denoising tasks [51]. The localization of color image splicing by a fully quaternion-valued convolutional network was explored by Chen et al. [9]. A deformable quaternion Gabor convolutional neural network for recognition of color facial expression was proposed by Jin et al. [22]. Takahashi et al. have merged histograms of oriented gradients (HOG) for human detection with a QVNN to determine human facial expression [47]. Quaternion multi-layer perceptron has been successfully applied to polarimetric synthetic aperture radar (PolSAR) land classification [24,43].

### 1.2    Contributions and the Organization of the Paper

Corroborating with the development of hypercomplex-valued neural networks, we present a quaternion-valued convolutional neural network (QVCNN) development to classify isolated white cells as lymphoblasts. Precisely, the QVCNN receives a white cell image like the one shown in Fig. 1 and classifies it as a lymphoblast or not. The classification of lymphoblast is essential for diagnosing acute lymphoblastic leukemia, a kind of blood cancer. The performance of the QVCNN is compared with a real-valued convolutional neural network with a similar architecture.

The paper is structured as follows: Sect. 2 presents the medical problem of acute lymphoblastic leukemia and presents a literature review on the computer-aided diagnosis of leukemia. Section 3 addresses real-valued and quaternion-valued convolutional neural networks. The experimental results are detailed in Sect. 4. The Sect. 5 presents the concluding remarks and future works.

## 2    Acute Lymphoblastic Leukemia (ALL)

According to the national cancer institute of the United States, acute lymphoblastic leukemia (ALL) is a type of leukemia, cancer in the blood, that

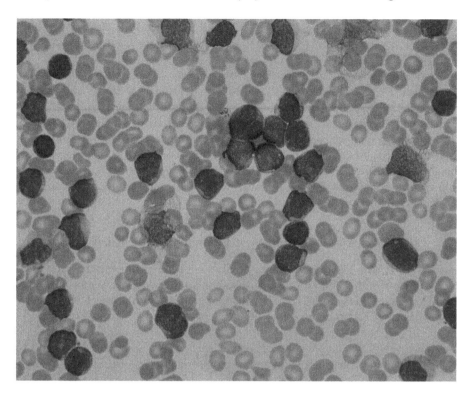

**Fig. 2.** Blood smear image from ALL-IDB dataset [28].

appears and multiplies rapidly [32]. ALL is characterized by the presence of many lymphoblasts in the blood and also in the bone marrow. In this context, a lymphoblast is an immature cell that can be converted into a mature lymphocyte [33].

There are several methods used for the diagnosis of ALL that can be found in the literature [34], including the peripheral blood smear technique [23]. The peripheral blood smear technique allows observing the information of a blood sample taken from the patient through a microscope. A specialist (hematologist) counts the number of lymphoblasts observed by microscope and, based on that, makes a diagnosis [45]. Figure 2 shows a picture of a blood smear that a hematologist sees for analysis. It is worth mentioning that the white cells appear stained with a bluish-purple coloration, which serves as a guide to find lymphoblasts.

The manual counting of lymphoblasts under the microscope is a somewhat dull task that takes much time from a professional who could be more productive in other matters. In effect, the time spent analyzing the microscope image has an economical cost because a specialist has significant value in the labor market. In addition, the analysis can be affected by human factors such as tiredness and stress. The operator's experience also plays an important role, and therefore, there is a subjectivity component affecting the results of the lymphoblast count. For these reasons, computational models to perform automatic lymphoblast counting in a blood smear image have been proposed in the literature [42].

Many methods divide the problem of automatic lymphoblast counting into two stages. The first stage, usually called the identification phase, aims to find white cells to be lymphoblast. Labeling a candidate cell as a lymphoblast or healthy cell is performed in the second stage, referred to as the classification phase. In this paper, we use real-valued and quaternion-valued convolutional neural networks to classify white cells, that is, in the second stage of the blood smear image analysis. In the following sections, we review real-valued and quaternion-valued neural networks. Before, however, we provide a literature review on automatic leukemia diagnosis methods.

## 2.1    Computer-Aided Diagnosis of Leukemia: Literature Review

Current literature has shown a large number of studies on computer-aided leukemia diagnosis with different approaches, including support vector machines (SVM), k-nearest neighbor (k-NN), principal component analysis (PCA), naive Bayes classifier, and random forest [8].

In [26], the authors used 60 sample images to develop a model to detected ALL using kNN and naive Bayes classifier with 92.8% accuracy. A method to extract features of microscopic images using discrete orthogonal Stockwell transform (DOST) and linear discriminant analysis (LDA) has been proposed in [31]. The paper [50] applies three pre-trained CNN architectures to extract features for image classification. In [2], a CNN reached 88.25% of accuracy in classifying ALL versus healthy cells. To distinguish between the four subtypes of leukemia, this CNN hits 81.74% accuracy. Using ALL-IDB dataset, [1] presents a k-medoids algorithm with 98.60% accuracy to classify white blood cells. Furthermore, a method based on generative adversarial optimization (GAO) [49], a neural network with statistic features [5], and a deep CNN with chronological sine-cosine algorithm (SCA) [21] have been proposed for ALL detection with 93.84%, 97.07%, and 98.70% accuracy, respectively.

A table summarizing the results from 16 papers on automated detection of leukemia and its subtypes can be found in [8]. This reference also presents a framework for automated leukemia diagnosis based on the ResNet-34 [15] and the DenseNet-121 [19]. The accuracy reported was 99.56% for the ResNet-34 and 99.91% for the DenseNet-121 [8].

# 3    Convolutional Neural Networks

In many machine learning applications, identifying appropriate representations of a large amount of data is usually challenging. A successful model must efficiently encode local relations within the input resources and their structural relations. Moreover, an adequate representation of data also offers a positive side effect by reducing the number of neural parameters needed to well-learn the input features, leading to a natural solution to the overfitting phenomenon [38].

Convolutional neural networks (CNN) are feed-forward neural networks with a robust feature representation method widely applied in machine learning. For example, the ResNet set a milestone in 2015 by outperforming humans in the ImageNet competition [10,15]. The successful AlexNet [25] also inspired the development of many novel CNNs including the VGG [44] and the DenseNet [19]. In addition, deep neural networks have been successfully used, for example, for segmentation tasks as well as for the automatic classification of objects in images [14,18].

One crucial aspect of the deep networks is the convolution layer, which extracts features from high-dimensional data through a set of convolution kernels [51]. Although convolutions perform well in many practical situations, it has some drawbacks in color image processing tasks. Firstly, a convolution layer sums up the outputs corresponding to different channels and ignores their complicated interrelationships. As a consequence, it may eventually lose important information of a color image. Secondly, simply summing up the outputs gives too many degrees of freedom, and thus, the network has a high risk of overfitting even when imposing heavy regularization terms [51]. Accordingly, García-Retuerta et al. argue that quaternion-valued neural networks may have a significant advantage in color image processing tasks because of quaternion's four-dimensional algebraic structure [10]. The following section reviews the basic concepts of quaternion-valued convolutional neural networks.

### 3.1   Quaternion-Valued Convolutional Neural Networks

Quaternions are a four-dimensional extension of complex numbers. Developed by Hamilton in 1843, the set of all quaternions is defined by

$$\mathbb{H} = \{q = q_0 + q_1\boldsymbol{i} + q_2\boldsymbol{j} + q_3\boldsymbol{k} : q_0, q_1, q_2, q_3 \in \mathbb{R}\} \tag{1}$$

where $q_0$ is the real part of a quaternion, $q_1$, $q_2$, and $q_3$ denote the imaginary components while $\boldsymbol{i}$, $\boldsymbol{j}$, $\boldsymbol{k}$ are the hypercomplex units. The product of the hypercomplex units is governed by the following identities, knows as Hamilton rules:

$$\boldsymbol{i}^2 = \boldsymbol{j}^2 = \boldsymbol{k}^2 = \boldsymbol{ijk} = -1. \tag{2}$$

Alternatively, a quaternion can be written as

$$q = (q_0 + q_1\boldsymbol{i}) + (q_2 + q_3\boldsymbol{i})\boldsymbol{j} = z_0 + z_1\boldsymbol{j}, \tag{3}$$

where $z_0 = q_0 + q_1\boldsymbol{i}$ and $z_1 = q_2 + q_3\boldsymbol{j}$ are complex numbers.

The addition of quaternions is performed adding the real and imaginary components. Precisely, given $p = p_0 + p_1\boldsymbol{i} + p_2\boldsymbol{j} + p_3\boldsymbol{k}$ and $q = q_0 + q_1\boldsymbol{i} + q_2\boldsymbol{j} + q_3\boldsymbol{k}$, their sum is

$$p + q = (p_0 + q_0) + (p_1 + q_1)\boldsymbol{i} + (p_2 + q_2)\boldsymbol{j} + (p_3 + q_3)\boldsymbol{k}. \tag{4}$$

The main result in quaternion algebra is the Hamilton product between two quaternions $p = p_0 + p_1 i + p_2 j + p_3 k$ and $q = q_0 + q_1 i + q_2 j + q_3 k$, denoted by $p \otimes q$ and defined by

$$\begin{aligned} p \otimes q = (p_0 q_0 - p_1 q_1 - p_2 q_2 - p_3 q_3) &+ (p_0 q_1 + p_1 q_0 + p_2 q_3 - p_3 q_2) \, i \\ + (p_0 q_2 - p_1 q_3 + p_2 q_0 + p_3 q_1) \, j &+ (p_0 q_3 + p_1 q_2 - p_2 q_1 + p_3 q_0) \, k \end{aligned}$$
(5)

Quaternions and quaternion algebra allow building processing entities composed of four elements that share information via the Hamilton product.

According to Gaudet and Maida [11], a quaternion-valued convolutional layer is obtained convolving a quaternion-valued filter matrix $W = W_0 + W_1 i + W_2 j + W_3 k$ by a quaternion-valued vector $h = h_0 + h_1 i + h_2 j + h_3 k$. Here, $W_0$, $W_1$, $W_2$, and $W_3$ are real-valued matrices while $h_0$, $h_1$, $h_2$, and $h_3$ are real-valued vectors. Details on the implementation of quaternion-valued convolutional layers can be found in [11].

## 4   Computational Experiments

Let us compare real-valued and quaternion-valued convolutional neural networks' performance for classifying a white cell image as a lymphoblast. Both real-valued and quaternion-valued neural networks have been implemented in python using the Keras and Tensorflow libraries.

The real-valued model is a sequential feed-forward network composed of three convolutional layers, three max-pooling layers, and a dense layer. Precisely, the first convolutional layer has 32 filters with a $(3, 3)$ kernel and ReLU activation function. A max-pooling follows the convolutional layer with a $(2, 2)$ kernel. The

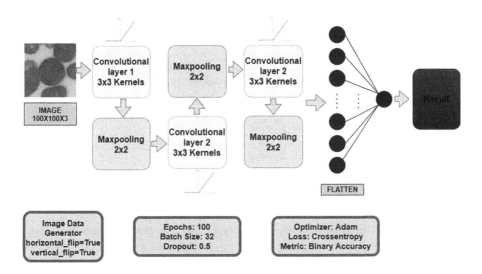

**Fig. 3.** RVCNN and QVCNN architectures.

second and third two-dimensional convolutional layers have 64 and 128 filters and have ReLU activation functions. Furthermore, they are also followed by max-pooling layers with $(2, 2)$ kernels. Figure 3 shows the architecture of the real-valued convolutional neural network. The total number of trainable parameters of the real-valued convolutional neural network is $106, 049$.

The quaternion-valued convolutional neural network has been designed similarly. Precisely, to maintain the same parameter budget among the real and quaternion-valued models, the number of filters per layer of the real-valued network was divided by four to build a quaternion-valued convolution. Thus, the quaternion-valued convolutional neural network has the same structure as the real-valued network depicted in Fig. 3, but with a quarter of the number of filters per layer. The number of trainable parameters of the quaternion-valued CNN model is $36, 353$. Table 1 summarizes the number of trainable parameters of both neural networks per layer.

**Table 1.** Parameters of real and quaternion-valued neural networks

| | Conv layer 1 | | Conv layer 2 | | Conv layer 3 | | Dense layer | |
| --- | --- | --- | --- | --- | --- | --- | --- | --- |
| | RVCNN | QVCNN | RVCNN | QVCNN | RVCNN | QVCNN | RVCNN | QVCNN |
| Filters (3,3) | 32 | 8 | 64 | 16 | 128 | 32 | 1 | 1 |
| Activation | ReLU | | ReLU | | ReLU | | None | |
| Max pooling | (2,2) | | (2,2) | | (2,2) | | - | |
| Parameters | 896 | 320 | 18,496 | 4,672 | 73,856 | 18,560 | 12,801 | 12,801 |

The dense layer of both real-valued and quaternion-valued networks has a single output neuron without activation function. Such a single neuron is used to classify the input image as a lymphoblast or not. Moreover, the parameters of all layers have been initialized according to Glorot and Bengio [12]. The optimizer used was *Adam*, an algorithm based on the stochastic gradient descent method with adaptive estimation of first-order and second-order moments.

To evaluate the performance of the RVCNN and QVCNN classifiers, we used the *ALL-IDB: The Acute Lymphoblastic Leukemia Image Database for Image Processing* provided by the "Università Degli Studi di Milano" [28]. This image database contains 260 images of white blood cells with $257 \times 257$ pixels, labeled by experts and evenly distributed among lymphoblast and health cells. Figure 1 shows an example of a color image used in the computational experiment.

We resized the $257 \times 257$ white blood cells images to $100 \times 100$ pixels. Also, the set of 260 color images was randomly divided into training and test images with different ratios. Data augmentation has been applied on the training set to improve the accuracy of the convolutional neural networks. Precisely, the images used for training were all submitted to a pre-processing data generation, which consists of obtaining new images through horizontal and vertical flips.

In our experiments, images were converted to RGB (red, green, and blue) and HSV (hue, saturation, and value) color spaces and used as input to neural networks. As a consequence, we performed the four experiments detailed in Table 2. The first experiment considers a real-valued CNN whose input is obtained by concatenating the three RGB channels in a single tensor with values in the unit interval $[0, 1]$. The second experiment also considers real-valued CNNs, but the input is obtained by concatenating the three HSV channels. Here, hue is arranged in a radial slice $H \in [0, 2\pi)$ while saturation and value belong to the unit interval, i.e., $S, V \in [0, 1]$.

**Table 2.** Experiments with real and quaternion-valued neural networks

| Neural network | Input | Input structure |
|---|---|---|
| Real-valued CNN | RGB | Concateneted channel |
| Real-valued CNN | HSV | Concateneted channel |
| Quaternion-values CNN | RGB | Quaternions encoded using (6) |
| Quaternion-valued CNN | HSV | Quaternions encoded using (7) |

The last two experiments were performed using quaternion-valued CNN. Specifically, in the third experiment, the RGB image is encoded in a quaternion structure with real part null, and each channel as one imaginary part of a quaternion as follows:

$$q = 0 + R\,\boldsymbol{i} + G\,\boldsymbol{j} + B\,\boldsymbol{k}. \tag{6}$$

Finally, in the fourth experiment, a color is encoded in a quaternion through the following expression using the HSV representation:

$$q = S\cos(H) + S\sin(H)\,\boldsymbol{i} + V\cos(H)\,\boldsymbol{j} + V\sin(H)\,\boldsymbol{k}. \tag{7}$$

The dataset has been divided into training and test sets with 5 different training/test ratios and trained by 100 epochs. One hundred simulations were performed for each different training/test ratio and, the average and standard deviation of the accuracy was calculated. Figure 4 presents the average accuracy of both real-valued and quaternion-valued convolutional neural networks for different percentages used for testing the networks in the four experiments. This figure also presents the interval between the 25% and the 75% quantiles of accuracy as shaded area.

Note from Fig. 4 that the quaternion-valued convolutional neural network with images in HSV color space (QVCNN-HSV) obtained the best performance, reaching 98.2% of accuracy in the test phase with 10% of training/test ratio.

The real and quaternion-valued networks with RGB encoded images exhibited similar performance, with accuracy between [93.6%, 97.1%] and [94.4%, 97.3%], respectively, depending on the ratio training/test. The real and quaternion-valued CNN models with RGB encoded images exhibited statistically equivalent performances. The real-valued neural network with HSV encoded images yielded the worst performance, reaching an average accuracy of 95.3% in the best case.

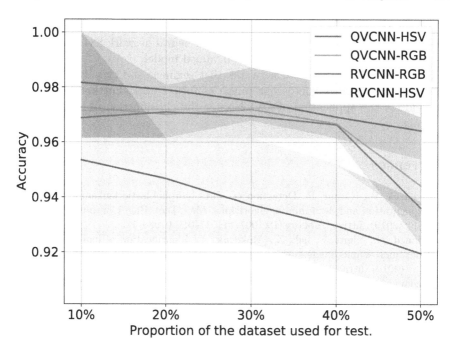

**Fig. 4.** Accuracy by the percentage of the dataset used for testing.

Concluding, the QVCNN-HSV exhibits a better generalization capability than the QVCNN-RGB, RVCNN-RGB, and RVCNN-HSV models. Moreover, the performance of the quaternion-valued convolutional neural network with images encoded using the HSV color space and (7) compares well with the results reported in the literature (see Sect. 2.1). However, the quaternion-valued convolutional neural network is much simpler than many of the architectures considered previously.

## 5   Concluding Remarks and Future Works

Acute lymphoblastic leukemia is characterized by many lymphoblasts in the blood and the bone marrow. Such disease can be diagnosticated by counting the number of lymphoblasts in a blood smear microscope image. This paper investigated the application of convolutional neural networks for classifying a white cell as lymphoblast or not. Precisely, we compared the performance of real-valued and quaternion-valued models. The QVCNN with input images encoded using the HSV color space showed the best result in our experiments. Also, the performance of the QVCNN is comparable with other deeper neural networks from the literature, including the ResNet and the DenseNet [8]. This computational experiment suggests that quaternion-valued neural networks exhibit better generalization capability than the real-valued convolutional neural network, possibly because it treats colors as single quaternion entities. Furthermore, it is noticeable that the quaternion-valued convolutional neural network has about 34% of the parameters of the corresponding real-valued model.

We plan to develop neural networks that segment and classify white blood cells on a blood smear microscope image as future work. Further research can also address the application of QVCNN for the classification of other types of leukemia.

# References

1. Acharya, V., Kumar, P.: Detection of acute lymphoblastic leukemia using image segmentation and data mining algorithms. Med. Biol. Eng. Comput. **57**(8), 1783–1811 (2019). https://doi.org/10.1007/s11517-019-01984-1
2. Ahmed, N., Yigit, A., Isik, Z., Alpkocak, A.: Identification of leukemia subtypes from microscopic images using convolutional neural network. Diagnostics (Basel) **9**(3) (2019). https://doi.org/10.3390/diagnostics9030104
3. Aizenberg, I., Alexander, S., Jackson, J.: Recognition of blurred images using multilayer neural network based on multi-valued neurons. In: 2011 41st IEEE International Symposium on Multiple-Valued Logic, pp. 282–287 (2011)
4. Aizenberg, I., Gonzalez, A.: Image recognition using MLMVN and frequency domain features. In: 2018 International Joint Conference on Neural Networks (IJCNN), pp. 1–8 (2018). https://doi.org/10.1109/IJCNN.2018.8489301
5. Aljaboriy, S., Sjarif, N., Chuprat, S., Abduallah, W.: Acute lymphoblastic leukemia segmentation using local pixel information. Pattern Recogn. Lett. **125**, 85–90 (2019). https://doi.org/10.1016/j.patrec.2019.03.024
6. Arena, P., Fortuna, L., Muscato, G., Xibilia, M.G.: Multilayer perceptrons to approximate quaternion valued functions. Neural Netw. **10**(2), 335–342 (1997). https://doi.org/10.1016/S0893-6080(96)00048-2
7. Bayro-Corrochano, E., Lechuga-Gutiérrez, L., Garza-Burgos, M.: Geometric techniques for robotics and hmi: interpolation and haptics in conformal geometric algebra and control using quaternion spike neural networks. Robot. Auton. Syst. **104**, 72–84 (2018)
8. Bibi, N., Sikandar, M., Din, I.U., Almogren, A., Ali, S.: Iomt-based automated detection and classification of leukemia using deep learning. J. Healthc. Eng. (2020). https://doi.org/10.1155/2020/6648574
9. Chen, B., Gao, Y., Xu, L., Hong, X., Zheng, Y., Shi, Y.Q.: Color image splicing localization algorithm by quaternion fully convolutional networks and superpixel-enhanced pairwise conditional random field. Math. Biosci. Eng. **6**(16), 6907–6922 (2019). https://doi.org/10.3934/mbe.2019346
10. García-Retuerta, D., Casado-Vara, R., Martin-del Rey, A., De la Prieta, F., Prieto, J., Corchado, J.M.: Quaternion neural networks: state-of-the-art and research challenges. In: Analide, C., Novais, P., Camacho, D., Yin, H. (eds.) IDEAL 2020. LNCS, vol. 12490, pp. 456–467. Springer, Cham (2020). https://doi.org/10.1007/978-3-030-62365-4_43
11. Gaudet, C.J.; Maida, A.: Deep quaternion networks. In: International Joint Conference on Neural Networks (IJCNN), pp. 1–8 (2018)

12. Glorot, X., Bengio, Y.: Understanding the difficulty of training deep feedforward neural networks. In: Teh, Y.W., Titterington, M. (eds.) Proceedings of the Thirteenth International Conference on Artificial Intelligence and Statistics. Proceedings of Machine Learning Research, vol. 9, pp. 249–256. PMLR, Chia Laguna Resort, Sardinia, Italy (13–15 May 2010). http://proceedings.mlr.press/v9/glorot10a.html
13. Greenblatt, A., Mosquera-Lopez, C., Agaian, S.: Quaternion neural networks applied to prostate cancer Gleason grading. In: 2013 IEEE International Conference on Systems, Man, and Cybernetics, pp. 1144–1149 (2013). https://doi.org/10.1109/SMC.2013.199
14. He, K., Gkioxari, G., Dollár, P., Girshick, R.: Mask r-cnn (2018)
15. He, K., Zhang, X., Ren, S., Sun, J.: Deep residual learning for image recognition. In: 2016 IEEE Conference on Computer Vision and Pattern Recognition (CVPR), pp. 770–778 (2016). https://doi.org/10.1109/CVPR.2016.90
16. Hirose, A.: Complex-Valued Neural Networks. Studies in Computational Intelligence, 2nd edn. Springer, Heidelberg (2012). https://doi.org/10.1007/978-3-642-27632-3
17. Hirose, A., Yoshida, S.: Generalization characteristics of complex-valued feedforward neural networks in relation to signal coherence. IEEE Trans. Neural Netw. Learn. Syst. **23**(4), 541–551 (2012). https://doi.org/10.1109/TNNLS.2012.2183613
18. Hu, J., Shen, L., Sun, G.: Squeeze-and-excitation networks. In: 2018 IEEE/CVF Conference on Computer Vision and Pattern Recognition, pp. 7132–7141 (2018). https://doi.org/10.1109/CVPR.2018.00745
19. Huang, G., Liu, Z., Van Der Maaten, L., Weinberger, K.Q.: Densely connected convolutional networks. In: 2017 IEEE Conference on Computer Vision and Pattern Recognition (CVPR), pp. 2261–2269 (2017). https://doi.org/10.1109/CVPR.2017.243
20. Isokawa, T., Matsui, N., Nishimura, H.: Quaternionic neural networks: fundamental properties and applications. In: Complex-Valued Neural Networks: Utilizing High-Dimensional Parameters, pp. 411–439 (2009)
21. Jha, K.K., Sekhar Dutta, H.: Mutual information based hybrid model and deep learning for acute lymphocytic Leukaemia detection in single cell blood smear images. Comput. Methods Program. Biomed. **179**, 104987 (2019). https://doi.org/10.1016/j.cmpb.2019.104987
22. Jin, L., Zhou, Y., Liu, H., Song, E.: Deformable quaternion Gabor convolutional neural network for color facial expression recognition. In: 2020 IEEE International Conference on Image Processing (ICIP), pp. 1696–1700 (2020). https://doi.org/10.1109/ICIP40778.2020.9191349
23. Kasvi: Hematologia: Como é realizada a técnica de esfregaço de sangue? https://kasvi.com.br/esfregaco-de-sangue-hematologia/ (2021). Accessed 18 Feb 2021
24. Kinugawa, K., Shang, F., Usami, N., Hirose, A.: Isotropization of quaternion-neural-network-based PolSAR adaptive land classification in Poincare-sphere parameter space. IEEE Geosci. Remote Sens. Lett. **15**(8), 1234–1238 (2018). https://doi.org/10.1109/LGRS.2018.2831215
25. Krizhevsky, A., Sutskever, I., Hinton, G.E.: Imagenet classification with deep convolutional neural networks. Commun. ACM **60**(6), 84–90 (2017). https://doi.org/10.1145/3065386
26. Kumar, S., Mishra, S., Asthana, P.: Pragya: automated detection of acute leukemia using k-mean clustering algorithm. In: Bhatia, S.K., Mishra, K.K., Tiwari, S., Singh, V.K. (eds.) Advances in Computer and Computational Sciences, pp. 655–670. Springer, Singapore (2018). https://doi.org/10.1007/978-981-10-3773-3_64

27. Kusamichi, H., Isokawa, T., Matsui, N., Ogawa, Y., Maeda, K.: A new scheme for color night vision by quaternion neural network. In: Proceedings of the 2nd International Conference on Autonomous Robots and Agents (ICARA 2004), pp. 101–106 (2004)

28. Labati, R.D., Piuri, V., Scotti, F.: All-idb: the acute lymphoblastic leukemia image database for image processing. In: 2011 18th IEEE International Conference on Image Processing (2011). https://doi.org/978-1-4577-1303-3

29. Mandic, D.P., Goh, V.S.L.: Complex Valued Nonlinear Adaptive Filters: Noncircularity, Widely Linear and Neural Models, vol. 59. Wiley, New York (2009)

30. Matsui, N., Isokawa, T., Kusamichi, H., Peper, F., Nishimura, H.: Quaternion neural network with geometrical operators. J. Intell. Fuzzy Syst. **15**(3), 149–164 (2004)

31. Mishra, S., Majhi, B., Sa, P.K.: Texture feature based classification on microscopic blood smear for acute lymphoblastic leukemia detection. Biomed. Sig. Process. Control **47**, 303–311 (2019). https://doi.org/10.1016/j.bspc.2018.08.012

32. NCI: Acute lymphoblastic leukemia. https://www.cancer.gov/publications/dictionaries/cancer-terms/def/acute-lymphoblastic-leukemia (2021). Accessed 18 Feb 2021

33. NCI: Lymphoblast. https://www.cancer.gov/publications/dictionaries/cancer-terms/def/lymphoblast (2021). Accessed 18 Feb 2021

34. NHS: Acute lymphoblastic leukemia diagnosis. https://www.nhs.uk/conditions/acute-lymphoblastic-leukaemia/diagnosis/ (2021). Accessed 18 Feb 2021

35. Nitta, T.: On the critical points of the complex-valued neural network. In: Proceedings of the ICONIP 2002 9th International Conference on Neural Information Processing: Computational Intelligence for the E-Age, pp. 411–439. Singapore (2002)

36. Ogawa, T.: Neural network inversion for multilayer quaternion neural networks. Comput. Technol. Appl. **7**, 73–82 (2016)

37. Onyekpe, U., Palade, V., Kanarachos, S., Christopoulos, S.R.: A quaternion gated recurrent unit neural network for sensor fusion. Information (2021). https://doi.org/10.3390/info12030117

38. Parcollet, T., Morchid, M., Linarès, G.: A survey of quaternion neural networks. Artif. Intell. Rev. **53**(4), 2957–2982 (2020). https://doi.org/10.1007/s10462-019-09752-1

39. Parcollet, T., Morchid, M., Linarès, G.: Quaternion Convolutional Neural Networks for Heterogeneous Image Process. (2018). https://doi.org/arXiv:1811.02656v1

40. Parcollet, T., et al.: Quaternion convolutional neural networks for end-to-end automatic speech recognition. In: Proceedings of the Interspeech 2018, pp. 22–26 (2018). https://doi.org/10.21437/Interspeech.2018-1898

41. Pavllo, D., Feichtenhofer, C., Auli, M., Grangier, D.: Modeling human motion with quaternion-based neural networks. Int. J. Comput. Vis. **128**(4), 855–872 (2019). https://doi.org/10.1007/s11263-019-01245-6

42. Shafique, S., Tehsin, S.: Computer-aided diagnosis of acute lymphoblastic Leukaemia. Comput. Math. Methods Med. **2018**, 6125289 (2018). https://doi.org/10.1155/2018/6125289

43. Shang, F., Hirose, A.: Quaternion neural-network-based PolSAR land classification in Poincare-sphere-parameter space. IEEE Trans. Geosci. Remote Sens. **52**, 5693–5703 (2014)

44. Simonyan, K., Zisserman, A.: Very deep convolutional networks for large-scale image recognition (2015)

45. Terwilliger, T., Abdul-Hay, M.J.B.C.J.: Acute lymphoblastic leukemia: a comprehensive review and 2017 update. Blood Cancer J. (2017). https://doi.org/10.1038/bcj.2017.53

46. Takahashi, K., Isaka, A., Fudaba, T., Hashimoto, M.: Remarks on quaternion neural network-based controller trained by feedback error learning. In: IEEE/SICE International Symposium on System Integration, pp. 875–880 (2017)

47. Takahashi, K., Takahashi, S., Cui, Y., Hashimoto, M.: Remarks on computational facial expression recognition from HOG features using quaternion multi-layer neural network. In: Mladenov, V., Jayne, C., Iliadis, L. (eds.) EANN 2014. CCIS, vol. 459, pp. 15–24. Springer, Cham (2014). https://doi.org/10.1007/978-3-319-11071-4_2

48. Trabelsi, C., et al.: Deep complex networks (May 2017)

49. Tuba, M., Tuba, E.: Generative adversarial optimization (goa) for acute lymphocytic leukemia detection. Stud. Inf. Control **28**, 245–254 (2019). https://doi.org/10.24846/v28i3y201901

50. Vogado, L.H., Veras, R.M., Araujo, F.H., Silva, R.R., Aires, K.R.: Leukemia diagnosis in blood slides using transfer learning in CNNs and SVM for classification. Eng. Appl. Artif. Intell. **72**, 415–422 (2018). https://doi.org/10.1016/j.engappai.2018.04.024

51. Zhu, X., Xu, Y., Xu, H., Chen, C.: Quaternion convolutional neural networks. In: Ferrari, V., Hebert, M., Sminchisescu, C., Weiss, Y. (eds.) ECCV 2018. LNCS, vol. 11212, pp. 645–661. Springer, Cham (2018). https://doi.org/10.1007/978-3-030-01237-3_39

# Sea State Estimation with Neural Networks Based on the Motion of a Moored FPSO Subjected to Campos Basin Metocean Conditions

Gustavo A. Bisinotto[(✉)] [ID], Lucas P. Cotrim[ID], Fabio Gagliardi Cozman[ID], and Eduardo A. Tannuri[ID]

Escola Politécnica of University of São Paulo, São Paulo, Brazil
gustavo.bisinotto@usp.br

**Abstract.** Important information for the design and operation of oceanic systems can be obtained by assessing local sea state parameters such as significant height, peak period and incidence direction. Techniques for motion-based inference and their possible drawbacks have been extensively discussed in the literature (their motivation coming from the simplicity of the required instrumentation when compared to traditional measuring systems), and machine learning approaches are now appearing in a few investigations. This paper addresses the estimation problem through supervised learning, using time series with the movement of a moored vessel to train neural networks models so as to estimate the sea state. Such time series are obtained through simulations, that consider a model of a spread-moored FPSO (Floating Production Storage and Offloading) platform with constant draft, out of a set of metocean conditions observed at Brazil's Campos Basin. A sensitivity analysis for different classes of neural networks was run, based on the significant height estimation, to choose the network architecture with the best results with respect to the mean absolute error metric. That topology was trained and employed in the estimation of the remaining sea state parameter, separately. The outcomes of the proposed models were confronted with other neural networks-based methods and showed up a comparable or slightly better performance in the error metrics. A preliminary discussion of the ability of the approach to deal with some classical issues on motion-based estimation is presented.

**Keywords:** Sea state estimation · Neural networks · Moored FPSO · Metocean conditions

## 1 Introduction

The operation of ships and other oceanic structures, such as offshore platforms, is affected by loads induced by waves, wind and currents. Therefore, reliable ways to obtain information about those environmental effects provide essential

© Springer Nature Switzerland AG 2021
A. Britto and K. Valdivia Delgado (Eds.): BRACIS 2021, LNAI 13074, pp. 294–308, 2021.
https://doi.org/10.1007/978-3-030-91699-2_21

data for the design and engineering of installations, and they are also useful to support decision-making processes, assisting the crew in the evaluation of a particular operation, or in the need to interrupt it [17].

Over the last decades, wave measurement has been carried out mainly by moored wave-buoys, whose motions are measured so as to recover the conditions around the buoys (due to their negligible dynamics). However, the setup is prone to damage and loss, and suffers from deep water mooring setbacks [17].

Most marine vessels are equipped with sensors that gather vast amounts of data, such as inertial measuring units (IMU), accelerometers, anemometers. In this sense, those crafts are inherently equipped with sea state measuring systems, as their sensor data can be used to infer their on-site condition, similarly to what is done with traditional buoys [2].

When compared to other wave monitoring systems, estimation of sea state based on vessel's motions presents the main advantage of the simplicity of the required instrumentation (composed basically of accelerometers and rate-gyros), already available or easily installed on-board. On the other hand, the limitation is clear: only waves that impose a reasonable level of motion may be inferred, which means that the vessel acts as a low-pass filter, filtering the high-frequency components that do not excite its first-order response. The filter analogy also indicates that the range of frequencies where the estimation can be properly performed will depend on the size of the vessel. Large-displacement vessels, such as the Very Large Crude Carriers (VLCCs) on which the FPSO (Floating Production Storage and Offloading) units are usually based, will have lower cut-off frequencies if compared to smaller vessels [16].

During the past years, motion-based methods for wave inference have been widely studied, mainly focusing on the parametric and the Bayesian approaches.

The parametric method as applied to an FPSO platform can be found in Ref. [19]. The formulation considers the characterization of the directional wave spectrum by a set of parameters and a linear relation between the incident wave and the movements' spectra, which is modeled by the Response Amplitude Operators (RAOs). Thereafter, a nonlinear optimization problem can be defined to minimize the absolute difference between the measured spectra of motion and the one computed from crossing the RAOs and the parametrized wave spectrum.

The Bayesian approach can be found in Ref. [14], with application to a container ship with forward speed, and in Ref. [17] and Ref. [16], to a moored FPSO, among others, with a derivation that leads to a quadratic optimization problem. In this case the linearity assumption remains, but no closed-form is imposed on the wave spectrum. The estimation is performed by maximizing the product of the likelihood function by the prior distribution. The likelihood function represents the conditional probability of occurrence of a given measurement, given the directional spectrum, while the prior distribution corresponds to the previous information about the unknown spectrum coefficients.

Since then, variations have been made to the initial proposals, especially to the Bayesian method. For instance, take Ref. [4], with the analysis of the influence of the hyperparameters associated with the priors, along with a procedure for their selection, and Ref. [5], with a combination of data from wave probes to the Bayesian modeling, to attenuate the effect of the filtering problem.

More recent years have seen machine learning-based proposals. For instance, in Ref. [1], where a Quadratic Discriminant Analysis classification and Least Square Regression were used to estimate the set of wave parameters and in [20] with the definition of a classification problem based on random forests.

Some other efforts based on neural networks can be found in the literature. In Ref. [6], time series of movements from an in-service frigate type vessel and data from numerical simulation were considered to output wave height, period and direction. In Ref. [3], a classification problem was analyzed with the definition of a sea state from discretized wave heights and directions adding up to a total of 40 possibilities, that were classified from zigzag motions of a research vessel.

From the previous discussion, it can be noticed that a large interest has been devoted to motion-based wave estimation methods in the last couple of decades, with several applications in simulations, experiments and field campaigns. However, few works have been yet carried out with machine learning techniques, particularly when taking into account large moored vessels such as FPSOs.

This paper aims to address sea state estimation from motions of a moored FPSO using neural networks. The motion data was obtained through simulations of the vessel subjected to a dataset of environmental conditions observed at Brazil's Campos Basin.

The next section presents an explanation of ocean waves and their parameters, where directional and power wave spectra are introduced, and also the sea state. This is followed by a brief discussion of different classes of neural networks in Sect. 3. The sea state estimation procedure is detailed in Sect. 4, with a description of the data and the process to select the architecture of the estimation model. In Sect. 5, the outcomes of the proposed method are displayed and discussed. Finally, some conclusions drawn from this study are presented along with possible further steps.

# 2    Background: the Description of Ocean Waves

There are two main types of waves affecting the behavior of oceanic structures: wind waves and swell. In both cases, the waves start as small ripples but increase in size due to the sustained energy from the wind. Wind waves result from the local wind blowing over a fetch of water, while a swell is created by winds that are no longer blowing; such waves are been generated elsewhere from a distance and are not significantly influenced by the local wind [12,15].

The most applied theory of waves in the dynamical analysis of marine systems is the linear wave theory, whose basic element is the linear regular wave [12]. Its dimensions associated with the propagation through space are depicted in Fig. 1. Besides those parameters, others that should be mentioned are the main direction of propagation and the wave period, which defines the time interval between the arrival of consecutive crests at a stationary point, and that can be associated with the wave length by a dispersion relation [13].

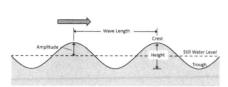

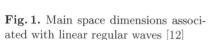

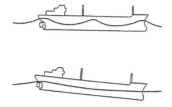

**Fig. 1.** Main space dimensions associated with linear regular waves [12]

**Fig. 2.** Illustration of the filtering problem with a regular incident wave

The regular wave is also useful to illustrate the filtering problem on motion-based wave inference, as shown in Fig. 2. Where for low-frequency incident waves (on bottom) oscillatory motions are generated in the wave frequency (first-order response). While it can be noticed that for high-frequency waves (on top) the vessel is mostly not responsive to the wave excitation, and hence little movement is induced, making the estimation more challenging.

However, that description is not faithful to the actual ocean environment, as real ocean waves are irregular and random. Despite that, they can be modeled by a suitable distribution of regular waves. Under a linearity assumption, a superposition method can be applied, in which irregular waves can be described as the sum of regular components with different amplitudes and periods [12,13].

With this simplification, waves can be represented by a power spectrum, $S(\omega)$, that gives the distribution of energy among different frequencies, $\omega$. To also account for the propagation of the components of the irregular wave in different directions, $\theta$, the power spectrum can be extended to the directional spectrum, $S(\omega,\theta)$, that defines the distribution of energy over frequencies and directions. Examples of power and directional spectra are shown in Fig. 3.

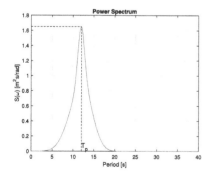

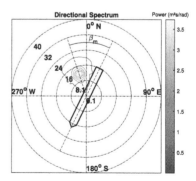

**Fig. 3.** Power and directional wave spectra

Due to the irregular nature of waves, it is not reasonable to assume a single wave height or wave period. Instead, wave statistics can be defined, such as the significant wave height $(H_s)$, that is computed as the average height of the highest one-third of the waves in the record, and the peak period $(T_p)$, that is the period of maximum energy of the spectrum, among other possible characteristic periods [10]. From the analysis of the power spectrum, Fig. 3 (left), those parameters can be obtained as follows:

$$H_s = 4\sqrt{\int_0^\infty S(\omega)d\omega} \quad \text{and} \quad T_p = \frac{2\pi}{\omega_p}, \quad \omega_p = \underset{\omega}{\operatorname{argmax}} S(\omega). \tag{1}$$

In the directional spectrum Fig. 3 (right), a contour plot is presented. Where the angular positions indicate the propagation direction, in degrees; the concentric lines correspond to periods, in seconds, of the wave components; and colors express the energy density of those components.

Because wind-generated waves are not uni-directional, an angular spread is adopted, thus defining a distribution of energy along the directions. Hence, two angular statistics can be defined to describe the wave propagation through space: the mean wave direction $(\beta)$ and the relative wave direction $(\beta_m)$. The mean wave incidence direction is usually measured clockwise from the vertical axis (from North), while the relative direction is a function of the incidence direction and the heading of the vessel $(\beta_{heading})$, depicted in Fig. 3 (right) and according to the following expression:

$$\beta_m = \pi + \beta_{heading} - \beta. \tag{2}$$

With the set of parameters $(H_s, T_p, \beta)$ or $(H_s, T_p, \beta_m)$, the sea state for a unimodal sea can be described. For multimodal seas, superposition can be applied with the individual wave spectra. And the sea state can be characterized by multiples sets of significant height, peak period and incidence direction.

## 3   Background: Neural Networks

Artificial Neural Networks (ANNs or simply NNs) essentially aim to approximate a function $y = f^*(x)$, that maps an input $x$ to a continuous value or a categorical output $y$, defining a relation $y = f(x; \vartheta)$. From data, one must learn the value of the parameters $\vartheta$ that results in the best function approximation [7].

Convolutional neural networks (CNNs) are a particular class of neural networks specialized in processing data with a known grid-like topology. Those networks use multiple sets of shared weights, called filters, to respond to different patterns in the data. To this end, the general matrix multiplication between input and weights is replaced by a convolution operation in the formulation of the neurons [7].

The basic structure of a CNN [11] consists of a series of convolutional layers, with different depths and kernel dimensions, each associated with an activation function (usually nonlinear). And pooling layers that are responsible for reducing the size of the data by keeping local information of the mapping, such as maximum or average values. In this process, it is possible to extract features from

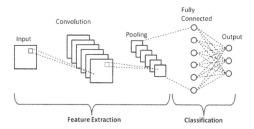

**Fig. 4.** CNN basic structure

the inputs by combining patterns underlined by each set of filters, which can be concatenated to feed an MLP for the final step of classification or regression.

Recurrent neural networks (RNNs) are a family of neural networks for sequential data processing, whose connections between layers model a dynamic temporal behavior for time-varying input series. However, traditional RNNs suffer from significant issues, the "vanishing or exploding gradients" effects, since it becomes difficult to backpropagate errors through a long-time span [7].

Long Short-Term Memory (LSTM) RNNs [9] deal with this problem by creating paths through time that have derivatives that neither vanish nor explode, with the application of a system of gating units to controls that data flow. In such a way that they can store information over extended time intervals.

## 4  An Estimation Procedure for Sea Parameters

The proposed estimation procedure was formulated as a supervised learning regression problem, where the goal is to compute each one of the sea state parameters (significant height, peak period and incidence direction) of a unimodal sea from time series of motion of a moored platform.

**Fig. 5.** FPSO platform at campos basin

Table 1. Information about the FPSO platform at campos basin

| Quantity | Value |
|---|---|
| Vessel type | FPSO |
| Mooring | Spread-Moored |
| Length ($L_{pp}$) | 320 m |
| Breadth | 54.5 m |
| Draft | 16 m |
| Heading | 206.16° |

Those time series were obtained from simulations of the model in 6°C of freedom (dofs) of a typical spread-moored FPSO unit, Fig. 5, with one loading condition (single draft) under a dataset of metocean conditions that were observed at Brazil's Campos Basin.

For data generation, the simulation model, along with the platform information, Table 1, and the environmental conditions were considered as inputs to the Dynasim simulator, a hydro-dynamical numerical simulator developed by a partnership between the Numerical Offshore Tank Laboratory of the University of São Paulo (TPN-USP) and Petrobras.

### 4.1 Metocean Data

The dataset of metocean information was observed from 2003 to 2009 and consists of 18006 different groups of environmental conditions with both unimodal and bimodal seas, defined by a total of up to 10 parameters by example: wind velocity and direction, current velocity and direction and up to 2 sets of wave related parameters.

As previously stated, in this paper only unimodal seas were considered, which are associated with just one set of parameters $(H_s, T_p, \beta)$ to specify the sea state, and represent a total of over 5000 observations. The distribution of each of those parameters over the dataset is shown in Figs. 6, 7 and 8.

The histograms indicate the most common ranges of values for each of the parameters. As a result, the training of the neural networks may favor those values over the less frequent ones, given that some of those sets have considerably fewer examples than others. On the other hand, the models may learn to identify patterns related to the statistical description of waves of that geographical region.

In the case of the wave significant height, most occurrences are around 1.5 m to 2.5 m, while examples with height less than 1 m or greater than 4.5 m are rarely observed. Taking into account the wave peak periods, a substantial amount of waves with periods lower than $7 - 8$ s can be noticed, which correspond to high-frequency incident waves for a large vessel like the FPSO under analysis. This condition may be an issue for the estimation method, due to the already mentioned filtering problem. For the incidence directions, the most remarkable aspect is the almost absence of occurrences over 200°, which can be justified by

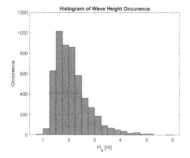

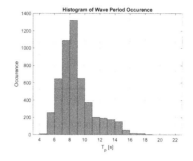

**Fig. 6.** Histogram of significant height

**Fig. 7.** Histogram of peak period

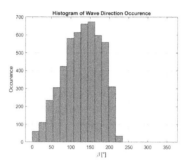

**Fig. 8.** Histogram of incidence direction

the geographical characteristic of the vessel's location. That is, waves with those incidence angles would be coming from the West, according to the polar plot of the directional spectrum in Fig. 3 (right), which would indicate waves coming from the Brazilian coast, and those situations are less frequent.

## 4.2   Data Processing

Before the actual training of estimators, a data treatment procedure was carried out on the time series obtained through the simulations. The output of the Dynasim simulator, for each set of conditions, is composed by time series of position, velocity and acceleration in the 6 dofs (surge, sway, heave, roll, pitch, yaw), which correspond to a time span of over 3 h (11400 s) with a sampling time of 1 s. From those series, just the 6 positional motions were selected, with respect to a fixed reference frame, and a time window of 30 min (1800 s), which is consistent with the regular dynamic of changes in the environment, was sampled in the middle of the total duration. Thereafter, each time series was centered by subtracting its mean value, and a dataset of over 5000 examples, each with 6 series of 1800 points, could be built.

The data was then divided into 3 different datasets, following a 70/20/10 split: the training data, to be used in the training of the network, the validation data, used for the evaluation of the model with the desired metrics and the test data, to verify the performance of the system on previously unseen data. Finally, each dataset was normalized using the statistical properties (mean value and standard deviation) of the training dataset.

### 4.3 Network Architecture

In this paper, a single neural network architecture was sought to address, separately, the estimation problems of each of the sea state parameters. From the literature review, it was observed that the significant height estimation was more challenging than period and direction. Therefore, a sensitivity study with different classes of neural networks and their hyperparameters was run to select the network configuration with best performance, whose architecture would be then repeated to estimate peak period and incidence direction. In this way, the overall estimation was divided into 3 distinct problems, each with the same network structure trained independently with distinct targets.

A general structure for the pursued network was chosen as being composed of one or more feature extracting blocks (FE blocks) followed by a regression block. The latter was kept unchanged during the evaluations, while the former varied according to the following scenarios:

- MLP: Each FE block was built from multilayer perceptrons with batch normalization and ReLU activation functions. The number of layers (or blocks) was chosen from 1 to 3 and the number of neurons on each layer was selected from the set $\{64, 128, 256, 512\}$.
- LSTM: Each block was composed of LSTM layers with returning sequences. The number of layers varied from 2 to 4, and the number of units was picked from $\{32, 64, 128, 256, 512\}$.
- CNN1D - single kernel: 1D convolutional layers were employed, each convolution was followed by batch normalization and ReLU activation. The number of blocks was either 2 or 3, the number of filters was selected from $\{32, 64, 128, 256, 512\}$, and the kernel dimension of those filters from $\{1, 3, 5\}$.
- CNN1D - multiple kernels: This scenario was motivated by the structure proposed in Ref. [18], where convolutions with different kernels were combined to extract features in image classification. The number of layers was either 2 or 3, two sets of kernel dimensions were evaluated $\{1, 3, 5\}$ and $\{1, 3, 5, 7\}$ and the number of filters in the first layer was selected from $\{64, 128, 256, 512\}$, for the remaining layers the number of filters was half of the previous layer.
- CNN1D - multiple kernels with residual connections: Residual connections, inspired by Ref. [8], were added to the CNN1D with multiple kernels, where the input information was passed forward in the data flow.

In all scenarios, the regression block was the same, with 3 MLP layers—the first two with batch normalization and ReLU activation functions, and the last with a linear activation. The number of neurons in the layers was, respectively, 128, 64 and 1.

**Table 2.** Sensitivity study for network parameters

|  | & Layers | & Units/Filters | Filter kernel | Validation MAE [m] |
|---|---|---|---|---|
| MLP | 2 | [256, 256] | – | 0.0608 |
| LSTM | 2 | [512, 512] | – | 0.1213 |
| CNN1D - single kernel | 2 | [128, 128] | 3 | 0.0442 |
| **CNN1D - multiple kernels** | **2** | **[256,128]** | **{1,3,5,7}** | **0.0369** |
| CNN1D - multiple kernels and residual connections | 2 | [128, 64] | {1, 3, 5, 7} | 0.0403 |

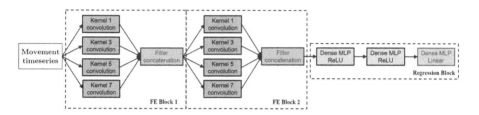

**Fig. 9.** Proposed network architecture

All experiments were carried out within a computational environment with Python 3.7.6. The layers were implemented by Keras 2.4.3, using TensorFlow 2.4.0 as the backend. The training process used the Adam optimizer, a batch size of 32 and a number of epochs of 1000. The selected loss function was the mean absolute error (MAE) between the actual significant wave height and the estimated one. The best model (based on the validation set) was stored during training.

The results of the sensitivity study are summarized in Table 2, where the best models obtained in each category, with respect to the validation MAE, along with their parameters, are presented.

From the analysis, it can be noted that the approaches based on convolutions presented a better performance compared to both MLP and LSTM. Furthermore, the association of filters with different kernels in a layer generated improvements, while the addition of residual connections did not bring benefits.

Those improvements can be justified by the definition of the convolutions, that were performed over windows of motions instead of time windows. The computations of each filter take into account all time samples and a number of movements equal to the kernel size; as a result, features related to the coupling of different combinations of motions can be extracted with multiple kernels. The proposed architecture is depicted in Fig. 9.

## 5    Motion-Based Estimation Results and Discussion

After selecting the network architecture through sensitivity analysis, the performance of the model was evaluated on the test dataset, with respect to the

**Table 3.** Comparison of wave height estimation results

|  | $\mu$ [m] | $\sigma$ [m] | $MAE$ [m] | $MAPE$ [%] | $R^2$ |
|---|---|---|---|---|---|
| Proposed | 0.0007 | 0.0644 | 0.0384 | 1.9087 | 0.9903 |
| SSENET (adapted from [3]) | 0.0000 | 0.1071 | 0.0675 | 3.3505 | 0.9733 |
| MLSTM-CNN [6] | 0.0063 | 0.0953 | 0.0561 | 2.6868 | 0.9788 |
| Sliding Puzzle [6] | −0.0002 | 0.0633 | 0.0400 | 1.9191 | 0.9907 |

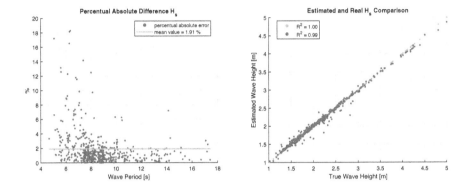

**Fig. 10.** Regression results - wave height

following metrics: mean value ($\mu$) and standard deviation ($\sigma$) of the error, mean absolute error ($MAE$), mean absolute percentual error ($MAPE$), and the coefficient of determination ($R^2$).

Moreover, the results attained by the proposed architecture were compared to other neural networks available in the literature for sea state estimation, that were implemented and trained with the same dataset. In particular, three networks were employed: SSENET, from Ref. [3], based on convolutions with residual connections; MLSTM-CNN, from Ref. [6], combining CNN and LSTM layers; and Sliding Puzzle, also from Ref. [6], with a purely convolutional architecture. Although the SSENET was designed for a classification task, its structure was adapted for the considered regression problem, which may provide illustrative results for comparison purposes. The MLSTM-CNN and the Sliding Puzzle remained unchanged since they were already designed for regression.

The summary of the results for the wave height estimation is presented in Table 3. There it can be observed that, except for mean value of the error, the architectures built only with convolutional layers (Proposed and Sliding Puzzle) presented a better performance when compared to the others, with a slightly better result of the Proposed in the MAE and MAPE, and slightly worse on the standard deviation and $R^2$. It is also worth pointing out that in both cases the average errors were low, with less than 2% error, 0.04 m of absolute error, and the $R^2$ was over 0.99.

**Table 4.** Comparison of wave period estimation results

|  | $\mu$ [s] | $\sigma$ [s] | $MAE$ [s] | $MAPE$ [%] | $R^2$ |
|---|---|---|---|---|---|
| Proposed | −0.0063 | 0.1074 | 0.0553 | 0.7210 | 0.9977 |
| SSENET (adapted from [3]) | −0.0060 | 0.0903 | 0.0552 | 0.7215 | 0.9984 |
| MLSTM-CNN [6] | 0.0017 | 0.0691 | 0.0446 | 0.5742 | 0.9990 |
| Sliding Puzzle [6] | −0.0040 | 0.0471 | 0.0283 | 0.3653 | 0.9996 |

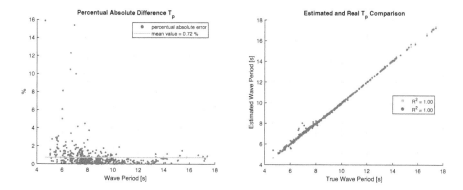

**Fig. 11.** Regression results - wave period

A further analysis is enabled by the (percentage) absolute difference plot and the comparison between actual and estimated values in Fig. 10.

From these plots, two main effects can be outlined: the filtering problem, given that the largest errors occurred at the low periods, and that true and estimated values on high height values, over 4 m, did not present large differences, despite few occurrences.

Similarly, for the peak period, the comparative results are shown in Table 4. From there it can be verified that all the architectures are able to present significant results, less than 0.8% of percentual error, and no more than 0.06 s of absolute error on average. However, for this sea state parameter, the proposed network was outperformed by the other approaches.

The plots in Fig. 11 show the same tendency of the height estimation: presence of filtering affecting the performance in low periods, and even though few examples with high periods are available, their estimation had small errors.

For the incidence direction, some differences from the previous cases are worth discussing. Given the circular characteristics of the target, a custom loss function was adapted considering the distance of two points $(P_1, P_2)$ in the unitary circle with angular coordinates $\beta_1$ (true value) and $\beta_2$ (estimation), which is stated as:

$$d(P_1, P_2) = \sqrt{(\sin \beta_1 - \sin \beta_2)^2 + (\cos \beta_1 - \cos \beta_2)^2}. \qquad (3)$$

**Table 5.** Comparison of wave direction estimation results

|  | $\mu$ [°] | $\sigma$ [°] | $MAE$ [°] | $R^2$ |
|---|---|---|---|---|
| Proposed | −0.1427 | 1.4533 | 0.5661 | 0.9991 |
| SSENET (adapted from [3]) | −0.0099 | 3.4532 | 0.8689 | 0.9951 |
| MLSTM-CNN [6] | −0.0458 | 2.8728 | 1.3340 | 0.9969 |
| Sliding Puzzle [6] | −0.2411 | 3.8300 | 1.2278 | 0.9939 |

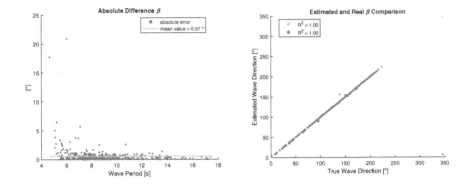

**Fig. 12.** Regression results - wave direction

And then, the absolute angular difference in the range $[0, \pi]$ can be obtained with the cosine law:

$$d(P_1, P_2)^2 = 1^2 + 1^2 - 2cos(\beta_1 - \beta_2) \Rightarrow |\beta_1 - \beta_2| = \arccos\left(1 - \frac{d(P_1, P_2)^2}{2}\right). \quad (4)$$

From the expression, it can be noted that the absolute angular error increases if $d(P_1, P_2)$ increases. Thus, the loss function was defined as the distance itself, in order to avoid computations of derivatives of the inverse cosine function.

The results of the direction estimation are shown in Table 5. As in the previous cases, the error metrics displayed low values in all methods—less than 1.5° in the MAE, for example. But for most of the metrics, except the mean value of the error, the proposed model generated better outcomes than other methods.

The plots in Fig. 12 highlight once again the difficulty in the estimation at low periods, with large deviations from the mean in those situations. And also the limited number of directions over 200°, which could still be properly estimated.

Overall, the proposed architecture produced significant results in the sea state estimation based on motions of a moored FPSO obtained through simulations; low errors metrics were attained and even less frequently observed parameters could be estimated. The well-known filtering problem was also observed in all evaluations. However, in most cases, either the errors in the high-frequency range were acceptable, less than 19% for height and period, or the number of occurrences with large deviations was very restricted, just 2 cases over 7° of absolute error in the direction. This may suggest that patterns were extracted from data related to the movement generated by those high-frequency waves, which may have led the network to use information not only from the first-order response but also from the slow varying motions (due to higher-order wave-induced effects) in the inference; or that the models were able to learn about the statistical distribution of the dataset of environmental conditions of the region—or some other feature that requires further analysis in the continuation of the work.

# 6 Conclusions

A supervised learning approach for motion-based sea state estimation with neural networks has been presented in this paper. Time series of movements, generated through simulations of a spread-moored FPSO with constant draft under environmental conditions observed at Brazil's Campos Basin, were applied to train the networks so as to estimate each of the sea state parameters. A single network architecture was obtained from a sensitivity study run on different classes of neural networks and their hyperparameters, based on the significant height estimation. Convolutional layers with multiple kernels concatenated were selected, allowing us to analyze coupling of motions among different sets of dofs.

Results obtained by the proposed architecture were compared to other networks designed for sea state estimation available in the literature and presented comparable or slightly better performance in the evaluated error metrics. The examination of the estimation outcomes in the individual examples displayed the classical filtering problem, in which high-frequency waves are filtered by the vessel. Despite that, the performance loss, although significant, did not completely compromise the estimation, which may lead one to question whether or not the network is able to extract features related to those settings—by the slow varying information present in the time series, by learning patterns of the statistical distribution of the environmental conditions of the region, or by some other aspect. Those circumstances motivate further developments on the work; for instance, the analysis for bimodal seas and multiple loading conditions, and the continuous search for possibly more suitable estimation models.

**Acknowledgments.** Authors acknowledge Petrobras for providing long-term support and motivation to this work. The authors also thank the Center for Artificial Intelligence (C4AI-USP) and the support from the São Paulo Research Foundation (FAPESP grant #2019/07665-4) and from the IBM Corporation. The first and second authors acknowledge the Higher Education Personnel Improvement Coordination (Capes) for the scholarship. The third author was supported in part by Brazilian National Council for Scientific and Technological Development (CNPq) under Grant 312180/2018-7. The last author acknowledges the CNPq for the research grant (310127/2020-3).

# References

1. Arneson, I.B., Brodtkorb, A.H., Sørensen, A.J.: Sea state estimation using quadratic discriminant analysis and partial least squares regression. IFAC-PapersOnLine **52**(21), 72–77 (2019)

2. Brodtkorb, A.H., Nielsen, U.D., Sørensen, A.J.: Sea state estimation using vessel response in dynamic positioning. Appl. Ocean Res. **70**, 76–86 (2018)
3. Cheng, X., Li, G., Ellefsen, A.L., Chen, S., Hildre, H.P., Zhang, H.: A novel densely connected convolutional neural network for sea-state estimation using ship motion data. IEEE Trans. Instrum. Meas. **69**(9), 5984–5993 (2020)
4. Da Silva Bispo, I.B., Simos, A.N., Tannuri, E.A., da Cruz, J.J., et al.: Motion-based wave estimation by a Bayesian inference method: a procedure for pre-defining the hyperparameters. In: The Twenty-second International Offshore and Polar Engineering Conference. International Society of Offshore and Polar Engineers (2012)
5. De Souza, F.L., Tannuri, E.A., de Mello, P.C., Franzini, G., Mas-Soler, J., Simos, A.N.: Bayesian estimation of directional wave-spectrum using vessel motions and wave-probes: proposal and preliminary experimental validation. J. Offshore Mech. Arctic Eng. **140**(4), 041102 (2018). https://doi.org/10.1115/1.4039263. ISSN 0892-7219
6. Duz, B., Mak, B., Hageman, R., Grasso, N.: Real time estimation of local wave characteristics from ship motions using artificial neural networks. In: Okada, T., Suzuki, K., Kawamura, Y. (eds.) PRADS 2019. LNCE, vol. 65, pp. 657–678. Springer, Singapore (2021). https://doi.org/10.1007/978-981-15-4680-8_45
7. Goodfellow, I., Courville, A., Bengio, Y.: Deep Learning, vol. 1. MIT Press, Cambridge (2016)
8. He, K., Zhang, X., Ren, S., Sun, J.: Deep residual learning for image recognition. In: Proceedings of the IEEE Conference on Computer Vision and Pattern Recognition, pp. 770–778 (2016)
9. Hochreiter, S., Schmidhuber, J.: Long short-term memory. Neural Comput. **9**(8), 1735–1780 (1997)
10. Journée, J.M., Massie, W.W.: Offshore Hydromechanics. Delft University of Technology, Delft, The Netherlands (2001)
11. LeCun, Y., Bengio, Y., et al.: Convolutional networks for images, speech, and time series. Handb. Brain Theor. Neural Netw. **3361**(10), 1995 (1995)
12. Ma, K.T., Luo, Y., Kwan, C.T.T., Wu, Y.: Mooring System Engineering for Offshore Structures. Gulf Professional Publishing, Houston (2019)
13. Newman, J.N.: Marine Hydrodynamics. The MIT press, Cambridge (1977)
14. Nielsen, U.D.: Estimations of on-site directional wave spectra from measured ship responses. Mar. Struct. **19**(1), 33–69 (2006)
15. Pecher, A., Kofoed, J.P. (eds.): Handbook of Ocean Wave Energy. OEO, vol. 7. Springer, Cham (2017). https://doi.org/10.1007/978-3-319-39889-1
16. Simos, A.N., Tannuri, E.A., da Cruz, J.J., Filho, A.N.Q., Da Silva Bispo, I.B., Carvalho, R.C.: Development of an on-board wave estimation system based on the motions of a moored FPSO: Commissioning and preliminary validation. In: International Conference on Offshore Mechanics and Arctic Engineering, vol. 44922, pp. 259–270. American Society of Mechanical Engineers (2012)
17. Simos, A.N., Tannuri, E.A., Sparano, J.V., Matos, V.L.: Estimating wave spectra from the motions of moored vessels: experimental validation. Appl. Ocean Res. **32**(2), 191–208 (2010)
18. Szegedy, C., et al.: Going deeper with convolutions. In: Proceedings of the IEEE Conference on Computer Vision and Pattern Recognition, pp. 1–9 (2014)
19. Tannuri, E.A., Sparano, J.V., Simos, A.N., Da Cruz, J.J.: Estimating directional wave spectrum based on stationary ship motion measurements. Appl. Ocean Res. **25**(5), 243–261 (2003)
20. Tu, F., Ge, S.S., Choo, Y.S., Hang, C.C.: Sea state identification based on vessel motion response learning via multi-layer classifiers. Ocean Eng. **147**, 318–332 (2018)

# Time-Dependent Item Embeddings
# for Collaborative Filtering

Pedro R. Pires[✉], Amanda C. Pascon, and Tiago A. Almeida

Department of Computer Science, Federal University of São Carlos, Sorocaba, Brazil
{pedro.pires,amanda.pascon}@dcomp.sor.ufscar.br, talmeida@ufscar.br

**Abstract.** Collaborative filtering recommender systems are essential tools in many modern applications. Their main advantage compared with the alternatives is that they require only a matrix of user-item interactions to recommend a subset of relevant items for a given user. However, the increasing volume of the data consumed by these systems may lead to a representation model with very high sparsity and dimensionality. Several approaches to overcome this problem have been proposed, neural embeddings being one of the most recent. Since then, many recommender systems were made using this representation model, but few consumed temporal information during the learning phase. This study shows how to adapt a pioneering method of item embeddings by adding a sliding window over time, in conjunction with a split in the user's interaction history. Results indicate that considering temporal information when learning neural embeddings for items can significantly improve the quality of the recommendations.

**Keywords:** Collaborative filtering · Distributed vector
representation · Item embeddings · Temporal data · Sliding window

## 1 Introduction

Personalized recommendations have become an increasingly common practice in our digital lives [5]. With the popularization of technology and ease of making information available, users have access to many items such as movies, music, and news, making it challenging for them to discover everything available and explore their interests. Recommender systems then emerged in the 1990s to overcome this problem, employing filtering techniques to direct the user to a restricted subset of relevant items [2].

Among several types of recommender systems, collaborative filtering is currently the most prolific in scientific literature and practical applications. Their popularity can be credited to its ease of application, since it depends only on

This study was financed by the Coordenação de Aperfeiçoamento de Pessoal de Nível Superior – Brasil (CAPES) Finance Code 88882.426978/2019-01, and Fundação de Amparo à Pesquisa do Estado de São Paulo (FAPESP) grant #2020/09354-3.

A. Britto and K. Valdivia Delgado (Eds.): BRACIS 2021, LNAI 13074, pp. 309–324, 2021.
https://doi.org/10.1007/978-3-030-91699-2_22

a matrix of interactions between users and items to generate recommendations based on similar tastes among users [5].

In early studies, the general approach uses item-based neighborhood algorithms for generating the recommendation [7]. However, the representation commonly adopted grows fast in size as the number of users and items increases; in real-world scenarios, these numbers grow constantly and much faster than the number of user-item interactions. Consequently, the traditional representation model became highly sparse and with an inflated dimensionality, demanding more and more computational power and reducing the quality of the results [18].

Many approaches have been presented to overcome this problem, such as matrix factorization [20] and neural models [36]. In the latter, methods based on neural embeddings have been gaining ground in recent literature. These methods aim to represent items or users as distributed vectors, resulting in a representation with reduced dimensionality while keeping its latent meaning [4,13].

Although many studies have proposed different methods based on neural embeddings [11,31], most of these studies do not consider the moment when the user interacted with the item [6]. The static approach – as it is known – while very present in the literature, has proven flaws [21]. Taking into account the timing and order of interactions can lead to significant improvements in results [3,6,33].

In this context, this study shows how to adapt Item2Vec [4] – a pioneering method of neural embeddings for a recommendation context – to consider temporal information during training by outlining an approach based on a sliding window over time, a strategy commonly employed in similar scenarios [33].

## 2   Related Work

Neighborhood algorithms became very popular in the first collaborative filtering recommender systems, given their relative low complexity and ability to produce satisfying results. Early neighborhood algorithms represented users as vectors and yielded recommendations based on the interactions history of the users closest to the target user [7]. Subsequent approaches began to represent items as vectors [28]. This strategy achieved better results, the training was more efficient, and the results were more stable over time having less need for retraining [17].

Gradually, the data used by recommender systems has grown, bringing new challenges to the area such as high sparsity and dimensionality of the commonly adopted representation [18]. Many algorithms for dimensionality reduction have been proposed to overcome this problem. Among different strategies, matrix factorization techniques have become state-of-the-art and are still very relevant to this day [25]. In this approach, users and items are represented as matrices of reduced dimensionality, and the recommendation is made using user-item similarities [20].

With the growth in research of neural networks, the use of neural models for recommender systems has increased significantly in recent years. Among several proposals for using neural networks for recommendation, neural embeddings have been gaining ground in the literature [13]. Inspired by Natural Language Processing (NLP) neural models capable of generating vector representations of words [24], these models were adapted to learn low-dimensional embeddings for items and users [27].

Grbovic *et al.* [13] addressed an ad recommendation problem based on receipts collected by email and proposed the Prod2Vec and User2Vec methods. The former is based on a skip-gram architecture [24] learning product embeddings and recommending through item similarity, while the latter is based on Paragraph Vector [22], learning embeddings of users and items concurrently and recommending through the similarities between users and items.

With an approach similar to Prod2Vec, Barkan & Koenigstein [4] proposed Item2Vec in the following year. The method was also inspired by consolidated techniques from the NLP area [24] and achieved promising results, surpassing state-of-the-art matrix factorization methods in different tasks.

In the ensuing years, different strategies for learning neural embeddings in recommender systems were proposed, such as *(i)* adapting existing models to leverage item metadata [11,31]; *(ii)* using content information during the embeddings training phase [14,35]; *(iii)* employing more complex neural models, e.g., LSTMs or CNNs [29,30]; *(iv)* training unaltered NLP models over textual data of items, users, or interactions [9,15]; and *(v)* considering different types of user-item interaction [37].

Few studies on neural embeddings in recommender systems explored the impact of using temporal information, i.e., *when* the interaction happened. The most common approach is session-based recommendation, in which only items consumed by the user in a short period are used for training the embeddings, considering an ordered relationship [12] or not [13].

The static approach is still customary in recommender systems as a whole, even though it has flaws [21]. User's interests change over time, and by not accounting for it, important information can be lost [6,33]. It is known that considering temporal aspects tends to improve the quality of the recommendation and generate greater confidence for the user [3]. Additionally, static algorithms trained in offline scenarios can suffer a drop in performance when applied in online and real scenarios with temporal properties [21]

Recommender systems capable of learning relevant information from temporal data have been proposed since the beginning of the field [1], but this has gained relevance when timeSVD++ [19], a temporal adaptation of the matrix factorization method SVD++, won one of the rounds of *The Netflix Prize*[1].

Two approaches can be applied to temporal information: using time as context, based on the idea of cyclical phenomena as it is done in Time-Aware Recommender Systems (TARS); or use time as a sequence, viewing temporal information as a chronologically ordered sequence, the strategy used in Time-Dependent Recommender Systems (TDRS) [33].

---

[1] The well-known competition of recommender systems, organized by the streaming company Netflix from 2006 to 2009: https://www.netflixprize.com/rules.html.

In TDRS two data interpretation methodologies are commonly adopted: the use of decay functions, which make newer interactions have more weight during the learning phase than older interactions [10]; and the use of sliding windows (also known as "forgetting techniques") in which interactions are sorted chronologically, and only a slice of the data is consumed during training, with the remaining information receiving less weight or being ignored [33].

In the last decade, some studies showed promising results using sliding window strategies for recommender systems. For instance, Vinagre & Jorge [32] employed two different sliding window techniques in a neighborhood-based recommender. Matuszyk *et al.* [23] proposed five forgetting strategies for matrix factorization using temporal windows or fading factors during data preprocessing and model training. Wang *et al.* [34] trained a neural network to predict shopping baskets in an e-commerce environment using a unit-size sliding window over past baskets. All studies above surpassed baseline algorithms or improved scalability without compromising accuracy.

In line with the positive results that have been presented in the literature, we propose SeqI2V, a sequential Item2Vec [4] adaptation using sliding windows over time. In our proposal, the embeddings learning phase is influenced by *when* interactions occur, increasing the context these item representations carry. The final recommendation is statically computed using an item-based neighborhood approach, just like the original method.

## 3    The Proposed Method

Methods based on neural embeddings are becoming state-of-the-art for recommender systems, presenting results comparable to established approaches, such as neighborhood techniques and matrix factorization. The Item2Vec was a pioneering technique in introducing neural embedding techniques from Natural Language Processing to the recommendation scenario, adapting the skip-gram network to generate item embeddings. As stated by the authors, the method outperformed the well-known SVD in different evaluated tasks.

Some subsequent studies adapted Item2Vec to specific scenarios or improved the embeddings training phase [11,31]. However, temporal information is still underexplored, limiting the application of Item2Vec to offline scenarios, in which pattern variations over time are ignored. To fill this important gap, we propose using sliding windows over time to introduce temporal information in the learning stage while keeping the elegant simplicity of Item2Vec.

In the following, we explain the traditional Item2Vec model and present SeqI2V – a sequential Item2Vec adaptation using sliding windows over time.

### 3.1    Item2Vec

Item2Vec is an artificial neural network composed of three layers: an input, a hidden and an output layer, as shown in Fig. 1.

Given a recommender system composed of a set $U$ of users, a set $I$ of items and multiple sets $I_u$ of items consumed by user $u$, the input layer $\mathcal{J}$ has a size $|I|$, as is comprised of items $i$ encoded as one-hot vectors (all elements in the array have a value of 0, except for the one that represents the item, which has a content value of 1). The middle layer $\mathcal{H}$ has size $M$, which corresponds to the desired dimensionality for the final vector representation of each item. Between the input and the middle layers, there is a weight matrix $\mathcal{W}$, of size $|I| \times M$, used to activate the initial layer through the operation $\mathcal{H} = \mathcal{J} \cdot \mathcal{W}$. The output layer $\mathcal{O}$ is made up of $|I_u| - 1$ vectors of size $|I|$ connected to the middle layer by the transpose of the same weight matrix $\mathcal{W}$ and a softmax activation function. Thus, $\mathcal{O} = \sigma(\mathcal{H} \cdot \mathcal{W}^T)$, where $\sigma$ represents the softmax function shown in Eq. 1.

$$\sigma(u,i) = \frac{e^{(\mathcal{W}_u \mathcal{W}_i^T)}}{\sum_{j \in I} e^{(\mathcal{W}_u \mathcal{W}_j^T)}} \tag{1}$$

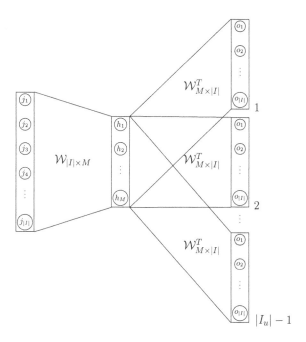

**Fig. 1.** Standard Item2Vec architecture

The network is trained over multiple epochs. For each epoch, each item $i \in I_u$ for every user $u$ is used as input. In the output layer $\mathcal{O}$, we have $|I_u| - 1$ one-hot encoded vectors (the number of items consumed by the user removing the target item), each associated with an item $j \in I_u \mid j \neq i$. In other words, the network receives an item and must predict another item consumed by the user, approximating them in the vector space. For every pair of input and output items, the network calculates the prediction error and updates the weights. The main goal of the network is to maximize the objective function given by Eq. 2.

$$\frac{1}{|U|} \sum_{u \in U} \sum_{i \in I_u} \sum_{\substack{j \in I_u \\ j \neq i}} log\ \sigma(i, j) \tag{2}$$

At the end of the learning phase, the weight matrix $\mathcal{W}$ will contain dense vector representations of dimensionality $M$ for every item processed.

Item2Vec come with some drawbacks that would be impractical in scenarios with many items, since it must predict a related item (when output is 1) and all unrelated items (when output is 0) for each target item. Thus, two strategies commonly used in NLP are adopted [24]: *(i)* negative sampling, i.e., the error is calculated over a small subset of $N$ negative items, randomly drawn so that frequent items are more likely to be selected according to Eq. 3; and *(ii)* sub-sampling of frequent items, i.e., a subset of the interactions of popular items are discarded with a probability of being kept shown in Eq. 4. In both equations, function $z(i)$ returns the frequency of item $i$, and the hyperparameters $\gamma$ and $\rho$ can be fine-tuned.

$$P(i \mid \gamma) = \frac{z(i)^{\gamma}}{\sum_{j \in I} z(j)^{\gamma}} \tag{3}$$

$$P(i \mid \rho) = \left( \sqrt{\frac{z(i)}{\rho}} + 1 \right) \cdot \frac{\rho}{z(i)} \tag{4}$$

### 3.2   Sequential Item2Vec

Standard Item2Vec assumes that all items consumed by a user are equally related, shuffling them at the beginning of training. Therefore, given a particular item, the network considers that another item consumed in the distant past (e.g., years ago) has the same similarity to the target item as an item consumed in the recent past (e.g., same day). In other words, all other items are considered contextually equal to the target item, as illustrated in Fig. 3 for the example shown in Fig. 2.

**Fig. 2.** User interactions in a chronological order.

We have adopted a sliding window of fixed and parameterizable size during training to restrict the context. In this way, only items consumed in sequence are considered to be related to the target item. In a first approach, we are not interested in the moment the interaction occurred, but only in the chronological order, as shown in Fig. 4.

The neural architecture for SeqI2V is very similar to Item2Vec, the only difference taking place in the number of vectors present in the output layer: instead of a vector for each of the other $|I_u| - 1$ items consumed by the user, the network must predict only $S$ items, where $S$ corresponds to the window size (Fig. 5).

Although this model considers the chronological order in which items are consumed, it fails to capture changes in users who spend long periods without interacting with the system. To overcome this problem, we propose splitting a user's interaction history into various chronological sequences using absolute and pre-defined time intervals to decide where to split. This approach allows that when two continuous interactions of the same user have an interval greater than $D$ days, their chronological sequence is then split into two. As we are only interested in the relationship between items, the network would interpret this single-user as different ones, restricting learning to its behavior in a defined time interval, as illustrated by Fig. 6. The value of the parameter controlling the number of days to define the binding time window is flexible and can be adjusted for each specific application scenario a user might want to use SeqI2V on. In this work, we opt for an absolute value of days when splitting as it is a less complex and humanly understandable strategy.

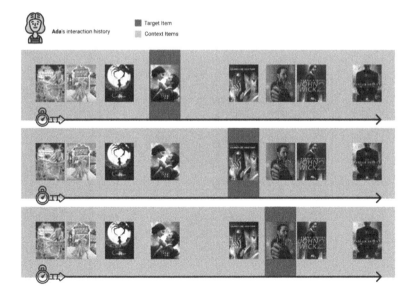

**Fig. 3.** Standard Item2Vec. Every item consumed by the user is equally related to the target item.

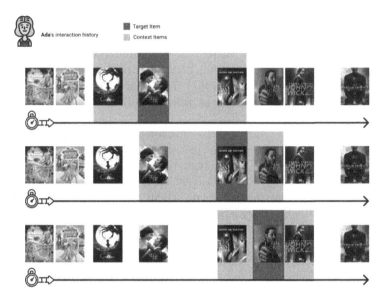

**Fig. 4.** Temporal sliding window during training.

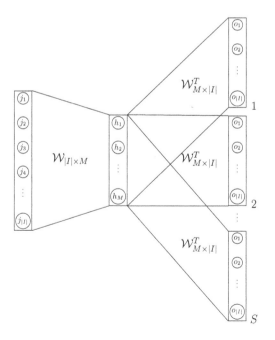

**Fig. 5.** Sequential Item2Vec architecture

During the learning phase and when generating the final recommendation, SeqI2V also employs all techniques used by standard Item2Vec, such as negative sampling and item subsampling during training, and also an item-based K-Nearest Neighbor when recommending.

## 4   Experiments and Results

In order to make the experiments reproducible, this section describes the experimental protocol conducted during the study. First, we introduce the datasets used, in conjunction with a description of how the training was carried out. Then, we present the achieved results.

### 4.1   Datasets

The datasets used in the experiment are listed in Table 1. All of them are publicly available and were selected based on their relevance within literature. DeliciousBookmarks and MovieLens belong to GroupLens repository[2]; BestBuy[3] and NetflixPrize[4] were datasets used in challenges conducted by, respectively,

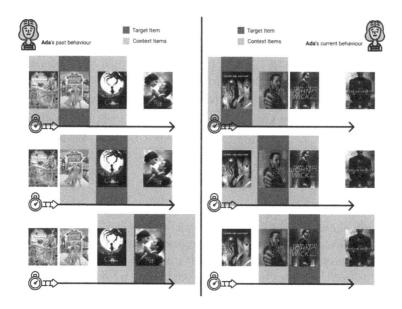

**Fig. 6.** Sequential Item2Vec. The user interaction history is split to capture the changes in its behavior.

---

[2] *GroupLens.* Available at: www.grouplens.org/datasets/. Access in August 31, 2021.
[3] *Data Mining Hackathon on BIG DATA (7 GB) Best Buy mobile web site.* Available at: www.kaggle.com/c/acm-sf-chapter-hackathon-big. Access in August 31, 2021.
[4] *Netflix Prize data.* Available at: www.kaggle.com/netflix-inc/netflix-prize-data. Access in August 31, 2021.

Association for Computing Machinery (ACM) and Netflix, Inc.; CiaoDVD[5] was crawled from Ciao website; RetailRocket is the database of the retention management platform with the same name[6]. In all these datasets, we removed users or items with a single interaction since most of the trained algorithms aim to learn relations between same-user or item interactions.

## 4.2    Experimental Protocol

We sorted the interactions chronologically in each dataset and separated them into a train, validation, and test partitions, with an 8:1:1 ratio, respectively. Then, we optimized the hyperparameters using grid search on the validation partition, aiming to maximize NDCG in a top-15 recommendation scenario. Finally, the final results were obtained on the test partition. Due to hardware limitations, we performed the parameter optimization/final experiment of larger datasets over a small and randomly comprised subset: 25%/100% for MovieLens and 5%/25% for NetflixPrize. Additionally, we removed cold-start cases, i.e., users or items with no interaction on the training set, since this is a problem beyond the scope of our study.

**Table 1.** Description of the datasets in terms of number of users ($|U|$), number of items ($|I|$), number of interactions ($|R|$), sparsity ($E$), and application domain.

| Dataset | $|U|$ | $|I|$ | $|R|$ | $E$ | Domain |
|---|---|---|---|---|---|
| BestBuy | 1,268,702 | 69,858 | 1,862,782 | 99.99% | Shopping |
| CiaoDVD | 17,615 | 16,121 | 72,345 | 99.97% | Movies |
| DeliciousBookmarks | 1,867 | 69,223 | 104,799 | 99.92% | Websites |
| MovieLens | 162,541 | 59,047 | 25,000,095 | 99.74% | Movies |
| NetflixPrize | 480,189 | 17,770 | 100,480,507 | 98.82% | Movies |
| RetailRocket | 11,719 | 12,025 | 21,270 | 99.98% | Shopping |

Although our main goal is to improve the results of Item2Vec, we also compared the performance achieved by the proposed Sequential Item2Vec (SeqI2V) with classical recommender algorithms. For this, we have implemented the established item-based version of K-Nearest Neighbors (KNN) [28] and two state-of-the-art matrix factorization methods: implicit singular value decomposition (ALS) [16] and Bayesian Personalized Ranking (BPR) [26]. In addition to the standard Item2Vec (I2V), we have also implemented User2Vec (U2V) [13], a user-item neural embeddings-method.

---

[5] *CiaoDVD Movie Ratings.* Available at: www.konect.cc/networks/librec-ciaodvd-movie_ratings/. Access in August 31, 2021.

[6] *Retailrocket recommender system dataset.* Available at: www.kaggle.com/retailrocket/ecommerce-dataset. Access in August 31, 2021.

For KNN we used the implementation of *turicreate library*, without requiring hyperparameter choices. Both matrix factorization methods were implemented using *implicit library*, with latent factors ranging in $\{50, 100, 200\}$, regularization factor in $\{10^{-6}, 10^{-4}, 10^{-2}\}$, number of epochs in $\{10, 20, 50, 100\}$, and learning rate in $\{0.0025, 0.025, 0.25\}$. All neural embeddings models, including Sequential Item2Vec, were implemented using *gensim library*, with hyperparameter being tuned according insights proposed by Caselles-Duprés *et al.* [8]. Thus, the dimensionality $M$ was fixed in 100 and 5 negative samples were randomly drawn for each item, with the number of epochs ranging in $\{50, 100, 150\}$, negative exponent for the negative sampling in $\{-1.0, -0.5, 0.5, 1.0\}$, and the subsampling factor in $\{10^{-5}, 10^{-4}, 10^{-3}\}$. Additionally, for the sequential adaptation, we tested different window sizes ranging in $\{1, 3, 5, 7, 9\}$, and the interval of days for splitting in $\{182, 365, 730, \text{no split}\}$.

## 4.3   Results

We evaluated the algorithms in a top-15 recommendation task, i.e. for each user, the methods must recommend 15 items in a ranked list. Then, we calculated the F1-Score (Table 2) and the Normalized Discounted Cumulative Gain, or NDCG (Table 3). All results are in grayscale, with darker tones representing better performances. The best value for each dataset is highlighted in **bold**.

To facilitate comparing the SeqI2V with its baseline (Item2Vec), Table 4 presents the improvements and worsenings resulting from the use of SeqI2V concerning the results obtained by Item2Vec in each database and performance mea-

Table 2. F1-Score obtained in a top-15 recommendation problem.

| Dataset | IS | ALS | BPR | U2V | I2V | SeqI2V |
|---|---|---|---|---|---|---|
| BestBuy | 0.0043 | 0.0078 | 0.0058 | 0.0007 | **0.0170** | 0.0153 |
| CiaoDVD | 0.0025 | 0.0062 | 0.0049 | 0.0050 | 0.0060 | **0.0075** |
| DeliciousBookmarks | 0.0548 | 0.0177 | 0.0446 | 0.0119 | 0.0382 | **0.0616** |
| MovieLens | **0.0613** | 0.0576 | 0.0445 | 0.0007 | 0.0311 | 0.0566 |
| NetflixPrize | 0.0175 | 0.0125 | 0.0101 | 0.0008 | 0.0181 | **0.0197** |
| RetailRocket | 0.0106 | 0.0058 | 0.0133 | 0.0041 | 0.0104 | **0.0252** |

Table 3. NDCG obtained in a top-15 recommendation problem.

| Dataset | IS | ALS | BPR | U2V | I2V | SeqI2V |
|---|---|---|---|---|---|---|
| BestBuy | 0.0117 | 0.0184 | 0.0145 | 0.0014 | **0.0324** | 0.0290 |
| CiaoDVD | 0.0030 | 0.0087 | **0.0106** | 0.0060 | 0.0066 | 0.0097 |
| DeliciousBookmarks | 0.1177 | 0.0444 | 0.1239 | 0.0211 | 0.0788 | **0.1347** |
| MovieLens | 0.1391 | **0.1422** | 0.1142 | 0.0018 | 0.0742 | 0.1219 |
| NetflixPrize | 0.0293 | 0.0207 | 0.0213 | 0.0011 | 0.0272 | **0.0298** |
| RetailRocket | 0.0179 | 0.0108 | **0.0469** | 0.0030 | 0.0157 | 0.0330 |

sure. In both metrics, the results obtained by Sequential Item2Vec are promising. In all datasets, except for BestBuy, the SeqI2V outperformed the I2V. On the RetailRocket dataset, the performance of SeqI2V was approximately 150% higher. The F1-Score achieved by SeqI2V was 52% and 43% higher than Item2Vec, in average and median, respectively. Moreover, the NDCG achieved by SeqI2V was 48% and 55% higher, in average and median.

When compared to the other established recommender algorithms, the results of Sequential Item2Vec remain auspicious. For the F1-Score, it attained the best result in 66% of the datasets. On the other hand, as BPR optimizes the ranking, it achieved the best performance when NDCG is used as an evaluation metric. Still, for both metrics, SeqI2V was the best or second-best in 83% of the cases.

It is important to highlight that regarding the number of days used to split the temporal sequences, RetailRocket was the only dataset in which sequences with no split achieved the best performance. For all the others datasets, the best performance was attained using sequences split between 182 and 730 days. These results evidence the effectiveness of splitting user sequences and the need to adapt the interval for each specific application. Moreover, even when the split was not necessary, using sliding windows significantly improved the results.

It is also important to highlight that, although SeqI2V demands an extra step of data preparation, training the embeddings is less costly than in Item2Vec. For each target item, it makes predictions only for a reduced set of items (the window size) instead of all items previously consumed by the user. Thus, the proposed method is more computationally efficient and presents better results without increasing implementation complexity.

**Table 4.** Improvements and worsenings provided by Sequential Item2Vec compared to Item2Vec.

| Dataset | F1-Score | NDCG |
|---|---|---|
| **BestBuy** | −10.0% | −10.5% |
| **CiaoDVD** | +25.0% | +47.0% |
| **DeliciousBookmarks** | +61.3% | +70.9% |
| **MovieLens** | +82.0% | +64.3% |
| **NetflixPrize** | +8.8% | +9.6% |
| **RetailRocket** | +147.1% | +110.2% |
| **Average** | **+52.4%** | **+48.6%** |
| **Median** | **+43.1%** | **+55.6%** |

The main limitation of the proposed method relies on exceptional cases in which the user always takes a long period between two interactions, greater than the defined window size. In this case, consumption contexts would be composed of unitary relationships, allowing sliding windows but making the interactions sequence splitting unfeasible.

# 5   Conclusion

Item2Vec is a well-known method capable of learning neural embeddings for items in a recommender system. This study presented Sequential Item2Vec – an adaptation of the original approach that uses a sliding window over time, giving temporal context awareness for the item embeddings. We also proposed splitting the user's interaction history into multiple sequences so that the network would not learn relationships between items consumed in considerably different moments, thus capturing changes in the user's behavior.

In order to assess whether the proposed approach was able to improve the results obtained with the standard Item2Vec, we compared both models with other established methods in the field, over six well-known and publicly available databases. Metrics of hit and ranking were calculated in a top-15 recommendation scenario. The results indicate that Sequential Item2Vec outperformed the results obtained by Item2Vec. It was superior to its predecessor in almost all of the datasets. The proposed approach was also competitive compared to the other methods, matching the Bayesian Personalized Ranking, a state-of-the-art matrix factorization method.

Although giving time awareness to the item embeddings, the recommendation generated by Sequential Item2Vec is still statically. In future research, we aim to consider time in the recommendation step, analyzing its impact. Additionally, we suggest studying other ways to include time during the learning phase. One promising approach can be the use of decay functions instead of - or in conjunction with - sliding windows.

# References

1. Adomavicius, G., Tuzhilin, A.: Multidimensional recommender systems: a data warehousing approach. Electron. Commer. **2232**, 180–192 (2001). https://doi.org/10.1007/3-540-45598-1_17
2. Adomavicius, G., Tuzhilin, A.: Toward the next generation of recommender systems: a survey of the state-of-the-art and possible extensions. IEEE Trans. Knowl. Data Eng. **17**(6), 734–749 (2005). https://doi.org/10.1109/TKDE.2005.99
3. Baltrunas, L., Amatriain, X.: Towards time-dependant recommendation based on implicit feedback. In: Proceedings of the RecSys 2009 Workshop on Context-Aware Recommender Systems, RecSys 2009, pp. 1–5. Association for Computing Machinery, New York (2009)
4. Barkan, O., Koenigstein, N.: Item2Vec: neural item embedding for collaborative filtering. In: IEEE 26th International Workshop on Machine Learning for Signal Processing, MLSP 2016, pp. 1–6. IEEE, Piscataway, NJ, USA (2016). https://doi.org/10.1109/MLSP.2016.7738886
5. Bobadilla, J., Ortega, F., Hernando, A., Gutiérrez, A.: Recommender systems survey. Knowl.-Based Syst. **46**, 109–132 (2013). https://doi.org/10.1016/j.knosys.2013.03.012
6. de Borba, E.J., Gasparini, I., Lichtnow, D.: Time-aware recommender systems: a systematic mapping. In: Kurosu, M. (ed.) HCI 2017. LNCS, vol. 10272, pp. 464–479. Springer, Cham (2017). https://doi.org/10.1007/978-3-319-58077-7_38

7. Breese, J.S., Heckerman, D., Kadie, C.: Empirical analysis of predictive algorithms for collaborative filtering. In: Proceedings of the 14th Conference on Uncertainty in Artificial Intelligence, UAI 1998, pp. 43–52. Morgan Kaufmann Publishers Inc., San Francisco, CA, USA (1998)

8. Caselles-Duprés, H., Lesaint, F., Royo-Letelier, J.: Word2vec applied to recommendation: hyperparameters matter. In: Proceedings of the 12th ACM Conference on Recommender Systems, RecSys 2018, pp. 352–356. Association for Computing Machinery, New York (2018). https://doi.org/10.1145/3240323.3240377

9. Collins, A., Beel, J.: Document embeddings vs. keyphrases vs. terms for recommender systems: a large-scale online evaluation. In: Proceedings of the 2019 ACM/IEEE Joint Conference on Digital Libraries, JCDL 2019, pp. 130–133. IEEE, New York (2019). https://doi.org/10.1109/JCDL.2019.00027

10. Ding, Y., Li, X.: Time weight collaborative filtering. In: Proceedings of the 14th ACM International Conference on Information and Knowledge Management, CIKM 2005, pp. 485–492. Association for Computing Machinery, New York (2005). https://doi.org/10.1145/1099554.1099689

11. Peng, F.U., LV, J.H. and LI, B.J.: Attr2vec: a neural network based item embedding method. In: Proceedings of the 2nd International Conference on Computer, Mechatronics and Electronic Engineering, CMEE 2017, pp. 300–307. DEStech Publications, Lancaster, PA, USA (2017). https://doi.org/10.12783/dtcse/cmee2017/19993

12. Grbovic, M., Cheng, H.: Real-time personalization using embeddings for search ranking at Airbnb. In: Proceedings of the 24th ACM SIGKDD International Conference on Knowledge Discovery and Data Mining, KDD 2018, pp. 311–320. Association for Computing Machinery, New York (2018). https://doi.org/10.1145/3219819.3219885

13. Grbovic, M., et al.: E-commerce in your inbox: product recommendations at scale. In: Proceedings of the 21th ACM SIGKDD International Conference on Knowledge Discovery and Data Mining, KDD 2015, pp. 1809–1818. Association for Computing Machinery, New York (2015). https://doi.org/10.1145/2783258.2788627

14. Greenstein-Messica, A., Rokach, L., Friedman, M.: Session-based recommendations using item embedding. In: Proceedings of the 22nd International Conference on Intelligent User Interfaces, IUI 2017, pp. 629–633. Association for Computing Machinery, New York (2017). https://doi.org/10.1145/3025171.3025197

15. Hasanzadeh, S., Fakhrahmad, S.M., Taheri, M.: Review-based recommender systems: a proposed rating prediction scheme using word embedding representation of reviews. Comput. J. 1–10 (2020). https://doi.org/10.1093/comjnl/bxaa044

16. Hu, Y., Koren, Y., Volinsky, C.: Collaborative filtering for implicit feedback datasets. In: Proceedings of the 8th IEEE International Conference on Data Mining, ICDM 2008, pp. 263–272. IEEE Computer Society, Washington, D.C., USA (2008). https://doi.org/10.1109/ICDM.2008.22

17. Karypis, G.: Evaluation of item-based top-n recommendation algorithms. In: Proceedings of the 10th International Conference on Information and Knowledge Management, CIKM 2001, pp. 247–254 (2001). https://doi.org/10.1145/502585.502627

18. Khusro, S., Ali, Z., Ullah, I.: Recommender systems: issues, challenges, and research opportunities. In: Information Science and Applications (ICISA) 2016. LNEE, vol. 376, pp. 1179–1189. Springer, Singapore (2016). https://doi.org/10.1007/978-981-10-0557-2_112

19. Koren, Y.: Collaborative filtering with temporal dynamics. In: Proceedings of the 15th ACM SIGKDD International Conference on Knowledge Discovery and Data Mining, KDD 2009, pp. 447–456 (2009). https://doi.org/10.1145/1557019.1557072

20. Koren, Y., Bell, R., Volinsky, C.: Matrix factorization techniques for recommender systems. Computer **42**(8), 30–37 (2009). https://doi.org/10.1109/MC.2009.263
21. Lathia, N., Hailes, S., Capra, L.: Temporal collaborative filtering with adaptive neighbourhoods. In: Proceedings of the 32nd International ACM SIGIR Conference on Research and Development in Information Retrieval, SIGIR 2009, pp. 796–797. Association for Computing Machinery, New York (2009). https://doi.org/10.1145/1571941.1572133
22. Le, Q., Mikolov, T.: Distributed representations of sentences and documents. In: Proceedings of the 31st International Conference on Machine Learning, ICML 2014, pp. 1188–1196. JMLR.org (2014). https://doi.org/10.5555/3044805.3045025
23. Matuszyk, P., Ao Vinagre, J., Spiliopoulou, M., Jorge, A.M., Ao Gama, J.: Forgetting methods for incremental matrix factorization in recommender systems. In: Proceedings of the 30th Annual ACM Symposium on Applied Computing, SAC 2015, pp. 947–953. Association for Computing Machinery, New York (2015). https://doi.org/10.1145/2695664.2695820
24. Mikolov, T., Sutskever, I., Chen, K., Conrado, G., Dan, J.: Distributed representations of words and phrases and their compositionality. In: Proceedings of the 26th International Conference on Neural Information Processing Systems, NIPS 2013, pp. 3111–3119. Curran Associates Inc., Red Hook, NY, USA (2013). https://doi.org/10.5555/2999792.2999959
25. Rendle, S.: Factorization machines. In: Proceedings of the 10th IEEE International Conference on Data Mining, ICDM 2010, pp. 14–17. IEEE, New York (2010). https://doi.org/10.1109/ICDM.2010.127
26. Rendle, S., Freudenthaler, C., Gantner, Z., Schmidt-Thieme, L.: BPR: Bayesian personalized ranking from implicit feedback. In: Proceedings of the 25th Conference on Uncertainty in Artificial Intelligence, UAI 2009, pp. 452–461. AUAI Press, Arlington, VA, USA (2009). https://doi.org/10.5555/1795114.1795167
27. Rudolph, M., Ruiz, F.J.R., Mandt, S., Blei, D.M.: Exponential family embeddings. In: Proceedings of the 30th International Conference on Neural Information Processing Systems, NIPS 2016, pp. 478–486. Curran Associates Inc., Red Hook, NY, USA (2016). https://doi.org/10.7916/D8NZ9RHT
28. Sarwar, B.M., Karypis, G., Konstan, J.A., Riedl, J.T.: Item-based collaborative filtering recommendation algorithms. In: Proceedings of the 10th International Conference on World Wide Web, WWW 2001, pp. 285–295. Association for Computing Machinery, New York (2001). https://doi.org/10.1145/371920.372071
29. Sidana, S., Trofimov, M., Horodnytskyi, O., Laclau, C., Maximov, Y., Amini, M.-R.: User preference and embedding learning with implicit feedback for recommender systems. Data Min. Knowl. Disc. **35**(2), 568–592 (2021). https://doi.org/10.1007/s10618-020-00730-8
30. Tang, J., Wang, K.: Personalized top-n sequential recommendation via convolutional sequence embedding. In: Proceedings of the 11th ACM International Conference on Web Search and Data Mining, WSDM 2018, pp. 565–573. Association for Computing Machinery, New York (2018). https://doi.org/10.1145/2939672.2939673
31. Vasile, F., Smirnova, E., Conneau, A.: Meta-prod2vec: product embeddings using side-information for recommendation. In: Proceedings of the 10th ACM Conference on Recommender Systems, RecSys 2016, pp. 225–232. Association for Computing Machinery, New York (2016). https://doi.org/10.1145/2959100.2959160
32. Vinagre, J., Jorge, A.M.: Forgetting mechanisms for scalable collaborative filtering. J. Braz. Comput. Soc. **18**(4), 271–282 (2012). https://doi.org/10.1007/s13173-012-0077-3

33. Vinagre, J., Jorge, A.M., Gama, J.: An overview on the exploitation of time in collaborative filtering. WIREs Data Min. Knowl. Disc. **5**, 195–215 (2015). https://doi.org/10.1002/widm.1160

34. Wang, P., Guo, J., Lan, Y., Xu, J., Wan, S., Cheng, X.: Learning hierarchical representation model for nextbasket recommendation. In: Proceedings of the 38th International ACM SIGIR Conference on Research and Development in Information Retrieval, SIGIR 2015, pp. 403–412. Association for Computing Machinery, New York (2015). https://doi.org/10.1145/2766462.2767694

35. Zhang, F., Yuan, N.J., Lian, D., Xie, X., Ma, W.Y.: Collaborative knowledge base embedding for recommender systems. In: Proceedings of the 22nd ACM SIGKDD International Conference on Knowledge Discovery and Data Mining, KDD 2016, pp. 353–362. Association for Computing Machinery, New York (2016). https://doi.org/10.1145/2939672.2939673

36. Zhang, S., Yao, L., Sun, A., Tay, Y.: Deep learning based recommender system: a survey and new perspectives. ACM Comput. Surv. **52**(1), 5:1–5:35 (2019). https://doi.org/10.1145/3285029

37. Zhao, X., Louca, R., Hu, D., Hong, L.: The difference between a click and a cart-add: learning interaction-specific embeddings. In: Companion Proceedings of the Web Conference 2020, WWW 2020, pp. 454–460. Association for Computing Machinery, New York (2020). https://doi.org/10.1145/3366424.3386197

# Transfer Learning of Shapelets for Time Series Classification Using Convolutional Neural Network

Alexandre Felipe Muller de Souza$^{(\boxtimes)}$ ⓘ, Mariane R. S. Cassenote ⓘ, and Fabiano Silva ⓘ

Informatics Department, Federal University of Paraná, Curitiba, Brazil
{afmsouza,mrscassenote,fabiano}@inf.ufpr.br

**Abstract.** Time series classification has a wide variety of possible applications, like outlines of figure types, signs of movement and sensor signals. This diversity may present different results with the application of machine learning techniques. Among the different ways to classify time series, two, in particular, are explored in this paper: the shapelet primitive and the neural network classification. A shapelet is a sub-sequence of the time series symbolic, like a high-level descriptor, that are representative for the class to which they belong. These features act as common knowledge used by domain experts. This paper proposes a CNN training protocol to achieve better results in the classification of time series. The idea consists of decomposing the original time series into shapelets and noise. Then, the shapelets are used to train a classifier while the no-shapelets ("signal noise") is used to train another classifier. The original time series is then used to train two final classifiers starting with the weights of shapelet and no-shapelet classifiers. This previous extraction of this representation can improve classification ability in a convolutional neural network using transfer learning. The experimental evaluation shows that the pre-selection of shapelets before the network training changes the classifier results for several databases and, consequently, improves classification accuracy.

**Keywords:** Machine learning · Shapelets · Time series · Transfer learning

## 1 Introduction

With the technology advancement and the mobile devices popularization, systems that generate real-time data have become disseminated. The amount of data generated is continuously growing and meaning attributions are needed to extract relevant information from this data. In addition to sensors, many other types of data can be represented in structures called time series. These structures can be handled as shapes, that can be projected in a one-dimensional plane or spectrogram [3]. Simply, any string of numerical values whose order forms a

A. Britto and K. Valdivia Delgado (Eds.): BRACIS 2021, LNAI 13074, pp. 325–339, 2021.
https://doi.org/10.1007/978-3-030-91699-2_23

sequence [10] can be called a time series. Naturally, the processing of these time series has applications in the most diverse areas of knowledge [7].

The scope of this work is limited to the problem of automated classification of time series: inputs are divided into two or more classes to be determined. In particular, the focus in this analysis is supervised classification, i.e., given a series whose classification is not known, the class to which it belongs must be inferred. This is accomplished through other examples previously classified among these classes, not exactly the same, but similar. Naturally, the series repository [3] already makes available these pre-classified (and other unclassified) examples by the domain expert.

Although there are several methods proposed for classifying time series, we will cover two of them in more details: symbolic representations, in particular the shapelet primitive extraction, and Convolutional Neural Networks (CNN). In the shapelet method, are extracted the sub-sequences of the time series that are partial and representative attribute (thus, symbolic) for the class to which they belong. The idea is to extract features from domain problem that allow to perform the classification.

In contrast to classification using symbolic representations paradigm, there are classifiers based on neural networks. These classifiers use a data model representing the memory in the form of weights of a network. Neural classifiers are known for their efficiency, as their model has already been trained, but learning is based purely on adjusting the weights of the network. This adjustment is given by an error minimization algorithm that can achieve different results depending on many factors such as network architecture, number of layers, filters, among others. CNN-based classifiers have many applications and are referred to by the term "Deep Learning" [11].

This paper proposes a pre-training method for time series classifiers using CNN. Figure 1 outlines the basic process of our method. Usually the network is started with random weights. However, in a different way, our proposal is to carry out an initial phase that extracts the relevant shapelets and separates the symbolic representations from the rest of the series, generating two new databases: one with only the parts of the series that represents shapelets, and other with only the remaining parts of the series. These databases are then used to train different models. Then a final model is generated with the original database, but starting the network with the information learned before by the previous trained models. The motivation of this approach refers to the duality between these symbolic and neural classifiers and how their performance improve by exchanging information.

Through this study, we observe that the pre-initialization of the network increases the accuracy of the final classification for most of the tested bases. There are two methods of improvement. The first consists in extracting the symbolic representations, in this case shapelets, and training only with these parts of the original series and then transferring the learned weights to the final model, which allows highlighting the symbolic representations. This case is being called "Classifier 4" in Fig. 1. Another method removes the shapelets and trains only with the "noisy part" of the original series and then apply the transfer the weights to the final model, called "Classifier 5" in the figure.

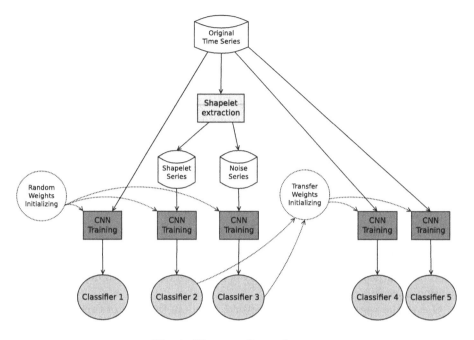

**Fig. 1.** Diagram of experiments.

The rest of this paper is organized as follows: related works are commented on in Sect. 2. The materials and method used are presented in Sect. 3. Section 4 contains the results and discussions, and finally, Sect. 5 concludes the paper and list some future works.

## 2   Related Work

In order to obtain the necessary conditions to compare classification models, researchers often use an openly available database of UCR Time Series [3]. This is a popular time series benchmark due to its diversity.

The time series classification is divided into several paradigms for generating models, whether symbolic or statistical. Most works based on symbolic paradigms use shapelets due to the intelligibility of the model. According to [20], shapelets can provide results that should help domain experts better understand their own data.

In [12] is presented an interface to visualize the extracted shapelets in an interactive way, which can also be used at different extraction methods. The first method was proposed by the same authors [13] and is based on intermediate symbolic representations, called *Symbolic Aggregate Approximation* (SAX). This concept is widely explored and was presented for the first time in [14]. It consists of discretizing the series into bands that become symbols of an alphabet and, consequently, each sub-sequence generate a word. In [13] the SAX words are converted into shapelets through a structure of weighted bitmaps of the SAX words to determine the quality of the shapelet candidates, transforming the shapelet selection problem into a heuristic search process. According to the authors, this process makes finding shapelets more efficient.

The main shapelet-based classification methods cited in [12] are: HIVE-COTE (*Hierarchical Vote Collective of Transformation based Ensembles*) [16], ELIS (*Efficient Learning Interpretable Shapelets*) [4] and LTS (*Learning Time-series Shapelet*) [8]. In addition, the BOSS method (*Bag of SFA Symbols*) of [17] is also referenced by [19] and [6]. Each of these will be explained in detail below.

One of the most popular time series classification algorithms is called BOSS. It generates a set of symbolic SFA representations (*Symbolic Fourier Approximation*) with different sliding window sizes and creates an ensemble based on a template similar to Bag of Words (BoW). This model is a set with occurrences counting of symbols, disregarding other elements such as the order in which they appear. Compared to shapelets, these representations are extremely short and have a wide range of sizes. Its classification is based on a histogram of occurrences rather than a decision tree. The BOSS is noise tolerant, scale independent, and position invariant.

One of the works that supports several others in the field of time series classification is the use of a collection of classifiers called COTE [1]. In this type of approach there are 35 classifiers [16]. Each classifier is trained individually and then the results are combined by assigning weights to the classifiers [15]. A later variation of this method, called HIVE-COTE, is based on a hierarchical vote between classifiers of the same nature. In this method there are a total of five modules. For example, one module would be based on shapelets and another module would be based on BoW. Superior results were obtained through this hierarchical voting process. However, despite both works showing positive results, they use classifiers from different paradigms, such as based on examples, symbolic, statistical and connectionist. This makes the final classification unintelligible.

Another work related to this paper that presents a time series classifier using shapelets is ELIS [4], which has a faster extraction method than the traditional one and shows good results. This method works in two phases: shapelet discovery and shapelet adjustment. In the first stage, the generation of sub-sequences occurs in a process called PAA (*Piecewise Aggregation Approximation*). This process is like a discretization that reduces the resolution of the series. For each class the PAAs, words are ranked and this information helps to adjust the shapelet numbers to be automatically extracted. Is created a model that tries to adjust the shapelet to the best shape. The main idea is that true shapelets shouldn't appear in exactly the best shape in the training set [4]. Finally, in the second stage, several classifiers are built, each with its specific shapelets. Then a regression process is used to better adjust the shapelet in the series and generate a final classifier. ELIS presents limitations in small databases, as well as the number of parameters that need to be adjusted. In order to outline these limitations, the authors recently proposed the ELIS++ method [21], which in addition to using data augmentation, also adjusts its parameters automatically.

Another very relevant work in the area of shapelets is LTS[8]. In that work, the authors obtain the shapelets not by candidate calculations, but through a gradient descent algorithm. In this way, the process becomes very similar to adjusting the weights of a neural network.

Although efficient, all these classifiers do not completely replace the use of a classifier based on a CNN. One work that managed to take CNN comparatives in time series was [6]. In this time series classification review, the authors reproduced the main implementations and compared deep learning methods with other methods. According to the authors, HIVE/COTE is currently considered the state-of-the-art algorithm for time series classification when evaluated in the 85 datasets of the UCR file. Through the empirical study carried out by the authors, ResNet came closest to COTE/HIVE in terms of accuracy.

On the other hand, when talking about time series, is a consensus that there is a lack of research on the use of CNN in this context[2,5]. Therefore, we have an important area to be explored, as learned symbolic representations (as they are in images) offer an important intelligibility that can also be used for time series. The implementation of the CNN presented in this paper was derived from [19], which has already obtained results close to the state-of-the-art in 2016.

Considering all this context, there seems to be an interesting research line to correlate classifiers based on CNN and shapelets. The motivation for this proposal is not new. Several authors focus on this theme, although each one has its own methodology and presentation. For example, in [2] the authors assume that learning LTS shapelets is a particular case of learning in convolutional networks. The authors explain that the measure of distance from shapelets can be transformed into a convolutional form and, thus, there is a relation between both methods. However, this specific study only aims to propose a multivalued classifier based on CNN. Thus, the study justifies its positive result by the ability to learn these representations similar to shapelets. Also in this work, the authors present a theoretical formalization, correlating the layers of a CNN with shapelets and calculating the Euclidean distance. Although the authors present this theoretical formalization, they do not deepen this relationship, showing it experimentally.

Although not directly related, some other knowledge is involved with this issue. Another relevant work to be cited is [5], which explores the issue of transfer learning. This concept is realized when the weights of a network previously trained in another series are used as initial training weights, instead of randomly assigned weights. This learning process is faster and has better generalization, which is due to the transfer of representations between the original series and those that received the knowledge. The article even mentions series based on symbols, as a particular case of good generator of models. Thus, it is evident that, when transferring knowledge from this series, the convergence of the neural network is faster, reinforcing the hypothesis that the neural network model learns symbolic representations (shapes). This experiment influences the development of our proposal, as we will see in Sect. 3.

# 3    Materials and Method

In this section, some implementation details of the experiments performed in this work are presented. The classifier, the source code and the method used are available for consultation[1]. This work aims to serve as a basis for derivative works, whether for reproduction of procedures, analysis or inspiration for other classifiers based on CNN.

The experiment that generates the classifier began by choosing the series that make up the database. The choice of the 20 series represented in Table 1 was due to their diversity, as well as to the results published in previous works of classifiers based on symbolic representations. The data are presented in text files with different formats, but already normalized and standardized. The chosen database has training and testing examples, i.e., each dataset has pre-classified examples in predetermined quantities to be used in model generation and validation.

**Table 1.** Selected time series from [3].

| #  | Dataset            | Training | Validation | Length | Classes | Type      |
|----|--------------------|----------|------------|--------|---------|-----------|
| 1  | BeetleFly          | 20       | 20         | 512    | 2       | IMAGE     |
| 2  | BirdChicken        | 20       | 20         | 512    | 2       | IMAGE     |
| 3  | ECGFiveDays        | 23       | 861        | 136    | 2       | ECG       |
| 4  | ECG200             | 100      | 100        | 96     | 2       | ECG       |
| 5  | CBF                | 30       | 900        | 128    | 3       | SIMULATED |
| 6  | FaceFour           | 24       | 88         | 350    | 4       | IMAGE     |
| 7  | FacesUCR           | 200      | 2050       | 131    | 14      | IMAGE     |
| 8  | Gun_Point          | 50       | 150        | 150    | 2       | MOTION    |
| 9  | ItalyPowerDemand   | 67       | 1029       | 24     | 2       | SENSOR    |
| 10 | Lightning7         | 70       | 73         | 319    | 7       | SENSOR    |
| 11 | Lightning2         | 60       | 61         | 637    | 2       | SENSOR    |
| 12 | MoteStrain         | 60       | 61         | 637    | 2       | SENSOR    |
| 13 | OliveOil           | 30       | 30         | 570    | 4       | SPECTRO   |
| 14 | DiatomSizeReduction| 16       | 306        | 345    | 4       | IMAGE     |
| 15 | Coffee             | 28       | 28         | 286    | 2       | SPECTRO   |
| 16 | Symbols            | 25       | 995        | 398    | 6       | IMAGE     |
| 17 | Beef               | 30       | 30         | 470    | 5       | SPECTRO   |
| 18 | SyntheticControl   | 300      | 300        | 60     | 6       | SIMULATED |
| 19 | Trace              | 100      | 100        | 275    | 4       | SENSOR    |
| 20 | TwoLeadECG         | 23       | 1139       | 82     | 2       | ECG       |

---

[1] https://github.com/alexandrefelipemuller/timeseries_shapelet_transferlearning, last accessed 16 Aug 2021.

### 3.1   Shapelet Extraction

This step is the differential of this work in relation to a conventional training using a classifier based on neural networks. The extraction of shapelets is a task that usually demands a lot of processing time and neural network training. Finding these sub-sequences is an additional step that allows to transfer them to the model to be used in the original series.

Given the set of series, the most relevant shapelets from each one were extracted. For this, we used the traditional method with a sliding window and candidate dictionary [20] with sizes from 5 to 18. This choice of size was adjusted to balance the proportion of what was shapelet and what was not in similar proportions in our database. In this method, an sorted list of all representations is generated with the computation of the gain. If we had to choose only one shapelet per class, choosing the first element from this list would be enough. In our case, the three most relevant are selected, discarding intersections. This is done by looking at the position in which the shapelet was extracted in the original series: if there is a conflict in the position (however different examples are involved), the deletion occurs. One to three most relevant shapelets from these candidates were chosen. The choice criterion is based on the gain and on having no intersection for most series.

The resulting shapelets serve to generate two extra supporting databases, totaling three databases named below:

- Original series;
- Shapelet series: where only the parts corresponding to the shapelets is mantained from the original series and everything else is replaced by the central value of the series. A central value is understood as the mean value of the extremes of the complete series;
- Noise series: where only the parts that do not match the shapelets were mantained from the original series, with the part corresponding to the shapelets replaced by the central value.

The process to generate these two databases is shown as example in Fig. 2. If we ignore the parts filled by the central value, the join between the shapelet series and the noise series corresponds to the original series.

### 3.2   Neural Network Training

As described in Sect. 2, the one-dimensional convolution training process is performed from the three databases. The initial training is based on the implementation of [19], which does not use the concept of shapelet. The only pre-processing performed was to shuffle the training base to improve neural network training.

The network architecture has been empirically adjusted to 3 one-dimensional layers. The first convolutional layer of the network has 32 filters and kernel length 8 (window equivalent concept), the second layer has 64 filters and kernel length 5 and the third convolutional layer has 32 filters and kernel length 3. At the end, there is a pooling layer and the output corresponds to the number of classes, thus

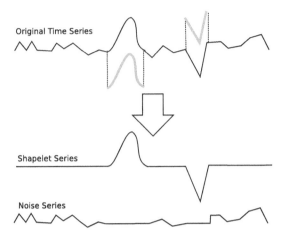

**Fig. 2.** Example of shapelet and noise series generation with 2 shapelets.

obtaining the probability of classification of each one. Regarding [19], the removal of "dropout" was performed. This technique consists of randomly removing some neurons to improve generalization and avoid overfitting [18].

To verify the impact of the transfer learning on classifier performance, we conducted the following experiments:

0. Process that precedes the training: extraction of shapelets and generation of support databases;
1. Original series training starting with random weights;
2. Shapelet series training starting with random weights;
3. Original series training starting with model imported from experiment 2;
4. Noise series training starting with random weights;
5. Original series training starting with model imported from experiment 4;
6. Cross validation, shapelet series training, importing model from 4;
7. Cross validation, noise series training, importing model from 2.

The objective of item 1 is to create a baseline comparison for the following tests. In this way, the results of this item should be similar to those obtained in [19]. Items 2 and 4 aim to obtain a training model formed by shapelets or by the rest of the series without shapelets (noise). Items 3 and 5 are the most important, as they aim to show the relevance of transferring the previously trained model. As all series have the same length filled with central value of the series, changing the initial model is possible. Finally, items 6 and 7 serve to elucidate and ratify the importance of transfer learning in each situation.

As the classification model is based on a neural network, if the same information is not put into training again, the weights suffer from loss of information during training. This means that if experiment 6 gives better results than 7, the shapelets are the most relevant piece of information. Thus, although all experiments have the same network architecture, only experiments 1, 3 and 5 use the complete data. All others use partial data.

### 3.3   Training and Transfer Learning

The extraction of symbolic representations, is performed by a deterministic algorithm, so its result is not changed in different executions. However, as the training process contains random factors related to weight adjustment, neural network training may vary. Therefore, experiments resulting from neural network training need to be statistically evaluated.

The selected databases from Table 1 are separated between training and validation (or testing). During neural network training, weights are adjusted with examples from the training base. At the end of each epoch (which corresponds to the end of the adjustment of the weights), the accuracy of the model in the validation base is verified, but this result is only a consultation. While training takes place, the error in the training base continues to be adjusted and decreased, but at the same time the error in the validation base increases. This difference is basically a form of over-adjustment.

Given the size of the time series bases, learning in 300 epochs was determined, with the best model between these epochs being saved for the validation step. For most of the tested series, the overfitting starts to happen between 150 and 250 epochs, remaining saved for the best model. We chose to run for 300 epochs because later models are discarded. As a rule, the model validated only on the training basis achieves 100% accuracy in this way. The best model is given by a checkpoint, i.e., as training continues and the error increases, the best model is saved until a better one is found. Therefore, there is no stopping criterion in this 250 epoch range because the best model is already saved.

As we transfer the model within the domain itself, it is expected that every experiment that receives a pre-trained model will rapidly evolve in number of epochs to reach a satisfactory result. The behavior in this transfer learn situation is the faster evolution of the model's accuracy [5]. For this reason, the greatest expectation in defining the experiments was that experiment 3, in addition to evolving quickly, would have better accuracy. This expectation is also due to the theoretical context exposed in Sect. 2.

## 4   Experimental Evaluation

As explained in Sect. 3, a total of 30 training rounds were carried out. For comparison with other works, it is expressed as means in Table 2.

The average accuracy of experiment 1 is equivalent to that presented in [19] in the databases used in both works. This validate our similar implementation of the proposed model.

Experiment 4 outperformed experiment 2 (Fig. 3). This suggests that there is still a lot of information relevant to classification that is comprised outside of extracted shapelets. In part, this is due to the size of the extracted shapelets that have absolute lengths of at most 18 values, which for most bases is a small length. An increase in this length would adjust this result, but at the cost of not making sense to highlight a very large segment. As the experiment extracts the segment from the original series, making the shapelet segment too large would

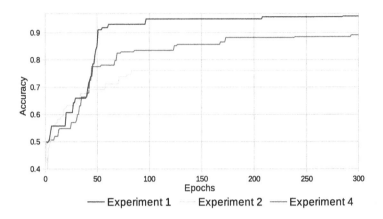

**Fig. 3.** Accuracy evolution for experiments 1, 2 and 4.

make the initial premise of putting the shapelet in evidence compromised, as the shapelet could be almost the entire length of the series. It becomes evident that setting parameters like the size of the extracted shapelets, the quantity of the extracted shapelets and the relevance of the shapelet is a difficult task.

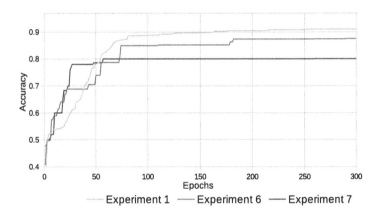

**Fig. 4.** Accuracy evolution for experiments 1, 6 and 7.

Another indicator of shapelet quality are the two cross-validation experiments 6 and 7. Both are inferior to experiment 1 at all epochal amounts (Fig. 4). Even so, experiment 6 was superior to experiment 7.

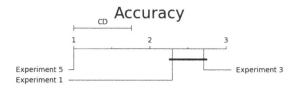

**Fig. 5.** Critical difference diagram for Nemenyi test.

Experiments 3 and 5 with transfer learn from the shapelet and noise series constitute the final objective. The result of the accuracy in the validation basis for experiments 1, 3 and 5 is described in Table 2 for each series (Fig. 6). For comparison, other 4 related classifiers in evidence were chosen, as described before. Table 2 is expressed as means (of 30 measurements), each series of measurements has a standard variation in the order of $10^{-5}$. The Student's t-test of both between experiments 1 vs 3 and separately experiments 1 vs 5 obtained p-values in the order of $10^{-15}$ each, so it is a high degree of reliability that the series present statistically relevant differences along the training epochs. After rejecting the null hypothesis, we then proceed with a post-hoc analysis in the best classifier as possible to see in diagram Fig. 5. The significance level of the tests is alpha=0.050 and critical distance of 0.76. We can see that on final result experiment 3 and experiment 1 have no significant differences and experiment 5 is significant different.

An important result is that of these 20 sets, at least 15 sets (in experiments 3 and 5) were better when compared to experiment 1 (baseline). Another relevant factor is that the accuracy of the classification overtaken what is equivalent to the state-of-the-art in half of the cases.

When evaluating the state-of-the-art on the theme of symbolic representations, it was expected that the model trained with the shapelets series would be similar to the training model of the original series started from scratch. However, there were situations where transfer learning showed superior results when started from shapelets and in some other cases where the final result was better when training started by the noise set. In these, it seems that there is an external knowledge towards symbolic representations that support a more precise classification with less overfitting.

In many cases, the results obtained in terms of accuracy of the time series classifier reach the reference works. The same results in simple base training, using the implementation of [19], would be repeatedly similar. However, by including the symbolic representations (which, in most cases, are the classification criteria of domain experts), the weights adjust more quickly (which is expected) and improve the generalization of learning, two relevant benefits.

**Table 2.** Accuracy of the main methods with the best result in bold.

| # | Datasets | Exp. 1 | Exp. 3 | Exp. 5 | LTS | ELIS | BOSS | HIVE-COTE |
|---|----------|--------|--------|--------|-----|------|------|-----------|
| 1 | BeetleFly | 0.9500 | 0.9500 | **1.0000** | **1.0000** | 0.8500 | 0.9490 | 0.9590 |
| 2 | BirdChicken | 1.0000 | 1.0000 | **1.0000** | **1.0000** | 0.9000 | 0.9840 | 0.9505 |
| 3 | ECGFiveDays | 0.9978 | 0.9954 | **1.0000** | 0.9954 | **1.0000** | 0.9830 | 0.9895 |
| 4 | ECG200 | 0.9100 | **0.9300** | 0.9000 | 0.9200 | – | 0.8900 | 0.8819 |
| 5 | CBF | 0.9933 | 0.9956 | 0.9978 | 0.9967 | - | 0.9980 | **0.9994** |
| 6 | FaceFour | 0.9318 | 0.9091 | 0.9659 | 0.9432 | 0.9545 | **0.9960** | 0.9495 |
| 7 | FacesUCR | 0.9268 | 0.9273 | 0.9210 | 0.9434 | – | 0.9510 | **0.9836** |
| 8 | Gun_Point | **1.0000** | **1.0000** | **1.0000** | **1.0000** | 0.9333 | 0.9940 | 0.9967 |
| 9 | ItalyPowerDemand | 0.9718 | **0.9974** | 0.9689 | – | 0.9757 | 0.8660 | 0.9678 |
| 10 | Lightning7 | 0.8904 | 0.8493 | 0.8630 | **0.9178** | 0.8082 | 0.8100 | 0.8111 |
| 11 | Lightning2 | 0.7869 | 0.7869 | **0.8197** | 0.7869 | – | 0.6660 | 0.7970 |
| 12 | MoteStrain | 0.9393 | 0.9377 | 0.9090 | 0.9361 | 0.8978 | 0.8460 | **0.9468** |
| 13 | OliveOil | 0.8000 | 0.7000 | 0.6667 | **0.9667** | – | 0.8700 | 0.8977 |
| 14 | DiatomSizeRed | 0.6536 | 0.5850 | 0.5850 | – | 0.8987 | 0.9390 | **0.9419** |
| 15 | Coffee | **1.0000** | **1.0000** | **1.0000** | **1.0000** | 0.9643 | 0.9890 | 0.9982 |
| 16 | Symbols | 0.9598 | 0.9545 | 0.9618 | **0.9889** | 0.7829 | 0.9610 | 0.9650 |
| 17 | Beef | 0.6333 | 0.7000 | 0.7000 | **0.9330** | 0.6333 | 0.6150 | 0.7227 |
| 18 | SyntheticControl | 0.9933 | 0.9933 | 0.9900 | – | – | 0.9680 | **0.9996** |
| 19 | Trace | **1.0000** | **1.0000** | **1.0000** | **1.0000** | **1.0000** | **1.0000** | **1.0000** |
| 20 | TwoLeadECG | **1.0000** | **1.0000** | **1.0000** | **1.0000** | 0.9982 | 0.9850 | 0.9935 |

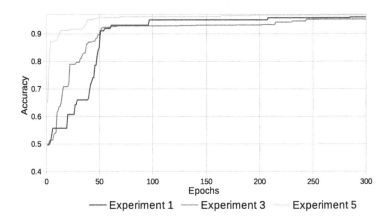

**Fig. 6.** Accuracy evolution for experiments 1, 3 and 5.

Figures 3, 4, 6, 7 and 8 show the accuracy evolution graphs of all experiments in comparison with experiment 1 as baseline.

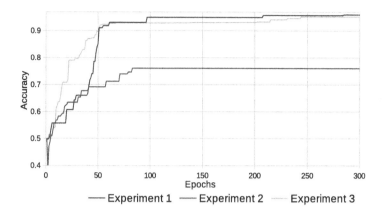

**Fig. 7.** Accuracy evolution for experiments 1, 2 and 3.

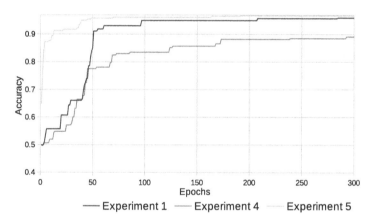

**Fig. 8.** Accuracy evolution for experiments 1, 4 and 5.

## 5   Conclusion

By exploring shapelets we obtained important results for time series classification
in most of the tested databases. We believe that the objectives of this work
have been achieved, since the performed experiments presented better results
than training purely started from scratch. Thus, the importance of extracting
symbolic representations in time series classifiers is evident, as they can be useful
even in classifiers based on convolutional networks.

Learning based on neural networks is not trivial, as it requires the data
analyst to adjust their experiments with different parameters. Only the continued
training of the model, without parameter changes, would invariably lead to an
increase in error. The proposed method, therefore, has a great advantage in this
type of classifier.

Throughout this work, some points identified as limitations have already been pointed. Among them are experiments, whose results were less than expected, such as specific domains. Furthermore, there seems to be a need to resolve a question not yet fully answered: are there non-symbolic components relevant to classification that can be captured by a neural network? The quality of the extracted shapelets still needs to be separated from the external factors in every symbolic representation. By pointing out the limitations of this work, it is evident that derived studies are still needed. The results from the experiments allow us to believe that the quality of the extracted shapelets can be improved, making the proposed method more refined. Furthermore, due to the number of parameters, the tests need to be replicated in order to confirm that the results persist in different contexts, such as other neural network architectures.

The analysis of the model already trained in a convolutional neural network is also a necessary development. Given the complexity of an already adjusted set of weights, unsupervised learning can be applied to segment the concepts in the learned model, such as identifying symbolic representations in the activated weights of a neural network. This would give a non-experimental, more analytical perspective on what happens during the transfer learn process. This can lead to the suppression of the training stage of the shapelet series using a neural network and creating a new model from scratch.

Another interesting future work would be comparison with [9], the authors search for a shapelet using neural network architecture. The implementation presented in this paper extracts shapelets using neural network adjustment directly. According to authors this hybrid approach have similar results than extracting shapelets using traditional extraction. Likely mutual contributions are possible to get better results.

# References

1. Bagnall, A., Lines, J., Hills, J., Bostrom, A.: Time-series classification with cote: the collective of transformation-based ensembles. IEEE Trans. Knowl. Data Eng. **27**(9), 2522–2535 (2015)
2. Cui, Z., Chen, W., Chen, Y.: Multi-scale convolutional neural networks for time series classification. CoRR abs/1603.06995 (2016). http://arxiv.org/abs/1603.06995
3. Dau, H.A., et al.: The UCR time series classification archive (October 2018). https://www.cs.ucr.edu/~eamonn/time_series_data_2018/
4. Fang, Z., Wang, P., Wang, W.: Efficient learning interpretable shapelets for accurate time series classification. In: 2018 IEEE 34th International Conference on Data Engineering (ICDE), pp. 497–508 (April 2018). https://doi.org/10.1109/ICDE.2018.00052
5. Fawaz, H.I., Forestier, G., Weber, J., Idoumghar, L., Muller, P.: Transfer learning for time series classification. CoRR abs/1811.01533 (2018). http://arxiv.org/abs/1811.01533
6. Ismail Fawaz, H., Forestier, G., Weber, J., Idoumghar, L., Muller, P.-A.: Deep learning for time series classification: a review. Data Min. Knowl. Disc. **33**(4), 917–963 (2019). https://doi.org/10.1007/s10618-019-00619-1

7. Gamboa, J.C.B.: Deep learning for time-series analysis. arXiv preprint arXiv:1701.01887 (2017)
8. Grabocka, J., Schilling, N., Wistuba, M., Schmidt-Thieme, L.: Learning time-series shapelets. In: Proceedings of the 20th ACM SIGKDD International Conference on Knowledge Discovery and Data Mining, KDD 14, pp. 392–401. ACM (2014). https://doi.org/10.1145/2623330.2623613, http://doi.acm.org/10.1145/2623330.2623613
9. Guijo-Rubio, D., Gutiérrez, P.A., Tavenard, R., Bagnall, A.: A hybrid approach to time series classification with shapelets. In: Yin, H., Camacho, D., Tino, P., Tallón-Ballesteros, A.J., Menezes, R., Allmendinger, R. (eds.) IDEAL 2019. LNCS, vol. 11871, pp. 137–144. Springer, Cham (2019). https://doi.org/10.1007/978-3-030-33607-3_16
10. Längkvist, M., Karlsson, L., Loutfi, A.: A review of unsupervised feature learning and deep learning for time-series modeling. Pattern Recogn. Lett. **42**, 11–24 (2014)
11. LeCun, Y., Bengio, Y., Hinton, G.: Deep learning. Nature **521**(7553), 436–444 (2015)
12. Li, G., Choi, B., Bhowmick, S.S., Wong, G.L.H., Chun, K.P., Li, S.: Visualet: visualizing shapelets for time series classification. In: Proceedings of the 29th ACM International Conference on Information & Knowledge Management, pp. 3429–3432 (2020)
13. Li, G., Choi, B.K.K., Xu, J., Bhowmick, S.S., Chun, K.P., Wong, G.L.: Efficient shapelet discovery for time series classification. IEEE Trans. Knowl. Eng. (2020)
14. Lin, J., Keogh, E., Wei, L., Lonardi, S.: Experiencing sax: a novel symbolic representation of time series. Data Min. Knowl. Disc. **15**(2), 107–144 (2007)
15. Lines, J., Bagnall, A.: Time series classification with ensembles of elastic distance measures. Data Min. Knowl. Disc. **29**(3), 565–592 (2014). https://doi.org/10.1007/s10618-014-0361-2
16. Lines, J., Taylor, S., Bagnall, A.: Time series classification with hive-cote: The hierarchical vote collective of transformation-based ensembles. ACM Trans. Knowl. Discov. Data **12**(5), 52:1–52:35 (July 2018). https://doi.org/10.1145/3182382, http://doi.acm.org/10.1145/3182382
17. Schäfer, P.: The boss is concerned with time series classification in the presence of noise. Data Min. Knowl. Disc. **29**(6), 1505–1530 (2015)
18. Srivastava, N., Hinton, G., Krizhevsky, A., Sutskever, I., Salakhutdinov, R.: Dropout: a simple way to prevent neural networks from overfitting. J. Mach. Learn. Res. **15**(1), 1929–1958 (2014)
19. Wang, Z., Yan, W., Oates, T.: Time series classification from scratch with deep neural networks: A strong baseline. CoRR abs/1611.06455 (2016). http://arxiv.org/abs/1611.06455
20. Ye, L., Keogh, E.: Time series shapelets: a new primitive for data mining. In: Proceedings of the 15th ACM SIGKDD International Conference on Knowledge Discovery and Data Mining, KDD 2009, pp. 947–956. ACM, New York (2009). https://doi.org/10.1145/1557019.1557122, http://doi.acm.org/10.1145/1557019.1557122
21. Zhang, H., Wang, P., Fang, Z., Wang, Z., Wang, W.: Elis++: a shapelet learning approach for accurate and efficient time series classification. World Wide Web **24**(2), 511–539 (2021)

# Text Mining and Natural Language Processing

# A Deep Learning Approach for Aspect Sentiment Triplet Extraction in Portuguese

José Meléndez Barros$^{(\boxtimes)}$ and Glauber De Bona

Universidade de São Paulo, São Paulo, SP 05508-010, Brazil
{jose.melendez,glauber.bona}@usp.br

**Abstract.** Aspect Sentiment Triplet Extraction (ASTE) is an Aspect-Based Sentiment Analysis subtask (ABSA). It aims to extract aspect-opinion pairs from a sentence and identify the sentiment polarity associated with them. For instance, given the sentence "Large rooms and great breakfast", ASTE outputs the triplet T = {(rooms, large, positive), (breakfast, great, positive)}. Although several approaches to ASBA have recently been proposed, those for Portuguese have been mostly limited to extracting only aspects without addressing ASTE tasks. This work aims to develop a framework based on Deep Learning to perform the Aspect Sentiment Triplet Extraction task in Portuguese. The framework uses BERT as a context-awareness sentence encoder, multiple parallel non-linear layers to get aspect and opinion representations, and a Graph Attention layer along with a Biaffine scorer to determine the sentiment dependency between each aspect-opinion pair. The comparison results show that our proposed framework significantly outperforms the baselines in Portuguese and is competitive with its counterparts in English.

**Keywords:** Deep learning · Natural Language Processing · Aspect Sentiment Triplet Extraction

## 1 Introduction

Sentiment analysis, also known as opinion mining, is a field of Natural Language Processing (NLP) that analyzes people's opinions, sentiments, and attitudes towards entities such as products, services, organizations, individuals, among others [21]. There are three granularity levels in sentiment analysis: document level, sentence level and aspect level. Aspect-Based Sentiment Analysis (ABSA) is the term used to denote a set of tasks that aim to resolve aspect level granularity problems [21,25], i.e., given a review, the model should select specific words corresponding to *aspect terms* and *opinion terms* and identify their *sentiment polarity*. In turn, ABSA subtasks may focus only on extracting/classifying one or more of these elements. In this work, we deal with Aspect Sentiment Triplet Extraction (ASTE), which is a relatively new subtask [24].

© Springer Nature Switzerland AG 2021
A. Britto and K. Valdivia Delgado (Eds.): BRACIS 2021, LNAI 13074, pp. 343–358, 2021.
https://doi.org/10.1007/978-3-030-91699-2_24

M. Barros and G. De Bona

Consider for instance the sentence *"Large rooms and great breakfast"*. Aspects are word sequences describing attributes or features of the targets (e.g., rooms, breakfast), opinions are those expressions carrying subjective attitudes or (un)desirable characteristics (e.g., large, great) and sentiments are the polarities associated with aspect-opinion pair, which can be positive, negative or neutral. ASTE aims to extract not only the aspects and its sentiment, but also the corresponding opinion spans expressing the sentiment for each aspect, as the example in Fig. 1 illustrates.

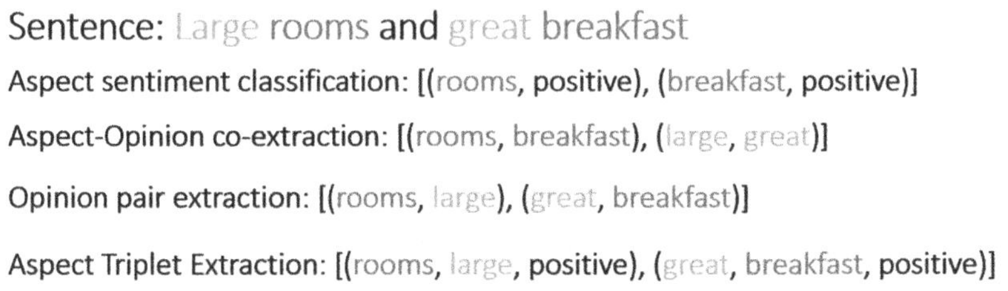

**Sentence:** Large rooms **and** great breakfast

Aspect sentiment classification: [(rooms, positive), (breakfast, positive)]

Aspect-Opinion co-extraction: [(rooms, breakfast), (large, great)]

Opinion pair extraction: [(rooms, large), (great, breakfast)]

Aspect Triplet Extraction: [(rooms, large, positive), (great, breakfast, positive)]

**Fig. 1.** Differences among ABSA subtasks.

ABSA tasks tackled in Portuguese include aspect term extraction [2,23], aspect sentiment classification [1,26] and aspect opinion co-extraction [4], but the proposed solutions employs methods that are considerably behind the state of the art in reference languages [25]. Besides, these works are focused on identifying aspects or opinions separately. Our work aims to extract aspects, opinions and sentiment polarity simultaneously. This not only provides richer context output, but also explains why a specific sentiment polarity was assigned.

We develop a framework based on deep learning to perform the Aspect Sentiment Triplet Extraction task in Portuguese. Our framework is based the state-of-the-art models for English, building on the work of Zhang et al. [32]. The main improvements proposed by our work are: we use BERT instead of Glove for sentence encoding, with word-vectors capturing a richer context; we add a Graph Attention layer to capture more complex relationships between two word vectors. The comparison results show that our proposed framework outperforms the baselines by more than 10%. Besides, the ablation study demonstrates the effectiveness of Graph Attention layers and BiLSTM layers for dimensionality reduction. The main contributions of this paper can be summarized as follows:

- We propose the first model to deal with ASTE tasks in Portuguese. To the best of our knowledge, all works in Portuguese-ABSA have been limited to Aspect Extraction.
- We provide a new dataset in Portuguese to work with ASTE tasks. Additionally, we adapt an existing dataset for this task (ReLi Corpus [12]). Other datasets [11,13,28] related to ABSA in Portuguese do not have the proper labeling for ASTE tasks.

## 2 Related Work

ABSA includes several subtasks that vary according to the domain of the target term. Xu et al. [31] developed a model based on BiLSTM networks, Attention and Conditional Random Fields (CRF), aiming to extract an opinion term given an aspect term as input. Their main contribution is the model's capability of capturing variable-length opinion spans. This model cannot manage overlapped aspects/opinions. He et al. [17] work on aspect-sentiment pair extraction task. They created a model using CNN layers and an attention mechanism. It incorporates two document-level classification tasks to be jointly trained with Aspect Extraction and aspect-level sentiment classification, allowing aspect-level tasks to benefit from document-level information. This model requires outputs intensively annotated to validate the results.

Aspect/target term sentiment classification is another subtask commonly addressed in ABSA, approached for instance by Cui and Maojie [5] and Han et al. [16]. Both works employed BiGRU/LSTM and attention mechanisms to attenuate irrelevant information, but neither of them can manage overlapped sentiments. Meanwhile, Fan et al. [10] focused their work on target-oriented opinion words-extraction (TOWE), which aims to extract aspect-opinion tuples given an aspect(s) as input. To achieve that, they proposed an Inward-Outward LSTM to get information from the left and the right contexts of the target. This work can handle overlapped aspect/opinion.

Aspect Sentiment Triplet Extraction was recently proposed by Peng et al. [24], and they put forward a two-stage framework to extract opinion triplets. In the first stage, they initially used a neural network based on BiLSTM and Graph Convolutional Networks to extract aspects-sentiments pairs and opinion terms separately. Then, to detect the relationship between aspect terms and opinion terms in the second stage, a LSTM network and pretrained word embeddings are employed. This pipeline approach might suffer from error propagation.

To handle error propagation problems in multi-stage frameworks, Wu et al. [30] proposed a tagging scheme model, which is implemented in three variants, using CNN, BiLSTM or BERT. Advantages of this approach include the following: only raw reviews are required as input; this model can extract all opinion factors of opinion pair extraction in one step, instead of pipelines; and it is easily extended to other pair/triplet extraction tasks from text. The most important limitation is again that outputs must be intensively annotated for the results to be validated.

Zhang et al. [32] developed a framework that can handle overlapping sentences, only requires raw review as input, and that is not multi-stage like the above one. The model structure consists of a word embedding (Glove) attached to a BiLSTM layer, which they use as a context sentence encoder. The BiLSTM output $h$ is passed to ReLU layers, which apply dimension-reduction to strip away irrelevant features. Finally, two independent softmax layers obtain distributions over the labels that denote an aspect-opinion term. A biaffine scorer [9] to determine if the sentiment dependency between each word pair is neutral, negative, positive, or null.

Unlike the works developed for English, in Portuguese, no available models were found in ASTE. The most remarkable works are focused on Aspect Extraction and Aspect-sentiment pair extraction. Cardoso and Pereira [4] used CRF and opLexicon to deal with aspect sentiment classification. Aires et al. [1] developed two models, one based on SVM and one employing an LSTM network. Saias et al. [26] opted for three methods: Maximum Entropy classifier, Sentiment lexicon SentiLex-PT and Rule-based methods, with the last two focusing on Aspect-sentiment pair extraction. Finally, Balage F. [2] used clustering techniques, word2vec embeddings and CRF to implement an unsupervised model.

## 3    Proposed Framework

Our framework[1] (BERT for Opinion Triplet Extraccion - BOTE) consists of 4 modules. The overall architecture is shown in Fig. 2. The sentence encoder module generates a set of word vectors, which encode semantic and context information. The aspect-opinion representation module extracts the aspect and opinion features from word vectors. Then, the aspect-opinion tagging module takes as input this feature vector to label the word as an aspect or an opinion or neither of them. Finally, the sentiment dependency between aspect and opinion vectors is detected by the dependency parsing module.

### 3.1    Problem Definition

Our Aspect Sentiment Triplet Extraction (ASTE) [24] problem is defined as, given a sentence $S = \{w_1, w_2, w_3, ..., w_n\}$ consisting of $n$ words, extracting all possible triplets $T = \{(a, o, p)_m\}_{m=1}^{|T|}$ from $S$, where $a$, $o$ and $p$ respectively denote an $n$-gram aspect term, an $n$-gram opinion term and a sentiment polarity; $a_m$ and $o_m$ can be represented as their start and end positions $(s_m, e_m)$ in $S$ and $p_m \in \{Positive, Negative, Neutral\}$. Note that this task involves dealing with One-to-One, One-to-Many and Many-to-Many relationships between aspects and opinions, as well as overlapped sentences.

### 3.2    Sentence Encoding

We adopt BERT [7] to encode sentences. Given a sentence $S = \{w_i\}_{i=1}^{|S|}$ we get a word-vectors set $V = \{v_i | v_i \in \mathbb{R}^{d_B}\}_{i=1}^{|S|}$ from the $n^{th}$ BERT hidden state, where $d_B$ denote the dimensionality of the BERT word-vector. The capability of BERT to generate different word embeddings depending on the context allows us to obtain feature vectors with better semantic information; for example, BERT vectors can deal with homonyms. Additionally, BERT can handle long reviews better than LSTM networks, thanks to attention mechanisms.

The BERT model works with WordPiece [7], therefore, from the sentence $S$, we obtain token vectors $t_i$ instead of word vectors $v_i$. A word can be formed by

---

[1] Source code available at https://github.com/josemelendezb/bote.

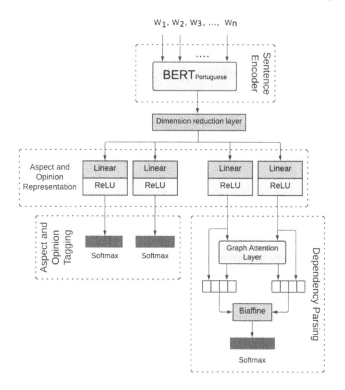

**Fig. 2.** Architectures of our model.

two or more tokens. To obtain a vector $v_i$ of a word $w_i$, we average the token vectors $(u_{i1}, u_{i2}, ..., u_{il})$ that form that word; formally, $v_i = \frac{1}{m}\sum_{l=1}^{m} u_{i,l}$ for all $v_i \in V$. A custom Average Pooling2D layer calculates the averages.

Finally, we apply a BiLSTM dimension-reducing layer to the word vectors. Since a BERT vector can have 758 or 1024 dimensions and machine learning does not understand causality, models map any input feature to the target variable, even if there is no causal relation. Many features demand a more complex model and increase the risk of overfitting. Dimensionality reduction removes multi-collinearity and irrelevant features, making our model more straightforward, less data-hungry, and reducing the risk of overfitting.

### 3.3 Aspect and Opinion Representation

Following Zhang et al. [32], we apply linear layers and nonlinear functions on $V$ before the opinion and aspect tagging operation in order to attenuate the noise of irrelevant information. Formally, let $\mathbf{r}_i^{(ap)}$ and $\mathbf{r}_i^{(op)}$ ($\mathbf{r}_i^{(ap)\prime}$ and $\mathbf{r}_i^{(op)\prime}$) denote the aspect and opinion representations employed in aspect and opinion tagging (sentiment dependency parsing), with $\mathbf{r}_i^{(ap)}, \mathbf{r}_i^{(op)}, \mathbf{r}_i^{(ap)\prime}, \mathbf{r}_i^{(op)\prime} \in \mathbb{R}^{d_r}$, where $d_r$ is the dimensionality of the representation. The linear layers employ a ReLU family function $g(.)$ and have parameters $\mathbf{W}_r^{(ap)}, \mathbf{W}_r^{(op)}, \mathbf{W}_r^{(ap)\prime}, \mathbf{W}_r^{(op)\prime} \in \mathbb{R}^{d_r \times d_B}$ and $\mathbf{b}_r^{(ap)}, \mathbf{b}_r^{(op)}, \mathbf{b}_r^{(ap)\prime}, \mathbf{b}_r^{(op)\prime} \in \mathbb{R}^{d_r}$:

$$\mathbf{r}_i^{(ap)} = g(\mathbf{W}_r^{(ap)} v_i + \mathbf{b}_r^{(ap)}) \tag{1}$$

$$\mathbf{r}_i^{(op)} = g(\mathbf{W}_r^{(op)} v_i + \mathbf{b}_r^{(op)}) \tag{2}$$

$$\mathbf{r}_i^{(ap)\prime} = g(\mathbf{W}_r^{(ap)\prime} v_i + \mathbf{b}_r^{(ap)\prime}) \tag{3}$$

$$\mathbf{r}_i^{(op)\prime} = g(\mathbf{W}_r^{(op)\prime} v_i + \mathbf{b}_r^{(op)\prime}) \tag{4}$$

### 3.4   Aspect and Opinion Tagging

Words are tagged by using two taggers built on a softmax layer as follows:

$$\mathbf{p}_i^{(l)} = softmax(\mathbf{W}_t^{(l)} \mathbf{r}_i^{(l)} + \mathbf{b}_t^{(l)}) \tag{5}$$

Above, $l \in \{ap, op\}$, $\mathbf{W}_t^{(l)} \in \mathbb{R}^{3 \times d_r}$ and $\mathbf{b}_t^{(l)} \in \mathbb{R}^3$ are trainable parameters. The softmax outputs two series of distributions over {B, O, I}, tagging aspect and opinion terms via the probability of each word $w_i$ being the Beginning/Inside/Outside of an aspect/opinion term. For example, in the sentence *"Large rooms and great breakfast. Room service was awesome."*, after decoding $\mathbf{p}_i^{(ap)}$ and $\mathbf{p}_i^{(op)}$ outputs, the result should be as in Table 1.

Table 1. Tagging result.

| | 0 | 1 | 2 | 3 | 4 | 5 | 6 | 7 | 8 | 9 |
|---|---|---|---|---|---|---|---|---|---|---|
| | Large | rooms | and | great | breakfast | . | Room | service | was | awesome |
| $\mathbf{p}_i^{(ap)}$ | O | B | O | O | B | O | B | I | O | O |
| $\mathbf{p}_i^{(op)}$ | B | O | O | B | O | O | O | O | O | B |

### 3.5   Sentiment Dependency Parsing

In this module, the aim is to identify the sentiment polarity of every word pair $(w_i, w_j)$. Our model uses four tags (NEU, NEG, POS, NO-DEP) to denote these dependencies. The tags respectively indicate neutral, negative, positive, and non-existent sentiment dependency. There are $|S|^2$ possible word pairs in each sentence since, during the training process, the target triplets induce ordered pairs. To avoid redundant relations, following [3,32], sentiment dependency between an aspect and opinion term is assigned via the pair formed by their last word.

Formally, we have a 3D-tensor $\mathbf{T} \in \mathbb{R}^{|S| \times |S| \times 4}$, where each element $t_{ijk}$ denotes the probability that the polarity in $(w_i, w_j)$ is $k$, with $k \in \{$NEU, NEG, POS, NO-DEP$\}$. Finally, we get an asymmetric square matrix $\mathbf{D} \in \mathbb{R}^{|S| \times |S|}$ as shown in Fig. 3.

|  | Large | rooms | and | great | breakfast |
|---|---|---|---|---|---|
| Large | NO-DEP | NO-DEP | NO-DEP | NO-DEP | NO-DEP |
| rooms | **POS** | NO-DEP | NO-DEP | NO-DEP | NO-DEP |
| and | NO-DEP | NO-DEP | NO-DEP | NO-DEP | NO-DEP |
| great | NO-DEP | NO-DEP | NO-DEP | NO-DEP | NO-DEP |
| breakfast | NO-DEP | NO-DEP | NO-DEP | **POS** | NO-DEP |

**Fig. 3.** A parsing example for sentiment dependency.

A Biaffine scorer [9] is used to obtain word-level sentiment dependencies. This mechanism is widely used and has shown success in various parsing-related tasks [19,20]. The score $s_{ijk}$ for a pair $(w_i, w_j)$ that have a dependency $k$ is computed using syntax-aware vectors $\mathbf{h}_i^{(ap)\prime}$ and $\mathbf{h}_j^{(op)\prime}$ obtained from a Graph Attention Layer (GAL). Using ; to represent the concatenation operation and $\mathbf{W}^{(k)}$ and $\mathbf{b}^{(k)}$ to denote trainable weight and bias, the scores can be defined as:

$$s_{ijk} = [\mathbf{W}^{(k)}\mathbf{z}_i^{(ap)\prime} + \mathbf{b}^{(k)}]^\top \mathbf{z}_j^{(op)\prime} \tag{6}$$

$$\mathbf{z}_i^{(ap)\prime} = [\mathbf{r}_i^{(ap)\prime}; \mathbf{h}_i^{(ap)\prime}], \quad \mathbf{z_i} \in \mathbb{R}^{2d_r} \tag{7}$$

$$\mathbf{z}_j^{(op)\prime} = [\mathbf{r}_j^{(op)\prime}; \mathbf{h}_j^{(op)\prime}], \quad \mathbf{z_j} \in \mathbb{R}^{2d_r} \tag{8}$$

An example of how to calculate $s_{ijk}$ is shown in Fig. 4. The aspect-vector $\mathbf{z}_i$ representing the word $w_i$ is inputted into the linear layer $\mathbf{W}^{(k)}(.) + \mathbf{b}^{(k)}$ (Eq. 6). The purpose of this linear layer is to generate a vector $\mathbf{z}_i$ for each $k$-polarity. Therefore, by multiplying $\mathbf{z}_{ik}$ and $\mathbf{z}_j$, we obtain a score that measures the polarity between $w_i$ and $w_j$. In our example, the score vector of $(\mathbf{w}_1, \mathbf{w}_0) = $ ("rooms", "large") is $s_{10} = \langle s_{100}, s_{101}, s_{102}, s_{103}\rangle = \langle -0.32, -0.39, -0.55, 1.98\rangle$. Once we apply the Softmax function, we obtain the probability vector $s_{13} = \langle 0.08, 0.07, 0.06, 0.79\rangle$, indicating that the dependency between "quartos" and "rooms" is positive.

Although BERT contains implicit syntactic information, its ability to capture explicit syntactic features is limited [15]. A common problem in ABSA when feature vectors are generated from a sequence, without considering explicitly the knowledge about the language, is that they may incorrectly locate specific targets in sentences with multiple aspects and opinions [22].

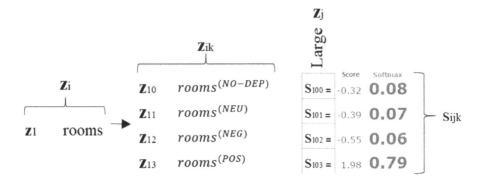

**Fig. 4.** A biaffine scoring example for sentiment dependency.

### 3.6 Syntax-Aware Vector

Unlike Zhang et al., we concatenate a syntax-aware vector $\vec{h}$ with $\vec{r}$ before inputting the features vector into the Biaffine scorer. As mentioned earlier, this vector $\vec{h}$ is obtained from a Graph Attention Layer (GAL), which can to capture linguistic structures like dependency trees other than only sequential data [18]. The GAL receives the vector $\vec{r}$ and an adjacency matrix that represents the syntactic dependency graph of the sentence[2]. GAL then embed the graph structure into the vector by performing masked attention – it computes self-attention between node $i$ and node $j$ if and only if $j$ is a neighbor of $i$.

Figure 5 shows the syntactic dependency of "The hotel has an awesome room service" and its adjacency matrix. In $\vec{r}_6$, for example, self-attention is applied between $\vec{r}_6$ and its neighbors (green region) instead of all tokens. In a dependency tree, the aspect-opinion pair will generally be related. By applying the mechanism of attention following the connections of the tree, more important nodes receive higher weight during neighborhood aggregation. Therefore, there will be more chances of identifying a sentiment dependency relationship in the selected pair. Although there are some useless dependency relationships for ASTE, aspect and opinion tagging outputs serve to counteract the noise produced by these irrelevant dependencies.

We take the syntactic dependency as an undirected graph. In directed graphs, self-attention is computed following the direction of the edge, however, edges do not always connect aspects and opinions directly, and if it does, the direction is not necessarily aspect $\rightarrow$ opinion. If we use a directed graph, we could lose information.

---

[2] We obtain the syntactic dependency graph of a sentence using Spacy parser.

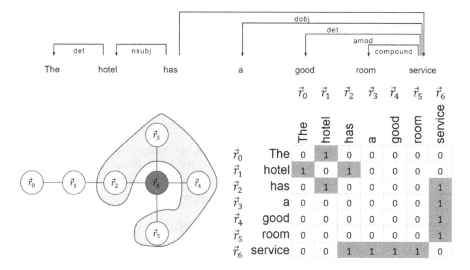

**Fig. 5.** A biaffine scoring example for sentiment dependency.

## 4   Experiments

### 4.1   Datasets

We conduct experiments in Portuguese and English datasets. Portuguese datasets include ReLi Corpus [12], which is composed of 1600 reviews from 14 different books with about 200 comments each. Besides, a new dataset was produced by us from hotel reviews collected from TripAdvisor (Table 2). Both datasets were manually annotated. These datasets are referenced in this work as ReLi and ReHol and they are available at https://dx.doi.org/10.21227/0ej1-br13.

Since there are no Portuguese models for ASTE tasks, English baselines were adapted to Portuguese-ASTE to compare with our model. Additionally, our model was trained in English to compare with the actual performance of these baselines. We used four English datasets[3] in the Laptop and Restaurant domain from Semeval 2014, 2015 and 2016 (Task 4, 12 and 5 respectively).

**Table 2.** Information regarding the composition of the ReHol dataset.

| # Reviews | 1514 | # Non-overlapped sentences | 941 |
|---|---|---|---|
| # Triplets | 3198 | # Overlapped sentences | 573 |
| # Positive triplets | 1845 | Average words per sentence | 16 |
| # Negative triplets | 1242 | Minimum sentence size (words) | 8 |
| # Neutral triplets | 111 | Maximum sentence size (words) | 38 |

---

[3] Datasets are available by Zhang et al. at https://github.com/GeneZC/OTE-MTL.

## 4.2 Baselines

Existing Portuguese-ABSA solutions do not provide enough information to reproduce their models/experiments. The lack of information includes: the source code is not available, there is insufficient information on the hyperparameters used, or the datasets are not available. The baselines were adapted to Portuguese by replacing the English pre-trained word embedding with a Portuguese pre-trained word embedding[4]. No further changes were made.

- **OTE-MTL** [32] is a model that encodes the sentences using Glove and BiLSTM networks, then, it applies dimension-reducing linear layers and non-linear functions on the hidden states to identify aspects and opinion and finally, the biaffine scorer [9] is used to get aspect-opinion pairs along with the associated sentiment with each other.
- **CMLA-MTL** [29] is an aspect-opinion co-extraction system, which is based on multi-layer attentions. It was adapted by Zhang et al. for ASTE task.

## 4.3 Experiment Settings

For the BERT encoder, we use the pre-trained cased BERT developed by Neural-Mind [27]. To compare our model with the baselines in English, we use uncased BERT base model developed by Google Research[5]. The maximum sequence length is 512 with a batch size of 32. We train our model for a maximal of 60 epochs using Adam optimizer. The learning rate is set to 1e−5. BiLSTM dimension reducing vector is 300-dimensional. Aspect and opinion representation vectors and syntax-aware vectors are 150-dimensional with a single hidden layer. Dropout is applied to avoid overfitting and the drop rate is 0.3. The development set is used for early stopping.

## 4.4 Evaluation

Following the previous works [24,30,32], F1-Score, recall, and precision measurements were used to evaluate the results and compare our model to the baselines. A triplet is correct if and only if the aspect span, the opinion span, the parsing and the sentiment polarity are all correct. The $5 \times 2$-nested cross-validation technique [8] was used to generate sufficient data from the selected metrics. Lilliefors, Anderson – Darling, and Shapiro – Wilk tests were used to validate the assumption of normality, and the Mauchly's test for the assumption of Sphericity [6]. Because cross-validation process generates repeated measures, appropriate tests should be used to deal with within-subjects. Based on the evaluation of the assumptions, non-parametric tests were selected. Comparing our model with the baselines, we used Friedman's test to identify if there was a statistically significant difference between the models [6]. Finally, we applied Hommel post-hoc procedure to identify if our model was better than the baselines [14]. The significance level used in all tests was 0.05.

---

[4] http://nilc.icmc.usp.br/nilc/index.php/repositorio-de-word-embeddings-do-nilc.
[5] https://github.com/google-research/bert.

# 5 Results and Analysis

## 5.1 Comparison with Baselines

The results are shown in Table 3. Our framework consistently achieves the best scores, both for the aspect and opinion extraction task and triplet extraction task in Portuguese. The average difference between our model and the Portuguese baselines in aspect extraction is 6.68%, opinion extraction is 7.87% and triplet extraction is 12.58%. In aspect extraction in English, the results are not conclusive. However, in opinion and triplet extraction in English, the framework outperforms the baselines significantly in three of the four datasets. In Rest 14, there is no statistically significant difference between BOTE and OTE-MTL. Detailed information about precision, recall, and how the errors affect the application can be found at https://dx.doi.org/10.21227/0ej1-br13.

**Table 3.** Results F1-score (%). * indicates difference is not statistically significant between flagged models. Bold indicates statistically significant superior performance.

| Task | Model | ReLi | ReHol | Rest14 | Rest15 | Rest16 | Lap14 |
|---|---|---|---|---|---|---|---|
| Aspect Ext. (AT) | OTE-MTL | 71.48 | 78.70 | 76.11* | 77.95* | 72.95 | 71.99 |
| | CMLA-MTL | 72.14 | 74.31 | 72.80 | 73.55 | 71.22 | 68.72 |
| | BOTE (ours) | **79.49** | **82.20** | 76.07* | 77.61* | **77.77** | 72.29* |
| Opinion Ext. (OT) | OTE-MTL | 68.61 | 72.93 | 77.91* | 74.27 | 76.19 | 65.62 |
| | CMLA-MTL | 62.16 | 69.45 | 74.46 | 74.72 | 74.69 | 63.82 |
| | BOTE (ours) | **70.52** | **81.10** | 77.98* | **77.69** | **78.88** | **68.66** |
| Triplet Ext. (TR) | OTE-MTL | 49.92 | 60.91 | 57.26* | 52.46 | 53.01 | 39.67 |
| | CMLA-MTL | 40.61 | 47.03 | 45.57 | 39.70 | 42.45 | 32.05 |
| | BOTE (ours) | **57.49** | **66.65** | 56.49* | **55.12** | **55.79** | **44.04** |

Additionally, experiments were carried out to test the models in domains for which they were not trained. The tests were performed in both Portuguese and English. The models in Portuguese were trained in the Books domain and tested in the Hotels domain. The English models were trained in the restaurant domain and tested in the laptop domain. The results are displayed in Table 4. BOTE shows significantly better performance than baselines in all three tasks, although lower when compared with BOTE results in the same domain. This indicates that, comparing with the baselines, our model responds better to new information, relationships and objects that were shown to it during training.

Finally, several tests were run to evaluate the performance of the proposed model based on the number of triples per sentence (Table 5). The results indicate that the greater the number of triplets in a sentence, the higher the hit rate (except between 3-triplets and 4-triplets in ReHol). Since the greater the number of triplets, the more complex are the relationships between aspects and opinion

**Table 4.** F1-score (%) transfer learning between different domains.

| Model | Train: rest14, Test: lap14 | | | Train: reli, Test: rehol | | |
|---|---|---|---|---|---|---|
| | AT | OT | TR | AT | OT | TR |
| OTE-MTL | 37.41 | 55.67 | 23.56 | 34.82 | 48.57 | 17.15 |
| CMLA-MTL | 33.38 | 54.44 | 15.27 | 20.18 | 43.93 | 4.37 |
| BOTE | **67.24** | **66.10** | **33.91** | **54.26** | **64.99** | **37.78** |

**Table 5.** BOTE F1-score (%) according to number of triplets per sentence.

| | 1-triplet | 2-triplets | 3-triplet | 4-triplets |
|---|---|---|---|---|
| Rest14 | 36.36 | 50.60 | 56.14 | 65.82 |
| Rest16 | 41.86 | 50.60 | 60.41 | 68.18 |
| ReHol | 33.33 | 56.34 | 75.62 | 68.03 |

terms, further experiments are needed to identify the underlying cause of this behavior.

## 5.2 Ablation Study

We examine the effectiveness of two components of our BOTE model, namely the reduction layer and graph attention layer (GAL). Table 6 presents the ablation results on Reli and ReHol datasets. BOTE-NoReduction does not use any type of reduction, BOTE-Linear uses a Linear layer, BOTE-ReLu uses a ReLU layer and BOTE-NoGraph uses a BiLSTM layer but does not use graph attention. The original BOTE uses a BiLSTM layer to reduce the size of the word vectors and graph attention layer to parse aspect and opinion terms. Regarding Aspect Extraction (AT) and Opinion Extraction (OT) tasks, there is no statistically significant difference between linear, nonlinear and no reduction. However, we can observe a significant improvement when the model uses a BiLSTM layer to reduce the dimensionality of the word vectors. Since GAL is not involved in AT and OT, it is not expected to be any significant difference between BOTE-NoGraph and BOTE. Regarding Triplet Extraction (TR), nonlinear and BiLSTM reduction show a significant improvement in the sentiment parsing process compared to no reduction. Likewise, when we use GAL we obtain better results compared to the other variants.

**Table 6.** Ablation study F1-score (%).

| Model | Reli | | | ReHol | | |
|---|---|---|---|---|---|---|
| | AT | OT | TR | AT | OT | TR |
| BOTE-NoReduction | 75.64 | 63.56 | 46.36 | 78.69 | 74.32 | 56.67 |
| BOTE-Linear | 74.83 | 62.97 | 47.84 | 78.24 | 74.13 | 58.22 |
| BOTE-ReLu | 74.14 | 63.17 | 50.15 | 78.14 | 73.41 | 57.66 |
| BOTE-NoGraph | 78.42 | 69.50 | 55.31 | 81.06 | 80.67 | 63.21 |
| BOTE | **79.49** | **70.52** | **57.49** | **82.20** | **81.10** | **66.65** |

# 6 Conclusions and Future Work

In this work, we proposed a Machine Learning framework to deal with Aspect Sentiment Triplet Extraction in Portuguese. Our model used a BERT model to obtain context-aware word vectors, a Graph Attention Layer to exploit the syntactic information contained in the sentence, and a Biaffine scorer as a sentiment parser. The model achieved an average F1-score of 62.07% in the datasets in ASTE Portuguese. When the model was trained in one domain and tested in another, it achieved an F1-score of 37.78% compared to 17.15% of the best baseline performance. Besides, the results showed the higher the number of triplets, the more accurate the model. The ablation study proved that performance is better when a dimensionality reducer is applied to BERT word vectors.

The experimental results verify the effectiveness of our framework compared to the baselines. To the best of our knowledge, we have developed the most fine-grained model to deal with aspect sentiment tasks in Portuguese. The proposed model even outperforms its English counterparts in some cases. Ablation study validates the effectiveness of applying dimensionality reduction in BERT word vectors, especially when using a BiLSTM layer. Besides, syntactic information improves sentiment parsing. Finally, our model shows a greater capacity of transfer learning across different domains, responding better to new information.

Future works include developing an opinion dependency tree where the relationship between words is based not on syntax, but on sentiment, as syntax trees usually ignore many connections between aspects and opinion words. Other possible research directions could aim at improving the classification ability of the model in multiple domains or determining the reason why the higher the number of triplets per sentence, the better is the model performance.

**Acknowledgments.** This work was supported by CAPES and Ministerio de Ciencia from Colombia.

# References

1. Aires, J.P., Padilha, C., Quevedo, C., Meneguzzi, F.: A deep learning approach to classify aspect-level sentiment using small datasets. In: 2018 International Joint Conference on Neural Networks (IJCNN), pp. 1–8. IEEE (2018)

2. Balage Filho, P.P.: Aspect extraction in sentiment analysis for Portuguese language. Ph.D. thesis, Universidade de Sao Paulo (2017)
3. Bekoulis, G., Deleu, J., Demeester, T., Develder, C.: Joint entity recognition and relation extraction as a multi-head selection problem. Expert Syst. Appl. **114**, 34–45 (2018)
4. Cardoso, B., Pereira, D.: Evaluating an aspect extraction method for opinion mining in the Portuguese language. In: Anais do VIII Symposium on Knowledge Discovery, Mining and Learning, pp. 137–144. SBC (2020)
5. Cui, Z., Maojie, Z.: Aspect level sentiment classification based on double attention mechanism. In: Proceedings of the 2019 2nd International Conference on E-Business, Information Management and Computer Science. EBIMCS 2019. Association for Computing Machinery, New York (2019). https://doi.org/10.1145/3377817.3377834
6. Demšar, J.: Statistical comparisons of classifiers over multiple data sets. J. Mach. Learn. Res. **7**(1), 1–30 (2006). http://jmlr.org/papers/v7/demsar06a.html
7. Devlin, J., Chang, M.W., Lee, K., Toutanova, K.: BERT: pre-training of deep bidirectional transformers for language understanding. In: Proceedings of the 2019 Conference of the North American Chapter of the Association for Computational Linguistics, Minneapolis, Minnesota, pp. 4171–4186. Association for Computational Linguistics, June 2019. https://doi.org/10.18653/v1/N19-1423
8. Dietterich, T.G.: Approximate statistical tests for comparing supervised classification learning algorithms. Neural Comput. **10**(7), 1895–1923 (1998)
9. Dozat, T., Manning, C.D.: Deep biaffine attention for neural dependency parsing. In: 5th International Conference on Learning Representations, ICLR 2017, Toulon, France, 24–26 April 2017, Conference Track Proceedings. OpenReview.net (2017). https://openreview.net/forum?id=Hk95PK9le
10. Fan, Z., Wu, Z., Dai, X.Y., Huang, S., Chen, J.: Target-oriented opinion words extraction with target-fused neural sequence labeling. In: Proceedings of the 2019 Conference of the North American Chapter of the Association for Computational Linguistics, Minneapolis, Minnesota, pp. 2509–2518. Association for Computational Linguistics, June 2019. https://doi.org/10.18653/v1/N19-1259
11. Farias, D.S., Matsuno, I.P., Marcacini, R.M., Rezende, S.O.: Opinion-meter: a framework for aspect-based sentiment analysis. In: Proceedings of the 22nd Brazilian Symposium on Multimedia and the Web, pp. 351–354. ACM (2016). https://doi.org/10.1145/2976796.2988214
12. Freitas, C., Motta, E., Milidiú, R., César, J.: Vampiro que brilha... rá! desafios na anotaçao de opiniao em um corpus de resenhas de livros. Encontro de Linguística de Corpus **11**, 22 (2012)
13. Freitas, L.A., Vieira, R.: Exploring resources for sentiment analysis in Portuguese language. In: Brazilian Conference on Intelligent Systems, pp. 152–156. IEEE (2015)
14. García, S., Herrera, F.: An extension on "statistical comparisons of classifiers over multiple data sets" for all pairwise comparisons. J. Mach. Learn. Res. **9**(89), 2677–2694 (2008). http://jmlr.org/papers/v9/garcia08a.html
15. Goldberg, Y.: Assessing Bert's syntactic abilities. arXiv (2019). http://arxiv.org/abs/1901.05287
16. Han, H., Li, X., Zhi, S., Wang, H.: Multi-attention network for aspect sentiment analysis. In: Proceedings of the 2019 8th International Conference on Software and Computer Applications, ICSCA 2019, pp. 22–26. Association for Computing Machinery, New York (2019). https://doi.org/10.1145/3316615.3316673

17. He, R., Lee, W.S., Ng, H.T., Dahlmeier, D.: An interactive multi-task learning network for end-to-end aspect-based sentiment analysis. In: Proceedings of the 57th Annual Meeting of the Association for Computational Linguistics, Florence, Italy, pp. 504–515. Association for Computational Linguistics, July 2019
18. Huang, B., Carley, K.: Syntax-aware aspect level sentiment classification with graph attention networks. In: Proceedings of the 2019 Conference on Empirical Methods in Natural Language Processing, Hong Kong, China, pp. 5469–5477. Association for Computational Linguistics, November 2019. https://doi.org/10.18653/v1/D19-1549
19. Li, Y., Li, Z., Zhang, M., Wang, R., Li, S., Si, L.: Self-attentive biaffine dependency parsing. In: Proceedings of the Twenty-Eighth International Joint Conference on Artificial Intelligence, IJCAI, pp. 5067–5073. ijcai.org (2019). https://doi.org/10.24963/ijcai.2019/704
20. Li, Z., et al.: Dependency or span, end-to-end uniform semantic role labeling. In: Proceedings of the AAAI Conference on Artificial Intelligence, vol. 33, no. 01, pp. 6730–6737 (2019). https://doi.org/10.1609/aaai.v33i01.33016730
21. Liu, B.: Sentiment analysis and opinion mining. Synthesis Lect. Hum. Lang. Technol. **5**(1), 1–167 (2012)
22. Lu, Z., Du, P., Nie, J.-Y., et al.: VGCN-BERT: augmenting BERT with graph embedding for text classification. In: Jose, J.M. (ed.) ECIR 2020. LNCS, vol. 12035, pp. 369–382. Springer, Cham (2020). https://doi.org/10.1007/978-3-030-45439-5_25
23. Machado, M.T., Pardo, T.A.S., Ruiz, E.E.S.: Analysis of unsupervised aspect term identification methods for Portuguese reviews. In: Anais do XIV Encontro Nacional de Inteligncia Artificial e Computacional (ENIAC), SBC, pp. 239–249 (2017)
24. Peng, H., Xu, L., Bing, L., Huang, F., Lu, W., Si, L.: Knowing what, how and why: a near complete solution for aspect-based sentiment analysis. In: Proceedings of the AAAI Conference on Artificial Intelligence, vol. 34, no. 05, pp. 8600–8607 (2020). https://doi.org/10.1609/aaai.v34i05.6383
25. Pereira, D.A.: A survey of sentiment analysis in the Portuguese language. Artif. Intell. Rev. **54**(2), 1087–1115 (2020). https://doi.org/10.1007/s10462-020-09870-1
26. Saias, J., Mourão, M., Oliveira, E.: Detailing sentiment analysis to consider entity aspects: an approach for Portuguese short texts. Trans. Mach. Learn. Artif. Intell. **6**, 26–35 (2018)
27. Souza, F., Nogueira, R., Lotufo, R.: BERTimbau: pretrained BERT models for Brazilian Portuguese. In: Cerri, R., Prati, R.C. (eds.) BRACIS 2020. LNCS (LNAI), vol. 12319, pp. 403–417. Springer, Cham (2020). https://doi.org/10.1007/978-3-030-61377-8_28
28. Vargas, F.A., Pardo, T.A.S.: Hierarchical clustering of aspects for opinion mining: a corpus study. In: Finatto, M.J.B., Rebechi, R.R., Sarmento, S., Bocorny, A.E.P. (eds.) Linguística de Corpus: Perspectivas, pp. 69–91 (2018)
29. Wang, W., Pan, S.J., Dahlmeier, D., Xiao, X.: Coupled multi-layer attentions for co-extraction of aspect and opinion terms. In: Proceedings of the AAAI Conference on Artificial Intelligence, vol. 31 (2017)
30. Wu, Z., Ying, C., Zhao, F., Fan, Z., Dai, X., Xia, R.: Grid tagging scheme for aspect-oriented fine-grained opinion extraction. In: Findings of the Association for Computational Linguistics, pp. 2576–2585. Association for Computational Linguistics, November 2020. https://doi.org/10.18653/v1/2020.findings-emnlp.234

31. Xu, L., Bing, L., Lu, W., Huang, F.: Aspect sentiment classification with aspect-specific opinion spans. In: Proceedings of the 2020 Conference on Empirical Methods in Natural Language Processing (EMNLP), pp. 3561–3567. Association for Computational Linguistics, November 2020. https://doi.org/10.18653/v1/2020.emnlp-main.288

32. Zhang, C., Li, Q., Song, D., Wang, B.: A multi-task learning framework for opinion triplet extraction. In: Findings of the Association for Computational Linguistics, pp. 819–828. Association for Computational Linguistics, November 2020. https://doi.org/10.18653/v1/2020.findings-emnlp.72

# Aggressive Language Detection Using VGCN-BERT for Spanish Texts

Errol Mamani-Condori$^{(\boxtimes)}$ and José Ochoa-Luna

Department of Computer Science,
Universidad Católica San Pablo, Arequipa, Peru
{errol.mamani,jeochoa}@ucsp.edu.pe

**Abstract.** The increasing influence from users in social media has made that aggressive content disseminates over the internet. To tackle this problem, recent advances in Aggressive Language Detection have demonstrated a good performance of Deep Learning techniques. Recently Transformer based architectures such as Bidirectional Encoder Representations from Transformer (BERT) outperformed previous aggressive text detection baselines. However, most of the Transformers-based approaches are unable to properly capture global information such as language vocabulary. Thus, in this work, we focus on aggressive content detection using the combination of Vocabulary Graph Convolutional Network (VGCN) to capture global information and BERT to model local information. This combined approach called VGCN-BERT allows us to improve the feature level representation in Spanish aggressive language detection. Our experiments were performed on a benchmark called MEX-A3T aggressiveness dataset which is composed of aggressive and non-aggressive Tweets written in the Mexican Spanish variant. We report 86.46% in terms of F1-score using this VGCN-BERT approach which allows us to obtain comparable results with the current state-of-the-art, ensemble BERT, so as to detect aggressive content regarding the track MEX-A3T 2020.

**Keywords:** Aggressiveness detection · BERT · Graph Convolutional Networks

## 1 Introduction

The exponential growth of social media such as Twitter, community forums, and blogging platforms has revolutionized communication and content publishing, but it has also increased the dissemination of hate speech [6,32]. Thus,

This research was supported by National Fund for Scientific and Technological Development and Innovation (Fondecyt-Perú) within the framework of the "Project of 50 E038-2019-01-BM Improvement and Expansion of the Services of the National System of Science, Technology and Technological Innovation" [Grant 028-2019-FONDECYT-BM-INC.INV].

© Springer Nature Switzerland AG 2021
A. Britto and K. Valdivia Delgado (Eds.): BRACIS 2021, LNAI 13074, pp. 359–373, 2021.
https://doi.org/10.1007/978-3-030-91699-2_25

nowadays offensive and aggressive language is pervasive in social media. The content which has profanity, abusive, aggressive, or any kind of words that disparages a person or a group is considered hate speech. Seemingly, the language is considered aggressive if encourages any kind of hostility or intention to be harmful, conveying a violent message.

Social media platforms and technology companies have heavily invested in ways to cope with this offensive language to prevent abusive behavior in social media [29]. One of the first approaches to tackle this problem was human control on text content. This manual filtering is very time-consuming as it can cause post-traumatic stress disorder-like symptoms to human annotators. Thus, the most effective strategy is to use computational methods to identify offense, aggression, and hate speech in user-generated content. This topic has attracted significant attention as evidenced in recent publications [11,28].

In this context, we address the automated task of aggressive language identification in Spanish texts. To do so, we use the combination of BERT model and Vocabulary Graph Convolutional Network which improves local information encoded in BERT embeddings by adding global information between words and concepts (Vocabulary GCN). This combination has been previously applied to other tasks [20,30].

We argue that VGCN-BERT is better suited to identify aggressive language in Spanish because it allows integrating the global notion of a specific domain language. That is, in addition to being able to capture the context of a word within a sentence with BERT, we can also catch the semantic relationships between words which can be replaced with other words in the same category using VGCN.

Basically, we incorporate the feature of a word and its relationship to other words that may replace it in meaning. For example, the phrase "read a book" would be replaced with "study a book" or "understand a book". It is worth noting that some aggressive words are composed by two or more tokens. One single word rarely appears as aggressive in the corpus, and most of the deep learning models cannot even find the word in their pre-trained vocabulary. Whereby, adding an extra feature of the connected "read a book" to "study a book" meaning will add a piece of global context information to the model.

Connecting those expressions more explicitly with their meanings allows to take into account the knowledge about the language (vocabulary). For instance, let consider the following tweet of aggressive content:

*Las fans de odisseo se ven bien bonitas en sus fotos de twitter y estan bien feas en persona.*
**(Odisseo fans look really pretty in their twitter photos and they are pretty ugly in person.)**

The sentence "they are pretty ugly" can be related to "disgusting" and "nasty" through the connections in a GCN graph. In this example, both positive and negative words appear in the sentence and the component "Odisseo fans look really pretty" denotes a strong positive opinion. Thus, the overall text would be wrongly classified as non-aggressive due to the first part overweights the classifier.

On the contrary, if we connect explicitly the last part of the sentence "pretty ugly" with the meaning of "really nasty" taking into account the knowledge of the aggressive tweet content (vocabulary), then it would be classified more accurately.

This last correlation between words and concepts in GCN has demonstrated to have a good performance capturing global information [30]. In brief, the combination of the local (embedding) and global information (graph) through self-attention is feed into a BERT model. In this sense, the word and graph embeddings interact with each other through the attention mechanism while learning the classifier.

In our experiments using VGCN-BERT, we report 0.8646 in terms of macro F1-score. This result outperforms slightly the state-of-the-art ensemble BERT model and other deep learning techniques [15], including the baselines reported during the Mexican Spanish Aggressive detection (MEX-A3T) task [3].

Overall, the contribution of the paper can summarized as:

- Combining the local an global information using VGCN-BERT without any external word embeddings or knowledge which is suitable and novel to detect the aggressiveness words with a global notion for the Spanish language.
- The combination of VGCN with a BERT model (a Spanish pre-trained version called BETO [9]) allows to obtain comparable results regarding the ensemble BERT models in Spanish Aggressiveness detection.

The paper is organized as follows. Related works are presented in Sect. 2. The methodology is described in Sect. 3. Experiments and conclusions are presented in Sects. 5 and 6.

## 2   Related Work

The English Offensive Language detection problem has been increasingly researched in the last years [11,31], this task is closely related to Spanish Aggressive identification.

Although many classification approaches have been applied to hate speech [5], offensive language, and aggressive, there still very few approaches applied to the Spanish aggressive language [2] compared to English [31]. Among them, the first attempts to detect offensive language were mostly based on the surface features techniques such as *uni-grams* and a larger *n-grams*. Later Badjatiya et al. [6] found out that the character n-grams had better performance than word tokens for hate speech detection.

Unlike feature extraction approaches, classification methods for Offensive Language detection have been predominantly supervised [23]. First works focused on manual feature engineering used for Machine learning algorithms such as Support Vector Machine (SVM) [11], Naive Bayes [11], and Logistic Regression [29]. Recent Deep Learning approaches [21] have demonstrated that automated feature learning representation allows to obtain better results. Also, pre-trained Word Embeddings have been applied successfully [6].

Nowadays, the best approach for the task and related NLP tasks has been the Bidirectional Encoder Representation from Transformer called BERT [12]. Although all of those techniques have been applied to the English language, they can also be "transferred" to other languages such as Spanish. Recently, to encourage the NLP community to develop this task for the Spanish language, IberEval and IberLEF (Iberian Languages Evaluation workshops) released the Aggressive identification task[1]. Related works on Spanish are mostly based on SVM and Convolutional Neural Network (CNN) [2]. It is also worth noting that good results were obtained using SVM and Bag of Words [4] and Long Short Term Memory (LSTM) and Gate Recurrent Unit [14].

### 2.1   Transfer Learning with BERT

With the recent emergence of the attention mechanism in 2017 [26], many improvements began to be noted in the field of Natural Language Processing (NLP). The same could be observed with the proposal of the revolutionary BERT [12]; that proved to be good and obtained outstanding results for 10 NLP downstream tasks.

Using BERT for identifying offensive language in the English language has proven to be effective [31], obtaining results that far exceed traditional models. However, since the transformers architecture and the attention mechanism appeared, attempts to combine BERT with one extra layer of attention were proposed [22]. In more recent related works multi-task BERT and ensemble BERT models showed good results to the detection of aggressive, offensive, and misogyny language in English, as reported by TRAC in ACL[2] [18].

Seemingly, the last MEX-A3T 2020 recently reported the use of BERT transformer-based models for aggressive language in Spanish. The best results were obtained using a pre-trained BERT version for the Spanish called BETO. Fine-tuning BETO for the aggressive has proved to be useful especially if we use an ensemble of different BETO [9] models for classification. Furthermore, BETO has been integrated with AutoEncoder representation [27], and a XGBoost classifier [10]. Tanase et al. [25] tried to fine-tune BETO with different dataset and multilingual transformer models. Additionally, as evidenced in the last MEX-A3T at IberLEF 2020, 9 teams used BERT, especially BETO, and 5 obtained the best results [3].

### 2.2   Graph Convolutional Networks (GCN)

Throughout the development of research in natural language processing, graphs have served as a representation of documents and texts. Very recently, this idea

---

[1] MEX-A3T: Authorship and aggressiveness analysis in the Mexican Spanish case study.

[2] Association for Computer Language conference.

inspired to search for the relationship of words in a language. There are many studies combining graphs with neural networks which is commonly called Graph Neural Networks (GNN) [7]. Graphs proved to be good at capturing general knowledge about words in a language. Thus, numerous studies and variations of GNNs have been proposed and applied to text classification tasks [17,24].

One of the most outstanding recent works showed the use of Graph Convolutional Networks (GCN) based on the spectrum of graph theory [17]. Kipf built a symmetric adjacency matrix denoting relationships in graphs. Thus, the representation of a node is also affected by its neighbors and its relationship in the graph during the convolution. Based on Kipf's work, Yao et al. [30] recently proposed a special case of GCN for text classification called text GCN. The authors denoted words and documents as nodes in a graph and their relationships as edges. Weights in edges can be calculated using three alternatives: the co-occurrence relationship between the words, tf-idf between documents and words and the similarity between documents. The work showed that GCNs are good at convolving global information from an input graph. [20] would later demonstrate the effectiveness of combining BERT with GCN using the co-occurrence measure and the relationship between words which is called Vocabulary Graph Convolutional Networks (VGCN) at the feature level.

## 3   Methodology

The goal of this paper is to identify whether a Spanish tweet content is aggressive or not. To do that, we carefully fine-tune the bidirectional encoder representation from transformers (BERT-Spanish version) and combine that with the VGCN.

Our design choice for BERT is due to its good performance in the English offensive detection [31]. Thus, to identify aggressive language in Spanish we have used the BERT model. However, we have noted this model is not suitable to lead with Spanish vocabulary which took us to explore other ways to improve it.

BERT is good at capturing the words' order and the local context information, but it also unable to capture global information. This missing information could be relevant to recognize aggressiveness specially in long text sequences. Starting from this point, we have already seen that GCNs for text classification are good at extracting global information [30]. Intuitively we thought of combining both approaches to join local and global text information. Fortunately, Yao et al. [30] focused on the feature level of BERT adding GCN features. In this sense, to address the missing global information in BERT, an additional embeddings graph would be needed.

Having said that, in this work we improve the BERT (BETO) model with a GCN. We aim to capture global notion and semantic correlation between words using the graph as a vocabulary of words following the previous proposals for text classification [16]. Thereby, the GCN-BERT architecture based on a vocabulary graph was deemed into the pipeline of our system.

The Vocabulary graph enables the lexical relationship between words in a language. The graph is built using the co-occurrence of words with documents such as Lu did [20]. The local information of a tweet is captured by BERT and is enriched by adding a graph embedding. We also must highlight that the construction of the vocabulary graph is based on the vocabulary of BERT, in such a way that the size is reduced. At the same time, the added embedding can have an efficient interaction and improve local context information of BERT.

By doing so, the relevant part of the global vocabulary graph is selected according to the input sentence and transformed into an embedding representation. Then VGCN-BERT uses multiple layers of attention mechanism to concatenate both embeddings representations allowing the interaction between BERT embeddings and graph embeddings. Finally, the classifier uses the fully connected layers, more details are depicted in Fig. 1.

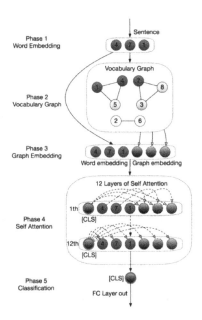

**Fig. 1.** Illustration of VGCN-BERT. (Blue) represents the input words, (green) are the related words in the graph, and the (blue-green) blend is the convolutional representation. The embeddings of the input sentence (Phase 1) are combined with the vocabulary graph (Phase 2) to produce a graph embedding, which is concatenated to the input sentence (Phase 3). Phase 2 produces three (hyperparameter) graph embeddings which have the same shape as the word embeddings. Note that from the vocabulary graph, the relevant part from input is extracted and embedded. In this case (3,5,8) will be convoluted but (2,6) will not. (Phase 4), several layers of self-attention are applied to the concatenated representation, allowing interactions between word embeddings and graph embeddings. The final embedding at the last layer is fed in a fully connected layer (Phase 5) for classification [20]. (Color figure online)

By applying the VGCN-BERT we aim to add carefully the global information of a language using vocabulary (of BERT) graph embedding to the classical embedding BERT (Spanish pre-trained BETO) in the features level. The system we used obtained good results improving the detection of the aggressiveness words in contrast to the other ensemble models using multiple BERT models at the same time. The Vocabulary graph knowledge from global information and its background concepts of the words will be added to the local information throughout multiple self-attention mechanisms. The VGCN and the integration to BERT will further explained in next sections.

### 3.1 VGCN

Our system follows the implementation and the model proposed by Lu [20], which uses a vocabulary graph based on the word co-occurrences in documents. This graph is built using normalized point-wise mutual information (NPMI) [8] to measure the relationship between words in a document. Then, they create an edge between two words if their NPMI is larger than a threshold and the performance is better when the threshold is between 0.0 and 0.3.

The GCN is generally based on Kipf's model [17], i.e., it has two multi-layer neural networks that convolve directly on the graph and create embedding vectors of nodes based on the neighborhoods. In this case, the convolution is made from related words instead of documents and the GCN is constructed in the vocabulary. Thus, for a single document, assuming the document is a row vector $x$ consisting of words in the vocabulary, a layer of convolution is defined as (1).

$$h = (Ax^T)^T W = xAW \tag{1}$$

where $A^T = A$ is the vocabulary graph. $xA$ extracts the part of vocabulary graph relevant to the input sentence $x$. $W$ holds the weights of the hidden state vector for the single document, whose dimension is $|v|h$. We could define the two layers VGCN with ReLU as follows:

$$VGCN = ReLU(X_{mv}A_{vv}W_{vh})W_{hc} \tag{2}$$

where $m$ is the number of documents in mini-batch size. $v$ is the vocabulary size, $h$ is the hidden layer size, $c$ the class size or sentence embedding size [17].

### 3.2 Integrating VGCN into BERT

In this section, we want to integrate VGCN embeddings with BERT and take advantage of its attention mechanism [26]. When using the attention mechanism one gets weighted vectors that encode the context information. Thus, instead of using only word embeddings of the input sentences, we feed both the vocabulary graph embedding obtained with the Eq. (2) and the sequence word embeddings to the BERT transformer.

In this sense, not only the order of the words in the sentence is retained (local context information), but also the background information obtained by VGCN (global information of the language). After that, the local and global embedding are fully integrated through layers interacting them with 12-layers and 12-heads of the self-attention encoder.

## 4    Dataset

Since our goal is to identify the aggressiveness content in social media for Spanish, we worked with the Mexican Spanish dataset MEX-A3T track[3]. We also noted that this track on detecting aggressive language is not new; however, it is still a challenge for the Spanish language as shown in the previous workshops: TRAC2020[4], iberLEF2020[5] and the track at iverEval2018.

The dataset was collected considering Twitter as a main source media since it is open and its anonymity allows people to write judgments about others. While building the corpus they use some rude words and controversial hashtags to narrow the search that ranged from August until November of 2017. They also used around 143 terms that served as a seed to extract tweets [13]. Additionally, the MEX-A3T contains 10.475 tweets 3143 for testing and 7332 for training (see Table 1) and we also noted that the test set does not contain labels in the dataset.

It is worth noting that the data (tweets) contains a dictionary of Mexican words "Mexicanisms" with at least one of vulgar or insulting words; then they were manually labeled with "Aggressive" and "Non Aggressive". The criteria used while tagging was on the promise that offensive content is disparaging or humiliating a person or a group of persons [3]. The linguistic criteria are the approach of using "vulgar, Aggressive and offensive" as an identifier. Diaz et al. [13] used a new annotation scheme based on the linguistic characteristics and intent of the message.

**Table 1.** MEX-A3T tweets with Aggressive data set distribution of classes.

| Class | Train corpus | Test corpus |
|---|---|---|
| Non Aggressive | 5222 | 2238 |
| Aggressive | 2110 | 905 |
| **Total** | **7332** | **3143** |

The aggressive content samples are shown below, we use # symbol to hide the aggressive word in purpose to avoid any offensive words for the reader.

**Aggresssive Samples:**
*"Sólo a las Pu#..aS MOCOS#S GORDAS Y feas les gusta ese al%man xd"*
*"Profe hijo de las mil pu#..as 6 de calificación como es posible. "*

---

[3] mex-a3t site: https://mexa3t.wixsite.com/home.
[4] II Trolling Aggressive and Cyberbylling workshop.
[5] Iberian Languages Evaluation Forum 2020.

**Non Aggressive Samples:**
*"Put#s Madres ahora comprendo todo, tu tan lava y yo tan frio "*
*" Segunda vez que me pasa. Estoy hasta la madre"*

We follow [15] to split the data, i.e., 80% for training and 20% for testing.
The picture below describes this distribution. We can see that the amount of non-aggressive content is greater which means our data is imbalanced (Fig. 2), but also it reflects the true distribution of data (more detailed in [1]).

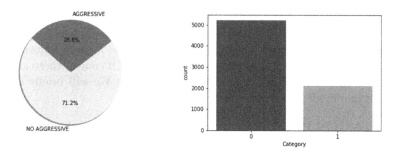

**Fig. 2.** MEX-A3T DataSet with 5222 labeled distribution, left: 28.8% (green) AGGRESSIVE, 71.2% NO AGGRESSIVE (pink), right: bar shows the majority class of the "non-aggressive" (blue) class 0 and 2110 for "aggressive" (orange) class 1. (Color figure online)

## 5    Experiments

This section presents the baselines models, pre-processing techniques, experiments, evaluation methodology, and results. We also discuss how we address the issue of vocabulary performance within Aggressive identification.

### 5.1    Baselines and Task

In order to investigate the Aggressiveness detection for Mexican Spanish Language, we studied the previous techniques and research lines. According the literature and the best performance models, we re-implement the current state of the art model proposed during the MEX-A3T 2020 track [15]. We also took other baselines [3]. Besides BERT there are others neural network models that we will detail below:

– **BOW with SVM** (base-line): The approach is presented as a traditional machine learning approach. The model uses a bag-of-words representation with TF and TF-IDF weights. One of their good results is obtained when applying a SVM and other neural network [4].

- **BI-LSTM** (base-line): This deep learning model approach is a bi-directional GRU model that uses words as inputs. The model also combines the predictions of gender and occupation of users obtained by a reference model, it uses a simple concatenation and one-hot-encodings [14].
- **Transformers** (State-of-the-art): the approach uses the novel pre-trained BERT and performs fine-tuning to accomplish the detection of aggression for Spanish. The BERT variation used is the Spanish transformer-based BERT called BETO[6]. There are also BETO improvements using multiple ensembles of these models, weighting vote schemes and different Data augmentation techniques [15].

Most of the models above work well; however, we also explore deep learning classification models in other languages. Thus, we found a good performance of the VGCN-BERT for English text classification task. Of course, there are other attempts to combine VGCN with BERT (see Sect. 2). We will briefly describe the vanilla model we based on:

- **vanilla-VGCN-BERT**: Our system is mainly based on this model which combines BERT and VGCN. First, the model produces two separate representations through BERT and GCN. Both features are concatenated. Then, fully connected layer and Rectified Linear Unit (ReLU) are applied to classify [16].

There is a large number of models that obtained good results for the task of aggressive content detection on Twitter. We were also able to describe some other scopes that were given for the classification of text in the English language. However, we noted that multi-tasking models or combined models have not yet been proposed to improve the detection of aggressive language especially for Spanish Language. Thereby, we took as a baseline the works described above for the aggressive language detection for Mexican Spanish.

### 5.2 Pre-processing and Model Setting

When using a dataset that came from social media usually has a lot of noise and every tweet needs a pre-processing technique. To implement this work we first noted that there are URL strings to be removed as well as "@", i.e., we retain word text content and remove all unnecessary symbols. After cleaning, we also convert all the text into lower case and tokenized using social media *tweetTokenizer* library from NLTK[7]. We also use the BERT Tokenizer to split the text, so the vocabulary of GCN is always a subset of the BERT vocabulary.

We fine-tune VGCN-BERT model and train the model for the Spanish Aggressive language detection because we want to capture the global context. To get the best performance we are using VGCN with NPMI for measuring the

---

[6] **BETO** is a pre-trained BERT on a large Spanish corpus [9].
[7] http://www.nltk.org/api/nltk.tokenize.html.

correlation between words in the vocabulary such we reduce the range of the meaningful relationship up to 0.2.

The graph embedding size used in the VGCN is set 16 and the hidden graph embedding dimension is 128. Whereas, the pre-trained BERT model use 200 length max of the sequence. Then, the whole model is trained in 8 epoch with a dropout of 0.2. Furthermore, due to the limitation of our GPU memory we use mini batches of 8 to seed the data and a learning rate of 8e−6, $L_2$ loss weight decay of 0.01.

It is worth to mention that all these parameters were defined based on our experimental test results. We also follow the parameter setting of $L_2$ loss weight and the learning rate according to the paper [20]. We also opted to use cross-entropy to optimize the classification. On the other hand, Adam optimizer and class weights were estimated to handle the unbalanced data using *compute_class_weight*[8].

### 5.3   Evaluation Metrics

As we are going to compare VGCN BERT against baselines approaches, we adopt the widely used metric F1-score for text classification, which was also used by [13]. The weighted average F1-score and the macro F1-score were defined as follows [19].

$$F1 = 2 * \frac{precision * recall}{precision + recall} \tag{3}$$

$$\text{Weigthed avg F1} = \sum_{i=1}^{C} F1_{ci} * W_{ci}, \qquad \text{Macro F1} = \frac{1}{C} \sum_{i=1}^{C} F1_{ci} \tag{4}$$

where C: is the each individual different class.

### 5.4   Experimental Results

In this section, we show the results of our VGCN-BERT system and to compare it against the best models for the Mexican Spanish aggressive detection task. We carefully selected the previous outstanding approaches considered as baselines for this task. We also highlight the implementation of the BERT (multi-language) combined with VGCN comparing to the best (SOTA) Spanish pre-trained BERT (BETO). We also found that 5 of the best winning models were based on BETO and clearly outperformed traditional deep learning methods [3]. Those methods are references to compare results under the same criteria. However, to the best of our knowledge, there are very few BERT models combined with other models. Also, the BERT multi-lingual was not much used during the MEX-A3T aggressiveness analysis track at iberLEF 2020 competition. Thereby, our BERT with

---

[8]  https://scikit-learn.org/.../sklearn.util..._weight.compute_class_weight.html.

VGCN system becomes a good alternative for the detection of aggressiveness, since our results show that it clearly outperformed the baselines models as shown in Table 2.

The table shows the "macro F1-score" evaluated with the test set for every model. To compare our proposal against the others, we use the average F1-macro score. We have also shown the scores for the aggressiveness and non-aggressiveness detection tasks. In addition, we also report the best model performed using ensembled BETO models. We noted that the closest score to ours is the BERT ensemble (20 BETOS). Another good classifier is BETO+XGBoost referred to as BETO+msg. On the other hand, we also re-implemented the single BERT-multi-language, the single BERT (Spanish pre-trained BETO), and the aforementioned ensembled BETO following Guzman et al. paper's [15]. This last model varies from 1 BETO to 20 BETOs and was used a voting scheme to compare them against our results.

**Table 2.** Results of the aggressive detection using F1-score in test set.

| Model | F1 aggressive | F1 non-aggressive | F1 macro |
|---|---|---|---|
| BoW-SVM | 0.6760 | 0.8780 | 0.7770 |
| BI-GRU | 0.7124 | 0.8841 | 0.7983 |
| BETO+msg | 0.7720 | 0.9042 | 0.8381 |
| bert (**multi\***) | 0.7809 | 0.9094 | 0.8452 |
| bert (**1 BETO**) | 0.7998 | 0.9195 | 0.8596 |
| bert (20 BETOs) | <u>0.7994</u> | 0.92.23 | <u>0.8608</u> |
| **VGCN-BERT\*** | **0.8124** | **0.9169** | **0.8642** |

\* means our developed system model.

Those results demonstrate that our system which combined VGCN with the fine-tuned BERT (*BETO-uncased*) effectively identifies whether a given tweet contains Aggressive content or not. Furthermore, we see that all models (except ours) have low values when they classify the minority aggressive class.

It is worth emphasizing that even in the case we are using a multi-language BERT model (Not BETO) with VGCN, referred to as **bert multi\***, we are still able to outperform BETO+XGBoost. That shows the improvement over pre-trained BERT model for Spanish text. We also noted that our system obtained a high F1-score on the aggressive class. We obtained the third score on the non-aggressive class. We argue that those results are due to the global information which adds attention to the aggressive class with the vocabulary. One interesting thing that we found is that the VGCN-BERT, without any additional external embedding, obtained comparable results to BERT (20 BETOs).

Preliminary studies for English text classification did not show impressive improvements using VGCN and BERT. However, in this paper we have shown that this model is suitable and fits better in the multi-language scenario. Despite all apparent disadvantage, we have shown that Global information captured using VGCN can contribute to the classification task. Likewise, if we add global to the local context information from BERT then the result is very good at detecting Aggressive language.

## 6 Conclusion

In this paper, we have explored the tight combination of the transfer learning fine-tuning BERT (Spanish pre-trained BETO) model and the Graph Convolutional Network to identify aggressive content for Spanish tweets. We have shown that adding a vocabulary graph, even in a small set of vocabulary for Spanish BERT, could improve the context local information. That was possible since the GCN has proven to be good at capturing the global information of a language. Our experimental results allowed us to state that using VGCN-BERT could be beneficial to detect Aggression content, specially for the Spanish language.

On the other hand, although our system used the original classic BERT version, with disadvantages compared to ensembled BETOs, it is still able to perform well when combined with another neural network such as GCN. Thus, BERT could be improved using the Vocabulary Graph Convolutional Network as our promising results show.

We have also demonstrated that it is still possible to improve the original BERT with models that increase the global knowledge information about the domain-specific language.

Based on our results, we also argue that, for detecting the aggressiveness in tweets, a vocabulary and global information of a language is a path for improving the BERT model as a classifier. Furthermore, we believe that a word within a sentence could contribute a lot if its relationship within a tweet contributes to detect aggressiveness. We also leave open another way to explore GCN for text classification.

## References

1. Álvarez-Carmona, M.Á., et al.: Overview of MEX-A3T at IberEval 2018: authorship and aggressiveness analysis in Mexican Spanish tweets. In: Notebook Papers of 3rd SEPLN Workshop on Evaluation of Human Language Technologies for Iberian Languages (IBEREVAL), Seville, Spain, vol. 6 (2018)
2. Aragón, M.E., Álvarez-Carmona, M.Á., Montes-y Gómez, M., Escalante, H.J., Villasenor-Pineda, L., Moctezuma, D.: Overview of MEX-A3T at IberLEF 2019: authorship and aggressiveness analysis in Mexican Spanish tweets. In: Notebook Papers of 1st SEPLN Workshop on Iberian Languages Evaluation Forum (IberLEF), Bilbao, Spain (2019)
3. Aragón, M., et al.: Overview of MEX-A3T at IberLEF 2020: fake news and aggressiveness analysis in Mexican Spanish. In: Notebook Papers of 2nd SEPLN Workshop on Iberian Languages Evaluation Forum (IberLEF), Malaga, Spain (2020)
4. Arce-Cardenasa, S., Fajardo-Delgadoa, D., Álvarez-Carmonab, M.Á.: TecNM at MEX-A3T 2020: Fake news and aggressiveness analysis in Mexican Spanish (2020)

5. Plaza-del Arco, F.M., Molina-González, M.D., Ureña-López, L.A., Martín-Valdivia, M.T.: Comparing pre-trained language models for Spanish hate speech detection. Expert Syst. Appl. **166**, 114120 (2021)
6. Badjatiya, P., Gupta, S., Gupta, M., Varma, V.: Deep learning for hate speech detection in tweets. In: Proceedings of the 26th International Conference on World Wide Web Companion, pp. 759–760. International World Wide Web Conferences Steering Committee (2017)
7. Battaglia, P.W., et al.: Relational inductive biases, deep learning, and graph networks. arXiv preprint arXiv:1806.01261 (2018)
8. Bouma, G.: Normalized (pointwise) mutual information in collocation extraction. In: Proceedings of GSCL, pp. 31–40 (2009)
9. Canete, J., Chaperon, G., Fuentes, R., Pérez, J.: Spanish pre-trained BERT model and evaluation data. In: PML4DC at ICLR 2020 (2020)
10. Casavantes, M., López, R., González, L.: UACh at MEX-A3T 2020: detecting aggressive tweets by incorporating author and message context. In: Notebook Papers of 2nd SEPLN Workshop on Iberian Languages Evaluation Forum (IberLEF), Malaga, Spain (2020)
11. Davidson, T., Warmsley, D., Macy, M., Weber, I.: Automated hate speech detection and the problem of offensive language. In: Eleventh International AAAI Conference on Web and Social Media (2017)
12. Devlin, J., Chang, M.W., Lee, K., Toutanova, K.: BERT: pre-training of deep bidirectional transformers for language understanding. arXiv preprint arXiv:1810.04805 (2018)
13. Díaz-Torres, M.J., Morán-Méndez, P.A., Villasenor-Pineda, L., Montes, M., Aguilera, J., Meneses-Lerín, L.: Automatic detection of offensive language in social media: defining linguistic criteria to build a Mexican Spanish dataset. In: Proceedings of the Second Workshop on Trolling, Aggression and Cyberbullying, pp. 132–136 (2020)
14. Garrido-Espinosa, M., Rosales-Pérez, A., López-Monroy, A.: GRU with author profiling information to detect aggressiveness. In: Notebook Papers of 2nd SEPLN Workshop on Iberian Languages Evaluation Forum (IberLEF), Malaga, Spain (2020)
15. Guzman-Silverio, M., Balderas-Paredes, A., López-Monroy, A.: Transformers and data augmentation for aggressiveness detection in Mexican Spanish. In: Notebook Papers of 2nd SEPLN Workshop on Iberian Languages Evaluation Forum (IberLEF), Malaga, Spain (2020)
16. Jeong, C., Jang, S., Park, E., Choi, S.: A context-aware citation recommendation model with BERT and graph convolutional networks. Scientometrics **124**(3), 1907–1922 (2020)
17. Kipf, T.N., Welling, M.: Semi-supervised classification with graph convolutional networks. arXiv preprint arXiv:1609.02907 (2016)
18. Kumar, R., et al.: Proceedings of the second workshop on trolling, aggression and cyberbullying (2020)
19. Lever, J., Krzywinski, M., Altman, N.: Classification evaluation (2016)
20. Lu, Z., Du, P., Nie, J.-Y., et al.: VGCN-BERT: augmenting BERT with graph embedding for text classification. In: Jose, J.M. (ed.) ECIR 2020. LNCS, vol. 12035, pp. 369–382. Springer, Cham (2020). https://doi.org/10.1007/978-3-030-45439-5_25
21. Park, J.H., Fung, P.: One-step and two-step classification for abusive language detection on twitter. arXiv preprint arXiv:1706.01206 (2017)

22. Samghabadi, N.S., Patwa, P., Srinivas, P., Mukherjee, P., Das, A., Solorio, T.: Aggression and misogyny detection using BERT: a multi-task approach. In: Proceedings of the Second Workshop on Trolling, Aggression and Cyberbullying, pp. 126–131 (2020)

23. Schmidt, A., Wiegand, M.: A survey on hate speech detection using natural language processing. In: Proceedings of the Fifth International Workshop on Natural Language Processing for Social Media, pp. 1–10 (2017)

24. Shang, J., Ma, T., Xiao, C., Sun, J.: Pre-training of graph augmented transformers for medication recommendation. arXiv preprint arXiv:1906.00346 (2019)

25. Tanase, M.A., Zaharia, G.E., Cercel, D.C., Dascalu, M.: Detecting aggressiveness in Mexican Spanish social media content by fine-tuning transformer-based models (2020)

26. Vaswani, A., et al.: Attention is all you need. arXiv preprint arXiv:1706.03762 (2017)

27. Villatoro-Tello, E., Ramırez-de-la Rosa, G., Kumar, S., Parida, S., Motlicek, P.: Idiap and UAM participation at MEX-A3T evaluation campaign. In: Notebook Papers of 2nd SEPLN Workshop on Iberian Languages Evaluation Forum (IberLEF), Malaga, Spain (2020)

28. Waseem, Z., Davidson, T., Warmsley, D., Weber, I.: Understanding abuse: a typology of abusive language detection subtasks. arXiv preprint arXiv:1705.09899 (2017)

29. Waseem, Z., Hovy, D.: Hateful symbols or hateful people? Predictive features for hate speech detection on Twitter. In: Proceedings of the NAACL Student Research Workshop, pp. 88–93 (2016)

30. Yao, L., Mao, C., Luo, Y.: Graph convolutional networks for text classification. In: Proceedings of the AAAI Conference on Artificial Intelligence, vol. 33, pp. 7370–7377 (2019)

31. Zampieri, M., Malmasi, S., Nakov, P., Rosenthal, S., Farra, N., Kumar, R.: SemEval-2019 task 6: identifying and categorizing offensive language in social media (OffensEval). arXiv preprint arXiv:1903.08983 (2019)

32. Zhang, Z., Luo, L.: Hate speech detection: a solved problem? the challenging case of long tail on twitter. Semant. Web **10**(5), 925–945 (2019)

# An Empirical Study of Text Features for Identifying Subjective Sentences in Portuguese

Miguel de Oliveira[✉] and Tiago de Melo

Intelligent Systems Laboratory, Superior School of Technology, Amazonas State University, Manaus, AM, Brazil
{mvo.snf18,tmelo}@uea.edu.br

**Abstract.** Studies in sentiment analysis have examined how different features are effective in identifying subjective sentences. Several studies on sentiment analysis exist in the literature that have already performed some evaluation of NLP classifications. However, the vast majority of them did not handle texts in the Brazilian Portuguese language, and there is no one to consider the combination of sets of text features of NLP tasks with classifiers. Therefore, in our investigation, we combined empirical features to identify subjective sentences in Portuguese and provide a comprehensive analysis of each set of features' relative importance using a representative set of user reviews.

**Keywords:** Sentiment analysis · Natural language processing · Data mining

## 1 Introduction

A vast quantity of user reviews is constantly published on the Web every day in recent years, thanks to the rapid development of social media. These reviews assist other users in making decisions, such as purchasing new products, as they are also useful for companies to improve their products. Sentiment analysis (SA) is an area of study that aims to find computational techniques to extract and analyze people's opinions and to identify the sentiment expressed in those opinions. Subjectivity identification is an essential task of SA because most polarity detection tools are optimized for distinguishing between positive and negative texts. Subjectivity identification hence ensures that factual information is filtered out and only opinionated information is passed on to the polarity classifier [9]. Several studies have demonstrated that information provided by some textual features is valuable for sentiment classification [2,11,20]. Many types of text features have been proposed and evaluated in the literature, such as syntactic features and part-of-speech features.

SA for the English language is well advanced. However, the linguistic resources available for sentiment analysis in other languages are still limited [23].

© Springer Nature Switzerland AG 2021
A. Britto and K. Valdivia Delgado (Eds.): BRACIS 2021, LNAI 13074, pp. 374–388, 2021.
https://doi.org/10.1007/978-3-030-91699-2_26

Portuguese is one of the languages with few linguistic resources available, despite being among the top five languages used online. Thus, the small number of specific works and resources for Portuguese-focused sentiment analysis provides a scenario with great challenges and opportunities.

Given this scenario, our study aims to present research regarding the use of machine learning algorithms for subjectivity identification of user reviews published in Portuguese. In addition, we will also investigate which text features are more important to address during this task. In particular, we will show that certain features play a more important role than others under different circumstances. In this way, this work contributes to an analysis of these combinations for the SA task from texts written in the Portuguese language, with the objective of answering the following research questions:

RQ1: Is there a single machine learning algorithm for subjectivity identification that is always the best for a diversified set of datasets?

RQ2: Given a set of feature groups, is there a group that is always the best regardless of the algorithm used?

RQ3: How do different feature combinations affect the predictive performance of a classifier?

We carried out an exhaustive evaluation of combinations considering five classifiers for four sentiment analysis datasets in the Brazilian Portuguese language, with the aim being to answer these research questions. We chose four well-known algorithms used in text classification: Gradient Boosting Trees (GBT), Maximum Entropy (ME), Random Forest (RF), and Support Vector Machine (SVM). We also used AutoML, a machine learning algorithm where the model finds the solution to the given data and produces results automatically. Specifically, we used AutoGluon[1] because it was one of the most recently released AutoML frameworks [14]. We didn't focus on presenting the best combinations or even improving the state-of-the-art predictive performance for each dataset. Instead, the goal was to raise the importance of text features for subjectivity identification.

Our main contribution is to report an extensive set of experiments aimed to evaluate the relative effectiveness of different linguistic features for subjectivity identification.

The remainder of this paper is organized as follows. Section 2 provides a brief description of the main related works. Then, the method and materials are described in Sect. 3. Experiments are reported in Sect. 4, where we also describe the evaluation and discuss the results. Finally, we draw the conclusion and future works in Sect. 5.

# 2   Related Work

In this section, we discuss prior works related to subjectivity identification on user reviews. The main approach is using machine learning techniques with different linguistic features. There are many types of classifiers for this task using

---

[1] https://auto.gluon.ai.

supervised learning algorithms, but the most popular classifiers are Support Vector Machine (SVM), Naive Bayes (NB), and Maximum Entropy [2,3]. Previous studies [2,11] also have explored the use of English features, such as adjectives, nouns and phrases, and have applied these features to identify subjective sentences. Chenlo and Losada [11] in their survey paper evaluated a wide range of features that have been employed to date for subjectivity classification. Some of the prominent features include POS, lexicon, number and proportion of subjective terms in the sentence, and so on. The subjectivity classification part is relevant to our study.

Moraes et al. [19] investigate the problem of subjectivity classification for the Portuguese language. They created a corpus of tweets on the area of technology called *ComputerBR*. Inspired by the methods for English, the evaluated methods were based on the use of sentiment lexicons and machine learning algorithms, such as SVM and Naive Bayes. Carvalho *et al.* [7] proposed a comparative study test between three learning algorithms (Naive Bayes, SVM and Maximum Entropy) and three feature selection methods for classifying texts of election-related news in Brazil. Belisário et al. [5] focused specifically on the task of subjectivity classification. The authors reported the study and comparison of machine learning methods of different paradigms (Naive-Bayes and SVM) to perform subjectivity classification of book review sentences in Portuguese. The authors also evaluated lexical and discourse features.

In summary, most methods for subjectivity identification are supervised and use different subsets of text features for English. Therefore, there is not a clear picture of the impact of every feature set for the most common machine learning algorithms. Thus, there is room for further studies in Portuguese. In our work, we evaluate a large set of text features with machine learning algorithms, including a recent automatic machine learning approach, for subjectivity identification from texts written in the Brazilian Portuguese language. We evaluated all features and algorithms across four different datasets.

## 3　Materials and Methods

We deal with a binary classification task: factual *versus* subjective sentences. This task can be performed by text classifiers composed of training data in a supervised strategy.

### 3.1　Features

The characteristics of user reviews will be encoded as features in vector representation. These vectors and the corresponding labels feed the classifiers. To build our classifiers, we considered the following sets of feature groups.

**POS Features.** Part-Of-Speech (POS) information is used to locate different types of information of interest inside text documents. For instance, adjectives usually represent opinions, while adverbs are used as modifiers to represent the degree of expressiveness of opinions. For the extraction of POS tags, the sentences were initially tokenized. Then the tokens were tagged with their respective word classes using spaCy[2] POS tagger [16]. The tokens were then lowercased. The following POS features[3] were extracted from the processed sentences: adjective (ADJ), conjunction (ADP), adverb (ADV), verb auxiliary (AUX), coordinating conjunction (CCONJ), determiner (DET), interjection (INTJ), noun (NOUN), cardinal number (NUM), pronoun (PRON), proper noun (PROPN), punctuation mark (PUNCT), subordinating conjunction (SCONJ), symbol (SYM), verbs (VERB), comparative (COMP), superlative (SUP), and other tags (X). The latter is used for words that can not be assigned a real POS category for any reason. In Table 1, each POS feature is described with an example and its feature values (FV).

**Syntactic Patterns.** Natural language texts are based on syntactic patterns which create a sequence of words based on grammar rules. In our study, we used syntactic patterns as indicative of subjective sentences. The patterns were originally proposed by Turney [25] and we adapted them to use spaCy toolkit. In Table 2, each syntactic pattern is described with an example and its feature values (FV). The rules are described in Table 2 with arrows ($\rightarrow$) denoting immediate sequence between two POS tags, while *Not* indicates that the absence of a given tag is expected. In feature 23, the verb can be in different forms such as participles (PCP), gerund (GER), perfect simple (PS), and imperfect (IMPF).

**Sentiment Lexicons.** Some of the most important indicators in the analysis of subjective text are sentiment lexicons. These features are based on counting the sentiment-bearing terms that occur in the sentence [1,10]. We consider the following terms: subjectives, positives, and negatives. The sentiment lexicon is a Portuguese translation of the lexicon from Pennebaker et al. [22], a well-known subjective classifier [4]. We include the number and percentage of opinionated terms in a sentence as features for our classifiers. We also consider the number and percentage of exclamation marks "!" and question marks "?" in the sentences because they usually indicate the strength of sentiment. In Table 3, each sentiment lexicon feature is described with an example and its feature values (FV).

**Concept-Level Features.** Concept-level features can help with a semantic analysis of text through web ontologies or semantic networks. Hence, they allow for aggregating conceptual and affective information associated with natural language opinions [24]. We adopted the same set of concept-level features used in [11], which in turn, measured different aspects of these concepts, including:

---

[2] The Python package version was v3.0.0 with model pt_core_news_lg, except for the COMP and SUP POS tags, which were extracted with v2.2.0 and model pt_core_news_sm.

[3] https://universaldependencies.org/u/pos.

**Table 1.** Set of POS features.

| #Feat. | Description | Example | FV |
|---|---|---|---|
| 1 | Number of ADJ | *Local* **agradável.** (**Nice** place.) | 1 |
| 2 | Number of ADP | *Sucos* **com** *frutas locais além* **dos** *tradicionais.* (Juices **with** local fruits beyond **the** traditional.) | 2 |
| 3 | Number of ADV | *O melhor fondue que* **já** *comi!!!!* (The best fondue I've **ever** had!!!!) | 1 |
| 4 | Number of AUX | *O preço* **é** *mais salgado mas* **é** *justo.* (The price **is** salty but it **is** fair.) | 2 |
| 5 | Number of CCONJ | *Funciona para almoço* **e** *jantar.* (Opens for lunch **and** dinner.) | 1 |
| 6 | Number of DET | **No** *geral,* **um** *bom restaurante!* (**In** general, it's **a** good restaurant!) | 2 |
| 7 | Number of INTJ | **Ah** *outra mega decepção.* (**Oh** another mega disappointment.) | 1 |
| 8 | Number of NOUN | **Buffet** *variado de* **pratos** *quentes e frios.* (Varied hot and cold **plates buffet.**) | 2 |
| 9 | Number of NUM | *Nota* **zero!** (A **zero** grade!) | 1 |
| 10 | Number of PRON | **Isso** *verdadeiramente* **me** *impressiona!* (**This** truly impresses **me!**) | 2 |
| 11 | Number of PROPN | **Coco Bambu** *é maravilhoso em qualquer lugar!* (**Coco Bambu** is awesome everywhere!) | 1 |
| 12 | Number of PUNCT | *Muito bom**!!!*** (Very good**!!!**) | 3 |
| 13 | Number of SCONJ | **Para** *quem não conhece ainda, recomendo.* (**For** those who don't know it yet, I recommend it.) | 1 |
| 14 | Number of SYM | *Os pratos tem os valores médios de* **R$***50,00.* (The plates have an average prices of **R$**50,00.) | 1 |
| 15 | Number of VERB | **Vim comer** *nessa pizzaria no domingo.* (I **came** to **eat** at this pizza parlor on Sunday.) | 2 |
| 16 | Number of COMP | *A* **melhor** *peixaria da cidade!* (The **best** fish restaurant in the city!) | 1 |
| 17 | Number of SUP | **Ótimo** *ambiente e atendimento.* (**Great** ambiance and service.) | 1 |
| 18 | Number of X | *Um* **fast food** *que cumpre o que promete.* (A **fast food** store that delivers what it promises.) | 1 |

**Table 2.** Set of syntactic patterns.

| #Feat. | Description | Example | FV |
|---|---|---|---|
| 19 | ADJ → NOUN | *O melhor fondue que já comi!!!!*<br>(The **best fondue** I've ever had!!!!) | 1 |
| 20 | ADV → ADJ → Not (NOUN) | *Vergonhoso cobrarem tão caro.*<br>(It's shameful they charge **so expensive**.) | 1 |
| 21 | ADJ → ADJ → Not (NOUN) | *Uma explosão de sabores regionais inigualável!*<br>(An **unequaled** explosion of **regional**<br>flavors!) | 1 |
| 22 | NOUN → ADJ → Not (NOUN) | *Preços bem salgados por sinal.*<br>(**Very salty prices** by the way.) | 1 |
| 23 | ADV → VERB + {PCP \| GER \| PS \| IMPF} | *Fomos muito bem atendidos!*<br>(We were **very well served**!) | 1 |

**Table 3.** Set of lexicon features.

| #Feat. | Description | Example | FV |
|---|---|---|---|
| 24 | Number of subjecticve terms | *Comida boa por um bom preço.*<br>(**Good** food for a **good** price.) | 3 |
| 25 | Number of positve terms | *As comidas são excelentes.*<br>(The food is **excellent**.) | 1 |
| 26 | Number of negative terms | *Atendimento da recepcionista da porta ruim.*<br>(**Bad** door receptionist service.) | 1 |
| 27 | Number of marks | *Foi tudo muito gostoso!*<br>(It was all very tasteful!) | 1 |
| 28 | Proportion of subjective terms | *Comida boa por um bom preço.*<br>(**Good** food for a **good** price.) | 0.429 |
| 29 | Proportion of positive terms | *As comidas são excelentes.*<br>(The food is **excellent**.) | 0.2 |
| 30 | Proportion of negative terms | *Atendimento da recepcionista da porta ruim.*<br>(**Bad** door receptionist service.) | 0.143 |
| 31 | Proportion of mark terms | *Foi tudo muito gostoso!*<br>(It was all very tasteful!) | 0.2 |

*pleasantness, attention, aptitude, sensitivity,* and *polarity.* To do this, we used the SenticNet corpus [6]. We have represented this group of features considering only each concept's absolute score since highly opinionated concepts tend to have higher absolute values. In Table 4, each concept-level feature is described with an example and its feature values (FV).

**Structural Features.** Structural features encode the number of words, words with an upper letter, and the number of upper letters. Intuitively, the number of words could be indicative of subjectivity. For instance, factual sentences may be shorter [11]. We include the ratio of the number of uppercase words and uppercase characters in a sentence as features for our classifiers. In Table 5, each structural feature is described with an example and its feature values (FV).

**Twitter Features.** Because the language used on Twitter is often informal and differs from traditional text types, we used the number of URLs, mentions and elongated words as features [18]. We also include emoji sentiment scores provided

**Table 4.** Set of concept-level features.

| #Feat. | Description | Example | FV |
|---|---|---|---|
| 32 | Sum of scores of pleasantness | *O ambiente é bem amplo, iluminado.* (The place is **very** spacious, **illuminated**.) | 1.530 |
| 33 | Sum of scores of sensitivity | *Comida muito boa.* (**Very** good **food**.) | 0.610 |
| 34 | Sum of scores of aptitude | *Tudo com qualidade.* (**Everything** with **quality**.) | 1.160 |
| 35 | Sum of scores of attention | *Vale a pena conhecer.* (It's **worth knowing**.) | 1.058 |
| 36 | Sum of scores of polarity | *O delivery é bem rápido.* (Delivery is **very fast**.) | 1.392 |
| 37 | Avg. of scores of pleasantness | *O ambiente é bem amplo, iluminado.* (The place is **very** spacious, **illuminated**.) | 0.191 |
| 38 | Avg. of scores of sensitivity | *Comida muito boa.* (**Very** good **food**.) | 0.153 |
| 39 | Avg. of scores of aptitude | *Tudo com qualidade.* (**Everything** with **quality**.) | 0.290 |
| 40 | Avg. of scores of attention | *Vale a pena conhecer.* (It's **worth knowing**.) | 0.212 |
| 41 | Avg. of scores of polarity | *O delivery é bem rápido.* (Delivery is **very fast**.) | 0.232 |

**Table 5.** Set of text structural features.

| #Feat. | Description | Example | FV |
|---|---|---|---|
| 42 | Number of words of the sentence | *O restaurante fica dentro do hotel Vila Amazônia* (The restaurant is inside the Vila Amazonia hotel) | 8 |
| 43 | Number of words with upper letter | *Comemos um prato Camarões Beira mar!* (**We** ate a dish **Shrimps Sea** shore!) | 3 |
| 44 | Number of upper letters | *Ou seja, simplesmente DIVINOOO!* (That is, simply **DIVIIINE!**) | 9 |
| 45 | Ratio of words with upper letters to lower letters | *Comemos um prato Camarões Beira mar!* (**We** ate a dish **Shrimps Sea** shore!) | 0.5 |
| 46 | Ratio of the uppercase characters to the sentence length | *Ou seja, simplesmente DIVINOOO !* (That is, simply **DIVIIINE!**) | 0.29 |

in [17] and emoticons sentiment scores provided in [15]. In Table 6, each Twitter feature is described with an example and its feature values (VoF).

**Miscellaneous Features.** We adopted a set of miscellaneous features that did not belong to the aforementioned groups. As adopted by Palshikar et al. [21], we include the number of named entities and datetimes. The intuition is that factual information generally has lots of dates and entities. We also include the number of words that are present in a dictionary [18]. Therefore, misspelled words were not counted. We used a list of more than 300,000 words[4]. In Table 7, each miscellaneous feature is described with an example and its feature values (FV).

---

[4] https://www.ime.usp.br/~pf/dicios/index.html.

**Table 6.** Set of Twitter features.

| #Feat. | Description | Example | FV |
|---|---|---|---|
| 47 | Number of URLs | *Vendo! Compartilha aí gente!* http://fb.me/24tl16IwA<br>(Selling! Share it folks! http://fb.me/24tl16IwA) | 1 |
| 48 | Number of mentions (@user) | *Comprei um notebook da **@Dell** vamos ver se eu vou gostar!!!*<br>( I bought a notebook from **@Dell** let's see if I will like it!!!) | 1 |
| 49 | Number of elongated words | *Essa Dell é demais... Note **chegooooou** ?*<br>(Dell is awesome... Note **arriiiived** ?) | 1 |
| 50 | Polarity of emojis | *O cara da dell vem amanha arrumar meu not*<br>(The guy from dell comes tomorrow to fix my *not* ) | 0.693 |
| 51 | Polarity of emoticons | *Notebook #dell sem teclado #abnt2 desanima... :-(*<br>(#Dell notebook without #abnt2 keyboard discourages... **:-()** | -1 |

**Table 7.** Set of miscellaneous features.

| #Feat. | Description | Example | FV |
|---|---|---|---|
| 52 | Number of named entities | *As pizzas da **Forneria** são ótimas!!*<br>(The pizzas from **Forneria** are great!!) | 1 |
| 53 | Number of datetime | *Cheguei no local na noite do dia **25/04/2019**.*<br>(I arrived at the place on the evening of **04/25/2019**.) | 1 |
| 54 | Number of correct words | ***Boas** pixzzas **e boas massas**.*<br>(**Good** pixzzas **and good pasta**.) | 4 |

## 3.2   Models

We chose four conventional methods frequently used in text classification when the features set was selected to investigate which feature groups are best between: Gradient Boosting Trees (GBT), Maximum Entropy (ME), Random Forest (RF), and Support Vector Machine (SVM). We also used AutoGluon because it is one of the most recently released AutoML frameworks. We used the Python Scikit-Learn[5] library to build conventional methods.

## 3.3   Recursive Feature Elimination

Recursive Feature Elimination (RFE) is considered a kind of wrapper feature selection method [8]. Initially, all the features are selected for feature selection. At every iteration, some features will be removed from the full features set, based on the inference of the training model. The goal is to repeatedly build a model and choose the best-performing feature. This procedure is repeated until all features in the dataset are evaluated. Features are then ranked according to the elimination order. As such, it is a greedy optimization for finding the best performing subset of features. The coefficients of features are generally used as the index of importance evaluation. The closer the coefficient to 0, the smaller effect on the target variable is. The importance ranking of the candidate features

---

[5] https://scikit-learn.org/stable.

is finally achieved by following the sequence order of elimination of features during every iteration.

# 4     Experiments

## 4.1     Setup

Table 8 presents the datasets we have used in our experiments. Dataset ReLi contains 2,000 sentences from user reviews of books taken from [12]. Dataset ComputerBR consists of 2,281 sentences of tweets regarding computers taken from [19]. Dataset Tripadvisor contains 1,049 sentences from user reviews of restaurants taken from [20]. Dataset Hotel consists of 840 sentences from user reviews of hotel services taken from [13]. Note that only dataset ReLi is well-balanced.

Table 8. Summary of the datasets.

| Dataset | #Sentences | | #Total |
|---------|------------|---------------|--------|
|         | Factual | Subjective |        |
| ReLi | 1,000 (50.00%) | 1,000 (50.00%) | 2,000 |
| ComputerBR | 1,677 (73.52%) | 604 (26.48%) | 2,281 |
| Tripadvisor | 458 (43.67%) | 591 (56.33%) | 1,049 |
| Hotel | 311 (37.03%) | 529 (62.97%) | 840 |

## 4.2     Metrics

For a particular sentence, the class predicted by a model is considered correct if it matches the class assigned in the datasets described previously. We use traditional metrics for evaluating the performance of models - macro-averaged Precision (P), Recall (R) and F-score (F1). For macro-averaged metrics, we compute the metrics for each class separately, then take their average to prevent bias towards high-frequency classes.

## 4.3     Comparison of Classifier Performances

To answer the research question RQ1, we conducted experiments to confirm whether there is a single, best-suited machine learning algorithm for subjectivity identification for a diversified set of datasets. Table 9 shows each classifier's performance in terms of F-measure $(F_1)$ and accuracy (A) along with its standard deviation. The bold values indicate the best scores. In this experiment, each result denotes an average of 5-fold cross-validation.

**Table 9.** Classification performance of each classifier on the four datasets.

| | ComputerBR | | TripAdvisor | | ReLi | | Hotel | | Average | |
|---|---|---|---|---|---|---|---|---|---|---|
| | $F_1$ | A | $F_1$ | A | $F_1$ | A | $F_1$ | A | F1 | A |
| SVM | 0.701 ± 0.002 | 0.726 ± 0.002 | 0.784 ± 0.004 | 0.789 ± 0.004 | 0.662 ± 0.002 | 0.663 ± 0.002 | 0.695 ± 0.005 | 0.718 ± 0.005 | 0.711 ± 0.003 | 0.724 ± 0.003 |
| GBT | 0.695 ± 0.002 | 0.773 ± 0.002 | 0.791 ± 0.004 | 0.796 ± 0.004 | 0.653 ± 0.002 | 0.654 ± 0.002 | 0.732 ± 0.005 | 0.758 ± 0.005 | 0.718 ± 0.003 | 0.745 ± 0.003 |
| ME | 0.682 ± 0.002 | 0.772 ± 0.002 | 0.783 ± 0.004 | 0.786 ± 0.004 | 0.662 ± 0.002 | 0.662 ± 0.002 | 0.690 ± 0.005 | 0.718 ± 0.005 | 0.704 ± 0.003 | 0.735 ± 0.003 |
| RF | 0.664 ± 0.002 | 0.768 ± 0.002 | 0.784 ± 0.004 | 0.790 ± 0.004 | 0.654 ± 0.002 | 0.655 ± 0.002 | 0.738 ± 0.005 | 0.771 ± 0.005 | 0.710 ± 0.002 | 0.746 ± 0.003 |
| AG | 0.696 ± 0.002 | 0.776 ± 0.002 | 0.776 ± 0.004 | 0.784 ± 0.004 | 0.636 ± 0.002 | 0.637 ± 0.002 | 0.709 ± 0.005 | 0.746 ± 0.005 | 0.704 ± 0.003 | 0.736 ± 0.003 |

The results in Table 9 reveal the following trends. Overall, the GBT model achieved the best average $F_1$ among all the datasets. The difference in the results with the best classifier (RF) in terms of the accuracy measure is only 0.001 on average. We also note that although the models used in our experiments were considerably different, there is minimal difference in their final results. For example, the difference between the best (GBT) and worst (ME and AG) classifier was only 0.014 for $F_1$ average. Meanwhile, the difference between the best (GBT) and worst (SVM) classifier was only 0.021 for accuracy average.

To ensure that the results were not achieved by chance, the Friedman test was performed on the results. The Friedman test is a non-parametric test used to measure the statistical differences of methods over multiple datasets. For each dataset, the methods were ranked based on the results of classifier metrics. We adopted $F_1$ metrics to rank the results.

Let $M$ be the number of models evaluated and $N$ be the number of datasets. The Friedman test is distributed according to the Fisher distribution with $M-1$ and $(M-1)(N-1)$ degrees of freedom. The null hypothesis in the Friedman test means that all methods perform equivalently at the significance level $\alpha$. The null hypothesis is accepted when the value of Fisher distribution is less than the critical value; otherwise, it is rejected. For a confidence interval $\alpha=0.05$, $M=5$, and $N=4$, the critical value was 3.259. Therefore, the null hypothesis is accepted as 1.764.

### 4.4  Feature Ablation Study

To answer the research question RQ2, we conducted a *feature ablation* study to evaluate the importance of the proposed features in the performance of the classifiers.

An ablation study is performed by removing sets of features individually and evaluating the classifier's performance to identify which of those features impact the most on the results. For each feature group, we retrained and retested the best performing classifier overall (GBT, as shown in Sect. 4.3), evaluating its performance with 5-fold cross-validation and $F_1$ score as a metric.

In Table 10, each row labeled as *All - F* represents the results obtained by training the classifier with all groups of features, except $F$. The row labeled as *All* shows the results for all groups of features together. For each dataset, we show the average $F_1$ achieved between the two classes (*factual* and *subjectivity*), and the $F_1$ for each class.

We also provide the difference of each $F_1$ measure from the score obtained by all groups of features together, labeled as *Loss*. A positive *Loss* indicates that a group $F$ of features contributes significantly to the overall performance. A negative *Loss* indicates that removing $F$ from the features set, in fact, improves the classifier's performance.

We observed that different groups of features perform differently in each dataset. However, it is noticeable that the POS features always contribute to all datasets. This may indicate that Part-of-Speech tags are very relevant information for subjectivity classification in the Portuguese language, being the only group in our experiments shown to be neither structure nor domain-specific.

It is interesting to mention that the Syntactic Patterns group have a low contribution for ReLi, TripAdvisor, and Hotel datasets, and a negative performance for ComputerBR which contains only tweets. Since Syntactic Patterns tend to be language-specific, many of the chosen rules potentially do not represent opinions in Portuguese texts. Likewise, the whole group of concept-level features only contributed to the Hotel dataset. Interestingly, this is the smallest dataset used in our experiments. Thus, concept-level features may work better in smaller scopes.

We also observed that, as expected, the most contributing group in the ComputerBR dataset was the *Twitter* group. This indicates that extracting specific features of Twitter texts is a better strategy than relying on language-specific resources such as sentiment lexicons and language patterns.

**Table 10.** Results obtained by the feature ablation study.

| | ComputerBR | | | | ReLi | | | | TripAdvisor | | | | Hotel | | | |
|---|---|---|---|---|---|---|---|---|---|---|---|---|---|---|---|---|
| | $F_1$ score | | | Loss (Avg.) | $F_1$ score | | | Loss (Avg.) | $F_1$ score | | | Loss (Avg.) | $F_1$ score | | | Loss (Avg.) |
| | Fact. | Subj. | Avg. | | Fact. | Subj. | Avg. | | Fact. | Subj. | Avg. | | Fact. | Subj. | Avg. | |
| All - POS | .844 | .519 | .681 | .013 | .650 | .625 | .638 | .015 | .718 | .794 | .756 | .035 | .616 | .801 | .708 | .023 |
| All - Synt. Patterns | .850 | .555 | .702 | -.007 | .649 | .611 | .653 | .000 | .739 | .805 | .790 | .001 | .637 | .810 | .723 | .008 |
| All - Sent. Lexicons | .851 | .539 | .695 | .000 | .599 | .608 | .603 | .050 | .740 | .827 | .783 | .007 | .656 | .819 | .737 | -.005 |
| All - Concept-level | .853 | .562 | .707 | -.012 | .655 | .655 | .655 | -.001 | .758 | .825 | .792 | -.001 | .625 | .757 | .691 | .040 |
| All - Structural | .844 | .524 | .687 | .007 | .658 | .635 | .646 | .007 | .764 | .825 | .794 | -.003 | .577 | .781 | .729 | .003 |
| All - Twitter | .839 | .513 | .676 | .018 | .664 | .643 | .653 | .000 | .760 | .655 | .793 | -.001 | .658 | .803 | .730 | .001 |
| All - Miscellaneous | .849 | .542 | .696 | -.001 | .665 | .645 | .655 | -.001 | .754 | .820 | .787 | .004 | .635 | .803 | .719 | .012 |
| All | .849 | .540 | .695 | .000 | .664 | .643 | .653 | .000 | .760 | .823 | .791 | .000 | .647 | .816 | .732 | .000 |

## 4.5   Feature Ranking

To answer the research question RQ3, we performed the *Recursive Feature Elimination* (RFE) algorithm to evaluate how different combinations of features affect the predictive performance of a classifier. Firstly, all 54 features are used to train the GBT model. The performance of each feature is separately maintained. GBT was chosen because it achieved the best performance as a learning algorithm (see Sect. 4.3). The evaluation is performed using 5-fold cross-validation and macro $F_1$ score as the metric. Secondly, the features with the lowest coefficients will be omitted during every epoch and retrained after removing each feature from the input set and continued until the required number of features are retained. As an outcome of RFE, features with the worst coefficients are eliminated individually during every iteration of the training process.

Figure 1 shows the performance of the GBT model using different sizes of feature subsets. The best result in each dataset is identified with a star. First of all, we can see that using all the features does not produce the best results. Therefore, using a technique of feature selection is necessary to remove unnecessary features. Interestingly, the best results in the Hotel dataset were achieved with just 8 features. In addition, we observed an improvement in the results when using feature selection. For example, using feature selection yielded gains of $F_1$ of approximately 10.9% for ComputerBR and 2.6% for the Hotel dataset.

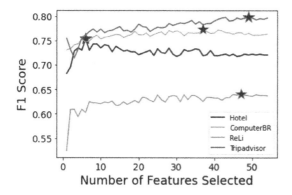

**Fig. 1.** Number of features against the $F_1$ score plot for each dataset.

Figure 2 lists the top 10 features for each dataset. Individually, the number of adjectives (*Feat. 1* - Table 1) is the most important feature in three datasets (ComputerBR, ReLi, and Tripadvisor). This feature is still the eleventh most important feature in the Hotel dataset. Concept-level features (Table 4) are the most important group of features. Concept-level features represent 65% among the top 10 features of the four datasets.

It can be concluded that RFE as a feature selection assists in increasing the classification accuracy by generating a more significant feature-weighted ranking. The number of features plays an important role in text classification. A large number of features does not guarantee the best classification performances and vice-versa. Yet, the best number of features will generate optimum classification accuracy.

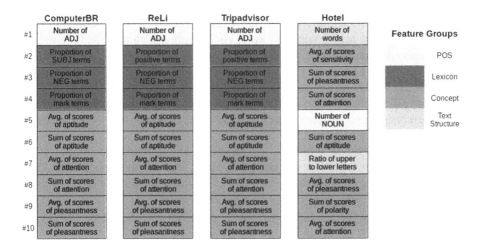

**Fig. 2.** Ranking of the top 10 features for each dataset.

## 5    Conclusion

In this paper, we have presented an empirical study of a vast set of text features for identifying subjective sentences for the Portuguese language. We examined the performance of these features within supervised learning methods along with four different datasets.

Firstly, we examined the performance of well-known machine learning algorithms for subjectivity identification. The experimental results showed that, although the classifiers used in our experiments were considerably different, there is minimal difference between the results obtained. This indicates that choosing the correct set of features is the most important factor for identifying subjective sentences. Secondly, we conducted a feature ablation study to evaluate the importance of the proposed features in the performance of the classifiers. The experimental results showed that POS features always contribute to all datasets. This indicates that POS tags are the most relevant feature group for subjectivity classification. Finally, we performed the recursive feature elimination algorithm to evaluate how different combinations of individual features affect the performance of a classifier. The experimental results showed that the number of adjectives is the most important feature in three out of four datasets. It was also possible to conclude that feature selection assists in increasing the classification accuracy.

In future works, we will try to evaluate the same set of text features against other NLP tasks, such as identifying comparative sentences and calculating the polarity of subjective sentences.

**Acknowledgments.** The authors are thankful for the financial and material support provided by the Amazonas State Research Support Foundation (FAPEAM) through Project PPP 04/2017 and for the assistance of the Intelligent Systems Laboratory (LSI) of the Amazonas State University (UEA). We also gratefully acknowledge the support provided by the *Gratificação de Produtividade Acadêmica* (GPA) of the Amazonas State University (Portaria 086/2021).

# References

1. Agarwal, A., Xie, B., Vovsha, I., Rambow, O., Passonneau, R.J.: Sentiment analysis of twitter data. In: Proceedings of the Workshop on Language in Social Media (LSM 2011), pp. 30–38 (2011)
2. Almatarneh, S., Gamallo, P.: Linguistic features to identify extreme opinions: an empirical study. In: Yin, H., Camacho, D., Novais, P., Tallón-Ballesteros, A.J. (eds.) IDEAL 2018. LNCS, vol. 11314, pp. 215–223. Springer, Cham (2018). https://doi.org/10.1007/978-3-030-03493-1_23
3. Almatarneh, S., Gamallo, P.: Comparing supervised machine learning strategies and linguistic features to search for very negative opinions. Information **10**(1), 16 (2019)
4. Balage Filho, P., Pardo, T.A.S., Aluísio, S.: An evaluation of the Brazilian Portuguese liwc dictionary for sentiment analysis. In: Proceedings of the 9th Brazilian Symposium in Information and Human Language Technology (2013)
5. Belisário, L.B., Ferreira, L.G., Pardo, T.A.S.: Evaluating richer features and varied machine learning models for subjectivity classification of book review sentences in portuguese. Information **11**(9), 437 (2020)
6. Cambria, E., Li, Y., Xing, F.Z., Poria, S., Kwok, K.: Senticnet 6: ensemble application of symbolic and subsymbolic ai for sentiment analysis. In: Proceedings of the 29th ACM International Conference on Information & Knowledge Management, pp. 105–114 (2020)
7. Carvalho, C.M.A., Nagano, H., Barros, A.K.: A comparative study for sentiment analysis on election Brazilian news. In: Proceedings of the 11th Brazilian Symposium in Information and Human Language Technology, pp. 103–111 (2017)
8. Chai, Y., Lei, C., Yin, C.: Study on the influencing factors of online learning effect based on decision tree and recursive feature elimination. In: Proceedings of the 10th International Conference on E-Education, E-Business, E-Management and E-Learning, pp. 52–57 (2019)
9. Chaturvedi, I., Cambria, E., Welsch, R.E., Herrera, F.: Distinguishing between facts and opinions for sentiment analysis: survey and challenges. Inf. Fusion **44**, 65–77 (2018)
10. Chenlo, J.M., Losada, D.E.: A machine learning approach for subjectivity classification based on positional and discourse features. In: Lupu, M., Kanoulas, E., Loizides, F. (eds.) IRFC 2013. LNCS, vol. 8201, pp. 17–28. Springer, Heidelberg (2013). https://doi.org/10.1007/978-3-642-41057-4_3
11. Chenlo, J.M., Losada, D.E.: An empirical study of sentence features for subjectivity and polarity classification. Inf. Sci. **280**, 275–288 (2014)
12. Freitas, C., Motta, E., Milidiú, R., César, J.: Vampiro que brilha... rá! desafios na anotaçao de opiniao em um corpus de resenhas de livros. Encontro de Linguística de Corpus 11, 22 (2012)
13. Freitas, L.A.D., Vieira, R.: Ontology-based feature-level sentiment analysis in Portuguese reviews. Int. J. Bus. Inf. Syst. **32**(1), 30–55 (2019)
14. Ge, P.: Analysis on approaches and structures of automated machine learning frameworks. In: 2020 International Conference on Communications, Information System and Computer Engineering (CISCE), pp. 474–477. IEEE (2020)

15. Hogenboom, A., Bal, D., Frasincar, F., Bal, M., De Jong, F., Kaymak, U.: Exploiting emoticons in polarity classification of text. J. Web Eng. **14**(1 & 2), 22–40 (2015)
16. Honnibal, M., Montani, I.: spacy 2: natural language understanding with bloom embeddings, convolutional neural networks and incremental parsing. To appear **7**(1), 411–420 (2017)
17. Kimura, M., Katsurai, M.: Investigating the consistency of emoji sentiment lexicons constructed using different languages. In: Proceedings of the 20th International Conference on Information Integration and Web-based Applications & Services, pp. 310–313 (2018)
18. Mansour, R., Hady, M.F.A., Hosam, E., Amr, H., Ashour, A.: Feature selection for twitter sentiment analysis: an experimental study. In: Gelbukh, A. (ed.) CICLing 2015. LNCS, vol. 9042, pp. 92–103. Springer, Cham (2015). https://doi.org/10.1007/978-3-319-18117-2_7
19. Moraes, S.M.W., Santos, A.L.L., Redecker, M., Machado, R.M., Meneguzzi, F.R.: Comparing approaches to subjectivity classification: a study on Portuguese tweets. In: Silva, J., Ribeiro, R., Quaresma, P., Adami, A., Branco, A. (eds.) PROPOR 2016. LNCS (LNAI), vol. 9727, pp. 86–94. Springer, Cham (2016). https://doi.org/10.1007/978-3-319-41552-9_8
20. Oliveira, M., Melo, T.: Investigando features de sentenças para classificação de subjetividade e polaridade em português do brasil. In: Anais do XVII Encontro Nacional de Inteligência Artificial e Computacional, pp. 270–281. SBC (2020)
21. Palshikar, G., Apte, M., Pandita, D., Singh, V.: Learning to identify subjective sentences. In: Proceedings of the 13th International Conference on Natural Language Processing, pp. 239–248 (2016)
22. Pennebaker, J.W., Francis, M.E., Booth, R.J.: Linguistic inquiry and word count: Liwc 2001. Mahway: Lawrence Erlbaum Assoc. **71**(2001), 2001 (2001)
23. Pereira, D.A.: A survey of sentiment analysis in the Portuguese language. Artif. Intell. Rev. **54**(2), 1087–1115 (2021)
24. Poria, S., Cambria, E., Winterstein, G., Huang, G.B.: Sentic patterns: dependency-based rules for concept-level sentiment analysis. Knowl.-Based Syst. **69**, 45–63 (2014)
25. Turney, P.: Thumbs up or thumbs down? semantic orientation applied to unsupervised classification of reviews. In: Proceedings of the 40th Annual Meeting of the Association for Computational Linguistics, pp. 417–424 (2002)

# Comparing Contextual Embeddings for Semantic Textual Similarity in Portuguese

José E. Andrade Junior[1,2(✉)], Jonathan Cardoso-Silva[3,4],
and Leonardo C. T. Bezerra[1]

[1] IMD, Universidade Federal do Rio Grande do Norte, Natal, RN, Brazil
`jose.andrade.099@ufrn.edu.br, leobezerra@imd.ufrn.br`
[2] iFood, Osasco, SP, Brazil
[3] Data Science Brigade, Porto Alegre, RS, Brazil
[4] London School of Economics and Political Science, London, UK

**Abstract.** Semantic textual similarity (STS) measures how semantically similar two sentences are. In the context of the Portuguese language, STS literature is still incipient but includes important initiatives like the ASSIN and ASSIN 2 shared tasks. The state-of-the-art for those datasets is a contextual embedding produced by a Portuguese pre-trained and fine-tuned BERT model. In this work, we investigate the application of Sentence-BERT (SBERT) contextual embeddings to these datasets. Compared to BERT, SBERT is a more computationally efficient approach, enabling its application to scalable unsupervised learning problems. Given the absence of SBERT models pre-trained in Portuguese and the computational cost for such training, we adopt multilingual models and also fine-tune them for Portuguese. Results showed that SBERT embeddings were competitive especially after fine-tuning, numerically surpassing the results of BERT on ASSIN 2 and the results observed during the shared tasks for all datasets considered.

**Keywords:** Deep learning · Natural language processing · Semantic textual similarity · Word embeddings

## 1 Introduction

Semantic textual similarity (STS) is the task of measuring how semantically similar a pair of sentences is [11]. The importance of this task to the natural language processing (NLP) field is endorsed by the creation of STS shared tasks, such as the ones proposed by the International Workshop on Semantic Evaluation (*SemEval* [5,12]). Shared tasks like SemEval led to great advancements in STS, but there is still a reduced number of studies in the context of the Portuguese language. To foster this research, the ASSIN [9] and ASSIN 2 [15] workshops hosted

**Supplementary Information** The online version contains supplementary material available at https://doi.org/10.1007/978-3-030-91699-2_27.

shared tasks for STS and natural language inference (NLI) in Portuguese. The models developed during ASSIN 2 used more recent NLP approaches, including contextual embeddings like BERT [7]. Recent works addressing these datasets have since been continuously proposed, with the state-of-the-art being a BERT model pre-trained in Portuguese fine-tuned for STS [8].

Though competitive, training BERT models on STS demands that all pairs of sentences be used as input to the network. This approach can cause a massive computational overhead, even for a moderate-size corpus. To address this problem, Reimers and Gurevych [17] proposed Sentence-BERT (SBERT), a siamese architecture with shared weights that can reduce the cost of BERT models. Since its proposition, SBERT has been used successfully in tasks where BERT had obtained good results [17,18]. However, to the best of our knowledge, these applications do not yet include STS in Portuguese.

The goal of this work is to evaluate contextual embeddings generated by SBERT models for STS in Portuguese, which we investigate in two stages. First, we compare the performance of pre-trained SBERT models with the state-of-the-art BERT models for the ASSIN datasets [8]. In addition, we include other baseline models, such as the best-performing works assessed in the workshops and other multilingual contextual embeddings. Later, we evaluate the benefits of fine-tuning SBERT models for STS in Portuguese, also comparing them with all baseline and state-of-the-art models.

Results from the first part of our investigation showed that multilingual SBERT models are competitive, outperforming the best results of the ASSIN shared task. Even if at this stage fine-tuning was not considered, SBERT results were second only to the results achieved by the state-of-the-art BERT model [8]. In the second part of our work, results were improved with the fine-tuning, numerically surpassing the performance of the state-of-the-art model for the ASSIN 2 dataset, at a much lower computational cost. For the ASSIN datasets, even if the state-of-the-art results were not matched, the contextual embeddings generated by multilingual SBERT models with fine-tuning remained competitive and, as mentioned before, required a reduced computational cost. Finally, we discuss the impacts of fine-tuning and language variants with a qualitative assessment that demonstrates that results can be further improved in the future.

The remainder of this work is structured as follows. Section 2 briefly reviews preliminary concepts, namely contextual embeddings and the most relevant architectures used to produce them, and deep learning training approaches such as fine-tuning and knowledge distillation. Next, Sect. 3 defines the STS problem, details the ASSIN and ASSIN 2 shared tasks, and briefly discusses the state-of-the-art for these datasets. In Sect. 4, we detail the experimental setup adopted in this investigation, and discuss results in Sects. 5 and 6. We conclude and discuss future work in Sect. 7.

## 2    Background

In this section, we briefly review the main preliminary concepts required to understand contextual embeddings, an important tool for problem solving in

NLP. Initially, we discuss transfer learning [25], the training paradigm that motivated the proposal of embeddings in general. Next, we discuss contextual embeddings and the main algorithms adopted in this work, namely BERT [7] and Sentence-BERT [17]. Finally, we briefly detail knowledge distillation [10], the deep learning training paradigm that enables the multilingual training used to produce the models we adopt in this work.

## 2.1 Transfer Learning

Transfer learning is a training paradigm that enables models fit to a general problem to be reused for a separate, and usually more specific problem [25]. When solving the new problem, two main strategies can be adopted.

**Pre-trained models** can be applied directly to the problem at hand when adjustments to match different input and/or output dimensionalities are feasible. Though pre-trained models are not expected to perform as well as problem-specific models, they are reusable across different problems.
**Fine-tuned models** are pre-trained models that are subject to additional training on a target specific problem. In detail, fine-tuning uses the pre-trained model as a starting point and runs additional training iterations on the new data.

Given the benefits of transfer learning, pre-trained models have become increasingly publicly available. Combined with fine-tuning, the same pre-trained model can become multiple specialized models without training from the ground up, saving both computing and time resources. In the context of NLP problems, this has motivated researchers to propose general models and make their pre-trained versions available, the most relevant example being the contextual and word embeddings we discuss next.

## 2.2 Contextual and Word Embeddings

A statistical language model is a probability distribution function of word sequences in a given language. Training language models is a very computationally intensive task, easily plagued by the curse of dimensionality, for two main reasons. First, the number of word co-occurrence is typically large. Second, the word sequences vary considerably across multiple text datasets, and even from training to test sets. These challenges motivated the distributed word representation [3], models in which both the distributed representation of each word and the probability function for the word sequence are learned simultaneously. Distributed representations can achieve better generalization since these models are able to attribute a high probability of occurrence to word sequences it had never seen before if similar sequences have been provided during training.

Popular word embeddings like Word2Vec [13], GloVe [14], and FastText [4] consider all sentences in which a given word appear to build a global vector representation for each word in the corpus. However, a word can have different meanings depending on the sentence and context it is in. To solve this problem, different contextual embeddings were proposed. Next, we discuss the two contextual approaches we use in this work, namely BERT and Sentence-BERT.

## 2.3 BERT

The *bidirectional encoder representations from Transformers* (BERT) architecture brought great advances to the NLP field, lately becoming the current state-of-the-art in different tasks [7]. BERT is a language model designed to create deep bidirectional vector representations from unsupervised texts. The bidirectional approach models context both to the right and to the left of each token in the input sequence. The BERT architecture can be seen on Fig. 1, where the pre-trained scenario is seen on the left and the fine-tuning scenario is illustrated for different tasks on the right.

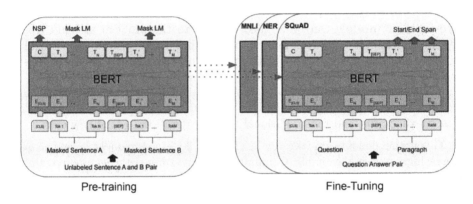

**Fig. 1.** The BERT architecture [7] for pre-training (left) or fine-tuning (right).

An improvement over other architectures is that BERT can be applied to tasks that take as input either individual sentences or pairs thereof. In the latter case, both sentences are separated by a special token dubbed [SEP]. Whether for individual or sentence pairs, the first token fed to the network is a special token dubbed [CLS], which serves as encoding for supervised tasks after training. Alternatively, a BERT embedding can be obtained by aggregating the three types of internal BERT embeddings, namely token, segment, and position.

## 2.4 Sentence-BERT (SBERT)

Although BERT has become the state-of-the-art for several NLP tasks, the algorithm faces scalability issues in tasks such as STS where there is the need to feed the network with sentence pairs. According to Reimers and Gurevych [17], even a moderate sized training corpus of 10000 sentences requires 50 million computational inferences, rendering BERT impractical for STS. As an alternative, SBERT was proposed as a more efficient approach to this type of tasks.

SBERT [17] is a siamese architecture in which the sentence pairs are fed to two parallel but connected network pathways to produce an estimate of the similarity between the sentences (Fig. 2a). The first layers consist of regular

BERT networks followed by a pooling operation to ensure embeddings produced for each sentence have the same vector size. The network outputs the cosine similarity between these embeddings. Since both BERT networks take a single sentence and their weights are shared, the number of computational inferences is much reduced [17].

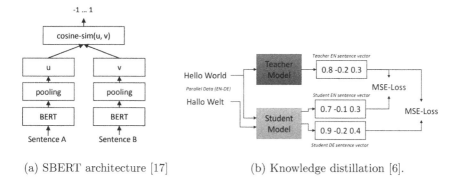

(a) SBERT architecture [17]                    (b) Knowledge distillation [6].

**Fig. 2.** SBERT architecture (left) and multilingual knowledge distillation (right).

## 2.5  Knowledge Distillation

Another concept relevant to this study is knowledge distillation, one of the deep learning training approaches where one model is trained to learn the knowledge encoded by another [10]. In this training approach, a *student* model attempts to emulate a *teacher* model with similar (or even higher) performance.

A knowledge distillation-based approach has been proposed by Reimers and Gurevych [17] to produce multilingual SBERT models and is illustrated in Fig. 2b. The teacher model is an English pre-trained SBERT model and the student model is trained to produce multilingual embeddings. Training is structured as follows. First, the input for teacher and student models are different, since the original sentence fed to the teacher is enriched with parallel, translated versions for the student. Second, the objective function is to reduce the mean squared error losses comparing every student embedding produced with the original embedding produced by the teacher. Effectively, translated sentences are mapped to the same location in the Euclidean space of the original sentence.

Two other aspects of that work are further worth mentioning. First, the student models are trained with parallel data for 50 languages including Portuguese. Second, the student model is learned by a XLM-R algorithm [6], a *cross-lingual* version of BERT. In detail, authors claim XLM-R is better suited for multilingual learning than BERT given its ability to handle non-latin alphabets.

As reviewed in this section, the literature on contextual embeddings has matured over recent years. Still, models are usually developed and made available for NLP applications in English. In the next section, we discuss the STS problem in the context of the Portuguese language.

# 3   Semantic Textual Similarity in Portuguese

As previously discussed, semantic textual similarity (STS) is a relevant NLP application with international efforts to foster its research. STS can be defined as a regression task where one wants to numerically measure the similarity between two sentences. Higher scores indicate a stronger similarity between a sentence pair. Among the main international efforts concerning STS, the *International Workshop on Semantic Evaluation* (SemEval [1]) is a series of workshops focused on semantic NLP problems. Each year, several shared tasks are hosted, in which high-quality datasets are used to benchmark submissions from participating research teams. Several similarity tasks have been defined at SemEval, including *cross-lingual* and *multilingual* STS [5].

The first dataset that included semantic textual similarity between pairs of sentences in Portuguese was ASSIN [9]. Later, ASSIN 2 [15] proposed a new dataset, based on sentences from the SICK-BR dataset [16]. Next, we describe each shared task, its associated datasets, and the best results observed for each.

**ASSIN** stands for *evaluation of semantic textual similarity and natural language inference* [9], a shared task organized at the PROPOR 2016 conference. The ASSIN datasets comprise (i) PT-PT, containing sentences in European Portuguese, and (ii) PT-BR, containing sentences in Brazilian Portuguese. Each dataset (PT-PT and PT-BR) has 5,000 sentences: 2,500 for training, 500 for validation, and 2,000 for testing. Sentences in each dataset were obtained from Google News, processed in three steps. First, vectorial space models [21] were used to select similar sentences from different documents. Second, these sentences were filtered manually, and noisy pairs were removed. Finally, filtered sentence pairs were annotated by four human judges. Scoring rules are describe below:

1. Sentences are completely different. They may talk about the same fact, but this cannot be determined without context.
2. Sentences refer to different facts and are not similar, but are about the same subject (e.g. a soccer match or elections).
3. The sentences present some similarity; can refer to the same fact or not.
4. Sentence content is very similar, but one (or both) has some exclusive information (e.g. a date or locality).
5. Sentences have practically the same meaning, possibly with a minimal difference (e.g. an adjective that does not change interpretation).

**ASSIN 2** was the second edition of ASSIN [15], held at the STIL 2019 symposium in Brazil. The dataset is a translation and manual adaptation of the SICK dataset [12], the SICK-BR dataset [16]. In addition, ASSIN 2 also includes manually-generated sentence pairs, which were reviewed by human judges. Each pair of sentences in ASSIN 2 was annotated by at least four native Brazilian Portuguese speakers with linguistic training background. For STS, the final score was the average of the scores of each annotator. The final dataset has 10000 pairs of sentences: 6500 used for training, 500 for validation, and 3000 for testing.

**Table 1.** Results using baseline, pre-trained, and fine-tuned models.

| | ASSIN PT-BR | | ASSIN PT-PT | | ASSIN 2 | |
|---|---|---|---|---|---|---|
| | Pearson | MSE | Pearson | MSE | Pearson | MSE |
| **Baseline models** | | | | | | |
| Solo Queue (Workshop) | 0.70 | 0.38 | 0.70 | 0.66 | — | — |
| L2F/INESC-ID (Workshop) | — | — | 0.73 | 0.61 | — | — |
| IPR (Workshop) | — | — | — | — | 0.82 | 0.52 |
| ptBERT-Base$_{ft}$ [8] | 0.83 ±0.00 | 0.25 | 0.85 ±0.00 | 0.47 | 0.84 ±0.01 | 0.50 |
| ptBERT-Large$_{ft}$ [8] | **0.84** ±0.01 | **0.23** | **0.85** ±0.01 | **0.40** | **0.84** ±0.01 | **0.43** |
| BERTimbau-Base [20] | 0.44 | 1.97 | 0.38 | 2.46 | 0.62 | 1.78 |
| BERTimbau-Large [20] | 0.55 | 3.32 | 0.52 | 4.16 | 0.27 | 2.49 |
| **Pre-trained models** | | | | | | |
| BERTimbau-Base (SBERT) | 0.57 | 1.60 | 0.53 | 2.22 | 0.68 | 1.24 |
| BERTimbau-Large (SBERT) | 0.58 | 2.69 | 0.49 | 3.57 | 0.71 | 1.92 |
| ⟨XLM-R, SBERT, NLI+STS⟩ | 0.67 | 0.65 | 0.71 | 0.68 | 0.79 | 0.63 |
| ⟨XLM-R, SBERT, Paraphrases⟩ | 0.71 | **0.42** | 0.74 | 0.65 | 0.79 | **0.50** |
| ⟨XLM-R, SBERT, Cross-EN-DE⟩ | **0.73** | 0.59 | **0.77** | **0.48** | **0.80** | 0.64 |
| **Fine-tuned models** | | | | | | |
| BERTimbau-Base (SBERT)$_{ft}$ | 0.76 ±0.01 | 0.35 | 0.74 ±0.00 | 0.61 | 0.83 ±0.00 | 0.52 |
| BERTimbau-Large (SBERT)$_{ft}$ | 0.78 ±0.01 | 0.32 | 0.76 ±0.01 | 0.68 | 0.84±0.00 | 0.53 |
| ⟨XLM-R, SBERT, NLI+STS⟩$_{ft}$ | 0.76 ±0.00 | 0.35 | 0.74 ±0.00 | 0.54 | 0.84 ±0.00 | 0.42 |
| ⟨XLM-R, SBERT, Paraphrases⟩$_{ft}$ | **0.79** ±0.00 | **0.30** | **0.77** ±0.00 | **0.52** | **0.85** ±0.00 | 0.43 |
| ⟨XLM-R, SBERT, Cross-EN-DE⟩$_{ft}$ | 0.78 ±0.00 | 0.31 | **0.77** ±0.00 | 0.55 | **0.85** ±0.00 | **0.41** |

**Baseline results** for the ASSIN and ASSIN 2 datasets are listed at the top of Table 1. Pearson correlation coefficient (to be maximized) is considered as the primary metric for the comparison, complemented by the mean squared error (MSE, to be minimized). The three topmost works are the best results obtained during the shared tasks, whereas the following two models were proposed in a work published after ASSIN 2 [8].[1] For brevity, the models we assess in this work are also given in Table 1, and are described in the next section.

**Baseline Results.** The work of Fialho, Coheur, and Quaresma [8] considerably advanced the state-of-the-art for both ASSIN PT-PT and ASSIN PT-BR, and to a lesser extent also for ASSIN 2. Specifically, the authors experimentally assessed BERT models for STS and NLI in Portuguese using the datasets ASSIN, ASSIN 2, and SICK-BR. For STS, two approaches were considered: BERT as a regressor or BERT embeddings as input for regression algorithms. Three models fine-tuned for STS were evaluated, namely (i) one multilingual and (ii) two monolingual versions pre-trained in Brazilian Portuguese differing in size (ptBERT-Base$_{ft}$ and ptBERT-Large$_{ft}$). ptBERT-Large$_{ft}$ used as a regressor achieved the best results.

As discussed in this section, ASSIN and ASSIN 2 are relevant Portuguese STS datasets for which BERT models are the state-of-the-art. Yet, the computational

---

[1] For brevity, other relevant works such as [19] comparing Word2Vec, FastText, ELMO, and BERT on ASSIN are not included as their results are surpassed by [8].

overhead incurred for BERT training limits its applicability to problems with a moderate size sentence collection. In the next section, we discuss how we employ and assess SBERT models on the Portuguese STS datasets reviewed here.

## 4 Experimental Assessment

SBERT models have been successfully employed on NLP applications where BERT models had state-of-the-art performance [17]. Furthermore, multilingual pre-trained SBERT models have been made available in an open source SBERT repository (https://www.sbert.net). In this section, we describe our experimental analysis in which we assess the performance of SBERT models with and without fine-tuning for STS in Portuguese. Initially, we detail the models we consider, following the order given in Table 1.[2] Later, we discuss the two stages of our experiments, differing as to whether fine-tuning is employed.

### 4.1 Models Assessed

As listed in Table 1, the top-most five models we consider as baseline are (i) the best-performing algorithms of the ASSIN and ASSIN 2 shared tasks, and (ii) the state-of-the-art BERT models [8], already described in the previous section. In addition, we also include as baseline two Portuguese pre-trained BERT models called BERTimbau [20]. Remaining models given in Table 1 are used within the SBERT architecture. The first two reuse BERTimbau weights, given the compatibility between BERT and SBERT. The remaining three models are multilingual pre-trained models open sourced by SBERT proponents.

We choose to employ pre-trained models instead of training models from scratch for two major reasons. First, the computational cost required for training deep learning NLP models from scratch is considerable. Second, the pre-trained models have often been trained on very rich corpora, whether in Portuguese or multilingual. Below, we describe the BERTimbau and multilingual models.

**BERTimbau** models were trained by *Neuralmind* and are available in two sizes, namely BERTimbau-Base and BERTimbau-Large. Pre-training BERT requires a vocabulary and a training corpus. *Neuralmind* produced a vocabulary from the Brazilian Portuguese version of the Wikipedia, and used the *brWac* corpus [22]. Pre-training followed the original BERT paper [7]. BERTimbau-Base and BERTimbau-Large were respectively warm-started with the *multilingual BERT-Base* and *English BERT-Large* checkpoints.

**SBERT** models pre-trained in Portuguese are not openly available. Instead, we adopt two sets of models, given in Table 1 on the five rows that follow baseline models. The first two models, labeled BERTimbau-Base (SBERT) and

---

[2] Though models based on other relevant architectures such as the multilingual universal sentence encoder [23] were available at the SBERT repository, we did not include them in our work due to the lack of training setup details.

BERTimbau-Large (SBERT), reuse the trained weights provided by BERTimbau models. The remaining three models are multilingual models open-sourced by SBERT proponents, having been trained using the knowledge distillation process. Among the models available, we used the ones for which the student-model was learned by the XLM-R algorithm [6]. Different teacher-models were used, described below under the notation ⟨student, teacher, task⟩, indicating the student-model and the task for which the teacher-model was originally trained.

- ⟨XLM-R, SBERT, NLI+STS⟩: XLM-R learned a multilingual model from an SBERT model fine-tuned for NLI and STS in English.
- ⟨XLM-R, SBERT, Paraphrases⟩: XLM-R learned a multilingual model from an SBERT model trained on an English paraphases dataset.
- ⟨XLM-R, SBERT, Cross-EN-DE⟩: fine-tuned ⟨XLM-R, SBERT, Paraphrases⟩ model for the STSbenchmark [5], with English and/or German sentences.

Training multilingual versions used a range of datasets, and so contextual embeddings produced by SBERT were generalized by XLM-R for 50 different languages. Further information about their training is available in the original paper [18].

## 4.2 Experimental Setup

As previously discussed, we split our experiments in two parts to isolate the effect of fine-tuning. This is reflected in Table 1, where we label results obtained from a given model after fine-tuning with the subscript *ft*. Each part of the investigation is further detailed next.

**Experiments Without Fine-Tuning.** In the first part of our experiments, we employed the pre-trained models on ASSIN and ASSIN 2 datasets without fine-tuning. Concretely, labels provided by the datasets were used only to validate the results. For the baseline BERTimbau models (BERTimbau-Base and BERTimbau-Large), each input sentence was fed individually to the model and the corresponding embedding was obtained from the [CLS] token. The similarity score for a pair of sentences was calculated as the cosine distance between the sentence embeddings produced. Then, we compare the cosine similarity directly with the labels of ASSIN and ASSIN 2 using Pearson correlation. Though cosine distance ranges differs from the STS score range, normalization and scaling is not necessary since Pearson correlation only considers the linear relationship between the variables.

**Experiments with Fine-Tuning.** In the second part of our experimental analysis, we assessed the impact in performance when pre-trained models are fine-tuned for the ASSIN and ASSIN 2 datasets. In detail, we use the available validation labels to fine-tune the pre-trained models. The developers of SBERT made available a standard fine-tuning script, with recommended hyperparameters we adopted. For each dataset and model, we ran fine-tuning ten times and report mean and standard deviation results. Regarding baseline BERTimbau results, fine-tuning would be computationally unfeasible in the context of this work. Yet, we remark that the state-of-the-art models [8] are ptBERT-Base and ptBERT-Large networks that have been fine-tuned for the ASSIN and ASSIN 2 datasets. As such, these models serve as reference for BERT results, though mean and standard deviation have been reported only for five repetitions.

Given the large number of models we consider, our complete set of results is provided as supplementary material [2]. In the next sections, we discuss the most relevant insights we observe in our assessment.

## 5   Results

As previously discussed, contextual embeddings are usually produced from pre-trained or fine-tuned language models. In our setup, we have isolated experiments without and with fine-tuning for STS in Portuguese. Below, we discuss the most relevant insights observed for each part of our investigation.

### 5.1   Pre-trained Models Without Fine-Tuning for STS in Portuguese

In order of appearance in Table 1, literature results are given at the top, as previously detailed. The following two models are also taken as baseline. In detail, BERTimbau-Base and BERTimbau-Large are the BERTimbau models that have been pre-trained in Portuguese. Remaining models are SBERT approaches. Given the compatibility between BERT and SBERT, we include SBERT results where weights were obtained from BERTimbau models, which we refer to as ptBERT-Base (SBERT) and ptBERT-Large (SBERT). Finally, Table 1 lists the multilingual SBERT models, namely ⟨XLM-R, SBERT, NLI+STS⟩, ⟨XLM-R, SBERT, Paraphrases⟩ and ⟨XLM-R, SBERT, Cross-EN-DE⟩. Next, we discuss the main insights observed in this part of our investigation.

**Portuguese pre-trained models** did not produce competitive results w.r.t. workshop or literature results. A direct comparison between models that use BERTimbau weights showed that SBERT models in general achieved better results than their BERT counterparts. This result is interesting considering that the only difference between them is that embeddings from BERT models are obtained from the [CLS] special token, whereas SBERT is average pooling all BERT output embeddings. Another important insight is that not always the Large version outperformed its Base counterpart. This is likely explained by the checkpoints used by *Neuralmind* for BERTimbau model training. As discussed in Sect. 4, a multilingual BERT checkpoint was used to warm start Base training, whereas Large models were warm-started with an English BERT checkpoint.

**Multilingual pre-trained models** produced competitive results w.r.t. results from the participating teams of the shared tasks. This is true for nearly all datasets and multilingual models considered, with two major exceptions. First, the ⟨XLM-R, SBERT, NLI+STS⟩ model is unable to match workshop results for any of the datasets considered, though its teacher-model had been originally trained for NLI and STS tasks. Second, no model is able to match the performance of ASSIN 2 workshop results. Among the SBERT versions, the one that

shows the most consistent performance is the one fine-tuned for Cross-EN-DE
STS. This indicates that fine-tuning for multilingual tasks is helpful, as expected.
Yet, without a specific fine-tuning for STS in Portuguese, even this model can-
not match state-of-the-art results [8]. Indeed, in this part of the investigation all
SBERT results fall short of the state-of-the-art for all datasets considered.

## 5.2   Pre-trained Models with Fine-Tuning

Results obtained with fine-tuned models are displayed at the bottom part of
Table 1. Models are given in the same order as the pre-trained models. Below,
we discuss the main insights from this analysis.

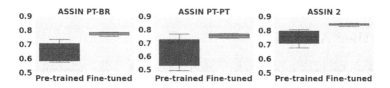

**Fig. 3.** Performances of pre-trained models with and without fine-tuning.

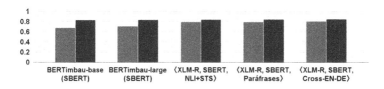

**Fig. 4.** Homogeneity of results with (blue) and without (red) fine-tuning (Color figure
olnine)

**Benefits of Fine-Tuning.** The performance gains provided by fine-tuning are
considerable for all algorithms. In fact, all models now (numerically) outperform
the best results achieved during the ASSIN and ASSIN 2 tasks. To evidence the
performance gains provided by fine-tuning, the boxplots in Fig. 3 show the average performance of all SBERT models with and without fine-tuning, grouped by
dataset. In addition to improving average performance, fine-tuning also reduces
variability to a significant extent, especially on ASSIN PT-PT.

**Comparison with the State-of-the-Art.** Results differ as a function of shared
task. Multilingual SBERT models numerically surpass the state-of-the-art results
according to Pearson correlation and/or MSE on ASSIN 2. Remaining models
also get closer to the state-of-the-art for this task, confirming the expected benefits from SBERT and fine-tuning. For ASSIN PT-BR and ASSIN PT-PT, the
best results showed by SBERT models are not yet competitive.

**Homogeneity of Results.** In the absence of fine-tuning (*pre-trained* section in Table 1) results were very contrasting among different models. Conversely, all fine-tuned models have produced results that are much closer to each other. We illustrate this increased homogeneity for ASSIN 2 results in Fig. 4, where average pre-trained model performance is given in red and average fine-tuned model performance is given in blue, grouped by model and sorted by fine-tuned performance. For this dataset, even BERTimbau models lead to a competitive performance after fine-tuning.

Overall, results discussed in this section confirmed the benefits of adopting SBERT and fine-tuning for STS in Portuguese. For the ASSIN 2 dataset, multilingual models even numerically surpass the current state-of-the-art. In the next section, we further investigate results to understand these benefits.

## 6   Further Analysis

To better understand some of the insights observed in the previous section, we initially conduct a qualitative assessment, regarding both (i) fine-tuning and (ii) language variant effects. Moreover, we run additional experiments to assess the benefits of multiple language variants in the fine-tuning setup.

**Table 2.** ASSIN 2 sentence pair examples with their scores illustrating changes in cosine similarity before and after fine-tuning ⟨XLM-R, SBERT, Paraphrases⟩.

| Sentence pairs | Score | Before | After |
|---|---|---|---|
| Examples of sentence similarities that **improved** after fine-tuning | | | |
| S1: "A senhora está pegando o canguru." | 2.0 | 3.9 | 2.0 |
| S2: "Um canguru está pegando o bebê da senhora." | | | |
| S1: "Uma senhora asiática está colocando maquiagem." | 4.0 | 2.2 | 4.1 |
| S2: "A senhora está se maquiando." | | | |
| S1: "A senhora está limpando um camarão" | 4.0 | 2.6 | 4.1 |
| S2: "Alguém está limpando um animal" | | | |
| Examples of sentence similarities that deteriorated after fine-tuning | | | |
| S1: "Um homem está colocando um dispositivo eletrônico." | 1.9 | 1.9 | 3.4 |
| S2: "O homem está tirando uma foto dele mesmo e de outro cara." | | | |
| S1: "Um homem está dançando." | 1.2 | 1.1 | 2.4 |
| S2: "Não tem nenhuma mulher se exercitando." | | | |
| S1: "A senhora está andando de elefante." | 3.8 | 3.5 | 4.8 |
| S2: "O elefante está sendo montado pela senhora." | | | |

## 6.1   Fine-Tuning Effects

We select a few sentence pairs to illustrate fine-tuning effects on ⟨XLM-R, SBERT, Paraphrases⟩ results, the SBERT model that performed best in our experiments. Table 2 gives six sentence pair examples with their expected scores and cosine similarities before and after fine-tuning for STS in Portuguese. For the first three pairs, results were improved by fine-tuning. Indeed, fine-tuned results become very close to the expected score, whereas pre-trained results were very off.

By contrast, results obtained with fine-tuning for the latter three sentence pairs in Table 2 are worse than when fine-tuning is not adopted. In the first deterioration example, we believe the model misinterprets the terms *"colocando"* (putting) e *"tirando"* (taking), which can be used as antonyms but not in the context *"tirando uma foto"* (taking a picture). In the second example, we believe the model misinterprets a negation quantifier *"Não tem nenhuma mulher"* (no woman) with an opposition adverb (not a woman), which renders both sentences less semantically different. Future analysis could also investigate the impact of double negatives in this case, as multilingual models need to deal with such differences between languages. Finally, in the last example the only differences between sentences regard (i) active versus passive sentence form, and (ii) whether *"montando"* refers to getting on or riding an animal. Since both interpretations are possible, we believe that the ASSIN 2 example could be considered noisy.

## 6.2   Language Variant Effects

With the exception of the state-of-the-art, all algorithms assessed for ASSIN datasets in the literature and also here are unable to perform their best for the European and Brazilian Portuguese variants at the same time. We illustrate this with sentence pairs given in Table 3. The two top-most sentence pairs are obtained from ASSIN PT-BR, and the two bottom-most from ASSIN PT-PT. Sentences selected in European Portuguese respectively illustrate vocabulary and grammatical differences between the language variants. Beside expected scores, similarities computed by ⟨XLM-R, SBERT, Paraphrases⟩ when fine-tuned for ASSIN PT-BR and ASSIN PT-PT are also given. Results for the model fine-tuned for ASSIN PT-BR are better on that dataset. The symmetrical situation is observed for the ASSIN PT-PT dataset.

The better performance of models fine-tuned for the given language variant is expected. We then conduct additional experiments to understand the impact of fine-tuning ⟨XLM-R, SBERT, Paraphrases⟩ for the three ASSIN and ASSIN 2 datasets altogether. We report mean values for ten repetitions, and provide standard deviations as supplementary material [2] given the very low variability observed in the results. Results differ as a function of the target testing dataset. For ASSIN PT-BR and ASSIN 2, results are not changed, except for MSE on the latter, reduced from 0.43 to 0.41. Regarding ASSIN PT-PT, results are strongly improved, with Pearson coefficient correlation increasing from 0.77 to 0.81 and MSE reducing from 0.52 to 0.49.

**Table 3.** ASSIN PT-BR (top) and PT-PT (bottom) pairs with their scores illustrating fine-tuning ⟨XLM-R, SBERT, Paraphrases⟩ for different language variants.

| Sentence pairs | Score | BR | PT |
|---|---|---|---|
| ASSIN PT-BR examples | | | |
| "O show está previsto para começar às 17h." "A atração acontece a partir das 12h." | 1.8 | 1.5 | 3.0 |
| "Já para 2016, a previsão dos economistas recuou de 5,6% para 5,51%." "A mediana das estimativas passou de 5,76% para 5,71%." | 2.2 | 2.2 | 3.5 |
| ASSIN PT-PT examples | | | |
| "Noruega e Roménia defrontam-se ainda esta quinta-feira no Pavilhão Municipal da Póvoa de Varzim "Os bilhetes para os jogos que decorrerão no Pavilhão Muncipal da Póvoa do Varzim são gratuitos." | 2.0 | 1.5 | 2.5 |
| "A companhia aérea brasileira Azul lança a 4 de maio o seu primeiro voo regular para a Europa." "O voo inaugural da Azul acontece já a 4 de maio." | 4.0 | 3.1 | 3.9 |

The qualitative assessment conducted in this section helped further understand the benefits of fine-tuning and the potential impacts of different language variants. Even if improved results did not match the state-of-the-art for the ASSIN PT-PT dataset, they shed light into promising future work directions.

# 7   Conclusions

Semantic textual similarity (STS [11]) is a core research problem in natural language processings (NLP) studies. This is evidenced by the (i) international efforts promoting STS shared tasks [5,12] and (ii) the fact that several novel contextual embedddings recently proposed have been benchmarked on this problem [17]. In the context of the Portuguese language and its variants, ASSIN and ASSIN 2 are the most relevant shared tasks identified [9,15], for which BERT embeddings comprise the current state-of-the-art [8]. In this work, we have investigated the application of the Sentence-BERT (SBERT [17]) architecture to STS in Portuguese. SBERT addresses scalability issues in BERT networks, and has been successfully applied and open-source also for multilingual applications [18].

Our contributions were two-fold. In the first part of this work, we assessed Portuguese and multilingual SBERT models, demonstrating that the latter present competitive performance w.r.t. shared task results even without fine-tuning. This can be very useful to data professionals who need to address this problem in unsupervised learning scenarios, as typical in real-world applications. In the second part, we demonstrated that fine tuning SBERT led to improvements in all previous results. The multilingual models of SBERT once again stood out and this time surpassed the state-of-the-art for the ASSIN 2 dataset.

Further analysis indicated promising future work possibilities. In detail, we have observed situations where fine-tuning worsened results, an indication that pre-training SBERT models in Portuguese could lead to yet better results. More importantly, we have discussed the impact of language variants, which we believe should be taken into consideration either for pre-training or fine-tuning. We evidenced this possibility with additional experiments that further improved the performance on European Portuguese for the best-performing SBERT multilingual model.

The contributions discussed in this paper further highlight that other contextual *embeddings* such as XLNet [24] need to be assessed in the context of STS in Portuguese. In this sense, we believe our work is instrumental to motivate more research groups addressing NLP problems in Portuguese. This is the purpose of shared tasks, especially given the computational cost of the experimental campaigns involved in deep learning assessment for NLP applications. Even more interesting is stirring the interest of researchers proposing novel NLP models to the Portuguese language, given that the differences between Portuguese variants impacts on the results for most models considered.

# References

1. Agirre, E., Diab, M., Cer, D., Gonzalez-Agirre, A.: SemEval-2012 task 6: a pilot on semantic textual similarity. In: SemEval, pp. 385–393. ACL, USA (2012)
2. Andrade, J., Bezerra, L.C.T., Cardoso-Silva, J.: Comparing contextual embeddings for semantic textual similarity in portuguese (supplementary material) (2021). https://github.com/andradejunior/bracis-2021-supp-material
3. Bengio, Y., Ducharme, R., Vincent, P., Janvin, C.: A neural probabilistic language model. J. Mach. Learn. Res. **3**, 1137–1155 (2003)
4. Bojanowski, P., Grave, E., Joulin, A., Mikolov, T.: Enriching word vectors with subword information. Trans. ACL **5**, 135–146 (2017)
5. Cer, D., Diab, M., Agirre, E., Lopez-Gazpio, I., Specia, L.: SemEval-2017 task 1: Semantic textual similarity multilingual and crosslingual focused evaluation. In: SemEval, pp. 1–14. ACL, Vancouver (2017)
6. Conneau, A., et al.: Unsupervised cross-lingual representation learning at scale. In: ACL, pp. 8440–8451. ACL (2020)
7. Devlin, J., Chang, M.W., Lee, K., Toutanova, K.: BERT: pre-training of deep bidirectional transformers for language understanding. In: NAACL, pp. 4171–4186. ACL, Minneapolis (2019)
8. Fialho, P., Coheur, L., Quaresma, P.: Benchmarking natural language inference and semantic textual similarity for Portuguese. Information **11**, 484 (2020)
9. Fonseca, E.R., Borges dos Santos, L., Criscuolo, M., Aluísio, S.M.: Visão geral da avaliação de similaridade semântica e inferência textual. Linguamática **8**(2), 3–13 (2016)
10. Gou, J., Yu, B., Maybank, S.J., Tao, D.: Knowledge distillation: a survey. Int. J. Comput. Vis. **129**(6), 1789–1819 (2021)
11. Jurafsky, D., Martin, J.H.: Speech and Language Processing, 2nd edn. Prentice-Hall Inc., Upper Saddle River (2009)

12. Marelli, M., Bentivogli, L., Baroni, M., Bernardi, R., Menini, S., Zamparelli, R.: SemEval-2014 task 1: evaluation of compositional distributional semantic models on full sentences through semantic relatedness and textual entailment. In: SemEval, pp. 1–8. ACL, Dublin (2014)
13. Mikolov, T., Sutskever, I., Chen, K., Corrado, G., Dean, J.: Distributed representations of words and phrases and their compositionality. In: NeurIPS, pp. 3111–3119. Curran Associates Inc., Red Hook (2013)
14. Pennington, J., Socher, R., Manning, C.: GloVe: global vectors for word representation. In: EMNLP, pp. 1532–1543. ACL, Doha, Qatar (2014)
15. Real, L., Fonseca, E., Gonçalo Oliveira, H.: The ASSIN 2 shared task: a quick overview. In: Quaresma, P., Vieira, R., Aluísio, S., Moniz, H., Batista, F., Gonçalves, T. (eds.) PROPOR 2020. LNCS (LNAI), vol. 12037, pp. 406–412. Springer, Cham (2020). https://doi.org/10.1007/978-3-030-41505-1_39
16. Real, L., et al.: SICK-BR: a Portuguese corpus for inference. In: Villavicencio, A. (ed.) PROPOR 2018. LNCS (LNAI), vol. 11122, pp. 303–312. Springer, Cham (2018). https://doi.org/10.1007/978-3-319-99722-3_31
17. Reimers, N., Gurevych, I.: Sentence-BERT: sentence embeddings using siamese BERT-networks. In: EMNLP, pp. 3973–3983. ACL (2019)
18. Reimers, N., Gurevych, I.: Making monolingual sentence embeddings multilingual using knowledge distillation. In: EMNLP, pp. 4512–4525. ACL (2020)
19. Rodrigues, R.C., Rodrigues, J., de Castro, P.V.Q., da Silva, N.F.F., Soares, A.: Portuguese language models and word embeddings: evaluating on semantic similarity tasks. In: Quaresma, P., Vieira, R., Aluísio, S., Moniz, H., Batista, F., Gonçalves, T. (eds.) PROPOR 2020. LNCS (LNAI), vol. 12037, pp. 239–248. Springer, Cham (2020). https://doi.org/10.1007/978-3-030-41505-1_23
20. Souza, F., Nogueira, R., Lotufo, R.: BERTimbau: pretrained BERT models for Brazilian Portuguese. In: Cerri, R., Prati, R.C. (eds.) BRACIS 2020. LNCS (LNAI), vol. 12319, pp. 403–417. Springer, Cham (2020). https://doi.org/10.1007/978-3-030-61377-8_28
21. Turney, P.D., Pantel, P.: From frequency to meaning: vector space models of semantics. J. Artif. Int. Res. **37**(1), 141–188 (2010)
22. Wagner Filho, J.A., Wilkens, R., Idiart, M., Villavicencio, A.: The brWaC corpus: a new open resource for Brazilian Portuguese. In: LREC. ELRA, Miyazaki, Japan (2018)
23. Yang, Y., et al.: Multilingual universal sentence encoder for semantic retrieval. In: ACL: System Demonstrations, pp. 87–94. ACL, Online, July 2020
24. Yang, Z., Dai, Z., Yang, Y., Carbonell, J., Salakhutdinov, R.R., Le, Q.V.: XLNet: generalized autoregressive pretraining for language understanding. In: Wallach, H., Larochelle, H., Beygelzimer, A., d' Alché-Buc, F., Fox, E., Garnett, R. (eds.) NeurIPS, vol. 32. Curran Associates, Inc. (2019)
25. Yosinski, J., Clune, J., Bengio, Y., Lipson, H.: How transferable are features in deep neural networks? In: Ghahramani, Z., Welling, M., Cortes, C., Lawrence, N., Weinberger, K.Q. (eds.) NIPS, vol. 27. Curran Associates, Inc. (2014)

# Deep Active-Self Learning Applied to Named Entity Recognition

José Reinaldo C. S. A. V. S. Neto$^{(\boxtimes)}$ and Thiago de Paulo Faleiros

University of Brasilia, Brasilia, DF, Brazil
thiagodepaulo@unb.br

**Abstract.** Deep learning models have been the state-of-the-art for a variety of challenging tasks in natural language processing, but to achieve good results they often require big labeled datasets. Deep active learning algorithms were designed to reduce the annotation cost for training such models. Current deep active learning algorithms, however, aim at training a good deep learning model with as little labeled data as possible, and as such are not useful in scenarios where the full dataset must be labeled. As a solution to this problem, this work investigates deep active-self learning algorithms that employ self-labeling using the trained model to help alleviate the cost of annotating full datasets for named entity recognition tasks. The experiments performed indicate that the proposed deep active-self learning algorithm is capable of reducing manual annotation costs for labeling the complete dataset for named entity recognition with less than 2% of the self labeled tokens being mislabeled. We also investigate an early stopping technique that doesn't rely on a validation set, which effectively reduces even further the annotation costs of the proposed active-self learning algorithm in real world scenarios.

**Keywords:** Deep active learning · Self learning · Named entity recognition · Deep learning

## 1 Introduction

The task of named entity recognition (NER) is widely used for information extraction with trained models being able to directly extract named entities from unstructured text. The named entities can be used to create databases of structured information, as well as to improve the performance of models in more challenging natural language processing tasks. Deep neural models have been the state of the art for solving NER tasks, but to be trained to achieve it they often require big labeled sets of data. In many practical scenarios it's not realistic to expect big amounts of data to be manually annotated. Active learning (AL) algorithms are often used to reduce the cost of annotation by identifying a small and representative subset of samples to be labeled. It's expected that a model trained on this representative subset, and on the whole dataset, should achieve similar performances. Thus, by labeling the small representative subset, it is possible to reduce the annotation costs while training a good machine learning model.

A. Britto and K. Valdivia Delgado (Eds.): BRACIS 2021, LNAI 13074, pp. 405–418, 2021.
https://doi.org/10.1007/978-3-030-91699-2_28

**Deep Active Learning.** (DAL) applied to sequence tagging tasks (e.g. NER, POS-tagging) has only recently appeared in the literature [15], even though traditional active learning strategies applied to such tasks have appeared much earlier [14]. The use of neural-based models in active learning scenarios, instead of classic shallow models, brings with it challenges that need to be addressed. For once, deep learning models are slow to be retrained from scratch for each active learning iteration when compared to shallow models. Shen et al. [15] proposes the first DAL algorithm applied to a sequence tagging task. It proposes to use iterative training where the neural model's training continues from where it stopped in the previous iteration of the active learning process. This iterative training coupled with early stopping based on the validation set incurs in a reduction of execution time. This may be justified by the fact that as the subset of labeled samples becomes more representative of the whole dataset, new unlabeled samples are less likely to bring new relevant information to it. Thus, the iteratively trained model is more likely to require fewer training epochs to assimilate the newer samples that were recently labeled. They also propose the CNN-CNN-LSTM model, a neural model which is lightweight to train and the Maximum Normalized Log-Probability (MNLP) sampling function which normalizes the confidence of the model's predictions based on the sentence's length. The AL algorithm of Shen et al. [15] trained a neural model to peak performance using just over 25% of labeled data from the training set of the OntoNotes 5.0 [11] dataset.

Siddhant and Lipton [16] extend the previous work by Shen et al. [15]. They rely on the Bayesian Active Learning through Disagreement (BALD) [4] sampling technique, which queries unlabeled samples that generate the most disagreement from multiple passes on bayesian neural models and apply it to sequence tagging problems. They also use early stopping based on the performance of the model on the validation set, but limit the size of the validation set for it to be proportional to the size of the labeled set used to train the model. The experiments performed investigate the performance of the bayesian DAL algorithm proposed using the CNN-CNN-LSTM [15] and the CNN-biLSTM-CRF [7] models on the OntoNotes 5.0 and CoNLL 2003 [13] datasets. The results indicate that the proposed bayesian sampling functions consistently outperform the MNLP function, but with marginal improvement.

Current works on deep active learning applied to NER rely on validation sets for early stopping of the model training. In real world scenarios, active learning algorithms are used to reduce annotation costs, and separating a part of the labeled dataset to be used as a validation set seems to go against the core idea of AL in general.

**Active-Self Learning.** (ASL) combines traditional active learning with self-training techniques, where an oracle (i.e. human annotator) annotates the most informative samples queried by a sampling function (e.g. least confidence, MNLP) while the trained model labels samples for which it has the highest confidence in its predictions. The ASL algorithm comes to further reduce the costs of labeling a dataset, when compared to the pure active learning process. Tran et al. [17] shows that the symbiotic relationship created by both the human and a trained Conditional Random Field model, labeling samples from the unlabeled set, increases the performance of the model while significantly reduce labeling costs. One major drawback of the ASL algorithm appears in its sensitivity to the quality of the initial labeled set, where a model trained on an ill-sampled initial labeled set can have its performance significantly reduced throughout the ASL process.

**In This Work,** we propose a deep active-self learning algorithm, that builds upon previous works from the literature [6,17]. We propose some key changes to the algorithm from the literature in order to try and minimize its sensitivity to the initial set of labeled samples. We also propose an early stopping strategy based on the model's confidence on an unlabeled set, which renders the use of a validation set unnecessary.

## 2    Methodology

This section presents the proposed deep active-self learning algorithm, which extends previous works from the literature [6,17] with the use of deep learning models and key changes to alleviate the sensitivity of the self learning process to the initial labeled set. Along with the ASL algorithm, we also propose an early stopping criterion based on the model's confidence on its predictions for the unlabeled samples, effectively dismissing the use of a validation set throughout the ASL procedure. Sections 2.1 and 2.2 present the proposed ASL algorithm and the early stopping criterion, respectively. Section 2.3 presents the experiments to be performed to evaluate the proposed strategies, as well as the baselines for comparison and hardware setup used for simulations.

### 2.1    Deep Active-Self Learning Algorithm

The active-self learning algorithms from the literature require the human and the trained model to cooperatively annotate samples from the unlabeled set. This process is very sensitive to the initial labeled set, which is used to train the initial machine learning model [17]. We argue that this sensitivity comes from the fact that samples annotated by the model in early rounds of the ASL algorithm may add a permanent bias to the labeled set, if poorly annotated. This stems from the fact that the samples annotated by the model are considered as reliable as those annotated by the oracle. Based on that, we propose an active-self learning algorithm that separates samples labeled by the model from those labeled by the human annotator, with the former having less impact on the model's parameters during training. We also propose to return the samples labeled by the model to the unlabeled set at the end of each iteration of the ASL algorithm. We expect these two changes to reduce the risk of adding permanent bias to both the trained model and the labeled sets. The proposed algorithm can be thought as an iterative semi-supervised learning process, as for each iteration it identifies a set of unlabeled samples that can be reliably used for self-training, an approach that resembles current semi-supervised works from the literature [1]. Figure 1 presents a comparison between the labeling process and training of the model by the ASL algorithms presented in the literature and the one proposed here. Algorithm 1 presents a more detailed explanation of the proposed active-self learning algorithm.

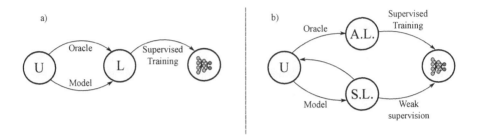

**Fig. 1.** In the diagrams, $U$ and $L$ represent the unlabeled and labeled sets, respectively. $A.L.$ is the active labeled set, which contains samples labeled by the oracle. $S.L.$ stands for self-labeled, meaning the set containing the samples labeled by the trained model. Figure (a) presents the ASL algorithm found in the literature, where both the oracle and the trained model cooperatively annotate unlabeled samples and add them to the same labeled set, which is then used to train the machine learning model. Figure (b) shows the proposed ASL algorithm, where samples labeled by the oracle and by the trained model are separated into different labeled sets, which are used for further training of the model, but with the self-labeled set having a lesser impact on the model's parameters during training. It also shows that after training, all samples labeled by the model are returned to the unlabeled set, thus reducing the risk of introducing permanent bias to the model throughout the ASL process.

Note that in the Algorithm 1, $m$ represents the machine learning model, $Q$ is the query budget, $min\_confidence$ is the minimum confidence the model must have to annotate an unlabeled sample, $A.L.$ stands for active labeled set which contains samples annotated by the oracle, $S.L.$ contains the samples labeled by the trained model, and $U$ represents the set of unlabeled data.

The active learning procedure, represented by the $Active\_Learning\_Query(\cdot)$ function in Algorithm 1, identifies the most informative unlabeled samples to be annotated by the oracle. For this work we selected the Maximum Normalized Log-Probability (MNLP) [15] as the sampling function, as it was shown to be competitive with more sophisticated sampling techniques [16] while being less expensive to be computed. The MNLP of a sequence $X$ of length $N$ can be computed as:

$$MNLP(X) = \max_{y_1,\dots,y_{N-1}} \frac{1}{N} \sum_{i=0}^{N} log\ P(y_i|x_i, y_0, y_1, \dots, y_{i-1}). \qquad (1)$$

**Algorithm 1.** Proposed active-self learning algorithm

1: **procedure** ASL($U$, $m$, $Q$, $min\_confidence$, $epoch$)
2:    $AL \leftarrow$ init_labeled_set($U$)
3:    Train_model($m$, $A.L.$, $epoch$)
4:    **while** Stopping Criterion not True **do**
5:       $A.L. \leftarrow$ Active_Learning_Query($U$, $m$, $Q$)
6:       $S.L. \leftarrow$ Self_Learning_Query($U$, $m$, $min\_confidence$)
7:       Train_model($m$, $A.L.$, $S.L.$, $epoch$)
8:       $U \leftarrow S.L.$

For the experiments, we follow previous works from the literature [16] and define a query budget as the number of tokens that can be selected by the sampling function to be manually annotated by the human annotator in a single iteration of the active learning process. We chose a query budget of approximately 2% of the tokens from the whole training set. Thus, the query budget was *20,000*, *6,000* and *4,000* words for the datasets OntoNotes5.0, *Aposentadoria*, and CoNLL 2003, respectively.

The *Self_Learning_Query*($\cdot$) function in Algorithm 1 identifies the samples for which the current trained model has a confidence higher than a predefined threshold. These samples are considered to be reliable and, therefore, can be used for self-training. A minimum confidence of 0.99 was selected in this work as the threshold, based on experiments performed using the validation set. The learning rate for training the model with self-labeled samples is one tenth of the learning rate used for training with the active-labeled samples, with this value being selected from initial experiments using the validation set.

For the model training, represented as *Train_model*($\cdot$) in Algorithm 1, we used classic supervised training. The single difference is that during training, we alternate using minibatches from the *A.L.* and *S.L.* sets.

## 2.2   Dynamic Update of Training Epochs - DUTE

Inspired by the *overall uncertainty* stopping criterion for active learning algorithms, proposed by Zhu et al. [18], we propose the *Dynamic Update of Training Epochs (DUTE)*, an early stopping strategy that reduces the number of training epochs based on the mean confidence of the trained model on its predictions for the unlabeled set. We hypothesize that the model's mean confidence indicates how well the labeled set represents the whole dataset, meaning that adding more unlabeled samples to the labeled set incurs in little change of the labeled set's label distribution. Because of that, we argue that fewer training epochs are required as the model's confidence on the unlabeled set increases.

To measure the model's confidence on the unlabeled set, we propose to use the harmonic mean of the model's normalized confidence for each unlabeled sample. The harmonic mean was used to emphasize those unlabeled samples for which the trained model has lower confidence in its predictions. The normalized confidence of a sequence of elements X can be computed as

$$NC(X) = e^{MNLP(X)},$$ (2)

where $MNLP(.)$ is the Maximum Normalized Log-Probability, presented in Eq. 1. The harmonic mean for the model's confidence on the unlabeled set $U$ is computed as

$$MC(U) = \frac{|U|}{\sum_{s \in U} NC^{-1}(s)}.$$ (3)

Given the mean confidence of the trained model on the unlabeled set, the DUTE strategy computes the number of training epochs to be used at the k-th iteration of the active learning algorithm, as presented in Eq. 4.

$$
epoch(k) = Round\Big[(1.0 - momentum) \times (1.0 - MC(U)) \times epoch(k-1)
$$
$$
+ (momentum) \times epoch(k-1)\Big]
$$ (4)

In this work, a momentum of 0.9 was selected based on initial experiments performed using the validation sets of the datasets presented in Sect. 2.3.

## 2.3   Experiments

This section describes the experiments designed in order to validate the proposed ASL algorithm and DUTE strategy. This validation was done in two separate experiments. The first experiment compares the proposed ASL algorithm with the DUTE strategy to the AL algorithm proposed by Shen et al. The second experiment is an ablation study, where we investigate the impact that the DUTE strategy has on both the execution time of the algorithm and the trained model's performance. The NER datasets, neural models and baselines used on both experiments are presented in the following sections.

### Datasets

For the experiments, we used two english NER datasets frequently used in the literature, namely the OntoNotes 5.0 [11] and the CoNLL 2003 [13]. Additionally, we also experimented on a novel legal domain NER dataset in portuguese, named *aposentadoria* (retirement, in direct translation) dataset. The *aposentadoria* dataset contains named entities from 10 distinct classes related to retirement acts of public employees published in the *Diário Oficial do Distrito Federal* (Brazilian Federal District official gazette, in direct translation). It's a part of a major dataset created by collaborators of project *KnEDLe*[1]. More information about the dataset as well as a download link to it are available at the github repository[2].

---

[1] http://nido.unb.br/.

[2] https://avio11.github.io/resources/aposentadoria/.

Table 1 presents the datasets used in the experiments, along with relevant information such as domain area and language.

**Table 1.** Datasets to be used for experiments on NER.

| Dataset | | CoNLL03 | OntoNotes5.0 | Aposentadoria |
|---------|-------|-------------|-------------|---------------------|
| Domain | | Reuters news | Variety | Brazilian legal texts |
| Language | | English | English | Portuguese |
| Train set | Sent. | 14,987 | 59,924 | 3,860 |
| | Token | 203,621 | 1,088,503 | 311,231 |
| Valid set | Sent. | 3,466 | 8,528 | 828 |
| | Token | 51,362 | 147,724 | 68,740 |
| Test set | Sent. | 3,684 | 8,262 | 827 |
| | Token | 46,435 | 152,728 | 65,912 |

For the experiments, all datasets were preprocessed by converting them to the IOBES notation which is frequently adopted by works on NER in the literature [1,5,7] for being capable of significantly improving the model's performance [12]. Also, numeric characters were replaced by # and 0 characters for english and portuguese datasets, respectively. Both replacements were made in order to enable the use of pretrained word embeddings used by the neural models, which are better described next.

**Neural Models**

The models to be used are those that appear in the work by Siddhant and Lipton [16], namely the CNN-CNN-LSTM introduced by Shen et al. [15] and the CNN-biLSTM-CRF designed by Ma and Hovy [7]. The hyperparameters used for both models were similar to those from their original papers for the experiments performed in the english NER datasets, and a grid-search was performed using the validation set on the *aposentadoria* dataset to find the best performing parameters for both models.

The parameters for the CNN-CNN-LSTM to be trained on the english NER datasets were similar to those presented in the experiments of Siddhant and Lipton [16], where the character-level CNN uses 25 dimensional character embeddings, the 1-d convolution layer has 50 filters, kernel size of 3, stride and padding of 1. The word-level CNN has two blocks, where each block has a 1-d convolutional layer with 800 filters, kernel size of 5, stride of 1 and padding of 2. The LSTM tag decoder consists of an LSTM layer of size 256. All dropout layers for the CNN-CNN-LSTM model have probability 0.5. For the portuguese NER dataset, a grid-search was performed using the validation set and the final architecture chosen had the following hyperparameters: The character-level CNN had the same parameters as those used for the english datasets. The word-level CNN has one block, consisting of a 1-d convolution layer with 400 filters, kernel size of

5, stride of 1 and padding of 2. The LSTM tag decoder has size 128. All dropout probabilities are still of 0.5.

The CNN-biLSTM-CRF model trained on the english NER datasets has a character-level CNN with 30 dimensional character embeddings, a 1-d convolution layer with 30 filters, kernel size of 3, padding of 1 and stride of 1. The biLSTM layer has size 300. All dropout probabilities are set to 0.5. For the portuguese dataset, a grid-search was employed to define the model's best parameters. The chosen model had the same parameters for the character-level CNN as that used for english datasets, while the biLSTM layer has size 256.

The pretrained embeddings used for both models for the english datasets were the GloVe embeddings of 100 dimensions pretrained on an english newswire corpus [10]. For the portuguese dataset, the GloVe embeddings of 300 dimensions pretrained on a multi-genre portuguese corpus [2] was used.

For optimization of the models throughout training, we used stochastic gradient descent of the cross entropy loss for the CNN-CNN-LSTM and the negative log-likelihood for the CNN-biLSTM-CRF. A constant momentum of 0.9 was selected and gradient was clipped at 5.0. Learning rates were 0.015 for both models trained on english datasets. For the portuguese dataset, learning rates of 0.010 and 0.0025 were selected for the CNN-CNN-LSTM and CNN-biLSTM-CRF models, respectively.

**Baselines and Evaluation Metrics**
For the first experiment, the baseline to compare the performance of the proposed ASL algorithm with the DUTE strategy is the deep active learning algorithm proposed by Shen et al. [15], using the MNLP sampling function. One key change is that we do not employ early stopping based on a validation set as the original work, instead we train the machine learning model for the full number of training epochs at each iteration of the DAL process. This change is justified by the fact that the early stopping is applied mainly to avoid overfitting of the models during training, and throughout all the experiments performed this phenomenon didn't occur. The f1-scores will be computed on the test set at the end of the training process. Query budget, number of training epochs, and initial labeled set size will be the same as those used by the ASL algorithm.

For the second experiment, the ablation study, we wish to investigate the impact of the proposed DUTE strategy. As such, the baseline will be the proposed ASL algorithm without the DUTE strategy.

A trained model's performance will be evaluated using the exact-match (i.e. span-based) micro-averaged f1-score on the test set.

**Experiment Setup**
All experiments reported were implemented and executed on the Google Colab platform with a pro subscription using the PyTorch [9] framework. GPUs available were the Tesla P100, the Tesla V100, and the Tesla T4 all with 16GB.

# 3   Results

The results for the experiments on the proposed deep active-self learning algorithm along with its baselines are presented in this section. We also show an ablation study conducted to investigate the impact of the DUTE strategy on the performance and execution time of the proposed ASL algorithm.

## 3.1   Deep Active-Self Learning with DUTE Strategy

Figure 2 shows the performance curves comparing the traditional deep active learning algorithms found in the literature and the proposed deep active-self learning algorithm with DUTE strategy. Each experiment was executed six times with unique initial labeled sets, and we report the mean performance curve for each of them. The same six initial labeled sets were used for experiments on the same dataset for all training algorithms and neural models. The algorithms were executed until at least 50% of the training set had been annotated by the oracle, in a similar setup used in previous works [15,16]. It has been observed that the proposed ASL algorithm achieved similar performance to the deep active learning baseline for most experiments.

One advantage of the active-self learning algorithm is its capabilities of allowing for self-labeling, thus potentially reducing human annotation efforts. Figure 3

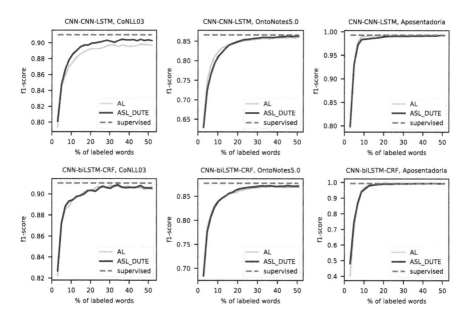

**Fig. 2.** Comparison between the proposed ASL algorithm with the DUTE strategy (ASL_DUTE) and the deep active learning algorithm (AL). Experiments were performed across all datasets with both neural models. The x axis represents the percentage of the whole training set that has been annotated by the oracle.

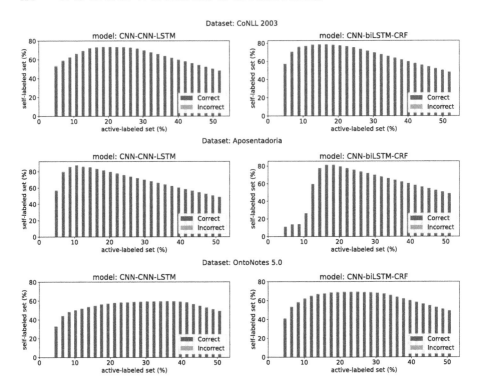

**Fig. 3.** Comparison between the correctly and wrongly self-annotated samples, at token level, for the experiments performed on all three datasets. Note that the Y-axis on each graph presents the percentage of the whole training set that has been self-labeled by the trained model in a given iteration of the ASL algorithm, while the X-axis presents the percentage of the whole training set that has been labeled by the human annotator.

reports the performance of the self-labeling process throughout the active-self learning algorithm. The figures present the percentage of self-labeled samples by the percentage of actively labeled samples (i.e. human annotation) and discriminates the amount of correctly and wrongly self-labeled tokens. In general, the trained model predicted most tokens correctly at all iterations of the algorithm. Across all experiments performed, 1.31% was the highest percentage of tokens to be mislabeled by the trained model in any given iteration of the ASL process. Even though most tokens were correctly self-labeled, little impact has been observed on the trained model's performance due to self-training. This may be justified by the fact that NER datasets are imbalanced, with most tokens not being a part of a named entity, and entity level annotations being unreliable at earlier rounds.

## 3.2 Ablation Study

Next we conduct an ablation study to investigate the impact of the proposed DUTE strategy on the performance and execution time of the proposed deep active-self learning algorithm. Differently from the previous experiment, in this ablation study we executed the algorithms until at least 30% of the training set had been annotated by the oracle. Figure 4 compares the performance of the ASL algorithm with and without the DUTE strategy, while Table 2 reports the mean and standard deviation for the execution times of the simulations. It has been observed that for all the experiments conducted, the DUTE strategy is capable of significantly reducing execution time, while maintaining similar model performance.

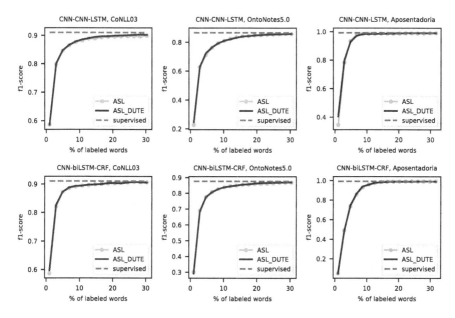

**Fig. 4.** Comparison of the performance of a model trained through the proposed deep active-self learning algorithm with and without the DUTE strategy. The x axis represents the percentage of the whole training set that has been annotated by the oracle.

**Table 2.** Mean and standard deviation for the execution time of the proposed active-self learning algorithm with and without the DUTE strategy, reported in units of minutes. Execution times are measured with algorithms being stopped when the set of samples annotated by the human annotator reaches 30% of the entire training set. ASL_DUTE and ASL refer to the proposed active-self learning algorithm with and without the DUTE strategy, respectively.

|  |  | ASL | | ASL_DUTE | |
|---|---|---|---|---|---|
|  |  | Mean (min) | Std (min) | Mean (min) | Std (min) |
| CNN-CNN-LSTM | CoNLL03 | 211.18 | 0.71 | 66.24 | 1.97 |
|  | OntoNotes5 | 366.61 | 2.20 | 148.87 | 1.80 |
|  | Aposentadoria | 342.20 | 50.36 | 79.17 | 1.94 |
| CNN-biLSTM-CRF | CoNLL03 | 178.55 | 2.14 | 67.29 | 11.42 |
|  | OntoNotes5 | 429.10 | 8.37 | 109.93 | 0.73 |
|  | Aposentadoria | 270.94 | 50.98 | 72.15 | 2.82 |

# 4    Conclusion

From the experiments conducted, we noticed that the proposed deep active-self learning algorithm is capable of self-annotating unlabeled samples reliably. The self-training hasn't, however, shown significant impact on the model's performance. The proposed DUTE strategy has also shown promising results, being capable of significantly reducing the execution times for simulations of the proposed algorithm with little impact on the model's performance, while not relying on a validation set.

One of the main limitations of the proposed ASL algorithm still continues to be its reliance on labeled data for hyperparameter tuning. While our DUTE strategy effectively avoids using validation sets throughout the ASL process, we still used training and validation sets for tuning of the hyperparameters for the neural models and others such as learning rates and batch sizes. This still poses one of the biggest limitations to the use of active learning algorithms in real-world low-resource scenarios.

Another observation made is that the self-training technique employed here wasn't able to improve the model's performance. Future works may investigate more sophisticated self-training techniques, such as consistency regularization techniques, which are often employed by current state-of-the-art semi-supervised methods [1]. These more recent self-training techniques also tend to use soft targets for training, instead of hard targets (i.e. one hot encoded vectors) [1,8], in a setup similar to knowledge distillation [3].

**Acknowledgements.** The authors are supported by the *Fundação de Apoio a Pesquisa do Distritio Federal (FAP-DF)* as members of the *Knowledge Extraction from Documents of Legal content (KnEDLe)* project from the University of Brasilia.

# References

1. Clark, K., Luong, M.T., Manning, C.D., Le, Q.: Semi-supervised sequence modeling with cross-view training. In: Proceedings of the 2018 Conference on Empirical Methods in Natural Language Processing, pp. 1914–1925. Association for Computational Linguistics, Brussels, October–November 2018. https://doi.org/10.18653/v1/D18-1217
2. Hartmann, N.S., Fonseca, E.R., Shulby, C.D., Treviso, M.V., Rodrigues, J.S., Aluísio, S.M.: Portuguese word embeddings: evaluating on word analogies and natural language tasks. In: Anais do XI Simpósio Brasileiro de Tecnologia da Informação e da Linguagem Humana, pp. 122–131. SBC, Porto Alegre, RS, Brasil (2017). https://sol.sbc.org.br/index.php/stil/article/view/4008
3. Hinton, G., Vinyals, O., Dean, J.: Distilling the knowledge in a neural network (2015)
4. Houlsby, N., Huszár, F., Ghahramani, Z., Lengyel, M.: Bayesian active learning for classification and preference learning (2011)
5. Lample, G., Ballesteros, M., Subramanian, S., Kawakami, K., Dyer, C.: Neural architectures for named entity recognition. In: Proceedings of the 2016 Conference of the North American Chapter of the Association for Computational Linguistics: Human Language Technologies, pp. 260–270. Association for Computational Linguistics, San Diego, June 2016. https://doi.org/10.18653/v1/N16-1030, https://www.aclweb.org/anthology/N16-1030
6. Lin, Y., Sun, C., Xiaolong, W., Xuan, W.: Combining self learning and active learning for Chinese named entity recognition. J. Softw. 5, May 2010. https://doi.org/10.4304/jsw.5.5.530-537
7. Ma, X., Hovy, E.: End-to-end sequence labeling via bi-directional LSTM-CNNs-CRF. In: Proceedings of the 54th Annual Meeting of the Association for Computational Linguistics (Volume 1: Long Papers), pp. 1064–1074. Association for Computational Linguistics, Berlin, August 2016. https://doi.org/10.18653/v1/P16-1101
8. Miyato, T., Dai, A.M., Goodfellow, I.: Adversarial training methods for semi-supervised text classification. In: International Conference on Learning Representations (ICLR) (2017)
9. Paszke, A., et al.: Pytorch: an imperative style, high-performance deep learning library. In: Wallach, H., Larochelle, H., Beygelzimer, A., d'Alché-Buc, F., Fox, E., Garnett, R. (eds.) Advances in Neural Information Processing Systems 32, pp. 8024–8035. Curran Associates, Inc. (2019). http://papers.neurips.cc/paper/9015-pytorch-an-imperative-style-high-performance-deep-learning-library.pdf
10. Pennington, J., Socher, R., Manning, C.: GloVe: global vectors for word representation. In: Proceedings of the 2014 Conference on Empirical Methods in Natural Language Processing (EMNLP), pp. 1532–1543. Association for Computational Linguistics, October 2014. https://doi.org/10.3115/v1/D14-1162
11. Pradhan, S., et al.: Towards robust linguistic analysis using OntoNotes. In: Proceedings of the Seventeenth Conference on Computational Natural Language Learning, pp. 143–152. Association for Computational Linguistics, Sofia, August 2013
12. Ratinov, L., Roth, D.: Design challenges and misconceptions in named entity recognition. In: Proceedings of the Thirteenth Conference on Computational Natural Language Learning (CoNLL-2009), pp. 147–155. Association for Computational Linguistics, Boulder, June 2009. https://www.aclweb.org/anthology/W09-1119

13. Sang, E.F.T.K., Meulder, F.D.: Introduction to the CoNLL-2003 shared task: Language-independent named entity recognition. In: Proceedings of the Seventh Conference on Natural Language Learning at HLT-NAACL 2003, pp. 142–147 (2003)

14. Settles, B., Craven, M.: An analysis of active learning strategies for sequence labeling tasks. In: Proceedings of the Conference on Empirical Methods in Natural Language Processing, EMNLP 2008, pp. 1070–1079. Association for Computational Linguistics, USA (2008)

15. Shen, Y., Yun, H., Lipton, Z., Kronrod, Y., Anandkumar, A.: Deep active learning for named entity recognition. In: Proceedings of the 2nd Workshop on Representation Learning for NLP, pp. 252–256. Association for Computational Linguistics, Vancouver, August 2017. https://doi.org/10.18653/v1/W17-2630

16. Siddhant, A., Lipton, Z.C.: Deep Bayesian active learning for natural language processing: results of a large-scale empirical study. In: Proceedings of the 2018 Conference on Empirical Methods in Natural Language Processing, pp. 2904–2909. Association for Computational Linguistics, Brussels, October–November 2018. https://doi.org/10.18653/v1/D18-1318

17. Tran, V.C., Nguyen, N.T., Fujita, H., Hoang, D.T., Hwang, D.: A combination of active learning and self-learning for named entity recognition on twitter using conditional random fields. Knowl.-Based Syst. **132**, 179–187 (2017). https://doi.org/10.1016/j.knosys.2017.06.023

18. Zhu, J., Wang, H., Hovy, E., Ma, M.: Confidence-based stopping criteria for active learning for data annotation. ACM Trans. Speech Lang. Process. **6**(3), April 2010. https://doi.org/10.1145/1753783.1753784

# DEEPAGÉ: Answering Questions in Portuguese About the Brazilian Environment

Flávio Nakasato Cação$^{(\boxtimes)}$ ⓘ, Marcos Menon Joséⓘ, André Seidel Oliveiraⓘ,
Stefano Spindolaⓘ, Anna Helena Reali Costaⓘ,
and Fabio Gagliardi Cozmanⓘ

Escola Politécnica, Universidade de São Paulo, Sao Paulo, Brazil
{flavio.cacao,marcos.jose,andre.seidel,stefano.spindola,
anna.reali,fgcozman}@usp.br

**Abstract.** The challenge of climate change and biome conservation is one of the most pressing issues of our time—particularly in Brazil, where key environmental reserves are located. Given the availability of large textual databases on ecological themes, it is natural to resort to question answering (QA) systems to increase social awareness and understanding about these topics. In this work, we introduce multiple QA systems that combine in novel ways the BM25 algorithm, a sparse retrieval technique, with PTT5, a pre-trained state-of-the-art language model. Our QA systems focus on the Portuguese language, thus offering resources not found elsewhere in the literature. As training data, we collected questions from open-domain datasets, as well as content from the Portuguese Wikipedia and news from the press. We thus contribute with innovative architectures and novel applications, attaining an F1-score of 36.2 with our best model.

**Keywords:** Question answering · Environment in Brazil · Natural language processing in Portuguese

## 1 Introduction

Developing technologies and public policies to address the challenges of climate change is a multifaceted task. The United Nations (UN) Resolution with 17 Sustainable Development Goals, whose focus is on the protection of the global environment and increased general prosperity, contains a call for "Climate Action", with five urgent goals to fight climate change; raising collective awareness belongs to these goals. Brazil has a central role in that debate as it has some of the richest and most important biomes in the world, and at the same time, it faces difficulties in curbing deforestation and illegal forest fires [20]. There is much to

---

F. N. Cação and M. M. José—These authors contributed equally to the work.

© Springer Nature Switzerland AG 2021
A. Britto and K. Valdivia Delgado (Eds.): BRACIS 2021, LNAI 13074, pp. 419–433, 2021.
https://doi.org/10.1007/978-3-030-91699-2_29

be done still in informing a poorly educated but interested population on issues related to the environment [16].

We can take advantage of the latest advances in natural language processing (NLP) and question answering (QA) so as to better inform the population on environmental issues. While natural language processing of textual databases has been used to deal with environmental challenges [3,8,12], exploration of such databases in Brazilian Portuguese remains underdeveloped, to say the least.

On the dataset availability side, [1] recently released *Pirá*, the first Bilingual Portuguese-English crowdsourced QA dataset about the ocean and, in particular, the Brazilian coast, based on UN reports and abstracts from scientific papers. In English, *CLIMATE-FEVER* is intended to serve as a fact-checking dataset for claims related to climate change [5]. For topic detection, *ClimaText* is a dataset that leverages manual annotation of labels on texts extracted from Wikipedia and the official U.S. documents via Active Learning [17]. Furthermore, there is a large gap in the availability of annotated NLP datasets focused on environmental or climate issues, despite the urgency of the topic.

In this work, we start to fill this gap by putting together QA systems that enhance existing architectures and that are built from a knowledge base (KB) consisting of 17K Wikipedia articles in Portuguese[1] and 29K news.[2] The combination of encyclopedic knowledge and recent news lets us capture the public's changing interests as they are reflected in newspapers. Due to the scarcity of QA datasets specifically related to environment and climate in Brazil and the high cost of manually generating such a dataset, we have also filtered the PAQ (*Probably Asked Questions*) dataset [11], a massive open-domain QA dataset with 65 million automatically-generated question/answer pairs (QA-pairs); we thus obtained a large set of QA-pairs that was then translated.

We leverage insights from the transformer architecture [18] and self-attention mechanisms [2], as well as insights on domain-specific fine-tuning [14].

Our reader model is based on PTT5 architecture [4], a sequence-to-sequence T5 network [14] model pre-trained in a corpora in Portuguese. To incorporate the databases in the production of answers, we used the BM25 algorithm [15], the state-of-the-art in sparse information retrieval, to add context blocks to the question then submitted to T5 for fine-tuning. This dual system, composed of a retrieval module and a neural reader model, has been explored in the QA literature [7,10] and has some advantages over systems with only a neural module. First, it reduces the document load that the reader needs to process because the retrieval system pre-selects the $k$ best passages in the corpus before submitting them further. Second, the possibility of including new factual information as input from the subsequent reader. Third, it potentially generates less hallucination, a very common problem in text generated by neural networks.

---

[1] Articles about the "Environment of Brazil" taken from the following category of Wikipedia: https://pt.wikipedia.org/wiki/Categoria:Meio_ambiente_do_Brasil.

[2] Published between January 2018 to June 2021, and scraped from the three biggest newspapers in circulation in Brazil on different topics related to environmental issues in the country (such as deforestation, the status of indigenous peoples).

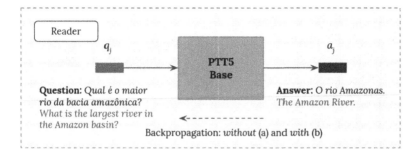

**Fig. 1.** QA system with only PTT5 as a Reader, without a retriever module. Two versions of this reader were tested: *(a)* without fine-tuning, in which the model could only rely on knowledge saved in the network's own weights *(b)* another with fine-tuning on the QA-pair training set.

In short, our main contribution is a QA system focused on the environment in Brazil in Portuguese, developed in two schemes. One scheme consists of only a Reader module containing a language model; the other consists of a Reader equipped with a powerful Retriever with access to documents indicated previously (Wikipedia, news, etc.). Another contribution is the filtered and translated corpus of QA-pairs related to our domain; the fundamental idea there was to extract these pairs from a massive open-domain dataset, thus avoiding the manual creation of a new set of QA-pairs[3]. As far as we know, we are the first to design a QA system and a dataset on the Brazilian environment in this way.

In the following sections, we explain how the models work and which settings we used in our experiments. We describe the process of building and filtering the knowledge bases: Wikipedia categories in Portuguese, and newspaper content. We also explain how we enhanced our QA dataset on the environment of Brazil using a massive open-domain QA dataset. Then we present the different experiments we ran, discuss the main results, and analyze possible improvements as future work.

## 2    Models and Architectures

In this work, we have two basic model architectures. The first one is illustrated in Fig. 1: without any additional supporting documents, the model answers the posed question by only accessing the information stored in its own parameters. We call this architecture a *Reader*-only one. So, for each question $q_j$, the Reader generates another sequence, the answer, $a_j$. The Reader can thus answer questions without text support; in our implementation, it is based on T5, a language model that can generate its own responses from scratch (that is, it does not rely on extracting it from a passage of text).

---

[3] All relevant code, checkpoints, and data (except for the scrapped news, in respect of copyright laws) are available or referenced in the Github repository: https://github.com/C4AI/deepage.

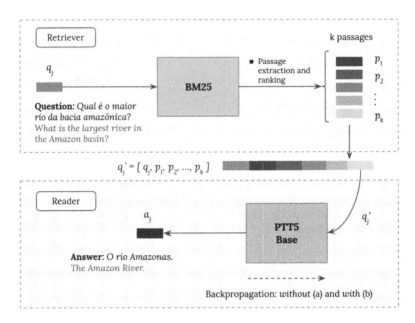

**Fig. 2.** QA system with both the Retriever (BM25) and the Reader (PTT5) modules working together. Again, two versions of this system were tested: *(a)* without fine-tuning *(b)* with fine-tuning on the QA-pair training set.

In the second architecture, we add a *Retriever* module before the Reader. In this case, the Reader has access to an external knowledge base, in addition to the information saved in its parameters. We resorted to Wikipedia and news from mainstream newspapers. For each question $q_j$, the Retriever searches for the most relevant $k$ passages $\{p_1, p_2, ..., p_k\}$ in the corpus. Then the original question is concatenated to these passages, producing a reformulated question $q'_j = [q_j, p_1, p_2, ..., p_k]$, which, finally, serves as input to the Reader, in place of $q_j$, to generate an answer $a_j$. The scheme is represented in Fig. 2.

In either case, the Reader may or may not be fine-tuned with the QA-pairs $(q_j, a_j)$ from the problem domain. This is expressed by options (b) and (a) presented at the bottom of the Figs. 1 and 2.

We next discuss in more detail the technical aspects of the Reader and the Retriever we have implemented.

## 2.1  BM25 as the Retriever

BM25 [15] is an algorithm that estimates the relevance of documents from a set given a query. It is the state-of-the-art *sparse* retrieval technique, defined as a function of query terms frequency, document length, average document length, and the number of documents containing the query term. We applied BM25 to retrieve sentences of about 100 words from all sentences of the KB. The query is defined as the posed question $q_j$.

## 2.2  PTT5 as the Reader

PTT5 [4], an encoder-decoder transformer, was pre-trained on the BrWaC Brazilian Portuguese website corpus [19] for the task of masked language modeling, where tokens from the corpus are masked so that the model has to predict them. The model is based on T5, which is derived from the original encoder-decoder transformer by Vaswani et al. [18], characterized by several blocks of self-attention layers concatenated to feed-forward networks. We applied the "base" version of PTT5 with a Portuguese vocabulary[4], with 12 layers and 12 attention heads, with a total of 220M trainable parameters.

# 3  Dataset Generation

We built a dataset based on a set of textual documents and a set of QA-pairs. The KB has two main sources of texts, the Brazilian Portuguese Wikipedia, and newspapers. We describe next how they were collected (as depicted in Fig. 3).

## 3.1  Filtering Articles from Wikipedia in Portuguese

Wikipedia is divided in such a way that articles are associated with categories. A category, on the other hand, is associated with articles and other categories that restrict even more the subject, called subcategories.

To access this information, a SQL table associating article and subcategory identifiers to category names is available for download at Wikimedia's dumps page.[5] Thus, to obtain several articles associated with the Brazilian Environment, we applied a recursive script that performs a breadth-first search of articles on subcategories, starting from an arbitrary category title. The algorithm stops when the desired number of articles is reached.

We searched by taking the starting point "Environment of Brazil" (freely translated from "Meio Ambiente do Brasil") and obtained 17K Wikipedia articles associated with the subject (hereafter abbreviated as "Wiki" for simplicity).

## 3.2  Scraping and Filtering News from the Biggest Brazilian Newspapers

To build the news base, we scraped and processed news linked to pre-selected keywords in the three biggest newspapers in the country: *Folha de S.Paulo*, *Estadão* and *O Globo*. Due to the limited value of this type of text over time, we kept only news from January 2018 on, as this is the beginning of the current federal government in Brazil. We downloaded the headline and body of each article and, after final cleaning and pre-processing, we ended up with 29K news (we will refer to this database as "News").

---

[4] The pre-trained model is available at https://huggingface.co/unicamp-dl/ptt5-base-portuguese-vocab.

[5] Available at https://dumps.wikimedia.org/.

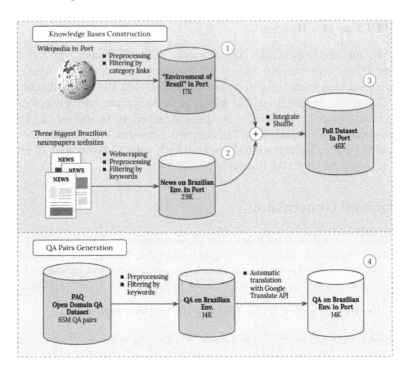

**Fig. 3.** To build the KBs (upper blue section), Wikipedia articles in Portuguese from the category "Environment of Brazil" were processed, filtered and loaded into a database (1); Newspaper news were filtered by keyword, scraped and also loaded into a database (2). Finally, the two databases were integrated and shuffled to produce a third database (3), the "full" version. All three were used in different experiments. At the bottom of the figure (orange section), the PAQ filtering process, QA massive open-domain dataset, is described. Using regex with key phrases related to the environment in Brazil, we filtered 14K QA-pairs and then translated them into Portuguese using Google Translation API (4). (Color figure online)

To select the news that would be scraped, we first carefully crafted a list of keywords that are strongly related to the environment in the country. We then use the native search engines on each newspaper's website to inject these keywords, list the search results, and download them via webscraping techniques. To minimize the number of false positives, i.e. news that is related to a certain keyword but is linked to news from a different subject that is not of our interest, we also excluded articles related to a set of specific words for some keywords. More details on this selection can be found in Appendix B.

Due to latencies and limitations inherent to the scraping process of websites, there is no guarantee that all news related to a particular term has been downloaded. However, we obtained large numbers related to each keyword, which suggests good coverage, as illustrated in the Fig. 4.

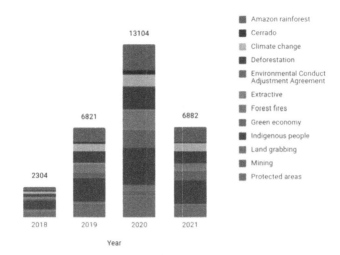

**Fig. 4.** Citation count of each environmental category per year since 2018, considering the three biggest newspapers in Brazil.

### 3.3  Filtering and Translating the PAQ QA Dataset

To obtain an appreciable number of QA-pairs to fine-tune the models, we chose to filter a large-scale open-domain QA dataset with keywords that should and should not be in the questions or answers; this query with multiple rules was carefully hand-crafted and searches were done with regex expressions.[6]

Initially, we applied this query to filter the MS MARCO v1 [13] training dataset, which is composed of questions from real users made in Bing, with human-annotated answers and contained 80.142 QA-pairs after eliminating unanswered questions. However, due to many constraints we imposed on the filter to avoid false positive and false negative pairs[7], we obtained a return rate of only 0.037%, which corresponded to 30 pairs, an insufficient amount of data to fine-tune our models. Relaxing the QA-pair filter did not generate a significant increase in this value.

Assuming this rate would be similar to other QA datasets based on user queries on search engines, such as Google's Natural Questions [9], we decided to filter the PAQ dataset, as it would be the only one capable of providing several training pairs of about three orders of magnitude greater than the one obtained from MS MARCO v1, which was what we desired at least. In fact, with a rate of return of about 0.024%, we got 14,386 QA-pairs after the filter. As shown in the plot 5, the filtering process did not generate a significant loss of quality for the QA-pairs when compared to the original PAQ.

---

[6] The query we developed is described in the Appendix A.

[7] For example, if the word "biome" were a substring of a certain question or its answer, the word "Brazil" or other names of states in the country should also be so, so as not to include QA-pairs about biomes from other countries in our selection.

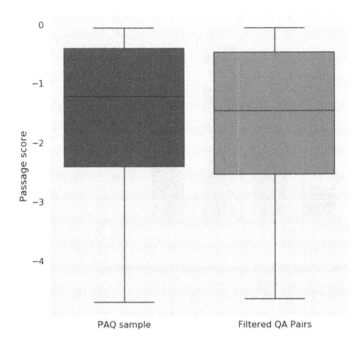

**Fig. 5.** Comparison between the distribution of passage scores of a random sample of the PAQ with the ones of QA-pairs filtered for the Brazilian environmental domain. The passage score is a logprob score calculated in the PAQ dataset that measures how likely a given QA-pair is in practice; the closer to zero, the better. Note that the filtering process did not cause a significant loss of quality.

In addition to the quantitative evaluation that demonstrates that our filtered QA-pairs are as good as those in the general PAQ base (which already have high-quality [11]), we also performed a manual, qualitative inspection on a sample of 50 instances of our set of QA-pairs. They were evaluated by a human annotator, who answered three questions for each filtered and translated QA-pair: "Is the domain adherent?", "Does the QA-pair make sense?" and "Is the answer correct?". The annotator could answer all questions with only one of the following possibilities: "Yes", "Admissible" and "No". As shown in Fig. 6, the results show that got at least admissible were: 70% for domain adherence, 82% for sense, and 80% for the correctness of the answer, and even considering just perfect QA-pairs, all categories got more than 50% of occurrence.

Finally, to fine-tune our QA system entirely on the same language, we applied the Google Translate API (Application Programming Interface) to translate these pairs into Portuguese.

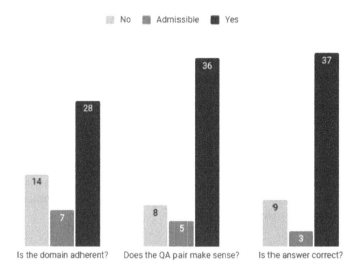

**Fig. 6.** Manual evaluation of a sample of 50 QA-pairs from our domain-specific QA dataset, which got at least 70% of admissible and 50% perfect results in all three categories

## 4   Experiments

To measure the impact of the retrieval module, each base of supporting documents, and the fine-tuning of the system, we performed three groups of experiments:

1. Reader-only and Retriever+Reader, both without fine-tuning;
2. Reader-only, with fine-tune;
3. Retriever+Reader, with fine-tune.

The filtered QA-pairs dataset was randomly split into 3 groups: 70% for training, 15% for validation, and 15% for the test. The models in experiments 2 and 3, which depended on a training phase, were trained for 30 epochs, with a batch size equal to 16, weight decay equal to 0.01 and a learning rate of $2e-5$; the same training and validation sets were used for the fine-tuning. For all models, we report the F1-score, the Exact Match (EM), and the Rouge-L (R-L) metrics, also obtained in the same test set. In all cases, we used the ptt5-base-portuguese-vocab T5 pre-trained model in Portuguese, since it was the recommended one by the original work [4] in comparison to the other versions of PTT5, including its large version. In cases where we used the BM25-based retrieval module, we preprocessed all the supporting documents by removing special characters, eliminating line breaks, and splitting them into chunks of 100-word passages.

### 4.1   Experiment 1: Systems Without Fine-Tune

Experiment 1 aimed to provide a baseline and demonstrate the impact of the lack of a fine-tuning step with the filtered QA base for the problem domain. Therefore, we place the two models, Reader-only and Retriever+Reader, directly to answer the test set questions, without any previous fine-tune, as indicated in Figs. 1(a) and 2(a), respectively.

### 4.2   Experiment 2: Reader-Only, with Fine-Tune

As in Experiment 1, in this case, we abdicated the retrieval module but performed the fine-tuning of PTT5 in our domain-specific QA dataset. All other parameters are identical to those of the Reader in the previous subsection. Figure 1(b) illustrates the procedure.

### 4.3   Experiment 3: Retriever+Reader with Fine-Tune

In this experiment, the model was composed of the two modules, Retriever and Reader, as in the second case discussed in Experiment 1, with the difference that now PTT5 is submitted to a fine-tuning on our domain-specific QA dataset, as shown in Fig. 2(b). In this experiment, we explore the impact on the quality of model answers to:

1. A larger number of passages retrieved by the retriever;
2. Each KB (Wiki, News and Wiki+News).

Thus, we trained the model with $k = 5$ retrieved passages and 512 entry tokens for PTT5 three times, once with each distinct KB (Wiki, News, and Wiki+News). Then, we repeated the same 3 pieces of training but considering $k = 10$ and 1024 entry tokens for PTT5.

## 5   Results and Discussion

The results of all the experiments described in the previous section are consolidated in Table 1. As the metrics are highly correlated, we will focus on the F1-score from now on. Information on training and inference times, as well as the machine settings used, can be found in Appendix C.

### 5.1   Importance of Fine-Tune on the Specific Domain

As expected, the models from Experiment 1, without fine-tune, had the worst results of all. This demonstrates the importance of this training phase and the construction of the domain-specific dataset we performed: the Reader-only from Experiment 2, fine-tuned in our QA dataset, performed 11 times better than the Reader+Retriever system from Experiment 1, which had access to a KB composed of all the news and Wikipedia articles collected, and achieved scores comparable to models that were fine-tuned and had access to one KB. Then, in short, the presence of the retrieval module does not compensate for the absence of the model's fine-tune.

**Table 1.** Main results of the tests conducted analysed by the metrics F1-score, Exact Match and Rouge-L. The best model was the one with a reader and a retriever backed only on the Wiki database, with 10 passages retrieved.

| Supporting documents | Model | Number of Passages $k$ | F1 | EM | R-L |
|---|---|---|---|---|---|
| None | Reader w/o FT | – | 3.5 | 0.0 | 3.9 |
| News + Wiki | Retriever + Reader w/o FT | 5 | 2.9 | 0.0 | 3.2 |
| None | Reader w/ FT | – | 32.2 | 24.8 | 32.8 |
| News | Retriever + Reader w/ FT | 5 | 32.9 | 25.2 | 33.5 |
| Wiki | Retriever + Reader w/ FT | 5 | 34.7 | 26.9 | 35.4 |
| Wiki + News | Retriever + Reader w/ FT | 5 | 34.4 | 26.8 | 35.0 |
| News | Retriever + Reader w/ FT | 10 | 32.2 | 24.9 | 32.7 |
| Wiki | Retriever + Reader w/ FT | 10 | **36.2** | **28.2** | **37.0** |
| Wiki + News | Retriever + Reader w/ FT | 10 | 35.4 | 27.5 | 36.2 |

## 5.2   Impact of Different KBs on Scores

Experiment 3 allowed us to compare the effect of each KB on the quality of the systems' responses with the Retriever. For both $k = 5$ and for $k = 10$, we observed that the systems supported *only* by the Wiki KB performed better than those that have access to the expanded KB with newspaper news (Wiki+News), which was contrary to what we expected at the beginning. Also, in both cases, the least competitive results occurred when the KB is composed only by the News KB, still, however, surpassing the Reader-only model.

A possible explanation for this phenomenon may lie in the PAQ construction process, which is automatically generated on Wikipedia passages in English. This can generate a bias in favor of the KB formed by a specific category of Wikipedia, even though it is, here, in Portuguese.

## 5.3   Influence of Distractors on the Reader

Finally, it is remarkable that doubling the number of retrieved passages to $k = 10$ improves the performance of the models with Wiki, even when integrated with the News, but simultaneously the worst model among those that have access to a KB is the one composed *solely of news*. It is slightly inferior even to the same model configured with $k = 5$. Arguably, this is because, when we concatenate the initial question $q$ with the 10 passages instead of 5, we end up diluting the weight of $q$ in the reformulated question $q'$ (a much longer text), making the original question more diffuse among heterogeneous news articles, which does not compensate for the information gain brought by the retrieved passages $\{p_1, p_2, ..., p_k\}$. Still, the News KB can be helpful due to the contemporaneity it aggregates to the KB, which can be particularly relevant for reasons of explainability.

**Table 2.** Comparison between a case in which the presence of the Retriever is useful to prevent the Reader from making mistakes (first case), and another in which the retrieved passages otherwise mislead it due to the presence of distractors.

| Question | True answer | Reader-only | Retriever+Reader |
|---|---|---|---|
| Quando Fernando de Noronha se tornou um Patrimônio Mundial da UNESCO? *(When did Fernando de Noronha become a UNESCO World Heritage Site?)* | 2001 | 1997 | **2001** |
| Qual é o maior rio da bacia amazônica? *(What is the largest river in the Amazon basin?)* | Rio Amazonas *(Amazon river)* | **Rio Amazonas** *(Amazon river)* | Tocantins *(Tocantins)* |

The same probably does not occur as often with the Wiki KB perhaps because of the generational bias of PAQ. Nevertheless, it does not make it immune to distractors. Table 2 illustrates two emblematic cases, comparing a QA system with only the Reader and another with the Retriever+Reader. In the first question, whose correct answer is "2001", the Reader-only was wrong, but the system composed also of a Retriever was right. The retrieved passage that contains the answer is:

"*...Today Fernando de Noronha's economy depends on tourism (...)* **In 2001 the archipelago was declared a World Heritage Site**, *including the Atol das Rocas, as Sítio das Ilhas...*".

Thus, we see that the information extracted by the Retriever was essential for the Reader not to incur the same error again.

However, in the second question, the opposite occurs: the Reader gets it right, but the Retrieve+Reader system gets it wrong. When observing the recovered passages, we noticed a potential distractor that could have induced the system to error:

*...On March 8 of that year, Marabá was practically submerged. Occupying an area of 803 250 square kilometers, it is the largest hydrographic basin entirely in Brazil, even though it belongs to the Amazon Basin (...)* **The Tocantins, the main river in this basin**, *rises in the north of Goiás and flows into the Marajoara Gulf...*".

Despite these occasional problems, all tests we performed indicated that a system consisting of a Retriever and a Reader always surpasses one with only a Reader.

# 6    Conclusion

We presented the first QA system focused on environmental issues in Brazil—more importantly, a QA system based on the Portuguese language, a language that has received remarkably low attention when it comes to automatic question answering. We combined PTT5 as the Reader, the state-of-the-art among pre-trained language models, and BM25 as the Retriever, the state-of-the-art sparse retrieval technique. Also, we collected documents and QA-pairs by filtering articles related to "Environment of Brazil" in the Wikipedia dump in Portuguese; scraped environmental news from January 2018 to June of 2021 in the three most important newspapers in the country; filtered and translated a recently released massive open-domain QA dataset to obtain a substantial domain-specific set of QA pairs. Despite potential generation biases found in this last step, our trained QA systems demonstrated competitive scores. We hope that this work can stimulate similar initiatives on a topic that is so relevant to Brazilian environmental efforts.

To DEEPAGÉ increase social awareness and understanding about the environment and the climate of Brazil, the system must be tested with human subjects. Integration with other modules such as a social chatbot can certainly make the system more appealing for users [6]. Another further improvement would be the construction of a system that gives more complete and elaborate answers. As our training was ran using the PAQ dataset, with a majority of factual and short responses, the system is not prepared to give long and detailed answers. Also, generative models such as the PTT5 can hallucinate when giving answers, especially when there is no retriever. Hence, another useful future extension to DEEPAGÉ would be a filtering module to avoid absurd answers.

**Acknowledgements.** This work was financed in part by the *Coordenação de Aperfeiçoamento de Pessoal de Nível Superior* (CAPES, Finance Code 001) and by the *Itaú Unibanco S.A.*, through the *Programa de Bolsas Itaú* (PBI) of the *Centro de Ciência de Dados* (C$^2$D) of *Escola Politécnica* of *Universidade de São Paulo* (USP). We also gratefully acknowledge support from *Conselho Nacional de Desenvolvimento Cientíífico e Tecnológico* (CNPq) (grants 312180/2018-7 and 310085/2020-9) and the *Center for Artificial Intelligence* (C4AI-USP), with support by the *Fundação de Amparo à Pesquisa do Estado de São Paulo* (FAPESP, grant 2019/ 07665-4) and by the *IBM Corporation*.

# 7    Appendix A

To filter QA-pairs in PAQ, we created four sets of keywords: $M$ (from "Must have": "brazil*" and other states names), $G$ (from "Good to have"; e.g. "deforestation"), $U$ (from "Unique expressions"; e.g. "ibama" or "amazon rainforest") and $E$ (from "to Exclude"; e.g. "soccer"). For a pair to be selected, it must contain, in its question or answer, at least one expression belonging to $M$ or $U$. If it was from $U$, it would already be selected; if it was from $M$, it could not contain any $E$ expressions. Finally, if the QA-pair contains any keyword from $G$, it should also contain at least one from $M$, but none from $E$ either.

# 8    Appendix B

We performed queries associated with the following keywords (here, translated into English): *Amazon rainforest, Cerrado, Climate change, Deforestation, Environmental Conduct Adjustment Agreement, Extractive* (from *"Extractivism"*), *Forest fires, Funding for conservation, Green economy, Land grabbing, Mining* and *Protected areas.* It should be noted that the decision to exclude some words is only understandable in Portuguese, since there is no reasonable parallel in English, as with the word "fist" for the keyword "Cerrado" - in Portuguese, the expression "punho cerrado" ("clenched fist") is common, but it is clearly not directly related to the Cerrado biome. Also for more significant results, we eliminated news related to "agrobusiness" in the *Green economy* keyword and "militias" in the *Land grabbing* one.

# 9    Appendix C

To perform the experiments, we leverage a machine with an AMD Ryzen 9 3950X Processor with 32 CPUs, 64 GB of RAM, 2 NVIDIA RTX 3090 GPUs of 24GB each, on an Ubuntu 20 LTS. Under these conditions, the training of each model lasted between 5h and 8h, with the best model being trained in about 7h40. The inference time – that is, the time it took to a model to generate an answer to a single question from the test set – was around 0.006s.

# References

1. Paschoal, A.F.A., et al.: A Bilingual Portuguese-English dataset for question-answering about the ocean. In: 30th ACM International Conference on Information and Knowledge Management (CIKM 2021) (2021). https://doi.org/10.1145/3459637.3482012
2. Bahdanau, D., Cho, K.H., Bengio, Y.: Neural machine translation by jointly learning to align and translate. In: 3rd International Conference on Learning Representations, ICLR 2015 - Conference Track Proceedings, pp. 1–15 (2015)
3. Bhatia, S., Lau, J.H., Baldwin, T.: Automatic Classification of Neutralization Techniques in the Narrative of Climate Change Scepticism, pp. 2167–2175 (2021)
4. Carmo, D., Piau, M., Campiotti, I., Nogueira, R., Lotufo, R.: PTT5: pretraining and validating the T5 model on Brazilian Portuguese data, pp. 1–12 (2020). http://arxiv.org/abs/2008.09144
5. Diggelmann, T., Boyd-Graber, J., Bulian, J., Ciaramita, M., Leippold, M.: CLIMATE-FEVER: a dataset for verification of real-world climate claims, pp. 1–16 (2020). http://arxiv.org/abs/2012.00614
6. Gao, J., Galley, M., Li, L.: Neural approaches to conversational AI. In: ACL 2018–56th Annual Meeting of the Association for Computational Linguistics, Proceedings of the Conference Tutorial Abstracts, pp. 2–7 (2018). https://doi.org/10.18653/v1/p18-5002
7. Guu, K., Lee, K., Tung, Z., Pasupat, P., Chang, M.W.: REALM: retrieval-augmented language model pre-training. In: 37th International Conference on Machine Learning, ICML 2020 Part F16814, pp. 3887–3896 (2020)

8. Kim, Y., Sohn, J., Bang, S., Kim, H.: Deep learning-based question answering system for proactive disaster management. In: Proceedings of the 37th International Symposium on Automation and Robotics in Construction (ISARC) (Isarc), 2020 (2020). https://doi.org/10.22260/isarc2020/0181
9. Kwiatkowski, T., et al.: Natural questions: a benchmark for question answering research. Trans. Assoc. Comput. Linguistics **7**, 453–466 (2019). https://doi.org/10.1162/tacl_a_00276
10. Lewis, P., et al.: Retrieval-Augmented Generation for Knowledge-Intensive NLP Tasks. arXiv (NeurIPS) (2020)
11. Lewis, P., Wu, Y., Liu, L., Minervini, P., Küttler, H., Piktus, A., Stenetorp, P., Riedel, S.: PAQ: 65 Million Probably-Asked Questions and What You Can Do With Them (2021). http://arxiv.org/abs/2102.07033
12. Luccioni, A., Baylor, E., Duchene, N.: Analyzing Sustainability Reports Using Natural Language Processing (2020). http://arxiv.org/abs/2011.08073
13. Nguyen, T., Rosenberg, M., Song, X., Gao, J., Tiwary, S., Majumder, R., Deng, L.: MS MARCO: a human generated Machine reading Comprehension dataset. In: CEUR Workshop Proceedings 1773 (Nips 2016), pp. 1–11 (2016)
14. Raffel, C., et al.: Exploring the limits of transfer learning with a unified text-to-text transformer. arXiv 21, pp. 1–67 (2019)
15. Robertson, S., Zaragoza, H.: The probabilistic relevance framework: BM25 and beyond, vol. 3 (2009). https://doi.org/10.1561/1500000019
16. Severo, E.A., De Guimarães, J.C.F., Dellarmelin, M.L.: Impact of the COVID-19 pandemic on environmental awareness, sustainable consumption and social responsibility: evidence from generations in Brazil and Portugal. J. Clean. Prod. **286** (2021). https://doi.org/10.1016/j.jclepro.2020.124947
17. Varini, F.S., Boyd-Graber, J., Ciaramita, M., Leippold, M.: ClimaText: a dataset for climate change topic detection, pp. 1–13 (2020). http://arxiv.org/abs/2012.00483
18. Vaswani, A., et al.: Attention is all you need. Advances in Neural Information Processing Systems 2017-Decem(Nips), pp. 5999–6009 (2017)
19. Wagner Filho, J.A., Wilkens, R., Idiart, M., Villavicencio, A.: The BRWAC corpus: a new open resource for Brazilian Portuguese. In: LREC 2018–11th International Conference on Language Resources and Evaluation, pp. 4339–4344, May 2019
20. West, T.A.P., Börner, J., Fearnside, P.M.: Climatic benefits from the 2006–2017 avoided deforestation in Amazonian Brazil. Front. Forests Global Change **2**(September), 1–11 (2019). https://doi.org/10.3389/ffgc.2019.00052

# Enriching Portuguese Word Embeddings
# with Visual Information

Bernardo Scapini Consoli[1]([✉])[ID] and Renata Vieira[2][ID]

[1] Pontifical Catholic University of Rio Grande do Sul, PUCRS. School of Technology,
Porto Alegre, Brazil
bernardo.consoli@edu.pucrs.br
[2] CIDEHUS, University of Évora, Évora, Portugal
renatav@uevora.pt

**Abstract.** This work focuses on the enrichment of existing Portuguese word embeddings with visual information in the form of visual embeddings. This information was extracted from images portraying given vocabulary terms and imagined visual embeddings learned for terms with no image data. These enriched embeddings were tested against their text-only counterparts in common NLP tasks. The results show an increase in performance for several tasks, which indicates that visual information fusion for word embeddings can be useful for word embedding based NLP tasks.

**Keywords:** Word embedding models · Multimodality · Portuguese language

## 1 Introduction

Language modelling technologies have been dominated by semantic embedding models ever since Mikolov et al. (2013b) and Mikolov et al.'s (2013a) [11,12] popularization of Word Embeddings, a concept which revolutionized the field of Natural Language Processing (NLP). The architecture presented by the authors, Word2Vec, has been used as basis for many works across the spectrum of NLP tasks, as attested by nearly 45,000 citations when accounting both of the aforementioned papers (as recorded by Google Scholar), mainly because of the fact that training this architecture only requires raw text, and no human-made annotation (the main obstacle in training machine learning models).

Many architectures based on the original intuition behind Word2Vec have become popular since 2013. The most prevalent, besides the original Word2Vec, are fastText [7] and GloVe [14]. An evolution upon the concept, taking into account the current context of a word, not just an amalgamation of all contexts

Financially supported by the Brazilian National Council for Scientific and Technological Development (CNPq) and by the Portuguese Foundation for Science and Technology (FCT) under the projects CEECIND/01997/2017, UIDB/00057/2020.

with which it was trained, was introduced by Peters et al. (2018) [15], with their ELMO architecture, and popularized by Devlin et al.'s (2019) [4] BERT architecture.

All of the mentioned embedding architectures have at least one model trained on Portuguese language corpora. The *Núcleo Interinstitucional de Linguística Computacional* (NILC), from the *Universidade de São Paulo* (USP), for example, has several Word2Vec, fastText and GloVe models for the Portuguese language available within their Word Embedding repository[1]. The Allen Institute for AI maintains an ELMO model repository which includes a Portuguese language model[2]. BERTimbau [19], a Portuguese language BERT model, was recently developed and added to the Hugging Face[3] library. These models, and others, have been used to advance the state-of-the-art in several Portuguese language NLP tasks [6,9,17].

Beyond these efforts to further enhance the usage of text in the training of word embedding models, be it Portuguese language text or otherwise, an effort to enrich these embeddings with other modes of information also arose. The most studied modes of information used to enhance Word Embeddings are the visual mode (composed of images and video), and the aural mode (composed of sounds, spoken language, music, etc.). These efforts spurred the creation of multimodal embedding fusion architectures, used to join embeddings of disparate modes into a single embedding representing all fused knowledge. An example of this is the concatenation based architecture of Bruni et al. (2014) [1], which arrived at promising results after proposing that multiple embeddings of different modes could be concatenated, resulting in a higher-dimensional space, for them to be enhanced for better use in NLP tasks.

The goal of this work is to study the usage of visual data to enrich textual data within word embeddings for NLP tasks in the Portuguese language. The main hypothesis is that fusing textual information with visual information will enhance results for text-only tasks. To test it, experiments in four NLP tasks were performed using text-only and multimodal embedding models. These tasks were: Word Relatedness, Analogy Prediction, Semantic Similarity in Short Sentences, and Named Entity Recognition.

The following sections are arranged in the following manner: Sect. 2 delves into related work within the literature; Sect. 3 explains the methodology used in creating the multimodal embeddings; Sect. 4 explains the testing methodology and presents the results for these tests; Sect. 5 presents the conclusions and future work that can be done to expand upon this topic.

## 2   Related Work

The literature reveals two main ways in which multimodal embeddings are constructed: individually and simultaneously. That is, either learning is performed

---

[1] http://www.nilc.icmc.usp.br/embeddings.
[2] https://allennlp.org/elmo.
[3] https://huggingface.co/.

individually (an embedding is learned for each modality, and then these are fused) [3], or simultaneously (all modalities are learned at the same time in the same space). Henceforth, the former method will be referred to as *Post-Learning Fusion*, while the latter method will be referred to as *Simultaneous Learning*.

Post-learning fusion is divided into two further methods: early fusion and late fusion. Early fusion is performed at the representation level, and three methods of early fusion were found in the literature: feature concatenation, auto-encoder fusion, and cross-modal mapping. Feature concatenation is performed through the concatenation of all single modality fusion embedding vector pairs (that is, a textual feature vector representing a concept will be concatenated with a visual feature vector representing that same context) into a single, longer, multimodal feature vector [8]. Auto-encoder fusion is performed through the use of auto-encoders fed with pre-trained single modality embeddings, thus generating a single feature vector which can then be extracted from the auto-encoder's last hidden layer [18]. Cross-modal mapping is performed through the learning of a certain amount of pre-mapped multimodal inputs and predicting those that do not have examples in both modalities [3]. Late fusion is performed at the level of prediction scores, and it is performed through an averaging of single modality predictions [8].

Lazaridous et al. (2015) [10] introduced the first instance found during the review of simultaneous learning semantic embedding model, based on Mikolov et al.'s (2013) [12] skip-gram architecture. They extended Mikolov et al.'s (2013) models to present relevant visual feature vectors alongside textual data during training for a subset of target words. This model has been shown to further propagate visual information to representations of words which were not trained with visual features.

As for evaluation methodologies, most of the literature consisted of using multimodality to improve the performance of downstream tasks. As such, the evaluation of the embeddings was extrinsic. That is, the evaluation metric was whether or not its addition to the systems performing the downstream task affected their performance.

Lazaridou et al. (2015) [10] were the only ones to perform intrinsic tests, using general semantic benchmarks such as concept relatedness (also known as semantic relatedness) [1] or semantic similarity. These are usually used to evaluate word embeddings, but multimodal embeddings were shown by Lazaridou et al. (2015) to outperform word embeddings on these tasks.

# 3   Resources and Methodology

Several choices had to be made prior to developing this work's methodology. It was decided that these first tests would use static word embeddings based on the Word2Vec and FastText architectures, and use a translated version of the image embeddings released by Collell et al. (2017) [3]. These readily available resources made post-learning fusion methods an obvious choice for developing our own fusion architectures. Since the tasks we intended to use these models for were strictly textual, late post-learning fusion was not an option, as there would be no visual data to input into the system during tests, which left early post-learning fusion techniques.

The resources and architectures mentioned in the above paragraph are elaborated upon in the following subsections. This section also explains the multimodal model development methodology.

## 3.1 Unimodal Embeddings

The text embeddings used for this work were NILC's word embeddings[4] [9] and BBP corpus word embeddings[5] [17]. Three versions of NILC's embeddings were used: the 100 feature word2vec version and the 100 and 300 feature fastText versions. These three were deemed to be adequate for studying the effect of different parameters when adding multimodality to textual models. Only the 300 feature fastText version of BBP was used, as it was the only one readily available for download. This final BBP model was chosen as a means to study how different text embedding training corpora within the same domain affected multimodal fusion.

**Table 1.** Corpora and token totals for each of the text corpora used for training text embedding models.

| Corpus | Sources | Vocabulary | Token number |
|---|---|---|---|
| NILC | LX-Corpus, Wikipedia, GoogleNews, SuIMDB-PT, G1, PLN-Br, Public domain literature Lacio-web, e-books, Mundo Estranho, CHC, FAPESP, Digitalized Textbooks, Folhinha, NILC subcorpus, Para Seu Filho Ler, SARESP | 929,605 | 1,395,926,282 |
| BBP | BlogSet-BR, brWaC, Portuguese Wikipedia | 553,637 | 4,900,352,063 |

The visual embedding, henceforth referred to as the ImageNet embedding, is derived from Collell et al.'s (2017) [3] work, as they made their original visual embeddings created using ImageNet freely available[6]. The individual embeddings were paired with English language terms from the English language WordNet, however, and so needed to be translated before use with Portuguese language textual embeddings. In order to translate the English terms, OpenWordNet-PT [13], an open Brazilian WordNet available online[7], was used. Since the codes used to refer to each term in both WordNets were the same, and Collell et al. (2017) also

---

[4] http://www.nilc.icmc.usp.br/embeddings.
[5] https://github.com/jneto04/ner-pt.
[6] https://liir.cs.kuleuven.be/software_pages/imagined_representation_aaai.php.
[7] http://wn.mybluemix.net/.

shared the WordNet code for each term, about 5000 of the 18000 original text-visual embedding pairs were successfully translated into Brazilian Portuguese unigrams. This resulted in what we believe to be the first visual embedding dataset paired with Brazilian Portuguese terms, made available through our GitHub page[8].

## 3.2   Dealing with the Information Gap

The great imbalance between visual embeddings and text embeddings becomes clear when comparing the roughly 5000 terms of the ImageNet embedding to the textual embedding vocabularies shown in Table 1. In order to ameliorate this problem, the "imagined embeddings" architecture described in Collell et al. (2017) [3] was used. As exemplified in Fig. 1, textual embedding-visual embedding pairs are created for the terms present in the visual embedding vocabulary, $w$, and used to train a feed-forward neural network. It does this by inputting the textual embedding $\vec{l_x}$ into the NN, and expecting the visual embedding $\vec{v_x}$ as an output, where the $w_x$ is the term being learned. Once this textual-visual translation, $f$, is learned by the network, it can be extrapolated into terms without visual counterparts, creating "Imagined" visual embeddings for the entire vocabulary represented by the textual embedding that was translated.

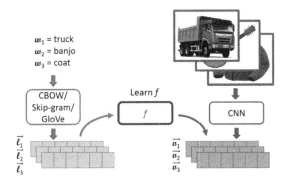

**Fig. 1.** Example of the architecture used by Collell et al. (2017). The imagined representations are the outputs of a text-to-vision mapping, $f$. Image created by Collell et al. (2017) [3]

Our imagined embedding networks used the following parameters: 0.25 dropout; 0.1 learning rate, SGD optimization; MSE based loss; 1 hidden layer with 200 nodes; and a TanH activation function. As was done in Collell et al. (2017), we chose certain epoch thresholds to test. These were 25, 50, 100, and 150 epochs for each model. The translated ImageNet embeddings were used to train these imagined embeddings for each text model.

---

[8] https://github.com/bsconsoli/Enriching-Portuguese-Word-Embeddings-with-Visual-Information.

Notably, the work discusses that while these imagined embeddings are valuable aggregates to common embeddings, substituting the textual embeddings completely with these "imagined embeddings" yields worse results. Additionally, in a follow-up paper, Collell et al. (2018) [2] highlighted several problems with this architecture, such as the fact that they do not fully mimic the behaviour of proper visual embeddings to the desired degree. It remains, however, that when combined with the original textual embeddings, these "imagined embeddings" do positively affect results in intrinsic tasks such as Word Relatedness.

### 3.3   Fusion Techniques

Two fusion techniques were tested in this work: Concatenation and Auto-encoding. Concatenation was performed as detailed in Collell et al. (2017), but for the Portuguese language, while Auto-encoding was inspired by the work of Silberer and Lapata (2014) [18] and adapted to work with our resources.

Furthermore, in order to perform this kind of fusion, it is helpful to ensure that all fused embeddings are in the same scale, so that none can overly influence the result simple because it is presented in a larger scale than another. To do this, a mathematical process called Standardization was performed on the embeddings, making it so all features were scaled according to a standard deviation of 1 and had a mean of 0.

**Concatenation Fusion.** This technique is simple: concatenate one mode's embeddings to the end of another mode's embeddings. This effectively packages all necessary data into a single vector space by expanding the dimensionality of that space.

This fusion technique's greatest weakness is the fact that should one embedding in a certain mode not have a counterpart in another mode (as often happens with text-image multimodality, e.g. the presence of a textual embedding with no counterpart visual embedding) it is not possible to create the multimodal embedding. This problem is solved with the use of Imagined Embeddings, which, though not perfectly representative of an actual image embedding, allows for the concatenation of the entire vocabulary.

As such, the development of this embedding required the prediction of an imagined visual embedding for each word in the vocabulary, which was then concatenated with its originating word embedding. This resulted in multimodal embeddings with larger feature pools with which to draw from. Figure 2 presents the architecture of the concatenated fusion used for every word embedding in this work.

**Auto-Encoding Fusion.** This technique is performed by a Neural Network trained to predict an output by using the output itself as an input. Once this is done, one of the hidden layers of this network with less features than the original input is extracted to serve as an embedded version of the input. This serves to both shorten the final embedding, and to fuse several embeddings together. This

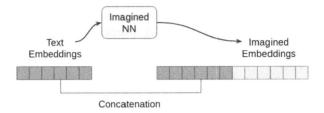

**Fig. 2.** Simplified concatenation fusion architecture.

fusion, in theory, keeps the most important features and fuses less important features together to make them more impactful.

This architecture has been used to lessen the impact of the gap between textual and visual information in the literature [18]. In this instance, whenever there was no visual pair for the textual embedding, a zeroed vector was appended to the textual embedding for the purposes of auto-encoding. The architecture presented below is a bit different, as it offers a new possibility: using imagined embeddings to fill the knowledge gap and offer complete feature vectors for auto-encoding. Figure 3 presents the architecture of the Auto-encoded fusion used for every multimodal word embedding in this work

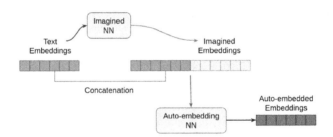

**Fig. 3.** Simplified auto-encoding fusion architecture.

The hidden layers are divided into two encoding layers and two decoding layers. The first encoding layer has the initial input node size of the concatenated textual-visual feature vector and an output node size of the feature vector of the textual model plus half the feature vector of the visual model. The second layer has the input node size of the previous output, and an output the size of the feature vector of the textual embedding. The output of this second layer is extracted and used as the Auto-encoded textual-visual embedding. The decoder is used only during training, and its two hidden layers are the same as the encoder's, but in reverse order. The auto-encoding networks used the following parameters: 0.001 learning rate; ADAM optimization; MSE based loss; four hidden layers, as explained above; and ReLU activation funtions between layers with a TanH function as a final output.

### 3.4   Multimodal Embeddings

Several different textual-visual multimodal embeddings were created using the unimodal embeddings and multimodal fusion techniques explained above. Four text corpora were used for training: a 300-dimensional fastText model using the BBP text corpus (BBPFT300); a 300-dimensional fastText model using the NILC text corpus (NILCFT300); a 100-dimensional fastText model using the NILC text corpus (NILCFT100); and a 100-dimensional word2vec model using the NILC text corpus (NILCFT100). The Imagined Embeddings were trained from the 5000 available word-image pairs to four epoch thresholds: 25, 50, 100, and 150. Finally, each of the four text corpora were fused with all Imagined Embedding epoch threshold models, meaning a total of 16 models, four for each text corpus. Since we used two different fusion architectures, this total is doubled to a final roster of 32 tested models, with 16 for the Concatenation fusion architecture and 16 for the Auto-encoding fusion architecture.

Note that the act of training to different epochs was simply due to a lack of time and computational resources that would be required to train the best model for each individual task. As such, the best performing model out of each group can be taken to best represent the capabilities of the multimodal embedding fusion in question.

## 4   Tests and Results

Four tests were performed on the 32 models created for his work. These were Word Relatedness, Analogy Prediction, Semantic Similarity in Short Sentences, and Named Entity Recognition. These tests and their results are presented in that order within this section. Note that for each model, all four training epochs were tested for each fusion architecture of each model, but only the results for the best performing training epoch for each model are displayed for comparison in the below tables.

### 4.1   Word Relatedness

Word Relatedness is the intrinsic task of giving a score to how closely related two terms are. These tasks are usually scored via Spearman correlation, which assigns a Real number score between $-1$ and 1. The score approaches -1 the more inversely correlated the predictions are to the annotation; it approaches 0 the more unrelated the predictions are to the annotation; and it approaches 1 the more directly correlated the predictions are to the annotation. The more representative of human understanding of the terms an embedding is, the closer the Spearman score comes to 1.

A custom code was written for this task. It uses the Gensim python library to extract the Cosine distance between each word pair as a relatedness measurement, and compares them to their respective annotated relatedness scores using the Spearman Correlation method. The code can be accessed in the GitHub page for this project[9].

The test set is a collection of 3000 word pairs annotated with a relatedness score from 50 (most related) to 0 (least related). The objective of the semantic models is to score each word pair in order to rank them from most related to least related. The closer to the original ranking the model gets, the higher its Spearman Correlation, the chosen method for scoring these kinds of tests. Table 2 presents some examples from this test set.

**Table 2.** Four examples of word pairs from the translated MEN corpus.

| Word 1 | Word 2 | Relatedness |
|---|---|---|
| rio (river) | água (water) | 49.0 |
| répteis (reptiles) | serpente (serpent) | 45.0 |
| banda (band) | metal (metal) | 27.0 |
| recém-nascido (newborn) | construção (construction) | 6.0 |

The test corpus used for word relatedness testing, MEN [1], was translated from the English language to the Portuguese language with the help of DeepL Translate[10]. The machine translations were checked individually to ensure some

**Table 3.** The best Spearman Correlation results for each multimodal model and the results for their text-only counterparts for the MEN test set.

| MEN | | |
|---|---|---|
| Model | Architecture | Correlation |
| BBPFT300 | Text-Only | 0.610 |
| | Concatenated | 0.648 |
| | Auto-encoded | **0.649** |
| NILCFT100 | Text-Only | 0.615 |
| | Concatenated | 0.648 |
| | Auto-encoded | **0.649** |
| NILCW2V100 | Text-Only | 0.493 |
| | Concatenated | 0.518 |
| | Auto-encoded | **0.528** |
| NILCFT300 | Text-Only | 0.570 |
| | Concatenated | 0.586 |
| | **Auto-encoded** | **0.597** |

---

[9] https://github.com/bsconsoli/Enriching-Portuguese-Word-Embeddings-with-Visual-Information.

[10] https://www.deepl.com/translator.

degree of uniformity, but the corpora should be considered Silver standard nonetheless. Table 3 shows the results of this test, with the best overall model and the best architecture for each model marked in bold.

This table shows that multimodal fusion enhances model performance for this task by an average of 3% points, and that the best overall architecture is the Auto-encoded architecture. It should be said, however, that between the multimodal models, the average difference is 0.5% point in favor of the Auto-encoded architecture, so neither fusion architecture has an overwhelming advantage over the other in this task.

## 4.2   Analogy Prediction

Hartmann et al. (2017) [9] published an analogy prediction test set, divided into Brazilian Portuguese and European Portuguese halves, alongside their initial publication of their NILC word embeddings. The test gives a related word pair and a single word from which it must predict a pair analogous to the first.

The code used to run these tests was made available alongside the test set itself. It can be found in the associated paper's GitHub page[11]. It measures accuracy by counting how many correct predictions were achieved by the model against the total number of predictions.

This test focuses on two kinds of analogies: Semantic and Syntactic. These are each divided into a Brazilian Portuguese set and an European Portuguese set. To reiterate, the objective of this task is to accurately predict the second word of a pair, when given an example pair and the first word of the prediction pair (e.g. Berlin/Germany, Prediction: Paris/?). The accuracy of the model is then measured in a percentage, from 0 (completely inaccurate) to 100 (completely accurate). Table 5 shows the results of this test, with the best overall model and the best architecture for each model marked in bold. Table 4 presents some examples for this test set.

**Table 4.** Four examples, two semantic and two syntactic, of word pairs from the Analogy Prediction corpus, translated to English.

| Analogy | Example | Prediction |
|---|---|---|
| Capital city/nation | Berlim (Berlin)/Alemanha (Germany) | Roma (Rome)/? |
| National currency/nation | Euro (Euro)/Alemanha (Germany) | Real (Real)/? |
| Singular/plural | maçã (apple)/ maçãs (apples) | carro (car)/? |
| Present continuous/past simple | dançando (dancing)/ dançou (danced) | caindo (falling)/? |

The results, presented in Table 5, show that the two language-specific test sets were corroborative, with similar results being achieved in all test set pairs. On average, there was a 0.01% point difference between text-only and the best

---

[11] https://github.com/nathanshartmann/portuguese_word_embeddings.

multimodal results, which leads to the conclusion that the task of Analogy Prediction was mostly unaffected by the addition of visual information through the multimodal fusion methods tested herein. That said, the Auto-encoding architecture tended to underperform when compared to the Concatenated architecture in all cases but those in which the NILCFT100 semantic model was used.

These results were not outside expectations, as the image data used for the visual embeddings focused mostly on objects, while the Analogy Prediction tests focused on abstracts such as parentage, countries, currency and word forms. It is promising, however, that the previously mentioned best overall model achieved the best multimodality results when compared to their text-only counterpart. Perhaps with further testing, it might be ascertained that the better the original text-embedding, the more effective the imagined visual embedding fusion is.

**Table 5.** The best accuracy results for each multimodal model and the results for their text-only counterparts for the Brazilian Portuguese and European Portuguese Analogy Prediction test sets.

| Analogy prediction | | | | | | | | | |
|---|---|---|---|---|---|---|---|---|---|
| Brazilian Portuguese | | | | | European Portuguese | | | | |
| Model | Modality | Syn. | Sem. | Total | Model | Modality | Syn. | Sem. | Total |
| BBPFT300 | **Textual** | **0.447** | **0.064** | **0.257** | BBPFT300 | **Textual** | **0.451** | **0.058** | **0.255** |
| | Concatenated | 0.441 | 0.063 | 0.254 | | Concatenated | 0.444 | 0.057 | 0.251 |
| | Auto-encoded | 0.382 | 0.047 | 0.216 | | Auto-encoded | 0.387 | 0.042 | 0.216 |
| NILCFT100 | Textual | 0.510 | 0.302 | 0.406 | **NILCFT100** | Textual | 0.509 | 0.293 | 0.401 |
| | Concatenated | 0.505 | 0.292 | 0.398 | | Concatenated | 0.505 | 0.284 | 0.394 |
| | **Auto-encoded** | **0.511** | **0.311** | **0.411** | | **Auto-encoded** | **0.509** | **0.298** | **0.403** |
| NILCW2V100 | **Textual** | **0.255** | **0.080** | **0.167** | NILCW2V100 | **Textual** | **0.252** | **0.074** | **0.163** |
| | **Concatenated** | **0.254** | **0.081** | **0.167** | | **Concatenated** | **0.250** | **0.075** | **0.163** |
| | Auto-encoded | 0.235 | 0.080 | 0.157 | | Auto-encoded | 0.231 | 0.074 | 0.152 |
| NILCFT300 | **Textual** | **0.332** | **0.158** | **0.245** | NILCFT300 | **Textual** | **0.324** | **0.143** | **0.233** |
| | Concatenated | 0.331 | 0.157 | 0.244 | | **Concatenated** | **0.322** | **0.144** | **0.233** |
| | Auto-encoded | 0.299 | 0.143 | 0.221 | | Auto-encoded | 0.292 | 0.123 | 0.208 |

### 4.3    Semantic Similarity in Short Sentences

Semantic similarity requires that a model give a numerical value to how semantically similar two sentences are, with the lower similarity extreme being that the sentences are completely different, and the higher similarity extreme being that the sentences are paraphrases. The ASSIN [5] sentence similarity corpus was used for this task in this work.

The code used for the tests is the same as was used by Hartmann et al. (2017) [9], available in the publication's GitHub page[12]. The architecture uses a linear regression algorithm trained on two features: the cosine similarity of the TF-IDF of each sentence and the cosine similarity between the sum of each sentence's word embeddings.

---

[12] https://github.com/nathanshartmann/portuguese_word_embeddings.

The ASSIN Semantic Similarity dataset is divided into two tracks, European Portuguese and Brazilian Portuguese. The objective of the task is to predict a number between 1 (unrelated sentences) and 5 (paraphrasing sentences) to represent the similarity between two short sentences. The task was evaluated using Pearson's Correlation and Mean Standard Error (MSE), as it was during the original ASSIN task. Table 6 shows the results of this test, with the best overall model and the best architecture for each model marked in bold. Figure 4 presents some examples for this test set.

```
<pair entailment="Entailment" id="2504" similarity="4.25">
    <t>A estreia do Brasil na Copa América está marcada para o dia 14 de junho, contra o Peru.</t>
    <h>O time estreia na Copa América contra o Peru.</h>
</pair>
<pair entailment="None" id="2505" similarity="2.25">
    <t>Funcionamento normal, lojas e praça de alimentação de 10h às 22h.</t>
    <h>Já na segunda-feira do feriado, o shopping abrirá das 9h às 19h.</h>
</pair>
```

**Fig. 4.** Example of sentence pairs from the ASSIN corpus.

The results found with these Semantic Similarity tests are very similar to those found during the Word Relatedness tests presented previously in this section. These tests found that multimodal models outperform text-only models by an average of 2% points and that the Auto-encoding architecture is generally superior to the Concatenation architecture within these test conditions.

**Table 6.** The best results for the Brazilian Portuguese and European Portuguese tracks of the ASSIN Semantic Similarity task.

| Assin semantic similarity test set | | | | | | | |
|---|---|---|---|---|---|---|---|
| Brazilian Portuguese | | | | European Portuguese | | | |
| Model | Architecture | Pearson | MSE | Model | Architecture | Pearson | MSE |
| BBPFT300 | Text-Only | 0.56 | 0.52 | **BBPFT300** | Text-Only | 0.59 | 0.79 |
| | Concatenated | 0.57 | 0.51 | | Concatenated | 0.60 | 0.78 |
| | **Auto-encoded** | **0.58** | **0.50** | | **Auto-encoded** | **0.60** | **0.76** |
| NILCFT100 | Text-Only | 0.53 | 0.54 | NILCFT100 | Text-Only | 0.53 | 0.86 |
| | **Concatenated** | **0.54** | **0.54** | | Concatenated | 0.54 | 0.85 |
| | **Auto-encoded** | **0.54** | **0.54** | | **Auto-encoded** | **0.55** | **0.85** |
| NILCW2V100 | Text-Only | 0.45 | 0.61 | NILCW2V100 | Text-Only | 0.47 | 0.93 |
| | Concatenated | 0.46 | 0.60 | | Concatenated | 0.48 | 0.92 |
| | **Auto-encoded** | **0.47** | **0.60** | | **Auto-encoded** | **0.49** | **0.91** |
| NILCFT300 | Text-Only | 0.49 | 0.58 | NILCFT300 | Text-Only | 0.50 | 0.90 |
| | Concatenated | 0.50 | 0.57 | | Concatenated | 0.51 | 0.90 |
| | **Auto-encoded** | **0.52** | **0.55** | | **Auto-encoded** | **0.52** | **0.88** |

### 4.4   Named Entity Recognition

Named Entity Recognition (NER) requires that, given a set of classes for named entities, a model recognize and classify these entities within raw text, usually by use of tags. Word embeddings can be used to parse the text input into the model, using the feature vectors in its tagging predictions. The HAREM [16] NER corpus was used to test the models.

The code used for the NER tests was developed by Santos et al. (2019) [17], available in the paper's GitHub page[13]. It uses an LSTM-CRF neural network architecture to train a sequence tagger using the Flair Toolkit to perform a NER task based on the supplied training and test corpora.

The HAREM test set is composed of two tracks: the Selective track; and the Total track. The Selective track is the smaller of the two, including only the five most populated named entity categories within the test set. The Total track is the larger of the two, including all ten named entity categories present in the First HAREM test set. Table 7 shows the results of this test, with the best overall model and the best architecture for each model highlighted in bold. Figure 5 presents some examples for this test set.

<EM ID="556" CATEG="PESSOA" TIPO="INDIVIDUAL">Leonardo</EM> nasceu a <EM ID="557" CATEG="TEMPO" TIPO="DATA">15 de Abril de 1452</EM> , na pequena cidade de <EM ID="558" CATEG="LOCAL" TIPO="HUMANO">Vinci</EM> (...)

**Fig. 5.** A snippet of a sentence from the First HAREM, to exemplify its annotation.

On average, the multimodal models outperform text-only models by 0.25% point in the Selective track, and are outperformed by the text-only models by 0.08% point in the Total track. These results show that the addition of visual information through multimodal fusion does not have much effect on the results for our models in this test set.

**Table 7.** The best results for the Selective and Total tracks of the HAREM task.

| HAREM test set | | | | | | | | | |
|---|---|---|---|---|---|---|---|---|---|
| Selective track | | | | | Total Track | | | | |
| Model | Architecture | Precision | Recall | F1 | Model | Architecture | Precision | Recall | F1 |
| BBPFT300 | **Text-Only** | **0.734** | **0.680** | **0.706** | BBPFT300 | **Text-Only** | **0.685** | **0.602** | **0.641** |
| | Concatenated | 0.738 | 0.668 | 0.701 | | Concatenated | 0.675 | 0.586 | 0.627 |
| | Auto-encoded | 0.728 | 0.653 | 0.688 | | Auto-encoded | 0.678 | 0.571 | 0.619 |
| NILCFT100 | Text-Only | 0.716 | 0.691 | 0.703 | NILCFT100 | **Text-Only** | **0.682** | **0.602** | **0.640** |
| | Concatenated | 0.735 | 0.679 | 0.706 | | Concatenated | 0.686 | 0.594 | 0.637 |
| | **Auto-encoded** | **0.731** | **0.691** | **0.710** | | Auto-encoded | 0.693 | 0.594 | 0.639 |
| NILCW2V100 | Text-Only | 0.727 | 0.690 | 0.708 | NILCW2V100 | Text-Only | 0.675 | 0.595 | 0.633 |
| | **Concatenated** | **0.746** | **0.686** | **0.715** | | **Concatenated** | **0.686** | **0.592** | **0.635** |
| | Auto-encoded | 0.733 | 0.697 | 0.714 | | Auto-encoded | 0.676 | 0.597 | 0.634 |
| NILCFT300 | Text-Only | 0.740 | 0.690 | 0.714 | **NILCFT300** | Text-Only | 0.667 | 0.599 | 0.631 |
| | **Concatenated** | **0.741** | **0.691** | **0.715** | | **Concatenated** | **0.680** | **0.606** | **0.641** |
| | Auto-encoded | 0.737 | 0.665 | 0.699 | | Auto-encoded | 0.690 | 0.591 | 0.637 |

---

[13] https://github.com/jneto04/ner-pt.

# 5   Conclusion and Future Work

This work presented the results of a study into the usefulness of visual data when used in conjunction with textual data for NLP tasks in a general news domain. It involved the development of word embedding models which were then put through a test battery for multimodal Word Embedding models which included the following tasks: Word Relatedness, Sentence Similarity, Analogy Prediction and Named Entity Recognition. These results revealed some aspects of textual-visual multimodal fusion for Word Embeddings within NLP tasks for the Portuguese language, a field in which it is most common to study purely textual Word Embedding models.

It took inspiration from the works of Bruni et al. (2014) [1], and their concatenation based multimodal fusion architecture; Silberer et al. (2014) [18], and their auto-encoding multimodal fusion architecture; and Collell et al. (2017) [3], and their Imagined Embeddings cross-modal mapping neural network, for visual vocabulary expansion. It took a different tack from previous work by exploring the possibility of use of this technology beyond the English language, using resources for the Portuguese language and in previously unexplored combinations.

Testing revealed that in tasks which require broader semantic meaning judgements, such as word relatedness and semantic similarity, multimodal fusion with visual information enhances results. For the specific test sets within these tasks explored in this work, the average increase in correlation with human scoring was of 2% points. For the tasks of analogy prediction and named entity recognition, however, the fusion resulted in little to no impact in the final results. This might be explained by the fact that these annotations in particular make use of knowledge that is not present within the visual modality, and thus were not enhanced by its addition.

As future work, we have planned testing multimodal fusion techniques on Contextual Embeddings such as BERT and ELMO. We also plan to expand testing into inherently multimodal tasks such as text-image pairing and cross-modal retrieval, both for the Portuguese Language.

# References

1. Bruni, E., Tran, N., Baroni, M.: Multimodal distributional semantics. J. Artif. Intell. Res. **49**, 1–47 (2014)
2. Collell, G., Moens, M.: Do neural network cross-modal mappings really bridge modalities? In: Proceedings of the 56th Annual Meeting of the Association for Computational Linguistics, pp. 462–468 (2018)
3. Collell, G., Zhang, T., Moens, M.: Imagined visual representations as multimodal embeddings. In: Proceedings of the 31st AAAI Conference on Artificial Intelligence, pp. 4378–4384 (2017)
4. Devlin, J., Chang, M., Lee, K., Toutanova, K.: BERT: pre-training of deep bidirectional transformers for language understanding. In: Proceedings of the 17th Conference of the North American Chapter of the Association for Computational Linguistics on Human Language Technologies, pp. 4171–4186 (2019)

5. Fonseca, E.R., Santos, L.B., Criscuolo, M., Aluísio, S.M.: Visão geral da avaliação de similaridade semântica e inferência textual. Linguamática **8**, 3–13 (2016)

6. Gomes, D.S.M., et al.: Portuguese word embeddings for the oil and gas industry: development and evaluation. Comput. Ind. **124**, 1–44 (2021)

7. Grave, E., Mikolov, T., Joulin, A., Bojanowski, P.: Bag of tricks for efficient text classification. In: Proceedings of the 15th Conference of the European Chapter of the Association for Computational Linguistics, pp. 427–431 (2017)

8. Habibian, A., Mensink, T., M., S.C.G.: Video2vec embeddings recognize events when examples are scarce. IEEE Trans. Pattern Anal. Mach. Intell. **39**, 2089–2103 (2017)

9. Hartmann, N., Fonseca, E.R., Shulby, C., Treviso, M.V., Rodrigues, J.S., Aluísio, S.M.: Portuguese word embeddings: evaluating on word analogies and natural language tasks. In: Proceedings of the 11th Brazilian Symposium in Information and Human Language Technology, pp. 122–131 (2017)

10. Lazaridou, A., Pham, N.T., Baroni, M.: Combining language and vision with a multimodal skip-gram model. In: Proceedings of the 13th Conference of the North American Chapter of the Association of Computational Linguistics on Human Language Technologies, pp. 153–163 (2015)

11. Mikolov, T., Chen, K., Corrado, G., Dean, J.: Efficient estimation of word representations in vector space. In: Proceedings of the 1st International Conference on Learning Representations, p. 12 (2013)

12. Mikolov, T., Sutskever, I., Chen, K., Corrado, G.S., Dean, J.: Distributed representations of words and phrases and their compositionality. In: Proceedings of the 27th Annual Conference on Neural Information Processing Systems, pp. 3111–3119 (2013)

13. Paiva, V., Rademaker, A., Melo, G.: Openwordnet-pt: an open brazilian wordnet for reasoning. In: Proceedings of the 24th International Conference on Computational Linguistics, pp. 353–360 (2012)

14. Pennington, J., Socher, R., Manning, C.D.: Glove: Global vectors for word representation. In: Proceedings of the 19th Conference on Empirical Methods in Natural Language Processing, pp. 1532–1543 (2014)

15. Peters, M.E., Neumann, M., Iyyer, M., Gardner, M., Clark, C., Lee, K., Zettlemoyer, L.: Deep contextualized word representations. In: Proceedings of the 16th Conference of the North American Chapter of the Association for Computational Linguistics on Human Language Technologies, pp. 2227–2237 (2018)

16. Santos, D., Cardoso, N.: A golden resource for named entity recognition in portuguese. In: Proceeding of the 7th International Conference on the Computational Processing of Portuguese, pp. 69–79 (2007)

17. Santos, J., Consoli, B.S., Santos, C.N., Terra, J., Collovini, S., Vieira, R.: Assessing the impact of contextual embeddings for portuguese named entity recognition. In: Proceedings of the 8th Brazilian Conference on Intelligent Systems, pp. 437–442 (2019)

18. Silberer, C., Lapata, M.: Learning grounded meaning representations with autoencoders. In: Proceedings of the 52nd Annual Meeting of the Association for Computational Linguistics, pp. 721–732 (2014)

19. Souza, F., Nogueira, R., Lotufo, R.: Bertimbau: pretrained BERT models for Brazilian Portuguese. In: Proceedings of the 9th Brazilian Conference on Intelligent Systems, pp. 403–417 (2020)

# Entity Relation Extraction from News Articles in Portuguese for Competitive Intelligence Based on BERT

Daniel De Los Reyes[1]([envelope]) [iD], Douglas Trajano[1] [iD], Isabel Harb Manssour[1] [iD], Renata Vieira[2] [iD], and Rafael H. Bordini[1] [iD]

[1] Pontifical Catholic University of Rio Grande do Sul, PUCRS, School of Technology, Porto Alegre, Brazil
{daniel.reyes,douglas.trajano}@edu.pucrs.br,
{isabel.manssour,rafael.bordini}@pucrs.br
[2] CIDEHUS, University of Évora, Évora, Portugal
renatav@uevora.pt

**Abstract.** Competitive intelligence (CI) is a relevant area of a corporation and can support the strategic business area by showing those responsible, helping decision making on how to position an organization in the market. This work uses the Bidirectional Transformer Encoding Representations (BERT) to process a sentence and its named entities and extract the parts of the sentences that represent or describe the semantic relationship between these named entities. The approach was developed for the Portuguese language, considering the financial domain and exploring deep linguistic representations without using other lexical-semantic resources. The results of the experiments show a precision of 73.5% using the Jaccard metric that measures the similarity between sentences. A second contribution of this work is the manually constructed dataset with more than 4.500 tuples (phrase, entity, entity) annotated.

**Keywords:** Competitive intelligence · Entity relation classification · Relation extraction

## 1 Introduction

The Relation Extraction (RE) task aims to identify and classify the semantic relationships that occur between (pairs of) recognized entities in a given text. Extracting relationships between named entities from text is a major challenge in Information Extraction (IE), given the necessary language knowledge and the sophistication of the language processing techniques employed. At the same time, this task can contribute to the development of several areas, such as Question and Answer Systems, summarization, among others [7].

Financially supported by the Brazilian National Council for Scientific and Technological Development (CAPES) and the by Portuguese Foundation for Science and Technology (FCT)under the projects CEECIND/01997/2017, UIDB/00057/2020.

© Springer Nature Switzerland AG 2021
A. Britto and K. Valdivia Delgado (Eds.): BRACIS 2021, LNAI 13074, pp. 449–464, 2021.
https://doi.org/10.1007/978-3-030-91699-2_31

There is a growing interest in RE, mainly motivated by the exponential growth of the information available on the Web, which can make the task of searching and using such a large amount of data manually unfeasible. This context makes RE an even more complex and relevant research area [10]. In relation to the financial market, a domain addressed in this work, the news brings information about sectors of the economy, industrial policies, acquisitions, and company partnerships, among others. Automating the process of analyzing this data, in the form of financial reports, headlines, and corporate announcements can support personal and corporate economic decision making [30].

Thus, for example, it is possible to extract an acquisition relationship between entities of the organization type, where a certain organization (the first entity) was purchased (relationship) by another organization (second entity) [20]. Therefore, RE research among financial entities is the basis for the automatic extraction of financial information that can be used to assist with individual economic activities and national economic decision making [30].

Research on RE for the English language is at a more advanced stage than for Portuguese. While much work can be found in the literature on RE for English [4,12,15,16,22,25], very few papers focus on RE for Portuguese. Unlike the English language, which has a larger number of datasets available to produce research, the Portuguese language lacks this type of resource; in fact, we were unable to find any large dataset prepared for this task. Considering that we had to build such a dataset for the validation of our experiments, it should be clear the difficulties for advancement in this area of research.

There are numerous techniques aimed at the area of IE and among them, deep learning techniques have recently stood out, mainly due to their ability to discover patterns implicit in the data. The literature has presented deep learning algorithms such as Transformers [23], Recurrent Neural Networks [15,24] and Convolutional Neural Networks [28,29] as good alternatives, as they have been efficiently applied in several sequential text processing tasks, including the RE task.

In this context, this work aims to propose an approach to the extraction of any semantic relationship between Named Entities (NEs) in the Financial Market domain for the Portuguese language. To achieve this goal, we use BERT, a pre-trained model with the transformers [23] architecture, so it is possible to harness the power of BERT and get sentence semantics without the use of enhanced feature selection or other external resources. For the validation of the experiment, we also created a dataset composed of 4,641 sentences and semantic relations annotated manually. Therefore, the contributions of this work are:

- An entity relation extraction approach for the Portuguese language in the financial context, based on BERT.
- A corpus with more than 4,500 manually annotated tuples formed from financial market news, available on GitHub[1].

---

[1] https://github.com/DanielReeyes/financial-market-corpus.

This work is organized as follows. Section 2 analyzes the context of automated information processing for the area of Competitive Intelligence (CI) and brings the concept about the transformers BERT. Section 3 discusses related work. Section 4 provides a detailed description of the proposed solution. The experimental process and its results are detailed in Sects. 5 and 6, respectively. Finally, Sect. 7 presents our conclusions, as well as possibilities for future work.

## 2  Background

This section presents a theoretical basis on the main concepts related to the work: Financial market news processing as a problem addressed, presented in Subsect. 2.1; BERT, presented in Subsect. 2.2.

### 2.1  Competitive Intelligence and News Processing

Nowadays, the largest companies in the financial segment have a CI sector and, through it, information from different sources is strategically worked, allowing them to anticipate market trends and enabling the evolution of the business in relation to its competitors. This sector is usually formed by one or more professionals dedicated specifically to monitoring the competitors' moves.

CI is a structured survey model for unstructured facts and data analysis to support the company's decision-making in its strategic planning. Essentially, CI, involves the legal collection of information on competitors and the overall business environment. The knowledge gained from this information is then used to enhance the organization's own competitiveness [26]. In times of competitiveness based on knowledge and innovation, CI allows companies to exercise proactivity. The conclusions obtained in this process allow the company to know if it really remains competitive and if there is sustainability for its business model. CI can bring some advantages to companies that use it, such as: minimizing surprises from competitors, identifying opportunities and threats, obtaining relevant knowledge for the formulation of strategic planning, understanding the repercussions of their actions on the market, among others.

The process of capturing information through news still requires a lot of manual effort. Most of the information in the financial field appears in the form of free text, relying on manual processing of these data, far from keeping up with the growth rate of data, and unable to make full use of this information [30]. It often depends on a professional responsible for carefully reading numerous news about organizations to highlight possible market movements, and this professional can also keep this knowledge for himself. It is expected then that, with a system that automatically filters the relationships between financial market entities, the effort and time spent on those activities can be reduced. Another benefit achieved is that this same system can feed Business Intelligence (BI) systems and establish a historical database with market events. Thus, knowledge about market movements can be stored and organized independently of the particular CI analysts currently working in the company.

## 2.2  BERT

BERT is a large pre-trained language model proposed by Google [9] in 2018. Since then, BERT has achieved leading-edge results in various Natural Language Processing (NLP) tasks [14,27]. BERT consists of a bidirectional multi-layer Transformer encoder based on the original implementation described in Vaswani et al. [23]. Each layer has two sub-layers. The first is a multi-head self-attention mechanism, and the second is a simple, position-wise fully connected feed-forward network. Residual connections are applied to both sub-layers.

The model trains by combining two tasks: *Masked LM* and Next Sentence Prediction. The first, *Masked LM*, involves masking 15% of the words in a given sentence, whose original value must then be predicted, considering the context of the sentence in which they appear. Out of these 15%, 80% is replaced by the symbol [MASK], 10% by a random word, and 10% is kept with the original word.

In the BERT training process, the model takes pairs of sentences as input and learns to predict whether the second sentence in the pair is the subsequent sentence in the original document. During training, 50% of the entries are pairs where the second sentence is the subsequent sentence in the original document, while in the other 50% a random sentence from the corpus is chosen as the second sentence. The assumption is that the random phrase will be disconnected from the first phrase.

## 3  Related Work

With the advancement of information and communication technology in recent times, it is possible to store data from different sources and massively process it, which can facilitate research. Due to its feasibility of use in several areas such as the one explored in this study, RE has become the subject of numerous studies in the literature [2,3,13,17,30]. Those studies differ in regards to the method used, the language of the trained dataset, and also the theme of the dataset itself. Thus, this section presents some of these works, exploring some peculiarities.

Recently, deep learning algorithms have been targeted for application in a wide range of areas, such as NLP, image processing, bioinformatics, crowd simulation, and many others. In the area of NLP, for example, there is work on named entities recognition (NER) (e.g., [19]) and also the tool used in this study for NER, SpaCy[2], which is based on deep learning.

Several approaches have been proposed for extracting relationships from unstructured sources. For some languages, such as English, there is extensive research and literature [8]. To get around the problem of lack of memory for very large sequences in Convolutional Neural Networks (CNN), some authors [12,15,16] adopted an approach using *Long short-term memory* (LSTM), which use memory cells for neural networks. In this direction, the work by Qingqing Li [15] uses recurrent neural networks *Bidirectional Long short-term*

---

[2] https://spacy.io/.

*memory* (Bi-LSTM), which are an extension of the traditional LSTMs for multitasking model, and presents a version with an attention mechanism that considerably improves the results in all tested datasets.

More recent work in the literature [13,17,30] uses attention mechanisms to improve the performance of their neural network models. These mechanisms assist in the automatic information filtering step that helps to find the most appropriate sentence passage to describe the relationship between the Named Entities (NEs). In [30], the authors also implement a model based on the Recurrent Neural Network (RNN) Bi-GRU with an attention mechanism to focus on the most important assumptions of the sentences for the financial market. Despite having great importance, the financial domain is little explored in the literature. The authors also created a corpus by manually collecting 3000 sentence records from major news sites, which was used for entity recognition and extraction of relationships such as learning and training as a whole.

Approaches to RE for the Portuguese language are still very limited and are often based on rules such as [2,3]. Such approaches applied simple heuristics that explore fragments of evidence of relationships between NEs in texts, comprising lexical, syntactic, and semantic analysis, types of entities, and information from external sources. Chaves [3] proposes an extraction system that deals with the NER task only for the Local category and its relations. The work by Batista et al. [1] proposes a distance-supervised RE approach between two entities in Portuguese-written Wikipedia articles.

More recently Collovini et al. [5] developed a CI approach using RE to collect and organize unstructured data in the Portuguese language. The authors proposed a joint framework for Named Entity Recognition and also their semantic relationships. For the Entity Recognition task, a neural network was used, and for the relation extraction, a model based in *Conditional Random Fields* (CRF) algorithm was used. This approach has shown good results on a small dataset, but it needs some additional lexical-semantic features of the sentences.

Most studies present RE solutions for texts in English, thus it is possible to find a greater number of datasets in that language. There are few datasets available in the Portuguese language, such as the Golden Collection HAREM. HAREM is a joint Portuguese language assessment event, organized by Linguateca [18]. The lack of this type of resource forces researchers to develop their own research corpora. In most cases, it is necessary to first create a set of sentences and manually annotate them when the classification is supervised in order to proceed with the RE task. In addition, the lack of public datasets also makes it difficult to compare with related work fairly, as well as requiring more time and effort on the part of the researcher.

It can also be noted that there is work related the RE task which already uses machine learning techniques for this purpose. However, although we have found some papers on the RE task, few of them are for the Portuguese language, and only one of them is related to the financial context [5]. Considering other languages, the work by Zhou [30] has similar goals to ours but proposes a joint model for NER and classifies the type of relationship between such named entities. Thus, it is clear that there is a gap in the literature for work that address

such tasks using deep learning techniques and having Portuguese as the main
language, especially in the economic-financial context as addressed in this work.

## 4    Relationship Extractor Model

Through the analysis of the records collected and used in the experiment, it
is possible to note that the data from the financial field contain relationships
composed of many tokens, in addition to the fact that the sentences can be long.
There are many ways to express relationships, and the same semantics can be
expressed in many ways. Thus, the problem we address can benefit from the use
of an attention mechanism.

In this section, we present our model based on transformers [23] BERT. We
used the pre-trained model in Portuguese based on the brWaC corpus provided
by Souza et al. [21]. The implementations of this version of transformers are
provided by Huggingface[3]; we have added and trained the last layers of the
model in order to extract a sub-sequence of the input text.

As in Fig. 1, the model architecture is composed of two main components,
*encoders* and *decoders*. This approach provides a slightly different representation
for the words as they are used in the sentences and their relationship to other
words. This allows the model to understand the word itself and the context in
which it is inserted.

In general terms, the sentences enter through the *encoder*, which has two
layers: an attention mechanism which then feeds into a *Feed Forward Neural
Network*; the output of the *encoder* is then sent to the *decoder*. The *decoder*
also has both those layers, but between them there is additionally an attention
mechanism that helps focusing on the relevant parts of the input sentence. Below,
we describe in more detail some of these concepts.

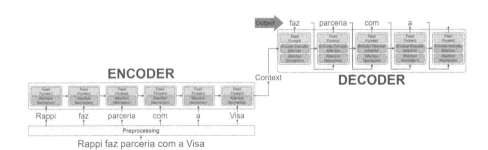

**Fig. 1.** Model architecture

**Attention Mechanism:** An attention mechanism can be described as mapping a query and a set of key-value pairs to an output, where the query, keys,

---

[3] https://github.com/huggingface/transformers.

values, and output are all vectors. As per Eq. 1, the output is calculated as a weighted sum of values, where the weight assigned to each value is calculated by a query matching function with the corresponding key. In the BERT pre-trained model, *Multi-Head Attention* is used, which allows the model to serve together information from different representations in different positions.

$$MultiHead(Q, K, V) = Concat(head_1, ..., head_h)W^O, \tag{1}$$

where

$$head_i = Attention(QW_1^Q, KW_i^K, VW_i^V). \tag{2}$$

**Feed-Forward Layer:** In addition to the attention mechanism, each of the layers in our *encoders* and *decoders* contains a fully connected feed-forward layer, which is applied to each position separately and identically. This consists of two linear transformations with a ReLU activation between them which are calculated according to Eq. 3.

$$FFN(x) = max(0, xW_1 + b_1)W_2 + b_2. \tag{3}$$

## 5    Experiments

This section aims to evaluate the performance of the proposed model in experiments using the corpus for the financial domain. The proposed approach follows the *Knowledge Discovery in Databases* (KDD) process created by Fayyad [11]. This process contains five steps ranging from data collection and creation, as described in Sect. 5.1, to the evaluation of results. The next sections aim to explain how each of these steps was employed in this work.

### 5.1    Selection

As in the selection step it is necessary to indicate which data will be used during the experiments for the RE [11] task, we start by searching for corpora. However, there was no evidence of open datasets in the context of extracting relationships in the financial area in the Portuguese language. Therefore, for this work, a corpus with 4,641 manually annotated tuples was created.

More than 1,500 financial market news from 2018 was provided by a partner company. Those news articles were collected from various media outlets, such as financial market websites, newspapers, and corporate balance sheets. Those articles gave rise to more than 10,000 sentences that were analyzed manually.

Another 7,097 tweets with dates from January 2021 were also collected. Those tweets were selected from 10 communication media users focused on the financial market and the economy in general. The selected users were: *infomoney, EstadaoEconomia, UOLEconomia, g1economia, OGlobo_Economia, folha_mercado, InvestingBrasil, leiamoneytimes, valoreconomico, br_economico.* Sentences that contained co-references were removed because handling them would require additional processing.

## 5.2    Pre-processing

The pre-processing step is intended to apply cleaning, correction, or removal procedures for inconsistent or missing data. In this work, we carried out a manual spell-checking process for each sentence, using Excel's spell-checker. Acronyms have also been expanded, such as *BC* being replaced by *Banco Central*.

Standardization can be done manually, but in a real work scenario, this task becomes massive and can be automated by creating a base of named entities and their acronyms. Thus, it is possible to design a process that validates the acronyms contained in the sentence and replaces them with their extensions or even an approach that focuses only on some specific entities informed by the CI analyst.

In this same phase, the named entities are also identified, through a single NER tool, called SpaCy[4], ensuring that the same criteria were used for all sentences.

The data cleaning process was done automatically through a script available at Github (See Footnote 1) that removes special characters and acronyms that follow the description itself. Phrases that have only one recognized named entity or none at all are removed from the dataset. At the end of this cleaning step, just over 5,000 sentences were selected for the next step.

The named entities in question are those related to the person, place, and organization categories, as they were considered the most relevant to the domain of organizations [6]. The focal point is information about organizations as well as their relationships with other organizations, people, and places.

## 5.3    Transformation

The data transformation or formatting step analyzes the data obtained from the previous step and reorganizes them in a specific way so that they can be analyzed and interpreted by the algorithm in the next step. In the case of this work, after identifying the Named Entities in the previous phase, the first step of the transformation step is to combine all entities present in the sentence in order to create a tuple (sentence, entity, entity) for each combination. It is important to emphasize that sentences with more than two entities generate more than one tuple for the same sentence, as it is necessary to create a pair for each combination of entities.

Then, the semantic relationships between the highlighted named entities are manually annotated. In this case, only positive tuples are considered and negative combinations are discarded. A tuple is considered positive when there is any semantic relationship between two named entities from the categories defined in Sect. 5.2. Finally, the two named entities are concatenated at the end of the sentence.

Finally, after removing sentences without the semantic relationship between the named entities, the corpus was left with a total of 4,641 records, containing a

---

[4] https://spacy.io/.

sentence, its entities, and the semantic relationship between them. Table 1 exemplifies some records that have combinations of entities that can generate more than one tuple per sentence and also examples of tuples with positive annotations that contain relationships between named entities of the organization type.

**Table 1.** Examples of positive tuples with annotations showing the relationships between named entities. The entities to be evaluated appear in bold font and the text representing the semantic relationship between them is underlined.

| Relation instance | Semantic relation |
|---|---|
| O estudo na britânica Nature é de autoria de **Neil M. Ferguson**, do **Imperial College**, de Londres, e mais sete colaboradores | do |
| O estudo na britânica Nature é de autoria de Neil M. Ferguson, do **Imperial College**, de **Londres**, e mais sete colaboradores | de |
| **Rappi** faz parceria com a **Visa** e anuncia cartão pré-pago no Brasil | faz parceria com a |
| **Rappi** faz parceria com a Visa e anuncia cartão pré pago **Brasil** | anuncia cartão pré-pago no |

As sentences are naturally composed of words and characters, the transformation step of the methodology also includes the transformation of tokens into numerical representations by the BERT encoder. As BERT is a pre-trained model that expects input data in a specific format, this step also adds the special tokens [CLS] and [SEP] properly encoded in each sentence, finishing the transformation of the natural language sentence into the input for the extractor model. The special token [SEP] is used to mark the end of a sentence or the separation between two sentences. The special token [CLS] is used to mark the beginning of our text.

### 5.4   Mining

The mining step contemplates the prediction task, in which a behavioral pattern of the data is searched in order to predict the behavior of a future entity [11]. The corpus was randomly divided into two parts, 90% of which were used to train the model and 10% for testing; This proportion rate was chosen so that it would be possible to provide more samples for training the two models used in the approach. The first set was used so that the algorithm could search for the particular pattern in the data related to the relationship label. Thus, after the training stage, from which the model is able to recognize this pattern, it is possible to apply it to the test set data.

The adjustment of the BERT hyper-parameters used was done using the combination of all the values indicated by Jacob Devlin when he proposed the new BERT language model in [9]. In that work, Jacob Devlin used most hyper-parameters with default values, except for batch size, learning rate, and a number of training epochs. We also added two more test values, referring to the optimizer parameter. The dropout rate was always kept at 0.1. Thus, the values analyzed for this task were:

- **Batch Size:** 16, 32;
- **Learning Rate:** 2e−5, 3e−5, 5e−5;
- **Epochs:** 2, 3, 4, 5;
- **Optimizer:** AdamW;

In the end, we ran a total of 24 experiments with all possible combinations of the parameters described above. After analyzing the results, the model that presented the best results was selected according to the parameters in Table 2.

**Table 2.** Combination of hyper-parameters that presented the best results.

| Hyper-parameter | Value |
|---|---|
| Batch Size | 32 |
| Learning Rate | 2e−5 |
| Epochs | 5 |
| Optimizer | AdamW |

### 5.5   Evaluation

The last step of KDD methodology presented in this section aims to evaluate the performance of the model we built. The experimental evaluation was carried out by applying, in the test data, the model based on a deep neural network built in the learning stage based on the defined parameters. For the implementation of the neural network, the TensorFlow Keras[5] library was used to adapt the last layer of BERT.

The evaluation metric used in this work is the Jaccard Similarity Coefficient or simply Jaccard Coefficient. Jaccard's coefficient measures the similarity between two sets and is defined as the size of the intersection divided by the size of the union of the sample sets. We chose this metric as it can present a more realistic view of the model's efficiency when recognizing the tokens present in the relationship. If we only considered completely correct extractions, the model would be penalized by not extracting just a token for example. Equation 4 shows how the coefficient is calculated and Table 3 an example of evaluation.

$$jaccard(A, B) = \frac{|A \bigcap B|}{|A \bigcup B|} \tag{4}$$

For the above two relations, we get a Jaccard similarity of $3/(3 + 1) = 0.75$, which is the size of the intersection of the set divided by the total size of the set.

---

[5] https://www.tensorflow.org/.

**Table 3.** Evaluation example for extracting relationships between Named Entities. The evaluated named entities are in bold font.

| Sentence | True Relationship | Extracted Relationship | Jaccard Score |
|---|---|---|---|
| **Havanna** abrirá cafeteria dentro do **Santander** | abrirá cafeteria dentro do | abrirá cafeteria dentro | 0.75 |

# 6    Results and Discussion

After the training step, the model was applied to the test data set. In this evaluation step, the model obtained good results, indicating an overall Jaccard metric of 73.5% for all the prediction cases. In terms of correctly extracted relationships, it was possible to extract 212 completely correct relationships from a total of 465 samples available for testing; that is when the extracted relationship is exactly the same as that manually annotated. We consider a relationship partially correct when the extracted relationship reaches a Jaccard score of at least 50%. As for partially correct relationships, our approach was able to extract 176 relationships. In only 40 occurrences the model was not able to extract any token present in the relation to be extracted. These results are summarized in Table 4.

**Table 4.** Results obtained by the proposed model.

| Number of relationships | Jaccard sscore | % Totally correct | % Partially correct | % Totally + Partially Correct |
|---|---|---|---|---|
| 465 | 73,5% | 46% | 38% | 84% |

In general, the extracted relationships express information relevant to the CI focus, for example, partnership formation relationships between Organizations; financial investment relationships between Organizations; relations between People and Organizations; entry of organizations into the market in certain locations, among others. Table 5 illustrates instances of extracted relationships that are completely correct. From this RE approach, it is possible to create a historical knowledge base, easily accessible and interpreted by CI analysts. Thus, it is possible to provide information so that everyone can extract value quickly and clearly.

We claim that the model was able to respond well to the complexity of sentence length and the size of the relation to be extracted. It was able to recognize patterns and indicate which tokens belong to the semantic relations contained in the same sentence in the financial domain. Figure 2 illustrates the average score according to sentence length.

**Table 5.** Completely correct relationships extracted by the proposed model.

| Sentence | Entities | Relationship |
|---|---|---|
| 1. A B2W dona da Americanas.com e do Submarino estuda separar o braço da Ame Digital de suas operações | B2W, Ame Digital | estuda separar o braço da |
| 2. Bolsonaro volta a criticar pesquisa de emprego do IBGE | Bolsonaro, IBGE | volta a criticar pesquisa de emprego do |
| 3. O Banco BMG e o Clube Atlético Mineiro se uniram para marcar a história mineira mais uma vez com o lançamento do Meu Galo BMG | Clube Atlético Mineiro, Banco BMG | se uniram |
| 4. O Brasil é um país foco para o Google com alto nível de engajamento diz diretor de dispositivos para a América Latina | Google , Brasil | é um país foco para o |

It can also be inferred that the model has greater difficulty when trying to extract relations composed of only one token, which ends up penalizing the model and its performance. This particular type of relationship is the third largest group within the test dataset, and in most cases there are only two score possibilities, 0 or 1. On these prediction errors, the model had more difficulty in inferring composite relationships just by a preposition (e.g. *da, de, na, no*) as shown in Table 6.

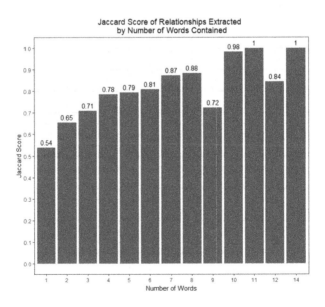

**Fig. 2.** Average score grouped by the number of words contained in the relation to be extracted.

**Table 6.** Examples of relationships not extracted by the model. In bold and underlined, the semantic relationship to be extracted.

| Sentence | Entities | Extracted Relationship |
|---|---|---|
| 1. Nubank chama Daniel Goldberg <u>**da**</u> Farallon para seu conselho de administração | Farallon, Daniel Goldberg | *None* |
| 2. Doria ataca intervenção de Bolsonaro **na** Petrobras desnecessário e condenável | Petrobras, Bolsonaro | *None* |
| 3. Com sinal verde para venda de estatais Guedes e Onyx <u>**disputam**</u> programa de privatização do governo | Onyx, Guedes | disputa |
| 4. O Mercado Pago <u>**fintech do grupo**</u> Mercado Livre e a Hub Fintech startup fornecedora de soluções de negócios em meios de pagamento firmaram parceria para criação de uma oferta compartilhada | Mercado Livre, Mercado Pago | fintech |

# 7    Conclusion and Future Work

In this work, we provide an approach to the RE task and a manually annotated corpus from news provided by a market intelligence company and also news collected from Twitter on the subject of Competitive Intelligence. More than 1,500 news about the financial market and more than 7,000 *tweets* were selected to build a knowledge base. The model proved to be able to recognize semantic relationships and is therefore useful for discovering events and facts related to the financial market.

From the section on related work, it is possible to note that there is little research on techniques for extracting relationships between named entities for the financial domain in Portuguese. This domain lacks practical solutions, in part because of the large amount of information in the financial area, so manual analysis becomes difficult to meet the needs and make full use of this information. Due to this lack of approaches to the RE task, it is also difficult to present comparative results at this stage, since there is still no dataset available for comparison.

As the main contributions of this work, we can mention the development of a Relation Extraction model between named entities based on BERT, which replaces the explicit linguistic resources, required by other methods, such as rule-based approaches or that use Parts-Of-Speech (PoS). This approach becomes much simpler as it only needs the phrase information and the pair of concatenated entities. Thus, it allows more than one entry to be sent, as a sentence can have N pairs of named entities. Therefore, the approach adopted allows us to infer that the sentence and the pair of entities are sent separately. Another contribution of this work is found in the development of a large corpus related to the financial market, with manually annotated text from *tweets* and news provided by CI analysts to support decision making. The results demonstrate that the approach used has reasonable results, reaching a Jaccard score of 73.5%. This score is interesting since the model was able to extract relationships of different sizes. As shown in Sect. 6 it was more penalized when extracting relations from just a token, usually formed by prepositions.

As future work, a method in pipeline format containing two models for extracting relationships between named entities will be developed. The first model will determine whether an entry containing the phrase and entity pair has a semantic relationship between the named entities to be tested. The output of this model, when it indicates that there is a semantic relationship, will be the input of the model here presented, which will highlight the parts of the sentences that represent or describe the relationship between the selected named entities.

# References

1. Batista, D.S., Forte, D., Silva, R., Martins, B., Silva, M.: Extracçao de relaçoes semânticas de textos em português explorando a dbpédia e a wikipédia. Linguamatica **5**(1), 41–57 (2013)
2. Bruckschen, M., De Souza, J.G.C., Vieira, R., Rigo, S., Mota, C., Santos, D.: Sistema serelep para o reconhecimento de relaçoes entre entidades mencionadas (2008)
3. Chaves, M.: Geo-ontologias e padrões para reconhecimento de locais e de suas relações em textos: o sei-geo no segundo harem. Cristina Mota; Diana Santos (ed) Desafios na avaliação conjunta do reconhecimento de entidades mencionadas: O Segundo HAREM Linguateca 2008 (2008)
4. Cheng, W., Xiong, J.: Entity relationship extraction based on bi-channel neural network. In: 2020 2nd International Conference on Machine Learning, Big Data and Business Intelligence (MLBDBI), pp. 349–352. IEEE (2020)
5. Collovini, S., Gonçalves, P.N., Cavalheiro, G., Santos, J., Vieira, R.: Relation extraction for competitive intelligence. In: Quaresma, P., Vieira, R., Aluísio, S., Moniz, H., Batista, F., Gonçalves, T. (eds.) PROPOR 2020. LNCS (LNAI), vol. 12037, pp. 249–258. Springer, Cham (2020). https://doi.org/10.1007/978-3-030-41505-1_24
6. Collovini, S., Grando, F., Souza, M., Freitas, L., Vieira, R.: Semantic relations extraction in the organization domain. In: Proceedings of IADIS International Conference on Applied Computing, Rio de Janeiro, pp. 99–106 (2011)
7. Collovini, S., Pugens, L., Vanin, A.A., Vieira, R.: Extraction of relation descriptors for Portuguese using conditional random fields. In: Bazzan, A.L.C., Pichara, K. (eds.) IBERAMIA 2014. LNCS (LNAI), vol. 8864, pp. 108–119. Springer, Cham (2014). https://doi.org/10.1007/978-3-319-12027-0_9
8. Cruz, C.G.A., Weitzel, L.: Evaluation of relation extraction systems for Portuguese language pt-br. In: 2018 13th Iberian Conference on Information Systems and Technologies (CISTI), pp. 1–6. IEEE (2018)

9. Devlin, J., Chang, M.W., Lee, K., Toutanova, K.: Bert: Pre-training of deep bidirectional transformers for language understanding. preprint arXiv:1810.04805 (2018)
10. Etzioni, O., Fader, A., Christensen, J., Soderland, S., et al.: Open information extraction: the second generation. In: Twenty-Second International Joint Conference on Artificial Intelligence, pp. 3–10 (2011)
11. Fayyad, U., Piatetsky-Shapiro, G., Smyth, P.: From data mining to knowledge discovery in databases. AI Mag. **17**(3), 37 (1996)
12. Florez, E., Precioso, F., Pighetti, R., Riveill, M.: Deep learning for identification of adverse drug reaction relations. In: Proceedings of the 2019 International Symposium on Signal Processing Systems, pp. 149–153 (2019)
13. GAN, T., GAN, Y., HE, Y.: Subsequence-level entity attention lstm for relation extraction. In: 2019 16th International Computer Conference on Wavelet Active Media Technology and Information Processing, pp. 262–265. IEEE (2019)
14. Han, X., Wang, L.: A novel document-level relation extraction method based on bert and entity information. IEEE Access **8**, 96912–96919 (2020)
15. Li, Q., et al.: A multi-task learning based approach to biomedical entity relation extraction. In: 2018 IEEE International Conference on Bioinformatics and Biomedicine (BIBM), pp. 680–682. IEEE (2018)
16. Pandey, C., Ibrahim, Z., Wu, H., Iqbal, E., Dobson, R.: Improving RNN with attention and embedding for adverse drug reactions. In: Proceedings of the 2017 International Conference on Digital Health, pp. 67–71 (2017)
17. Qin, P., Xu, W., Guo, J.: Designing an adaptive attention mechanism for relation classification. In: 2017 International Joint Conference on Neural Networks (IJCNN), pp. 4356–4362. IEEE (2017)
18. Santos, D., Cardoso, N.: Reconhecimento de entidades mencionadas em português: Documentação e actas do harem, a primeira avaliação conjunta na área (2007)
19. Santos Neto, J.F.d, et al.: Reconhecimento de entidades nomeadas para o português usando redes neurais (2019)
20. Sarawagi, S.: Information extraction. Now Publishers Inc. (2008)
21. Souza, F., Nogueira, R., Lotufo, R.: BERTimbau: pretrained BERT models for Brazilian Portuguese. In: 9th Brazilian Conference on Intelligent Systems, BRACIS, Rio Grande do Sul, Brazil, October 20–23 (to appear) (2020)
22. Tang, Y.: An extended sequence labeling approach for relation extraction. In: 2019 IEEE International Conference on Power, Intelligent Computing and Systems (ICPICS), pp. 121–124. IEEE (2019)
23. Vaswani, A., et al.: Attention is all you need. preprint arXiv:1706.03762 1 (2017)
24. Wang, C., Wang, Y., Mo, J., Wang, S.: End-to-end relation extraction based on part of speech syntax tree. In: 2020 2nd International Conference on Machine Learning, Big Data and Business Intelligence (MLBDBI), pp. 5–9. IEEE (2020)
25. Wang, Y., Sun, Y., Ma, Z., Gao, L., Xu, Y., Wu, Y.: A method of relation extraction using pre-training models. In: 2020 13th International Symposium on Computational Intelligence and Design (ISCID), pp. 176–179. IEEE (2020)
26. Weiss, A.: A brief guide to competitive intelligence: how to gather and use information on competitors. Bus. Inf. Rev. **19**(2), 39–47 (2002)
27. Xue, K., Zhou, Y., Ma, Z., Ruan, T., Zhang, H., He, P.: Fine-tuning bert for joint entity and relation extraction in chinese medical text. In: 2019 IEEE International Conference on Bioinformatics and Biomedicine (BIBM), pp. 892–897. IEEE (2019)
28. Yin, B., Sun, Y., Wang, Y.: Entity relation extraction method based on fusion of multiple information and attention mechanism. In: 2020 IEEE 6th International Conference on Computer and Communications (ICCC). IEEE (2020)

29. Yu, H., Cao, Y., Cheng, G., Xie, P., Yang, Y., Yu, P.: Relation extraction with bert-based pre-trained model. In: 2020 International Wireless Communications and Mobile Computing (IWCMC), pp. 1382–1387. IEEE (2020)
30. Zhou, Z., Zhang, H.: Research on entity relationship extraction in financial and economic field based on deep learning. In: 2018 IEEE 4th International Conference on Computer and Communications (ICCC), pp. 2430–2435. IEEE (2018)

# Experiments on Kaldi-Based Forced Phonetic Alignment for Brazilian Portuguese

Cassio Batista$^{(\boxtimes)}$ and Nelson Neto

Computer Science Graduate Program, FalaBrasil Group, Federal University of Pará,
Augusto Corrêa 1, Belém 66075–110, Brazil
{cassiotb,nelsonneto}@ufpa.br

**Abstract.** Forced phonetic alignment (FPA) is the task of associating a given phonetic unit to a timestamp interval in the speech waveform. Phoneticians are able mark the boundaries with precision, but as the corpus grows it becomes infeasible to do it by hand. For Brazilian Portuguese (BP) in particular, only three tools appear to perform FPA: EasyAlign, Montreal Forced Aligner (MFA), and UFPAlign. Therefore, this work aims to develop resources based on Kaldi toolkit for UFPAlign, including their release alongside all scripts under open licenses; and to bring forth a comparison to the other two aforementioned aligners. Evaluation took place in terms of the phone boundary metric over a dataset of 385 hand-aligned utterances, and results show that Kaldi-based aligners perform better overall, and that UFPAlign models are more accurate than MFA's. Furthermore, complex deep-learning-based approaches did not seem to improve performance compared to simpler models.

**Keywords:** Forced phonetic alignment · Speech segmentation · Acoustic modeling · Kaldi · Brazilian Portuguese

## 1  Introduction

The analysis of the prosodic structure of speech very often requires the alignment of the speech recording with a phonetic transcription of the speech, a task known as forced phonetic alignment (FPA). However, transcribing and aligning several hours of speech by hand is very time-consuming, even for experienced phoneticians. As several approaches have been applied to automate this process, some of them brought from the automatic speech recognition (ASR) domain, the combination of hidden Markov models (HMM) and Gaussian mixture models (GMM) has been for long the most widely explored for FPA.

With respect to ASR-based frameworks, we found only three forced aligners that provide pre-trained models for Brazilian Portuguese (BP): EasyAlign [9], Montreal Forced Aligner (MFA) [16] and UFPAlign [6,32]. To the best of our knowledge, EasyAlign is the only HTK-based aligner that ships with a model for

© Springer Nature Switzerland AG 2021
A. Britto and K. Valdivia Delgado (Eds.): BRACIS 2021, LNAI 13074, pp. 465–479, 2021.
https://doi.org/10.1007/978-3-030-91699-2_32

BP, MFA is the only Kaldi-based one, and UFPAlign has been evolving through time to work with both HTK and Kaldi as back-end.

It should be remarked that UFPAlign was born in [32] as an early effort to mitigate the gap for Brazilian Portuguese, providing a package with grapheme-to-phoneme (G2P) converter, syllabification system and GMM-based acoustic models trained over the HTK toolkit [34]. As usual, tests comparing the automatic versus manual segmentations were performed. An extra comparison was made to EasyAlign [9], which to our knowledge was the only aligner that supported BP at that moment. It was observed that the tools achieved equivalent behaviors, considering two metrics: boundary-based and overlap rate.

Later on, following Kaldi's success as the *de facto* open-source toolkit for ASR [25] due to its efficient implementation of deep neural networks (DNN) for hybrid HMM-DNN acoustic modeling, UFPAlign was updated in [6] w.r.t. its older HTK-based version, yielding better results with both monophone and triphone GMM-based models, as well as with a standard feed-forward network trained using **nnet2** recipes. Both HTK- and Kaldi-based versions of UFPAlign were then evaluated over a dataset containing 181 utterances spoken by a male speaker, whose phonemes were manually aligned by an expert phonetician.

Therefore, as **nnet2** recipes became outdated, this work builds upon [6] by updating training scripts to Kaldi's **nnet3** recipe, which contains the current state-of-the-art scripts for ASR. Up-to-date versions of the acoustic models, phonetic and syllabic dictionaries were released to the public under the MIT license on FalaBrasil's GitHub account[1], as well as the scripts to generate them. Assuming Kaldi is pre-installed as a dependency, UFPAlign pipeline's works fine under Linux environments via command line, but also provides a graphical interface as a plugin to Praat [3], a popular free software package for speech analysis.

Additionally, some intra- and inter-evaluation procedures were performed, the former considering all acoustic models trained within the Kaldi's default GMM and DNN pipeline, while the latter applied the HTK former version of UFPAlign [32], EasyAlign [9], and MFA [16] aligners over the same dataset for the sake of a fair comparison. The evaluation dataset was extended from 193 utterances spoken by a male individual to include 192 sentences spoken by a female speaker, i.e., 385 manually aligned audio files in total. The similarity measure is given by the absolute difference between the forced alignments with respect to manual ones, which is called phonetic boundary [16].

In summary, the contributions of this work include:

- Release of monophone-, triphone-, and DNN-based (**nnet3**) acoustic models, which comprise a total of five pre-trained, Kaldi-compatible models included as part of UFPAlign. Scripts used to train such models are also available.
- Generation of multi-tier TextGrid files for Praat, based on phonetic and syllabic dictionaries built over a list of words in BP collected from multiple sources and post-processed by GNU Aspell [2] spell checker.

---

[1] https://github.com/falabrasil.

– Comparison to the only two ASR-based phonetic aligners that exist for Brazilian Portuguese (to the best of our knowledge), regarding the phone boundary metric [16] over a dataset of 385 hand-aligned utterances.

The remainder of this paper is as follows. Section 2 presents the FPA procedure with Kaldi, and some other resources used for training and evaluation. Evaluation tests and results are reported and discussed on Sects. 3 and 4, respectively. Finally, Sect. 5 presents the conclusion and plans for future work.

## 2   Methodology

This section details the forced phonetic alignment process within UFPAlign, which is similar to a traditional decoding stage in speech recognition where one needs an acoustic model and a phonetic dictionary (or lexicon) to decide among senones, except the language model is not necessary in such case.

UFPAlign uses Kaldi as the ASR back-end, and FalaBrasil's grapheme-to-phoneme (G2P) and syllabification tools to provide phonemes and syllables from regular words (also known as graphemes), given that users themselves provide such transcriptions as input alongside with the corresponding audio file. The output is stored in a TextGrid file—a well-known file format for Praat users.

### 2.1   Kaldi, Grapheme-to-Phoneme and Syllabification Tools

Kaldi [25] is an open-source toolkit developed to support speech recognition researchers. The DNN training framework is provided by Kaldi in three distinct setups[2]: nnet1 [14], nnet2 [27,35] and nnet3. Unlike nnet1 and nnet2, nnet3 offers an easier access to more specialized kinds of networks other than simple feed-forward ones, including long short-term memory (LSTM) [21] and time-delay neural networks (TDNN) [22,24], for example.

Scripts in Kaldi's nnet3 setup use factorized time-delay neural networks (TDNN-F) as default architecture [22], which are a type of feed-forward network that has a behavior similar to recurrent topologies like LSTMs in the sense of capturing past and future temporal contexts w.r.t. the current speech frame to be recognized, but with an easier procedure for parallelization. This opposes to previous nnet2 recipes, for instance, which are pure vanilla networks.

As Kaldi requires a lexicon to serve as the target being modeled by HMMs, this work uses a G2P converter provided by the FalaBrasil Group as an open-source library written in Java [18,30]. This tool relies on a stress determination system to provide only one pronunciation per word, which means it does not consider co-articulation between words (i.e., cross-word events are ignored). The phonetic alphabet is composed by 38 phonemes plus a silence phone, inspired by the Speech Assessment Methods Phonetic Alphabet (SAMPA) [7].

The syllabification tool, on the other hand, is not a requirement when training acoustic models for ASR, but rather just a feature of UFPAlign for composing

---

[2] http://www.kaldi-asr.org/doc/dnn.html.

another tier in the TextGrid output file. It is also provided by the FalaBrasil Group within the same library as the G2P [19].

## 2.2 Training Speech Corpora and Lexicon

To build an effective acoustic model (AM), a relatively large amount of labeled data is required, apart from a language model (LM) and a pronunciation model (a.k.a. phonetic dictionary or lexicon). An LM is necessary for speech recognition despite not being explicitly used during phonetic alignment itself. The model used here was built in [18] using SRILM [33] toolkit over approximately 1.5 million sentences from the CETENFolha dataset [12]. The FalaBrasil speech corpora, on the other hand, consists of seven datasets in Brazilian Portuguese with a total of approximately 170 h of transcribed audio, the same as in [6].

Finally, the phonetic dictionary was created via FalaBrasil G2P tool [18,30] based on a list of words collected from multiple sources on the Internet, including University of Minho's Projecto Natura [1], LibreOffice's VERO dictionary [17], NILC's CETENFolha dataset [12], and FrequencyWords repository based on subtitles from OpenSubtitles [8,20]. GNU Aspell [2] is responsible for checking out the spelling and consequently filtering the huge number of words collected, resulting in approximately 200,000 words in the final list.

## 2.3 Acoustic Models

The deep-learning-based training approach in Kaldi actually uses the GMM training as a pre-processing stage. For this work, AMs were trained by adapting the recipe for Mini-librispeech dataset [23]. For details on the GMM training pipeline, the reader is referred to [6]. The DNN is trained on the top of the last GMM model of the pipeline, which comprises a speaker-adapted training (SAT).

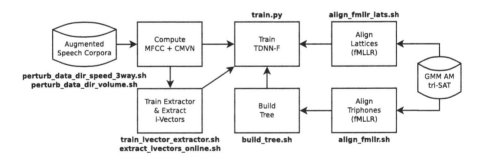

**Fig. 1.** Stages for training a TDNN-F following Kaldi's Mini-librispeech recipe. On the left side, high-resolution, cepstral-normalized MFCCs (40 features instead of 13) are extracted from an augmented corpora after applying speed and volume perturbation [15], as are the speaker-related 100-dimensional i-vector features [5,31]; to be used as input to the neural network. On the right side, training labels are provided by a GMM tri-SAT acoustic model.

Figure 1 details how the DNN model is obtained as a final-stage AM by using the neural network to model the state likelihood distributions as well as to input those likelihoods into the decision tree leaf nodes [10]. The implementation in Kaldi uses a sub-sampling technique that avoids the whole computation of a feed-forward's hidden activations at all time steps and therefore allows a faster training of TDNNs. The "factorized" term distinguishes a TDNN-F from a traditional TDNN architecture by a singular value decomposition (SVD) that is applied at the hidden layer's weight matrices in order to reduce the number of model parameters without degrading performance [24].

## 2.4   Kaldi Forced Phonetic Alignment

Kaldi's FPA procedure performs several steps for obtaining the time-marked conversation (CTM) files, which contains a list of numerical indices corresponding to phonemes with both their start times and durations in seconds. After Kaldi scripts extract some features from time-domain audio data, the forced alignment step, that employs the aforementioned pre-trained acoustic models, is computed by Kaldi using Viterbi beam search algorithm [11]. Figure 2 shows an overview of the stages within UFPAlign.

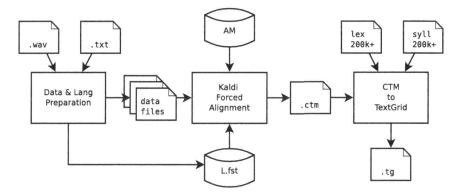

**Fig. 2.** Pipeline followed by UFPAlign. When a user feeds the system with an audio (.wav) and its respective transcription (.txt), they should expect a Praat's TextGrid file (.tg) as output. Time marks are provided by Kaldi, which relies on the knowledge of the acoustic model (AM) and tokens of the lexicon (L.fst).

The data and language preparation stage in particular also creates some "data files" on the fly, which contain information regarding the specifics of the audio file and its transcription, namely text, wav.scp, utt2spk, and spk2utt. The language preparation stage, on the other hand, is given by a script provided by Kaldi to create another set of important files, the main one being the lexicon parsed into a finite-state transducer (FST) format, called L.fst.

For data preparation, the first step consists in checking whether there are any new words in the input data that were not seen during the acoustic model training. If any word in the transcriptions is not found in the pronunciation dictionary (lexicon), it calls the grapheme-phoneme conversion module (G2P) [18,30] to extend the lexicon with each new word along with its respective phonemic pronunciation. For Praat's final visualization purposes, the word is also divided into syllables through the embedded syllabification tool [19]. As the original phonetic and syllabic dictionaries contain approximately 200,000 entries, they both become `lex 200k+` and `syll 200k+` files after the insertion of missing words.

The last block of the phonetic alignment process handles the conversion of both CTM files to a Praat's TextGrid (`.tg`), a text file containing the alignment information. Therefore, CTM files are read by a Python script that in the conversion process uses the `lex 200k+` and `syll 200k+` extended dictionaries to generate the output five-tier TextGrid that can be displayed by Praat's editor.

## 3   Evaluation Tests

The evaluation procedure takes place by comparing a bunch of TextGrid files: the hand-aligned reference and the ones automatically annotated by the forced aligners (i.e., by inference), as the phone boundary metric considers the absolute difference between the ending time of both phoneme occurrences [16]. The calculation is performed for each acoustic model, and it takes place over all utterances from the evaluation dataset composed by one male and one female speaker.

### 3.1   Evaluation Speech Corpus

The automatic alignment was estimated on the basis of the manual segmentation. The original dataset used for assessing the accuracy of the phonetic aligner is composed of 200 and 199 utterances spoken by a male and a female speaker, in a total of 15 min and 32 s of hand-aligned audio, as shown in Table 1. Praat's TextGrid files, whose phonetic timestamps were manually adjusted by a phonetician, are available alongside audio and text transcriptions.

**Table 1.** Speech corpus used to evaluate the automatic phonetic aligners. Actual duration and number of files after discard are shown between parentheses, as well as the number of unique words.

| Dataset | Duration | # Files | # Words | # Tokens |
|---------|----------|---------|---------|----------|
| Male | 7 m:58 s (7 m:40 s) | 200 (193) | 1,260 (665) | 5,275 |
| Female | 7 m:34 s (7 m:18 s) | 199 (192) | 1,258 (664) | 5,262 |
| Total | 15 m:32 s (14 m:58 s) | 399 (385) | 2,518 (686) | 10,537 |

This dataset was aligned with a set of phonemes inspired by the SAMPA alphabet, which in theory is the same set used by the FalaBrasil's G2P software that creates the lexicon during acoustic model training. Nevertheless, there are some problems of phonetic mismatches, and some cross-word phonemes between words, which makes the mapping between both phoneme sets challenging, given that FalaBrasil's G2P only handles internal-word conversion [30].

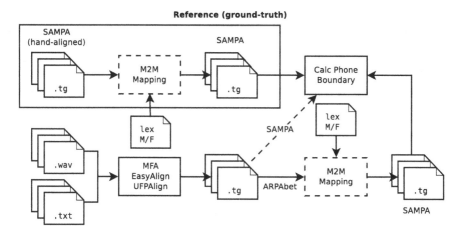

**Fig. 3.** Evaluation takes place by comparing the output of all forced aligners to a hand-aligned ground-truth. The M2M mapping is applied to make different phone sets match the SAMPA version used by FalaBrasil's G2P, which is provided by the lexicon generated over transcriptions of the corpus (`lex M/F`).

The example in Table 2 shows the phonetic transcription for a sentence given by the original dataset (top) and the acoustic model (bottom) which then suppress vowel sounds altogether due to cross-word rules (usually elision and apocope) when they occur at the end of the current word and at the beginning at the next. Such mismatches occur because the dataset was aligned by a phonetician considering acoustic information (i.e., listening), which cannot be done by the G2P tool that creates the acoustic model's lexicon, since it is provided only with textual information. Situations like these of phonetic information loss led to the removal of such audio files from the dataset before evaluation.

**Table 2.** Cross-word mismatches between transcriptions manually aligned by a phonetician (top) vs. generated by our G2P software (bottom). Word boundary losses are represented by the empty set symbol (∅).

(a) "*às novi meia, pairum ar no rio*" → "*às nove e meia, paira um ar no rio*"

```
6 ∅ Z n O v i ∅ ... p a j 4 ∅ u~ m a h/ ...
a j s n O v i i ... p a j r a u~ ∅ a X ...
```

In the end, fourteen files were excluded from the dataset, so about 34 s of audio was discarded, and 193 and 192 utterances remained in the male and female datasets, respectively. The filtering also ignored intra- and inter-word pauses and silences, resulting in 2,518 words (686 unique, since the utterances' transcriptions are identical for both speakers, i.e., they speak the very same sentences) and 10,537 phonetic segments (tokens) (c.f. Table 1).

## 3.2 Simulation Overview

Figure 3 shows a diagram of the experiments where EasyAlign, UFPAlign and MFA forced aligners receive the same input of audio files (.wav) with their respective textual transcriptions (.txt). These are the files whose manual annotation is available. All three aligners output one TextGrid file (.tg) for each audio given as input, which then serve as the inference inputs to the phone boundary calculation. The reference ground-truth annotations, on the other hand, are provided by the 385 TextGrid files that contain the hand-aligned phonemes corresponding to the transcriptions in the evaluation dataset.

However, for computing phone boundaries, there must exist a one-to-one mapping between the reference and the inference phones, which was not possible at first due to the nature of the phonetic alphabets: UFPAlign and EasyAlign share the same SAMPA-inspired lexicon generated by FalaBrasil's G2P tool, while MFA is based on ARPAbet [29]. Furthermore, the hand-aligned utterances fall on a special case where the phonetic alphabet used (referred here as "original") is also SAMPA-inspired, but not exactly the same as FalaBrasil's.

Apart from the fact that cross-word rules can insert or delete phones, some phonemes do not have an equivalent, such as /tS/ and /dZ/. Besides, there are also usual swaps between phonetically similar sounds: /h//, /h\/, /h/ and /4/, for instance, might be almost deliberately mapped to either /r/, /R/ or /X/. This is worse in MFA, where the set of phonemes is entirely different.

Thus, since the situation seemed to require a smarter approach than a simple one-to-one tabular, static mapping, it was necessary to employ a many-to-many (M2M) mapping procedure (c.f. dashed blocks on Fig. 3) based on statistical frequency of occurrence, e.g., how many times phones /t/ and /S/ from the original evaluation dataset were mapped to a single phone /tS/ in the lex M/F file representing FalaBrasil's G2P SAMPA-inspired alphabet. This mapping also works when dealing with MFA's ARPAbet phonemes, and will be further discussed in Sect. 3.3.

## 3.3 Many-to-Many (M2M) Phonetic Mapping

By taking another look at Table 2, one might have also reasoned that the mapping between the two sets of phonemes is not always one-to-one. The usual situation is where a pair of phonemes from the dataset (original) is merged into a single one for the AM (FalaBrasil G2P), such as /i~/ /n/ → /i~/ and /t/ /S/ → /tS/. However, a single phoneme can also be less frequently split into two or more, such as /u/ /S/ → /u/ /j/ /s/.

To deal with these irregularities, we used the many-to-many alignment (m2m-aligner) software [13] in the core of a pipeline that converts the original TextGrid from the evaluation dataset to a TextGrid that is compatible with the FalaBrasil's lexicon used to train the acoustic models. We took advantage of the same pipeline to convert MFA's ARPAbet-based phonemes to SAMPA as well.

The m2m-aligner works in an unsupervised fashion, using an edit-distance-based algorithm to align two strings from a file in the **news** format, in order for them to share the same length [13]. All 385 TextGrid files from our evaluation dataset (`.tg`) are used to compose a single **news** file, as exemplified in Table 3. Notice the file is composed by the phonemes of the whole sentence rather than by isolated words, in order to mitigate the effects of the cross-word boundaries. The string mapping is finished after a certain number of iterations when the m2m-aligner provides a one-to-one mapping in a file we called **m2m** that joins some phonemes together, as shown by shades of gray in Table 3.

**Table 3.** Example of a single **news** file with phonemes from three out of 385 TextGrid files for sentences *"é bom pousar"* and *"os lindos jardins"*. Each line contains a whole phonetic sentence to be converted, and different phone sets are separated into two distinct columns divided by a tabular '`\t`' character, so every other token is separated by a single space. Groups of phonemes which are supposed to be later merged by m2m-aligner in the **m2m** file are shaded in gray.

(a) Original dataset phone set (original SAMPA) vs. FalaBrasil's (SAMPA)

| Dataset phonemes (SAMPA, original) | AM phonemes (SAMPA, FB) |
| --- | --- |
| E b o~ n p o w z a h | E b o~ p o w z a X |
| u S l i~ n d u S Z a h\ dZ i~ n S u j s l i~ d u s Z a R dZ i~ s | |

(b) MFA phone set (ARPAbet) vs. FalaBrasil's (SAMPA)

| MFA phonemes (ARPAbet) | AM phonemes (SAMPA, FB) |
| --- | --- |
| E+ B O~+ W~ P O Z A+ RR | E b o~ p o w z a X |
| UX S L I~+ D UX S Z A RR DJ I~ S u j s l i~ d u s Z a R dZ i~ s | |

Finally, as the m2m-aligner provides the mapping for phonemes, another script provides the time stamps calculations prior to creating the converted TextGrid file. Table 4 illustrates how the phonetic time stamps, in milliseconds, are mapped accordingly. Basically if two or more phonemes are mapped into a single one (merging), as in /o~/ /n/ → /o~/ or /d/ /Z/ → /dZ/ (marked with an *), the time stamp of the last phoneme is considered. However, if one phoneme is mapped to two or more (splitting) as in /e~/ → /e~/ /j~/, then linearly spaced time stamps are generated in between the phone to be split (†) and its immediate predecessor (‡).

# 4    Results and Discussion

Results will be reported in terms of statistics such as mean ($\mu$), median and standard deviation ($\sigma$) over the distribution of phone boundary values, and a tolerance threshold that shows how many phonetic tokens were more precisely aligned with respect to the manual alignments. Numerical values, in milliseconds, are presented in Table 5. The best ones are highlighted in bold.

**Table 4.** Conversion of time stamps for the sentence "*onde existem*".

| 494 | 533* | 558 | 565* | 583 | 682 | 748 | 854 | 929 | 979‡ | 1042† |
|-----|------|-----|------|-----|-----|-----|-----|-----|------|-------|
| o~  | n    | d   | Z    | i   | i   | z   | i   | S   | t    | e~    |       |
| o~  |      | dZ  |      | i   | e   | z   | i   | s   | t    | e~    | j~    |
| 533* |     | 565* |     | 583 | 682 | 748 | 854 | 929 | 979‡ | 1010  | 1042† |

As far as MFA train-and-align (T&A) feature is concerned, roughly only 1% of phoneme tokens aligned by Kaldi-based aligners are off the 100 ms tolerance, against 3% of tokens aligned by HTK-based tools. In fact, approximately 96%–97% of phonemes were under the 50 ms tolerance when aligned by acoustic models trained with MFA and UFPAlign, considering an average of all models. Unfortunately, this is not true for MFA's pre-trained model for Brazilian Portuguese (in align-only mode), which on the other hand, for larger tolerance threshold values, performed a little worse than HTK.

Among HTK-based aligners, EasyAlign performed best considering all statistics and tolerance thresholds for both male and female speakers. However, as already pointed out in [32], the same ground-truth dataset used for evaluation in this work was also used to train the BP acoustic model shipped with EasyAlign, so this might have had some bias during the comparison. Overall, UFPAlign (HTK) achieved very similar values across metrics for both speakers of the dataset, while EasyAlign's behavior shows a greater accuracy on the female voice. Nevertheless, the parcel of phonetic tokens whose difference to the manual segmentation was less than 10 ms stayed below the 40% even for EasyAlign.

In align-only (A) mode, MFA models performed slightly better until 10 ms than EasyAlign's, but increasingly worse for larger values of tolerance for both male and female speakers. These poor results may be due to the nature of the dataset used to generate MFA's pre-trained acoustic models (GlobalPhone [28]), which contains only 22 h of transcribed audio. In contrast, training and aligning (T&A) on the same evaluation dataset with MFA proved better than HTK for the male speaker, and the results are similar for the female speaker.

The monophone- and triphone-based GMM models we trained with Kaldi for UFPAlign achieved the best performance with respect to phone boundary when compared to both MFA and HTK-based aligners. On average, approximately 45% of tokens were accurately aligned within the 10 ms margin for all GMM models. Mean and median values are the lowest (except for tri-SAT on the male

**Table 5.** Results regarding mean ($\mu$), median (med.), standard deviation ($\sigma$), and cumulative percentage below a tolerance threshold, in milliseconds, of the differences between forced aligned audio and ground-truth (hand aligned) phonemes, also known as phone boundary. Notations on MFA stand for align-only (A) and train-and-align (T&A) procedures, while on UFPAlign they denote either the nature of the toolkit or the acoustic model.

| | Toolkit | $\mu$ | med. | $\sigma$ | Cumulative tolerance (%) | | | |
|---|---|---|---|---|---|---|---|---|
| | | | | | <10 ms | <25 ms | <50 ms | <100 ms |
| Female dataset | UFPAlign (HTK) | 26.44 | 17.00 | 38.31 | 31.40 | 63.94 | 88.19 | 97.08 |
| | EasyAlign | 18.42 | 13.00 | 20.30 | 36.59 | 78.12 | 94.06 | 98.91 |
| | MFA ( A ) | 23.62 | 12.00 | 34.16 | 39.34 | 75.99 | 87.77 | 95.65 |
| | MFA (T&A) | 17.60 | 13.00 | 18.62 | 37.65 | 78.69 | 95.16 | 99.08 |
| | UFPAlign (mono) | 13.58 | 10.00 | 15.02 | 47.47 | 87.70 | 97.55 | 99.57 |
| | UFPAlign (tri-$\Delta$) | 12.43 | 9.00 | 13.28 | **50.44** | **89.88** | **98.34** | 99.62 |
| | UFPAlign (tri-LDA) | 12.99 | 10.00 | 12.62 | 47.48 | 89.22 | 98.27 | 99.76 |
| | UFPAlign (tri-SAT) | 13.43 | 10.00 | 12.75 | 45.69 | 88.20 | 98.15 | 99.77 |
| | UFPAlign (TDNN-F) | 17.18 | 14.00 | 13.87 | 34.41 | 75.94 | 97.61 | **99.87** |
| Male dataset | UFPAlign (HTK) | 26.86 | 17.00 | 32.61 | 30.73 | 62.45 | 86.55 | 96.42 |
| | EasyAlign | 24.35 | 17.00 | 30.70 | 31.53 | 67.51 | 89.69 | 96.95 |
| | MFA ( A ) | 34.28 | 16.00 | 46.70 | 32.81 | 64.85 | 78.49 | 90.61 |
| | MFA (T&A) | 14.65 | 11.00 | 14.37 | 45.12 | 83.34 | **97.23** | **99.66** |
| | UFPAlign (mono) | 15.25 | 11.00 | 15.70 | 43.51 | 83.42 | 96.29 | 99.42 |
| | UFPAlign (tri-$\Delta$) | 14.16 | 10.00 | 14.06 | **46.28** | **85.55** | 97.13 | 99.74 |
| | UFPAlign (tri-LDA) | 14.66 | 11.00 | 13.82 | 43.49 | 84.50 | 97.19 | 99.74 |
| | UFPAlign (tri-SAT) | 14.96 | 12.00 | 13.77 | 42.14 | 83.51 | 97.19 | 99.78 |
| | UFPAlign (TDNN-F) | 18.58 | 16.00 | 14.26 | 32.02 | 70.62 | 96.65 | 99.94 |

dataset, which was greater than MFA's T&A) and at most ~4 ms distant from each other. With respect to the speakers' gender, UFPAlign (Kaldi) performed approximately 4% better for the woman's voice until the 50 ms of tolerance, and about 2 ms more accurate according to the average mean.

Finally, TDNN-F simulation was definitely disappointing. We expected that results from a nnet3 DNN-based setup would be at least similar to GMM-based ones, as it was in [6] with nnet2, but cumulative tolerance values were instead just slightly better than EasyAlign. Therefore, even though one can say that the best result was achieved by tri-delta ($\Delta$) models on both male and female datasets, since it holds the rows with most boldface values in Table 5 (except MFA was better off after 50 ms on the man's voice, but the values compared to UFPAlign's tri-$\Delta$ model are fairly and virtually the same), we would rather prefer to state that all GMM-based AMs in UFPAlign achieved similar results. Even monophone models, the simplest ones, had a close performance on tri-SAT, the most complex.

### 4.1   Discussion

A possible reason for such a difference between HTK- and Kaldi-based aligners might be that HTK uses Baum-Welch algorithm for training HMMs while Kaldi uses Viterbi training [4]. On the other hand, among Kaldi models, tri-$\Delta$ stands out as being virtually the best one. However, with just a $\sim$1–3% difference in tolerance, and $\sim$1 ms difference in both mean and median values, we cannot tell whether it is significant enough to classify one model into being better than the others, as they appear pretty close at glance. The linear sequence of model training just does not result in lower errors in phonetic boundaries as it resulted in lower word error rates for speech recognition.

The somewhat shocking results were produced by the DNN. For the state of the art for ASR to perform so poorly in phonetic alignment problems, it certainly needs careful investigation. We suspect the HMM topology used in nnet3 chain models, which can be traversed in one frame rather than in three on the traditional left-to-right [26], may have had some unfavorable influence. Moreover, data insufficiency could even have been the problem for the DNN in the first place, since the $\sim$171 h in our training dataset are far from the ideal volume to train a neural network efficiently. Other reasons include the possible high number of hidden layers in the TDNN-F, and the use of frame subsampling, which requires an extra normalization value to be passed to Kaldi's ali-to-phones script for compensation.

Besides, navigating through all the burden to train a DNN model with Kaldi (which requires at least one GPU card) may not be the more appropriate move if the final task's goal is to align phonemes rather than to recognize speech. As MFA seem to have dropped support to DNN models, and our previous results with a nnet2 neural network setup only took tolerance values so far as to match tri-$\Delta$ models [6], we feel discouraged to invest so much time computer power to train a DNN model. Nevertheless, conjectures still need to be experimented.

## 5   Conclusion

This paper presented contributions for the problem of forced phonetic alignment (FPA) in Brazilian Portuguese (BP). An update to UFPAlign [6] was offered by providing adapted Kaldi recipes for training acoustic models on BP datasets, as well as properly releasing all the acoustic models for free under an open-source license on the GitHub of the FalaBrasil Group[3]. UFPAlign works either via command line (Linux) or in a graphical interface as a plugin to Praat. Up-to-date phonetic and syllabic dictionaries created over a list of 200,000 words for BP are also provided, as well as standalone grapheme-to-phoneme and syllabification systems for handling out-of-vocabulary words.

For evaluation, a comparison among the Kaldi-based acoustic models trained with an updated version of the scripts from [6] was performed, as well as a comparison to an outdated HTK-based version of UFPAlign from [32]. Results

---

[3] https://github.com/falabrasil.

regarding the absolute difference between forced and manual aligned utterances (phone boundary metric) showed that the HTK-based aligner performed worse when compared to any of the Kaldi-based models, and that our acoustic models we trained from scratch performed better than MFA's pre-trained models.

## 5.1   Future Work

As future work, there are a couple of experiments to be investigated. The simplest one would be to train GMM-based tri-$\Delta$, tri-LDA, tri-SAT and even monophone-based acoustic models with a higher number of Gaussian mixtures per senone. Training a DNN on the top of tri-$\Delta$, since that was the one that yielded the most accurate results according to phone boundary, should be also worth trying. Besides, training a DNN on the top of context-independent monophones does not sound so absurd either, given the proximity of the results.

Regarding the DNN, one thing to verify is whether removing the i-vectors and leaving just normalized MFCCs as input features would result in more accurate alignments. Splicing cepstral features with LDA would also be a valid test. By the way, the TDNN-F setup has not been altered from Mini-librispeech's default recipe, which means some parameters such as layer dimension, number of layers, context width, and the application of frame subsampling could still undergo tuning. Finally, other architectures like LSTMs should have its use evaluated.

Another idea might be the employment of transfer learning techniques to take advantage of models pre-trained on larger volumes of audio data and just make some adaptations to make it work on our evaluation dataset. That way, an acoustic model trained over LibriSpeech dataset, for example, could be downloaded from OpenSLR [23] to serve as a starting point, and GMM-based models would be trained from scratch over the male/female evaluation dataset to play the role of the new tri-SAT reference alignments. One impediment, however, is that most of the pre-trained TDNN-F-based models available on the Internet are chain models (i.e., a simplified HMM topology is used to model phonemes), which suggests a new, chain-free model would have to be trained from scratch on English data, which is also freely available.

At last, although UFPAlign can be used as a plugin to Praat, we plan in the future to train models compatible with MFA under the same licensing, as to avoid open-source competition. The provision of a train-and-align feature for UFPAlign is also an ongoing plan.

**Acknowledgment.** We gratefully acknowledge NVIDIA Corporation with the donation of the Titan Xp GPU used for this research. The authors also would like to thank CAPES for providing scholarships and FAPESPA (grant 001/2020, process 2019/583359) for the financial support.

# References

1. Almeida, J.J., Simões, A.: Projecto natura (2021). https://natura.di.uminho.pt/wiki/doku.php

2. Atkinson, K.: Gnu aspell (2021). https://aspell.net
3. Boersma, P., Weenink, D.: Praat: doing phonetics by computer (version 6.1.15) [computer program] (2020). https://www.fon.hum.uva.nl/praat/
4. Buthpitiya, S., Lane, I., Chong, J.: A parallel implementation of viterbi training for acoustic models using graphics processing units. In: 2012 Innovative Parallel Computing (InPar), pp. 1–10 (2012). https://doi.org/10.1109/InPar.2012.6339590
5. Dehak, N., Kenny, P.J., Dehak, R., Dumouchel, P., Ouellet, P.: Front-end factor analysis for speaker verification. IEEE Trans. Audio Speech Lang. Process. **19**(4), 788–798 (2011). https://doi.org/10.1109/TASL.2010.2064307
6. Dias, A.L., Batista, C., Santana, D., Neto, N.: Towards a free, forced phonetic aligner for Brazilian Portuguese using kaldi tools. In: Cerri, R., Prati, R.C. (eds.) BRACIS 2020. LNCS (LNAI), vol. 12319, pp. 621–635. Springer, Cham (2020). https://doi.org/10.1007/978-3-030-61377-8_44
7. Gibbon, D., Moore, R., Winski, R.: Sampa computer readable phonetic alphabet (2021). https://www.phon.ucl.ac.uk/home/sampa/
8. GitHub: Frequencywords (2020). https://github.com/hermitdave/FrequencyWords
9. Goldman, J.P.: Easyalign: An automatic phonetic alignment tool under praat. In: Proceedings of the Annual Conference of the International Speech Communication Association, INTERSPEECH, pp. 3233–3236 (2011)
10. Guiroy, S., de Cordoba, R., Villegas, A.: Application of the kaldi toolkit for continuous speech recognition using hidden-markov models and deep neural networks. In: IberSPEECH'2016 On-line Proceedings, IberSPEECH 2016, Lisboa, Portugal, pp. 187–196 (2016)
11. Huang, X., Acero, A., Hon, H.W.: Spoken Language Processing: A Guide to Theory, Algorithm, and System Development, 1st edn. Prentice Hall PTR, Upper Saddle River (2001)
12. Interinstitutional Center for Computational Linguistics: Cetenfolha dataset (2021). https://www.linguateca.pt/cetenfolha/index_info.html
13. Jiampojamarn, S., Kondrak, G., Sherif, T.: Applying many-to-many alignments and hidden markov models to letter-to-phoneme conversion. In: Human Language Technologies 2007: The Conference of the North American Chapter of the Association for Computational Linguistics; Proceedings of the Main Conference, pp. 372–379. Association for Computational Linguistics, Rochester, New York (2007). http://www.aclweb.org/anthology/N/N07/N07-1047
14. Vesely, K., Ghoshal, A., Burget, L., Povey, D.: Sequence-discriminative training of deep neural networks. In: INTERSPEECH 2013, pp. 2345–2349 (2013)
15. Ko, T., Peddinti, V., Povey, D., Khudanpur, S.: Audio augmentation for speech recognition. In: Proceedings of Interspeech (2015)
16. McAuliffe, M., Socolof, M., Mihuc, S., Wagner, M., Sonderegger, M.: Montreal forced aligner: Trainable text-speech alignment using kaldi. In: Proceedings of Interspeech, pp. 498–502 (2017). https://doi.org/10.21437/Interspeech.2017-1386
17. Moura, R.: Libreoffice's vero dictionary (2021). https://github.com/LibreOffice/dictionaries/tree/master/pt_BR
18. Neto, N., Patrick, C., Klautau, A., Trancoso, I.: Free tools and resources for Brazilian Portuguese speech recognition. J. Braz. Comput. Soc. **17**(1), 53–68 (2010). https://doi.org/10.1007/s13173-010-0023-1
19. Neto, N., Rocha, W., Sousa, G.: An open-source rule-based syllabification tool for Brazilian Portuguese. J. Braz. Comput. Soc. **21**(1), 1–10 (2015). https://doi.org/10.1186/s13173-014-0021-9

20. Opensubtitles.org: Opensubtitles (2021). https://www.opensubtitles.org/
21. Peddinti, V., Wang, Y., Povey, D., Khudanpur, S.: Low latency acoustic modeling using temporal convolution and LSTMs. IEEE Signal Process. Lett. **25**(3), 373–377 (2018). https://doi.org/10.1109/LSP.2017.2723507
22. Peddinti, V., Povey, D., Khudanpur, S.: A time delay neural network architecture for efficient modeling of long temporal contexts. In: Proceedings of Interspeech, pp. 3214–3218 (2015)
23. Povey, D.: Openslr: open speech and language resources (2021). https://openslr.org/index.html
24. Povey, D., et al.: Semi-orthogonal low-rank matrix factorization for deep neural networks. In: Proceedings of Interspeech 2018, pp. 3743–3747 (2018). https://doi.org/10.21437/Interspeech.2018-1417
25. Povey, D., et al.: The kaldi speech recognition toolkit. In: In IEEE 2011 workshop (2011)
26. Povey, D., et al.: Purely sequence-trained neural networks for ASR based on lattice-free mmi. In: Interspeech 2016, pp. 2751–2755 (2016). https://doi.org/10.21437/Interspeech.2016-595
27. Povey, D., Zhang, X., Khudanpur, S.: Parallel training of DNNs with natural gradient and parameter averaging (2015)
28. Schultz, T., Vu, N.T., Schlippe, T.: Globalphone: a multilingual text speech database in 20 languages. In: 2013 IEEE International Conference on Acoustics, Speech and Signal Processing, pp. 8126–8130 (2013). https://doi.org/10.1109/ICASSP.2013.6639248
29. Shoup, J.E.: Phonological aspects of speech recognition. Trends Speech Recogn., 125–138 (1980)
30. Siravenha, A., Neto, N., Macedo, V., Klautau, A.: Uso de regras fonológicas com determinação de vogal tônica para conversão grafema-fone em português brasileiro (2008)
31. Snyder, D., Garcia-Romero, D., Povey, D., Khudanpur, S.: Deep neural network embeddings for text-independent speaker verification. In: Proceedings of Interspeech 2017, pp. 999–1003 (2017). https://doi.org/10.21437/Interspeech.2017-620
32. Souza, G., Neto, N.: An automatic phonetic aligner for Brazilian Portuguese with a praat interface. In: Silva, J., Ribeiro, R., Quaresma, P., Adami, A., Branco, A. (eds.) PROPOR 2016. LNCS (LNAI), vol. 9727, pp. 374–384. Springer, Cham (2016). https://doi.org/10.1007/978-3-319-41552-9_38
33. Stolcke, A.: Srilm - an extensivle language modeling toolkit. In: Proceedings of the 7th International Conference on Spoken Language Processing (ICSLP), vol. 2, pp. 901–904 (2002)
34. Young, S., Ollason, D., Valtchev, V., Woodland, P.: The HTK Book. Cambridge University Engineering Department, version 3.4, Cambridge, UK (2006)
35. Zhang, X., Trmal, J., Povey, D., Khudanpur, S.: Improving deep neural network acoustic models using generalized maxout networks. In: 2014 IEEE International Conference on Acoustics, Speech and Signal Processing (ICASSP), pp. 215–219 (2014). https://doi.org/10.1109/ICASSP.2014.6853589

# Incorporating Text Specificity into a Convolutional Neural Network for the Classification of Review Perceived Helpfulness

Beatriz Lima[✉] and Tatiane Nogueira

Federal University of Bahia, Salvador, Brazil
{beatriz.santana,tatiane.nogueira}@ufba.br

**Abstract.** Reviews are valuable sources of information to support the decision making process. Therefore, the task of classifying reviews according to their helpfulness has paramount importance to facilitate the access of truly informative content. In this context, previous studies have unveiled several aspects and architectures that are beneficial for the task of review perceived helpfulness prediction. The present work aims to further investigate the influence of the text specificity aspect, defined as the level of details conveyed in a text, with the same purpose. First, we explore an unsupervised domain adaptation approach for assigning text specificity scores for sentences from product reviews and we propose an evaluation measure named Specificity Prediction Evaluation (SPE) in order to achieve more reliable specificity predictions. Then, we present domain-oriented guidelines on how to incorporate, into a CNN architecture, either hand-crafted features based on text specificity or the text specificity prediction task as an auxiliary task in a multitask learning setting. In the experiments, the perceived helpfulness classification models embodied with text specificity showed significant higher precision results in comparison to a popular SVM baseline.

**Keywords:** Review helpfulness · Text specificity · Opinion mining

## 1 Introduction

Reviews written by consumers on e-commerce platforms are valuable resources in the decision making process of product purchase. Nowadays, it is hard to imagine buying a product without reading at least some reviews first. Moreover, online product reviews are an essential part of the acquisition of business intelligence and market advantage for the retailers [17,22] once they can retrieve informative evaluations about several aspects of a product.

Due to the great number of reviews constantly posted, many websites provide a voting system through which consumers can express whether they perceive a review as helpful or not. These votes are frequently summarized to the users

© Springer Nature Switzerland AG 2021
A. Britto and K. Valdivia Delgado (Eds.): BRACIS 2021, LNAI 13074, pp. 480–495, 2021.
https://doi.org/10.1007/978-3-030-91699-2_33

with a message next to the review, similar to *"H of T people found this helpful"*. This message means that from T people who evaluated this comment, H found the review helpful.

From the helpfulness votes, the perceived helpfulness of a review can be derived, which is characterized as the majority impression of the consumers about the review utility during the purchase decisions. The name "perceived helpfulness" is used to emphasize that we are tackling a definition obtained from the helpfulness votes rather than some expert judgment [1,12,17]. Given this concept, the helpfulness score of a review is calculated as $\theta = \frac{H}{T}$. Having all posted comments with a helpfulness score assigned is beneficial for consumers and merchants in several ways, including as a dimension to rank them.

Since most of the reviews do not receive any votes at all [13], especially for less popular and recently released products, several reviews cannot be graded with a perceived helpfulness score. Therefore, this scenario has been fruitful for researchers to study what makes a review helpful and how to build intelligent systems that can distinguish reviews with different levels of helpfulness. These studies have mainly concentrated their efforts on feature engineering since several complex factors can contribute to the performance of a model in the helpfulness prediction task. Subjectivity [1,6,8] and readability [6,7] are some of the many aspects that have been investigated in the last years.

More recently, hand-crafted features based on text specificity, which is defined as the level of details about a subject expressed in a text [14], also proved to be interesting attributes for the classification of reviews according to their helpfulness [12]. Text specificity has been widely used to assess the writing quality of a text. In the field of automatically generated summaries, [15] argued that the quantity of specific and general sentences, as well as how sequences of them are disposed, affect the writing quality of a text.

The quality of a text is also related to how easy it is to understand its content, i.e. what is its level of readability. This aspect has also been considered important for the helpfulness prediction task [6,7]. Based on the aforementioned points, we argue that text specificity may play an important role in helpfulness prediction.

The first part of our proposal aims to combine the specificity based features proposed in [12] into a well known Convolutional Neural Network (CNN) architecture [9]. CNNs have been successfully employed in some earlier helpfulness prediction studies by reducing the need for labor-intensive feature engineering and by achieving good performance [1,3,4,20]. Secondly, we propose to integrate the specificity prediction as an auxiliary task in a Multitask learning (MTL) version of the same CNN architecture used in the first part. MTL can be used to improve model generalization and learning efficiency by sharing underlying common structures between complementary tasks [2]. The multitask paradigm has recently also shown promising results in the helpfulness prediction task [4].

The specificity based features are derived from the specificity degree, which is assigned to each review using an unsupervised domain adaptation technique [10]. Although [12] proposed these features, the study did not discuss how different experimental setups, beyond the recommended by the authors of the domain adaptation method, can affect the specificity degree predictions of online product reviews. Therefore, the present study also aims to bridge this gap by empirically finding more suitable experimental settings for our domains. To evaluate the specificity scores predicted in this unsupervised context, we also propose a measure named Specificity Prediction Evaluation (SPE), which is calculated as the average length of general sentences over the average length of specific sentences.

In a nutshell, our contribution is three-fold: 1) a better understanding of how to obtain more reliable specificity prediction results in the domain of product reviews; 2) proposing a method for the evaluation of specificity predictions of unlabeled sentences, and 3) presenting domain-oriented guidelines on how to incorporate the specificity aspect into a CNN architecture. The experiments showed that the CNN-based models embodied with text specificity could achieve significant higher precision results in comparison to a popular SVM baseline.

The rest of this paper is structured as follows. Section 2 presents some of the related studies on perceived helpfulness prediction. Section 3 explains how did the review specificity predictions were obtained and how they were evaluated using the SPE. Our proposed perceived helpfulness classification model using a CNN architecture and text specificity is presented in Sect. 4. Details about the experiments are defined in Sect. 5 and their results are discussed in Sect. 6. Section 7 summarizes the concluding remarks and future work.

## 2    Related Work

One of the first studies to investigate the helpfulness prediction task is in [8]. This work proposed a regression task in which the target was the helpfulness score based on the votes received by the review. One of its main goals was to analyze the performance of five categories of features for this task: structural, lexical, syntactic, semantic, and metadata. They reported that the best combination of features was the length of the review, the lemmatized unigrams, and the star rating score given by the review author to the product.

The effect of review length on perceived helpfulness prediction has also been much explored by past researches [6–8,17]. According to [8], in the reviews used in their experiments, among the longest reviews the average helpfulness score was 0.82 while the average score among the shortest ones was only 0.23. [17] also empirically demonstrated that reviews with more words have a higher helpfulness degree. Therefore, the researchers have been arguing that longer reviews are likely to contain more information and, consequently, can influence more readers to vote them as "helpful" [18].

Besides the review extensiveness, how well the text is organized and written, to facilitate the understanding of its content, has also been considered an important factor. In [7] the behavior of the review length as a determinant of review helpfulness was further investigated and they revealed some factors that moderate the relation between length and helpfulness. According to their experiments, review length has a positive influence on helpfulness only when the readability is high. Additionally, [6] reported that not only review readability has an impact on review helpfulness, but also it influences the product sales. In their experiments, for some types of products, having reviews with higher readability scores is related to higher sales of such products. This elucidates the importance of studying the influence of factors related to writing quality on review helpfulness.

Based on the previous studies, [12] started to investigate the influence of text specificity in the perceived helpfulness context. This work reported that combining lemmatized unigrams with three hand-crafted features, derived from text specificity, either outperformed or showed similar performance on more than 80% of the results, when compared to models using only the unigrams. At the opposite side, using only the features based on sentence specificity achieved the lowest results. The ideas developed in this work have inspired the present study and, therefore, the features proposed by its authors are used to evaluate our proposal to incorporate them into a CNN architecture.

Several machine learning algorithms have been used to model the helpfulness prediction task, including CNNs. [3] proposed a novel end-to-end cross-domain architecture for helpfulness prediction using word-level and character-based representations. Their CNN architecture is based on the one designed by [9] which they further adjusted with auxiliary domain discriminators to transfer knowledge between domains, using large datasets as the source domains and small ones as the target domains. In their experiments, the CNN models yielded better results than known baselines which used hand-crafted features.

Likewise, [1] proposed a helpfulness classification model by combining convolutional layers and Gated Recurrent Units. Instead of using embeddings, they selected 100 linguistic and meta data features, based on prior work, to form the input review representation. Their approach outperformed other classification methods by 0.04 and 0.02 in terms of F1-measure and accuracy, respectively.

Due to the successful usage of MTL on a wide range of tasks, [4] introduced an end-to-end MTL architecture to learn at the same time the helpfulness classification of online product reviews and the star rating given by the reviewer to the product. The architecture consists of convolutional layers, equipped with an attention mechanism, which receives as input the concatenation of word embeddings and their character-level encoding. The main purpose of this model is to jointly learn the helpfulness classification task (main task) by using the hints learned from the star rating prediction task (auxiliary task). Using Amazon reviews, the study empirically validated that the model achieved a superior performance than single-task learning (STL) models similar to the proposed MTL model, as well as prior techniques using hand-designed features.

# 3    Specificity Prediction on Sentences from Reviews

The text specificity prediction task aims to build machine learning models that can learn, from examples, to assign a specificity degree to a text representation, usually on sentence-level [10, 11, 14, 15]. Even though different approaches have been proposed in the last years, the majority of them had tackled the problem in a supervised way, which requires extensive manual annotation. To overcome this matter, a robust unsupervised domain adaptation solution was proposed in [10] to predict the specificity score of unlabeled domains.

The unsupervised domain adaptation technique consists of using labeled sentences from a source domain to assign reliable specificity scores (between 0 and 1) to unlabeled sentences from a different target domain, without access to any labeled example from the target domain. [10] reported good generalization results when evaluated their approach with social media posts, restaurant reviews, and movie reviews as the target domains. The source data is a publicly available dataset with about 4,300 labeled news sentences [14].

This approach is based on the self-ensembling of a single base model, which combines hand-crafted features (sentence length, average word length, percentage of strongly subjective words, etc.), word embeddings and BiLSTM (Bidirectional Long Short-term Memory) to encode the input sentences. Because of the good performance of this technique on review domains (restaurant and movie reviews), it was employed by the present work to infer the specificity degree of the unlabeled sentences from our product reviews.

Although this solution was also exploited in [12] to predict the specificity of reviews' sentences, the study did not report any broader analysis about these experiments. In summary, for each dataset (for example, reviews about books), they have sampled 4,300 sentences as the training data (the same amount of sentences of the source news data) and trained the model for 30 epochs, which is the same value that [10] reported for their best results. However, during our experiments, we detected more robust specificity degrees when increasing the training set and the number of epochs. The best settings regarding these two aspects for our domains are further discussed in Sect. 6, along with more details about the experiments.

One of the features used in the base model introduced in [10] is the sentence length. Their labeled and unlabeled datasets (source and target data) have sentences with lengths varying between 15 and 23 tokens, on average. Therefore, despite coming from different domains, the sentences used in their experiments have close lengths. Likewise, the datasets used in our experiments contain reviews with sentences varying, on average, between 17 and 22 tokens.

However, while the longest sentence from the target domains used by [10] has 202 tokens, there are many much longer sentences within our datasets. This may be caused by noises in the reviews, which, even after several preprocessing techniques, may be harming the sentence splitting process. Still, we are assuming, for now, this is an intrinsic characteristic of these datasets. We noticed that this aspect was negatively affecting the specificity prediction results when training for few epochs or with few sentences. In many cases, the longest sentences were scored with the lowest specificity degrees and the opposite for the shortest sentences. After trying different experimental settings, the models could achieve more robust results by increasing the training size and the number of epochs.

Given the problems observed in the experiments, to systematically choose a trained model that could designate the most reliable specificity scores for each target domain of product reviews, we propose a measure called Specificity Prediction Evaluation (SPE). Considering $\sigma$ as the specificity degree of a sentence, general sentences having $\sigma < 0.5$, and specific sentences having $\sigma \geq 0.5$. SPE is based on one assumption: on average, reliable specific sentences tend to be longer than reliable general sentences [11]. This assumption is supported by related past studies and by examining the datasets used in the experiments performed in [10]. Therefore, SPE is calculated as follows:

$$SPE = \begin{cases} 0, & \text{if } |G| = 0 \text{ or } |S| = 0 \\ \frac{L_{avg}(G)}{L_{avg}(S)}, & \text{otherwise} \end{cases} \tag{1}$$

where G is the set of general sentences, S is the set of specific sentences, $|G|$ denotes the quantity of general sentences, $|S|$ refers to the quantity of specific sentences, $L_{avg}(G)$ denotes the average length of general sentences, and $L_{avg}(S)$ is the average length of general sentences.

We assume $SPE < 1$ is a satisfactory value because, in this case, the average length of specific sentences is longer than the general ones. In fact, the datasets from [10] have SPE values varying between 0.52 and 0.74. In addition to that, it is important to highlight that the text specificity aspect is composed by several other text characteristics beyond the length. For that reason, SPE is a first effort to evaluate the specificity scores without having labeled sentences and, in future endeavors, it should be applied along with other evaluation approaches.

After the improvements performed to get more reliable specificity predictions, we extracted the same three hand-crafted features proposed in [12]: **SpecificityDegree**, the review-level specificity degree; **SpecificSents%**, the percentage of specific sentences in the review; and **SpecificityBalance**, which is a balance measure between the number of specific and general sentences in the review. The values of all these features lie in the range $[0, 1]$.

The next section explains how these features were incorporated into a CNN architecture for the perceived helpfulness classification task.

## 4   Perceived Helpfulness Classification Model

For a review $r$, let $H_r$ be the number of helpful votes received by the review and $T_r$ be the total number of votes given to $r$. The helpfulness ratio of the review $r$ is calculated as $\theta_r = \frac{H_r}{T_r}$. To transform the helpfulness ratio into binary labels, we set the threshold value to 0.5, which is a common value used on related studies [4]. If $\theta_r > 0.5$, $r$ is categorized as "very helpful", otherwise if $\theta_r \leq 0.5$, $r$ is said to be "poorly helpful". In summary, the task consists of classifying reviews into two categories: "very helpful" and "poorly helpful".

Based on the successful application of CNN architectures on previous related works [1,3,4,20], this type of neural network was employed here to validate the influence of text specificity on perceived helpfulness. The usage of convolutional and pooling layers is known to be successful in several text classification tasks when there are strong local clues (sequence of tokens) that could appear in different locations of the texts. For example, in the context of product reviews, expressions such as "I did not like" or "I recommend" could be frequent sequences that are important to distinguish reviews with different levels of helpfulness.

Our helpfulness classification models have a base CNN classification architecture which is the single channel architecture proposed in [9] for sentence classification. This architecture has achieved good performance across many different tasks, including sentiment classification. It consists of a single convolutional layer, with 3 types of filter of kernel sizes 3, 4, and 5 and 100 filters each, followed by a max-pooling layer. Each filter processes all the possible windows of words, according to its kernel size, from the input review representation, and generates a feature map. Then, the max-pooling operation captures, for each feature map, the feature with the highest value, which is presumably the most important feature in the map. Finally, the learned pooled vector is passed to a fully connected layer that computes the model output.

Figure 1 illustrates a review representation at different steps of the classification process using this CNN design. The input representation is a $L \times D$ matrix where D is the dimension of the embedding vectors used to represent each word in the review and L is the text length which is a fixed value for all the reviews. Truncation and zero padding is applied to the reviews when necessary.

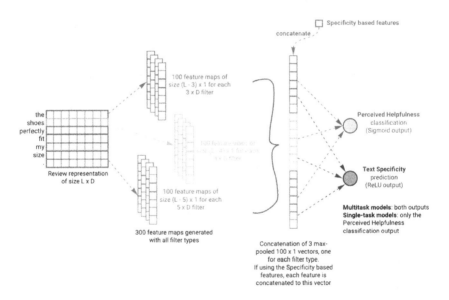

**Fig. 1.** The input, outputs, and intermediate representations in the CNN architecture proposed on [9] and adjusted for our proposal.

To incorporate the text specificity aspect into the base CNN structure, we propose two approaches: i) using the specificity based features, and ii) jointly learning the specificity prediction and the helpfulness classification task in a MTL setting. Concerning the features, they are simply concatenated into the pooled vector. Then, the classification output is computed using not only the CNN learned representation but also the specificity hand-crafted features.

Regarding the MTL scheme, the goal of the model is to learn all the network parameters by minimizing the joint loss presented on Eq. 2. Here the weights $\lambda_h$ and $\lambda_s$ were empirically set to 1 after some initial experiments.

$$\mathcal{L} = \lambda_h \mathcal{L}_h(\hat{y}_h, y_h) + \lambda_s \mathcal{L}_s(\hat{y}_s, y_s) \qquad (2)$$

where $\mathcal{L}_h(\hat{y}_h, y_h)$ is the loss of the helpfulness classification task and $\mathcal{L}_s(\hat{y}_s, y_s)$ is the loss of the specificity prediction task.

Review specificity prediction is a regression task that consists of learning to predict a specificity score between 0 and 1 for each review. We tackled this problem as a supervised task by using, as the true labels, the review specificity degrees obtained with the approach explained in Sect. 3. After assigning specificity scores for each sentence in the review, the review specificity degree is calculated as the average sentence specificity degree.

# 5   Experimental Setup

## 5.1   Data and Preprocessing

The experiments were performed with public datasets of Amazon reviews written in English from 9 different product categories [16]. Each dataset originally contains at least five reviews per product and per user. We decided to use Amazon reviews in the experiments to be consistent with most of the studies from the related literature [1,3–8,12,17,20]. Table 1 shows some relevant characteristics of these datasets.

**Table 1.** Characteristics of the Amazon datasets after preprocessing. The column # reviews is the total amount of reviews, V is the vocabulary size, $L_{avg}$ is the average review length, $L_{min} - L_{max}$ is the range of review length, $P_{avg}$ is the average amount of sentences, $P_{min} - P_{max}$ is the minimum and maximum amount of sentences in the reviews, and % very helpful is the percentage of reviews with the class "very helpful". All values, except from the last column, were computed after data balancing.

| Category | # reviews | V | $L_{avg}$ | $L_{min} - L_{max}$ | $P_{avg}$ | $P_{min} - P_{max}$ | % very helpful |
|---|---|---|---|---|---|---|---|
| Beauty | 28,052 | 35,009 | 113 | 1–2,635 | 6 | 1–176 | 68.81% |
| Books | 107,066 | 200,057 | 252 | 2–7,474 | 11 | 1–301 | 76.86% |
| CDs and Vinyl | 98,328 | 208,190 | 237 | 1–6,329 | 11 | 1–331 | 73.09% |
| Electronics | 34,496 | 93,555 | 241 | 1–6,978 | 12 | 1–319 | 84.37% |
| Health and Personal Care | 55,316 | 64,967 | 122 | 1–5,105 | 6 | 1–208 | 69.16% |
| Home and Kitchen | 50,170 | 56,031 | 130 | 1–6,276 | 7 | 1–320 | 81.68% |
| Kindle Store | 97,476 | 94,595 | 128 | 1–4,551 | 7 | 1–258 | 79.55% |
| Movies and TV | 149,934 | 286,920 | 270 | 1–10,037 | 12 | 1–294 | 66.70% |
| Sports and Outdoors | 37,104 | 53,776 | 121 | 1–6,570 | 6 | 1–275 | 72.91% |

Before using these collections as inputs to our classification models, some cleaning procedures were applied to reduce the negative effect of noisy data in the experiments. This preprocessing step is specially important to improve tokenization and splitting the comments into sentences, which were done here with the help of the spaCy library[1]. The procedures employed to clean the datasets and to improve sentence boundaries are listed below:

- Replace URLs by the placeholder token "URL";
- Remove ASCII symbols, double quotes, simple emoticons (e.g. "=)"), and empty brackets (e.g. "()");
- Replace ellipsis by a single period mark ( "..." $\longrightarrow$ ".")
- Add a blank space after every comma or period mark when it was followed by a word, a special symbol or a number (if the token is a number, the token before the comma or the period must not be a number as well);
- Replace dots by hyphens on enumerations (e.g.: "1. item" $\longrightarrow$ "1 - item").

Besides the previous steps, invalid reviews with more helpful votes than the total amount of votes ($H > T$) were discarded. Also, it was removed the reviews with $T = 0$ because the helpfulness score $\theta$ cannot be calculated for such reviews.

Regarding the datasets with the largest sizes in their original form (Books, CDs and Vinyl, Electronics, and Movies and TV), reviews with $T < 5$ were removed in order to increase the confidence in the perceived helpfulness scores as more people has evaluated the selected reviews. This type of cut-off is a known approach among the prior related studies [8]. Additionally, reviews with $0.3 < \theta < 0.7$ were removed because this approach seems to avoid dealing with reviews that received almost the same number of helpful and not helpful votes, i.e. the reviews with a more uncertain perception of helpfulness [12].

These Amazon datasets are known to be highly imbalanced [12,13] in which the class "very helpful" is the majority one. Handling the challenges related to learning on imbalanced scenarios is out of the scope of the present work, so data balancing was applied by undersampling the majority class.

## 5.2 Training

Even though all collections have product reviews from Amazon, each dataset was analyzed as a distinct domain because past studies showed that the product type influences how people perceive helpfulness [17]. Therefore, in the experiments, the models were independently trained for each domain. The code was developed with the aid of Keras[2], Tensorflow[3] and scikit-learn[4] libraries. All the random seeds were set to 42 during the experiments.

The results reported in Sect. 6 were obtained using stratified 5-fold cross-validation. The classifiers embodied with the text specificity aspect were also statistically compared against two baselines with the non-parametric Friedman test, considering $p - value < 0.05$, and the post-hoc Nemenyi test.

---

[1] https://spacy.io/.
[2] https://keras.io/.
[3] https://www.tensorflow.org/.
[4] https://scikit-learn.org/.

Regarding the CNN hyperparameters, valid padding was performed and the stride was set to 1. In comparison to the original proposal [9], we used much less regularization, a dropout of 0.1 in the penultimate layer and l2-norm regularization of 0.01, because of observed performance improvements after some initial experiments. Consequently, the number of training epochs was decreased to two since the models would overfit beyond this point. Training was performed with the Adam optimizer using $\eta = 0.001$. For the helpfulness classification task, it was used the Binary Cross Entropy loss and the ReLU activation function. For the auxiliary specificity prediction task, it was used Mean Squared Error and sigmoid. ReLU was also the chosen activation in the convolutional layers.

For every CNN-based model, similar to experiments performed in [4,9], we tested two ways of initializing the 300-dimensional embeddings: randomly and by using pretrained GloVe [19] embeddings which were trained on a large 42 billion token corpus. In either approach, the word embeddings were fine-tuned during training time. The dimension size of 300 was defined because of its good performance when using CNN on other text classification tasks [21].

Due to the broad range of review sizes among the Amazon datasets, it was also tested two maximum input length values for each domain: the mean review length and 512 tokens. In fact, other values were tested but we noticed more interesting results when comparing these two values. The batch size was set to 32 when using the mean length and to 16 when using a length of 512 due to memory constraints.

## 5.3   Model Variations

The following models were compared during our experiments:

- Baselines:
  - **SVM**: A linear SVM model trained with all the lemmatized unigrams weighted with tf-idf. This is a popular baseline based on previous works on helpfulness prediction [1,4,8,12,13].
  - **STL CNN**: The single-task CNN model, without the specificity features.
- CNN combined with text specificity (CNN+SPECIFICITY):
  - **MTL CNN**: The multitask CNN model, without the specificity features.
  - **SpecificityDegree**: The CNN model embodied with the SpecificityDegree feature.
  - **SpecificSents%**: The CNN model embodied with the SpecificSents% feature.
  - **SpecificityBalance**: The CNN model embodied with the SpecificityBalance feature.
  - **All features**: The CNN model embodied with all the three features (SpecificityDegree, SpecificSents%, SpecificityBalance).

With respect to the models **SpecificityDegree**, **SpecificSents%**, **SpecificityBalance**, and **All features**, both STL and MTL architectures were tested.

# 6  Results and Discussion

## 6.1  Perceived Helpfulness Classification

Table 2 summarizes the best F1 results obtained with the STL CNN and the MTL CNN models. Together with the F1 measure, we also report which combination of embeddings initialization approach (randomly or with GloVe pretrained vectors) and maximum input length (mean length or 512 tokens) yielded such performance. Finally, the table also shows the GloVe embeddings coverage for each domain, i.e. the percentage of all words for which a pre-trained GloVe embedding was found. The closer this coverage is to 100%, the smaller is the amount of out-of-vocabulary (OOV) words, which may affect the performance.

**Table 2.** Comparison results of the STL CNN and MTL CNN models

| Dataset | GloVe coverage | STL CNN | | MTL CNN | |
|---|---|---|---|---|---|
| | | Best settings | F1 | Best settings | F1 |
| Beauty | 85% | GloVe+mean | 0.5759 | GloVe+mean | **0.5929** |
| Books | 74% | GloVe+512 | 0.7697 | Glove+512 | **0.7763** |
| CDs and Vinyl | 65% | GloVe+512 | **0.8343** | Glove+512 | 0.8281 |
| Electronics | 70% | GloVe+512 | **0.7733** | Glove+512 | 0.7501 |
| Health and Personal Care | 78% | GloVe+512 | 0.5377 | Random+512 | **0.632** |
| Home and Kitchen | 80% | Random+mean | 0.5792 | Random+mean | **0.605** |
| Kindle Store | 80% | Random+512 | **0.6801** | Random+mean | 0.6618 |
| Movies and TV | 62% | Random+512 | 0.8009 | Random+512 | **0.8017** |
| Sports and Outdoors | 82% | GloVe+mean | **0.6667** | Random+512 | 0.6309 |

The results indicate that jointly learning the text specificity prediction task with the perceived helpfulness classification task could enhance the classifier performance for most of the datasets. This reveals some evidence regarding the benefit of incorporating text specificity into a CNN architecture, at least for 5 out of 9 domains. Apart from this performance comparison between STL CNN and MTL CNN, the purpose of this first part of the experiments was to investigate the effect of embeddings initialization and maximum input length.

Learning the word embeddings from the GloVe pre-trained weights seemed overall a good strategy for both STL and MTL approaches, even for domains with a considerable proportion of OOV words, such as the CDs and Vinyl dataset (35%). Besides that, except for Health and Personal Care and Sports and Outdoors, the choice of embeddings initialization did not appear to be influenced by the learning paradigms (single-task or multitask).

Likewise, the results in Table 2 also reveal that the maximum input length seemed to be more related to the domain than to the type of learning paradigm. For most of the datasets, the best input length was the same for STL CNN and MTL CNN. Additionally, even though there is not a clear relation between these best input lengths to the data characteristics presented on Table 1, the datasets with higher average review length showed better performance when using 512 as the maximum input length. All of these observations demonstrate that there may be a suitable domain-oriented choice of embeddings initialization and maximum input length, considering the single-task and multitask CNN approaches here presented. This finding may be used as a starting point on future experiments.

Even though having a good F1 score is desirable, having a high precision is crucial for the helpfulness classification problem. Considering a real-world application, either for recommendation [5] or for automatic summarization of the opinions expressed on helpful reviews [13], it is preferable to correctly identify very helpful reviews, even if they are few, and to avoid misclassifying poorly helpful reviews. In other words, we expect the number of false positive instances to be as close to zero as possible. That's why the best results achieved with the CNN+SPECIFICITY models were compared against the baseline models using both F1 (Table 3) and precision (Table 4). As most of the best results from the first part of the experiments (Table 2) were obtained with GloVe initialization, and to simplify the amount of settings to vary, the subsequent experiments were conducted without testing the random embeddings initialization.

**Table 3.** Comparison **F1** results of SVM, STL CNN and the best of all CNN+SPECIFICITY models

| Dataset | SVM | STL CNN | Best CNN+SPECIFICITY | | |
| | | | Model | Best settings | F1 |
|---|---|---|---|---|---|
| Beauty | 0.6268 | 0.5759 | All features | MTL+mean | **0.6731** |
| Books | **0.7868** | 0.7697 | MTL CNN | 512 | 0.7763 |
| CDs and Vinyl | **0.8501** | 0.8343 | MTL CNN | 512 | 0.8281 |
| Electronics | **0.7947** | 0.7733 | SpecificityBalance | MTL+512 | 0.7892 |
| Health and Personal Care | **0.64** | 0.5377 | SpecificityDegree | STL+mean | 0.6378 |
| Home and Kitchen | **0.6437** | 0.5792 | MTL CNN | mean | 0.605 |
| Kindle Store | 0.6772 | 0.6801 | All features | STL+512 | **0.6842** |
| Movies and TV | **0.8234** | 0.8009 | SpecificityDegree | STL+512 | 0.803 |
| Sports and Outdoors | 0.649 | **0.6667** | SpecificityDegree | MTL+mean | 0.6531 |

**Table 4.** Comparison **precision** results of SVM, STL CNN and the best of all CNN+SPECIFICITY models

| Dataset | SVM | STL CNN | Best CNN+SPECIFICITY | | |
| | | | Model | Best settings | Precision |
|---|---|---|---|---|---|
| Beauty | 0.6099 | 0.626 | SpecificityDegree | STL+512 | **0.6456** |
| Books | 0.772 | 0.781 | SpecificSents% | MTL+mean | **0.8002** |
| CDs and Vinyl | 0.8474 | 0.8198 | SpecificSents% | MTL+512 | **0.8634** |
| Electronics | 0.7891 | 0.7936 | All features | STL+mean | **0.8578** |
| Health and Personal Care | 0.6302 | 0.653 | SpecificityBalance | MTL+512 | **0.6615** |
| Home and Kitchen | 0.6277 | 0.6643 | MTL CNN | mean | **0.6788** |
| Kindle Store | **0.6582** | 0.6429 | SpecificityDegree | MTL+512 | 0.6401 |
| Movies and TV | 0.8231 | 0.8246 | SpecificityDegree | STL+mean | **0.8548** |
| Sports and Outdoors | 0.6379 | **0.677** | All features | MTL+512 | 0.666 |

Even though the SVM baseline seemed to outperform the other two approaches, the F1 results are not statistically significantly different, according to Friedman test at $p - value < 0.05$. On the other hand, when comparing the models using precision, CNN+SPECIFICITY greatly outperformed SVM with significant difference. This might indicate that incorporating the text specificity into a CNN classifier, whether as features or as an auxiliary prediction task, can specially reduce the amount of misclassified poorly helpful reviews.

All the five CNN+SPECIFICITY model variations appeared in the best results, therefore any of them should be worth testing when doing experiments with perceived helpfulness classification on other domains. Regarding the best settings, the results suggest that they seemed to vary according to both the domain and the classifier architecture, which do not indicate a clear domain-oriented behavior. Nevertheless, multi-task was a popular approach among most of the best results, across several datasets.

### 6.2    Sentence Specificity Prediction

Besides analyzing the performance of the helpfulness classification models with and without incorporating the text specificity aspect, we also present here the main points regarding our experiments with the sentence specificity prediction approach proposed in [10]. Therefore, the SPE (explained in Sect. 3) results are reported considering the specificity predictions on sentence-level. In other words, for each dataset containing product reviews, their sentences were extracted, then some or all of them were used as the target source to train the unsupervised domain adaptation model, and finally, the trained model was used to assign the specificity scores for all of these sentences.

Concerning the size of the training set, two variations were tested: a random sample of 100k sentences and all of the sentences in the dataset. After some preliminary experiments, better results were observed using a bigger training set rather than just 4.3k instances, as it was set in [12]. We decided to experiment with 100k sentences because this is about the amount of unlabeled sentences in the restaurant reviews domain used in the experiments performed in [10].

By increasing the training set, superior SPE results were also observed when training the models for more epochs. Therefore, using a training set with 100k instances, the model was trained for 80, 100, 120, 140, 160, and 180 epochs, and with all the sentences, it was trained for 60, 80, 100, and 120 epochs.

The best and worst SPE results for each dataset are summarized in Table 5. Beauty and Books domains were the only ones that achieved a truly satisfactory SPE score ($< 1$), according to what was discussed in Sect. 3. Nevertheless, when comparing the worst and the best results we can see that testing different training settings was important to achieve more reliable specificity predictions in our product domains. In addition to that, it is interesting to note that the size of the training set was crucial for the performance because, for every dataset, when the sample of 100k sentences achieved the preferred result, using all sentences to train the model presented an inferior performance, and vice-versa.

Some datasets, even the ones with more than 1M sentences, required all the sentences to be used as the target source to train the domain adaptation model. Furthermore, the results show that training with more data requires fewer epochs

**Table 5.** The best and the worst SPE results obtained in the specificity prediction experiments. The settings consist of the amount of sentences used for training + the quantity of training epochs.

| Dataset | # sentences | Best results | | Worst results | |
|---|---|---|---|---|---|
| | | SPE | Settings | SPE | Settings |
| Beauty | 185,709 | 0.58 | 100k+160 | 2.07 | All+60 |
| Books | 1,278,510 | 0.71 | All+80 | 2.58 | 100k+180 |
| CDs and Vinyl | 1,138,296 | 1.12 | 100k+180 | 2.56 | All+120 |
| Electronics | 421,788 | 1.03 | 100k+160 | 2.15 | All+100 |
| Health and Personal Care | 376,909 | 1.37 | 100k+180 | 2.32 | All+120 |
| Home and Kitchen | 372,036 | 1.19 | All+120 | 2.51 | 100k+180 |
| Kindle Store | 734,936 | 1.92 | All+60 | 2.53 | 100k+160 |
| Movies and TV | 1,922,349 | 1.31 | All+120 | 2.70 | 100k+120 |
| Sports and Outdoors | 252,402 | 1.13 | All+120 | 2.61 | 100k+120 |

to achieve better results. However, choosing a suitable training set size for this specificity prediction approach depends on the domain.

# 7  Conclusion

The present study aims to contribute to the perceived helpfulness prediction literature by exploring the text specificity aspect of product reviews. It is not a trivial activity to access truly valuable online reviews due to an overwhelming volume of poor quality comments. This elucidates the need for intelligent systems with the ability to identify helpful reviews. In this sense, we argue that text specificity may play an important role to improve such systems. Therefore, we empirically validated the usefulness of different ways to incorporate the text specificity aspect into a CNN architecture. In summary, the results revealed that the proposed models seem to have the desired ability to reduce the amount of false positive (increasing precision) in comparison to a SVM baseline.

In future endeavors, we plan to carry out analysis about the influence of the text specificity in the helpfulness prediction, using, among other solutions, explainability methods. Besides that, we aim to empirically evaluate incorporating the text specificity aspect into other modern architectures (e.g. Transformers) due to their successful application on a variety of text classification problems.

# References

1. Basiri, M.E., Habibi, S.: Review helpfulness prediction using convolutional neural networks and gated recurrent units. In: 2020 6th International Conference on Web Research (ICWR), pp. 191–196 (2020)
2. Caruana, R.: Multitask learning. Mach. Learn. **28**(1), 41–75 (1997)

3. Chen, C., Yang, Y., Zhou, J., Li, X., Bao, F.S.: Cross-domain review helpfulness prediction based on convolutional neural networks with auxiliary domain discriminators. In: Proceedings of the 2018 Conference of the North American Chapter of the Association for Computational Linguistics: Human Language Technologies, vol. 2 (Short Papers), pp. 602–607 (2018)

4. Fan, M., Feng, Y., Sun, M., Li, P., Wang, H., Wang, J.: Multi-task neural learning architecture for end-to-end identification of helpful reviews. In: 2018 IEEE/ACM International Conference on Advances in Social Networks Analysis and Mining (ASONAM), pp. 343–350 (2018)

5. Fan, M., Feng, C., Sun, M., Li, P.: Reinforced product metadata selection for helpfulness assessment of customer reviews. In: Proceedings of the 2019 Conference on Empirical Methods in Natural Language Processing and the 9th International Joint Conference on Natural Language Processing, pp. 1675–1683 (2019)

6. Ghose, A., Ipeirotis, P.G.: Estimating the helpfulness and economic impact of product reviews: mining text and reviewer characteristics. IEEE Trans. Knowl. Data Eng. **23**(10), 1498–1512 (2011)

7. Kang, Y., Zhou, L.: Longer is better? a case study of product review helpfulness prediction. In: Americas Conference on Information Systems (2016)

8. Kim, S.M., Pantel, P., Chklovski, T., Pennacchiotti, M.: Automatically assessing review helpfulness. In: Conference on Empirical Methods in Natural Language Processing, pp. 423–430 (2006)

9. Kim, Y.: Convolutional neural networks for sentence classification. In: Proceedings of the Conference on Empirical Methods in Natural Language Processing, pp. 1746–1751 (2014)

10. Ko, W.J., Durrett, G., Li, J.J.: Domain agnostic real-valued specificity prediction. In: Proceedings of the AAAI Conference on Artificial Intelligence (2019)

11. Li, J.J., Nenkova, A.: Fast and accurate prediction of sentence specificity. In: Proceedings of the AAAI Conference on Artificial Intelligence, pp. 2281–2287 (2015)

12. Lima, B., Nogueira, T.: Novel features based on sentence specificity for helpfulness prediction of online reviews. In: 2019 8th Brazilian Conference on Intelligent Systems (BRACIS), pp. 84–89 (2019)

13. Liu, J., Cao, Y., Lin, C.Y., Huang, Y., Zhou, M.: Low-quality product review detection in opinion summarization. In: Conference on Empirical Methods in Natural Language Processing, vol. 7, pp. 334–342 (2007)

14. Louis, A., Nenkova, A.: Automatic identification of general and specific sentences by leveraging discourse annotations. In: Proceedings of 5th International Joint Conference on Natural Language Processing, pp. 605–613 (2011)

15. Louis, A., Nenkova, A.: Text specificity and impact on quality of news summaries. In: Proceedings of the Workshop on Monolingual Text-To-Text Generation, pp. 34–42 (2011)

16. McAuley, J., Targett, C., Shi, Q., Van Den Hengel, A.: Image-based recommendations on styles and substitutes. In: Proceedings of the ACM SIGIR Conference on Research and Development in Information Retrieval, pp. 43–52 (2015)

17. Mudambi, S.M., Schuff, D.: What makes a helpful online review? a study of customer reviews on amazon.com. MIS Q. **34**(1), 185–200 (2010)

18. Ocampo Diaz, G., Ng, V.: Modeling and prediction of online product review helpfulness: a survey. In: Proceedings of the 56th Annual Meeting of the Association for Computational Linguistics, vol. 1: Long Papers, pp. 698–708 (2018)

19. Pennington, J., Socher, R., Manning, C.: GloVe: global vectors for word representation. In: Proceedings of the 2014 Conference on Empirical Methods in Natural Language Processing, pp. 1532–1543 (2014)

20. Saumya, S., Singh, J.P., Dwivedi, Y.K.: Predicting the helpfulness score of online reviews using convolutional neural network. Soft Comput. **24**(15), 10989–11005 (2019). https://doi.org/10.1007/s00500-019-03851-5
21. Zhang, Y., Wallace, B.: A sensitivity analysis of (and practitioners' guide to) convolutional neural networks for sentence classification. In: Proceedings of the Eighth International Joint Conference on Natural Language Processing, vol. 1: Long Papers, pp. 253–263. Asian Federation of Natural Language Processing (2017)
22. Zhang, Y., Lin, Z.: Predicting the helpfulness of online product reviews: a multilingual approach. Electron. Commer. Res. Appl. **27**, 1–10 (2018)

# Joint Event Extraction with Contextualized Word Embeddings for the Portuguese Language

Anderson da Silva Brito Sacramento[ID] and Marlo Souza[✉][ID]

Federal University of Bahia - UFBA, Salvador-Bahia, Brazil
{andersonsacramento,msouza1}@ufba.br

**Abstract.** Event Extraction (EE) is the task of identifying mentions of particular event types and their arguments in text, and it constitutes an important and challenging task within the area of Information Extraction (IE). However, in the context of the Portuguese language, very little work has been conducted on this topic. In this paper, we propose a neural-based method for EE, as well as a data resource to mitigate this research gap. We also present a data augmentation strategy for EE, employing an Open Information Extraction (OIE) system, aiming to overcome the shortage in annotated data for the problem in the Portuguese language. Our experimental results show that our method is able to predict event types and arguments automatically, and the proposed method of data augmentation, in one of the two evaluated samples, contributes to the performance of the tested models in the subtask of argument role prediction. Further, an implementation of our method is available to the community, as the models trained in our experiments (https://github. com/FORMAS/TEFE).

**Keywords:** Event Extraction · Information Extraction · Natural Language Processing · Portuguese language

## 1  Introduction

Event Extraction (EE) is an important and challenging task of Information Extraction (IE) in the field of Natural Language Processing (NLP). The task comprises identifying the mentions of particular event types and their arguments, i.e. mentions to entities participating in the event, and the roles of these arguments in relation to an event type.

The term event has different, definitions in the literature [6,23]. While events are undeniably temporal entities, they also may possess a rich non-temporal structure that is important for intelligent information access systems [1]. In this work, we consider events as things that happen or occur involving participants and attributes, most notably spatio-temporal attributes. To be more precise, we adopt the definition presented in the ACE 2005 annotation guidelines [6]: an

© Springer Nature Switzerland AG 2021
A. Britto and K. Valdivia Delgado (Eds.): BRACIS 2021, LNAI 13074, pp. 496–510, 2021.
https://doi.org/10.1007/978-3-030-91699-2_34

event is a specific occurrence involving participants; it is something that happens and can frequently be described as a change of state.

Based on the event annotation guideline ACE 2005 [6], and related literature on EE [18,20], EE can be divided into two main subtasks: Event Detection (ED), i.e. the task of identifying and classifying event triggers, and Argument Role Prediction (ARP), i.e. the task of identifying the arguments of an even and labeling their roles.

In this context, an event trigger consists of an expression denoting the occurrence of the event and each event mention in a sentence is identified by a trigger term. An event trigger may be expressed primarily through verbs and nominalizations but also by other word classes such as adjectives and prepositions. As such, one of the challenging aspects of the EE task is that the same trigger term can express different events in different contexts. That is, trigger words may be ambiguous. To illustrate, consider the following sentences:

$s_1$: *"... os árabes teriam de apoiar o Iraque numa **luta** contra o seu inimigo comum israelita."*[1]

$s_2$: *"Ambas as empresas são aliadas da Navigation Mixte na **luta** contra uma OPA hostil ..."*[2]

Both of $s_1$ and $s_2$ contain a word, *"**luta**"* (fight), functioning as an event trigger. However, in s1, *"**luta**"* means a hostile encounter between opposing forces, which denotes a *Hostile encounter* event. In s2, *"**luta**"* means a dispute between parties with incompatible opinions, and denotes an event of type *Quarreling* [2].

On the other hand, the same event can be described by various different expressions, by means of different trigger words. For example, we observe in the annotated TimeBankPT Event Frame Annotation (TEFA) corpus that the following trigger words denote an occurrence of an event of type *Statement*: *"dito"*, *"disse"*, *"referiu"*, *"anunciado"*, *"acrescentou"*, etc.[3]

Furthermore, when dealing with multiple event mentions in the same sentence, it is possible that different events share arguments with different roles. Consider the following sentence:

*"A Meridian National Corp. **disse** que **vendeu** 750.00 ações oridinárias ao grupo da família McAlpine, por 1 milhão de dólares, ou 1,35 dólares por ação."*[4]

the entity mention *"Meridian National Corp."* takes two different (and not related) argument roles: *Speaker* and *Seller*, respectively, in the events *Statement* and *Commerce_sell* denoted by the event triggers "disse" (said) and "vendeu" (sold).

---

[1] s1: *"... the Arabs would have to support Iraq in a **fight** against their common Israeli enemy."*.

[2] s2: *"Both companies are allies of Navigation Mixte in its **fight** against a hostile takeover bid ..."*.

[3] "said", "referred", "announced", "added".

[4] "Meridian National Corp. **said** it **sold** 750,000 shares of its common stock to the McAlpine family interests, for $1 million, or $1.35 a share."

Event mentions in natural language text are ubiquitously present in different domains and genres and encompass a great amount of information encoded in a sentence.

As noted by Ahn [1], solutions for EE can benefit the development of other NLP applications, such as text summarization, question answering and information retrieval.

Notably, there are two variations of the task of EE regarding the types of target event that are considered [30]: open domain, when no schema and list of target event types are defined for the task; and closed domain, when the set of target event types and their respective schemata are pre-defined. In this paper, we will discuss a method for closed domain EE for the Portuguese language. We developed a method to identify and classify a closed set of event types whose arguments and their roles were previously specified based on machine learning.

As there is no publicly available dataset and corpus for the task of closed domain EE for the Portuguese language that we are aware, we built a dataset by enriching the TimeBankPT [8] corpus with event annotation schemata from the FrameNet project [2]. TimeBankPT is the first corpus of Portuguese with rich temporal annotations, i.e. it includes annotations not only of temporal expressions but also about events and temporal relations [8].

In this work, we propose a method to the task of EE developed and evaluated over a newly created data set with event types and argument roles annotations, labeled over the TimeBankPT corpus, from which we maintain only the event trigger annotations. Our method jointly performs ED and ARP by learning a shared intermediary representation for the ED and ARP subtasks.

Our main contributions are: (1) We propose a novel method for the EE task, simultaneously tackles the ED and ARP subtasks. (2) We demonstrate the usefulness of the application of OIE systems as a strategy to data augmentation for EE annotated sentences. (3) We have conducted experiments on a proposed enriched TimeBankPT corpus, achieving modest performance with low feature engineering effort.

## 2    Related Work

Most work on the literature on EE have focused on languages such as English and Chinese, for which there are standard corpora for the task [30], such as the ACE 2005 corpus [27]. Regarding the approaches adopted in the literature, there are two main categorizations with respect to the input features and the modularization of the methods, respectively divided between discriminative featured-based [1,15] and representation learning-based methods [10,17], and the pipeline [15] versus the joint approach [20].

Recently, however, methods based on the application of deep neural networks, more specifically, the use of representation learning to address the task of EE [4,19], have achieved good performance improvement for the task compared to earlier feature-based approaches and, as such, we will focus on a neural-based approach in this work.

While ED is a much well-established task, if we consider the ARP subtask, very few works on the literature focused on both argument identification and argument role labeling [20]. Most of the related work assumes that argument identification is a previously resolved problem and focus only on the task role classification. Among the work on argument identification and role labeling, the works of Nguyen et al. [18,20] propose the use of recurrent neural networks (RNNs) for the ARP, achieving good performance for the task. These works will be the main inspiration for our method. It is also important to notice that the use of contextualized word embeddings is also a recent development [26].

To our knowledge, very little work has been done on event extraction for the Portuguese language. Notably, this task has been addressed in a limited scope in the HAREM [3] named entity recognition evaluation, which included temporal named entities of the type event. From a more general perspective, the work of Costa and Branco [7] and Quaresma [22] are some of the only works on the literature on this problem for the Portuguese language, to our knowledge.

Costa e Branco [7] proposed a method for event identification and classification using an approach based on feature engineering and a decision tree trained over the TimeBankPT corpus. The corpus, however, only contains annotation on a very broad event classification typology, e.g. *REPORTING, OCCURRENCE, STATE, I_STATE*, and *I_ACTION*, and does not contain annotation on event structure, i.e. its arguments and their roles in the event.

Quaresma et al. [22] focus on the task of event extraction proposing an algorithm that relies on the output of a semantic role labeling (SRL) system. In doing so, the authors assumed that only predicates are event trigger candidates. In their work, the authors did not classify events by type, and they also limited the classification of event arguments, considering only the roles provided by SRL schemas. Unfortunately, the data set provided by the authors[5] contains only the information on trigger output predictions of their systems, without a gold reference that would allow comparison at least for event identification.

## 3  Task Definition

In this work, we are concerned with the task of Event Extraction for the Portuguese language. Throughout this work, we will employ the following terminology:

- Event mention: a phrase or sentence in which an event occurs, including one trigger and an arbitrary number of arguments.
- Event trigger: the main word that most clearly expresses an event occurrence.
- Event argument: an entity mention, temporal expression or value (e.g. Money) that servers as a participant or attribute with a specific role in an event mention.

---

[5] https://github.com/kraiyani/Automated-Event-Extraction-Model-for-Multiple-Linked-Portuguese-Documents.

– Argument role: the relationship between an argument to the event in which it participates.

The corpus that we employ in our experiments contains 514 event types (e.g., Statement, Commerce_buy, Firing) that correspond to the types of event triggers associated with each event mention. Each event type has its own set of roles that can be performed by one of the entities participating in the event, i.e. its arguments. For instance, some of the roles of the event type *Statement* are *Speaker*, *Message*, *Topic*, *Addresse* and *Time*. The total number of roles for all the event types on the annotated corpus is 1936.

Following this terminology, we explicitly define the standard evaluation procedures as follows, as presented by [30]:

– Trigger identification: A trigger is correctly detected if its offsets (viz., the position of the trigger word in the text) match a reference trigger
– Trigger classification: An event type is correctly classified if both the trigger's offset and event type match a reference trigger and its event type.
– Argument identification: An argument is correctly identified if its offsets match any of the reference argument mentions (viz., correctly recognizing participants in an event)
– Argument role classification: An argument role is correctly classified if its event type, offsets, and role match any of the reference argument mentions.

## 4   Model

We propose a model that jointly performs ED and ARP at the sentence level. As such, let $W = \langle w_1, w_2, ..., w_n \rangle$ be a sentence, where $n$ is the number of words/tokens and $w_i$ is its $i$-th token. We will model the ED problem, as a multi-class word classification problem, following prior works [10,16,26] in assuming that event triggers are single words/tokens in the sentences. This definition leads to a sequence classification problem on the input sentence $W$, in which we predict the event type $t_i$ for each $w_i \in W$ - where $t_i$ can be "None" to indicate the word $w_i$ is not a trigger, or it is not any of the target event types. It is assumed that a trigger candidate cannot refer to more than one event mentioned in the same sentence.

For event argument identification and role prediction, we need to recognize the entity mentions that act as an argument for each of the event mentions occurring in $W$ (argument identification) and classify their associated role. So, for the sake of explanation, considering that each sentence has only one event mention, this task is cast as a sequence labeling task in which for each word/token in the sentence, we predict a sequence of labels $E = e_1, e_2, ..., e_n$. In summary, for each trigger candidate word $w_i$ we must predict the corresponding argument role labels for each word/token in $W$. An illustration of the architecture of our model with the joint prediction of event mentions and their arguments is depicted in Fig. 1.

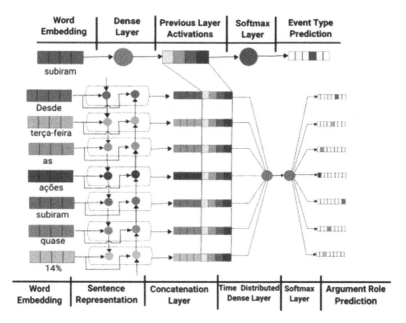

**Fig. 1.** The joint EE model for the two subtasks with an input sentence. "subiram" (risen) is the current trigger word candidate, and all the other word tokens are transformed into vector representations to predict their roles given the current trigger candidate.

## 4.1 Trigger and Sentence Encoding

In the component of trigger encoding, every trigger candidate word $w_i \in W$ is transformed into a word vector $c_i$ using the pre-trained word embedding $d_i$ of $w_i$. We employ the BERTimbau model [25], a transformer model trained over Portuguese language data, for obtaining these representations.

For the sentence encoding step, we only use the respective word embedding for each word/token of the sentence. Since BERTimbau applies WordPiece [28] tokenizations, possibly generating subword units, we choose to compose the respective word embeddings by summing the vector representation of each word's subword units.

## 4.2 Sentence Representation

After the sentence encoding step, the input sentence $W$ is transformer in a sequence of word embedding vectors $X = \langle x_1, x_2, ..., x_n \rangle$. To produce the sentence representation, we feed the sequence $X$ into a bidirecional recurrent neural network [24], which produces the hidden representation vector for each input vector $x_t$ from $X$. We obtain the sequence $H = \langle [\overrightarrow{h_1}; \overleftarrow{h_1}], [\overrightarrow{h_2}; \overleftarrow{h_2}], \cdots , [\overrightarrow{h_n}; \overleftarrow{h_n}] \rangle$ of two hidden states at each time-step $t$, one for the left-to-right propagation $\overrightarrow{h_t}$ and another for the right-to-left propagation $\overleftarrow{h_t}$. At each step $t$, we employ a

LSTM network [13] that accepts a current input $x_t$ and a previous hidden state $h_{t-1}$ to compute the current hidden state $h_t = LSTM(x_t, h_{t-1})$.

### 4.3   Trigger Representation

For the trigger representation, we feed the word embedding vector of the current trigger candidate $c_i$ into a feed-forward layer $FF(c_i)$. The feature representation from this layer is shared between the two next prediction states to perform ED and ARP simultaneously. The value of this layer activations is computed as: $R_i^{ED} = ReLU(W_{tr}c_i + b_{tr})$ where $W_{tr}$ is a weight matrix and $b_{tr}$ a bias term.

### 4.4   Event Detection and Argument Role Prediction

The predictions of the event trigger classifier and argument role classifier components are done sequentially over the sentence from left to right. At the current word/step $i$, we attempt to compute the probability

$$P(a_i, t_i | \Gamma) = P(t_i|\Gamma)P(a_{i,1}|\Gamma, t_i)P(a_{i,2}|\Gamma, a_{i,<1}, t_i) \cdots P(a_{i,n}|\Gamma, a_{i,<n}, t_i),$$

where $\Gamma = \langle W, a_{<i}, t_{<i} \rangle$, and $a_{i<j} = a_{i,1}, a_{i,2}, \cdots, a_{i,j-1}$.

In the argument role prediction classifier, at each time step $j$, we generate the feature representation vector $R_{i,j}^{ARP}$ for the word/token $w_j$ by concatenating the hidden layer representation $h_j$ of the sentence representation stage with the shared vector of activations of the current trigger candidate, the trigger representation vector $R_i^{ED}$, to obtain: $R_{i,j}^{ARP} = [h_j, R_i^{ED}]$.

In order to compute the probability $P(t_i|W, t_{<i})$, we feed the feature representation $R_i^{ED}$ into a feed-forward neural network with a softmax layer $FF^{ED}$, resulting in the a probability distribution over the possible event types: $P(t_i|W, t_{<i}) = FF^{ED}(R_i^{ED})$. The event type of the trigger candidate $i$ is selected by a greedy decoder: $t_i^p = argmax P(t_i|W, t_{<i})$.

For the argument role distribution $P(a_{i,j}|W, a_{i,<j}, t_{<i+1})$, we follow similar procedure. We feed the feature representation $R_{i,j}^{ARP}$ into a feed-forward neural network with a $ReLU$ activation function, followed by a softmax layer: $P(a_{i,j}|W, a_{i,<j}, t_{<i+1}) = FF^{ARP}(ReLU(R_{i,j}^{ARP}))$. We apply the greedy strategy to predict the argument role: $a_{i,j}^p = argmax P(a_{i,j}|W, a_{i,<j}, t_{<i+1})$.

### 4.5   Training

We train the network by minimizing the loss function values. The optimization objective function is defined as multi-class cross-entropy loss:

$$C(A, T, W) = -\sum_{i=1}^{n} \log P(t_i|W, t_{<i}) - \sum_{i=1}^{n}\sum_{j=1}^{n} \log P(a_{i,j}|W, a_{i,<j}, t_{<i+1}).$$

The gradients are computed with backpropagation with the stochastic gradient descent with mini-batches applying RMSProp [12] weights-average.

# 5   Corpus

To our knowledge, there is no currently publicly available dataset for EE in the Portuguese language that encompasses annotation both on event occurrences and their arguments, which include event types and argument roles.

Between the two public available corpora found in the literature [8,22], the TimeBankPT meets most of our requirements, as it was annotated following a well-defined guideline, which is well-known and used to guide the annotation of corpora in other languages [23]. Also, it provides others annotation information, besides event mentions, that can be used to perform related tasks, such as event ordering. It is important to notice that the notion event in TimeBankPT guidelines agrees with that of ACE 2005 guidelines, which we adopt in this work. Thus, we consider this corpus as an interesting resource to base our work. While TimeBankPT describes classes attributes, it does not provide a fine-grain distinction of the semantics of events by means of a semantically relevant typology of events. More yet, it does not contain annotations of event arguments and their roles, which are necessary for our problem.

As such, we enrich the TimeBankPT corpus with annotation about event type and argument roles. In this annotation, we employ the event type schemata from the FrameNet project to define event types and argument roles. We adopted a semi-automatic annotation process, in which firstly, the LOME [29] frame parser automatically annotated all the sentences in the corpus, followed by a manual validation and correction by two human annotators. From the 7887 events originally annotated in TimeBankPT, 6220 (79%) were automatically identified by LOME and analyzed by the human annotators. We measured the inter-annotator over 10% of a common set of event type annotations to assess the reliability of the annotation process. The annotators achieved an inter-annotator agreement of 0.78 as measured by the Cohen's Kappa [5] coefficient, which is considered a good value.

We evaluate the proposed model for EE on this TEFA (TimeBankPT Event Frames Annotation) dataset obtained as a result of our annotation process. The TEFA corpus contains annotation of 6620 event mentions of 514 different types and 1936 arguments.

# 6   Experiments

In the following, we describe our empirical investigation on EE for the Portuguese language, based on the joint identification and classification model proposed in Sect. 4 and evaluated on the TEFA corpus described in the previous section.

## 6.1   Dataset, Parameters, and Resources

For all the experiments, in the trigger and sentence encoding phase, we use 768 dimensions for the word embeddings. We extracted these embeddings from the

BERTimbau Base model, where we compose the resulting WordPiece sub-tokens by adding them.

We use 350 units in the hidden layers for the LSTMs. For the trigger representation, during training, we use a dropout layer of 25% rate over the input word embedding followed by a feed-forward neural network with 700 units with ReLU activation function. After this layer, we employed a batch normalization layer [14], and another dropout layer of 50% rate.

Regarding the argument prediction phase, at each time step of the BiLSTM, of the sentence representation phase, we concatenate the trigger representation with the two hidden unit vectors, constructing a vector representation of 1400 activations, and applied a time distributed feed-forward layer with 700 units with ReLU activation function followed by a final softmax layer for probability distribution prediction for the argument role labels. For the ED part of the model, we apply a softmax dense layer over the shared event trigger representation. Finally, during training, we use a mini-batch of size 128. These parameter values were selected according to the validation data.

We applied the pre-trained language representations from BERTimbau-Base in a feature-based approach. We follow Devlin et al. [9], applying a feature-based approach by extracting the activations from one or more layers without fine-tuning any parameters of BERTimbau-Base. During the model development, we evaluated three different strategies: capturing the last hidden layer activations, summing the last four, and summing all the twelve. From now on we will refer to these strategies as Last Hidden, Sum Last 4, and Sum All 12, respectively.

Regarding the event types and argument roles labels, we consider a set of 514 event types from FrameNet [2] plus the None type, which identifies a word as not denoting an event, and a set of 1936 argument roles types as defined in FrameNet [2]. We adopted the BIO annotation schema to assign argument role labels to each token in the sentence, achieving a total of 3873 labels (two times the number of argument role types, corresponding to the labels Begin and In for each argument role type, plus one Outside label).

To evaluate our method, we defined two scenarios considering the amount of annotated examples for each event type. The first consisted only of event mentions of target types containing more than 100 examples in the training corpus, consisting of 7 event types with 93 argument roles. The second consisted of all event types annotated in the corpus, containing 514 event types with 1936 argument roles. The purpose of this procedure was to investigate the influence of the number of training examples in the performance of the method and possibly infer the effort to further support new event types.

We use the criteria for evaluation described on Sect. 3. To provide a meaningful comparison with possible future work, we employ the precision (P), recall (R), and $F_1$ Score ($F_1$) evaluation metrics. We report the micro-average scores for event type classification and argument role prediction as in previous work [18]. We also show the $F_1$ micro-average score for argument role label prediction on the test set.

## 6.2   Data Augmentation via OIE

In order to obtain more annotated data and possibly increase the robustness of our method, we explore the use of a data augmentation method for the task of EE using new sentences formed by Open Information Extraction (OIE) triples over the event annotated sentences from the original corpus. To the best of our knowledge, this strategy of data augmentation for the task of EE has not been mentioned in the literature.

OIE is the task of extracting facts, or simple propositions, from text without limiting the analysis to a predefined set of relationships or predicates [11]. As described by Oliveira *et al.* [21], OIE systems usually extract facts from a sentence in the form of triples $t = (arg1, rel, arg2)$, where $arg1$ and $arg2$ are two arguments and $rel$ describes a semantic relationship between $arg1$ and $ag2$.

We argue that this technique of EE data augmentation can boost the model performance because it provides simpler syntactic realizations of event mentions to model the relationship between an event trigger and their arguments.

To make sense of the previous argument, consider the following sentence: *"Na Bolsa de Valores Americana, as ações da Citadel fecharam ontem nos 45,75 dólares, descendo 25 cêntimos."*[6]. One of the triples obtained by the execution of DptOIE [21][7], an OIE system for the Portuguese language, over the previous sentence was: ( *"As ações da Citadel"*, *"fecharam"*, *"nos 45,74 dólares"*).

If we consider as a new sentence, which we refer to as a synthetic sentence, simply the concatenation of $arg1, rel$ and $arg2$ from the extracted triple, we obtain the sentence: *"As ações da Citadel fecharam nos 45,74 dólares"*[8]. In most cases, this simple approach produces grammatical and semantic correct sentences.

The synthetic sentences obtained from the triples are at most the same length that the original sentences, and those that are equal we do not count as new ones. Our hypothesis is that this data augmentation approach will be beneficial when dealing with long sentences for which the synthetic sentences are shorter and include the relevant arguments because the new sentence will help reduce the number of long-term dependencies in the input sequence the model needs to remember. Also, as we maintain the original sentence it will not prohibit the model from learning these dependencies from more complex and real examples. We create the augmented dataset by iterating into the extractions from the OIE system, producing the synthetic sentences and selecting the one where the event trigger is part of the relation descriptor in the obtained triple. Following that, we transfer the annotations of the extracted sentence to the synthetic one.

The application of this data augmentation strategy over the original dataset produced an increase of 192% of annotated sentences (i.e. from 1962 to 5747 examples), 70% of event triggers, i.e. from 5345 to 9130 examples, and 56% of arguments, i.e. from 10727 to 16779 examples.

---

[6] "In American Stock Exchange composite trading, Citadel shares closed yesterday at $45.75, down 25 cents".

[7] Available at: https://github.com/FORMAS/DptOIE.

[8] "Citadel shares closed at $45.75".

### 6.3   Word Embedding Layers Selection

We evaluate different approaches to extract the activations from layers of BERTimbau to obtain the pretrained word embeddings, which we employ as input features to the joint model for EE. Table 1 presents the performance on the development set of the augmented training set when Last Hidden, Sum Last 4, and Sum All 12 layers extractions are used to obtain the word embeddings from the same corpus over the two different scenarios (more than 100 examples and more than 0 examples). The development set also contains sentences resulting from the data augmentation via OIE.

**Table 1.** Average performance of models over development set with augmentation using 10-fold *cross-validation* evaluation.

| Model | Event trigger classification (%) | | | Argument role classification (%) | | |
|---|---|---|---|---|---|---|
| | $P$ | $R$ | $F_1$ | $P$ | $R$ | $F_1$ |
| LastHidden/100 | 81.7 ± 3.2 | 83.1 ± 4.9 | 82.4 ± 3.5 | 43.5 ± 4.7 | **43.6 ± 5.8** | **43.4 ± 4.9** |
| SumLast4/100 | 83.2 ± 3.1 | 84.2 ± 5.4 | 83.6 ± 3.7 | **43.9 ± 6.3** | 42.9 ± 6.7 | 43.4 ± 6.2 |
| SumAll12/100 | 83.4 ± 3.7 | 85.7 ± 3.7 | **84.5 ± 2.8** | 41.7 ± 6.3 | 41.3 ± 5.7 | 41.4 ± 5.6 |
| LastHidden/0 | 60.1 ± 6.0 | 45.2 ± 5.6 | 51.5 ± 5.5 | **35.5 ± 6.7** | **19.0 ± 3.6** | **24.6 ± 4.0** |
| SumLast4/0 | 57.9 ± 4.3 | 46.7 ± 5.9 | 51.6 ± 5.1 | 31.7 ± 7.4 | 19.0 ± 4.3 | 23.7 ± 5.1 |
| SumAll12/0 | 59.2 ± 4.1 | 50.0 ± 5.3 | **54.2 ± 4.6** | 27.4 ± 4.7 | 18.0 ± 3.0 | 21.7 ± 3.5 |

We can observe from the results depicted in Table 1, that the Last Hidden input word embeddings performs best for the task of ARP, and the Sum All 12 performs best for the ED subtask. We observe the same pattern on the original development set evaluation, i.e. without data augmentation. From these results, we chose to prioritize the ARP subtask by choosing the Last Hidden combination as the input word embeddings to produce the final models on both original and augmented datasets.

### 6.4   Test Evaluation

Table 2 shows the results of the comparison between the proposed method trained in four different scenarios, where we compare the performance of the models trained on the original TEFA data (blstme) and over the augmented training set (blstmea). We notice that data augmentation strategy was beneficial to the task of ARP when the data per event type and argument role were more scarce, and the BIO tags labeling task performance does not match the performance on argument role classification. However, we did not notice the same benefit on event types and, consequently, arguments roles with a greater number of examples in the corpus. More than that, the augmentation appears to diminish the $F_1$ performance of the model, but in contrast, it raises the ARP individual labels classification.

**Table 2.** Performance of the four models over test set of trained over the original (blstme) and augmented training sets (blstmea) over two event types distributions.

| Model | Event trigger identification (%) | | | Event trigger classification (%) | | | Event argument identification (%) | | | Argument role classification (%) | | | ARP label (%) |
|---|---|---|---|---|---|---|---|---|---|---|---|---|---|
| | $P$ | $R$ | $F_1$ | $P$ | $R$ | $F_1$ | $P$ | $R$ | $F_1$ | $P$ | $R$ | $F_1$ | $F_1$ |
| *blstme-100* | **91.1** | 82.6 | **86.7** | **88.7** | 80.4 | **84.3** | **45.2** | **52.5** | **48.6** | **45.8** | **50.1** | **47.9** | 32.3 |
| *blstmea-100* | 86.1 | **83.0** | 84.5 | 85.6 | **82.6** | 84.1 | 41.0 | 48.8 | 44.6 | 40.9 | 45.8 | 43.2 | **73.8** |
| *blstme-0* | 85.8 | **69.9** | **77.0** | 57.2 | **46.6** | **51.3** | 31.6 | **17.3** | **22.4** | 30.9 | **15.3** | 20.4 | **43.4** |
| *blstmea-0* | **87.7** | 50.5 | 64.1 | **62.8** | 36.2 | 45.9 | **41.9** | 14.9 | 22.0 | **43.0** | 14.0 | **21.1** | 42.7 |

# 7  Error Analysis

We examine the outputs of *blstme-0* on the test set to find out the contributions of each event type to event detection errors. Following Nguyen et al. [20], we highlight two types of errors: (i) missing an event mention in the test set (called *MISSED*), and (ii) incorrectly detecting an event mention (called *INCORRECT*).

In Table 3, we list the top five event types appearing in these two types of errors and their corresponding percents over the total number of errors, and the number of available event mentions on the training and testing data sets. The total number of event types present on the test set amounts to 244.

These top five event types amount to 8.1% of the *MISSED* errors and 31.1% of the *INCORRECT* errors. The *MISSED* errors are more evenly distributed between the event types than the *INCORRECT* errors. Examples from the *Statement* event type appears in both top five type of errors, and it is ranked in the first place primarily due to the greater amount of examples on the test set. When we observe one of the *MISSED* errors from the *Statement* event type, even the trigger word "relata" being available on the training set, due to a different and somehow confusing context, the model failed to detect the event mention in the following sentence: "*A correspondente da BBC Karyn Coleman relata do Kosovo.*"[9]. When we change the word order of this sentence: "*Do Kosovo, a correspondente da BBC Karyn Coleman relata.*" the model was able to detect the *Statement* event mention. Despite this example, the *MISSED* errors were detected more frequently in cases where the trigger words are not present in the training data.

From the analysis of the *INCORRECT* errors, we notice that similar context, when the sentence contains event arguments common to different event types, the most predominant example event type hinder the performance of similar event types. As an example of such a case, in the sentence: "*Os funcionários americanos afirmam que já veem sinais de que Saddam Hussein está a ficar nervoso.*"[10], the model detected a *Statement* event type, instead of *Affirm_or_deny*

---

[9] "BBC correspondent Karyn Coleman reports from Kosovo.".

[10] "U.S. officials claim they already see signs Saddam Hussein is getting nervous.".

event type, despite a very indicative trigger word. This may indicate an over-reliance of the model on lexical information, as opposed to the semantic information we expect to be encoded in the word and sentence representation stages of our architecture. Another explanation may reside in the much fine-grained schemata that we employed and the imbalance between these two event type annotated examples.

**Table 3.** Top five event types for ED errors.

| MISSED | | | INCORRECT | | |
|---|---|---|---|---|---|
| Label | (%) | Train/Test | Label | (%) | Train/Test |
| Statement | 1.93 | 803/127 | Statement | 9.84 | 803/127 |
| Attempt_suasion | 1.71 | 30/9 | Intentionally_act | 6.98 | 69/11 |
| Criminal_investigation | 1.71 | 8/8 | Causation | 5.58 | 90/14 |
| Willingness | 1.49 | 9/7 | Change_position_on_a_scale | 4.91 | 316/41 |
| Awareness | 1.29 | 21/6 | Process_end | 3.93 | 33/4 |

## 8   Conclusion

In this paper, we have presented a method for event extraction in the Portuguese language over an enriched event frame annotated corpus constructed from the TimeBankPT corpus. Our approach requires less effort on feature engineering, using as input only contextualized word embeddings, and jointly performs ED and ARP. We also proposed and evaluated a method of data augmentation for the EE task using an OIE system. The annotation process required to produce the corpus turns out to be tested by this experimentation evaluation, validating the process of annotation, using three language resources already available: the TimebankPT corpus, the LOME frame parser, and the FrameNet schemata.

Our experimental results show that our method is able to learn and automatically predict with good precision some event types and argument roles over the annotated corpus. Also, we notice an improvement in the performance on the argument role prediction for the models that used the augmented data from OIE when dealing with event types and argument roles with scarce annotated examples, showing that this strategy may be valuable to improve the performance of EE systems for languages with little training data for the task, as is the case of the Portuguese language.

**Acknowledgments.** Anderson da Silva Brito Sacramento would like to thank Coordenação de Aperfeiçoamento de Pessoal de Nível Superior - CAPES for financial support (88887. 467864/2019-00).

# References

1. Ahn, D.: The stages of event extraction. In: Proceedings of the Workshop on Annotating and Reasoning about Time and Events, pp. 1–8 (2006)
2. Baker, C.F., Fillmore, C.J., Lowe, J.B.: The berkeley framenet project. In: 36th Annual Meeting of the Association for Computational Linguistics and 17th International Conference on Computational Linguistics, vol. 1, pp. 86–90 (1998)
3. Carvalho, P., Gonçalo Oliveira, H., Santos, D., Freitas, C., Mota, C.: Segundo harem: Modelo geral, novidades e avaliaçao. quot; In Cristina Mota; Diana Santos (ed) Desafios na avaliação conjunta do reconhecimento de entidades mencionadas: O Segundo HAREM Linguateca 2008 (2008)
4. Chen, Y., Xu, L., Liu, K., Zeng, D., Zhao, J.: Event extraction via dynamic multi-pooling convolutional neural networks. In: Proceedings of the 53rd Annual Meeting of the Association for Computational Linguistics and the 7th International Joint Conference on Natural Language Processing (Volume 1: Long Papers), pp. 167–176 (2015). https://doi.org/10.3115/v1/P15-1017
5. Cohen, J.: A coefficient of agreement for nominal scales. Educ. Psychol. Meas. **20**(1), 37–46 (1960). https://doi.org/10.1177/001316446002000104
6. Consortium, L.D.: Ace (automatic content extraction) English annotation guidelines for events. Version (5.4.3) (2005)
7. Costa, F., Branco, A.: Lx-timeanalyzer: a temporal information processing system for Portuguese (2012). http://hdl.handle.net/10451/14148
8. Costa, F., Branco, A.: Timebankpt: a timeml annotated corpus of portuguese. In: LREC, pp. 3727–3734 (2012)
9. Devlin, J., Chang, M.W., Lee, K., Toutanova, K.: Bert: pre-training of deep bidirectional transformers for language understanding (2018). https://doi.org/10.18653/v1/N19-1423
10. Ding, R., Li, Z.: Event extraction with deep contextualized word representation and multi-attention layer. In: Gan, G., Li, B., Li, X., Wang, S. (eds.) ADMA 2018. LNCS (LNAI), vol. 11323, pp. 189–201. Springer, Cham (2018). https://doi.org/10.1007/978-3-030-05090-0_17
11. Glauber, R., de Oliveira, L.S., Sena, C.F.L., Claro, D.B., Souza, M., et al.: Challenges of an annotation task for open information extraction in Portuguese. In: Villavicencio, A. (ed.) PROPOR 2018. LNCS (LNAI), vol. 11122, pp. 66–76. Springer, Cham (2018). https://doi.org/10.1007/978-3-319-99722-3_7
12. Hinton, G., Srivastava, N., Swersky, K.: Neural networks for machine learning lecture 6a overview of mini-batch gradient descent. Cited on **14**(8), 2 (2012)
13. Hochreiter, S., Schmidhuber, J.: Long short-term memory. Neural Comput. **9**(8), 1735–1780 (1997). https://doi.org/10.1162/neco.1997.9.8.1735
14. Ioffe, S., Szegedy, C.: Batch normalization: accelerating deep network training by reducing internal covariate shift. In: International Conference on Machine Learning, pp. 448–456. PMLR (2015)
15. Ji, H., Grishman, R.: Refining event extraction through cross-document inference. In: Proceedings of ACL-08: Hlt, pp. 254–262 (2008). https://aclanthology.org/P08-1030
16. Li, Q., Ji, H., Huang, L.: Joint event extraction via structured prediction with global features. In: Proceedings of the 51st Annual Meeting of the Association for Computational Linguistics (Volume 1: Long Papers), pp. 73–82. Association for Computational Linguistics (2013). https://www.aclweb.org/anthology/P13-1008

17. Liu, J., Chen, Y., Liu, K., Zhao, J.: Event detection via gated multilingual attention mechanism. In: Proceedings of the AAAI Conference on Artificial Intelligence, vol. 32 (2018)
18. Nguyen, T.H., Cho, K., Grishman, R.: Joint event extraction via recurrent neural networks. In: Proceedings of the 2016 Conference of the North American Chapter of the Association for Computational Linguistics: Human Language Technologies, pp. 300–309. Association for Computational Linguistics (2016). https://doi.org/10.18653/v1/N16-1034
19. Nguyen, T.H., Grishman, R.: Event detection and domain adaptation with convolutional neural networks. In: Proceedings of the 53rd Annual Meeting of the Association for Computational Linguistics and the 7th International Joint Conference on Natural Language Processing (Volume 2: Short Papers), pp. 365–371. Association for Computational Linguistics (2015). https://doi.org/10.3115/v1/P15-2060
20. Nguyen, T.M., Nguyen, T.H.: One for all: Neural joint modeling of entities and events. In: Proceedings of the AAAI Conference on Artificial Intelligence, vol. 33, pp. 6851–6858 (2019)
21. Oliveira, L.D., Claro, D.B.: Dptoie: a Portuguese open information extraction system based on dependency analysis (2019)
22. Quaresma, P., Nogueira, V.B., Raiyani, K., Bayot, R.: Event extraction and representation: a case study for the Portuguese language. Information 10(6), 205 (2019). https://doi.org/10.3390/info10060205
23. Saurı, R., Littman, J., Knippen, B., Gaizauskas, R., Setzer, A., Pustejovsky, J.: Timeml annotation guidelines version 1.2. 1 (2006)
24. Schuster, M., Paliwal, K.K.: Bidirectional recurrent neural networks. IEEE Trans. Sig. Process. 45(11), 2673–2681 (1997). https://doi.org/10.1109/78.650093
25. Souza, F., Nogueira, R., Lotufo, R.: BERTimbau: pretrained BERT models for Brazilian Portuguese. In: 9th Brazilian Conference on Intelligent Systems, BRACIS, Rio Grande do Sul, Brazil, October 20–23 (2020). https://doi.org/10.1007/978-3-030-61377-8_28
26. Wadden, D., Wennberg, U., Luan, Y., Hajishirzi, H.: Entity, relation, and event extraction with contextualized span representations. In: Proceedings of the 2019 Conference on Empirical Methods in Natural Language Processing and the 9th International Joint Conference on Natural Language Processing (EMNLP-IJCNLP), pp. 5788–5793 (2019). https://doi.org/10.18653/v1/D19-1585
27. Walker, C., Strassel, S., Medero, J., Maeda, K.: Ace 2005 multilingual training corpus. Linguist. Data Consortium Philadelphia 57, 45 (2006)
28. Wu, Y., et al.: Google's neural machine translation system: Bridging the gap between human and machine translation. arXiv preprint arXiv:1609.08144 (2016)
29. Xia, P., et al.: LOME: Large ontology multilingual extraction. In: Proceedings of the 16th Conference of the European Chapter of the Association for Computational Linguistics: System Demonstrations, pp. 149–159. Association for Computational Linguistics (2021). https://aclanthology.org/2021.eacl-demos.19
30. Xiang, W., Wang, B.: A survey of event extraction from text. IEEE Access 7, 173111–173137 (2019)

# mRAT-SQL+GAP: A Portuguese Text-to-SQL Transformer

Marcelo Archanjo José[1]([✉]) [ID] and Fabio Gagliardi Cozman[2] [ID]

[1] Instituto de Estudos Avançados, Universidade de São Paulo and Center for Artificial Intelligence (C4AI), São Paulo, Brazil
marcelo.archanjo@usp.br
[2] Escola Politécnica, Universidade de São Paulo and Center for Artificial Intelligence (C4AI), São Paulo, Brazil
fgcozman@usp.br

**Abstract.** The translation of natural language questions to SQL queries has attracted growing attention, in particular in connection with transformers and similar language models. A large number of techniques are geared towards the English language; in this work, we thus investigated translation to SQL when input questions are given in the Portuguese language. To do so, we properly adapted state-of-the-art tools and resources. We changed the RAT-SQL+GAP system by relying on a multilingual BART model (we report tests with other language models), and we produced a translated version of the Spider dataset. Our experiments expose interesting phenomena that arise when non-English languages are targeted; in particular, it is better to train with original and translated training datasets together, *even* if a single target language is desired. This multilingual BART model fine-tuned with a double-size training dataset (English and Portuguese) achieved 83% of the baseline, making inferences for the Portuguese test dataset. This investigation can help other researchers to produce results in Machine Learning in a language different from English. Our multilingual ready version of RAT-SQL+GAP and the data are available, open-sourced as mRAT-SQL+GAP at: https://github.com/C4AI/gap-text2sql.

**Keywords:** NL2SQL · Deep learning · RAT-SQL+GAP · Spider dataset · BART · BERTimbau

## 1 Introduction

A huge number of data is now organized in relational databases and typically accessed through SQL (Structured Query Language) queries. The interest in automatically translating questions expressed in natural language to SQL (often referred to as NL2SQL) has been intense, as one can observe through a number of excellent surveys in the literature [1–3]. Figure 1 depicts the whole flow from

Supported by IBM and FAPESP (São Paulo Research Foundation).

A. Britto and K. Valdivia Delgado (Eds.): BRACIS 2021, LNAI 13074, pp. 511–525, 2021.
https://doi.org/10.1007/978-3-030-91699-2_35

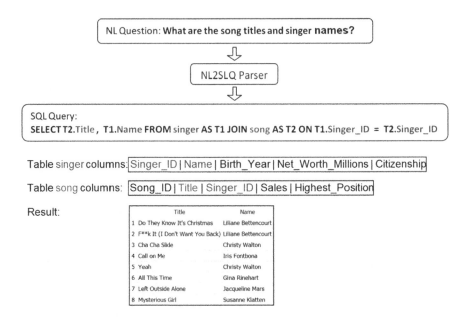

**Fig. 1.** From a natural language question to a SQL query and to the database query result. Database table names appear in blue (singer) and red (song), while the primary key appears in green (Singer_ID). (Color figure online)

a natural language question to a SQL query result; the SQL query refers to database tables and their columns, using primary and secondary keys as appropriate.

Existing approaches for NL2SQL can be divided into entity-based and machine learning ones, the latter dominated by techniques based on deep learning [3].

Entity-based approaches focus on the interpretation of input text based on rules so as to translate it to a SQL query. The translation often goes first to an intermediary state and later to a final SQL query. Relevant systems are Bela [4], SODA [5], NaLIR [6–8], TR Discover [9], Athena [10,11], Athena++ [12] and Duoquest [13,14] .

Machine learning approaches are based on supervised learning, in which training data contains natural language questions and paired SQL queries [3]. Several architectures can be trained or fine-tuned so as to run the translation. Relevant systems are EchoQuery [15], Seq2SQL [41], SQLNet [16], Dial-SQL [17], TypeSQL [18], SyntaxSQLNet [19], AugmentedBI [21], IRNet [22], RAT-SQL [23], RAT-SQL+GAP [24], GraPPa [25], BRIDGE [26], DBPal [27–29], HydraNet [30], DT-Fixup [32] and LGESQL [31].

There are also hybrid approaches that combine entity-based and machine learning [3]; relevant examples are Aqqu [34], MEANS [35] and QUEST [33].

The previous paragraphs contain long lists of references that should suffice to demonstrate that translation from natural language to SQL is a well explored

**Table 1.** NL2SQL benchmarks.

| Dataset | Questions | SQL queries | Databases | Domains | Tables/DB | References |
|---------|-----------|-------------|-----------|---------|-----------|------------|
| ATIS | 5,280 | 947 | 1 | 1 | 32 | [36, 42–45] |
| GeoQuery | 877 | 247 | 1 | 1 | 6 | [36–40] |
| WikiSQL | 80,654 | 77,840 | 26,521 | * | 1 | [41] |
| Spider | 10,181 | 5,693 | 200 | 138 | 5.1 | [20] |

* The WikiSQL has multiple domains, but the organization of one table per database does not allow exploring the complexity of the different domains.

research topic. The field is relatively mature and benchmarks for NL2SQL are now widely used, containing training and testing data and ways to evaluate new proposals. Table 1 shows a few important datasets in the literature, reporting their number of questions, number of SQL queries, number of databases, number of domain and tables per database [20]. Particularly, the Spider dataset is a popular resource that contains 200 databases with multiple tables under 138 domains.[1] The complexity of these tables allows testing complex nested SQL queries. A solid test suite evaluation package for testing against Spider [46] is available;[2] in addition, there is a very active leaderboard rank for tests that use Spider.[3]

Currently, the best result in the Spider leaderboard for *Exact set match without values*, whereby a paper and code are available, is the entry by RAT-SQL+GAP [24].[4] This system appears in the 6th rank position with Dev 0.718 and Test 0.697.[5] Note that the Spider leaderboard, as of August 2021, displays in the 1st rank position LGESQL [31] with Dev 0.751 and Test 0.720 for *Exact set match without values*. Thus RAT-SQL+GAP is arguably at the state-of-art in NL2SQL.

RAT-SQL+GAP is based on the RAT-SQL package (Relation-Aware Transformer SQL) [23]. RAT-SQL was proposed in 2019 as a text to SQL parser based on the BERT language model [47]. Package RAT-SQL version 3 with BERT is currently the 14th entry in the Spider leaderboard rank. RAT-SQL+GAP adds Generation-Augmented Pre-training (GAP) to RAT-SQL. GAP produces synthetic data to increase the dataset size to improve pre-training; the whole generative models are trained by fine-tuning a BART [48] large model.

Despite the substantial number of techniques, systems and benchmarks for NL2SQL, most of them focus on the English language. Very few results can be found for input questions in the Portuguese language, for example. The study by

---

[1] Spider dataset: https://yale-lily.github.io/spider.
[2] Spider test suite evaluation github:https://github.com/taoyds/test-suite-sql-eval.
[3] Spider leaderboard rank: https://yale-lily.github.io/spider.
[4] RAT-SQL+GAP gitHub: https://github.com/awslabs/gap-text2sql.
[5] Dev results are obtained locally by the developer; to get official score and Test results, it is necessary to submit the model following guidelines in "Yale Semantic Parsing and Text-to-SQL Challenge (Spider) 1.0 Submission Guideline" at https://worksheets.codalab.org/worksheets/0x82150f426cb94c17b861ef4162817399/.

Silva et al. [51] presents an architecture for NL2SQL in which natural language questions in Portuguese are translated to the English language on arrival, and are then shipped to NL2SQL existing packages.

The goal of this paper is simple to state: we present a translator for queries in Portuguese natural language into SQL. We intend to study the effect of replacing the questions in the Spider dataset with translated versions, and also to investigate how to adapt the RAT-SQL+GAP system to the needs of a different language. Using a new version of Spider with RAT-SQL+GAP to train models, we produce inferences and compare results so as to understand the difficulties and limitations of various ideas.

What we found is that, by focusing on Portuguese, we actually produced methods and results that apply to any multilingual NL2SQL task. An important insight (and possibly the main contribution of this paper) is dealing with a non-English language, such as Portuguese, *we greatly benefit from taking a multilingual approach that puts together English and the other language*—in our case, English and Portuguese. We later stress this idea when we discuss our experiments. We thus refer to our "multilingual-ready" version of RAT-SQL+GAP as mRAT-SQL+GAP; all code and relevant data related to this system are freely available[6].

## 2   Preliminary Tasks

The adaptation to language other than English demands at least the translation of the dataset and changing the code to read and write files UTF-8 encoding.

### 2.1   Translating the Spider Dataset

The translation to the Portuguese language in the NL2SQL task evolves the natural language part, the questions. The SQL queries must remain the same to make sense. To translate the questions, it is important to extract them from specific .json files. The Spider dataset has three files that contain input questions and their corresponding SQL queries: dev.json, train_others.json, and train_spider.json. We extracted the questions and translated them using the Google Cloud Translation API.[7]. Table 2 presents the number of questions and number of characters per file (just for the questions). The code that reads the original files and that generates translated versions relies on the UTF-8 encoding so as to accept Portuguese characters; several files were generated in the process (.txt just for the translated questions, .csv for the SQL queries and original/translated questions, .json for the translated questions).

We then conducted a revision process by going through the text file and looking for questions in the csv file (together with the corresponding SQL queries). After the revision, a new .json file was generated with these translated and revised questions. Table 3 shows four examples of translated questions.

---

[6]  mRAT-SQL+GAP Github: https://github.com/C4AI/gap-text2sql.
[7]  Cloud Translation API: https://googleapis.dev/python/translation/latest/index. html.

Table 2. Number of questions and characters per file.

| File | Number of questions | Number of characters |
|------|---------------------|----------------------|
| dev.json | 1,034 | 70,362 |
| train_others.json | 1,659 | 80,571 |
| train_spider.json | 7,000 | 496.054 |

Table 3. Translation examples.

| English question | Portuguese question |
|------------------|---------------------|
| How many singers do we have? | Quantos cantores nós temos? |
| Find the number of pets for each student who has any pet and student id. | Encontre o número de animais de estimação para cada aluno que possui algum animal de estimação e a identificação do aluno. |
| How many United Airlines flights go to City 'Aberdeen'? | Quantos voos da United Airlines vão para a cidade de 'Aberdeen'? |
| What is the name of the shop that is hiring the largest number of employees? | Qual é o nome da loja que está contratando o maior número de funcionários? |

**Adapting the RAT-SQL+GAP System.** We had to change the RAT-SQL+ GAP code to allow multilingual processing. For instance, the original Python code is not prepared to handle UTF-8 files; thus, we had to modify the occurrences of "open" and "json.dump" commands, together with a few other changes. We ran a RAT-SQL+GAP test and checked whether all the characters employed in Portuguese were preserved. We also noticed lemmatization errors in preprocessed files. As the original code for RAT-SQL+GAP relies on the Stanford CoreNLP lemmatization tool that currently does not support Portuguese, it was replaced by Simplemma.[8] The latter package supports multilingual texts, and particularly supports Portuguese and English.

**Training.** The original language model at the heart of RAT-SQL+GAP is BART-large[9] [48], a language model pretrained for the English language. We had to change that model to another one that was pretrained for the Portuguese language. A sensible option was to work with a multilingual Sequence-to-Sequence BART model; the choice was mBART-50[10] [50] because it covers Portuguese and English languages (amongst many others). Another language model we investi-

---

[8] Simplemma: a simple multilingual lemmatizer for Python at https://github.com/ adbar/simplemma.

[9] Facebook BART-large: https://huggingface.co/facebook/bart-large.

[10] FacebookmBART-50manyfordifferentmultilingualmachinetranslations:    https:// huggingface.co/facebook/mbart-large-50-many-to-many-mmt.

gated was the BERTimbau-base[11] [49], as RAT-SQL works with BERT; the move to BERTtimbau, a Portuguese-based version of BERT, seemed promising.

**Dataset.** A total of 8,659 questions were used for training (7,000 questions in train_spider.json and 1,659 questions in train_others.json). The 1,034 questions in dev.json were used for testing. We later refer to three scenarios:

- English train and test: questions are just in English for training and testing.
- Portuguese train and test[12]: questions are just in Portuguese for training and testing.
- English and Portuguese (double-size) train and test(see footnote 12): questions are in English and Portuguese for training and testing (in this case, we thus have twice as much data as in each of the two previous individual scenarios).

**Evaluation Metrics.** The main evaluation metric with respect to Spider is Exact Set Match (ESM). We here present results for Exact Set Match (ESM) without values, as most results in the Spider leaderboard currently adopt this metric. Some Spider metrics are also used to classify the SQL queries into 4 levels: easy, medium, hard and extra hard. Table 4 shows an example for each level; these queries correspond to the four questions in Table 3 in the same order.

To evaluate the results, we used the Spider test suite evaluation [46]. An aside: the suite must receive a text file with the SQL query generated and another one with the gold-standard SQL query. These files obviously do not change when we move from English to any other input language.

As a digression, note that it is possible to plug values during evaluation. A query with a value looks like this:

SELECT Count(*) FROM airlines JOIN airports WHERE airports.City = **"Abilene"**

A query without values has the word **"terminal"** instead of the value:

SELECT Count(*) FROM airlines JOIN airports WHERE airports.City = "terminal"

## 3 Experiments

Experiments were run in a machine with AMD Ryzen 9 3950X 16-Core Processor, 64 GB RAM, 2 GPUs NVidia GeForce RTX 3090 24 GB running Ubuntu 20.04.2 LTS. Figure 2 shows the architecture of the training, inference and evaluation processes described in this section.

---

[11] BERTimbau-base: https://huggingface.co/neuralmind/bert-base-portuguese-cased.
[12] Spider dataset translated to Portuguese and double-size (English and Portuguese together): https://github.com/C4AI/gap-text2sql.

**Table 4.** SQL query levels: easy/medium/hard/extra.

| Level | SQL Query |
|-------|-----------|
| Easy | SELECT count(*) FROM singer |
| Medium | SELECT count(*), T1.stuid FROM student AS T1 JOIN has_pet AS T2 ON T1.stuid=T2.stuid GROUP BY T1.stuid |
| Hard | SELECT count(*) FROM FLIGHTS AS T1 JOIN AIRPORTS AS T2 ON T1.DestAirport = T2.AirportCode JOIN AIRLINES AS T3 ON T3.uid = T1.Airline WHERE T2.City = "Aberdeen" AND T3.Airline = "United Airlines" |
| Extra | SELECT t2.name FROM hiring AS t1 JOIN shop AS t2 ON t1.shop_id = t2.shop_id GROUP BY t1.shop_id ORDER BY count(*) DESC LIMIT 1 |

Results can be found in Table 5. This table shows the results of Exact Set Match without Values for RAT-SQL+GAP trained locally for all models. We have 3 datasets, 5 trained model checkpoints and 7 distinct relevant results.

The first line corresponds to the original model BART and original questions in English. Note that the result in line #1 achieved the same performance reported by [24] for *Exact Set Match without values* in Spider: 0.718 (All) for Dev. This indicates that our testing apparatus can produce state-of-the-art results. Moreover, line #1 shows a well-tuned model in English that can be attained.

Our first experiment was to change the questions to Portuguese and the model to BERTimbau-base which is pretrained in Portuguese. In Table 5 the result in line #2 for BERTimbau 0,417(All) is quite low when compared to the result in line #1. This happens for many reasons. The model is BERT and the best result uses BART. Another important difference is that the Portuguese content used in fine-tuning has a mixture of Portuguese and English words because the SQL query inevitably consists of English keywords, see examples of SQL queries in Table 4. In fact, some questions demand untranslated words to make sense, for example "Boston Red Stockings" in the translated question: *Qual é o salário médio dos jogadores da equipe chamada "Boston Red Stockings"?*. This suggested that a multilingual approach might be more successful. The mBART-50 language model was then tested within the whole architecture.

mBART-50 was in fact fine-tuned in three different ways: with questions only in English, only in Portuguese, and with questions both in English and in Portuguese (that is, a dataset with questions and their translations). Inferences were run with English test questions and Portuguese test questions, while the model was fine-tuned with the corresponding training questions language. For the mBART-50 model fine-tuned with the train dataset with two languages, three inferences were made: only English, only Portuguese, and the combined English Portuguese test dataset.

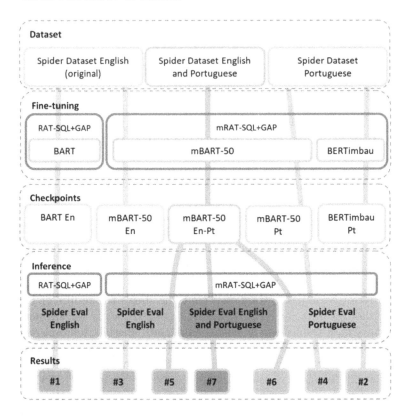

**Fig. 2.** Architecture of the training, inference, evaluation. Results related to Table 5: each line in that table appears here as a square at the bottom of the figure.

mBART-50 fine-tuned with questions in English in line #3 achieved 0.651 (All) when tested with questions in English. The same model mBART-50 fine-tuned with questions in Portuguese in line #4 achieved 0.588(All) when tested with questions in Portuguese.

A multilingual model such as mBART-50 can be trained with the two languages at the same time. This is certainly appropriate for data augmentation and to produce a fine-tuning process that can better generalize. The results in Table 5 lines #5, #6 and #7 were obtained with mBART-50 fine-tuned with the double-size training dataset (English and Portuguese); the three inferences were made using the same model checkpoint. The test datasets were in English for line #5, in Portuguese for line #6, and the double-size test dataset in English and Portuguese for line #7. The results demonstrate improvements, if we compare inferences with English test dataset lines #3 and #5. Results went up from 0.651 (All) to 0.664 (All), better for all levels of questions. If we compare inferences with the Portuguese test dataset in lines #4 and #6, the results went from 0.588 (All) to 0.595 (All). However, they are better just for an easy level of questions; this was enough to influence the overall results for line #6.

**Table 5.** Results.

| # | Model | Train | Infer | Easy 248 | Medium 446 | Hard 174 | Extra 166 | All **1034** |
|---|-------|-------|-------|----------|------------|----------|-----------|--------------|
| 1 | BART | En | En | 0.899 | 0.744 | 0.667 | 0.428 | **0.718** |
| 2 | BERTimbau | Pt | Pt | 0.560 | 0.422 | 0.333 | 0.277 | **0.417** |
| 3 | mBART-50 | En | En | 0.851 | 0.679 | 0.546 | 0.386 | **0.651** |
| 4 | mBART-50 | Pt | Pt | 0.762 | 0.599 | 0.529 | 0.361 | **0.588** |
| 5 | mBART-50 | En/Pt | En | 0.863 | 0.682 | 0.569 | 0.422 | **0.664** |
| 6 | mBART-50 | En/Pt | Pt | 0.827 | 0.596 | 0.511 | 0.331 | **0.595** |
|   | Model | Train | Infer | Easy 496 | Medium 892 | Hard 348 | Extra 332 | All **2068** |
| 7 | mBART-50 | En/Pt | En/Pt | 0.847 | 0.639 | 0.537 | 0.380 | **0.630** |

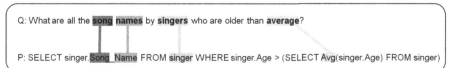

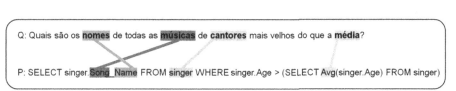

**Fig. 3.** Examples of keywords in the prediction of the SQL query in English and Portuguese languages. Top pair: question in English and corresponding SQL query predicted from it. Bottom pair: question in Portuguese and corresponding SQL query predicted from it.

The inference made with the double-size test dataset in English and Portuguese, in line #7, cannot be compared with the other inferences because they used just one language. Nevertheless, the model mBART-50 trained with English and Portuguese (double-size training dataset) produced good results with this rather uncommon testing dataset.

All the detailed results presented in this paper are openly available[13].

# 4 Analysis and Discussion

These experiments indicate that multilingual pretrained transformers can be extremely useful when dealing with languages other than English. There is

---

[13] mRAT-SQL+GAP Github: https://github.com/C4AI/gap-text2sql.

En Q: What is the series name of the TV Channel that shows the cartoon "The Rise of the Blue Beetle"?

Pt Q: Qual é o nome da série do canal de TV que mostra o desenho animado "The Rise of the Blue Beetle"?

P: SELECT TV_Channel.series_name FROM TV_Channel JOIN Cartoon WHERE Cartoon.Title = terminal

G: SELECT T1.series_name FROM TV_Channel AS T1 JOIN Cartoon AS T2 ON T1.id = T2.Channel
WHERE T2.Title = "The Rise of the Blue Beetle!";

**Fig. 4.** Example of words that represent the value in the prediction of the SQL query. En Q: English question, Pt Q: Question translated to Portuguese, P: SQL query predicted, and G: Gold SQL query.

always the need to integrate English processing with the additional languages of interest, in our case, with Portuguese.

Overall, questions in the English language have a closer similarity with SQL queries, thus simplifying inferences. Conversely, questions in Portuguese require further work. Figure 3 show a real example of correct predictions in English (Table 5 line #5) and in Portuguese (Table 5 line #6). In Fig. 3, words such as **song, names, singers, average** in the English question are keywords needed to resolve the query, and they are very close to the target word in the query. In Portuguese, the same keywords are **músicas, nomes, cantores, média** that must respectively match song, name, singer, and avg. This introduced an additional level of difficulty that explains the slightly worse results for inference with questions in Portuguese: 0.595 (Table 5 line #6). This is to be compared with questions in English: 0.664 (Table 5 line #5). In any case, it is surprising that the same model checkpoint resolved the translation with such different questions.

Some translations actually keep a mix of languages, because some words represent the value and cannot be translated. Figure 4 shows an example. There the show name "The Rise of the Blue Beetle" should not be translated to maintain the overall meaning of the question; these words in English must be part of the Portuguese question. This successful SQL query inference was produced with mBART-50 fine-tuned with the English and Portuguese training dataset (Table 5 line #6) and mBART-50 fine-tuned in the Portuguese-only training dataset (Table 5 line #4). The show name was then replaced with "terminal" during the RAT-SQL+GAP prediction process, as it is processed through the Spider Exact Set Match **without Values** evaluation. In any case, the show name is part of the input and will introduce difficulties in the prediction.

In addition, for real-world databases, it is a practice, at least in Brazil, to name tables and columns with English words even for databases with content in Portuguese. This practical matter is another argument in favor of a multilingual approach.

Figure 5 shows a sample of failed translations evaluated by the Spider Exact Set Match for inferences using mBART-50 (Table 5 line #6). It is actually difficult to find the errors without knowing the database schema related to every query. The objective of this figure is to show that even when the query is incorrect, it is not composed of random or nonsensical words. Our manual analysis indicates that this is true for queries failing with all other models.

**Easy**

Q: Encontre a classificação média dos vencedores em todas as partidas.

P: SELECT Avg(rankings.ranking) FROM rankings

G: SELECT avg(winner_rank) FROM matches

**Medium**

Q: Mostre o nome e o ano de lançamento da música do cantor mais jovem.

P: SELECT singer.Name, singer.Song_release_year FROM singer ORDER BY singer.Age Asc LIMIT 1

G: SELECT song_name , song_release_year FROM singer ORDER BY age LIMIT 1

**Hard**

Q: Descubra o número de shows ocorridos no estádio com maior capacidade.

P: SELECT Count(*) FROM stadium ORDER BY stadium.Capacity Desc LIMIT 1

G: select count(*) from concert where stadium_id = (select stadium_id from stadium order by capacity desc limit 1)

**Extra**

Q: Encontre o modelo do carro cujo peso está abaixo do peso médio.

P: SELECT cars_data.Cylinders FROM cars_data WHERE cars_data.Weight < (SELECT Avg(cars_data.Weight) FROM cars_data)

G: SELECT T1.model FROM CAR_NAMES AS T1 JOIN CARS_DATA AS T2 ON T1.MakeId = T2.Id WHERE T2.Weight < (SELECT avg(Weight) FROM CARS_DATA)

**Fig. 5.** Sample of failed queries evaluated by Spider Exact Set Match for inferences from mBART-50 (Table 5 line #6) . Q: question, P: SQL query predicted, and G: Gold SQL query.

# 5   Conclusion and Future Work

In sum, we have explored the possible ways to create a translator that takes questions in the Portuguese language and outputs correct SQL queries corresponding to the questions. By adapting a state-of-the-art NL2SQL to the Portuguese language, our main conclusion is that a multilingual approach is needed: it is not enough to do everything in Portuguese; rather, we must simultaneously work with English and Portuguese.

In Table 5, our best result is in line #5 0.664 (All) whereby we test with questions in English (original test set from Spider) using mBART-50 model fine-tuned with a double-size training dataset (English and Portuguese). This yields 92% of the English-only performance of 0.718 (All) in line #1. Testing with questions in Portuguese (using our translation) with the same BART-50 model fine-tuned with a double-size training dataset (English and Portuguese), we achieve instead 0.595 (All) line #6. Now this is 83% of the English-only performance of 0.718 (All). These results should work as a baseline for future NL2SQL research in Portuguese.

Our multilingual RAT-SQL+GAP, or mRAT-SQL+GAP for short, the translated datasets, the trained checkpoint, and the results; are open-source available[14].

Future work should try other multilingual transformers (and possibly other seq-to-seq models), always seeking ways to use English and Portuguese together. Another possible future work is to fine-tune BERTimbau-large[15] [49] so as to better understand the effect of the size of the language model. Lastly, a translation of the Spider dataset to other languages so as to work with several languages at the same time should produce valuable insights.

**Acknowledgment.** This work was carried out at the Center for Artificial Intelligence (C4AI-USP), supported by the São Paulo Research Foundation (FAPESP grant #2019/07665-4) and by the IBM Corporation. The second author is partially supported by the Conselho Nacional de Desenvolvimento Científico e Tecnológico (CNPq), grant 312180/2018-7.

# References

1. Kim, H., So, B.H., Han, W.S., Lee, H.: Natural language to SQL: where are we today? Proc. VLDB Endow. **13**, 1737–1750 (2020). https://doi.org/10.14778/3401960.3401970
2. Affolter, K., Stockinger, K., Bernstein, A.: A comparative survey of recent natural language interfaces for databases. VLDB J. **28**, 793–819 (2019). https://doi.org/10.1007/s00778-019-00567-8
3. Ozcan, F., Quamar, A., Sen, J., Lei, C., Efthymiou, V.: State of the art and open challenges in natural language interfaces to data. In: Proceedings of the ACM SIGMOD International Conference on Management of Data, pp. 2629–2636 (2020). https://doi.org/10.1145/3318464.3383128
4. Walter, S., Unger, C., Cimiano, P., Bär, D.: Evaluation of a layered approach to question answering over linked data. In: Cudré-Mauroux, P., et al. (eds.) ISWC 2012. LNCS, vol. 7650, pp. 362–374. Springer, Heidelberg (2012). https://doi.org/10.1007/978-3-642-35173-0_25
5. Blunschi, L., Jossen, C., Kossmann, D., Mori, M., Stockinger, K.: SODA: generating SQL for business users. Proc. VLDB Endow. **5**, 932–943 (2012). https://doi.org/10.14778/2336664.2336667
6. Li, F., Jagadish, H. V: Constructing an interactive natural language interface for relational databases. Proc. VLDB Endow. **8**, 73–84 (2014). https://doi.org/10.14778/2735461.2735468

---

[14] mRAT-SQL+GAP Github: https://github.com/C4AI/gap-text2sql.
[15] BERTimbau-large:    https://huggingface.co/neuralmind/bert-large-portuguese-cased.

7. Li, F., Jagadish, H. V.: NaLIR: an interactive natural language interface for query-ing relational databases. In: Proceedings of the 2014 ACM SIGMOD International Conference on Management of Data, New York, pp. 709–712. ACM (2014). https://doi.org/10.1145/2588555.2594519

8. Li, F., Jagadish, H.V.: Understanding natural language queries over relational databases. ACM SIGMOD Rec. **45**, 6–13 (2016). https://doi.org/10.1145/2949741.2949744

9. Song, D., et al.: TR discover: a natural language interface for querying and analyz-ing interlinked datasets. In: Arenas, M., et al. (eds.) ISWC 2015. LNCS, vol. 9367, pp. 21–37. Springer, Cham (2015). https://doi.org/10.1007/978-3-319-25010-6_2

10. Saha, D., Floratou, A., Sankaranarayanan, K., Minhas, U.F., Mittal, A.R., Özcan, F.: ATHENA: an ontology-driven system for natural language querying over rela-tional data stores. Proc. VLDB Endow. **9**, 1209–1220 (2016). https://doi.org/10.14778/2994509.2994536

11. Lei, C., et al.: Ontology-based natural language query interfaces for data explo-ration. IEEE Data Eng. Bull. **41**, 52–63 (2018)

12. Sen, J., et al.: ATHENA++: natural language querying for complex nested SQL queries. Proc. VLDB Endow. **13**, 2747–2759 (2020). https://doi.org/10.14778/3407790.3407858

13. Baik, C., Arbor, A., Arbor, A., Arbor, A., Jagadish, H.V: Constructing expressive relational queries with dual-specification synthesis. In: Proceedings of the 10th Annual Conference Innovations Data Systems Research (CIDR 2020) (2020)

14. Baik, C., Jin, Z., Cafarella, M., Jagadish, H. V.: Duoquest: a dual-specification system for expressive SQL queries. In: Proceedings of the ACM SIGMOD Inter-national Conference on Management of Data, pp. 2319–2329 (2020). https://doi.org/10.1145/3318464.3389776

15. Lyons, G., Tran, V., Binnig, C., Cetintemel, U., Kraska, T.: Making the case for query-by-voice with echoquery. In: Proceedings of the ACM SIGMOD International Conference on Management of Data, 26-June-20, pp. 2129–2132 (2016). https://doi.org/10.1145/2882903.2899394

16. Xu, X., Liu, C., Song, D.: SQLNet: generating structured queries from natural language without reinforcement learning. arXiv. pp. 1–13 (2017)

17. Gur, I., Yavuz, S., Su, Y., Yan, X.: DialSQL: dialogue based structured query gen-eration. In: ACL 2018–56th Annual Meeting of the Association for Computational Linguistics Proceedings of the Conference (Long Paper 1), pp. 1339–1349 (2018). https://doi.org/10.18653/v1/p18-1124

18. Yu, T., Li, Z., Zhang, Z., Zhang, R., Radev, D.: TypeSQL: knowledge-based type-aware neural text-to-SQL generation. In: NAACL HLT 2018 - 2018 Conference of the North American Chapter of the Association for Computational Linguistics: Human Language Technologies - Proceedings of the Conference, vol. 2, pp. 588–594 (2018). https://doi.org/10.18653/v1/n18-2093

19. Yu, T., Yasunaga, M., Yang, K., Zhang, R., Wang, D., Li, Z., Radev, D.R.: Syn-taxSQLNet: syntax tree networks for complex and cross-domain text-to-SQL task. In: Proceedings of the 2018 Conference on Empirical Methods in Natural Language Processing, pp. 1653–1663. Association for Computational Linguistics, Brussels, Belgium (2018)

20. Yu, T., et al.: Spider: A Large-Scale Human-Labeled Dataset for Complex and Cross-Domain Semantic Parsing and Text-to-SQL Task. arXiv:1809.08887v5 (2018)

21. Francia, M., Golfarelli, M., Rizzi, S.: Augmented business intelligence. In: CEUR Workshop Proceedings, vol. 2324 (2019)

22. Guo, J., et al.: Towards Complex Text-to-SQL in Cross-Domain Database with Intermediate Representation (2019)
23. Wang, B., Shin, R., Liu, X., Polozov, O., Richardson, M.: RAT-SQL: Relation-aware schema encoding and linking for text-to-SQL parsers. arXiv. (2019). https://doi.org/10.18653/v1/2020.acl-main.677
24. Shi, P., et al.: Learning Contextual Representations for Semantic Parsing with Generation-Augmented Pre-Training (2020)
25. Yu, T., et al.: GraPPa: Grammar-Augmented Pre-Training for Table Semantic Parsing (2020)
26. Lin, X.V., Socher, R., Xiong, C.: Bridging Textual and Tabular Data for Cross-Domain Text-to-SQL Semantic Parsing, pp. 4870–4888 (2020). https://doi.org/10.18653/v1/2020.findings-emnlp.438
27. Utama, P., et al.: DBPal: An End-to-end Neural Natural Language Interface for Databases (2018)
28. Basik, F., et al.: DBPal: a learned NL-interface for databases. In: Proceedings of the ACM SIGMOD International Conference on Management of Data, pp. 1765–1768 (2018). https://doi.org/10.1145/3183713.3193562
29. Weir, N., et al.: DBPal: a fully pluggable NL2SQL training pipeline. In: Proceedings of the 2020 ACM SIGMOD International Conference on Management of Data, New York, pp. 2347–2361. ACM (2020). https://doi.org/10.1145/3318464.3380589
30. Lyu, Q., Chakrabarti, K., Hathi, S., Kundu, S., Zhang, J., Chen, Z.: Hybrid ranking network for text-to-SQL. arXiv. pp. 1–12 (2020)
31. Cao, R., Chen, L., Chen, Z., Zhao, Y., Zhu, S., Yu, K.: LGESQL: Line Graph Enhanced Text-to-SQL Model with Mixed Local and Non-Local Relations, pp. 2541–2555 (2021). https://doi.org/10.18653/v1/2021.acl-long.198
32. Xu, P., et al.: Optimizing Deeper Transformers on Small Datasets, pp. 2089–2102 (2021). https://doi.org/10.18653/v1/2021.acl-long.163
33. Bergamaschi, S., Guerra, F., Interlandi, M., Trillo-Lado, R., Velegrakis, Y.: Combining user and database perspective for solving keyword queries over relational databases. Inf. Syst. **55**, 1–19 (2016). https://doi.org/10.1016/j.is.2015.07.005
34. Bast, H., Haussmann, E.: More accurate question answering on freebase. In: Proceedings of the International on Conference on Information and Knowledge Management, 19–23-October 2015, pp. 1431–1440 (2015). https://doi.org/10.1145/2806416.2806472
35. Ben Abacha, A., Zweigenbaum, P.: MEANS: a medical question-answering system combining NLP techniques and semantic Web technologies. Inf. Process. Manag. **51**, 570–594 (2015). https://doi.org/10.1016/j.ipm.2015.04.006
36. Iyer, S., Konstas, I., Cheung, A., Krishnamurthy, J., Zettlemoyer, L.: Learning a neural semantic parser from user feedback. In: ACL 2017–55th Annual Meeting of the Association for Computational Linguistics Proceeding Conference (Long Paper 1), pp. 963–973 (2017). https://doi.org/10.18653/v1/P17-1089
37. Giordani, A., Moschitti, A.: Translating questions to SQL queries with generative parsers discriminatively reranked. In: Coling, pp. 401–410 (2012)
38. Popescu, A.M., Etzioni, O., Kautz, H.: Towards a theory of natural language interfaces to databases. In: International Conference on Intelligent user Interfaces, Proceedings of the IUI, pp. 149–157 (2003). https://doi.org/10.1145/604050.604070
39. Zelle, J.M., Mooney, R.J.: Learning to parse database queries using inductive logic programming. In: Proceedings of the National Conference on Artificial Intelligence, pp. 1050–1055 (1996)

40. Zettlemoyer, L.S., Michael, C.: Learning to map sentences to logical form: structured classification with probabilistic categorial grammars. In: Proceedings of the 21st Conference on Uncertain Artificial Intelligence, UAI 2005, pp. 658–666 (2005)
41. Zhong, V., Xiong, C., Socher, R.: Seq2Sql: Generating Structured Queries From Natural Language Using Reinforcement Learning. arXiv:1709.00103v7. pp. 1–12 (2017)
42. Zettlemoyer, L.S., Collins, M.: Online learning of relaxed CCG grammars for parsing to logical form. In: EMNLP-CoNLL 2007 - Proceedings of the 2007 Joint Conference on Empirical Methods in Natural Language Processing and Computational Natural Language Learning, pp. 678–687 (2007)
43. Price, P.J.: Evaluation of spoken language systems. In: Proceedings of the workshop on Speech and Natural Language - HLT 1990, pp. 91–95. Association for Computational Linguistics, Morristown, NJ, USA (1990). https://doi.org/10.3115/116580.116612
44. Dahl, D.A., et al.: Expanding the scope of the ATIS task 43 (1994). https://doi.org/10.3115/1075812.1075823
45. Hemphill, C.T., Godfrey, J.J., George, R.D.: The ATIS spoken language systems pilot corpus. In: Proceedings of the DARPA Speech and Natural Language Workshop., Hidden Valley, Pennsylvania (1990)
46. Zhong, R., Yu, T., Klein, D.: Semantic evaluation for Text-to-SQL with distilled test suites. arXiv. (2020). https://doi.org/10.18653/v1/2020.emnlp-main.29
47. Devlin, J., Chang, M.W., Lee, K., Toutanova, K.: BERT: pre-training of deep bidirectional transformers for language understanding. In: NAACL HLT 2019–2019 Conference of the North American Chapter of the Association for Computational Linguistics: Human Language Technologies - Proceedings of the Conference, vol. 1, pp. 4171–4186 (2019)
48. Lewis, M., et al.: BART: Denoising Sequence-to-Sequence Pre-training for Natural Language Generation, Translation, and Comprehension (2019)
49. Souza, F., Nogueira, R., Lotufo, R.: BERTimbau: pretrained BERT models for Brazilian Portuguese. In: Cerri, R., Prati, R.C. (eds.) BRACIS 2020. LNCS (LNAI), vol. 12319, pp. 403–417. Springer, Cham (2020). https://doi.org/10.1007/978-3-030-61377-8_28
50. Tang, Y., et al.: Multilingual Translation with Extensible Multilingual Pretraining and Finetuning. arXiv:2008.00401 (2020)
51. da Silva, C.F.M., Jindal, R.: SQL query from portuguese language using natural language processing. In: Garg, D., Wong, K., Sarangapani, J., Gupta, S.K. (eds.) IACC 2020. CCIS, vol. 1367, pp. 323–335. Springer, Singapore (2021). https://doi.org/10.1007/978-981-16-0401-0_25

# Named Entity Recognition for Brazilian Portuguese Product Titles

Diego F. Silva[1(✉)], Alcides M. e Silva[1], Bianca M. Lopes[1],
Karina M. Johansson[1], Fernanda M. Assi[1], Júlia T. C. de Jesus[1],
Reynold N. Mazo[1], Daniel Lucrédio[1], Helena M. Caseli[1], and Livy Real[2]

[1] Federal University of São Carlos, São Carlos, SP, Brazil
{diegofs,daniel.lucredio,helenacaseli}@ufscar.br,
{alcidesms,biancalopes,karina.mayumi,fernanda.malheiros,
juliatcj,reynold.mazo}@estudante.ufscar.br
[2] americanas s.a. Digital Lab, São Paulo, SP, Brazil
livy.coelho@b2wdigital.com

**Abstract.** Improving the interaction between consumers and marketplaces, focusing on reaching higher conversion rates is one of the main goals of e-commerce companies. Offering better results for user queries is mandatory to improve user experience and convert it into purchases. This paper investigates how named entity recognition can extract relevant attributes from product titles to derive better filters for user queries. We conducted several experiments based on MITIE and BERT applied to smartphones/cellphones product titles from the largest Brazilian retail e-commerce. Both of our strategies achieve outstanding results with a general F1 score of around 95%. We concluded that using a classical machine learning pipeline is still more useful than relying on large pre-trained language models, considering the model's throughput and efficiency. Future work may focus on evaluating the scalability and reusability capacity of both approaches.

**Keywords:** Product titles · Named entity recognition · MITIE · BERT · Portuguese

## 1 Introduction

Improving the interaction between consumers and marketplaces, focusing on reaching higher conversion rates is one of the most significant challenges faced by e-commerce companies. In other words, the primary goal in this scenario is to guide the users to purchase the items they are searching in the platform. Therefore, due to the increasing specificity of search, the shopping experience becomes a bottleneck in this scenario, even for big e-commerce companies.

E-commerce shopping becomes a more daily activity than ever. In the pandemic scenario, Brazilian e-commerces saw an increase of 47% of purchases, according to Ebit|Nelson 2020 report[1]. Besides, the product assortment, partic-

---

[1] https://company.ebit.com.br/webshoppers/webshoppersfree.

© Springer Nature Switzerland AG 2021
A. Britto and K. Valdivia Delgado (Eds.): BRACIS 2021, LNAI 13074, pp. 526–541, 2021.
https://doi.org/10.1007/978-3-030-91699-2_36

ularly for marketplaces, is getting more complicated since e-commerce is replacing traditional retail settings, like groceries and health care supply. A traditional marketplace strategy to improve product assortment is to introduce more sellers into the marketplace platform. On the one hand, it makes the consumers' lives easier, since they can acquire their needs in only one platform. On the other hand, it makes the product assortment to be increasingly non-uniform. Product titles broadly vary, either by their sellers or their nature/category.

Consider the following examples from our data to illustrate these problems:

1. *Smartphone Samsung Galaxy A01, 32 GB, 2 GB RAM, Tela Infinita de 5.7",* *Câmera Dupla Traseira 13MP (Principal) + 2MP (Profundidade), Frontal de* *5MP, Bateria de 3000 mAh, Dual Chip, Android - Azul*[2]
2. *Smartphone Moto G9 Play 64 GB Dual Chip Android 10 Tela 6.5" Qualcomm* *Snapdragon 4G Câmera 48MP+2MP+ 2MP - Verde Turquesa*[3]
3. *iPhone SE 128 GB Preto iOS 4G Wi-Fi Tela 4.7" Câmera 12MP + 7MP -* *Apple*[4]

The first title offers the following information: WIT[5] (Smartphone); brand (Samsung); model (Galaxy A01); internal memory (32 GB); display size (5.7"); quality of the cameras (13MP and 5MP); SIM card capacity (Dual chips) and color (Azul – "Blue" in Brazilian Portuguese). In the second example, the brand name is not explicit, but we can find the operational system (Android 10) and processor (Qualcomm Snapdragon) specifications. The last example shows: brand (Apple); model (SE); internal memory (128 GB); color (preto – "black" in Portuguese); display size (4,7") and quality of the cameras (12MP and 7MP).

From these examples, we can see that the titles from a quite common category (Smartphone) do not follow a standard structure and are not even offering the same information. As a consequence, it is very difficult to specify standard search filters that could fit any title or query in this category.

In this scenario, increasing the products' retrieval becomes a difficult challenge. A syntax-based search engine is not enough to make all the assortment accessible to the customer. Commonly, e-commerces web pages offer facets to filter customer queries. It becomes a critical task for offering useful filters, having a uniform, vast, and high-quality product attribute extraction in place [11].

Hence, motivated by improving the human interaction with our e-commerce platform, we investigated how **named entity recognition** could be applied to

---

[2] In English: Samsung Galaxy A01 Smartphone, 32 GB, 2 GB RAM, 5.7" Infinite Screen, 13MP Dual Rear Camera (Main) + 2MP (Depth), 5MP Front, 3000 mAh Battery, Dual Chip, Android - Blue.

[3] In English: Moto G9 Play 64 GB Smartphone Dual Chip Android 10 Screen 6.5" Qualcomm Snapdragon 4G Camera 48MP+2MP+2MP - Turquoise Green.

[4] In English: iPhone SE 128 GB Black iOS 4G Wi-Fi Screen 4.7" 12MP + 7MP Camera - Apple.

[5] WIT stands for "What Is This" and is used to define the product being sold.

identify attributes in product titles of the Smartphone category[6]. We investigated two approaches: MITIE[7] and BERT [6].

From our experiments we found that models trained with MITIE and BERT had very similar results, achieving around 95% in F1 scores. MITIE was chosen as the best one for our scenario due to other advantages such as its prediction latency and required infra-structure.

Thus, the main contributions of this work are:

- The description of an end-to-end approach of corpus annotation, model building and evaluation for attribute-value pairs extraction from product titles;
- The careful comparison of two state-of-the-art models for named entity recognition – MITIE and BERT – in a not well explored domain (e/commerce);
- The addressing of a poorly explored scenario of e-commerce language for Brazilian Portuguese.

This paper is organized as follows. In Sect. 2 we describe the task of named entity recognition and the approaches proposed to perform it. In Sect. 3 we describe the set of attribute products that we found relevant for our problem. The experiments and results are presented in Sect. 4 and Sect. 5 finishes the paper with some final remarks.

## 2   Background and Related Work

**Named Entity Recognition.** (NER) is a subtask of natural language processing (NLP) or information extraction (IE) that tries to identify and classify "named entities" present in unstructured text. Named entities are well-known predefined categories such as people's names (e.g., Bill), organizations (e.g., United Nations), locations (e.g., Brazil), time expressions (e.g., yesterday), quantities (e.g., liter), monetary values (e.g., dollar), among others. In the scope of e-commerce, our named entities will be renamed to **attributes**, and the attributes that are of our interest will be specified in Sect. 3.

As noted by More [11], extracting attributes from product titles in e-/commerce is a difficult task since titles, in this context, lack syntactic structure. For this purpose, the author proposes a NER-based method and demonstrates results on the particular attribute "brand". More's proposal consists of combining Structured Perceptron and Conditional Random Fields to predict BIO (B = begin, I = in, O = out) tags in product titles in English. The author used an automatically labeled (by regex) dataset to train the models and increased its volume and quality by a post-processing step, which includes augmenting a normalization dictionary and manual feedback from domain experts. The author reports a F1-score of 92% for the attribute "brand".

Xu et al. [18] proposed an approach to support value extraction, scaling up to thousands of attributes with no loss of performance. The approach proposed by

---

[6] The Smartphone category encompasses cell phones, smartphones and iPhones sold by the largest Brazilian e-commerce marketplace, B2W Digital.

[7] https://github.com/mit-nlp/MITIE.

those authors uses: (i) a global set of BIO tags, (ii) a model of semantic representation for attributes and titles, and (iii) an attention mechanism to capture the semantic relations. The proposed model processes up to 8,906 attributes with an overall F1 score of 79.12%.

Cheng *et al.* [4] explored NER in the e-commerce context, proposing an end-to-end procedure to query annotation and extraction for English language, using BIO as a sequence tagging format and establishing two important entities to investigate: "brand" and "product type". The annotation process was carried out with 16k queries. The proposed model reached a F1 score of 99.49% for the validation data and 93.30% for the test data.

Real *et al.* [14] presented the use of NER in the process of title generation in the fashion e-commerce context. The experiments showed that using a context-specific human-annotated data set for training, even though small (only 358 examples), achieved an overall F1 score of 71%. The solution proposed uses MITIE.

Recently, one of the greatest revolutions in NLP area was the development of the contextualized language models such as the Bidirectional Encoder Representations from Transformers (BERT) [6]. This language model encodes the text to a vector space where words with similar meanings are close to each other through a series of bidirectional self-attention heads. Unlike other well-known word embedding models, such as GloVe [13] and Word2Vec [10], BERT is capable of embedding words considering their specific contexts. BERT has been used successfully in several NLP tasks as an off-the-shelf solution. To achieve these results, BERT was trained in an unsupervised procedure, using *corpora* that sum up billions of words.

Souza *et al.* [15] trained a BERT-CRF to the NER task on the Portuguese language, and explored feature-based and fine-tuning training strategies for the BERT model. Their fine-tuning approach obtained new state-of-the-art results on the HAREM I dataset [1], improving the F1-score by 1 point on the selective scenario (5 Named Entities classes) and by 4 points on the total scenario (10 classes of Named Entities).

Besides BERT, we also investigate how the well-known MIT Information Extraction tool (MITIE) perform for the extraction of attributes from product titles. Geyer *et al.* [7] used MITIE to recognize named entities on a *corpus* consisting of 5,991 tweets in English, which have been annotated on seven different categories: person, organization, location, event, product, character, and thing. They varied the number of training documents and tested on the remainder of the documents, utilizing 5-fold cross-validation and only in-domain data. Their results showed that training with in-domain data began to show diminishing returns with 500 training documents across all of the entity types other than character and thing.

To the best of our knowledge this is the first work to investigate, in depth, the attribute-value extraction for the e-commerce domain in Brazilian Portuguese.

## 3    Attribute Set

To define which attributes are relevant in Smartphone category, after an initial analysis of Smartphone titles, **10 attributes** were selected for being investigated in this work:

1. **WIT**: WIT stands for "What Is This" and is attached to the expression that better represents the product. In this work, the possible values for this attribute are: "smartphone", "celular" (cell phone), "iphone" and other spelling variations. For example[8]:

   | **Smartphone[wit]** Samsung Galaxy S6 Desbloqueado Preto |
   | --- |

2. **Brand**: The brand is one of the most relevant attributes in a customer query. Common values for this attribute are: "Motorola", "Apple", "Samsung", "Xiaomi", "Blu", among others. For example:

   | Smartphone **Samsung[brand]** Galaxy J7 Prime Dual Chip Android 6.0 Tela 5.5" Octa-Core 1.6 GHz 32GB 4G Câmera |
   | --- |

3. **Model**: The model is also an important attribute for queries in this category and should be extracted in its maximum extension. For example:

   | Sony **Xperia L2 H3321[model]** 32gb Lte 1sim Tela 5.5" Câm.13mp+8mp |
   | --- |

4. **Internal memory**: The internal memory capacity is usually an important attribute for this category and must be extracted together with its unit measure in gigabytes (GB). Common values for this attribute are: 4 GB, 8 GB, 16 GB, 32 GB, 64 GB, 128 GB, 256 GB and 512 GB. For example:

   | iPhone 6S plus Apple **64GB[internal_memory]** Prata Seminovo |
   | --- |

5. **Display size**: The display size should also be extracted with its unit measure in inches ("). The values for this attribute generally range from 4.7" to 6.1". For example:

   | Smartphone Positivo Twist Pro, Dual Chip, Preto Tela **5.7"[display_size]**, 3g+wifi, Android Oreo, 8mp, 32gb |
   | --- |

6. **Processor**: Common values for this attribute are: "Dual-Core", "Quad-Core", "Hexa-Core", "Octa-Core", "Helio", among others. For example:

   | Smartphone Alcatel Pixi4 5" Preto Com Dual Chip Memória 8gb Câmera 8mp 4g **Quad Core[processor]** |
   | --- |

7. **Camera quality**: The quality of the smartphone camera is usually an attribute of great interest to customers. Subsequently, the resolution in megapixels (MP) must be extracted with its unit measure. The values for this attribute usually range from 5.0 MP to 18.0 MP. For example:

---

[8] In this paper, the tags associated with the attributes are presented between brackets and the values associated to them, in bold.

Smartphone Multilaser Ms50g Dual Chip Android 8.1 Tela 5.5 8gb 3g Câmera **8mp[camera_quality]** Bivolt

8. **Color**: When the color of the product appears in the title, it must be extracted as a relevant attribute. For example:

Smartphone Nokia 6.1 dual Android 8.1 Tela 5.5 32GB 16MP - **Branco[color]**

9. **Operating system**: The operational system is an extremely relevant attribute for the smartphone category. The version of the operational system must also be extracted. Common values for this attribute are: "Android", "IOS", "Windows Phone", "Blackberry OS", among others. For example:

Smartphone Asus Zenfone GO Dual Chip **Android 5.1[operational_system]** Tela 5" 16GB 4G Câmera 13MP - Dourado

10. **SIM card capacity**: When the SIM card capacity is present in the title, it must be extracted. The most common value for this attribute is "Dual Chip". For example:

Smartphone Multilaser MS50S, **Dual Chip[sim_card_capacity]**, Branco, Tela 5", 3G+Wi-Fi, Android 6.0, 8MP, 8GB

These are the ten most relevant attributes for the Smartphone category that we found in our database. From this set, we built a small annotated sample and trained supervised named entity recognition approaches, aiming at automatically extracting attribute-value pairs from product titles for the Smartphone category as explained in the Sect. 4.

# 4 Experiments and Results

In this section we describe the corpus used in our experiments and the annotation process (Sect. 4.1) carried out to feed the supervised named entity recognition (NER) approaches we investigated in this work. These approaches are detailed in Sect. 4.2 and their results presented in Sect. 4.3.

It is worth mentioning that we used the source code available in the official open repositories of each specific tool applied here and that the corpus is not freely available due to the americanas s.a.'s police we worked with.

## 4.1 Corpus Pre-processing and Annotation

To analyze the viability of NER to extract attributes from product titles of the Smartphone category, we defined a criterion to select a subset from the original data set of around 7 million products of general categories. We removed from the data set all the products with WIT not labeled as "smartphone", "celular" (cell phone), or "iphone". This selection resulted in a data set of 7,432 products.

From this set, we extracted only the product titles. The titles were, then, pre-processed by performing the following tasks: (i) Conversion of the text to lowercase; (ii) Removal of special characters such as: bars, parentheses, brackets and hyphens; (iii) Tokenization by white space; (iv) Stop words[9] removal; and (v) Removal of duplicate titles.

Then, we removed the outliers[10] by excluding all titles that did not contain "smartphone", "celular" or "iphone" and some possible misspelling variations (such as "smatphone"). In the end, 58 outliers[11] were removed. Most of them were battery cells, biological cells or money bills probably wrongly categorized as "celular" due to the orthographic similarity between the word "celular" (cell phone) and the words "célula" (cell) or "cédula" (bill).

The remaining 7,374 product titles were then clusterized. To start the clustering task, the tokens "smartphone", "celular" and related spelling variants were removed from the data set[12]. Then, the titles were vectorized using the TF-IDF vectorizer, using default parameter values. Using the Elbow Method, the number of clusters was set to be 16 and the Mini Batch K-Means clustering method was executed to group the product titles of the same brand, with a few deviations. The clustering was performed using scikit-learn [12].

From each cluster, 26 items were selected: 13 being the closest to the centroid and 13 being other ones randomly selected. As a result, a total of 416 product titles were selected to be annotated by two linguists. The annotation was performed using the Prodigy [3] tool. A third linguist was responsible for resolving the discrepancy cases. The percentages[13] of agreement between the two annotators can be seen in Table 1.

The annotation of the title "Smartphone blu grand m dual sim 3g 5.0" 5mp 3.2mp prata" is illustrated in Fig. 1 using the Prodigy [3] tool. As a result, the following attributes were marked: WIT (Smartphone), brand (blue grand m), SIM card capacity (dual sim), internal memory (3g), display size (5.0"), camera quality (5mp 3.2mp) and color (prata).

---

[9] Stop words list in Portuguese: de, a, o, que, e, do, da, em, os, no, na, por, as, dos, ao, das, á, ou, ás, com.

[10] Outliers refers to those product titles that do not belong to the Smartphone category.

[11] Examples of removed outliers, in Portuguese: "célula vegetal ampliada aproximadamente 20 mil vezes", "celula carga 10 kg sensor peso arduino" and "cédula foleada ouro 100 euros coleção notas moedas euro".

[12] We didn't remove the token "iphone" and its spelling variations since the format of iPhone titles is very different from the other items in the data set and the experiments removing "iphone" led to results worse than those not removing it.

[13] Since how to measure the inter-annotator agreement of named entities annotation is a debatable task [5], we followed [1] and considered the percentages of agreement as our main metric.

**Fig. 1.** Annotation example using the annotation tool prodigy [3]

**Table 1.** Agreement between the two annotators for each attribute

|  | Equal | Different | Intersection | Total |
|---|---|---|---|---|
| WIT | 386 (93.23%) | 8 (1.94%) | 20 (4.83%) | 414 |
| Brand | 374 (92.41%) | 18 (3.93%) | 14 (3.66%) | 406 |
| Model | 314 (76.96%) | 25 (6.13%) | 69 (16.91%) | 408 |
| Internal memory | 225 (85.51%) | 18 (6.89%) | 20 (7.60%) | 263 |
| Display size | 188 (76.11%) | 12 (4.87%) | 47 (19.02%) | 247 |
| Processor | 28 (73.68%) | 9 (23.68%) | 1 (2.64%) | 38 |
| Camera quality | 164 (88.17%) | 9 (4.85%) | 13 (6.98%) | 186 |
| Color | 291 (91.79%) | 16 (5.04%) | 10 (3.17%) | 317 |
| Operating system | 131 (92.25%) | 7 (4.93%) | 4 (2.82%) | 142 |
| SIM card capacity | 207 (85.90%) | 31 (12.86%) | 3 (1.24%) | 241 |

As Table 1 makes evident, WIT was the attribute with the highest agreement, being labeled equally in 386 of the 414 instances. On the other hand, Processor, Model and Display size were the attributes with the highest disagreement between annotators, with about 73% to 76% of the instances annotated equally.

## 4.2   Experimental Setup

In this section, we describe the tools for NER investigated in this work: BERT and MITIE. BERT is a recent approach which has achieved significant results in many NLP tasks [6]. MITIE, in turn, is an earlier well-known and widely used tool for NER and binary relation extraction. While the former is a neural network based approach, which relies on contextualized word vectors, the latter applies traditional machine learning algorithms and static word embeddings to identify named entities.

**BERT.** (Bidirectional Encoder Representations from Transformers) [6] is a neural approach which outputs deep contextualized language representations derived from unlabeled text. Although training a big BERT model from scratch can be too computationally expensive, pre-trained BERT models can be fine-tuned to several NLP tasks without substantial task-specific architecture modifications.

Some freely available, pre-trained BERT models are: (i) the BERT-base Multilingual Cased[14], which is a pre-trained model for 104 languages including Portuguese; and (ii) BERTimbau-Base[15] [16], which was trained with the Brazilian Portuguese corpus brWaC [17], widely used in open-source projects.

Besides BERTimbau-Base, some pre-trained models are also available for NER [15], which use BERTimbau-Base as a start point and were optimized for NER using HAREM[16] dataset. Two approaches were applied for NER by the BERTimbau authors: the feature-based and the fine-tuning.

In the feature-based approach, a pre-trained model is used as a starting point, but the weights for the BERT's network layers did not change. A Long Short Term Memory (LSTM) layer, when possibly combined with a Conditional Random Fields (CRF) layer, is trained and used to classify the sentences.[17] In the fine-tuning approach, a pre-trained model is also used as a starting point, but its weights are adjusted during the training to achieve better results for NER. Following the fine-tuning approach, it is possible to add a CRF layer at the end of the network to help with sentence classification.

In this work we fine-tuned two models for NER in our dataset: one fine-tuning only with BERTimbau-Base (`BERTimbau`) and another one starting from the BERTimbau-Base trained for NER with HAREM dataset and also adding a CRF layer (`BERTimbau-HAREM`).[18]

To evaluate the robustness of these methods to random variations, two random seeds (`seed1` and `seed2`) were extracted from the data set for generating training (50%), validation (25%) and test (25%) partitions. In total, 4 models were trained using the BERT approach: `BERTimbau` in `seed1`, `BERTimbau` in `seed2`, `BERTimbau-HAREM` in `seed1` and `BERTimbau-HAREM` in `seed2`. For both pre-trained BERT models, the hyperparameters used were the default values.

**MITIE.** (MIT Information Extraction) framework[19] [9] was designed to be a simple, easy and intuitive tool with no parameters. The current version of MITIE includes tools for performing NER, binary relationship extraction, as well as tools for training custom models.

The MITIE NER model uses the WordRep benchmark for building word representations (word embeddings), word morphology and traditional machine

---

[14] https://huggingface.co/bert-base-multilingual-cased/tree/main.

[15] https://github.com/neuralmind-ai/portuguese-bert.

[16] https://www.linguateca.pt/HAREM/.

[17] From previous experiments, we concluded that the feature-based models as well as the ones trained with the multilingual BERT did not reach results as good as the fine-tuned models trained with BERTimbau-Base, so these options are not described here.

[18] These two configurations were the ones which achieved the best results in previous experiments with product tiles from Fashion category.

[19] https://github.com/mit-nlp/MITIE.

learning algorithms such as Structural Support Vector Machines [8]. MITIE comes with some previously generated word embeddings for English, Spanish and German. In our experiments we generated new word embeddings, using WordRep, which is publicly available in the MITIE repository [2]. We used a dataset containing around 7 thousand titles from the Smartphone category. This word representation was called `celular`.

The same seeds (`seed1` and `seed2`) used for training BERT NER models were also used for training MITIE NER models with one difference: MITIE does not explicitly use a validation set. Thus, the seeds were divided only into training and test, following the proportion of 75% for training and 25% for testing. In this way, the training instances of MITIE correspond to the training and the validation instances used by BERT, and the test cases are the same for both models.

In addition to the `celular` word representation created in this work, existing ones for English (`English`) and Spanish (`Spanish`) available with MITIE were also used. We also generated a huge word representation from 7.5 million titles for products from diverse categories (not only Smarthphone). This representation was called `all`. Finally, we also generated two versions of the `celular` word representation removing the titles from `seed1` (`cel-seed1`) and `seed2` (`cel-seed2`). Ergo, ten different models were trained in total using these 6 word representations.

### 4.3   Results

In this section we present the results for BERT and MITIE separately, then a comparison of both approaches will be made in the next section by drawing some conclusions about their performances on solving the investigated problem.

**BERT Results.** As described in Sect. 4.2, two BERT models were fine-tuned for NER (attribute extraction) in product titles: the original BERTimbau (`BERTimbau`) and the BERTimbau trained for NER with the HAREM dataset and a CRF layer (`BERTimbau-HAREM`).

Table 2 shows that the BERT models present F1 scores of around 94–95%, proving to be very robust independently of the random seed, indicating the absence of overfitting.

**Table 2.** F1 scores for BERT models in test set

|        |              | BERTimbau | BERTimbau-HAREM |
|--------|--------------|-----------|-----------------|
| seed 1 | Micro-AVG F1 | 0.9394    | 0.9325          |
|        | Macro-AVG F1 | 0.9399    | 0.9323          |
| seed 2 | Micro-AVG F1 | **0.9496** | 0.9387         |
|        | Macro-AVG F1 | **0.9495** | 0.9382         |

It is interesting to notice that, although by a little difference, the model fine-tuned from the BERTimbau-Base performed better than the one fine-tuned from a version trained for NER in HAREM dataset.

Table 3 provides the detailed results for the best scenario: the BERTimbau model in the test set of seed2. The "support" column indicates the amount of evaluated instances in each class. The classes with the worst F1 scores were *Model* and *Processor*. The former one, probably due to labelling errors for the boundaries of the entity and the latter one maybe due to the small amount of training instances (less than 40).

**MITIE Results.** As described in Sect. 4.2, ten MITIE models were trained using 6 different word representations: English, Spanish, all, celular, cel-/seed1 and cel/seed2. Table 4 shows the F1 scores for these models.

**Table 3.** Detailed evaluation of BERTimbau fine-tuned with seed2 in the test set

|  | Precision | Recall | F1 | Support |
|---|---|---|---|---|
| WIT | 1.0000 | 0.9905 | 0.9952 | 105 |
| Brand | 0.9898 | 0.9700 | 0.9798 | 100 |
| Model | 0.8224 | 0.8381 | 0.8302 | 105 |
| Internal memory | 0.9722 | 0.9859 | 0.9790 | 71 |
| Display size | 0.9571 | 0.9853 | 0.9710 | 68 |
| Processor | 1.0000 | 0.7500 | 0.8571 | 12 |
| Camera quality | 0.9394 | 0.9841 | 0.9612 | 63 |
| Color | 0.9778 | 0.9462 | 0.9617 | 93 |
| Operating system | 0.9744 | 0.9048 | 0.9383 | 42 |
| SIM card capacity | 0.9552 | 0.9697 | 0.9624 | 66 |
| Micro-AVG | 0.9515 | 0.9476 | 0.9496 | 725 |
| Macro-AVG | 0.9525 | 0.9476 | 0.9495 | 725 |

**Table 4.** F1 scores for the MITIE models in test set

|  |  | English | Spanish | all | celular | cel-seed1 | cel-seed2 |
|---|---|---|---|---|---|---|---|
| seed 1 | Micro-AVG F1 | **0.9359** | 0.9324 | 0.9290 | 0.9325 | 0.9351 | – |
|  | Macro-AVG F1 | **0.9352** | 0.9300 | 0.9328 | 0.9335 | 0.9306 | – |
| seed 2 | Micro-AVG F1 | 0.9396 | 0.9390 | 0.9378 | **0.9453** | – | 0.9397 |
|  | Macro-AVG F1 | 0.9428 | 0.9448 | 0.9441 | **0.9492** | – | 0.9466 |

From F1 scores we can see, again, that the values obtained for seed1 and seed2 are very close – again around 94–95%. Regarding the wordreps (word embeddings), the **English** and **celular** were the ones with best results and removing the titles from **seed1** or **seed2** did not significantly impact the results. Thus, it is possible to conclude that having the titles used in training for the generation of the word representations did **not** significantly bias the model. Therefore, the model trained with **celular** for **seed2** was the one chosen for further analysis.

In order to do that, Table 5 presents the detailed results for the evaluation of the MITIE model trained with **celular** and **seed2** in the test set. It can be noticed that, as happened with the BERT models, the MITIE model also performed poorly in the *Model* class. Again, we believe that this is due to entity labelling errors.

**Example.** To finish our results and discussion section, Table 6 shows the MITIE's predictions output by the model trained with **celular** and **seed2** for the three product titles:

1. *smartphone samsung galaxy j6, 32 GB, dual chip, android, tela 5.6 pol, octa core, 4g, 13mp, tv prat;*
2. *iphone 7 apple, ouro rosa, tela 4.7", 4g+wifi, ios 11, 12mp, 32 GB;*
3. *celular up 3 chip quad cam mp3 4 fm preto cinza p3274 multilaser*

**Table 5.** Detailed evaluation of the MITIE using **celular** and **seed2** in the test set

|                    | Precision | Recall | F1     | Support |
|--------------------|-----------|--------|--------|---------|
| WIT                | 0.9905    | 0.9905 | 0.9905 | 105     |
| Brand              | 0.9706    | 0.9900 | 0.9802 | 100     |
| Model              | 0.8462    | 0.8381 | 0.8421 | 105     |
| Internal memory    | 0.9571    | 0.9437 | 0.9504 | 71      |
| Display size       | 0.9848    | 0.9559 | 0.9701 | 68      |
| Processor          | 1.0000    | 0.9167 | 0.9565 | 12      |
| Camera quality     | 0.9677    | 0.9836 | 0.9756 | 61      |
| Color              | 0.9140    | 0.9140 | 0.9140 | 93      |
| Operating system   | 1.0000    | 0.9048 | 0.9500 | 42      |
| SIM card capacity  | 0.9420    | 0.9848 | 0.9636 | 66      |
| Micro-AVG          | 0.9472    | 0.9433 | 0.9453 | 723     |
| Macro-AVG          | 0.9573    | 0.9422 | 0.9492 | 723     |

The only differences between BERT and MITIE's outputs for these examples were: for title 1, BERT did not output a value for *Color* attribute; for title 2, in the *Internal Memory*, the only output of BERT was "32 GB" and the "ios 11" was tagged as *Operating system*. For title 3, "quad" token was tagged as *Brand*, the *Display size* attribute was left empty, and the *Model* attribute values were "up" and "p3274".

**Table 6.** Examples of MITIE's predictions using `celular` and `seed2`

|                   | Title 1       | Title 2              | Title 3             |
|-------------------|---------------|----------------------|---------------------|
| WIT               | Smartphone    | iphone               | Celular             |
| Brand             | Samsung       | Apple,               | Multilaser          |
| Model             | Galaxy j6,    | 7                    | "up","4 fm"         |
| Internal memory   | 32 GB,        | "4g+wifi", "32 GB"   | –                   |
| Display size      | 5.6 pol,      | 4.7",                | 4 fm                |
| Processor         | Octa core,    | –                    | quad                |
| Camera quality    | 13mp,         | 12mp,                | –                   |
| Color             | prat          | "ouro", "rosa"       | "preto", "cinza"    |
| Operating system  | Android,      | –                    | –                   |
| SIM card capacity | Dual chip,    | -                    | 3 chip              |

### 4.4   Comparison Between the Models

Figure 2 shows a graph of F1 scores for the best BERT (`BERTimbau` in `seed2`) and MITIE (trained with `celular` and `seed2`) models.

As we can see from Fig. 2, the performances are very close with little highlights to: `BERTimbau` in *Color* class and MITIE `celular` in *Processor* class. In fact, it is worth highlighting the good performance of the MITIE model in the *Processor* class, which has only less than 40 training instances.

Regarding the **training time**, we can point out that , when using the CPU, both MITIE and BERT took a considerable amount of time, however **MITIE was still faster than BERT**. BERT took around 7 h against 5 h from MITIE to train each model. However, the BERT training can be speed up using GPUs as accelerators: **with a median GPU, the fine-tuning of BERTimbau took only 28 min**.

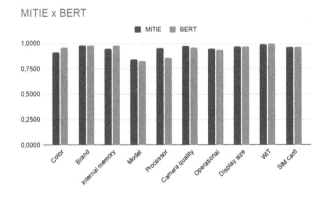

**Fig. 2.** Comparison of F1 scores for the best models (`BERTimbau` and MITIE trained with `celular`) trained with `seed2` in the test set

Regarding the **prediction latency** (that is, the time for inferring new enti-ties), the `BERTimbau` model took **97 min and 15 s** to infer all the entities in the dataset containing 7,374 titles running (only on CPU) in a machine with a Intel(R) Xeon(R) Silver 4210 CPU @ 2.20 GHz processor and 40 cores. Using a GPU Gigabyte NVIDIA GeForce RTX 2060 Windforce OC (6 GB), the time needed to finish all inferences decreased considerably: the model took only **11 min e 52 s** to complete the inference for the same set of 7,374 instances.

On the other hand, for the same dataset and the same CPU machine, the MITIE model trained with `celular` and `seed2` took approximately **3.64 s** to make all the inferences, showing an extremely better throughput when compared to BERT model. This mean 4 s from MITIE × 11 min from BERT. So, MITIE offers not only accuracy, but also efficiency as had already been pointed out as one of its great advantages by its developers.

Regarding the **size of the model** when stored on disk, BERT uses an average of 1.3 GB to store the model as a whole. For MITIE, the storage size of the model varies a lot and it is directly proportional to the size of the word representation used. For `English`, `Spanish` and `all` the model sizes are around 338 MB, for `celular`, `cel-seed1` and `cel-seed2`, the final size of the models is about 29 MB. In light of that, **the MITIE model wins again when the size of the model is considered**.

In general, both BERT and MITIE models achieved satisfactory results on the pursued task. The difference in F1 score between these methods is not signifi-cant. However, a few points need to be considered. First, MITIE performs better where BERT achieved the worst scores. Specifically in the processor and model classes. In the classes where BERT performs slightly better than MITIE, the differences are minor, and the scores obtained by MITIE were considered ade-quate. Moreover, the computational resources required by MITIE are notably lower than those demanded by BERT. Considering these points and, particularly, the fact that the prediction latency is crucial for the application, we considered the **MITIE model trained on `celular` and `seed2`** as the most appropriate to generate the standardization dictionary that will give rise to search filters for the Smartphone category.

## 5    Final Remarks

This paper addressed the problem of attribute-value extraction from product titles of the Smartphone category in Brazilian Portuguese. By automating this process, the e-commerce companies are able to have a unified treatment to their product assortment, improving query matching, product recommendation and the use of facets to enhance product discoverability.

Several models were investigated in this paper based on BERT and MITIE approaches. After a careful analysis based on accuracy and efficiency, we con-cluded that, for our scenario, a solution based on MITIE is still more interesting than one based on pre-trained language models.

As future work, we want to investigate how scalable our approach is: would a MITIE-based model still get competitive accuracy when applied to different categories? Considering a sparsely annotated data scenario, which approach would be quick to deploy, keeping high-quality predictions? All in all, a question that remains is, across the 35MI products americanas s.a. sells now, will a classical machine learning approach still be competitive with deep learning approaches?

**Acknowledgment.** This paper and the research behind it would not have been possible without the support of americanas s.a. Digital Lab, specially José Pizani, Ester Campos and Thiago Gouveia Nunes, who closely followed this research. This work is part of the project "Dos dados ao conhecimento: extração e representação de informação no domínio do e-commerce" (Projeto de extensão - UFSCar #23112.000186/2020-97).

# References

1. HAREM linguateca datasets. https://www.linguateca.pt/HAREM/. Accessed 08 Jan 2021
2. Repositório oficial - MITIE. https://github.com/mit-nlp/MITIE
3. Prodigy: An annotation tool for AI, machine learning, and NLP (2017). https://prodi.gy. Accessed 08 Jan 2021
4. Cheng, X., Bowden, M., Bhange, B.R., Goyal, P., Packer, T., Javed, F.: An end-to-end solution for named entity recognition in ecommerce search. arXiv preprint arXiv:2012.07553 (2020)
5. Deleger, L., et al.: Building gold standard corpora for medical natural language processing tasks. In: AMIA Annual Symposium Proceedings (2012)
6. Devlin, J., Chang, M.W., Lee, K., Toutanova, K.: BERT: pre-training of deep bidirectional transformers for language understanding. In: Conference of the North American Chapter of the Association for Computational Linguistics, pp. 4171–4186 (2019)
7. Geyer, K., Greenfield, K., Mensch, A.C., Simek, O.: Named entity recognition in 140 characters or less (2016)
8. Joachims, T., Finley, T., Yu, C.J.: Cutting-plane training of structural SVMs. Mach. Learn. **77**, 27–59 (2009)
9. King, D.E.: Dlib-ml: a machine learning toolkit. J. Mach. Learn. Res. **10**, 1755–1758 (2009)
10. Mikolov, T., Sutskever, I., Chen, K., Corrado, G.S., Dean, J.: Distributed representations of words and phrases and their compositionality. In: Burges, C., Bottou, L., Welling, M., Ghahramani, Z., Weinberger, K. (eds.) Advances in Neural Information Processing Systems 26, pp. 3111–3119 (2013)
11. More, A.: Attribute extraction from product titles in ecommerce. In: Workshop on Enterprise Intelligence - ACM SIGKDD Conference on Knowledge Discovery and Data Mining (2016)
12. Pedregosa, F., et al.: Scikit-learn: machine learning in Python. J. Mach. Learn. Res. **12**, 2825–2830 (2011)
13. Pennington, J., Socher, R., Manning, C.D.: GloVe: global vectors for word representation. In: Empirical Methods in Natural Language Processing, vol. 14, pp. 1532–1543 (2014)

14. Real, L., Johansson, K., Mendes, J., Lopes, B., Oshiro, M.: Generating e-commerce product titles in Portuguese. In: Anais do XLVIII Seminário Integrado de Software e Hardware, pp. 299–304. SBC, Porto Alegre, RS, Brasil (2021). https://doi.org/10.5753/semish.2021.15835. https://sol.sbc.org.br/index.php/semish/article/view/15835

15. Souza, F., Nogueira, R., Lotufo, R.: Portuguese named entity recognition using BERT-CRF. arXiv preprint arXiv:1909.10649 (2019). http://arxiv.org/abs/1909.10649

16. Souza, F., Nogueira, R., Lotufo, R.: BERTimbau: pretrained BERT models for Brazilian Portuguese. In: 9th Brazilian Conference on Intelligent Systems, BRACIS, Rio Grande do Sul, Brazil, October 20–23 (2020)

17. Wagner, J., Wilkens, R., Idiart, M., Villavicencio, A.: The brWaC corpus: a new open resource for Brazilian Portuguese. In: International Conference on Language Resources and Evaluation, pp. 4339–4344 (2018)

18. Xu, H., Wang, W., Mao, X., Jiang, X., Lan, M.: Scaling up open tagging from tens to thousands: comprehension empowered attribute value extraction from product title. In: Annual Meeting of the Association for Computational Linguistics, pp. 5214–5223 (2019). https://doi.org/10.18653/v1/P19-1514

# Portuguese Neural Text Simplification Using Machine Translation

Tiago B. de Lima[1][✉] [ID], André C. A. Nascimento[1][✉], George Valença[1],
Pericles Miranda[1][✉], Rafael Ferreira Mello[1][✉], and Tapas Si[2][✉]

[1] Universidade Federal Rural de Pernambuco, Rua Dom Manuel de Medeiros,
Recife, Pernambuco 52171-900, Brazil
{tiago.blima,andre.camara,george.valenca,rafael.mello}@ufrpe.br
[2] Bankura Unnayani Institute of Engineering, Subhankar Nagar, Bankura,
Pohabagan 722146, West Bengal, India

**Abstract.** Automatic Text Simplification (ATS) has played a significant
role in the Natural Language Processing (NLP) field. ATS is a sequence-
to-sequence problem aiming to create a new version of the original text
removing complex and domain-specific words. It can improve communication and understanding of documents from specific domains, as well
as support second language learning. This paper presents an empirical
study on the use of state-of-the-art ATS methods to simplify texts in
Portuguese. It is important to remark that the literature reports the challenge in analyzing Portuguese texts due to the lack of resources compared
to other languages (i.e., English). More specifically, this work evaluated
different Neural Machine Translation (NMT) techniques for ATS in Portuguese. The experiments showed that NMT achieved promising results
in Portuguese texts, obtaining 40.89 BLEU score using multiple parallel
corpora and raising the overall readability score by more than 5 points.

**Keywords:** Text simplification · Machine Translation · Deep
learning · Natural Language Processing

## 1 Introduction

Automatic Text Simplification (ATS) aims to transform complex sentences into
simpler ones, which supports second language learners and improves communication with people with poor literacy, among other benefits [4]. ATS can be
applied to multiple domains. For instance, it could simplify legal documents
transforming jargon-heavy and juridic terms into more accessible vocabulary,
making the document more understandable by the general public [9]. Hence,
there a lot of opportunities for ATS techniques in institutions from the public
sector, which needs to make their public documents more accessible and reinforce
their relevance and transparency.

ATS has been an active research topic over the years with several applications [28]. In this context, José and Finatto expressed that the demand for text

© Springer Nature Switzerland AG 2021
A. Britto and K. Valdivia Delgado (Eds.): BRACIS 2021, LNAI 13074, pp. 542–556, 2021.
https://doi.org/10.1007/978-3-030-91699-2_37

simplification in Brazil has increased over the years [16]. One of the main reasons for that is the growing need to make specific concepts accessible for a wider range of people. The authors also made an investigation about the language used in the documents provided by the Ministry of Health of Brazil. They found two kinds of documents describing the same disease. The first one is directed to health professionals and, therefore, has a particular domain-specific vocabulary. In the other class of documents, focused on the general public, a "simplified version" is provided. Nevertheless, there are still terms that are not usual among the less educated, such as "mucus". Besides that, the manual simplification of complex text is not scalable, thus, ATS alternatives should be investigated thoroughly [16].

In the past decade, Portuguese ATS had a significant expansion with systems using lexical and syntactical simplification and Statistical Machine Translation (SMT) methods [3,4,30]. For instance, Specia [30] proposed a SMT model to simplify text in Portuguese using only a few examples. It achieved acceptable adequacy and fluency [30]. However, these studies were developed more than ten years ago, before the advent of Neural Networks architectures for NLP tasks. Therefore, even though deep learning algorithms are a trend of the field, they still have limited applications in Portuguese ATS. For instance, Neural Machine Translation (NMT) is a recent method for text simplification which directly transforms complex sentences in simpler ones without any need of syntactical or lexical analysis [2]. NMT has gained popularity due to its well succeed results on simplification in a variety of domains [2]. Moreover, different companies have used NMT methods in their services, such as Google Translate, Microsoft Translator, IBM Watson Language Translator [13,27,37].

MT-based ATS methods, such as NMT, usually use a parallel corpus to map hard-to-read sentences to simpler ones. Besides, it is domain-independent, i.e., one can use a larger parallel corpus to train an ATS model and then apply the same model on texts from a different domain with regards to its performance [8, 12,32]. It is important to highlight that NMT methods have presented successful results and outperformed consolidated statistical methods [2]. According to our knowledge, no research has investigated the application of NMT methods to simplify Brazilian Portuguese texts.

Based on this scenario, this study investigates and assesses the use of state-of-the-art methods based on NMT to simplify documents written in Brazilian Portuguese automatically. This paper presents an empirical evaluation of NMT Models in a parallel corpus extracted from complex and simplified translations of the Bible to reach this goal. The results demonstrated that the use of NMT in Portuguese text simplification is promising, with a wide range of practical applications. These findings can improve text accessibility for more people, fostering the democratisation of information.

This paper is organised as follows. Section 2 introduces basic concepts about NMT and the methods adopted in this work. Section 3 presents works related to the ATS problem. In Sect. 4, materials and methods are detailed. Section 5 presents the results and discussion. Finally, Sect. 6 states the conclusion and future works.

## 2   Background

This paper explores the use of NMT models using mono language translation to simplify texts in Portuguese. Herein, we briefly introduce Recurrent Neural Networks (RNNs), NMT, and the methods considered in this work, i.e., an Attention-based model and a Bidirectional Recurrent Neural Network (B-RNN) with an Attention layer.

A RNN main advantage is to learn temporal information, even though it can be used in a non-temporal context [20]. In the case of machine translation, it usually works with a combination of encoder-decoder architectures in which both of them use RNN [20,34]. An encoder is responsible for transforming the input in a context vector summarising its information after T recursive updates [25]. The decoding process takes the dummy input and generates recursively the output feeding the next output with the previous output generated [25]. In this paper, we consider a specific RNN type called Bidirectional Recurrent Neural Network (B-RNN), in which the encoder is not only able to predict based on the past inputs but also in the future ones [20]. It produces a feed-forward sequence $(f_1, f_2, \ldots, f_n)$ and a backward sequence $(b_1, b_2, \ldots, b_n)$ such that h = [f, b] is the concatenation of them [20].

A significant advancement on RNN was the proposal of the attention mechanism [6]. This mechanism allows a sequence-to-sequence model to pay attention to key parts of the target sequence. Consequently, it permits the model to learn the correct alignment of the sentences [6]. Studies have stated that attention mechanisms significantly improve the model performance on long sentences and improve the model soft-alignment [6]. Consequently, it had a considerable impact on improving the results of machine translation [6]. In this work, we used a B-RNN using an attention layer as one of the algorithms to be analysed in the ATS problem for Portuguese.

More recently, it was proposed a method called *Transformer*, which is based solely on attention layers, dispensing with recurrence and convolutions entirely [33]. The *Transformer* follows a general sequence-to-sequence architecture based on encoder-decoder [33]. The basic encoder format is a stack of N layers followed by two sub-layers, the self-attention, and the multi-head attention. Also, the encoder has a normalization layer and a residual connection [33]. The decoder follows a similar design using a stack of N layers with sub-layers and normalization with multi-head attention and residual connections [33]. The attention implementation proposed by [33] consists of a scaled dot product attention where the key (K), queries (Q) are vectors (V) of dimension $d_k$ and values are vectors of dimension $d_v$ [33]. Therefore, the attention to each output is calculated as given by Eq. 2 where $\frac{1}{\sqrt{d_k}}$ is the scaling factor.

$$Attention(Q, K, V) = softmax(\frac{QK^T}{\sqrt{d_k}})V. \tag{1}$$

In practice, the model makes use of multi-head attention to learn different parts of the representation and in different positions [33]. Besides, attention is used both in decoder and encoder and in a self-attention manner [33]. In addition to attention, the models also use a fully connected position-wise feed-forward with positional encoding layer also [33].

The *Transformer* experimental results showed that only attention models overcame RNNs in quality and required significantly less time to train as in the on two machine English-French translation tasks [33]. The development of Transformer allowed the development of new promising models such as Bidirectional Encoder Representations from Transformers (BERT) and many others [33]. Due to its relevant results, the Transformer was considered in our experiments as one of the algorithms to be analysed in the ATS problem for Portuguese.

## 3  Related Works

ATS is a relevant task, with a growing interest in Natural Language Processing field in recent years. This section presents relevant methods developed, over the last decade, for the ATS problem for Brazilian Portuguese.

Recently, the ATS problem has been addressed as a monolingual machine translation problem, where a given text is translated into a simpler one. There are two relevant machine translation approaches: statistical machine translation (SMT) and neural machine translation (NMT). In the SMT, the translation of the original sentence $f$ (called the translation model) into a sentence $e$ (called the language model) is modelled on the Bayes Theorem as detailed in [1]. The research carried out by [30] treated the ATS problem of Portuguese texts as a translation task. The authors adopted the SMT approach to learning how to translate complex sentences into simple ones. The SMT was trained with a parallel corpus of original and simplified texts, aligned at the sentence level. The translations produced were evaluated using the metrics (Bilingual Evaluation Understudy) BLEU and manual inspection. According to both evaluations, the results were promising, and the overall sentence quality is not harmed. It was observed that some types of simplification operations, mainly lexical, are correctly captured.

In summary, despite all the advancements, there is still a gap in studies on the applications of NMT to Portuguese. NMT is a recently developed deep learning technique that has reached significant results over several complex tasks [2,6,23,34,39]. According to [2], NMT based methods have shown a better alternative than SMT techniques for translation problems. Although several works employed NMT for text simplification [2,10,23,26,32], no work has applied it in Portuguese texts. To the best of our knowledge, the last works in automatic text simplification in Portuguese was done more than ten years ago [3,4,30], and used SMT. Thus, this paper aims to explore state-of-the-art NMT methods for text simplification in Portuguese.

## 4  Materials and Methods

This section details the dataset, methods, experimental methodology and evaluation metrics of this work.

### 4.1 Data Description

This work adopted a parallel corpus based on different versions of the bible to evaluate the NMT methods. The first one is a traditional version called Almeida Revista e Corrigida (ARC), published in 1997, with a complex text style. The newer version, called Nova Almeida Atualizada (NAA), was launched in 2017, simplifying the traditional version[1]. In this paper, we also evaluated other versions of the bible, such as the Nova Tradução Linguagem de Hoje (NLTH), Nova Bíblia Viva (NBV) and the Nova Versão Internacional (NVI). Considering a diverse range of versions might provide different simplification types as explored in the *Porsimples* project [4].

Each dataset has 29070 aligned verses, which will be used to create the proposed sequence-to-sequence model. Table 1 provides more information about the corpora used in this study including number of tokens, sentences, readability and Lexical Diversity (extracted using pylinguistic library [7]). In that library, the readability ease (FRE) score was proposed by [17] and adapted to Portuguese by [22] (see Eq. 2).

$$FRE = 206.835 - (1.015 * ASL) - (84.6 * ASW) \qquad (2)$$

It adds 42 more points to the equation proposed by [22] because Portuguese words has more syllable then English ones and therefore, the score would be too penalised. ASL means the average sentence length and AWS means average number of syllables per word. Complex and Simplified Portuguese texts tend to have key differences. One of them is the size of each sentence and the number of tokens per sentence, as pointed out by a previous work, the *Porsimples* project, which manually simplified a newspapers corpus. The study found that, in most cases, the simplified versions had fewer words per sentence [4]. This was also observed in both versions of the bible.

In a random sample of 292 pairs of verses (0.01% of the original dataset), we analysed different aspects of the versions of the bible. The Table 1 and Fig. 1 shows the difference between the traditional ARC versions and the other ones.

Figure 1 shows the histograms stating the frequency of the number of tokens per sentence of each Bible. The simplified versions of the Bible have fewer tokens per sentence, with more sentences under the median. The distribution of tokens per sentence in the ARC is smoother, and it has a prevalence of longer sentences (i.e., more tokens per sentence). It is considerably different from the other versions, specially NLTH and NBV. The difference is even greater from the ARC to the NLTH version in almost all aspects, such as average tokens per sentence and median sentence length. Thus, both features indicate that the NLTH and the other versions are easier to read because it has fewer tokens per sentences and more sentences.

---

[1] versions are available at: http://altamiro.comunidades.net/biblias.

**Table 1.** The table shows descritive statistics on texts using the pylinguistic library in a random sample of 303 pairs of verses (0.01% of the original dataset). It is possible to see that simplified text has, in general, fewer tokens per sentence and more sentences.

| Version | Tokens | Sentences | Readability | Lexical diversity | Average number tokens per sentence of | Median sentence length |
|---------|--------|-----------|-------------|-------------------|----------------------------------------|------------------------|
| ARC  | 6975.0 | 296.0 | 66.48 | 0.27 | 23.56 | 26.0 |
| NAA  | 7084.0 | 357.0 | 68.57 | 0.28 | 19.84 | 19.0 |
| NBV  | 7619.0 | 426.0 | 67.82 | 0.28 | 17.88 | 18.0 |
| NLTH | 7479.0 | 457.0 | 72.05 | 0.26 | 16.37 | 17.0 |
| NVI  | 6791.0 | 370.0 | 67.36 | 0.3  | 18.35 | 18.0 |

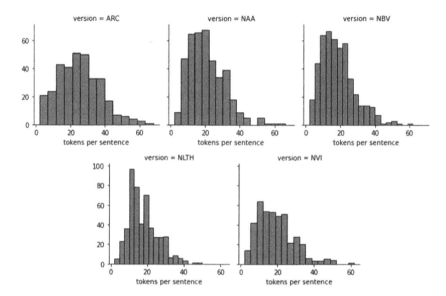

**Fig. 1.** The histogram shows the distribution of tokens per sentences in both versions of the Bible. In a random sample of 303 pairs of verses (0.01% of the original dataset), the split in sentences and tokens was made by using the Portuguese *sentencizer* and tokenizer from spacy [15].

Table 2 exemplifies the aligned versions of ARC and NLTH Bibles used in the experiments. It is important to remain that ARC is considered the complex version to be simplified. The other versions are considered a target in separated experiments and combined in a unique dataset afterward.

**Table 2.** The table exemplifies the aligned versions of the Bible used in the experiments. The passage is from Genesis Chapter 1.1-4.

| ARC | NLTH |
| --- | --- |
| No princípio, criou Deus os céus e a terra | No começo Deus criou os céus e a terra |
| E a terra era sem forma e vazia; e havia treva... | A terra era um vazio, sem nenhum ser vivente, ... |
| E disse Deus: Haja luz. E houve luz | Então Deus disse: - Que haja luz! E a luz come... |
| E viu Deus que era boa a luz; e fez Deus separ... | Deus viu que a luz era boa e a separou da escu... |
| E Deus chamou á luz Dia; e ás trevas chamou No... | Deus pôs na luz o nome de "dia" e na escuridão... |

## 4.2 Automatic Text Simplification

This section presents the details about the automatic text simplification architecture adopted in this study. We applied the Transformer and Bidirectional Recurrent Neural Network (B-RNN) architectures to simplify texts in Portuguese which are state-of-the-art methods.

**Table 3.** The table shows the hyperparameters used in both models.

| Optimization | | Preprocessing | |
| --- | --- | --- | --- |
| Model dtype | fp32 | Maximum source sequence length | 100 |
| Optim | adam | Truncate source sequence length | 100 |
| Batch size | 32 | Maximum target sequence length to keep | 100 |
| Warmup steps | 6000 | Truncate target sequence length | 100 |
| Decay method | Noam | Max length | 100 |
| Adam beta2 | 998 | – | – |
| Max grad norm | 0 | – | – |
| Label smoothing | 0.1 | – | – |
| Param init | 0 | – | – |
| Param init glorot | True | – | – |
| Normalization | tokens | – | – |
| Encoder dropout | [0.5] | – | – |

To perform the evaluation, we used the algorithms implemented at Open-NMT framework [18]. In OpenNMT, it is possible to train the model using different datasets. We considered each pair of SOURCE-TARGET a distinct corpus and assigned different weights based on the difference between the median sentence length from the ARC version to the target version of the corpus presented at Table 1. Further, the validation content received target examples in the same proportion of the weights. The main objective is to avoid over-fitting by increasing the training data. Also, it might allow the model to learn different simplification styles, which may improve the model generalisation. The combined corpus can be identified in the following tables as "multi-corpus".

Finally, the dataset was split into 17441 verses for training, 8139 verses for validation, and 3489 verses for test parallel examples. The experiments considered different target corpus where the ARC bible version is always the input. Also, different encoder-decoder architecture were considered (see Table 5). Two different experiments were performed for each model: with and without pre-trained word embeddings (Portuguese glove embedding with 300 dimensions [14]). At last, a total of 20 different experiments were performed: 5 to each encoder-decoder architecture for each corpus. All the experiments considered a shared embedding and vocabulary and allowed the execution of 10000 training epochs. Detailed information on the experiment setup is given in Tables 3 and 4.

**Table 4.** The table shows the hyperparameters specific for each model.

| Transformer | Value | Bidirectional Recurrent Neural Network (B-RNN) | Value |
|---|---|---|---|
| Encoder layers | 6 | Hidden size | 256 |
| Decoder layers | 6 | Word vector size | 300 |
| Heads | 6 | RNN size | 300 |
| Transformer feedforward | 2048 | – | – |
| Dropout steps | [0] | – | – |
| Encoder dropout | [0.5] | – | – |
| Attention dropout | [0.5] | – | – |
| Position encoding | True | – | – |

### 4.3 Evaluation

The evaluation used two metrics for translation and text simplification evaluation. The first one is the Bilingual Evaluation Understudy Score (BLEU score) [24]. The BLEU score is a widely used metric to evaluate machine translation between two languages based on a reference corpus. It also has been extensively used to assess automatic text simplification, especially the models based on mono language translation [5,35]. Another metric is the System output Against References and against the Input (SARI score) [35]. Unlike the BLEU score, the initial purpose of the SARI score is to evaluate text simplification, considering the system output and references and the source sentence. In summary, SARI score measure how well the words are maintained or changed by the system [35]. Herein, it was used the SARI and BLEU score implementation[2] proposed by [5].

---

[2] SARI and BLEU score implementation: https://github.com/feralvam/easse.

## 5   Results

This section presents the results obtained in the experiments. First, we discuss quantitative aspects of the supervised metrics, and then, a more in-depth discussion on the quality of the predictions is given. Table 6 synthesize the results from Table 5. Table 5 shows the detailed results of the text simplification for each architecture and pair of datasets analyzed. In this paper context, as long as it was not possible to find a massive, parallel corpus of Portuguese simplified texts and the experiment training time constraints, the B-RNN and B-RNN+Embedding achieved the best results. Despite the poor performance when compared with the BRNN model, the transformer model might improve its performance when trained with more epochs and with a larger corpus [11, 21, 29].

**Table 5.** The table shows the result of the text simplification to the different experiments. The B-RNN model outperforms all the other models when both metrics are considered.

| Source-target corpus | SARI score | BLEU score | Encoder-decoder |
|---|---|---|---|
| ARC-Multicorpus | 36.88 | **40.89** | BRNN |
| ARC-NAA | **46.89** | 32.17 | |
| ARC-NBV | 43.35 | 9.49 | |
| ARC-NLTH | 45.52 | 9.78 | |
| ARC-NVI | 44.91 | 16.85 | |
| ARC-Multicorpus | 40.32 | **37.49** | BRNN+Embedding |
| ARC-NAA | **48.45** | 31.70 | |
| ARC-NBV | 44.59 | 9.66 | |
| ARC-NLTH | 46.75 | 10.84 | |
| ARC-NVI | 46.60 | 16.99 | |
| ARC-Multicorpus | 38.58 | **34.77** | Transformer |
| ARC-NAA | **45.43** | 26.53 | |
| ARC-NBV | 43.58 | 7.68 | |
| ARC-NLTH | 44.49 | 07.06 | |
| ARC-NVI | 44.27 | 14.52 | |
| ARC-Multicorpus | 41.08 | 13.75 | Transformer+Embedding |
| ARC-NAA | 42.81 | **17.40** | |
| ARC-NBV | 41.79 | 3.90 | |
| ARC-NLTH | **43.07** | 3.59 | |
| ARC-NVI | 42.63 | 7.98 | |

## 5.1  Simplification Quality

One particular insight is that the simplification using multiple targets achieves a much higher BLEU score but has a lower SARI score in almost all experiments. This difference is due to the diverse nature of both metrics, i.e., the BLEU score measures the number of unigrams of the system prediction is part of the references. In other words, it calculates a "modified precision score", which decreases the incentive of an over-generation of a particular word to obtain a high score [24]. Therefore, the high BLEU score might mean that the model is sharing a significant overlap with the references in the prediction[3]. On the other hand, the SARI score rewards the words that are maintained in both reference and source sentence [5,36]. It also scores the addition of new words as long as

**Table 6.** The summary of metrics of Table 5.

| Score | Agg. metric | BRNN | BRNN+Embedding | Transformer | Transformer+Embedding |
|-------|-------------|------|----------------|-------------|-----------------------|
| SARI  | Mean | 43.51 | **45.34** | 43.27 | 42.28 |
|       | Min  | 36.88 | **40.32** | 38.58 | 41.08 |
|       | Max  | 46.89 | **48.45** | 45.43 | 43.07 |
|       | Std  | 3.92  | 3.12      | 2.7   | 0.82  |
| BLEU  | Mean | **21.84** | 21.34 | 18.11 | 9.32 |
|       | Min  | 9.49  | **9.66**  | 7.06  | 3.59 |
|       | Max  | **40.89** | 37.49 | 34.77 | 17.4 |
|       | Std  | 14.08 | 12.59     | 12.17 | 6.1  |

**Table 7.** The multi-corpus prediction was produced using the B-RNN model with and without pre trained embeddings. He both models removed a specific part of the sentence to try to make it shorter which is in bold text.

| Corpus | Sentence | BLEU |
|--------|----------|------|
| ARC | E o menino crescia e se **fortalecia** em espírito, **cheio de sabedoria;** e a graça de Deus estava sobre ele | |
| Multicorpus BRNN+Embedding | O menino se crescia em espírito, cheio de sabedoria; e a graça de Deus estava sobre ele | 63.04 |
| Multicorpus BRNN | O menino crescia e se fortalecia em espírito, e a graça de Deus estava sobre ele | 74.44 |
| NAA | O menino crescia e se fortalecia, enchendo-se de sabedoria; e a graça de Deus estava sobre ele | |
| NBV | Ali o menino começou a ficar forte e sadio, enchendo-se de sabedoria; e a graça de Deus estava sobre ele | |
| NVI | O menino crescia e se fortalecia, enchendo-se de sabedoria; e a graça de Deus estava sobre ele | |
| NLTH | O menino crescia e ficava forte; tinha muita sabedoria e era abençoado por Deus | |

---

[3] BLEU score scale: https://cloud.google.com/translate/automl/docs/evaluate.

they belong to at least one reference [5,36]. Further, the metric showed to be intuitive on how the simplification gain is calculated [5,36].

Figure 2 show that in the single training corpora, the metrics of readability is improve and it is even higher than the readability of the reference corpus. This means that the model was able to learn the style of the target corpus as it was pointed out by previous works [19,38]. Besides, although the predicted texts have more tokens per sentence in average, the high readability score might mean that it is predicting short words as it is one of the aspects considered in the readability metric [7].

Finally, the model trained with a single corpus achieved a higher SARI score, indicating a better simplification. Nonetheless, it could not produce a sentence with the same level of grammatical correctness and semantic meaning in this particular example as the one produced by the multi-corpus training approach. It was pointed by [31] that even though SARI scores can represent the quality of the simplified sentences, the BLEU score performs better on scoring the grammatical meaning of the sentences.

Table 7 presents an example of the outcome of the best text simplification method. It shows details about the potential of the application of the proposal in practice. As presented, the text after applying the algorithm contains more general words than the original text. Even though it did not produce an exact translation of the tokens, the model is able to maintain the original meaning of the sentence and grammatical correctness.

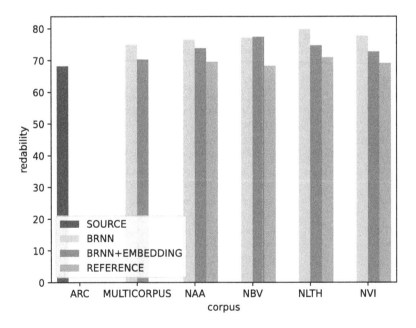

**Fig. 2.** Text readability scores, calculated by the pylinguistics library, of the text simplification made by the B-RNN model in different corpus.

**Table 8.** Different scores produced by the simplification made over different corpus from the best performing methods which are B-RNN with and without pre trained embeddings.

| Corpus | Origin | Tokens | Sentences | Readability | Lexical diversity | Average of number of tokens per sentence | Median sentence length |
|---|---|---|---|---|---|---|---|
| ARC | Source | 81886.0 | 3552.0 | 68.23 | 0.11 | 23.05 | 26.0 |
| Multicorpus | BRNN | 73200.0 | 2719.0 | 74.92 | 0.09 | 26.92 | 28.0 |
| Multicorpus | BRNN+Embedding | 82484.0 | 2427.0 | 70.32 | 0.07 | 33.99 | 32.0 |
| NAA | BRNN | 82103.0 | 2753.0 | 76.51 | 0.06 | 29.82 | 30.0 |
| | BRNN+Embedding | 81303.0 | 2831.0 | 73.85 | 0.07 | 28.72 | 29.0 |
| | Reference | 83201.0 | 4219.0 | 69.56 | 0.11 | 19.72 | 21.0 |
| NBV | BRNN | 86808.0 | 2547.0 | 77.12 | 0.05 | 34.08 | 31.0 |
| | BRNN+Embedding | 76387.0 | 2568.0 | 77.46 | 0.06 | 29.75 | 27.0 |
| | Reference | 90037.0 | 4942.0 | 68.31 | 0.1 | 18.22 | 19.0 |
| NLTH | BRNN | 81293.0 | 3454.0 | 79.85 | 0.04 | 23.54 | 24.0 |
| | BRNN+Embedding | 82348.0 | 3139.0 | 74.73 | 0.05 | 26.23 | 25.0 |
| | Reference | 87079.0 | 5164.0 | 70.99 | 0.09 | 16.86 | 19.0 |
| NVI | BRNN | 81589.0 | 2416.0 | 77.76 | 0.06 | 33.77 | 31.0 |
| | BRNN+Embedding | 82117.0 | 2479.0 | 72.74 | 0.06 | 33.13 | 30.0 |
| | Reference | 80250.0 | 4306.0 | 69.13 | 0.12 | 18.64 | 20.0 |

# 6   Conclusion

Neural Machine Translation (NMT) methods have achieved successful results for the Text Simplification problem in different languages, overcoming traditional statistical approaches. To the best of our knowledge, no research has investigated the application of NMT methods to simplify Brazilian Portuguese texts. The main contribution of this paper is the application of NMT methods for the simplification of Portuguese text. Two different state-of-the-art NMT methods were considered: the Transformer and Bidirectional Recurrent Neural Network (B-RNN). The results demonstrated that the B-RNN was able to obtain the best results, in average (BLEU = 21.84 without pre trained embedding and SARI = 45.34 with pre trained embedding), despite the small corpus size and limited training epochs constraints.

Another significant improvement was the use of multiple corpora presenting different possible simplifications for the same input. It achieved an improvement of over 8 points on the BLEU score. Despite of a lower SARI score, the higher BLEU score might mean the ability to preserve the sentence meaning and grammatical correctness.

As future works, we intend to: (i) perform an analysis on the parameters of each algorithm evaluated; (ii) use different embedding models, such as BERT [11, 21,29]; (iii) apply the NMT methods in text from different domains, such as law and health; (iv) explore the use of other methods such as lexical and syntactical simplification and pre-trained models for a mono-lingual translation approach.

# References

1. Al-Onaizan, Y., et al.: Statistical machine translation. In: Final Report, JHU Summer Workshop, vol. 30 (1999)
2. Al-Thanyyan, S.S., Azmi, A.M.: Automated text simplification: a survey. ACM Comput. Surv. (CSUR) **54**(2), 1–36 (2021)
3. Aluisio, S., Specia, L., Gasperin, C., Scarton, C.: Readability assessment for text simplification. In: Proceedings of the NAACL HLT 2010 5th Workshop on Innovative Use of NLP for Building Educational Applications, pp. 1–9 (2010)
4. Aluísio, S.M., Gasperin, C.: Fostering digital inclusion and accessibility: the Por-Simples project for simplification of Portuguese texts. In: Proceedings of the NAACL HLT 2010 Young Investigators Workshop on Computational Approaches to Languages of the Americas, pp. 46–53. Association for Computational Linguistics (2010)
5. Alva-Manchego, F., Martin, L., Scarton, C., Specia, L.: EASSE: easier automatic sentence simplification evaluation. In: Proceedings of the 2019 Conference on Empirical Methods in Natural Language Processing and the 9th International Joint Conference on Natural Language Processing (EMNLP-IJCNLP): System Demonstrations, Hong Kong, China, pp. 49–54. Association for Computational Linguistics (November 2019). https://www.aclweb.org/anthology/D19-3009
6. Bahdanau, D., Cho, K., Bengio, Y.: Neural machine translation by jointly learning to align and translate. arXiv preprint arXiv:1409.0473 (2014)
7. Castilhos, S., Woloszyn, V., Barno, D., Wives, L.K.: Pylinguistics: an open source library for readability assessment of texts written in Portuguese. Revista de Sistemas de Informação da FSMA **18**, 36–42 (2016)
8. Chu, C., Wang, R.: A survey of domain adaptation for neural machine translation. arXiv preprint arXiv:1806.00258 (2018)
9. Collantes, M., Hipe, M., Sorilla, J.L., Tolentino, L., Samson, B.: Simpatico: a text simplification system for senate and house bills. In: Proceedings of the 11th National Natural Language Processing Research Symposium, pp. 26–32 (2015)
10. Cooper, M., Shardlow, M.: CombiNMT: an exploration into neural text simplification models. In: Proceedings of the 12th Language Resources and Evaluation Conference, pp. 5588–5594 (2020)
11. Devlin, J., Chang, M.W., Lee, K., Toutanova, K.: Bert: pre-training of deep bidirectional transformers for language understanding. arXiv preprint arXiv:1810.04805 (2018)
12. Freitag, M., Al-Onaizan, Y.: Fast domain adaptation for neural machine translation. arXiv preprint arXiv:1612.06897 (2016)
13. Gao, Y., et al.: IBM MASTOR system: multilingual automatic speech-to-speech translator. Technical report, IBM Thomas J Watson Research Center Yorktown Heights, NY (2006)
14. Hartmann, N., Fonseca, E., Shulby, C., Treviso, M., Rodrigues, J., Aluisio, S.: Portuguese word embeddings: evaluating on word analogies and natural language tasks. arXiv preprint arXiv:1708.06025 (2017)
15. Honnibal, M., Montani, I., Van Landeghem, S., Boyd, A.: spaCy: industrial-strength Natural Language Processing in Python (2020). https://doi.org/10.5281/zenodo.1212303
16. José, M., Finatto, B.: Acessibilidade textual e terminológica: promovendo a tradução intralinguística. Estudos Linguísticos (São Paulo. 1978) **49**(1), 72–96 (2020). https://doi.org/10.21165/el.v49i1.2775

17. Kincaid, J.P., Fishburne, R.P., Jr., Rogers, R.L., Chissom, B.S.: Derivation of new readability formulas (automated readability index, fog count and flesch reading ease formula) for navy enlisted personnel. Technical report, Naval Technical Training Command Millington TN Research Branch (1975)
18. Klein, G., Kim, Y., Deng, Y., Senellart, J., Rush, A.: OpenNMT: open-source toolkit for neural machine translation. In: Proceedings of ACL 2017, System Demonstrations, Vancouver, Canada, pp. 67–72. Association for Computational Linguistics (July 2017). https://www.aclweb.org/anthology/P17-4012
19. Krishna, K., Wieting, J., Iyyer, M.: Reformulating unsupervised style transfer as paraphrase generation. arXiv preprint arXiv:2010.05700 (2020)
20. Liu, B., Lane, I.: Attention-based recurrent neural network models for joint intent detection and slot filling. arXiv preprint arXiv:1609.01454 (2016)
21. Liu, Y., et al.: Multilingual denoising pre-training for neural machine translation. Trans. Assoc. Comput. Linguist. **8**, 726–742 (2020)
22. Martins, T.B., Ghiraldelo, C.M., das Graças Volpe Nunes, M., de Oliveira Junior, O.N.: Readability formulas applied to textbooks in Brazilian Portuguese. Icmsc-Usp (1996)
23. Nisioi, S., Štajner, S., Ponzetto, S.P., Dinu, L.P.: Exploring neural text simplification models. In: Proceedings of the 55th Annual Meeting of the Association for Computational Linguistics (Volume 2: Short papers), pp. 85–91 (2017)
24. Papineni, K., Roukos, S., Ward, T., Zhu, W.J.: BLEU: a method for automatic evaluation of machine translation. In: Proceedings of the 40th annual meeting of the Association for Computational Linguistics, pp. 311–318 (2002)
25. Park, S.H., Kim, B., Kang, C.M., Chung, C.C., Choi, J.W.: Sequence-to-sequence prediction of vehicle trajectory via LSTM encoder-decoder architecture. In: 2018 IEEE Intelligent Vehicles Symposium (IV), pp. 1672–1678 (2018). https://doi.org/10.1109/IVS.2018.8500658
26. Qiang, J.: Improving neural text simplification model with simplified corpora. arXiv preprint arXiv:1810.04428 (2018)
27. Rescigno, A.A., Vanmassenhove, E., Monti, J., Way, A.: A case study of natural gender phenomena in translation a comparison of Google Translate, Bing Microsoft Translator and DeepL for English to Italian, French and Spanish. In: Association for Machine Translation in the Americas (AMTA): Workshop on the Impact of Machine Translation, iMpacT 2020, p. 62. Workshop on the Impact of Machine Translation (iMpacT 2020) at Association (2020)
28. Sikka, P., Singh, M., Pink, A., Mago, V.: A survey on text simplification. arXiv preprint arXiv:2008.08612 (2020)
29. Souza, F., Nogueira, R., Lotufo, R.: BERTimbau: pretrained BERT models for Brazilian Portuguese. In: 9th Brazilian Conference on Intelligent Systems, BRACIS, Rio Grande do Sul, Brazil, 20–23 October (2020, to appear)
30. Specia, L.: Translating from complex to simplified sentences. In: Pardo, T.A.S., Branco, A., Klautau, A., Vieira, R., de Lima, V.L.S. (eds.) PROPOR 2010. LNCS (LNAI), vol. 6001, pp. 30–39. Springer, Heidelberg (2010). https://doi.org/10.1007/978-3-642-12320-7_5
31. Sulem, E., Abend, O., Rappoport, A.: Semantic structural evaluation for text simplification. arXiv preprint arXiv:1810.05022 (2018)
32. Sulem, E., Abend, O., Rappoport, A.: Simple and effective text simplification using semantic and neural methods. arXiv preprint arXiv:1810.05104 (2018)
33. Vaswani, A., et al.: Attention is all you need. arXiv preprint arXiv:1706.03762 (2017)

34. Wang, T., Chen, P., Amaral, K., Qiang, J.: An experimental study of LSTM encoder-decoder model for text simplification. arXiv preprint arXiv:1609.03663 (2016)
35. Xu, W., Napoles, C., Pavlick, E., Chen, Q., Callison-Burch, C.: Optimizing statistical machine translation for text simplification. Trans. Assoc. Comput. Linguist. **4**, 401–415 (2016). https://cocoxu.github.io/publications/tacl2016-smt-simplification.pdf
36. Xu, W., Napoles, C., Pavlick, E., Chen, Q., Callison-Burch, C.: Optimizing statistical machine translation for text simplification. Trans. Assoc. Comput. Linguist. **4**, 401–415 (2016)
37. Yamada, M.: The impact of Google Neural Machine Translation on post-editing by student translators. J. Specialised Transl. **31**, 87–106 (2019)
38. Yang, Z., Hu, Z., Dyer, C., Xing, E.P., Berg-Kirkpatrick, T.: Unsupervised text style transfer using language models as discriminators. arXiv preprint arXiv:1805.11749 (2018)
39. Zaremba, W., Sutskever, I., Vinyals, O.: Recurrent neural network regularization. arXiv preprint arXiv:1409.2329 (2014)

# Rhetorical Role Identification for Portuguese Legal Documents

Roberto Aragy[1,2](✉) [ID], Eraldo Rezende Fernandes[1] [ID],
and Edson Norberto Caceres[1] [ID]

[1] Universidade Federal de Mato Grosso do Sul, Campo Grande, Brazil
{eraldo,edson}@facom.ufms.br
[2] Tribunal de Justiça de Mato Grosso do Sul, Campo Grande, Brazil
roberto.aragy@tjms.jus.br

**Abstract.** In this paper, we present a new corpus for Rhetorical Role Identification in Portuguese legal documents. The corpus comprises petitions from 70 civil lawsuits filed in TJMS court and was manually labeled with rhetorical roles specifically tailored for petitions. Since petition documents are created without a standard structure, we had to deal with several issues to clean the extracted textual content. We assessed classic and deep learning machine learning methods on the proposed corpus. The best performing method obtained an $F$-score of 80.50. At the best of our knowledge, this is the first work to deal with rhetorical role identification for petitions, given that previous works focused only on judicial decisions. Additionally, it is also the first work to tackle this task for the Portuguese language. The proposed corpus, as well as the proposed rhetorical roles, can foster new research in the judicial area and also lead to new solutions to improve the flow of Brazilian court houses.

**Keywords:** Rhetorical role identification · Legal sentence classification · Natural language processing · Corpus

## 1 Introduction

Brazilian judicial system has usually adopted a conservative stance regarding its lawsuit bureaucracy. However, in the last two decades, it started to adopt information technology systems to improve its underlying procedures. In 2006, Brazilian Congress passed a law[1] to rule electronic lawsuit systems. Since then, all Brazilian courts started to digitize their lawsuit bureaucracy. This process has greatly accelerated the filing and intermediary procedures of a lawsuit which, for instance, allowed a 22% increase in the number of cases filed in 2019 when compared to 2009 [18]. Although this effect is mostly beneficial, it presents its own challenges. One issue is that the main bottleneck of Brazilian judicial system has shifted from the intermediary procedures performed by civil registries to judges' offices.

---

[1] LeiFederal11.419de19/12/2006.

© Springer Nature Switzerland AG 2021
A. Britto and K. Valdivia Delgado (Eds.): BRACIS 2021, LNAI 13074, pp. 557–571, 2021.
https://doi.org/10.1007/978-3-030-91699-2_38

Nowadays, most documents in a lawsuit in Brazil are either originally digital or digitized before inclusion in the judicial system. Nevertheless, several tasks within a lawsuit procedure still depend on direct human intervention. In general, every time a party (judge, complainant, defendant, etc.) is requested to pronounce within a case, this party may need to carefully analyse different documents. In particular, the petition (*petição inicial*, in Portuguese) is the first document presented by the complainant in order to file a civil lawsuit in Brazilian courts. In this document, the complainant needs to identify the involved parties, expose facts that are relevant to the case, present the legal basis and relevant prior cases, describe the requested remedy, among other aspects. After a petition is filed, it needs to be carefully analysed by staff of a judge's office in order to verify different aspects. For instance, it is necessary to check if the petition presents the minimal requirements specified in the Brazilian civil procedure (*Código de Processo Civil*) [4]. Ultimately, the petition must be fully considered by the assigned judge, when another careful analysis is required. Although it is virtually impossible to mechanize all these manual analytic steps, in most of these cases if not all, machine learning (ML) and natural language processing (NLP) techniques can be leveraged to assist humans in such analyses.

Rhetorical role identification (RRI) is an NLP task that consists of labeling the sentences of a document according to a given set of semantic functions (rhetorical roles). This task is useful to applications like document summarization [11,19–21,26], semantic search [15], document analysis [22], among others. Different approaches have been proposed to solve this task for court decisions [2,20,21]. These previous works have proposed to segment a court decision into rhetorical roles such as facts, court arguments, prior related cases, ruling, among others. As far as we know, all previous RRI methods have tackled only court decisions and are limited to the English language. Although the benefits of analytic tools of judicial decisions are undisputed, it is also important to provide similar tools for other legal documents and languages, particularly petitions in Brazilian legal system. As mentioned before, a judge's office in Brazil handle a high volume of work, and petition analysis represents a substantial portion of it. Therefore, rhetorical role identification for petitions represents an opportunity to improve Brazilian judges' offices efficiency.

In this paper, we propose to segment petitions into eight rhetorical roles by mainly considering the analytic needs of judges' offices in Brazil. We present a corpus of 70 petitions comprising more than 10 thousand sentences manually labeled with the proposed rhetorical roles. These petitions were taken from civil lawsuits filed in the court of the Brazilian state of Mato Grosso do Sul (TJMS). Additionally, we report on experiments to assess classic and modern machine learning methods on the created corpus. In order to propose relevant rhetorical roles, we considered the Brazilian civil procedure [4] which defines the minimal requirements of a petition. The proposed rhetorical roles are: identification of parties, facts, arguments, legal basis, precedents, requests, remedy, and others. The corpus was anonymized and is publicly available. We trained and evaluated six machine learning methods, including classic and deep learning models, on the developed corpus. The best performing method was an end-to-end-trained BERT-based [6] method that obtained a sentence-level micro-averaged $F$-score of 80.50. This method outperformed a fixed-representation BERT-based model by five points and the best classic algorithm (SVM with TF-IDF representation) by 25 points of $F$-score.

As far as we know, this is the first paper to approach rhetorical role identification of petitions, instead of court decisions. Moreover, this is also the first work on this task that considers the Portuguese language and legal domain. We hope this paper will foster research about this important subject, especially in Brazil.

## 2   Related Work

One of the first works to deal with text segmentation based on rhetorical function was proposed by Teufel [25]. In this work, Teufel proposed a segmentation approached called *argumentative zoning* that is based on the rhetorical function that an excerpt plays within a scientific article. This approach was later applied to extractive summarization [5,12,26].

Hachey and Grover [11], inspired by Teufel's work, proposed a method to legal text summarization based on rhetorical role text segmentation. The proposed roles were: fact, proceedings, background, framing, disposal, textual, and other. They assessed the proposed method on the HOLJ dataset [10] which consists of 40 manually-labeled decisions from the House of Lords, the highest court in the United Kingdom until 2009. They employed a C4.5 classifier that achieved an accuracy of 65.4%.

Saravanam [19] also followed Teufel's work to study the generation of headnotes (a type of summary) for decisions from Indian courts. He argued that rhetorical roles proposed by Teufel were not appropriate in the legal domain. Thus, he proposed the following rhetorical roles for legal decisions: case identification, facts, arguments, chronology, argument analysis, ratio decidendi, and final decision. Later, based on these roles, Saravanam *et al.* [21] created a corpus out of 200 decisions from the Indian Court of Justice spanning three different domains. They developed and evaluated a Conditional Random Field (CRF) classifier to perform sentence-level rhetorical role identification which obtained the following $F$-scores on the considered domains: 84.9 on rent control, 81.7 on income tax, and 78.7 on sales tax domain.

Nejadgholi *et al.* [15] leveraged rhetorical role identification to perform semantic search. They defined eight rhetorical roles and manually labeled the sentences in 150 decisions taken from immigration and refugee cases from Canada's Federal and Supreme Court. They assessed a simple classifier based on fastText that obtained an accuracy of 90%.

Walker *et al.* [28] proposed six rhetorical roles to aid a system for argument mining. They produced a corpus of 50 decisions extracted from the U.S. Board of Veterans' Appeals comprising 6,153 sentences. They evaluated three different classification algorithms on this sentence classification corpus. The best performing classifiers (based on logistic regression and SVM) achieved 85.7% accuracy.

Bhattacharya *et al.* [2] annotated 50 decisions from the Supreme Court of India using the same rhetorical roles proposed by Saravanam [19]. They trained a hierarchical BiLSTM model with CRF on this corpus, obtaining an *F*-score of 82.0.

Yamada *et al.* [29] leveraged the argumentation structure in legal decisions from Japanese justice system to improve a summarization system. They manually annotated a corpus of 209 decisions based on seven rhetorical roles. By means of BiLSTM-CRF model, they obtained a macro-averaged *F*-score of 65.4 on this corpus.

All papers mentioned above are based on legal decisions. Although this kind of documents is of high importance, there are other types of documents that are also relevant to different applications in the legal domain. Another aspect that is worth mentioning is that all previous works on rhetorical role identification were performed on documents from legal systems based on the common law paradigm. However, the Brazilian legal system is based on the civil law paradigm, which implies some key differences in the structure of the documents within a legal case. Therefore, it is worth studying rhetorical role identification within the Brazilian legal system.

A few previous works [7–9] have tackled rhetorical role identification in Portuguese. However, as far as we know, there is no RRI work for legal documents in this language. Recently, some papers have proposed resources and systems to tackle NLP problems involving Portuguese legal documents, mainly for document classification [1] and named entity recognition [13,24]. As far as we know, our work is the first one on rhetorical role identification for Portuguese legal documents, and also the first one to perform this task on petitions regardless of language. Moreover, we propose some novel rhetorical roles that are specific for petitions.

## 3    Corpus and Rhetorical Roles

We created a corpus of petitions based on the court of the Brazilian State of Mato Grosso do Sul (TJMS) which receives hundreds of thousands of lawsuits every year. During 2017, for example, more than 340 thousand cases have been filed in TJMS among different types such as civil, criminal, fiscal, and others. We initially considered civil cases that were judged between 2014 and 2018 and are not under judicial secrecy. We then took the petitions of such cases which are usually written by a lawyer that represents the complainant. The system used to file cases in TJMS accepts a petition only as a PDF file. However, there is no requirement as how this document is created. It can even be produced by scanning a paper document. Therefore, such documents present great variation regarding encoding, content structure, background watermark, headings, footers, among others. Since these aspects may generate a lot of noise in the content extracted from the petitions, we selected 70 petitions and, after extracting its textual content by means of PDFBox[2], a manual inspection was performed in

---

[2] https://pdfbox.apache.org/.

order to remove noisy content. We split each petition into sentences and tokens by means of the NLTK library [3]. We obtained a total of 10,784 sentences comprising 249,105 tokens (20,914 unique tokens). The average length of a petition is 154 sentences, and the average length of a sentence is 23.1 tokens. In Fig. 1, to provide a better understanding of this corpus, we present the histogram of sentence length.

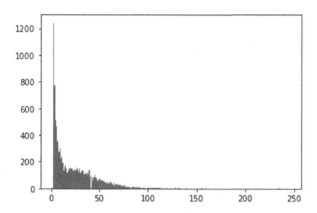

**Fig. 1.** Frequency of sentences per length

For all documents, personal information were manually identified and anonymized by means of random procedures. More specifically, names of people, institutions, streets and cities were replaced by random names taken from a database containing two thousand names. Personal identification numbers and telephone numbers were replaced by random numbers.

In order to define the rhetorical roles used to label sentences, we took some inspiration from the Brazilian civil procedure (Código de Processo Civil) [4]. More specifically, we considered articles 319, 320 and 321 from this law, which state the minimum requirements regarding the content of a petition within Brazilian legal system. In addition to these legal requirements, we considered two possible applications for this corpus: (i) support to staff of a judge's office (including the judge) when analysing a filed petition; and (ii) petition summarization to support the generation of headnotes that need to be included in the judge's pronouncement within the legal case.

In the following, we list the eight proposed rhetorical roles for sentences within a petition. The terms between parenthesis correspond to Portuguese translations of the rhetorical roles. For each rhetorical role, we also present some exemplary sentences.

1. *Identification* (identificação das partes): Identification of the parties (complainant, appellant, judge, among others) involved in the case. Usually such sentences occur at the beginning of the document.

- ADEMIR CANTAREIRA E PAULA, brasileiro, solteiro, auxiliar de produção, portador do CPF n⁰.
- 179.939.452 - 04 e do RG n⁰.
- 103673421 SSP/MS, residente e domiciliado sito á Rua do Carapicuibano, n⁰.

2. *Facts* (fatos): Factual account that gave rise to the lawsuit. Usually these sentences occur right after the identification, but they can be presented interspersed with the arguments.

   - No dia 28/01/2013 o funcionário da Requerida, Sr. Jorge, realizou serviços de substituição de válvulas no apartamento do síndico do condomínio, Sr. Ailton Cesar, que aproveitando o ensejo contratou verbalmente o profissional para verificar os hidrômetros do prédio e, se necessário, consertar ou substituir dois registros de água do condomínio.

3. *Arguments* (argumentos): Pronouncement to persuade the judge to adopt a certain line of thought. These are the sentences that present the greatest variation in linguistic styles. It is common to interconnect these sentences with facts and legal basis.

   - O presente pleito tem como objetivo, entre tantos outros, ressarcir o condomínio autor pelos danos morais, coibindo a atitude abusiva da Requerida, em razão do constrangimento sofrido pelo síndico, Sr. Leandro Musk, o qual se sente lesado porque ficou extremamente constrangido ao ter que pagar e explicar perante os condôminos do prédio um gasto exorbitante de R$ 1.660,00 para trocar apenas dois castelos de registros.

4. *Legal basis* (fundamentação legal): Description of legal doctrine that gives the ground for the decision making process. It usually includes citations to laws and texts by jurisprudential authors. This is usually interspersed with the arguments and precedents, but we decided to create this specific label since its nature is more objective than arguments.

   - CC. Art. 186.
   - Aquele que, por ação ou omissão voluntária, negligência ou imprudência, violar direito e causar dano a outrem, ainda que exclusivamente moral, comete ato ilícito.

5. *Precedents* (jurisprudência): This part is based on citations to headnotes of similar or relevant previous cases. Some sentences within this part are in capital letters since this is the typical format of headnotes in Brazilian legal system. It also occurs interspersed with the arguments.

   - (STJ - REsp 927727 / MG, RECURSO ESPECIAL, 2007/0038830-3, Dês.
   - Rel.
   - Ministro JOSÉ DELGADO, Primeira Turma, 06/05/2008).

6. *Requests* (pedidos): This corresponds to the main requests by the complainants about which the judge must pronounce. It is usually the last by one section of the petition.

   - Ante o exposto com supedâneo nos motivos de fato e nos fundamentos do direito pátrio, requer a Vossa Excelência se digne de.
   - a) citar a Ré, na pessoa de seu representante legal, para que, assim desejando, compareça á audiência designada e apresente defesa, sob pena de revelia e confissão (art.

**Table 1.** Basic statistics per rhetorical role

| Label | Rhetorical role | Sentences | Tokens/sent |
|-------|-----------------|-----------|-------------|
| Id    | Identification  | 235       | 48.5        |
| Fac   | Facts           | 1,573     | 27.9        |
| Arg   | Arguments       | 3,024     | 32.4        |
| LB    | Legal Basis     | 1,266     | 18.6        |
| Pre   | Precedents      | 3,032     | 14.1        |
| Req   | Requests        | 734       | 31.4        |
| Rem   | Remedy          | 71        | 22.3        |
| Oth   | Others          | 849       | 5.2         |
|       | Total           | 10,784    | 23.1        |

7. *Remedy* (valor da causa): Normally contained in one or two sentences in the
   end of the petition, this part provides a monetary estimate to remedy the
   complainant's claims. This is usually the last section of the petition.
   – Dá-se á presente o valor de R\$ 4.450,00 (quatro mil quatrocentos e cinquenta
   reais), para fins de alçada e fiscais.
8. *Others* (outros): Other textual elements like section and page headings.
   – DOS REQUERIMENTOS.
   – DO DIREITO.

In Table 1, we present the number of sentences and the average number of tokens
per sentence for each rhetorical role in our corpus. In the first column of this
table, we provide a label for each rhetorical role to ease further references.

By means of the *doccano* tool [14], an expert labeled each sentence of a
petition with one of the eight rhetorical roles aforementioned. The sequence of
sentences in a petition was preserved in the corpus, so that future approaches
can leverage this structure.

## 4    Text Representation and Machine Learning Approaches

Rhetorical role identification is usually modeled as a sentence classification task.
Following this modeling, there are two broad types of methods in literature: the
ones that treat each sentence independently, and the ones that treat a document
as a sequence of sentences leveraging the inter-dependencies among sentences.
Although the later type considers a relevant piece of information that is ignored
by the former, in this work we focus only on the former type of methods. Our
motivation for this decision is that our main goal here is to investigate the
feasibility of the proposed RRI task. And we indeed experimentally show that,
even ignoring the sequential aspect of the given sentences, it is possible to achieve
a highly effective rhetorical role classifier ($F$-score over 80%) for sentences within
petitions from a Brazilian court. Besides that, we also make progress on assessing
different text representations and machine learning algorithms on this task.

### 4.1   Baseline Methods

We considered some standard text classification approaches as baseline methods. More specifically, we combined Naive Bayes (NB) and Support Vector Machine (SVM) models with two standard text representation techniques, namely bag of words (BoW) and term frequency-inverse document frequency (TFIDF). BoW and TFIDF are among the most used text representation techniques. Although deep learning representations have dominated the latest advances in text processing tasks, BoW and TFIDF can still be competitive, mainly in text classification problems. Thus, these classic representations represent strong baselines in order to evaluate the incremental contribution of more complex methods, like the ones based on deep learning.

NB is a probabilistic ML model specially appropriate for text classification tasks. While linear SVM is an effective model to tackle problems with sparse input data like texts. Both models offer competitive performance in many text classification problems.

### 4.2   Deep Learning Methods

In the last decade, deep learning models have represented the most prominent approaches for NLP problems. And, following the proposal of the seminal Transformer architecture [27], models based on attention mechanisms [6,16,17] became the standard approach for text tasks. BERT [6] is probably the most popular model among such approaches. For instance, among the more than 10 thousand NLP models available in the popular Hugging Face library[3], approximately 25% are based on BERT or some of its variants. Among those BERT-based models, there are 18 models were trained with Portuguese data.

In this work, we assessed two BERT-based models for rhetorical role identification by training and evaluating them on our proposed corpus. Both models are based on the *BERTimbau Base* model [23], a BERT language model pretrained on Portuguese texts which is available in the Hugging Face library[4]. In Fig. 2, we depict these two models. Both of them employ a BERT language model (LM) to compute a sentence representation (black part of the figure). This part, which is the same for both models, is represented in black at the bottom of the figure. Before applying a BERT LM, the input sentence is first tokenized into $N$ tokens $(T_1, \ldots, T_N)$, then two special tokens [CLS] and [SEP] are added, respectively, at the beginning and in the end of the tokenized sentence. The resulting sequence of tokens ([CLS], $T_1, \ldots, T_N$, [SEP]) is then fed in the language model, which outputs a 768-dimensional representation for each input token: $(E_{[CLS]}, E_{T_1}, \ldots, E_{T_N}, E_{[SEP]})$. When dealing with sentence classification tasks, like is the case for rhetorical role identification, one needs to compute a fixed-length representation for the variable-length input sentence. In this work, we use a common sentence representation approach which consists of

---

[3] https://huggingface.co/models.
[4] https://huggingface.co/neuralmind/bert-base-portuguese-cased.

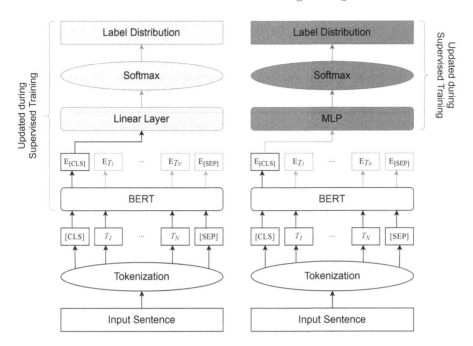

**Fig. 2.** Two BERT-based models for sentence classification. *Black*: BERT language model computes a sentence representation $E_{[CLS]}$. This part is identical in both models, except that, for the model on the left, the BERT LM is fine tuned during supervised training. On the other hand, for the model on the right, the BERT LM is kept fixed and only the remaining layers are updated during supervised training. *Blue*: The BERT-based sentence representation $E_{[CLS]}$ is fed to a single linear layer followed by a softmax function that outputs a probability distribution over the eight labels. This model is trained in an end-to-end fashion, i.e., the BERT model is fine-tuned together with the linear layer. *Red*: The sentence representation is fed to a MLP comprising two 512-neuron layers followed by a softmax function which outputs the label distribution. When training this model, the BERT LM is kept fixed and only the MLP parameters are updated. (Color figure online)

simply taking $E_{[CLS]}$, thus ignoring the representations of all remaining tokens. Since BERT is composed of a sequence of self-attention layers, the output $E_{[CLS]}$ is directly connected to all tokens of the sentence. Therefore, this representation is robust for sentence classification tasks, regardless of which part of the input sentence is more important for the task at hand.

In the upper part of Fig. 2, we present the remaining layers of the two sentence classification models used in our work. In blue (upper-left of the figure), we represent the model that takes the BERT-based sentence representation $E_{[CLS]}$, passes it through a linear layer and then applies a softmax activation function which outputs a probability distribution over the eight rhetorical roles proposed in our work. This corresponds to the original BERT architecture for text classification problems. This model is trained in an end-to-end fashion, i.e., during supervised training the parameters of both the output linear layer and the BERT language model are jointly learned. This approach performs the so called LM fine tuning because the BERT LM parameters are updated using labeled data for the final task.

The red part of Fig. 2 represents a model that feeds the BERT-based sentence representation $E_{[CLS]}$ to a two-layer Multi-Layer Perceptron (MLP). The output of this MLP is then passed to a softmax function that provides the output label distribution. When training this model, we keep fixed the parameters of the BERT language model. In that way, we can evaluate the benefit of fine tuning the BERT LM in the rhetorical role identification task.

## 5    Experimental Evaluation

In this section, we describe the experimental evaluation of the developed ML models on the proposed RRI corpus. We model RRI as a sentence classification problem. In order to perform model selection and still report meaningful performance estimates, we randomly split the proposed corpus into three splits: *train* containing 6, 901 sentences, *validation* containing 1, 726 sentences, and *test* containing 2, 157 sentences.

We use Naive Bayes and SVM models, combined with bag of words and TFIDF representations, to define meaningful baselines for this task. In these approaches, each sentence was preprocessed with *NLTK*[5], the Natural Language Toolkit, to tokenize and remove stopwords. We represent input sentences using BoW and TFIDF representations by means of the *scikit-learn* library[6]. Then, we train and evaluate NB and SVM models using both input representations, again making use of *scikit-learn*. The performances of these four baseline methods on our test set are reported in Table 2. We can observe that the best performing baseline method is SVM with TFIDF representation which obtains a *F*-score of 60.66. But this method is only slightly better than NB with the same representation.

We also evaluated the four NB/SVM-based models when the input comprised all words (including stopwords), but the achieved results were substantially worse (F-score values were 5% lower on average). Thus, we do not report these performances.

In order to train and evaluate the two BERT-based methods, we did not employ any preprocessing steps but the corresponding tokenization. By means of the Hugging Face (HF) library, we trained and evaluated the end-to-end-trained BERT-based model. For the MLP-based classifier, we again employed the HF library to extract sentence representations, but then we used the Keras

---

[5] https://www.nltk.org/.
[6] https://scikit-learn.org/.

**Table 2.** Test performances for different models and input representations. The column labeled **F** corresponds to micro-averaged F-score over the eight classes, and the remaining columns correspond to per-class F-score.

| Model | Repr. | F | Id | Fac | Arg | LB | Pre | Req | Rem | Oth |
|---|---|---|---|---|---|---|---|---|---|---|
| NB | BoW | 52.30 | 16.87 | 64.02 | 62.24 | 40.86 | 67.49 | 67.16 | 54.05 | 45.68 |
| | TFIDF | 60.47 | 13.29 | 58.49 | 61.68 | 55.63 | 67.80 | 66.66 | 96.00 | 64.17 |
| SVM | BoW | 59.28 | 13.39 | 54.71 | 57.80 | 54.25 | 70.69 | 64.00 | 92.30 | 67.14 |
| | TFIDF | 60.66 | 11.00 | 57.43 | 62.44 | 54.54 | 69.20 | 65.32 | 96.00 | 69.37 |
| MLP | BERT$^f$ | 75.50 | 88.00 | 69.40 | 70.80 | 67.30 | 83.10 | 80.10 | 76.90 | 82.10 |
| Linear layer | BERT | **80.50** | **91.60** | **71.40** | **74.70** | **74.20** | **88.40** | **86.40** | **96.00** | **89.70** |

library to train the MLP model, since the BERT LM is kept fixed. In Table 2, we refer to this *fixed* BERT LM as BERT$^f$. The MLP network comprises two hidden layers with 512 neurons each. This network was trained by the NAdam optimizer for 500 epochs using a batch size of 32 sentences and the categorical cross-entropy loss. The original (end-to-end) model was trained by the default HF AdamW optimizer for 10 epochs using a batch size of 4 sentences. From the results in Table 2, we can observe that fine-tuning the BERT LM brings a 5 point increase in $F$-score. The best performing method achieved an $F$-score of 80.50, which is almost 20 points higher than the performance achieved by the best baseline method.

In Table 2, we also report per-class $F$-scores. Untypically, the class with best results is *Remedy*, which is the least frequent class. Although there are only 71 sentences labeled as *Remedy* in the whole corpus (including the three splits), such sentences have a very specific vocabulary ("Dá-se o valor da causa ...", for instance). This characteristic obviously facilitates the identification of these sentences. Besides that, we also observe that some frequent classes – namely *Facts* (2), *Arguments* (3), and *Legal Basis* (4) – present the worst performances.

In order to investigate this fact, we present the confusion matrix for our best model predictions in Fig. 3. First, we can see that there are 73 sentences labeled as *Facts* (Fac) but classified by the model as *Arguments* (Arg). And other 73 sentences labeled as *Arguments* (Arg) but classified as *Facts* (Fac). We also see that there are 181 sentences labeled as *Arguments* (Arg), *Legal Basis* (LB) or *Precedents* (Pre) that are misclassified among these same three classes. As mentioned in Sect. 3, sentences from these four roles (Fac, Arg, LB and Pre) are frequently interspersed among them. Thus, these interspersed sentences are probably more difficult to classify.

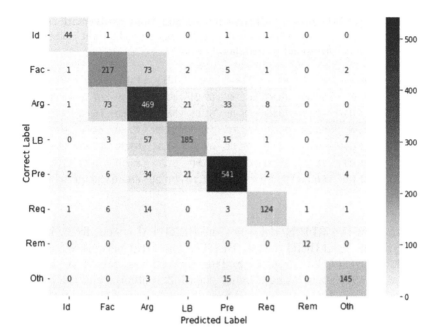

**Fig. 3.** Confusion matrix

## 6    Conclusions and Future Work

In this paper, we present a new corpus comprising 70 petitions (petiÇão inicial) from civil lawsuits filed in TJMS. Based on the Brazilian civil procedure, we proposed eight categories representing the rhetorical roles of text sentences within the petitions. We manually labeled the sentences of the proposed corpus using these eight categories. Since TJMS does not require any specific structure for the digital files of petitions, we had to deal with several issues to extract the textual content from these files. As far we know, this is the first work to consider rhetorical role identification of petitions in Portuguese language. The proposed corpus is available[7] and we hope that it can foster research on this important subject.

We also analysed the performance of classic and deep learning machine learn methods on the proposed Rhetorical Role Identification corpus. The best performing method was an end-to-end-trained BERT-based sentence classifier. This model achieved 80.50 of $F$-score on our test set.

As future work, we intend to pre-train a BERT language model on judicial documents. The models evaluated in this work classify sentences independently, i.e. disregarding the sequence of sentences within a petition. Thus, we also intend to improve the obtained classification performance by employing deep learning models that consider the sequential structure of sentences. Nevertheless, the

---

[7] https://bit.ly/rhetoricalrole.

obtained results are promising. Therefore, we are working on the development of a new corpus for summarization of petitions, which will leverage the rhetorical role labels in the proposed corpus.

As we have stated, the contributions of this paper can open new research possibilities for judicial NLP. Additionally, our work can lead to solutions with potential to relieve the current bottleneck in Brazilian judges' offices.

# References

1. de Araujo, P.H.L., de Campos, T.E., Braz, F.A., da Silva, N.C.: VICTOR: a dataset for Brazilian legal documents classification. In: Proceedings of the 12th Language Resources and Evaluation Conference, Marseille, France, pp. 1449–1458. European Language Resources Association (May 2020). https://www.aclweb.org/anthology/2020.lrec-1.181

2. Bhattacharya, P., Paul, S., Ghosh, K., Ghosh, S., Wyner, A.: Identification of rhetorical roles of sentences in Indian legal judgments. CoRR abs/1911.05405 (2019). http://arxiv.org/abs/1911.05405

3. Bird, S., Loper, E., Klein, E.: Natural Language Processing with Python. O'Reilly Media Inc. (2009)

4. Brasil: Lei n. 13.105 de 16 de março de 2015 (Código de Processo Civil)

5. Contractor, D., Guo, Y., Korhonen, A.: Using argumentative zones for extractive summarization of scientific articles. In: Proceedings of COLING 2012, Mumbai, India, pp. 663–678. The COLING 2012 Organizing Committee (December 2012). https://www.aclweb.org/anthology/C12-1041

6. Devlin, J., Chang, M.W., Lee, K., Toutanova, K.: BERT: pre-training of deep bidirectional transformers for language understanding. In: Proceedings of the 2019 Conference of the North American Chapter of the Association for Computational Linguistics: Human Language Technologies, Volume 1 (Long and Short Papers), Minneapolis, Minnesota, pp. 4171–4186. Association for Computational Linguistics (June 2019). https://doi.org/10.18653/v1/N19-1423. https://www.aclweb.org/anthology/N19-1423

7. Feltrim, V.D., Aluísio, S.M., Nunes, M.G.V.: Analysis of the rhetorical structure of computer science abstracts in Portuguese. In: Corpus Linguistics (2003)

8. Feltrim, V.D., Nunes, M.G.V., Aluísio, S.M.: Um corpus de textos científicos em português para a análise da estrutura esquemática (2001)

9. Feltrim, V.D., Teufel, S., das Nunes, M.G.V., Aluísio, S.M.: Argumentative zoning applied to critiquing novices' scientific abstracts. In: Shanahan, J.G., Qu, Y., Wiebe, J. (eds.) Computing Attitude and Affect in Text: Theory and Applications. The Information Retrieval Series, vol. 20. Springer, Dordrecht (2006). https://doi.org/10.1007/1-4020-4102-0_18

10. Grover, C., Hachey, B., Hughson, I.: The HOLJ corpus: supporting summarisation of legal texts. In: Proceedings of the 5th International Workshop on Linguistically Interpreted Corpora, Geneva, Switzerland, pp. 47–54. COLING, 29 August 2004. https://www.aclweb.org/anthology/W04-1907

11. Hachey, B., Grover, C.: A rhetorical status classifier for legal text summarisation. In: Text Summarization Branches Out, Barcelona, Spain, pp. 35–42. Association for Computational Linguistics (July 2004). https://www.aclweb.org/anthology/W04-1007

12. Liu, H.: Automatic argumentative-zoning using word2vec. CoRR abs/1703.10152 (2017). http://arxiv.org/abs/1703.10152
13. Luz de Araujo, P.H., de Campos, T.E., de Oliveira, R.R.R., Stauffer, M., Couto, S., Bermejo, P.: LeNER-Br: a dataset for named entity recognition in Brazilian legal text. In: Villavicencio, A., Moreira, V., Abad, A., Caseli, H., Gamallo, P., Ramisch, C., Gonçalo Oliveira, H., Paetzold, G.H. (eds.) PROPOR 2018. LNCS (LNAI), vol. 11122, pp. 313–323. Springer, Cham (2018). https://doi.org/10.1007/978-3-319-99722-3_32
14. Nakayama, H., Kubo, T., Kamura, J., Taniguchi, Y., Liang, X.: doccano: text annotation tool for human (2018). Software available from https://github.com/doccano/doccano
15. Nejadgholi, I., Bougueng, R., Witherspoon, S.: A semi-supervised training method for semantic search of legal facts in Canadian immigration cases. In: Wyner, A.Z., Casini, G. (eds.) The 30th Annual Conference on Legal Knowledge and Information Systems, JURIX 2017. Frontiers in Artificial Intelligence and Applications, Luxembourg, 13–15 December 2017, vol. 302, pp. 125–134. IOS Press (2017). https://doi.org/10.3233/978-1-61499-838-9-125
16. Radford, A., Narasimhan, K., Salimans, T., Sutskever, I.: Improving language understanding by generative pre-training. OpenAI (2018)
17. Radford, A., Wu, J., Child, R., Luan, D., Amodei, D., Sutskever, I.: Language models are unsupervised multitask learners. OpenAI (2019)
18. Rotta, M.J.R., Vieira, P., Rover, A.J., Sewald, E., Jr.: Aceleração processual e o processo judicial digital: Um estudo comparativo de tempos de tramitação em tribunais de justiça. Democracia Digital e Governo Eletrônico 1(8), 125–154 (2013)
19. Saravanan, M.: Ontology-based retrieval and automatic summarization of legal judgments. Ph.D. thesis, Indian Institute of Technology Madras (2008)
20. Saravanan, M., Ravindran, B.: Identification of rhetorical roles for segmentation and summarization of a legal judgment. Artif. Intel. Law 18(1), 45–76 (2010)
21. Saravanan, M., Ravindran, B., Raman, S.: Automatic identification of rhetorical roles using conditional random fields for legal document summarization. In: Proceedings of the 3rd International Joint Conference on Natural Language Processing: Volume-I (2008). https://www.aclweb.org/anthology/I08-1063
22. Savelka, J., Ashley, K.D.: Segmenting U.S. court decisions into functional and issue specific parts. In: Palmirani, M. (ed.) The 31st Annual Conference on Legal Knowledge and Information Systems, JURIX 2018. Frontiers in Artificial Intelligence and Applications, Groningen, The Netherlands, 12–14 December 2018, vol. 313, pp. 111–120. IOS Press (2018). https://doi.org/10.3233/978-1-61499-935-5-111
23. Souza, F., Nogueira, R., Lotufo, R.: BERTimbau: pretrained BERT models for Brazilian Portuguese. In: 9th Brazilian Conference on Intelligent Systems, BRACIS, Rio Grande do Sul, Brazil, 20–23 October (2020, to appear)
24. Souza, F., Nogueira, R.F., de Alencar Lotufo, R.: Portuguese named entity recognition using BERT-CRF. CoRR abs/1909.10649 (2019). http://arxiv.org/abs/1909.10649
25. Teufel, S.: Argumentative zoning: information extraction from scientific text. Ph.D. thesis, University of Edinburgh (1999). http://www.cl.cam.ac.uk/users/sht25/az.html
26. Teufel, S., Moens, M.: Sentence extraction and rhetorical classification for flexible abstracts. In: Intelligent Text Summarization, pp. 16–25 (1998)

27. Vaswani, A., et al.: Attention is all you need. In: Guyon, I., et al. (eds.) Advances in Neural Information Processing Systems, vol. 30. Curran Associates, Inc. (2017). https://proceedings.neurips.cc/paper/2017/file/3f5ee243547dee91fbd053c1c4a845aa-Paper.pdf

28. Walker, V.R., Pillaipakkamnatt, K., Davidson, A.M., Linares, M., Pesce, D.J.: Automatic classification of rhetorical roles for sentences: comparing rule-based scripts with machine learning. In: Ashley, K.D., et al. (eds.) Proceedings of the 3rd Workshop on Automated Semantic Analysis of Information in Legal Texts co-located with the 17th International Conference on Artificial Intelligence and Law, ICAIL 2019, Montreal, QC, Canada, 21 June 2019. CEUR Workshop Proceedings, vol. 2385. CEUR-WS.org (2019). http://ceur-ws.org/Vol-2385/paper1.pdf

29. Yamada, H., Teufel, S., Tokunaga, T.: Neural network based rhetorical status classification for japanese judgment documents. In: Araszkiewicz, M., Rodríguez-Doncel, V. (eds.) The 32nd Annual Conference on Legal Knowledge and Information Systems, JURIX 2019. Frontiers in Artificial Intelligence and Applications, Madrid, Spain, 11–13 December 2019, vol. 322, pp. 133–142. IOS Press (2019). https://doi.org/10.3233/FAIA190314

# Speech2Phone: A Novel and Efficient Method for Training Speaker Recognition Models

Edresson Casanova[1(✉)], Arnaldo Candido Junior[2], Christopher Shulby[3],
Frederico Santos de Oliveira[4], Lucas Rafael Stefanel Gris[2],
Hamilton Pereira da Silva[2], Sandra Maria Aluísio[1], and Moacir Antonelli Ponti[1]

[1] University of São Paulo, São Carlos, Brazil
edresson@usp.br
[2] Federal University of Technology - Paraná, Medianeira, Brazil
[3] DefinedCrowd Corp, Seattle, USA
[4] Federal University of Goiás, Goiânia, Brazil

**Abstract.** In this paper we present an efficient method for training models for speaker recognition using small or under-resourced datasets. This method requires less data than other SOTA (State-Of-The-Art) methods, e.g. the Angular Prototypical and GE2E loss functions, while achieving similar results to those methods. This is done using the knowledge of the reconstruction of a phoneme in the speaker's voice. For this purpose, a new dataset was built, composed of 40 male speakers, who read sentences in Portuguese, totaling approximately 3h. We compare the three best architectures trained using our method to select the best one, which is the one with a shallow architecture. Then, we compared this model with the SOTA method for the speaker recognition task: the Fast ResNet–34 trained with approximately 2,000 h, using the loss functions Angular Prototypical and GE2E. Three experiments were carried out with datasets in different languages. Among these three experiments, our model achieved the second best result in two experiments and the best result in one of them. This highlights the importance of our method, which proved to be a great competitor to SOTA speaker recognition models, with 500x less data and a simpler approach.

**Keywords:** Speaker verification · Speaker recognition · Speaker identification

## 1 Introduction

Voice recognition is widely used in many applications, such as intelligent personal assistants [14], telephone-banking systems [4], automatic question response [12], among others. In several of these applications, it is useful to identify the speaker, as is the case in voice-enabled authentication and meeting loggers. Speaker verification can be done in two scenarios: open-set and closed-set. In both scenarios, the objective is to verify that two audio samples belong to the same speaker. However, in the closed-set scenario, the verification is restricted only to speakers seen during the training of the models. On the other hand, in the open-set scenario, verification occurs with speakers not seen in model training [11,17]. The verification of speakers in an open-set scenario is especially

© Springer Nature Switzerland AG 2021
A. Britto and K. Valdivia Delgado (Eds.): BRACIS 2021, LNAI 13074, pp. 572–585, 2021.
https://doi.org/10.1007/978-3-030-91699-2_39

desired in applications such as meeting loggers, since in these applications speakers can be added frequently, thus, the use of closed-set models would imply the retraining of the model after the insertion of new speakers.

The first works to use deep neural networks in speaker recognition in an open-set scenario learned speaker embeddings were [30,31], using the Softmax function. Although the Softmax classifier can learn different embeddings for different speakers, it is not discriminatory enough [8]. To work around this problem, models trained with softmax were combined with back-ends built on Probabilistic Linear Discriminant Analysis (PLDA) [16] to generate scoring functions [27,31]. On the other hand, Softmax Angular [19] was proposed and it uses cosine similarity as a logit entry for the softmax layer, and it proved to be superior to the use of softmax only.

Thereafter, Additive Margins in Softmax (AM-Softmax) [35] was proposed to increase inter-class variance by introducing a cosine margin penalty in the target logit. However, according to [8] training with AM-Softmax and AAM-Softmax [10] proved to be a challenge, as they are sensitive to scale and margin value in the loss function. The use of Contrastive Loss [7] and Triplet Loss [5,28] also achieved promising results in speaker recognition, but these methods require careful choice of pairs or triplets, which costs time and can interfere with performance [8]. Finally, the use of Prototypical networks [36] for speaker recognition was proposed. Prototypical networks seek to learn a metric space in which the classification of open-sets of speakers can be performed by calculating distances to prototypical representations of each class. Generalized end-to-end loss (GE2E) [34] and Angular Prototypical (AngleProto) [8] follow the same principle and achieved state-of-the-art (SOTA) results recently in speaker recognition. Parallel with this work, [15] proposed the use of the AngleProto loss function in conjunction with Softmax, presenting a result superior to the use of AngleProto only. The authors proposed a new architecture presenting SOTA results.

In this work, we propose a new method for training speaker recognition models, called Speech2Phone. This method was trained with approximately 3.5 h of speech and surpassed a model trained with 2.000 h of speech using the GE2E loss function. Our method is based on the reconstruction of the pronunciation of a specific phoneme and has shown promise in scenarios with few available resources. In addition, the simplicity of its architecture makes our method suitable for real-time applications with low processing power.

Finally, to simplify the reproduction of this work, Python code and download links for the datasets used to reproduce all experiments are publicly available on the Github repository[1].

This work is organized as follows. Section 2 details the datasets used as well as the preprocessing performed to attend the proposed experiments. Section 3 presents the Speech2Phone method and experiments carried out to find the best model trained with this method for the identification of speakers in an open-set scenario. Section 4 compares the best model trained with the Speech2Phone method with the state of the art in the literature. Finally, Sect. 5 shows the conclusions of this paper.

---

[1] https://github.com/Edresson/Speech2Phone.

## 2    Datasets and Pre-processing

Section 2.1 presents the datasets used, as well as describes a new dataset created to attend the needs of our experiments. Sections 2.2 and 2.3 detail the pre-processing performed on the datasets to allow the execution of all the proposed experiments.

### 2.1    Audio Datasets

To train our method, it was necessary to build a specific dataset, which we call the Speech2Phone dataset. This dataset includes 40 male speakers, aged between 20 and 50 years. The dataset includes only Portuguese utterances, because that is the native language of the speakers. We chose to focus only on male speakers, because during the collection phase of our dataset we were able to collect only voices from 5 female speakers. To collect the data, each speaker was given a phonetically balanced text, according to the work of [29], which was comprised of 149 words. The reading time ranged from 42 to 95 s, totaling approximately 43 min of speech.

Additionally, we asked each speaker to say the phoneme /a/ for approximately three seconds. The central second of each capture was extracted and then used as expected output for the embedding models. The phoneme /a/ was chosen because it is simple to articulate and very frequent in the Portuguese language. The Speech2Phone dataset is publicly available on the Github repository[2]

To evaluate our method and compare it with related works, we use the VCTK [33] and Common Voice (CV) [2] datasets. The VCTK is an English language dataset with a total of 109 speakers. During its creation, the 109 speakers spoke approximately 400 sentences. The same phrases are spoken by all speakers. The dataset has approximately 44 h of speech and is sampled at 48 KHz. Common Voice is a massively multilingual transcribed speech dataset for research and development of speech technology. CV has 54 subsets and each of these sets have data from a language, currently the dataset has a total of 5,671 h. In this work, we use version 5.2 of the corpus.

### 2.2    Preprocessing of the Speech2Phone Dataset

To preprocess the Speech2Phone dataset we extracted five-second speech segments from the original audio length. The five-second window was defined after preliminary experiments, varying the input duration. In order to maximize the number of speech segments, we used the overlapping technique, in which the window was shifted one second each time and an instance was extracted during the total audio duration. The main dataset resulted in 2,394 speech segments totaling 3 h and 23 min of speech. The next step was to divide the dataset into smaller sets to attend the needs of each proposed experiment. Therefore, the original dataset was divided into four subsets. The Partitions $A_1$ and $B_1$ each have 20 different speakers and have approximately 1,097 samples each. Partitions $A_2$ and $B_2$ have approximately 100 speech segments each and have, respectively, speakers from the $A_1$ and $B_1$ partition. Thus, $A$ partitions do not have speakers in common with $B$ partitions.

---

[2] https://github.com/Edresson/Speech2Phone.

## 2.3 Pre-processing of Speaker Verification Datasets

We preprocessed the VCTK and CV datasets in order to use them for speaker verification. For the VCTK we chose to use the entire dataset and for CV we used the test subsets of the dataset in Portuguese (PT), Spanish (ES) and Chinese spoken in China (ZH).

The VCTK dataset has, in many of its samples, long initial and final silences. In order to ensure that this feature does not affect our analysis, we chose to remove these silences. So, we applied Voice Activity Detection (VAD) using the Python implementation of the Webrtcvad toolkit[3].

We used VCTK and CV to test our models. The datasets were used to build audio pairs. The positive class is composed from audio pairs from the same speaker, while negative class has pairs from different speakers. In this scenario, it is possible to build more examples from the negative class. To avoid class imbalance issues, we defined the maximum number of negative pairs analyzed as the number of positive samples divided by the number of speakers. We also removed speakers with less than two samples.

Table 1 shows the number of speakers, language and number of positive and negative speech segments of the datasets used to verify the speaker in our experiments. The Python code used for the preprocessing of the dataset, as well as the link to download the versions of the VCTK and CV datasets used are available in the Github repository[4].

**Table 1.** Preprocessed speaker verification datasets

| Dataset | Language | N° speakers | N° pos. samples | N° neg. samples |
|---|---|---|---|---|
| Common Voice | PT | 525 | 25,846 | 25,847 |
| | ES | 4,167 | 19,355 | 19,356 |
| | ZH | 1,968 | 14,656 | 14,657 |
| VCTK | EN | 109 | 9,084,638 | 9,001,368 |

# 3   Speech2Phone

Section 3.1 presents the experiments carried out to choose the best model trained with the Speech2Phone method to identify speakers in the open-set scenario. On the other hand, Sect. 3.2 presents the results of Speech2Phone experiments.

## 3.1 Proposed Method

The goal of open-set models is to be speaker independent; additionally, a desirable feature is to be multilingual and text independent. In pursuit of these goals, we propose that the neural network training uses five second speech fragments as input and, as expected output, the reconstruction of a second of a simple phoneme (/a/ in our experiments).

---

[3] https://github.com/wiseman/py-webrtcvad.

[4] https://github.com/Edresson/Speech2Phone/tree/master/Paper/EER-Experiments.

As the phoneme sounds differ according to each speaker, a good reconstruction would allow the model to distinguish between speakers. Focusing on a single phoneme allows for dimensionality reduction in the embedding layer.

In the Speech2Phone experiments, the model's input and the expected output is represented in the form of Mel Frequency Cepstral Coefficients (MFCCs) [20]. We extract MFCCs using the Librosa [21] library. The default sampling rate (22 KHz) was used and 13 MFCCs (empirically defined) were extracted. Windowed frames were used as defined by the default parameters in Librosa 0.6, namely, a 512 Hop Length and 2,048 as the window length for the Fast Fourier Transform [25]. In addition, as the models must reconstruct an MFCC segment they were induced using Mean Square Error (MSE) [13].

Several models using the Speech2Phone method, and consequently the Speech2Phone dataset, have been tested. We report the three most interesting ones in this section. To evaluate these experiments, we used the accuracy of the speaker identification.

To calculate the accuracy, we randomly chose and entered an embedding of a sample of each of the speakers in a database. For the calculation it is necessary to search the extracted embedding in an embeddings database. This is done by running the KNN [22] algorithm with $k = 1$ and using the Euclidean distance. If the embedding of a speaker has a Euclidean distance closer to its embedding registered in the database than the embedding of all other speakers, this will be counted as a hit, otherwise it will be counted as an error.

In the experiments, we compared the performance of the open-set models in a closed-set scenario. All of these experiments were trained with the Speech2Phone dataset $A_1$ subset, described previously in Sect. 2.2. Therefore, the models were trained with only 1,037 speech segments of 20 different speakers, approximately 1.5 h of speech.

Tensorflow [1] and TFlearn [32] were used to generate the neural networks for all Speech2Phone Experiments. All models were trained using the Adam Optimizer [18]. The convolutional layers in all experiments have a stride of 1. Hyperparameters used to train each model are presented in Table 2.

**Table 2.** Experiments hyperparameters

| Experiment | Epochs | Learning rate | Batch size |
|---|---|---|---|
| 1 (Dense) | 1,000 | 0.0007 | 128 |
| 2 (Conv) | 10 | 0.0010 | 16 |
| 3 (Recurrent) | 100 | 0.0050 | 256 |

To try to find the best topology for the Speech2Phone method, we propose the following experiments:

- **Experiment 1 (Dense):** this experiment consists of a fully connected feed-forward neural network with one hidden layer for embedding extraction. The architecture of the model used in this experiment is shown in the Fig. 1.

- **Experiment 2 (Conv):** This experiment is based on Experiment 1, but it uses a fully convolutional neural network. This network has only convolutional layers, in addition the decoder uses upsampling layer. Following [8] we use 2D convolutions. The speech segments can be seen as a bidimensional image matrix where columns are time steps and the rows are cepstral coefficients. Convolutions have the advantage of being translationally invariant in this matrix. As we try to reconstruct a specific phoneme, this is a desired property, since the location of the instance may contain the target phoneme may occur in different parts of the window. The model architecture used in this experiment is shown in the Fig. 2.

- **Experiment 3 (Recurrent):** This experiment is based on Experiment 1, but it consists of a recurrent fully-connected neural network for embedding generation. The five-second window is split into five segments containing one second each, in which the model analyzes one at a time. Considering that the recurrence window is small, we used classical recurrence instead of long term models like LSTM [13], since vanishing gradients are less prone to occur. If the phoneme of interest happens in one of the five fragments, the recurrence network should store it in its memory before reconstructing it in the final step, potentially improving the reconstruction accuracy. The approach reduces the number of learned parameters and, consequently, also improves training times. The model architecture used in this experiment is shown in the Fig. 3.

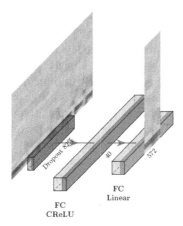

**Fig. 1.** Fully connected shallow neural network (experiment 1)

### 3.2 Speech2Phone Results

Table 3 shows the results of the Speech2Phone experiments, showing accuracy obtained in the open-set scenario, that is, evaluations using different speakers for training and testing the models and closed-set, where the training and test speakers are the same.

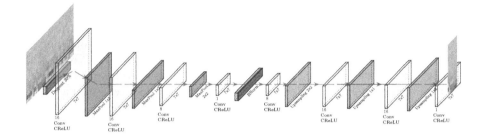

**Fig. 2.** Fully convolutional neural network (experiment 2)

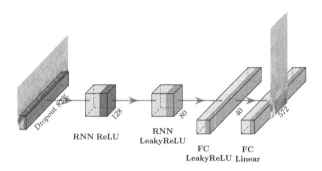

**Fig. 3.** Recurrent neural network (experiment 3)

In this set of experiments, the neural models received 5 s of audio from a specific speaker and were induced to reconstruct 1 s of the phoneme /a/ in the voice of that speaker. The goal is to obtain good results with little training data in contrast to the GE2E and AngleProto loss functions, which need a large data set for good performance. To conduct the proposed experiments, samples from 20 speakers were used for training and samples from another 20 speakers for testing, as previously discussed in Sect. 3.1.

Experiment 1 used a fully connected neural network. In an open-set scenario, it obtained an accuracy of 76.96%, the best accuracy in the open-set scenario for all experiments. On the other hand, in the closed-set scenario, it obtained 77.50% accuracy. This was the worst result for all closed-set experiments. We believe that the fully connected model achieved the best results on the open-set due to the low number of parameters, thus being less prone to overfit. In addition, the dataset is very small and in this way, deeper models are very likely to memorize features dependent on the speaker or noise artifacts. Apparently, the recurrent and convolutional models specialized in extracting particular features for the speakers in the training set in order to reconstruct the output. In this way, as the deeper models learn specific characteristics of the speakers, their generalization for new speakers is impaired, having good performance in the closed-set scenario and a drop in performance in the open-set.

Experiment 2, which explored the use of a fully convolutional neural network for generating embeddings, presented the second best result (64.43%) in the open-set scenario. On the other hand, in the closed-set, the model achieved the best result obtaining

**Table 3.** Results of Speech2Phone experiments

| Experiment | Scenario (subset) | Accuracy | Test speech segments |
|---|---|---|---|
| 1 (Dense) | Closed-set ($A_2$) | 77.50 | 100 |
| | Open-set ($B_1 + B_2$) | 76.96 | 1,197 |
| 2 (Conv) | Closed-set ($A_2$) | 100.00 | 100 |
| | Open-set($B_1 + B_2$) | 64.43 | 1,197 |
| 3 (Recurrent) | Closed-set ($A_2$) | 88.75 | 100 |
| | open-set ($B_1 + B_2$) | 50.28 | 1,197 |

an accuracy of 100%. Translational invariance is a useful feature from convolutional networks and can be used to detect specific phonemes independently of where their occur in the audio. We believe that convolutional models are suitable for this task; however, due to the low amount of data the models learn characteristics dependent on speakers, which leaves this model at a disadvantage in open-set scenario, having a worse performance than Experiment 1.

Experiment 3 explored the use of a recurrent neural network with fully connected layers for generating embeddings, resulting in the worst accuracy in the open-set scenario (50.28%) and the second worst in the closed-set scenario (88.75%). Recurrent models can perform a more detailed analysis on the input audio, searching patterns in one input fragment at a time. However, a problem may happen when this pattern is split in a different analysis window. The simple recurrent model tested could not overcome this issue. We also evaluated, in preliminary experiments, a recurrent LSTM network, but it did not perform as well as simple recurrence, as there is no need for long-term memory in a 5-step analysis process.

In the open-set scenario, the superiority of the fully connected model (Experiment 1) is noticeable. This is because they are able to generalize better for new speakers and have proven to be less prone to overfitting for the task. In addition, the fully connected model was able to maintain very close accuracy in the closed-set scenario (77.50%), compared to the open-set scenario (76.96%), while the other models had a great drop in performance. On the other hand, the fully convolutional model (Experiment 2) also showed promising results with a performance 12.53% below the fully connected model.

## 4    Application: Speaker Verification

Section 4.1 presents the proposed experiments to compare our method with the state of the art in the literature. On the other hand, Sect. 4.2 presents the results of speaker verification experiments.

### 4.1    Speaker Verification Experiments

An important question is how well a model trained with the Speech2Phone method performs in speaker verification. To answer this question we compared Speech2Phone with the Fast ResNet–34 model proposed by [8] trained using the Angular Prototypical [8] and GE2E [34] losses function. We chose this model because it presents state-of-the-art results in the VoxCeleb [23] dataset, in addition the authors made the pre-trained models available in the Github repository[5].

To compare the models, we chose two datasets, one of which is multi-language, presented in Sect. 2.3. As Speech2Phone receives 22 kHz sample rate audio, while Fast ResNet–34 16 kHz audio input. We cannot directly compare the results of the models in the VoxCeleb test dataset. As VoxCeleb is sampled at 16 kHz, it would not be a fair comparison to resample audios from 16 kHz to 22 kHz. Therefore, we chose other datasets with a sample rate greater than 22 kHz. In addition, using the dataset test that the Fast ResNet–34 model was trained on could put the Speech2Phone model at a disadvantage.

The audios for each dataset were resampled to 16 kHz for the test with the Fast ResNet–34 model and to 22 kHz for the test with Speech2Phone, thus making a fair comparison between the models. For comparison, we use the metric Equal Error Rate (EER) [6], the lower the EER is, the greater the accuracy becomes.

To compare the best model trained with the Speech2Phone method with the SOTA we propose the following experiments:

- **Experiment 4 (Speech2Phone):** This experiment uses the same model and hyperparameters as experiment 1; however, the model was trained with the entire Speech2Phone dataset. Therefore, the model was trained with 2,394 speech segments of 40 speakers totaling approximately 3 h and 23 min of speech.
- **Experiment 5 (Fast AngleProto):** This experiment uses the Fast ResNet–34 model, proposed in [8], this model is trained with the Angular Prototypical loss function in the Voxceleb dataset, which has approximately 2,000 h of speech by approximately 7,000 speakers. This model achieves an EER of approximately 2.2 in the voxceleb dataset test set, as reported in [8].
- **Experiment 6 (Fast GE2E):** This experiment also uses the Fast ResNet–34 model, and was also trained with the same number of speakers and hours of experiment 5. However the model is trained using the GE2E loss function.

For the evaluation of the Fast ResNet–34 model we followed the original work and sample ten 4-s temporal crops at regular intervals from each test segment. As the model accepts audios of variable size when the audio was less than 4-s, like the original work, we only used the audio without sample crops.

Unlike the Fast ResNet–34 model, which accepts audios of varying sizes, our model receives an MFCC of just 5 s of speech as input. However, in the VCTK and CV datasets we have audios with variable sizes. Therefore, for a fair comparison and each model to have access to all the audio content for calculating the EER of the Speech2Phone model, we proceed as follows. For audios longer than 5 s, we use the overlapping technique, as described in Sect. 2.2. Therefore, after applying the overlapping technique for a six-second audio, two five-second samples are obtained, the resulting embedding for that sample is the average between the predicted embedding for these two five-second samples. On the other hand, for sample less than 5 s, we repeat the audio frames until reaching at least 5 s, for example, a three-second audio is repeated once, thus obtaining

---

[5] https://github.com/clovaai/voxceleb_trainer.

a six-second audio, where the resulting audio applies the overlapping technique, since we audios longer than 5 s.

## 4.2 Speaker Verification Results

In this set of experiments we compared the performance of our best model trained with the Speech2Phone method with the Fast ResNet–34 model proposed by [8], trained with approximately 2,000 h of speech using the Angular Prototypical loss function [8] and GE2E [34]. Table 4 shows the EER of these experiments in English using the VCTK dataset, in Portuguese (PT), Spanish (ES) and Chinese (ZH) using the Common Voice dataset.

**Table 4.** Results for speaker verification experiments

| Experiment | Datasets | EER (%) |
|---|---|---|
| 4 (Speech2Phone) | VCTK | **22.7041** |
| | CV PT | 13.6805 |
| | CV ZH | 10.3909 |
| | CV ES | 7.7551 |
| 5 (Fast AngleProto) | VCTK | 23.8011 |
| | CV PT | **7.2468** |
| | CV ZH | **7.2666** |
| | CV ES | **2.8622** |
| 6 (Fast GE2E) | VCTK | 27.0647 |
| | CV PT | 14.0751 |
| | CV ZH | 12.9563 |
| | CV ES | 5.0530 |

Experiment 4 consisted of the best Speech2Phone result trained using the entire Speech2Phone dataset (approximately 3 h and 23 min of speech from 40 different speakers). This achieved the best EER of all experiments in the VCTK dataset. For the Common Voice dataset, the model achieved the second best result for the PT and ZH subsets, being surpassed only by the Fast ResNet–34 model trained with the Angular Prototypical loss function (Experiment 5). On the other hand, in the ES subset, this experiment had the worst performance of all experiments.

Experiment 5 used Fast ResNet–34 model trained with the Angular Prototypical loss function, obtaining the second best EER in the VCTK dataset, only surpassed by Speech2Phone. In addition, this experiment achieved the best result in all subsets of the Common Voice dataset.

Experiment 6, which consisted of using Fast ResNet–34 model trained with the GE2E loss function, obtained the worst EER in the VCTK dataset. This experiment also had the worst EER in the ZH and PT subsets of Common Voice. However, the model achieved the second best EER in the ES subset of Common Voice.

Experiment 4 showed the potential of the Speech2Phone approach, which despite having been trained with only 3 h and 23 min of speech from only 40 speakers, obtained better results than Fast ResNet–34 model trained with 2000 h of speech and approximately 7,000 speakers using the GE2E loss function. In addition, this experiment achieved better results than both Experiments 5 and 6 in the VCTK dataset.

In experiment 5 we observed better results in 3 of the 4 evaluated subsets, when compared with experiment 4. This was expected due to the model in experiment 5 having access to more than 1.996 h of speech and 6.960 speakers. In addition, the Experiment 4's training dataset has only male voices, as the reconstruction of a female voice is different and the VCTK and Common voice datasets have female speakers this should cause a decrease of performance at test time. Another point is that the training dataset used in Experiment 4 is a high quality dataset with low background noise, so the model probably did not learn to ignore or filter out noise, probably harming the reconstruction of the /a/ phoneme. Despite audio quality and low noise facilitate learning during training, the model may be impaired in a noisy situation which is a scenario observed in other domains such as images [24]. Its better overall performance in the VCTK dataset, also high quality and low noise, built for speech synthesis and voice transfer applications, is yet another evidence for this behavior. The performance of the model drops, compared to experiment 5, when the model is used in audios recorded in uncontrolled environments such as Common Voice.

In Experiments 5 and 6 we verified what has already been shown in [8], that the Fast ResNet–34 model trained with the AngleProto loss function in the Voxceleb dataset obtains an EER higher than the same model trained with the GE2E loss function. However, the authors in their work compared the models only in the VoxCeleb test dataset, we on the other hand, made a comparison using 4 different languages and different datasets, thus making a broader comparison.

An important consideration is that given the way we propose our experiments, we cannot say that language is a factor that decreases or increases the performance of the models. The high values of EER in the English language, for example, are due to the way the speaker verification dataset was set up. The VCTK has only 109 speakers and many samples were considered for each speaker as can be seen in Table 1. A greater number of test instances make the task more difficult and tend to increase the EER values. Therefore, we can only compare the individual performance of each model in the datasets and we cannot discuss decrease or increase in performance with the language change.

## 5   Conclusions and Future Work

In this article, we proposed a novel training method for speaker recognition models, called Speech2Phone. To enable the training of this method, we also built a novel dataset. Fully connected, fully convolutional and recurring models were explored. We observed that the fully connected models have a better performance in open-set scenarios, although they have had the worst performance for the closed-set scenario, while convolutional models have a better performance in the closed-set scenario, but they do not generalize well for the open-set scenario. The best model in our experiments was trained on 3 h and 23 min of speech and compared to two SOTA models in the Vox-Celeb dataset, which were trained with approximately 2000 h of speech. The results obtained were comparable to SOTA even with an amount of data approximately 500 times smaller.

This work contributes directly to the area of speaker recognition, presenting a promising method for training speaker recognition models. In addition, the model proposed here can be used in tasks such as speech synthesis [26], voice cloning [3] and multilingual speech conversion [37]. In these tasks, the speaker recognition system embeddings are used to represent the speaker. In addition, an advantage of Speech2Phone in relation to the models proposed in [8] is the speed of execution, as our best model is a fully connected shallow neural network, making it faster. This feature is very desirable for applications due to the need to run in real time.

As our model demands a specific dataset format, we were not able to evaluate its training in a large dataset. We plan to address this issue in future works. For this we intend to increase the model's training dataset as much as possible, and make it public. Additionally, we intend to explore the use of multispeaker speech synthesis [9] and voice cloning [3] to generate a dataset with more speakers and a larger vocabulary. On the other hand, we intend to investigate the possibility of a hybrid method that uses a Speech2Phone technique and Angular Prototypical loss function, thus being able to learn from a larger amount of data and at the same time guide the model's learning with the reconstruction of a phoneme[6]. Evaluating the limits of generalization across different languages is also a matter of future investigation. In addition, we intend to explore the insertion of noise in the training dataset in order to make the model more robust to noise[7].

**Acknowledgments.** This study was financed in part by the Coordenação de Aperfeiçoamento de Pessoal de Nível Superior – Brasil (CAPES) – Finance Code 001, as well as CNPq (National Council of Technological and Scientific Development) grant 304266/2020-5. Also, we would like to thank the CyberLabs and Itaipu Technological Park (Parque Tecnológico Itaipu—PTI) for financial support for this paper. We also gratefully acknowledge the support of NVIDIA Corporation with the donation of the GPU used in part of the experiments presented in this research.

# References

1. Abadi, M., et al.: TensorFlow: large-scale machine learning on heterogeneous distributed systems. arXiv preprint arXiv:1603.04467 (2016)
2. Ardila, R., et al.: Common voice: a massively-multilingual speech corpus. In: Proceedings of the 12th Language Resources and Evaluation Conference, pp. 4218–4222 (2020)
3. Arik, S., Chen, J., Peng, K., Ping, W., Zhou, Y.: Neural voice cloning with a few samples. In: Advances in Neural Information Processing Systems, pp. 10019–10029 (2018)
4. Bowater, R.J., Porter, L.L.: Voice recognition of telephone conversations. US Patent 6,278,772 (21 August 2001)
5. Bredin, H.: TristouNet: triplet loss for speaker turn embedding. In: 2017 IEEE International Conference on Acoustics, Speech and Signal Processing (ICASSP), pp. 5430–5434. IEEE (2017)

---

[6] https://cyberlabs.ai/.

[7] https://www.pti.org.br/.

6. Cheng, J.M., Wang, H.C.: A method of estimating the equal error rate for automatic speaker verification. In: 2004 International Symposium on Chinese Spoken Language Processing, pp. 285–288. IEEE (2004)
7. Chopra, S., Hadsell, R., LeCun, Y.: Learning a similarity metric discriminatively, with application to face verification. In: 2005 IEEE Computer Society Conference on Computer Vision and Pattern Recognition, CVPR 2005, vol. 1, pp. 539–546. IEEE (2005)
8. Chung, J.S., et al.: In defence of metric learning for speaker recognition. In: Proceedings of the Interspeech 2020, pp. 2977–2981 (2020)
9. Cooper, E., et al.: Zero-shot multi-speaker text-to-speech with state-of-the-art neural speaker embeddings. In: 2020 IEEE International Conference on Acoustics, Speech and Signal Processing (ICASSP), ICASSP 2020, pp. 6184–6188. IEEE (2020)
10. Deng, J., Guo, J., Xue, N., Zafeiriou, S.: ArcFace: additive angular margin loss for deep face recognition. In: Proceedings of the IEEE Conference on Computer Vision and Pattern Recognition, pp. 4690–4699 (2019)
11. Ertaş, F.: Fundamentals of speaker recognition. Pamukkale Üniversitesi Mühendislik Bilimleri Dergisi **6**(2–3) (2011)
12. Ferrucci, D., et al.: Building Watson: an overview of the DeepQA project. AI Mag. **31**(3), 59–79 (2010)
13. Goodfellow, I., Bengio, Y., Courville, A.: Deep Learning. MIT Press (2016). http://www.deeplearningbook.org
14. Gruber, T.: Siri, a virtual personal assistant-bringing intelligence to the interface (2009)
15. Heo, H.S., Lee, B.J., Huh, J., Chung, J.S.: Clova baseline system for the VoxCeleb speaker recognition challenge 2020. arXiv preprint arXiv:2009.14153 (2020)
16. Ioffe, S.: Probabilistic linear discriminant analysis. In: Leonardis, A., Bischof, H., Pinz, A. (eds.) ECCV 2006. LNCS, vol. 3954, pp. 531–542. Springer, Heidelberg (2006). https://doi.org/10.1007/11744085_41
17. Kekre, H., Kulkarni, V.: Closed set and open set speaker identification using amplitude distribution of different transforms. In: 2013 International Conference on Advances in Technology and Engineering (ICATE), pp. 1–8. IEEE (2013)
18. Kingma, D.P., Ba, J.: Adam: a method for stochastic optimization. arXiv preprint arXiv:1412.6980 (2014)
19. Liu, W., Wen, Y., Yu, Z., Li, M., Raj, B., Song, L.: SphereFace: deep hypersphere embedding for face recognition. In: Proceedings of the IEEE Conference on Computer Vision and Pattern Recognition, pp. 212–220 (2017)
20. Logan, B., et al.: Mel frequency cepstral coefficients for music modeling. In: ISMIR, vol. 270, pp. 1–11 (2000)
21. McFee, B., et al.: librosa: audio and music signal analysis in Python. In: Proceedings of the 14th Python in Science Conference, pp. 18–25 (2015)
22. Michalski, R.S., Carbonell, J.G., Mitchell, T.M.: Machine learning: an artificial intelligence approach. Springer Science & Business Media (2013). https://doi.org/10.1007/978-3-662-12405-5
23. Nagrani, A., Chung, J.S., Zisserman, A.: VoxCeleb: a large-scale speaker identification dataset. In: Proceedings of the Interspeech 2017, pp. 2616–2620 (2017)
24. Nazaré, T.S., da Costa, G.B.P., Contato, W.A., Ponti, M.: Deep convolutional neural networks and noisy images. In: Mendoza, M., Velastín, S. (eds.) CIARP 2017. LNCS, vol. 10657, pp. 416–424. Springer, Cham (2018). https://doi.org/10.1007/978-3-319-75193-1_50
25. Nussbaumer, H.J.: The fast Fourier transform. In: Fast Fourier Transform and Convolution Algorithms, vol. 2, pp. 80–111. Springer, Heidelberg (1981). https://doi.org/10.1007/978-3-662-00551-4_4
26. Ping, W., et al.: Deep Voice 3: scaling text-to-speech with convolutional sequence learning. In: International Conference on Learning Representations (2018)

27. Ramoji, S., Krishnan V, P., Singh, P., Ganapathy, S.: Pairwise discriminative neural PLDA for speaker verification. arXiv preprint arXiv:2001.07034 (2020)
28. Schroff, F., Kalenichenko, D., Philbin, J.: FaceNet: a unified embedding for face recognition and clustering. In: Proceedings of the IEEE Conference on Computer Vision and Pattern Recognition, pp. 815–823 (2015)
29. Seara, I.: Estudo Estatístico dos Fonemas do Português Brasileiro Falado na Capital de Santa Catarina para Elaboração de Frases Foneticamente Balanceadas. Ph.D. thesis, Dissertação de Mestrado, Universidade Federal de Santa Catarina ... (1994)
30. Snyder, D., Garcia-Romero, D., Povey, D., Khudanpur, S.: Deep neural network embeddings for text-independent speaker verification. In: Interspeech, pp. 999–1003 (2017)
31. Snyder, D., Garcia-Romero, D., Sell, G., Povey, D., Khudanpur, S.: X-vectors: robust DNN embeddings for speaker recognition. In: 2018 IEEE International Conference on Acoustics, Speech and Signal Processing (ICASSP), pp. 5329–5333. IEEE (2018)
32. Tang, Y.: TF.Learn: Tensorflow's high-level module for distributed machine learning. arXiv preprint arXiv:1612.04251 (2016)
33. Veaux, C., Yamagishi, J., MacDonald, K., et al.: Superseded-CSTR VCTK corpus: English multi-speaker corpus for CSTR voice cloning toolkit. University of Edinburgh, The Centre for Speech Technology Research (CSTR) (2016)
34. Wan, L., Wang, Q., Papir, A., Moreno, I.L.: Generalized end-to-end loss for speaker verification. In: 2018 IEEE International Conference on Acoustics, Speech and Signal Processing (ICASSP), pp. 4879–4883. IEEE (2018)
35. Wang, F., Cheng, J., Liu, W., Liu, H.: Additive margin Softmax for face verification. IEEE Sig. Process. Lett. **25**(7), 926–930 (2018)
36. Wang, J., Wang, K.C., Law, M.T., Rudzicz, F., Brudno, M.: Centroid-based deep metric learning for speaker recognition. In: 2019 IEEE International Conference on Acoustics, Speech and Signal Processing (ICASSP), ICASSP 2019, pp. 3652–3656. IEEE (2019)
37. Zhou, Y., Tian, X., Xu, H., Das, R.K., Li, H.: Cross-lingual voice conversion with bilingual Phonetic PosteriorGram and average modeling. In: 2019 IEEE International Conference on Acoustics, Speech and Signal Processing (ICASSP), ICASSP 2019, pp. 6790–6794. IEEE (2019)

# Text Classification in Legal Documents Extracted from Lawsuits in Brazilian Courts

André Aguiar[1] (ID), Raquel Silveira[2](✉) (ID), Vládia Pinheiro[1] (ID), Vasco Furtado[1] (ID),
and João Araújo Neto[1] (ID)

[1] University of Fortaleza, Fortaleza, Brazil
[2] Federal Institute of Education, Science and Technology of Ceará, Fortaleza, Brazil
raquel_silveira@ifce.edu.br

**Abstract.** Recently, Brazil's National Council of Justice (CNJ) highlighted the importance of robust solutions to perform automated lawsuit classification. A correct lawsuit classification substantially improves the assertiveness of (i) distribution, (ii) organization of the agenda of court hearing and sessions, (iii) classification of urgent measures and evidence, (iv) identification of prescription and (v) prevention. This paper investigates different text classification methods and different combinations of embeddings, extracted from Portuguese language models, and information about legislation cited in the initial documents. The models were trained with a Golden Collection of 16 thousand initial petitions and indictments from the Court of Justice of the State of Ceará, in Brazil, whose lawsuits were classified in the five more representative CNJ's classes - Common Civil Procedure, Execution of Extrajudicial Title, Criminal Action - Ordinary Procedure, Special Civil Court Procedure, and Tax Enforcement. Our best result was obtained by the BERT model, achieving 0.88 of F1 score (macro), in the experiment scenario that represents the lawsuit in an embedding formed by concatenating the texts of all the petitions that contain at least one citation to one legislation. Legal documents have specific characteristics such as long documents, specialized vocabulary, formal syntax, semantics based on a broad specific domain of knowledge, and citations to laws. Our interpretation is that the representation of the document through contextual embeddings generated by BERT, as well as the architecture of the model with bidirectional contexts, makes it possible to capture the specific context of the domain of legal documents.

**Keywords:** Text classification · Legal domain · Brazilian lawsuits · Language models

## 1 Introduction

Recently, Brazil's National Council of Justice (CNJ) highlighted in a public call [1] the need for implementing procedural automation with robotization resources and the use of Artificial Intelligence (AI) techniques, such as machine learning in legal proceedings in Brazil. These applications allow the replication of human activity, in order to save human resources that could be relocated to tasks that demand greater creativity and expertise.

© Springer Nature Switzerland AG 2021
A. Britto and K. Valdivia Delgado (Eds.): BRACIS 2021, LNAI 13074, pp. 586–600, 2021.
https://doi.org/10.1007/978-3-030-91699-2_40

Particularly in the field of jurisdictional efficiency, the CNJ calls the AI community in Brazil to develop robust solutions to perform automated lawsuit classification. A correct lawsuit classification substantially improves the assertiveness of (i) distribution, (ii) organization of the agenda of court hearing and sessions, (iii) classification of urgent measures and evidence, (iv) identification of prescription and (v) prevention, considering, also, issues such as the categorization in the CNJ's Unified Procedural Tables.

The classification of lawsuits is initially assigned by the lawyers and attorneys, manually, and recorded in the initial lawsuit documents. In Brazilian justice, these documents are commonly classified as initial petitions (civil lawsuits) and indictment (criminal lawsuits). Some benefits of the classification of petitions and indictimens, highlighted by the CNJ in [1], are: simplifying procedures for access to justice by citizens and/or their representatives, freeing them from carrying out the procedural classification; reduce the necessary structure of human resources in notary offices and departments responsible for processing the cases, in the different spheres of justice; drastically reduce the need for human intervention in the distribution and processing of cases; provide greater detail in the lawsuit classification, resulting in better organization of the judgment guidelines and opening the way for the development of productivity improvement tools.

In order to automate this task, text classification methods should be developed from language models [2, 3] from the Natural Language Processing (NLP) area and learning models [4, 5] from the AI area, and trained from a Golden Collection of documents extracted from lawsuits. Text classification, i.e., the process of assigning one or multiple categories from a set of options to a document [6], is a prominent and well-researched task in Natural Language Processing (NLP) and text mining. Text classification variants include simple binary classification (for example, deciding if a document is spam or not spam), multi-class classification (selection of one from a number of classes), and multi-label classification (where multiple labels can be assigned to a single document). Text classification methods have been successfully applied to a number of NLP tasks and applications ranging from plagiarism [7] and pastiche detection [8], in order to estimating the period in which a text was published [9], with commercial or forensic goals (e.g. identifying potential criminals [10], crimes [11, 12], or antisocial behavior [13]). However, in the legal domain, to the best of our knowledge, is relatively under-explored, mainly for the Brazilian lawsuits.

Text classification in the legal domain is used in a number of different applications. Katz et al. [14] use extremely randomized trees and extensive feature engineering to predict if a decision by the Supreme Court of the United State would be affirmed or reversed. In a similar fashion, [15] trained a model to predict, given the textual content of a case from the European Court of Human Rights, if there has been a violation of human rights or not. In [16], the authors trained traditional classifiers on text descriptions of cases from the French Supreme Court, in order to predict with high accuracy the ruling of the French Supreme Court (six classes), the law area to which a case belongs to (eight classes), and the influence of the time period in which a ruling was made. Undavia et al. [17] evaluated a series of classifiers trained on a dataset of cases from the American Supreme Court.

In the Brazilian legal domain, Araújo et al. [18] present a novel dataset built from Brazil's Supreme Court digitized legal documents, containing labeled text data and supports two types of tasks: document type classification; and theme assignment, a multilabel problem. Specifically for the problem stated by the CNJ in [1], we did not find any work that considered initial documents of lawsuits (petitions and complaints), especially those filed in lower courts of Brazilian Justice.

Considering the above, this paper investigates different text classification methods and different combinations of embeddings extracted from Portuguese language models, like BERTimbau [19], and information about legislation cited in the initial documents, validated by a Brazilian Legal Knowledge Graph, containing Brazilian Federal and Regional Legislation. The models were trained with a Golden Collection of 16 thousand initial petitions and indictments from the Court of Justice of the State of Ceará, in Brazil, whose lawsuits were classified in the five more representative CNJ's classes - Common Civil Procedure, Execution of Extrajudicial Title, Criminal Action - Ordinary Procedure, Special Civil Court Procedure, and Tax Enforcement. The lawsuits categorized in these classes represent more than 80% of lawsuits processed in 2019 in the state of Ceará Court of Justice. In addition, the Golden Collection contains a class "others" with a mix of initial petitions and indictments from several classes, which were selected to provide negative examples for the learning model.

Our best result was obtained by the BERT model, achieving 0.88 of F1 score (macro), in the experiment scenario that represents the lawsuit in an embedding formed by concatenating the texts of all the petitions that contain at least one citation to one legislation. Legal documents have specific characteristics such as long documents, specialized vocabulary, formal syntax, semantics based on a broad specific domain of knowledge, and citations to laws. Our interpretation is that the representation of the document through contextual embeddings generated by BERT, as well as the architecture of the model with bidirectional contexts, makes it possible to capture the specific context of the domain of legal documents. We also emphasize that by representing a lawsuit with only the text of petitions that have legislation, we are reducing the size of the text, but keeping only the excerpts that present reasons for the content of the lawsuit, which are therefore relevant for the classification of lawsuits.

## 2    Related Works

Text classification methods are investigated and applied with commercial or forensic goals (e.g. identifying potential criminals [10], crimes [11, 12], or antisocial behavior [13]). However, in the legal domain, these methods have been under-explored, mainly in Brazilian lawsuits.

Katz et al. [14] use extremely randomized trees and extensive feature engineering to pre- dict if a decision by the Supreme Court of the United State would be affirmed or reversed, achieving an accuracy of 69.7%. Aletras et al. [15], in a similar fashion, trained a model to predict, given the textual content of a case from the European Court of Human Rights, if there has been a violation of human rights or not. The paper employed n- grams and topics as inputs to a SVM, reaching an accuracy of 79%.

Sulea et al. [16] trained a linear SVM on text descriptions of cases from the French Supreme Court in order to predict with high accuracy the ruling of the French Supreme Court and the law area to which a case belongs to. The authors also investigate the influence of the time period in which a ruling was made. They report results of 98% average F1 score in predicting a case ruling, 96% F1 score for predicting the law area of a case, and 87.07% F1 score on estimating the date of a ruling.

Undavia et al. [17] proposed to classify US Supreme Court documents into fifteen different categories, comparing various combinations between feature representation and classification models, with better results through the application of Convolutional Neural Networks (CNN) to Word2Vec [3] representations and was able to achieve an accuracy of 72.4% when classifying the cases into 15 broad categories and 31.9% when classifying over 279 finer-grained classes.

In the Brazilian legal domain, Araújo et al. [18] present a novel dataset built from Brazil's Supreme Court digitized legal documents, containing labeled text data and supports two types of tasks: document type classification; and theme assignment, a multilabel problem. A similar model was applied to documents received by the Supreme Court in Brazil and reported in Silva et al. [20], which obtained a classifier using an embedding layer and a CNN applied to a problem involving six classes.

# 3 Corpus and Data Preparation

In this section, we describe the preparation and structuring of data used in the experiments that will be demonstrated in this paper. Initially, we present the dataset collected from lawsuits of the Court of Justice of the State of Ceará, in Brazil. Then, we presented the knowledge graph of federal and regional legislations, the Named Entity Recognition (NER) of these legislations and the validation process of legislations recognized in the legal documents.

## 3.1 Corpus and Golden Collection

Data processing was divided into phases, consisting of: (i) data cleaning phase, and (ii) data extraction phase. At the end of the data cleaning and extraction phases, a sample was produced with the lawsuits completed in 2019.

During the data cleaning phase, corrupt and inaccurate records were detected in their metadata, where an action to correct or remove these records was taken. In the metadata we can obtain the information of document date, document type, lawsuit number and lawsuit page. These data were relevant to organize the data extraction phase.

In the data extraction phase, Amazon's Optical Character Recognition (OCR) service was used, which refers to the branch of computer science that allows the translation of an optically digitized image of a printed or written text into manageable and editable text. We identified some errors after the data extraction phase, such as: special characters and additional spacing. With this, we carry out a data cleaning process to minimize these errors.

Finally, 7,103 lawsuits were selected, of which 16,668 petitions were used to build the dataset, distributed in 6 selected classes, which were defined by experts of the Court of Justice of the State of Ceará, in Brazil. These classes express the type of lawsuits and were defined by the National Council of Justice of Brazil[1].

---

[1] https://www.cnj.jus.br/sgt/consulta_publica_classes.php

### 3.2 Integration with the Brazilian Legal Knowledge Graph

A characteristic of legal documents is that they present citations to legislation, which are used to argue and present legal theories and arguments about the legal themes supporting the lawsuit. Considering that legislation can be important for classifying lawsuits, we use a Named Entity Recognizer (NER) to identify legislation in the text of the lawsuits. More specifically, we use a NER[2], structured in the Conditional Random Field model (CRF) Classifier of the Stanford JavaNLP API[3] and trained with the LENER-BR dataset [21] (a dataset for Named Entity Recognition in Brazilian legal text).

Additionally, a knowledge graph was built with federal and regional legislation of the state of Ceará, in Brazil. The laws were taken from the Federal Government Legislation Portal[4], Legislative and Legal Information Network[5] and from the Legislative Assembly of Ceará[6]. Table 1 demonstrates the legislation types, year of creation and quantity of legislation in the actual Brazilian Legal Knowledge Graph.

**Table 1.** Statistics and information about the Brazilian legal knowledge graph.

| Legislations | Quantity | Years of creation |
| --- | --- | --- |
| Ordinary Laws | 13,362 | 1891 a 2021 |
| Decrees | 28,128 | 1851 a 2021 |
| Complementary Laws | 162 | 1962 a 2021 |
| Decree-Laws | 3,785 | 1937 a 1946 e 1965 a 1988 |
| Delegated Laws | 13 | 1962 e 1992 |
| Provisional Measures PE32 | 1,054 | 2001 a 2021 |
| Provisional Measures AE32 | 615 | 1988 a 2001 |
| Federal Constitutions | 7 | 1824, 1891, 1934, 1937, 1946, 1967 e 1988 |
| Legislative Decrees | 5 | 1821 a 1935 |
| State Laws (CE) | 6,549 | 1984 a 2021 |
| Complementary State Laws (CE) | 237 | 1991 a 2021 |

The legislations extracted from the texts of the lawsuits by NER were validated in the knowledge graph of legislation, so that we consider only those present in the knowledge base as an entity "legislation".

From the identification and validation of the "legislation" entities in the text of the lawsuits, the lawsuits that have at least one citation to the legislation were selected, totaling 6,283 lawsuits, with 11,131 petitions in all. In Table 2 we can see the name

---

[2] https://github.com/MPMG-DCC-UFMG/M02
[3] https://nlp.stanford.edu/nlp/javadoc/javanlp/edu/stanford/nlp/ie/crf/CRFClassifier.html
[4] http://www4.planalto.gov.br/legislacao/
[5] https://www.lexml.gov.br/
[6] https://www.al.ce.gov.br/index.php/tividades-legislativas/leis

of the lawsuit classes of the dataset and the number of the National Council of Justice of Brazil (informed in parentheses in the Class column), and the distribution of dataset lawsuits in the 6 classes mentioned in Sect. 3.1.

**Table 2.** Distribution of lawsuits in legal classes.

| Classes | Lawsuits | | Lawsuits with citation of legislation | |
|---|---|---|---|---|
| | Number of lawsuits | Number of petitions | Number of lawsuits | Number of petitions |
| Others (*) | 1,486 | 3,286 | 1,325 | 2,116 |
| Common civil procedure (17) | 2,466 | 6,678 | 2,269 | 4,518 |
| Execution of extrajudicial title (12154) | 471 | 1,092 | 419 | 643 |
| Criminal action - ordinary procedure (283) | 772 | 2,511 | 735 | 1,765 |
| Special civil court procedure (436) | 824 | 1,637 | 770 | 1,187 |
| Tax enforcement (1116) | 1,084 | 1,464 | 765 | 902 |
| **Total** | **7,103** | **16,668** | **6,283** | **11,131** |

*This class represents a mix of several classes.

We investigate the legislation cited in the lawsuits for each class individually. Table 3 shows the amount of different legislations mentioned and in how many classes these legislations occur.

**Table 3.** Number of classes and the amount of legislation mentioned differently.

| Number of classes | Number of different legislations cited |
|---|---|
| 1 | 643 |
| 2 | 151 |
| 3 | 53 |
| 4 | 25 |
| 5 | 13 |
| 6 | 10 |
| **Total** | 895 |

In the text of the lawsuits' petitions, were identified 110,044 citations to Brazilian legislation. According to Table 3, these citations represent 895 different Brazilian laws and legal norms. We verified that only 1.2% (10 legislations) of these legislations are mentioned in lawsuits of all classes, being characterized as more generic legislations that do not distinguish the class of lawsuit, such as the Brazilian Civil Code (Law 10.406, of January, 01/10/2002), Brazilian Criminal Code (Decree-Law 2,848, of 07/12/1940), Code of Civil Procedure (Law 13.105, of 03/16/2015) and National Tax Code (Law 5.172, of 10/25/1966). While, 71.84% (643 legislations) are cited in lawsuits of a single class, which can be considered legislations that characterize the theme and, consequently, the class of the lawsuit. As, for example, Law 970, of 12/16/1949, which provides for the attributions, organization and functioning of the National Economy Council, is mentioned only in the lawsuits of the "Common Civil Procedure" class.

Table 4 shows the total of citations of legislation, the total of distinct legislations that occur in citations and the total of distinct legislations that occur by legal class. We analyzed the amount of different legislation mentioned in each of the classes of lawsuits and verified that there are laws that occur only in each class. For example, the 59,720 citations to the legislation present in the lawsuits of the "Common Civil Procedure" class correspond to 536 different legislations. In cases of this class, Law 8,078, of 09/11/1990, for example, is cited 8,560 times. We emphasize that, of the 536 distinct legislations cited in this class, 329 legislations are cited only in this class.

Likewise, for the "Criminal Action - Ordinary Procedure" class, the 12,610 citations that occur in this class correspond to 125 different legislations. For example, Law 11,343, of 23/08/2006, is cited 1,910 times in lawsuits of this class. We highlight that 43 different legislations are mentioned only in this class.

**Table 4.** Distribution of citations of legislation in total numbers and distinctly by legal class.

| Classes | Number of citations | Number of distinct legislations | Number of distinct legislations that occur only in the class |
|---|---|---|---|
| Others | 16,416 | 424 | 219 |
| Common civil Procedure | 59,720 | 536 | 329 |
| Execution of extrajudicial title | 5,041 | 72 | 14 |
| Criminal action - ordinary Procedure | 12,610 | 125 | 43 |
| Special civil court procedure | 13,401 | 142 | 31 |
| Tax enforcement | 2,856 | 30 | 7 |
| **Total** | 110,044 | 1,329 | 643 |

To complement the interpretation of citations in the lawsuits, we created a graph (shown in Fig. 1) that shows the relationship of the most frequent legislations with the lawsuits in which these legislations are cited. The nodes of this graph represent a law or a lawsuit and the edges represent the citation of the law in the lawsuit. We reinforce that some legislations are cited in many lawsuits, while other legislations are cited in few lawsuits, which suggests that the legislations cited in petitions can help in the identification of the class of lawsuits.

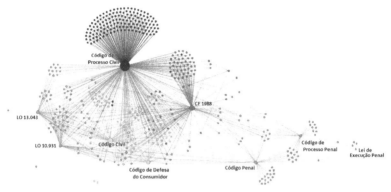

**Fig. 1.** Graph with nodes being legislations or lawsuits and edges being a lawsuit that cites legislation.

# 4  Lawsuit Classification

In this section, initially, we define the scenarios and algorithms used in the experiments for classifying lawsuits. Then, we present and discuss the results achieved.

## 4.1  Experiment Scenarios

Lawsuits classification experiments were conducted in different scenarios. In each scenario, we choose different features to represent a lawsuit. Below we present each scenario used in the experiments.

**Embeddings of the Lawsuit/Case Text (S1).** Each lawsuit is made up of a set of petition-type text documents. We define that the text of a lawsuit corresponds to the concatenation of the texts of all the petitions that comprise it. In this scenario, the lawsuit is represented by the embedding of the lawsuit text, generated from the pre-trained model BERTimbau [19] (a pre-trained model BERT for Brazilian Portuguese).

**Embeddings of the Lawsuit/Case Text with Citation (S2).** We assume that petitions that have citations to the legislation are more relevant to the lawsuit. In this way, for each petition in a lawsuit, we verify if it contains a citation for Brazilian legislation (according to the procedure described in Sect. 3.2). Then, a text is formed by concatenating the texts of all the petitions that contain at least one citation to one legislation. In this scenario, the lawsuit is represented by the embedding of this text, generated from the pre-trained BERTimbau model [19].

**Embeddings of the Cited Laws (S3).** We assume that in the case of legal documents, legislations are cited to represent and substantiate the subject of the document, therefore, the content of these legislations is relevant to define the class of a lawsuit. In this context, a text is formed by the concatenation of the legislation cited in the petitions of a lawsuit. In this scenario, the lawsuit is represented by the embedding of the text of the summary of the cited legislations (these summaries were retrieved from Brazilian Legal Knowledge Graph), generated from the pre-trained model BERTimbau [19].

**Embeddings of the Lawsuit/Case Text with Citation and Cited Laws (S4).** We assume that the laws cited are as important as the text of the lawsuit. In this scenario, a text is formed by the concatenation of the texts of all the petitions that contain at least one citation to the legislation and the texts of the summary of the cited legislations. The embedding of this text, generated from the pre-trained model BERTimbau [19], is used to represent the lawsuit.

**Embeddings of the Lawsuit/Case Text with Citation and Embeddings of Cited Laws (S5).** In this scenario, a lawsuit is represented by two embeddings: (i) embedding of the lawsuit text, generated according to S2, and (ii) embedding of the summary of the cited legislations, generated according to S3.

**TF-IDF$_{\text{Law}}$ (S6).** We assume that the relevance of cited legislations in lawsuit texts is an important information for the learning model: legislation cited only in lawsuits of the same class should be considered more important than legislation cited in lawsuits of several classes. Based on this, we define a feature named *TF-IDF$_{Law}$*, a variant of TF-IDF (*Term Frequency - Inverse Document Frequency*), which aims to measure the relevance of legislation for a lawsuit, according to the frequency of citations of legislation in the lawsuit and in other lawsuits in the corpus. *TF-IDF$_{Law}$(l,d)* is calculated according to Eq. (1) below:

$$TF - IDF_{Law}(l, d) = \frac{f_{l,d}}{\Sigma_{l \in d} f_{l,d}} \times log \frac{N}{|\{d \in D : l \in d\}|} \tag{1}$$

where $f_{l,d}$, the frequency of citation of the law $l$ in the lawsuit $d$, is divided by the total number of citations to the law in the lawsuit. $d$. Then, the number of lawsuits $N$ in the corpus $D$ is divided by the total frequency of the law $l$ in all lawsuits of the corpus. In this scenario, we represent a lawsuit as a bag-of-words with *TF-IDF$_{Law}$* features. In other words, given a vocabulary $V = \{cl_1, cl_2, ..., cl_v\}$ formed by the laws mentioned in the $N$ lawsuits of the train set, we represent each lawsuit $d_i$ as a length-$|V|$ vector $L(d_i)$, where $L(d_i)_j = TF\text{-}IDF_{Law}(cl_j, d_i)$, with $j = 0$ to $|V|-1$ and $cl_j \in V$.

**Embeddings of the Lawsuit/Case Text with Citation and TF-IDF$_{\text{Law}}$ (S7).** In this scenario, a lawsuit is represented by: (i) embedding of the lawsuit text with citation, generated according to S2, and (ii) bag-of-words with *TF-IDF$_{Law}$* features, generated according to S6.

**Embeddings of the Cited Laws and TF-IDF$_{Law}$ (S8).** In this scenario, a lawsuit is represented by: (i) embedding of the menus of the aforementioned laws, generated according to S3, and (ii) bag-of-words with *TF-IDF$_{Law}$* features, generated according to S6.

**Embeddings of the Lawsuit/Case Text with Citation and Cited Laws and TF-IDF$_{Law}$ (S9).** In this scenario, a lawsuit is represented by: (i) embedding of the lawsuit text and the summary of the cited laws, generated according to S4, and (ii) bag-of-words with *TF-IDF$_{Law}$* features, generated according to S6.

**Embeddings of the Lawsuit/Case Text with Citation, Embeddings of Cited Laws and TF-IDF$_{Law}$ (S10).** In this scenario, a lawsuit is represented by: (i) embedding of the lawsuit text, generated according to S2, (ii) embeddings of the summary of the cited laws, generated according to S3, and (iii) bag-of-words with *TF-IDF$_{Law}$* features, generated according to S6.

**Embeddings of the Lawsuit/Case Text and Topics (S11).** Given a set of text documents, a topic model is applied to find out interpretable semantic concepts, or topics, present in documents. We assume that the topics can suggest the main theme of the document, making it possible, therefore, to help in inferring the class of lawsuits. We choose Latent Dirichlet Allocation (LDA) [22] as the method for topic generation of the lawsuits. LDA is a probabilistic model generator of a corpus, where each document is represented as a mixture of latent topics. Each topic is, in turn, a distribution of words. In this way, we run LDA on corpus $D$ to find 6 topics (we set the number of topics as the same number of classes). To each document, we choose the most likely topic for each lawsuit and the top-10 words more representative to the lawsuit's topic. In this scenario, each lawsuit is represented by: (i) embedding of the lawsuit text, generated according to S1, and (ii) bag-of-words with the word distribution of the topics.

### 4.2 Models

We train four models on split-of-the-data training in the scenarios presented in Sect. 4.1: (i) Random Forest [23], (ii) Support Vector Machine (SVM) [24], (iii) Extreme Gradient Boosting (XGBoost) [25], and (iv) Bidirectional Encoder Representations from Transformers (BERT)[7] [2]. We train each model as a multiclass classification task, using the following parameters (obtained from an empirical evaluation):

**Random Forest.** We applied the Random Forest algorithm using Scikit-learn's Random Forest Classifier package[8]. We trained 1,000 trees with a maximum of 200 features to consider when looking for the best split.

---

[7] Given the specifics of the BERT's original architecture, this model was trained only in scenarios: (S1), (S2), (S3) and (S4).

[8] https://scikit-learn.org/stable/modules/generated/sklearn.ensemble.RandomForestClassifier. html

**Support Vector Machine (SVM).** We applied the SVM algorithm using Scikit-learn's SVM package[9] with default parameters.

**Extreme Gradient Boosting (XGBoost).** We applied the XGBoost algorithm using XGBoost Classifier package[10]. We trained 1,000 trees with a maximum depth of 4 and a learning rate of 0.1.

**Bidirectional Encoder Representations from Transformers (BERT).** We used the fine-tuning-based approach with the pre-trained model BERTimbau [19], 4 epochs and batch size of 4 samples for the classification task. For the optimizer, we used the ADAM optimizer with a learning rate of $1e - 5$.

### 4.3 Results and Discussion

To carry out the experiments in the scenarios and models described in Sects. 4.1 and 4.2, we divided the dataset into 85% for the train set and 15% for the test set. Table 5 shows the performance of the models in each experiment scenario, in terms of F1 score (macro) for the test set.

**Table 5.** Results in terms of F1 score macro for lawsuit classification in different scenarios and models.

| Experiments scenario | Random forest | SVM | XGBoost | BERT |
|---|---|---|---|---|
| S1 (embeddings of the lawsuit text) | 0.67 | 0.61 | 0.75 | 0.87 |
| S2 (embeddings of the lawsuit text with citation) | 0.71 | 0.66 | 0.77 | **0.88** |
| S3 (embeddings of the cited laws) | 0.68 | 0.67 | 0.71 | 0.73 |
| S4 (embeddings of the lawsuit text with citation and cited laws) | 0.71 | 0.65 | 0.77 | 0.87 |
| S5 (S2 + S3) | **0.75** | 0.73 | 0.82 | * |
| S6 (TF-IDF$_{Law}$) | 0.74 | 0.64 | 0.71 | * |
| S7 (S2 + S6) | **0.75** | 0.74 | **0.83** | * |
| S8 (S3 + S6) | 0.70 | 0.70 | 0.72 | * |
| S9 (S4 + S6) | **0.75** | 0.74 | **0.83** | * |
| S10 (S2 + S3 + S6) | **0.75** | **0.75** | **0.83** | * |
| S11 (embeddings of the lawsuit text and topics) | 0.71 | 0.62 | 0.77 | * |

*Given the specifics of the BERT's original architecture, whose input is a text, this model was trained only in scenarios: (S1), (S2), (S3) and (S4).

Based on the Kruskal-Wallis statistical test, we are able to claim that the results are statistically significant at a 99% confidence level, with p-value equal to 0.0008.

---

[9] https://scikit-learn.org/stable/modules/generated/sklearn.svm.SVC.html

[10] https://xgboost.readthedocs.io/en/latest/python/python_api.html

The BERT model outperforms the other models in all scenarios, achieving the best result of 0.88 of F1 score (macro) in the experiment scenario that represents the lawsuit from the petition texts that have citation. Legal documents have specific characteristics such as long documents, specialized vocabulary, formal syntax, semantics based on a broad specific domain of knowledge, and citations to laws. Our interpretation is that the representation of the document through contextual embeddings generated by BERT, as well as the architecture of the model with bidirectional contexts, makes it possible to capture the specific context of the domain of legal documents. We also emphasize that by representing a lawsuit with only the text of petitions that have legislation citation, we are reducing the size of the text, but keeping only the excerpts that present reasons for the content of the lawsuit, which are therefore relevant for the classification of lawsuits.

The second best model is XGBoost in S7, S9 and S10 scenarios. These scenarios use the feature $TF \times IDF_{Law}$, in addition to the embeddings of the texts of the petitions with legislation (in S7, S9 and S10) and the summary of the cited legislation (in S9 and S10). The characterization of the lawsuit with the petitions that have citations is complemented by the relevance of the legislation for the lawsuits, through the feature $TF \times IDF_{Law}$. This suggests that the legislation cited informs about the class, helping to classify the lawsuits.

Finally, in order to evaluate the results in a cross-validation approach, we employ a stratified 5-fold cross-validation setup for the best result experiment (model BERT with scenario S2) and obtained the F1 macro score of 0.88 (the same result for the dataset divided into 85% for training and 15% for testing).

Figure 2 shows the confusion matrix for the best result achieved in the experiments, a scenario with the representation of text embeddings of the petitions of the lawsuits that have citations with the model trained with BERT. We observe some patterns which may help us understand these results. The confusion matrix shows us that the lawsuits of the "Tax Enforcement" class have the best results, with a recall close to 1.0, while the lawsuits of the "Others" class are the most difficult to predict, with a recall close to 0.71. Lawsuits of class "Others" correspond to lawsuits of mixed classes grouped into a single class, thus making it difficult to classify these lawsuits. The second most difficult class to predict is the "Execution of Extrajudicial Title" class. This class contains the smallest number of samples in the dataset.

Table 6 presents the F1 score results of the BERT model trained with the texts of the petitions of the lawsuits without (S1) and with (S2) citation to the legislation, for each class.

The classes' F1 scores show variability from 0.78 to 1.00 in both scenarios. S2 scenario presents better F1 score results for the "Execution of Extrajudicial Title" and "Tax Enforcement" classes, with an increase of 3.6% and 2.0%, respectively. Whereas the S1 scenario has better results for the "Special Civil Court Procedure" and "Criminal Action - Ordinary Procedure" classes, with an increase of 2.4% and 1.5%, respectively. In the other classes, "Common Civil Procedure" and "Others", the F1 score values are the same for both scenarios.

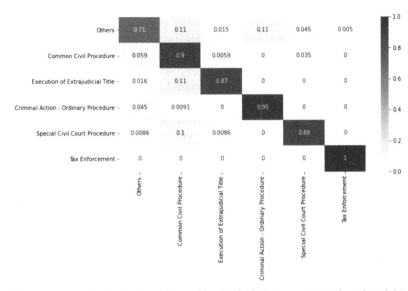

**Fig. 2.** Confusion matrix for the Lawsuit Classification in the best-case scenario and model (model BERT with scenario S2).

**Table 6.** Results in terms of F1 score for BERT model in S1 and S2 experiments scenario, considering the text of the lawsuits with and without citations to legislation, respectively.

| Class | S1 (embeddings of the lawsuit text) | S2 (embeddings of the lawsuit text with citation) |
|---|---|---|
| Others | **0.78** | **0.78** |
| Common civil procedure | **0.90** | **0.90** |
| Execution of extrajudicial title | 0.83 | **0.86** |
| Criminal action - ordinary procedure | **0.88** | 0.87 |
| Special civil court procedure | **0.87** | 0.85 |
| Tax enforcement | 0.98 | **1.00** |
| Average | 0.87 | **0.88** |

## 5   Conclusions

In this paper we investigate the application of different models and scenarios for classifying legal texts using a dataset of lawsuits from the Court of Justice of the State of Ceará, in Brazil. The best results are achieved by the BERT model (using the pre-trained BERTimbau model [19]) in the scenario in which the lawsuit is represented by the text of the petitions that have citations to Brazilian legislation.

The legal text has specific characteristics, in this way, we represent the text contextually from the BERTimbau (pre-trained model for Brazilian Portuguese) and provide only the petitions of the lawsuit that mention a Brazilian law. We argue that the contextual representation of the text and the citation to legislation help to identify the classes of a lawsuit.

As future work, we intend to investigate other features to characterize the lawsuits and to use other models, such as Recurrent Neural Network (RNN) and Convolutional Neural Network (CNN) for lawsuit classification. We also intend to develop a specific language model for the Brazilian legal domain, which can be used to improve the contextual representation of the texts of proceedings in the specific domain of the legal area. We also intend to investigate the accuracy of the model in lawsuits from other Courts of Justice in different Brazilian states.

# References

1. Conselho Nacional de Justiça: CONVOCAÇÃO nº 01/2021 – Desenvolvimento- piloto de soluções para a automação processual e uso de técnicas de inteligência artificial no Poder Judiciário. https://acessoexterno.undp.org.br/Public/Jobs/18062021164751_Resultado%20p ara%20publica%C3%A7%C3%A3o_Sinapses.pdf. Accessed 20 June 2021
2. Devlin, J., Chang, M.-W., Lee, K., Toutanova, K.: BERT: pre-training of deep bidirectional transformers for language understanding. In: Proceedings of the 2019 Conference of the North American Chapter of the Association for Computational Linguistics: Human Language Technologies, vol. 1 (Long and Short Papers), pp. 4171–4186. Association for Computational Linguistics, Minneapolis (2019)
3. Mikolov, T., Chen, K., Carrado, G., Dean, J.: Efficient Estimation of Word Representations in Vector Space. http://arxiv.org/pdf/1301.3781.pdf. Accessed 20 Nov 2015
4. Hochreiter, S., Schmidhuber, J.: Long short-term memory. Neural Comput. **9**(12), 1735–1780 (1997)
5. Conneau, A., Schwenk, H., Barrault, L., Lecun, Y.: Very deep convolutional networks for text classification. In: Proceedings of the 15th Conference of the European Chapter of the Association for Computational Linguistics, vol. 1, Long Papers, pp. 1107–1116. Association for Computational Linguistics, Valencia, Spain (2017)
6. Shaheen, Z., Wohlgenannt, G., Filtz, E.: Large Scale Legal Text Classification Using Transformer Models. arXiv preprint arXiv:2010.12871 (2020)
7. Barrón-Cedeño, A., Vila, M., Martí, M.A., Rosso, P.: Plagiarism meets paraphrasing: insights for the next generation in automatic plagiarism detection. Comput. Linguist. **39**(4), 917–947 (2013)
8. Dinu, L.P., Niculae, V., Sulea, O.-M.: Pastiche detection based on stopword rankings: exposing impersonators of a Romanian writer. In: Proceedings of the Workshop on Computational Approaches to Deception Detection (2012)
9. Niculae, V., Zampieri, M., Dinu, L.P., Ciobanu, A.M.: Temporal text ranking and automatic dating of texts. In: Proceedings of EACL (2014)
10. Sumner, C., Byers, A., Boochever, R., Park, G.J.: Predicting dark triad personality traits from twitter usage and a linguistic analysis of tweets. In: Proceedings of ICMLA (2012). https://doi.org/10.1109/ICMLA.2012.218
11. Pérez-Rosas, V., Mihalcea, R.: Experiments in open domain deception detection. In: Lluís, M., Chris, C.B., Jian, S., Daniele, P., Yuval, M. (eds.) Proceedings of EMNLP. Association for Computational Linguistics (2015). https://aclweb.org/anthology/D/D15/D15-1133.pdf

12. Pinheiro, V., Pequeno, T., Furtado, V., Nogueira, D.: Information extraction from text based on semantic inferentialism. In: Andreasen, T., Yager, R.R., Bulskov, H., Christiansen, H., Larsen, H.L. (eds.) FQAS 2009. LNCS (LNAI), vol. 5822, pp. 333–344. Springer, Heidelberg (2009). https://doi.org/10.1007/978-3-642-04957-6_29

13. Cheng, J., Danescu-Niculescu-Mizil, C., Leskovec, J.: Anti-social behavior in online discussion communities. In: Proceedings of ICWSM (2015)

14. Katz, D.M., Bommarito, M.J.I., Blackman, J.: Predicting the behavior of the supreme court of the United States: a general approach. In: arXiv e-prints, page arXiv:1407.6333 (2014)

15. Aletras, N., Tsarapatsanis, D., Preotiuc-Pietro, D., Lampos, V.: Predicting judicial decisions of the european court of human rights: a natural language processing perspective. Peer J. Comput. Sci. **10** (2016)

16. Sulea, O.M., Zampieri, M., Vela, M., vanGenabith, J. Predicting the law area and decisions of French Supreme Court cases. In: Proceedings of the International Conference Recent Advances in Natural Language Processing, RANLP, pp. 716–722. INCOMA Ltd. (2017)

17. Undavia, S., Meyers, A., Ortega, J.E.: A comparative study of classifying legal documents with neural networks. In: Federated Conference on Computer Science and Information Systems (FedCSIS), pp. 515–522 (2018)

18. Araújo, P.H.L., Campos, T.E., Braz, F.A.; Silva, N.C.: VICTOR: a dataset for Brazilian legal documents classification. In: Proceedings of the 12th Conference on Language Resources and Evaluation (LREC 2020), 11–16 May, pp. 1449–1458. Marseille (2020)

19. Fabio, S., Nogueira, R., Lotufo, R.: BERTimbau: pretrained BERT models for Brazilian Portuguese. In: 9th Brazilian Conference on Intelligent Systems, BRACIS, 20–23 October. Rio Grande do Sul, Brazil (2020)

20. Silva, N., Braz, F., Campos, T.: Document type classification for Brazil's supreme court using a convolutional neural network. In: The Tenth International Conference on Forensic Computer Science and Cyber Law-ICoFCS, vol. 10, pp. 7–11 (2018)

21. Luz de Araujo, P.H., de Campos, T.E., de Oliveira, R.R.R., Stauffer, M., Couto, S., Bermejo, P.: LeNER-Br: a dataset for named entity recognition in brazilian legal text. In: Villavicencio, A., et al. (eds.) PROPOR 2018. LNCS (LNAI), vol. 11122, pp. 313–323. Springer, Cham (2018). https://doi.org/10.1007/978-3-319-99722-3_32

22. Blei, D.M., Ng, A.Y., Jordan, M.I.: Latent dirichlet allocation. J. Mach. Learn. Res. **3**, 993–1022 (2003)

23. Breiman, L.: Random forests. Mach. Learn. **45**(1), 5–32 (2001)

24. Hearst, M.A.: Support vector machine. IEEE Intell. Syst. **13**(4), 18–28 (1998)

25. Chen, T., Guestrin, C.: XGBoost: a scalable tree boosting system. In: Proceedings of the 22nd ACM SIGKDD International Conference on Knowledge Discovery and Data Mining, pp. 785–794. New York (2016)

# Universal Dependencies-Based PoS Tagging Refinement Through Linguistic Resources

Lucelene Lopes$^{(\boxtimes)}$ [ID], Magali S. Duran[ID], and Thiago A. S. Pardo[ID]

Interinstitutional Center for Computational Linguistics (NILC),
Institute of Mathematical and Computer Sciences, University of São Paulo,
São Carlos, Brazil
`lucelene@gmail.com, taspardo@icmc.usp.br`

**Abstract.** This paper presents a technique that employs linguistic resources to refine PoS tagging using the Universal Dependencies (UD) model. The technique is based on the development and use of lists of non-ambiguous single tokens and non-ambiguous co-occuring tokens in Portuguese (regardless of whether they constitute multiword expressions or not). These lists are meant to automatically correct the tags for such tokens after tagging. The technique is applied over the output of two well-known state of the art systems - UDPipe and UDify - and the results for a real data set have shown a significant improvement of annotation accuracy. Overall, we improve tagging accuracy by up to 1.4%, and, in terms of the number of fully correct tagged sentences, our technique produces results that are 13.9% more accurate than the corresponding original system.

**Keywords:** PoS tagging · Linguistic resource · Universal dependencies

## 1 Introduction

The importance of the Part of Speech (PoS) tagging task is beyond discussion, as often the other Natural Language Processing (NLP) tasks rely on the outcome of PoS tagging. Furthermore, the current NLP applications are designed to process large amounts of texts, making the use of taggers a necessity. For well resourced languages, PoS tagging processes are usually dealt with consistent high accuracy [12]. The reason for such high accuracy relies mostly on the existence of large annotated corpora and powerful techniques, usually based on neural network inspired implementations [5].

For poorly resourced languages, or even specific dialects, PoS tagging may become challenging because of the lack of an appropriate training model [8]. This can be coped with reduced or slightly inadequate training models and the use of very powerful taggers/parsers based on performant solutions as the use of word embeddings and bidirectional RNNs [4]. One example of this is implemented in UDPipe, a trainable pipeline that performs sentence segmentation,

© Springer Nature Switzerland AG 2021
A. Britto and K. Valdivia Delgado (Eds.): BRACIS 2021, LNAI 13074, pp. 601–615, 2021.
https://doi.org/10.1007/978-3-030-91699-2_41

tokenization, lemmatization, PoS tagging and dependency parsing [11]. Other performant similar solutions are the ones based on the use of cutting edge technology as BERT [9], which is implemented in UDify, a multilingual multi-task model capable of accurately predicting universal part-of-speech, morphological features, lemmas, and dependency trees simultaneously for several Universal Dependencies (UD) treebanks [3].

Such approaches are very effective, basically because they are flexible enough to detect complex characteristics necessary to classify words and grammatical constructions that are present in the training set. Unfortunately, these high performant PoS taggers still make basic mistakes and misclassify simple words (as those belonging to closed classes). That leads to errors in PoS annotation that could be easily tackled by solutions that rely on linguistic resources that are not explicitly covered by current machine learning models [13].

One thing in common to the UDPipe and UDify taggers/parsers is the use of UD formalism for encoding the output representation [6]. UD is a de-facto standard for cross-linguistically comparable morphological and syntactic annotation that keeps evolving and provides a steadily growing and heavily multilingual collection of corpora [1]. UD has reshaped the initiatives in the area of tagging and parsing in the world, causing a significant movement from constituency to dependency analysis in NLP.

For Portuguese texts, the PoS tagging task using tools as UDPipe and UDify present some challenges because of the low availability of appropriate training sets with the right language style and a reasonable size. One of the few options is the Bosque-UD corpus, a Portuguese treebank based on the Constraint Grammar converted version of Bosque, which is part of the Floresta Sintá(c)tica treebank [7] that contains both European and Brazilian variants [14]. The Bosque-UD corpus has 9,364 sentences, totalizing 210,957 tokens.

In order to contribute to UD-based PoS tagging of Brazilian Portuguese texts, we propose a linguistic-based technique to improve tagging accuracy, which we specifically test over the output of UDPipe and UDify systems, which use Bosque-UD as training set. The proposed technique relies on building and employing linguistic resources to automatically correct the PoS tags produced by the cited systems. Our research claim is that explicit linguistic knowledge does help improving the result of modern machine learning-based models. To support our claim, we describe the process of building our linguistic resources for Brazilian Portuguese, and we conduct experiments illustrating our attempt of quality improvement.

Specifically, we propose the automatic correction of tags wrongfully assigned to non-ambiguous single tokens and non-ambiguous co-occuring tokens (regardless of whether they constitute MWE - multiword expressions - or not) from closed PoS classes in Portuguese. We consider in our linguistic resources three types of phenomena: single functional words (the pronoun *você* - "you" in English, for example); MWEs acting as functional words (the prepositional phrase *por meio de* - "through", for example); and co-occurring functional words that, although in isolation are ambiguous, together are not ambiguous (for example, *a* may be a determiner (DET), a preposition (ADP), or a pronoun (PRON), but in the co-occurrence *à de* may be unambiguously tagged as ADP PRON ADP). It is important to call the reader attention that, being functional words, they are naturally non-ambiguous, independently of the domain.

We show that the achieved gains by our proposed technique is significant and that this is a strategy worth to follow. Overall, we improve tagging accuracy in up to 1.4%, and, in terms of the number of fully correct tagged sentences, our technique produces results that increases the accuracy by 13.9% from the corresponding original system. Considering that PoS tagging annotation is the basis for other text analysis levels, such improvement may be really impactful for producing better NLP tools and applications.

This paper is organized as follows: the next section describes the process and the result of producing our linguistic resources composed by lists of non-ambiguous single tokens and non-ambiguous co-occuring tokens belonging to closed PoS tag classes, highly frequent in Portuguese written text; the third section presents the evaluation of our proposed correction technique on a data set of 2,000 sentences (43,483 tokens) from the Folha-Kaggle corpus [10] annotated by UDPipe [11] and UDify [3] systems; finally, the last section presents our concluding remarks and future works.

## 2 Linguistic Analysis of Non-ambiguous Tokens in Portuguese

In this section we analyze the possibility to establish a set of tokens that can only be annotated by one single possible PoS tag. Usually, very performant PoS taggers based on a training set knows no such boundaries as they try to capture very subtle interdependencies among the tokens and their representation. Linguistic knowledge of the target language, however, can provide such boundaries by establishing the specific tokens or expressions that are unambiguously capable to receive only one single PoS tag.

The knowledge of these non-ambiguous tokens can be a powerful and fully automatic tool to improve the quality for a very performant PoS tagger based on a training set. In this work, we adopt two linguistic groups to improve the PoS tagging:

- The single tokens belonging to a closed PoS tag class (in UD):
  - ADP (adposition), ADV (adverbs[1]), CCONJ (coordinating conjunction), DET (determiner), NUM (numeral - just cardinals), PRON (pronoun), SCONJ (subordinating conjunction), a subset of the class AUX (verbs *ser* and *estar*) and ADJ (ordinal numbers);

---

[1] The ADV class is not exactly a closed one as, similarly to English with the ending -ly, in Portuguese it is possible to turn adjectives into adverbs by adding *-mente* at the end (for example, the adjective *final* can be turned into the adverb *finalmente* - "finally"), but, for the purpose of our technique, we ignore such adverbs.

- Common co-occuring tokens that have always the same PoS tag classes, which include:
  - MWEs acting as functional words;
  - Co-occurring functional words that in isolation are ambiguous, but together become non-ambiguous.

### 2.1   Non-ambiguous Single Tokens for Closed PoS Classes

To establish this group, we started listing all tokens tagged to each of the targeted PoS classes (ADP, ADV, CCONJ, DET, NUM, PRON and SCONJ) in the Bosque-UD corpus [14], and the equivalent tags in the MacMorpho corpus [2]. The lists for each PoS class were analyzed and inappropriate tokens were removed throughout a manual linguistic analysis of each token individually. Similarly, some tokens were added to the lists, despite not being found in the corpora above mentioned. This was the case of ordinal and cardinal numerals, additional forms of auxiliary verbs (*ser* and *estar*), and functional rare words, as the adverb *adentro* ("inwards").

Table 1 presents the overall number of listed tokens and the final number of tokens retained for each class. In this table, only the tokens for ordinal numerals (annotated as ADJ in UD) are absent, since they were not searched in the Bosque-UD and MacMorpho as they are not distinguishable from other open class adjectives (all these tokens were added by the linguistic analysis only).

**Table 1.** Tokens for closed PoS classes.

| PoS classes | Tokens | |
|---|---|---|
| | Found | Retained |
| ADP | 158 | 31 |
| ADV | 327 | 100 |
| DET | 212 | 101 |
| PRON | 254 | 123 |
| CCONJ | 31 | 20 |
| SCONJ | 55 | 16 |
| AUX | 398 | 106 |
| NUM (cardinal) | 871 | 79 |
| NUM (ordinals - ADJ) | -- | 46 |

The main reason for a token being considered inappropriate was misannotation due to different annotation principles. An example of such difference of annotation principles can be found in MacMorpho corpus, where several MWEs, acting as functional words, were tagged as a whole and not by the words that compose them. This is the case of the *por fim* expression that is tagged in Mac-Morpho by assigning a tag ADV to *por* and another tag ADV to *fim*, since this expression plays the role of an adverb (this expression can be translated into English as "finally"). However, according to the UD guidelines, each token has to be tagged individually, not considering MWEs. Following this principle, *por* will be clearly tagged as an adposition (PREP in MacMorpho tagset, ADP in UD tagset). Therefore, the tokens *por* and *fim* were removed from the list of ADV despite appearing as such in the MacMorpho corpus. This is exemplified in the sentence of Fig. 1.

**Fig. 1.** Example of the difference between MacMorpho and UD annotation principles.

The next step was to cross-analyze the lists among themselves. For example, the token *se* can be found in the PRON and SCONJ lists, and, therefore, it was considered an ambiguous token regarding the PoS tag. In English, *se* could be translated to "yourself" for PRON or to "if" for SCONJ. Figure 2 exemplifies two sentences where the *se* token is employed either way.

| A | educação | global | tem | **se** | tornado | mais | importante | ? |
|---|---|---|---|---|---|---|---|---|
| DET | NOUN | ADJ | VERB | PRON | VERB | ADV | ADJ | PUNCT |

| **Se** | não | chegar | , | tem | algo | errado | ali | . |
|---|---|---|---|---|---|---|---|---|
| SCONJ | ADV | VERB | PUNCT | VERB | PRON | ADJ | ADV | PUNCT |

**Fig. 2.** Example of ambiguous token within closed PoS classes (PRON and SCONJ).

After crossing the tokens for the closed PoS tag classes, each token was also individually analyzed in relation to its other possible open classes. For example, the token *entre* can be an ADP, but also a conjugation of the verb *entrar* (therefore, a VERB). In English *entre* could be translated to "between" for ADP or to "enter" for VERB. Figure 3 presents two sentences where *entre* token is employed both ways.

After all those analyses, it was possible to identify all single tokens for the target closed PoS classes, as well as which ones are ambiguous or not. Tables 2 and 3 indicate the non-ambiguous tokens in bold face (269 tokens) and the ambiguous ones in italic.

**Table 2.** Tokens of closed PoS classes.

---

ADP (adposition)

*a, afora,* **ante, após,** *até,* **com,** *como, conforme,* **contra,** *dado,* **de, desde,** *devido,* **durante, em,** *entre,* **exceto,** *fora,* **mediante,** *menos, para,* **perante,** *por, pra, salvo, segundo,* **sem,** *senão,* **sob,** *sobre, visto*

---

ADV (adverbs)

**abaixo, acerca, acima, ademais,** *adentro, adiante,* **afinal,** *afora,* **agora, aí, ainda,** *algo, além,* **ali, aliás,** *amanhã,* **antes, apenas, apesar, aquém, aqui, assim,** *até,* **atrás, através,** *baixo, bastante, bem,* **cá,** *cedo, cerca, como,* **contanto, debaixo, decerto,** *demais,* **dentro, depois, depressa, detrás, devagar, diante,** *direito,* **eis, embaixo,** *embora,* **enfim,** *enquanto,* **então, etc., etc.,** *fora, frente, fundo, hoje,* **inclusive,** *já,* **jamais,** *junto,* **lá,** *logo,* **longe,** *mais, mal, meio, melhor, menos, mesmo, muito, nada,* **não, nem, nunca,** *onde, ontem, ora,* **perto,** *pouco, primeiro, próximo, quando, quanto,* **quão, quase,** *que, rápido,* **recém,** *segundo,* **sempre, sequer, sim,** *só,* **sobretudo, talvez, também, tampouco,** *tanto,* **tão,** *tarde,* **trás**

---

CCONJ (coordinating conjunction)

*como,* **contudo, e,** *enquanto,* **entretanto,** *já, logo,* **mas,** *nem,* **ou,** *pois,* **porém, porquanto,** *porque,* **portanto,** *que, quer, senão, seja,* **todavia**

---

DET (determiner)

*a, algum, alguma, algumas, alguns, ambas, ambos, aquela, aquelas, aquele, aqueles, as, cada, certa, certas, certo, certos,* **cuja, cujas, cujo, cujos,** *demais,* **diversas, diversos,** *essa, essas, esse, esses, esta, estas, este, estes, mais, menos, meu, meus, mesma, mesmas, mesmo, mesmos, minha, minhas, muita, muitas, muito, muitos, nenhum, nenhuma, nossa, nossas, nosso, nossos, o, os, outra, outras, outro, outros, pouca, poucas, pouco, poucos, própria, próprias, próprio, próprios, quais, quaisquer, qual, qualquer, quanta, quantas, quanto, quantos, que, seu, seus, sua, suas,* **tais,** *tal, tanta, tantas, tanto, tantos, teu, teu, toda, todas, todo, todos, um, uma, umas, uns, várias, vários, vossa, vossas, vosso, vossos*

---

PRON (pronoun)

*a, algo,* **alguém,** *algum, alguma, algumas, alguns, ambos, ambas, aquela, aquelas, aquele, aqueles,* **aquilo,** *as, cada, demais,* **ela, elas, ele, eles,** *essa, essas, esse, esses, esta, estas, este, estes,* **eu,** *gente,* **isso, isto, la, las, lhe, lhes, lo, los, me,** *mesma, mesmas, mesmo, mesmos, meu, meus,* **mim,** *minha, minhas, muita, muitas, muito, muitos, nada, nenhum, nenhuma,* **ninguém, nos, nós,** *nossa, nossas, nosso, nossos, o, onde, os, outra, outras, outro, outros, pouca, poucas, pouco, poucos, próprio, própria, próprios, próprias, próximo, quais, quaisquer, qual, qualquer, quando, quanta, quantas, quanto, quantos, que,* **quem,** *se, seu, seus,* **si,** *sua, suas, tal, tanta, tantas, tanto, tantos,* **te,** *teu,* **ti,** *toda, todas, todo, todos,* **tudo,** *um, uma, umas, uns, várias, vários,* **você, vocês, vos,** *vossa, vossas, vosso, vossos,* **vós**

---

SCONJ (subordinating conjunction)

*embora, caso, como, conforme,* **conquanto,** *embora, enquanto, para, pois, porque, pra, quando, quanto, que, se, segundo*

---

| A | porcentagem | é | maior | **entre** | os | mais | escolarizados | . |
|---|---|---|---|---|---|---|---|---|
| DET | ADV | VERB | ADJ | ADP | DET | ADV | ADJ | PUNCT |

| É | melhor | que | **entre** | em | pauta | em | breve | . |
|---|---|---|---|---|---|---|---|---|
| AUX | ADJ | SCONJ | VERB | ADP | NOUN | ADP | ADJ | PUNCT |

**Fig. 3.** Example of ambiguous token within a closed class (ADP) and as an open class PoS tag (VERB).

**Table 3.** Tokens of closed PoS classes (cont.).

| |
|---|
| AUX (auxiliary) - verb *ser* |
| é, *era*, **eram**, **éramos**, *eras*, **éreis**, **és**, *foi, fomos, for, fora, foram, fôramos, foras, fordes, fôreis, forem, fores, formos, fosse, fôsseis, fossem, fôssemos, fosses, foste, fostes, fui, são, sê, sede, seja*, **sejais**, **sejam**, **sejamos**, **sejas**, **sendo**, *ser*, **será, serão, serás, serdes, serei, sereis, serem, seremos**, *seres*, **seria, seriam, seríamos, serias, seríeis, sermos, sido, sois, somos, sou** |
| AUX (auxiliary) - verb *estar* |
| **está**, *estado*, **estais, estamos, estando, estão, estar, estará, estarão, estarás, estarei, estareis, estaremos, estaria, estariam, estaríamos, estarias, estaríeis, estás, estava, estavam, estávamos, estavas, estáveis, esteja, estejais, estejam, estejamos, estejas, esteve, estive, estivemos, estiver, estivera, estiveram, estivéramos, estiveras, estiverdes, estivéreis, estiverem, estiveres, estivermos, estivesse, estivésseis, estivessem, estivéssemos, estivesses, estiveste, estivestes, estou** |
| NUM (numerals) - cardinals |
| *um, uma*, **dois, duas, três, quatro, cinco, seis, sete, oito, nove, dez, onze, doze, treze, quatorze, catorze, quinze, dezesseis, dezessete, dezoito, dezenove, vinte**, *trinta*, **quarenta, cinquenta, sessenta**, *setenta*, **oitenta, noventa, cem, duzentos**, *trezentos*, **quatrocentos, quinhentos, seiscentos, setecentos, oitocentos, novecentos, mil**, *milhão, milião, bilhão*, **bilião**, *trilhão, trilião, quatrilhão, quatrilião, quintilhão, quintilião, sextilhão, sextilião, septilhão, septilião, octilhão, octilião, nonilhão, nonilião, decilhão, decilião, milhões, bilhões, biliões, trilhões, triliões, quatrilhões, quatriliões, quintilhões, quintiliões, sextilhões, sextiliões, septilhões, septiliões, octilhões, octiliões, nonilhões, noniliões, decilhões, deciliões* |
| ADJ (adjective) - numerals - ordinals |
| *primeiro, segundo*, **terceiro**, *quarto*, **quinto, sexto, sétimo, oitavo, nono, décimo, undécimo, duodécimo, vigésimo, trigésimo, quadragésimo, quinquagésimo, sexagésimo, septuagésimo, setuagésimo, octogésimo, nonagésimo, centésimo, ducentésimo, trecentésimo, tricentésimo, quadringentésimo, quingentésimo, sexcentésimo, seiscentésimo, septingentésimo, setingentésimo, octingentésimo, octogentésimo, noningentésimo, nongentésimo, milésimo, milionésimo, bilionésimo, trilionésimo, quatrilionésimo, quintilionésimo, sextilionésimo, septilionésimo, octilionésimo, nonilionésimo, decilionésimo** |

## 2.2   Non-ambiguous Co-occurring Tokens

The process to obtain the group of co-occurring tokens to be considered in our technique was somewhat similar to the one for single tokens of closed PoS classes. We started by searching in the available corpora the occurrences of a list of functional expressions that are commonly employed in Portuguese such as MWEs acting as functional words, as the prepositional phrase *de acordo com* ( "according to"). This list was suggested by a linguist dedicated to annotating a corpus following UD guidelines and it includes highly frequent functional expressions such as *desde que* ("since"), annotated as ADP SCONJ, and *mais ou menos* ("more or less"), annotated as ADV CCONJ ADV.

The linguistic analysis filtered out those expressions that appeared with different sets of PoS tags in the corpora. In other words, expressions that need context to be disambiguated were disregarded. The goal was to determine once more if that was an ambiguity due to context or just a misannotation due to different annotation principles. Table 4 shows some examples of non-ambiguous expressions and co-occurring tokens with their respective tags and number of occurrences in the Bosque-UD and MacMorpho corpora.

**Table 4.** Examples of non-ambiguous co-occuring tokens and respective PoS tags in different corpora.

| Expression | Bosque-UD | | MacMorpho | | Adopted tags |
|---|---|---|---|---|---|
| | Tags | Occ. | Tags | Occ. | |
| *cada um* | DET NUM | 13 | PROADJ PROSUB | 679 | DET PRON |
| *de longe* | ADP NOUN | 2 | ADV ADV | 153 | ADP ADV |
| *nada que* | PRON SCONJ | 1 | PROSUB PRO-KS | 189 | PRON PRON |
| *o bastante* | DET ADJ | 1 | ART ADJ | 21 | DET ADJ |

Observing the expressions in Table 4, we have simple cases as *o bastante* ("enough"), where all annotations converged to the same tags (DET ADJ), as MacMorpho uses ART for article, which is always mapped as DET in UD. However, other examples required the analysis of different annotation principles, for example, *de longe* ("from afar"), which is annotated in MacMorpho as an expression that plays a role of an adverb, but, following the UD principles to tag each token individually, *de* ("from" in this context) is undoubtedly an adposition (ADP), as agreed by Bosque-UD annotation. Furthermore, our decision to adopt the tag ADV to the word *longe* ("afar") relies on the fact that it is a non-ambiguous place adverb in Portuguese. Similar decisions based on linguistic concepts were adopted to each expression individually.

Some expressions, on the contrary, were considered ambiguous because they correctly appear with different PoS tags. Figure 4 illustrates two sentences with different tags associated to the co-occurring tokens *a mais* that can be tagged as ADP ADV or DET ADV according to the context. In English, *a mais* could be translated to "more" (or "extra") for ADP ADV or to "the more" (or "the most") for DET ADV. The co-occuring tokens considered ambiguous were left out of our technique.

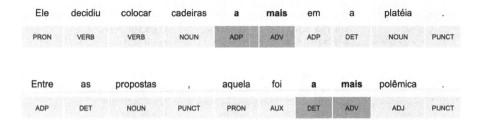

**Fig. 4.** Example of sentences with ambiguous co-occuring tokens.

This process of analysis of ambiguity was carried out to each candidate individually and, even thought we are aware that the resulting list is non-exhaustive, the 110 non-ambiguous expressions and co-occurring tokens with their respective PoS tags are representative of usual and highly frequent lexical phenomena in Portuguese given the observed corpora. The full list of expressions and co-occuring tokens used in our technique is presented in Table 5, where each expression is followed by its non-ambiguous associated PoS tags.

## 3    Evaluation

**The Test Data Set.** Once the set of non-ambiguous single and co-occuring tokens for closed PoS tag classes are defined, our proposed technique is experimented over a data set composed by 2,000 sentences randomly picked from Folha-Kaggle corpus [10]. The limit of 2,000 sentences for the data set is due to the fact that we proceeded a laborious manual annotation of these 2,000 sentences to serve as a gold standard for our experiments.

The Folha-Kaggle corpus is composed by news published at the electronic version of the Brazilian newspaper Folha de São Paulo from January 2015 and September 2017. This corpus holds 167,053 news articles with an approximate average of 22 sentences per news and 23 tokens per sentence, thus more than 3.6 million sentences and about 84 million tokens.

The major concern choosing the sentences to form our testing data set is to have sentences with at least one of the chosen non-ambiguous single or co-occurring tokens. Additionally, we restricted our choices to sentences from 7 to 40 tokens long.

The full random process consisted to pass sequentially for the sentences of the Folha-Kaggle corpus, until obtaining 2,000 sentences performing the following steps:

– To test if the sentence had from 7 to 40 tokens;
– To test if the sentence had either at least one token or one expression among the non-ambiguous ones (Tables 2, 3 or 5);
– To randomize a chance of 5% to keep the sentence in the test data set (so that the several sentences come from a wide variety of texts).

**Table 5.** Chosen non-ambiguous co-occuring tokens and their tags.

| | | | |
|---|---|---|---|
| *à toa* | ADP DET NOUN | *fazer com que* | VERB ADP SCONJ |
| *a despeito de* | ADP NOUN ADP | *frente a* | NOUN ADP |
| *a fim de que* | ADP NOUN ADP SCONJ | *já que* | ADV SCONJ |
| *a menos que* | ADP ADV SCONJ | *logo que* | ADV SCONJ |
| *a não ser que* | ADP ADV VERB SCONJ | *mais do que nunca* | ADV ADP PRON PRON ADV |
| *ao certo* | ADP DET ADJ | *mais do que* | ADV ADP PRON PRON |
| *ao passo que* | ADP DET NOUN CCONJ | *mais ou menos* | ADV CCONJ ADV |
| *ao todo* | ADP DET NOUN | *mais que* | ADV SCONJ |
| *ao vivo* | ADP DET NOUN | *menos do que* | ADV ADP PRON PRON |
| *aos poucos* | ADP DET NOUN | *menos que* | ADV SCONJ |
| *a partir de* | ADP VERB ADP | *muitos deles* | PRON ADP PRON |
| *a ponto de* | ADP NOUN ADP | *nada que* | PRON PRON |
| *a pouco mais de* | ADP ADV ADV ADP | *não obstante* | ADV ADJ |
| *a seguir* | ADP VERB | *nem ao menos* | ADV ADP DET NOUN |
| *ainda mais que* | ADV ADV SCONJ | *nem mesmo* | ADV ADV |
| *ainda que* | ADV SCONJ | *nem sequer* | ADV ADV |
| *algo de bom* | PRON DET ADJ | *no entanto* | ADP DET NOUN |
| *algo que* | PRON PRON | *o bastante* | DET ADJ |
| *antes que* | ADV SCONJ | *o quanto* | DET PRON |
| *apesar de que* | ADV ADP SCONJ | *o suficiente* | DET ADJ |
| *assim mesmo* | ADV ADV | *para baixo* | ADP NOUN |
| *assim que* | ADV SCONJ | *para cima* | ADP NOUN |
| *até então* | ADP ADV | *para frente* | ADP NOUN |
| *cada um* | DET PRON | *para quê* | ADP PRON |
| *cada vez que* | DET NOUN SCONJ | *para que* | ADP SCONJ |
| *caso contrário* | NOUN ADJ | *para trás* | ADP ADV |
| *de agora em diante* | ADP ADV ADP ADV | *por enquanto* | ADP ADV |
| *de cima* | ADP NOUN | *por isso que* | ADP PRON SCONJ |
| *de forma que* | ADP NOUN SCONJ | *por mais que* | ADP ADV SCONJ |
| *de frente* | ADP NOUN | *por muito que* | ADP ADV SCONJ |
| *de longe* | ADP ADV | *pelo menos* | ADP DET NOUN |
| *de maneira que* | ADP NOUN SCONJ | *por ora* | ADP ADV |
| *de modo que* | ADP NOUN SCONJ | *por outro lado* | ADP DET NOUN |
| *de outro lado* | ADP DET NOUN | *por pouco que* | ADP NOUN SCONJ |
| *de perto* | ADP ADV | *por que* | ADP PRON |
| *de sorte que* | ADP NOUN SCONJ | *por quê* | ADP PRON |
| *de tal forma que* | ADP DET NOUN SCONJ | *por sua vez* | ADP DET NOUN |
| *de trás* | ADP ADV | *por último* | ADP ADJ |
| *depois de* | ADV ADP | *por um lado* | ADP DET NOUN |
| *depois que* | ADV SCONJ | *pouco a pouco* | NOUN ADP NOUN |
| *desde então* | ADP ADV | *prestes a* | ADJ ADP |
| *desde que* | ADP SCONJ | *se bem que* | SCONJ ADV SCONJ |
| *devido a* | ADP ADP | *sem mais nem menos* | ADP NOUN CCONJ NOUN |
| *diante de* | ADV ADP | *sem que* | ADP SCONJ |
| *em aberto* | ADP ADJ | *sempre que* | ADV SCONJ |
| *em anexo* | ADP NOUN | *tudo de bom* | PRON ADP ADJ |
| *em branco* | ADP ADJ | *tudo quanto* | PRON PRON |
| *em comum* | ADP ADJ | *tudo que* | PRON PRON |
| *em frente* | ADP NOUN | *um a um* | NUM ADP NUM |
| *em geral* | ADP ADJ | *um por um* | NUM ADP NUM |
| *em razão de* | ADP NOUN ADP | *um pouco de* | DET NOUN ADP |
| *em relação a* | ADP NOUN ADP | *um pouco maior* | DET ADV ADJ |
| *em seguida* | ADP NOUN | *várias vezes* | DET NOUN |
| *em separado* | ADP NOUN | *vários de eles* | PRON ADP PRON |
| *em vão* | ADP ADJ | *volta e meia* | NOUN CCONJ NUM |

The resulting data set is composed by 2,000 sentences totalizing 43,483 tokens, therefore, an average of 22 tokens per sentence. The total number of non-ambiguous single tokens of closed PoS classes (Tables 2 and 3) within this data set is 8,544 tokens, and the total number of non-ambiguous co-occuring tokens (Table 5) is 273.

**The Automatic Annotation.** The test data set was processed by UDPipe [11] and UDify [3] systems using as training set the Bosque-UD [14]. The goal is to observe how each system annotated each token of the test data set and how our proposed technique could improve the tagging accuracy. It is important to notice that UDPipe and UDify are considered to be among the state of the art systems in the area for UD annotation.

**The Manually Produced Gold Standard.** A team of linguists performed the annotation of the test data set to provide a gold standard to evaluate the automatic annotation accuracy of each system. The annotation was conducted independently by 10 highly trained linguists, and the overall result was adjudicated by a chief linguist to provide a correct and homogeneous annotation.

### 3.1 Evaluation of the Non-ambiguous Single Tokens from Closed PoS Classes Corrections

Our goal here is to improve the tagging accuracy by applying an automatic correction of all non-ambiguous single tokens from closed PoS classes, by identifying and replacing the PoS annotation of all these tokens (hence, this process is denoted as ACS for Automatic Correction of Single tokens). The test data set has 8,544 tokens that are non-ambiguous tokens from closed PoS classes, and they are fairly distributed among all 2,000 sentences, since all sentences have at least one of those tokens. Comparing the systems' output with the gold standard, we observe a good overall accuracy for these tokens as stated in Table 6.

UDPipe annotation was wrong in 5.6% of these tokens, while UDify was wrong in 2.8%. However, considering that those tokens belong to sentences, and a wrongfully annotated token may jeopardize the whole sentence annotation because of a possible ripple effect, it is concerning that UDPipe and UDify outputs contain errors in 22.2% and 11.0% of the sentences, respectively.

By running our automatic correction (ACS), we successfully corrected all wrong annotations mentioned in Table 6 for both systems' outputs, as all tokens wrongfully annotated (482 by UDPipe, 239 by UDify) were corrected by us in accordance to the gold standard. This represented an improvement of, respectively, 22.2% and 11.0% in the number of correct sentences annotated by UDPipe and UDify concerning the non-ambiguous single tokens for closed PoS classes.

**Table 6.** Automatic annotation of the test data set for the non-ambiguous single tokens from closed PoS classes compared to the gold standard (ACS).

| System | Target single tokens | | | | | Sentences with target single tokens | | | | |
|---|---|---|---|---|---|---|---|---|---|---|
| | Total | Correct | | Wrong | | Total | Correct | | Wrong | |
| UDPipe | 8,544 | 8,062 | 94.4% | 482 | 5.6% | 2,000 | 1,556 | 77.8% | 444 | 22.2% |
| UDify | 8,544 | 8,305 | 97.2% | 239 | 2.8% | 2,000 | 1,779 | 89.0% | 221 | 11.0% |

## 3.2 Evaluation of the Non-ambiguous Co-occurring Tokens Corrections

Similarly to the process for the single tokens of closed PoS classes, we conducted an automatic correction of the chosen non-ambiguous functional expressions and co-occuring functional words (Table 5) (hence, this process is denoted as ACC for Automatic Correction of Co-occuring tokens). The 2,000 sentences test data set holds 273 occurrences of the chosen non-ambiguous co-occurring tokens that are distributed over 263 sentences. Both UDPipe and UDify have several expressions incorrectly annotated as shown in Table 7.

**Table 7.** Automatic annotation of the test data set for the non-ambiguous co-occurring tokens compared to the gold standard (ACC).

| System | Target co-occurring tokens (expressions) | | | | | Sentences with target co-occurring tokens | | | | |
|---|---|---|---|---|---|---|---|---|---|---|
| | Total | Correct | | Wrong | | Total | Correct | | Wrong | |
| UDPipe | 273 | 166 | 60.8% | 107 | 39.2% | 263 | 158 | 60.1% | 105 | 39.9% |
| UDify | 273 | 184 | 67.4% | 89 | 32.6% | 263 | 174 | 66.2% | 89 | 33.8% |

The observation of the results described in Table 7 shows in scale the same need for correction as the one for single tokens. An impressive number of wrong-fully annotated co-occurring tokens (39.2% for UDPipe and 32.6% for UDify) reflects in annotation errors of 39.9% and 33.8% of sentences, respectively.

After applying the automatic correction (ACC) to both systems' outputs, we were pleased to verify that all 107 and 89 expressions, respectively, were correctly reannotated by our technique, eliminating all system errors for the chosen non-ambiguous co-occurring tokens.

It is important to point out that the ACC carried out by our technique had a low overlap with ACS. For UDpipe, only 7 out of 107 co-occurring tokens corrections had an overlap with the corrections carried out for the single tokens: the token *de* in the expression *a ponto de* (twice); and the token *desde* in the expression *desde que* (five times). For UDify, only 2 out of 89 co-occurring tokens corrections had overlap and they both were for the token *desde* in the expression *desde que* (twice).

## 3.3   Evaluation of All Non-ambiguous Corrections

As seen in Sects. 3.1 and 3.2, both automatic corrections brought improvements considering the targeted tokens and expressions. Also, our experiments indicated an overall improvement in the accuracy of the systems' annotation when compared to the gold standard. Table 8 presents the obtained accuracy starting from the original system annotation, followed by the application of our automatic correction of non-ambiguous single tokens (ACS) and automatic correction of non-ambiguous co-occurring tokens (ACC). However, in this table, we indicate not only the numbers concerned by the tokens belonging to the target set (single and co-occurring tokens), but all tokens of the 2,000 sentences test data set, providing an overall picture of the situation.

**Table 8.** Automatic annotation of the test data set: overall analysis considering the original system annotation and our proposed automatic corrections (ACS and ACC) compared to the gold standard.

| Process | All tokens in the data set | | | | | All sentences in the data set | | | | |
|---|---|---|---|---|---|---|---|---|---|---|
| | Total | Correct | | Wrong | | Total | Correct | | Wrong | |
| UDPipe | 43,483 | 41,548 | 95.5% | 1,935 | 4.5% | 2,000 | 886 | 44.3% | 1,114 | 55.7% |
| UDPipe+ACC | 43,483 | 41,666 | 95.8% | 1,817 | 4.2% | 2,000 | 932 | 46.6% | 1,068 | 53.4% |
| UDPipe+ACS | 43,483 | 42,030 | 96.7% | 1,453 | 3.3% | 2,000 | 1,121 | 56.1% | 879 | 43.9% |
| UDPipe+ACS+ACC | 43,483 | 42,131 | **96.9%** | 1,352 | 3.1% | 2,000 | 1,163 | **58.2%** | 837 | 41.8% |
| UDify | 43,483 | 41,326 | 95.0% | 2,157 | 5.0% | 2,000 | 799 | 40.0% | 1,201 | 60.0% |
| UDify+ACC | 43,483 | 41,415 | 95.3% | 2,068 | 4.7% | 2,000 | 827 | 41.4% | 1,126 | 58.6% |
| UDify+ACS | 43,483 | 41,565 | 95.6% | 1,918 | 4.4% | 2,000 | 874 | 43.7% | 1,126 | 56.3% |
| UDify+ACS+ACC | 43,483 | 41,652 | **95.8%** | 1,828 | 4.2% | 2,000 | 907 | **45.4%** | 1,093 | 54.6% |

Observing the results in Table 8, it is clear that both automatic corrections presented consistent improvements by correcting wrongfully annotated tokens (1.4% and 0.8% for UDPipe and UDify, respectively). However, the gains in terms of the number of correctly annotated sentences is even more noticeable, as the initial system accuracy for fully correct tagged sentences was 44.3% and 40.0% for UDPipe and UDify, respectively, and the combined application of ACS and ACC brought an increase around 13.9% of fully correct sentences for UDPipe (from 44.3% to 58.2% of sentences) and 5.4% for UDify (from 40% to 45.4% of sentences). Such values are very relevant, as tagging results directly influence other automatic analyses that parsers and other NLP systems perform. Therefore, producing an error reduction in this scale is significant.

Another interesting observation from Table 8 is that the ACS and ACC corrections bring rather complementary gains. For instance, observing the reduction of wrongfully annotated tokens for UDPipe, the application of ACC over the UDPipe output corrected the tags of 118 tokens (1935 minus 1817), while the application of ACS corrected the tags of 482 tokens (1935 minus 1453), and the combined application of both ACS and ACC corrected 583 tokens (1935 minus

1352). This shows that the intersection of corrected tags between ACC and ACS was just over 17 tokens (which is the difference between 118+482 and 583). A similar relation was found for UDify output, and also for the gains in terms of sentences. These numbers reinforce our findings of the small overlap between ACS and ACC gains mentioned in Sect. 3.2.

## 4  Concluding Remarks

We proposed a technique for Universal Dependencies-based PoS tagging refinement through linguistic resources. Our goal was to show that such refinement could be accomplished by improving the annotation accuracy of two well-known systems (UDPipe and UDify) through tag corrections based on non-ambiguous single and co-occurring tokens. The overall impact of our proposed automatic corrections lead to a tagging accuracy improvement of up to 1.4%. More than this, in relation to the number of fully correct annotated sentences, the improvement was up to 13.9%.

We performed a verification over the entire Folha-Kaggle corpus with 3.6 million sentences and 84 million tokens, and we found nearly 28 million tokens that would be detected by our proposed approach. Given the results of our experiments, which indicate that about 2.5 million tokens would be wrongfully tagged by UDPipe and would be corrected by our approach, this represents the correction of about 20% of the sentences of the whole Folha-Kaggle corpus.

Another important contribution of our work is the construction and availability of the linguistic resources with the 269 non-ambiguous single token words from closed PoS classes and 110 non-ambiguous functional expressions and co-occuring functional words for Portuguese. These resources may help several linguistic efforts in Portuguese, which is still an under resourced language. For the interested reader, all the resources and the gold standard data are available at the POeTiSA project webpage[2].

Finally, tackling PoS tagging under the UD formalism is also an important contribution for the computational processing of the Brazilian Portuguese language, as UD model has become the standard in tagging and parsing in the world. Nowadays, the UD project has been adopted by over 100 languages, including Portuguese. This paper helps fostering UD research for this language.

Future work includes to possibly refine the current lists, in particular, to enlarge the lists of non-ambiguous tokens and functional expressions, as well as to look for possible disambiguation rules for some tokens from closed PoS classes and to include nominal and verbal MWEs.

**Acknowledgments.** This work was carried out at the Center for Artificial Intelligence (C4AI-USP), with support of the São Paulo Research Foundation (FAPESP grant #2019/07665-4) and the IBM Corporation.

---

[2] https://sites.google.com/icmc.usp.br/poetisa.

# References

1. Droganova, K., Zeman, D.: Towards deep universal dependencies. In: Proceedings of the 5th International Conference on Dependency Linguistics (Depling, SyntaxFest), pp. 144–152 (2019)
2. Fonseca, E.R., G Rosa, J.L., Aluísio, S.M.: Evaluating word embeddings and a revised corpus for part-of-speech tagging in Portuguese. J. Braz. Comput. Soc. **21**(1), 1–14 (2015)
3. Kondratyuk, D., Straka, M.: 75 languages, 1 model: parsing universal dependencies universally. In: Proceedings of the Conference on Empirical Methods in Natural Language Processing and the 9th International Joint Conference on Natural Language Processing (EMNLP-IJCNLP), pp. 2779–2795 (2019)
4. Ling, W., et al.: Finding function in form: compositional character models for open vocabulary word representation. In: Proceedings of the Conference on Empirical Methods in Natural Language Processing (EMNLP), pp. 1520–1530 (2015)
5. Nivre, J., Fang, C.T.: Universal dependency evaluation. In: Proceedings of the NoDaLiDa 2017 Workshop on Universal Dependencies (UDW), pp. 86–95 (2017)
6. Nivre, J., et al.: Universal Dependencies v1: a multilingual treebank collection. In: Proceedings of the 10th International Conference on Language Resources and Evaluation (LREC), pp. 1659–1666 (2016)
7. Rademaker, A., Chalub, F., Real, L., Freitas, C., Bick, E., De Paiva, V.: Universal dependencies for Portuguese. In: Proceedings of the 4th International Conference on Dependency Linguistics (Depling), pp. 197–206 (2017)
8. Rehbein, I., Hirschmann, H.: POS tagset refinement for linguistic analysis and the impact on statistical parsing. In: Henrich, V., Hinrichs, E., de Kok, D., Osenova, P., Przepiorkowski, A. (eds.) Proceedings of the 13th International Workshop on Treebanks and Linguistic Theories (TLT13), pp. 172–183. University of Tübingen (2018)
9. Rogers, A., Kovaleva, O., Rumshisky, A.: A primer in BERTology: what we know about how BERT works. Trans. Assoc. Computat. Linguist. **8**, 842–866 (2020)
10. Santana, M.: Kaggle - news of the Brazilian newspaper. https://www.kaggle.com/marlesson/news-of-the-site-folhauol. Accessed 14 June 2021
11. Straka, M.: UDPipe 2.0 prototype at CoNLL 2018 UD shared task. In: Proceedings of the CoNLL 2018 Shared Task: Multilingual Parsing from Raw Text to Universal Dependencies, pp. 197–207 (2018)
12. Straka, M., Straková, J.: Tokenizing, POS tagging, lemmatizing and parsing UD 2.0 with UDPipe. In: Proceedings of the CoNLL 2017 Shared Task: Multilingual Parsing from Raw Text to Universal Dependencies, pp. 88–99 (2017)
13. Sulubacak, U.: Implementing universal dependency, morphology, and multiword expression annotation standards for Turkish language processing. Turk. J. Electr. Eng. Comput. Sci. **26**(3), 1662–1672 (2018)
14. Universal Dependencies: UD Portuguese Bosque - UD version 2. https://universaldependencies.org/treebanks/pt_bosque/index.html. Accessed 14 June 2021

# When External Knowledge Does Not Aggregate in Named Entity Recognition

Pedro Ivo Monteiro Privatto$^{(\boxtimes)}$ and Ivan Rizzo Guilherme

Institute of Geosciences and Exact Sciences, UNESP - São Paulo State University, Rio Claro, SP, Brazil

**Abstract.** In the different areas of knowledge, textual data are important sources of information. This way, Information Extraction methods have been developed to identify and structure information present in textual documents. In particular there is the Named Entity Recognition (NER) task, which consists of using methods to identify Named Entities, such as Person, Place, among others, in texts, using techniques from Natural Language Processing and Machine Learning. Recent works explored the use of external sources of knowledge to boost the Machine Learning models with sets of domain specific relevant information for the NER task. This work aims to evaluate the aggregation of external knowledge, in the form of Gazetter and Knowledge Graphs, for NER task. Our approach is composed of two steps: i) generation of embeddings, ii) definition and training of the Machine Learning methods. The experiments were conducted on four English datasets, and their results show that the applied strategies for external knowledge integration did not bring great gains to the models, as expressed by F1-Score metric. In the performed experiments, there was an F1-score increase in 17 of the 32 cases where external knowledge was used, but in most cases the gains were lesser than 0.5% in F1-score. In some scenarios the aggregated external knowledge does not capture relevant content, thus not being necessarily beneficial to the methodology.

**Keywords:** Named entity recognition · Information extraction · Knowledge embeddings

## 1 Introduction

With the evolution of digital technologies and the internet users profile, the generation of unstructured data had a huge increase. According to [22], unstructured data are those that do not show a clear syntactic and semantic, machine-processable structure.

This way, methods have been developed to identify and structure information present in textual documents. In these methods, the data structuring process make use of Natural Language Processing, an area that uses concepts of Linguistics and Artificial Intelligence to process data and automate language related

© Springer Nature Switzerland AG 2021
A. Britto and K. Valdivia Delgado (Eds.): BRACIS 2021, LNAI 13074, pp. 616–627, 2021.
https://doi.org/10.1007/978-3-030-91699-2_42

tasks. Some of the Natural Language Processing tasks that we can mention are Machine Translation, Speech Recognition, Automatic Text Summarization, Information Extraction, among others.

Information Extraction methods have been developed to identify and structure information present in textual documents. In particular there is the Named Entity Recognition task, which consists of using methods to identify Named Entities, such as Person, Place, among others, in texts written in natural language and categorize them according to their nature. A Named Entity is a concept, formed by one or more words, that belongs to a previously defined semantic group [9–11,25,28,33].

Traditionally, NER approaches have used many techniques from Linguistics, such as syntactic labels, word lemmas, affixes, among others, to extract information present in texts. The use of traditional techniques is quite laborious, as it involves several stages of data preparation. In order to ease the work of traditional NER approaches, Machine Learning methods have been developed. Recently, numeric techniques that captures syntactic and semantic aspects of words has been gaining space for their similar results, sometimes even better, when compared to classical techniques, without requiring an extensive process of feature engineering.

As examples of Machine Learning approaches to Named Entity Recognition task we can cite [5,6,12,14,15,26], among many others. Distributed representations for words are some of the reasons for the popularization of Machine Learning methods in NLP, and as example of these representations there are word2vec [23,24], GloVe [27], fastText [3], Flair [1], BERT [7], and many others.

As stated by Ratinov and Roth [29], NER is knowledge-intensive task. Therefore, there are approaches that still perform feature engineering with Machine Learning methods in order to include features that cannot be captured by word vectors or texts. Even though part of the problems are solved by feature engineering, there is still a semantic gap that cannot be solved with lexical and syntactic attributes alone. In this sense, semantic repositories have been adopted.

In [5] external information is added to the CNN-LSTM model through the use of a lexicon. This lexicon is made of Wikipedia data and is used to add new features in the shape of Inside-Outside-Beginning tags to the input vectors.

A work using external knowledge from ontology is presented in [19], where the authors perform the Named Entity Recognition on bridge inspection reports. In order to do this, they use a semi-supervised Conditional Random Fields (CRF) whose inputs consists of syntactic features, like Stems and Part Of Speech tags, and semantic features from the domain ontology, named BridgeOnto.

Liu et al. [20] add external information from Gazetteers, but instead of using tags indicating the pertinence of the word to one or more Gazetteers, it uses Hybrid Semi-Markov CRF to generate a numeric value that express the degree of pertinence of the word to a Gazetteer. The reason for this is to find a better alternative to the hard match representation, which is commonly used when Gazetteers use is adopted.

In [18] the authors present an approach using external knowledge through use of lexicons together with syntactic features like Part Of Speech tags and n-grams.

Ratinov and Roth [29] enrich the Named Entity Recognition task by using a External Knowledge in the form of gazetteers on CoNLL03, MUC7, and a smaller dataset of webpages assembled and annotated by them. They also use other features, such as context aggregation, extended prediction history, among others, to boost the NER performance of their model.

Seyler et al. [30] divide external features in four categories to quantify the impact of each one in the NER task, using a Linear-Chain CRF on CoNLL03 and MUC7 datasets. The four categories are: i) Knowledge Agnostic - using only local features; ii) Name-Based Knowledge - using a list of named entities; ii) Knowledge-Base-Based Knowledge - using features extracted from a Knowledge Base or an annotated corpus; iv) Entity-Based Knowledge - using the results of a Named Entity Disambiguation. Authors show that incrementally adding more categories of knowledge yields better effectiveness, but sometimes at the cost of efficiency, stating that there is a trade-off between them.

In order to add external knowledge to a neural model, Ding et al. [8] propose the use of an adapted Gated Graph Sequence Neural Network to capture the information contained in multiple gazetteers. The role of the Gated Graph Sequence Neural Network is to serve as a embedding layer that learn how to combine the knowledge present in more than one gazetteer of the same or different type. The resulting embeddings are then fed to a standard BiLSTM-CRF to fulfill the NER task on Weibo-NER and OntoNotes 4, both in Chinese.

The gazetteer knowledge is aggregated to an Attentive Neural Network by Lin et al. [17] for the Nested Named Entity Recognition task. They leverage the knowledge contained in gazetteers by finding a representation for entity candidates through what they call a gazetteer network, that is concatenated with the representation learned by a region encoder. The experiments show that this strategy improves the model performance on ACE2005 dataset.

Xiaofeng et al. [32] propose a method to incorporate dictionary features to a BiLSTM-CRF model in order to evaluate their impact. Their differential is that the dictionaries used during the training phase are obtained from the train split data, whereas the dictionaries used in the testing phase are from SENNA. Their experiments are conducted on CoNLL2003 dataset, and show that the size of the dictionaries (partial or oversized) may lead to inferior results in some cases.

The purpose of this work is to evaluate the aggregation of external knowledge, in form of Gazetter and Knowledge Graphs from YAGO and Freebase, for Named Entity Recognition task using BiLSTM, BiGRU and CRF.

The paper is organized as follows: Sect. 2 presents our approach, details of the models, the input vectors and the external knowledge used. In Sect. 3 the experimental protocol and the datasets are explained, and the results are discussed. Section 4 presents conclusions and future work.

# 2    Approach

This work aims to investigate the use of external knowledge in some commonly used neural models for NER. The first step of our approach is to generate the embeddings for the datasets utilized by the methods, and add the sources of external knowledge. After the first step, the next one is to define the neural networks, with the architecture inspired by [5].

This section introduces the neural models used, as well as the sources of the external knowledge and how these knowledge sources are added to our model.

## 2.1    Neural Models

In this work we used two neural models: Bidirectional Long Short-Term Memory (BiLSTM) combined with Conditional Random Fields (CRF) [6], and Bidirectional Gated Recurrent Units (BiGRU) combined with CRF.

The aim of the models is to find a sequence of labels $\mathcal{Y} = \{\mathcal{Y}_1, \mathcal{Y}_2, ..., \mathcal{Y}_n\}$ for a given sequence of inputs $\mathcal{X} = \{\mathcal{X}_1, \mathcal{X}_2, ..., \mathcal{X}_n\}$ of length $n$. In this work, $\mathcal{X}_i$ are vector representations of each word and its features in a sentence. These vectors are used as input to the BiLSTM/BiGRU layers, and the purpose of these layers is to extract features and create a new feature vector for each word represented by $\mathcal{X}_i$ while considering the surrounding words present in the same sentence. The idea of bidirectional layers is to use the same input vectors for two LSTM/GRU layers, one layer with the word sequence from left to right, generating $\overrightarrow{h_i}$, and the other the sequence from right to left, generating $\overleftarrow{h_i}$, which are concatenated into one feature vector, $h_i = [\overrightarrow{h_i} : \overleftarrow{h_i}]$, that is used as input by the classification layer.

Following [14] and other works, we chose CRF as the classification layer of our models because it takes into account the previously assigned labels. This way, combining BiLSTM/BiGRU with CRF, the models make good use of the sequential characteristic of texts.

## 2.2    Embeddings

Inspired by [5], this work make use of common embeddings: Character embeddings, Casing embeddings and Word embeddings. Further, we also aggregate the aim of validation: External Knowledge embeddings. All these embedding techniques are explained below, with exception of the External Knowledge embedding that is shown in the next subsection.

**Character Embeddings:** To generate the Character embeddings we first create a vector, randomly initialized with $U(-0.5, 0.5)$, for each character in a set of 135 characters. After initialization, these vectors are then retrieved for each character on each word and used as input to a Convolutional Neural Network with max-pooling layer to generate a single vector with information from all the characters of a word, named *Character embedding*. To better capture character features, character vectors are trained with the rest of the model, and we use a Dropout layer to avoid Character embeddings overfitting.

**Casing Embeddings:** For the Casing embeddings generation, each input word is categorized in one of eight possible categories according to their composition, such as their capitalisation and presence of numbers and special characters. Then, each category is initialized as a one-hot vector that is further trained with the model.

**Word Embeddings:** As Word embeddings we decided to use pre-trained GloVe [27] Word embeddings with 50 dimensions. Other candidates were word2vec, fastText, Flair and BERT. Some of these maybe would yield better final results, but as the objective of the work is to analyze the impact of external knowledge in the chosen neural architecture, results below the state of the art do not invalidate this work.

### 2.3   External Knowledge

To aggregate external information to the input vectors, we chose to use two distinct sources: Gazetteers made from version 3.1 of Yet Another Great Ontology (YAGO) [21]; and Knowledge embeddings from Freebase, generated by TransE method [4] using OpenKE framework [13] with the latest Freebase dump[1].

To create the Gazetteers we picked all entities referring to four types of entities in YAGO (Person, Organization, Foundation, Place), which correspond to three of CONLL2003 types (Person, Organization, Place). Besides the chosen types, we also picked their sub-types (e.g. Abstract painters is a sub-type of People, Presidents is a sub-type of People) By the end of this process, we had three Gazetteer lists whose number of entities is shown in Table 1.

**Table 1.** Number of entities in each Gazetteer list.

| Type | # |
| --- | --- |
| Person | 1,743,625 |
| Organization/Foundation | 370,085 |
| Place | 507,599 |
| **Total** | 2,621,309 |

With the purpose of adding Gazetteer information to the input vectors, a strategy similar to the Casing Embedding was used, but instead of the eight categories related to the composition of the word, we used another eight categories that express the pertinence of the word in one or more Gazetteer. To do

---

[1] https://developers.google.com/freebase/.

this, we did a tagging stage where each word of the dataset was tagged according to their pertinence to a Gazetteer (e.g. Washington received PER/LOC tag, Kilimanjaro received only LOC tag). Then one-hot vectors are generated for each of the categories, which are then trained with the model, just as we did with Casing Embeddings.

As for the Knowledge embeddings from Freebase, we chose to use only single-word topics, but to compensate it we did not filter the topics by types. This way we used the Knowledge embeddings of all words in the text, and if the word doesn't have a knowledge embedding we used a vector full of zeros.

Regardless of the source, the addition of external knowledge is done by concatenating the semantic feature vector, that was generated by one of the method described above, to the other vectors (Word, Casing, Character) in order to present the resulting vector as input to the neural models used.

# 3   Experiments

We conducted experiments on four datasets in order to check the impact of external knowledge on chosen neural model for NER task. We executed each experimental setting a total of 10 times due to the stochastic elements present in each model initialization. For evaluation we decided to adopt the F1-score metric, shown in Eq. 1 that is the harmonic mean of Precision (P) and Recall (R), shown in Eq. 2 and Eq. 3, where TP stands for True Positive, FP for False Positive, and FN for False Negative.

$$F_1 - score = \frac{2 * P * R}{(P + R)} \tag{1}$$

$$P = \frac{TP}{TP + FP} \tag{2}$$

$$R = \frac{TP}{TP + FN} \tag{3}$$

So, the F1-score results presented in this section are the mean of 10 executions for each setting of the model.

## 3.1   Datasets

In this work we chose four distinct datasets, all of them in English, with different sizes and types of entities in order to validate our approach on different scenarios. The chosen dataset are CONLL2003 [31], OntoNotes5, MIT Movies [18], and MIT Restaurants [18]. We only used train/test split, leaving validation sets out of our experiments, thus not conducting a hyper-parameter optimization. All of the datasets use Inside-Outside-Beginning as entity annotation scheme. Table 2 shows in details the number of sentences and entities contained in datasets.

**Table 2.** Quantification of datasets.

| Dataset | # Sentences | # Entities |
|---|---|---|
| CONLL2003 train | 14,987 | 23,499 |
| CONLL2003 test | 3,684 | 5,648 |
| OntoNotes train | 115,812 | 128,738 |
| OntoNotes test | 12,217 | 12,586 |
| MIT movies train | 7,816 | 23,030 |
| MIT movies test | 1,953 | 5,686 |
| MIT restaurants train | 7,660 | 15,363 |
| MIT restaurants test | 1,521 | 3,151 |

## 3.2 Experimental Settings

The experiments consisted in using external embeddings, described on previous sections, to check their impact on the results of our models. To verify this, we conducted experiments in the same model with and without the external knowledge. The model without the external knowledge was used as Baseline for our modifications, this way, we executed both network models, BiLSTM-CRF and BiGRU-CRF, with and without the addition of the external embeddings and compared their F1-score.

The parameters used are shown in Table 3. The parameters are the same for all datasets, except for OntoNotes 5 dataset, which we decided to use a lower Learning Rate and fewer Epochs due its large amount of data.

**Table 3.** Parameters values. Values with * symbol refer to parameters used only for OntoNotes5.

| Parameter | Value |
|---|---|
| Epochs | 100/20* |
| Dropout | 0.5 |
| Recurrent dropout | 0.25 |
| LSTM/GRU units | 200 |
| Convolution filters | 30 |
| Convolution width | 3 |
| Convolution step | 1 |
| Learning rate | 0.0105/0.008* |

## 3.3 Experimental Results

Table 4 shows the results of the carried out experiments and the state-of-art (as stated by the authors in their papers) F1-score for the given dataset. The results show a an increase in all cases when we added Gazetteer information to BiLSTM-CRF. However, the addition of Knowledge Embedding to BiLSTM-CRF decreased the F1-score on every situation. On the experimental results using BiGRU there are two scenarios of increase in F1-score with the addition of Gazetteer information, and the use of Knowledge Embeddings also increased the F1-score in two scenarios. Regardless of whether the external knowledge increase or decreased the F1-score, the difference was not significant, representing on average 0,4%, with exception of OntoNotes 5 dataset, where the differences were very accentuated, averaging 6,76%.

Even though other works show an increase in F1-score when adding external knowledge to the models, our addition of external knowledge doesn't always brings positive impacts on F1-score, as shown by Table 4, and even when it does it not necessarily achieve the best result of our models. Furthermore, even our best results are far from the state of the art in some datasets.

**Table 4.** Comparison of F1-score between our models and state-of-art models, where Gaz stands for Gazetteer, and KE stands for Knowledge Embeddings. Each column represents the F1-score for that dataset, and the bold values represent the best result for that dataset.

| Model | CONLL2003 | ON5 |
|---|---|---|
| BiLSTM-CRF | 88.57 | 68.71 |
| BiLSTM-CRF+Gaz | 88.81 | 72.21 |
| BiLSTM-CRF+KE | 88.18 | 67.50 |
| BiGRU-CRF | 88.15 | 59.00 |
| BiGRU-CRF+Gaz | 88.39 | 69.53 |
| BiGRU-CRF+KE | 88.07 | 70.80 |
| Baevski et al. [2] | **93.50** | – |
| Li et al. [16] | – | **92.07** |
| Model | MIT-M | MIT-R |
| BiLSTM-CRF | 66.56 | 73.85 |
| BiLSTM-CRF+Gaz | 66.91 | 73.94 |
| BiLSTM-CRF+KE | 65.80 | 73.75 |
| BiGRU-CRF | 67.50 | 72.83 |
| BiGRU-CRF+Gaz | 67.25 | 72.80 |
| BiGRU-CRF+KE | 66.39 | 74.13 |
| Liu et al. [18] | **88.58** | **85.07** |

When compared to the results of other works, such as [29,30] our strategy doesn't seem to bring gains, however it is worth noting that the models we chose as baseline achieve good values of F1-measure (88.57% and 88.15% for CoNLL2003 using BiLSTM and BiGRU, respectively), which are very close, respectively, to their best and second best results. This choice of a good baseline may be one of the reasons behind the small gains.

## 4    Conclusion

This work aimed to evaluate the use of external knowledge used in machine learning methods for Named Entity Recognition. The methodology was composed of two steps: i) generation of embeddings, ii) definition and training of Machine Learning methods.

The defined models were trained and tested in four English dataset of different sizes and different types of entities in order to evaluate our methodology.

As our experiments show, in spite of an increase of F1-score in 17 of the 32 cases, the way external knowledge was integrated to the model did not bring much gains, most of them being lesser than 0.5%, and in some datasets the results were a way below the state-of-art methods (for the values stated by the authors in their papers). This may be explained because we haven't made any hyper-parameter optimization, which may have led the model to suffer from overfit, and underfit in the case of OntoNotes5, where there was an increase of 11.8% in one scenario.

Another point to consider in the gap between our results and the state-of-art is the choice of Word embeddings: while our choice was to use GloVe Word embeddings, most recent works use embeddings that better capture the context of words.

It is important to note that we haven't reproduced the state-of-art methods. Although we did not achieve state-of-art results, we were still able to check the impact of the addition of external knowledge in the used neural models.

The results and discussion show that the results of adding external knowledge are strongly linked to what information is used, as well as how it is used. We conjecture that in some cases the information present in external bases may be already integrated on the word representations, especially when the embeddings training set and the knowledge base share common data.

This way, adding external knowledge to the models does not always improve the results, and can even lead to performance decreases. So, in order to integrate external knowledge, a deep analysis is needed to capture all the semantic present in external knowledge bases.

## References

1. Akbik, A., Blythe, D., Vollgraf, R.: Contextual string embeddings for sequence labeling. In: Proceedings of the 27th International Conference on Computational Linguistics, Santa Fe, New Mexico, USA, pp. 1638–1649. Association for Computational Linguistics (August 2018). https://www.aclweb.org/anthology/C18-1139
2. Baevski, A., Edunov, S., Liu, Y., Zettlemoyer, L., Auli, M.: Cloze-driven pretraining of self-attention networks. In: Proceedings of the 2019 Conference on Empirical Methods in Natural Language Processing and the 9th International Joint Conference on Natural Language Processing (EMNLP-IJCNLP), Hong Kong, China, pp. 5360–5369. Association for Computational Linguistics (November 2019). https://doi.org/10.18653/v1/D19-1539. https://www.aclweb.org/anthology/D19-1539

3. Bojanowski, P., Grave, E., Joulin, A., Mikolov, T.: Enriching word vectors with subword information. Trans. Assoc. Computat. Linguist. **5**, 135–146 (2017). https://doi.org/10.1162/tacl_a_00051. https://www.aclweb.org/anthology/Q17-1010
4. Bordes, A., Usunier, N., Garcia-Durán, A., Weston, J., Yakhnenko, O.: Translating embeddings for modeling multi-relational data. In: Proceedings of the 26th International Conference on Neural Information Processing Systems, NIPS 2013, vol. 2, pp. 2787–2795. Curran Associates Inc., Red Hook (2013). https://doi.org/10.5555/2999792.2999923
5. Chiu, J.P., Nichols, E.: Named entity recognition with bidirectional LSTM-CNNs. Trans. Assoc. Comput. Linguist. **4**, 357–370 (2016). https://www.aclweb.org/anthology/Q16-1026
6. Collobert, R., Weston, J., Bottou, L., Karlen, M., Kavukcuoglu, K., Kuksa, P.: Natural language processing (almost) from scratch. J. Mach. Learn. Res. **12**, 2493–2537 (2011). https://doi.org/10.5555/1953048.2078186
7. Devlin, J., Chang, M.W., Lee, K., Toutanova, K.: BERT: pre-training of deep bidirectional transformers for language understanding. In: Proceedings of the 2019 Conference of the North American Chapter of the Association for Computational Linguistics: Human Language Technologies, Minneapolis, Minnesota, Volume 1 (Long and Short Papers), pp. 4171–4186. Association for Computational Linguistics (June 2019). https://doi.org/10.18653/v1/N19-1423. https://www.aclweb.org/anthology/N19-1423
8. Ding, R., Xie, P., Zhang, X., Lu, W., Li, L., Si, L.: A neural multi-digraph model for Chinese NER with gazetteers. In: Proceedings of the 57th Annual Meeting of the Association for Computational Linguistics, Florence, Italy, pp. 1462–1467. Association for Computational Linguistics (July 2019). https://doi.org/10.18653/v1/P19-1141. https://aclanthology.org/P19-1141
9. Freire, N., Borbinha, J., Calado, P.: An approach for named entity recognition in poorly structured data. In: Simperl, E., Cimiano, P., Polleres, A., Corcho, O., Presutti, V. (eds.) ESWC 2012. LNCS, vol. 7295, pp. 718–732. Springer, Heidelberg (2012). https://doi.org/10.1007/978-3-642-30284-8_55
10. Gorinski, P.J., et al.: Named entity recognition for electronic health records: a comparison of rule-based and machine learning approaches. CoRR abs/1903.03985. arXiv:1903.03985 (2019)
11. Goyal, A., Gupta, V., Kumar, M.: Recent named entity recognition and classification techniques: a systematic review. Comput. Sci. Rev. **29**, 21–43 (2018). https://doi.org/10.1016/j.cosrev.2018.06.001
12. Habibi, M., Weber, L., Neves, M., Wiegandt, D.L., Leser, U.: Deep learning with word embeddings improves biomedical named entity recognition. Bioinformatics **33**(14), i37–i48 (2017). https://doi.org/10.1093/bioinformatics/btx228
13. Han, X., et al.: OpenKE: an open toolkit for knowledge embedding. In: Proceedings of the 2018 Conference on Empirical Methods in Natural Language Processing: System Demonstrations, Brussels, Belgium, pp. 139–144. Association for Computational Linguistics (November 2018). https://doi.org/10.18653/v1/D18-2024. https://www.aclweb.org/anthology/D18-2024
14. Lample, G., Ballesteros, M., Subramanian, S., Kawakami, K., Dyer, C.: Neural architectures for named entity recognition. In: Proceedings of the 2016 Conference of the North American Chapter of the Association for Computational Linguistics: Human Language Technologies, San Diego, California, pp. 260–270. Association for Computational Linguistics (June 2016). https://doi.org/10.18653/v1/N16-1030. https://www.aclweb.org/anthology/N16-1030

15. Lange, D., Böhm, C., Naumann, F.: Extracting structured information from Wikipedia articles to populate infoboxes. In: Proceedings of the 19th ACM International Conference on Information and Knowledge Management, CIKM 2010, pp. 1661–1664. Association for Computing Machinery, New York (2010). https://doi. org/10.1145/1871437.1871698

16. Li, X., Sun, X., Meng, Y., Liang, J., Wu, F., Li, J.: Dice loss for data-imbalanced NLP tasks. In: Proceedings of the 58th Annual Meeting of the Association for Computational Linguistics, pp. 465–476. Association for Computational Linguistics (July 2020). https://doi.org/10.18653/v1/2020.acl-main.45. https://www.aclweb. org/anthology/2020.acl-main.45

17. Lin, H., Lu, Y., Han, X., Sun, L., Dong, B., Jiang, S.: Gazetteer-enhanced attentive neural networks for named entity recognition. In: Proceedings of the 2019 Conference on Empirical Methods in Natural Language Processing and the 9th International Joint Conference on Natural Language Processing (EMNLP-IJCNLP), Hong Kong, China, pp. 6232–6237. Association for Computational Linguistics (November 2019). https://doi.org/10.18653/v1/D19-1646. https://aclanthology.org/D19-1646

18. Liu, J., Pasupat, P., Cyphers, S., Glass, J.: Asgard: a portable architecture for multilingual dialogue systems. In: 2013 IEEE International Conference on Acoustics, Speech and Signal Processing, pp. 8386–8390 (2013). https://doi.org/10.1109/ICASSP.2013.6639301

19. Liu, K., El-Gohary, N.: Ontology-based semi-supervised conditional random fields for automated information extraction from bridge inspection reports. Autom. Constr. **81** (2017). https://doi.org/10.1016/j.autcon.2017.02.003

20. Liu, T., Yao, J.G., Lin, C.Y.: Towards improving neural named entity recognition with gazetteers. In: Proceedings of the 57th Annual Meeting of the Association for Computational Linguistics, Florence, Italy, pp. 5301–5307. Association for Computational Linguistics (July 2019). https://doi.org/10.18653/v1/P19-1524. https://www.aclweb.org/anthology/P19-1524

21. Mahdisoltani, F., Biega, J., Suchanek, F.M.: Yago3: a knowledge base from multilingual Wikipedias (2013). https://hal-imt.archives-ouvertes.fr/hal-01699874/

22. Manning, C.D., Raghavan, P., Schütze, H.: Introduction to Information Retrieval. Cambridge University Press (2008). https://doi.org/10.1017/CBO9780511809071

23. Mikolov, T., Chen, K., Corrado, G., Dean, J.: Efficient estimation of word representations in vector space. In: Bengio, Y., LeCun, Y. (eds.) 1st International Conference on Learning Representations, Workshop Track Proceedings, ICLR 2013, Scottsdale, Arizona, USA, 2–4 May 2013 (2013). arXiv:1301.3781

24. Mikolov, T., Sutskever, I., Chen, K., Corrado, G., Dean, J.: Distributed representations of words and phrases and their compositionality. CoRR abs/1310.4546. arXiv:1310.4546 (2013)

25. Nadeau, D., Sekine, S.: A survey of named entity recognition and classification. Lingvisticæ Investigationes **30**(1), 3–26 (2007). https://doi.org/10.1075/li.30.1. 03nad. https://www.jbe-platform.com/content/journals/10.1075/li.30.1.03nad

26. Nurdin, A., Maulidevi, N.U.: 5w1h information extraction with CNN-bidirectional LSTM. J. Phys. Conf. Ser. **978**, 012078 (2018). https://doi.org/10.1088/1742-6596/978/1/012078

27. Pennington, J., Socher, R., Manning, C.: GloVe: global vectors for word representation. In: Proceedings of the 2014 Conference on Empirical Methods in Natural Language Processing (EMNLP), Doha, Qatar, pp. 1532–1543. Association for Computational Linguistics (October 2014). https://doi.org/10.3115/v1/D14-1162. https://www.aclweb.org/anthology/D14-1162

28. Rais, M., Lachkar, A., Lachkar, A., Ouatik, S.E.A.: A comparative study of biomedical named entity recognition methods based machine learning approach. In: 2014 3rd IEEE International Colloquium in Information Science and Technology (CIST), pp. 329–334 (October 2014). https://doi.org/10.1109/CIST.2014.7016641
29. Ratinov, L., Roth, D.: Design challenges and misconceptions in named entity recognition. In: Proceedings of the 13th Conference on Computational Natural Language Learning, CoNLL 2009, USA, pp. 147–155. Association for Computational Linguistics (2009)
30. Seyler, D., Dembelova, T., Del Corro, L., Hoffart, J., Weikum, G.: A study of the importance of external knowledge in the named entity recognition task. In: Proceedings of the 56th Annual Meeting of the Association for Computational Linguistics (Volume 2: Short Papers), Melbourne, Australia, pp. 241–246. Association for Computational Linguistics (July 2018). https://doi.org/10.18653/v1/P18-2039. https://aclanthology.org/P18-2039
31. Tjong Kim Sang, E.F., De Meulder, F.: Introduction to the CoNLL-2003 shared task: language-independent named entity recognition. In: Proceedings of the 7th Conference on Natural Language Learning at HLT-NAACL 2003, CoNLL 2003, USA, vol. 4, pp. 142–147. Association for Computational Linguistics (2003). https://doi.org/10.3115/1119176.1119195
32. Xiaofeng, M., Wei, W., Aiping, X.: Incorporating token-level dictionary feature into neural model for named entity recognition. Neurocomputing **375**, 43–50 (2020). https://doi.org/10.1016/j.neucom.2019.09.005. https://www.sciencedirect.com/science/article/pii/S0925231219312652
33. Yadav, V., Bethard, S.: A survey on recent advances in named entity recognition from deep learning models. In: Proceedings of the 27th International Conference on Computational Linguistics, Santa Fe, New Mexico, USA, pp. 2145–2158. Association for Computational Linguistics (August 2018). https://www.aclweb.org/anthology/C18-1182

# Author Index

# Author Index

Printed in the United States
by Baker & Taylor Publisher Services